C++ HOW TO PROGRAM

INSTRUCTOR'S MANUAL
WITH PROGRAM DISK

INSTRUCTOR'S MANUAL WITH PROGRAM DISK

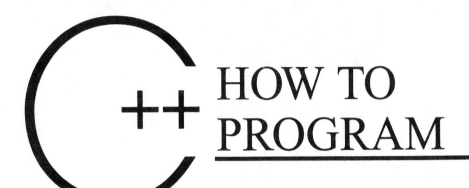

C++ HOW TO PROGRAM

H. M. Deitel
Nova University
Deitel and Associates

P. J. Deitel
Deitel and Associates

with **T. R. Nieto**

PRENTICE HALL, Englewood Cliffs, New Jersey 07632

©1994 by **PRENTICE-HALL, INC.**
A Simon & Schuster Company
Englewood Cliffs, NJ 07632

10 9 8 7 6

ISBN 0-13-142713-X
Printed in the United States of America

Preface

The old guy (H. M. D.) and the young guy (P. J. D.) would like to thank you for considering and/or adopting our text, C++ *How to Program*. We have worked hard to produce a textbook and ancillaries that we hope you and your students will find valuable.

Before designing this ancillary package, we spoke with college professors and professional seminar instructors who offer C++ courses worldwide. We asked what ancillaries would be most valuable to them.

The most frequent request was for a PC-compatible format disk containing all the C++ source code for the programs in the text. Instructors indicated this would help them prepare lectures faster and with the assurance that the programs really work. Many instructors said they would also like to make the programs available to their students.

The second most frequent request was for disks with answers to all the exercises in the book. Instructors indicated this would be helpful for assigning homework problems and distributing solutions in machine-readable format to students.

The enclosed PC-compatible format disk contains 189 programs from the text and 272 program solutions to the exercises. The disk includes two directories: EXAMPLES contains the text examples and SOLUTION contains the programming exercise solutions. The programs are separated into directories by chapter. All these materials have been tested in our classes and professional seminars.

A key feature of the text is the substantial problem introduced in the *Thinking About Objects* sections in Chapters 2 through 8. We carefully guide the student through the object-oriented design and programming of an elevator simulator. We have thoroughly class tested this problem with very positive results. The students enjoy the substantial challenge, reinforce their knowledge of C++ and OOP, and generally compete amongst themselves to develop the best implementations. We have grouped the solutions for the elevator simulator problems at the end of this instructor's manual.

Please let us know if there is anything else you need now or for future editions of this work. We would sincerely appreciate your comments, criticisms, and corrections. The best way to reach us is by email at

deitel@world.std.com

We will respond immediately.

We would like to thank the extraordinary team of publishing professionals at Prentice-Hall who made C++ *How to Program* and its ancillaries possible. Sondra Chavez worked closely with us to ensure the timely availability and professional quality of these ancillaries. If you find these materials valuable, it is due in large measure to the insights and careful guidance provided by our editor, publishing mentor, and friend—Alan Apt. We would also like to extend a special note of thanks to our associate Temujin Nieto who put many months of effort into writing a major portion of the solutions that appear in this instructor's manual.

Harvey M. Deitel
Paul J. Deitel

Contents

1

Introduction to Computers and C++ Programming: Solutions

Exercises

1.10 Categorize each of the following items as either hardware or software:
a) CPU
ANS: hardware.
b) C++ compiler
ANS: software.
c) ALU
ANS: hardware.
d) C++ preprocessor
ANS: software.
e) input unit
ANS: hardware.
f) an editor program
ANS: software.

1.11 Why might you want to write a program in a machine-independent language instead of a machine-dependent language? Why might a machine-dependent language be more appropriate for writing certain types of programs?
ANS: Machine independent languages are useful for writing programs to be executed on multiple computer platforms. Machine dependent languages are appropriate for writing programs to be executed on a single platform. Machine dependent languages tend to exploit the efficiencies of a particular machine.

1.12 Fill in the blanks in each of the following statements:
a) Which logical unit of the computer receives information from outside the computer for use by the computer? _____.
ANS: The input unit.
b) The process of instructing the computer to solve specific problems is called _____.
ANS: computer programming.
c) What type of computer language uses English-like abbreviations for machine language instructions? _____.
ANS: a high-level language.
d) Which logical unit of the computer sends information that has already been processed by the computer to various devices so that the information may be used outside the computer? _____.
ANS: The output unit.
e) Which logical unit of the computer retains information? _____.
ANS: memory unit and secondary storage unit.
f) Which logical unit of the computer performs calculations? _____.
ANS: arithmetic and logical unit.
g) Which logical unit of the computer makes logical decisions? _____.
ANS: arithmetic and logical unit.

h) The level of computer language most convenient to the programmer for writing programs quickly and easily is _____.

ANS: high-level language.

i) The only language that a computer can directly understand is called that computer's _____.

ANS: machine language.

j) Which logical unit of the computer coordinates the activities of all the other logical units? _____.

ANS: central processing unit.

1.13 Discuss the meaning of each of the following objects:

a) `cin`

ANS: This object refers to the standard input device that is normally connected to the keyboard.

b) `cout`

ANS: This object refers to the standard output device that is normally connected to the computer screen.

c) `cerr`

ANS: This object refers to the standard error device. Error messages are sent to this device that is normally connected to the computer screen.

1.14 Why is so much attention today focused on object-oriented programming in general and C++ in particular?

ANS: Object-oriented programming enables the programmer to build reusable software components that model items in the real world. Building software quickly, correctly, and economically has been an elusive goal in the software industry. The modular, object-oriented design and implementation approach has been found to increase productivity 10 to 100 times over conventional programming languages while reducing development time, errors, and cost. C++ is used for object-oriented programming because it is a superset of the C programming language and C is widely used.

1.15 Fill in the blanks in each of the following:

a) _____ are used to document a program and improve its readability.

ANS: Comments.

b) The object used to print information on the screen is _____.

ANS: `cout`.

c) A C++ statement that makes a decision is _____.

ANS: `if`.

d) Calculations are normally performed by _____ statements.

ANS: assignment.

e) The _____ object inputs values from the keyboard.

ANS: `cin`.

1.16 Write a single C++ statement or line that accomplishes each of the following:

a) Print the message `"Enter two numbers."`

ANS: `cout << "Enter two numbers." << endl;`

b) Assign the product of variables **b** and **c** to variable **a**.

ANS: `a = b * c;`

c) State that a program performs a sample payroll calculation (i.e., use text that helps document a program).

ANS: `// Sample payroll calculation program`

d) Input three integer values from the keyboard and place these values in integer variables **a**, **b**, and **c**.

ANS: `cout << "Enter three integers: ";    // prompt`
`    cin >> a >> b >> c;`

1.17 State which of the following are true and which are false. Explain your answers.

a) C++ operators are evaluated from left to right.

ANS: False. Some operators are evaluated from left to right and others are evaluated from right to left depending on their associativity (see Appendix C).

b) The following are all valid variable names: `_under_bar_`, `m928134`, `t5`, `j7`, `her_sales`, `his_account_total`, `a`, `b`, `c`, `z`, `z2`.

ANS: True. All these variable names begin with a letter or underscore.

c) The statement `cout << "a = 5;";` is a typical example of an assignment statement.

ANS: False. The statement prints the string literal `a = 5;` on the screen.

d) A valid C++ arithmetic expression with no parentheses is evaluated from left to right.

ANS: False. Multiplication, division, and modulus are evaluated first from left to right, then addition and subtraction are evaluated from left to right.

e) The following are all invalid variable names: `3g`, `87`, `67h2`, `h22`, `2h`.

ANS: False. Only those beginning with a number are invalid.

1.18 Fill in the blanks in each of the following:
  a) What arithmetic operations are on the same level of precedence as multiplication? _____.
  ANS: modulus (%) and division (/),
  b) When parentheses are nested, which set of parentheses is evaluated first in an arithmetic expression? _____.
  ANS: innermost.
  c) A location in the computer's memory that may contain different values at various times throughout the execution of a program is called a _____.
  ANS: variable.

1.19 What, if anything, prints when each of the following C++ statements is performed? If nothing prints, then answer "nothing." Assume `x = 2` and `y = 3`.
  a) `cout << x;`
  ANS: 2
  b) `cout << x + x;`
  ANS: 4
  c) `cout << "x=";`
  ANS: x=
  d) `cout << "x = " << x;`
  ANS: x = 2
  e) `cout << x + y << " = " << y + x;`
  ANS: 5 = 5
  f) `z = x + y;`
  ANS: Nothing. Value of `x + y` is assigned to `z`.
  g) `cin >> x >> y;`
  ANS: Nothing. Two integer values are read into the variable `x` and the variable `y`.
  h) `// cout << "x + y = " << x + y;`
  ANS: Nothing. This is a comment.
  i) `cout << "\n";`
  ANS: A newline character is output to position the cursor at the beginning of the next line on the screen.

1.20 Which of the following C++ statements contain variables whose values are destroyed?
  a) `cin >> b >> c >> d >> e >> f;`
  b) `p = i + j + k + 7;`
  c) `cout << "variables whose values are destroyed";`
  d) `cout << "a = 5";`
  ANS: (a) and (b).

1.21 Given the equation $y = ax^3 + 7$, which of the following, if any, are correct C++ statements for this equation?
  a) `y = a * x * x * x + 7;`
  b) `y = a * x * x * (x + 7);`
  c) `y = (a * x) * x * (x + 7);`
  d) `y = (a * x) * x * x + 7;`
  e) `y = a * (x * x * x) + 7;`
  f) `y = a * x * (x * x + 7);`
  ANS: (a), (d), and (e).

1.22 State the order of evaluation of the operators in each of the following C++ statements, and show the value of `x` after each statement is performed.
  a) `x = 7 + 3 * 6 / 2 - 1;`
  ANS: `*` is first, `/` is second, `+` is third, and `-` is fourth. Value of `x` is 15.
  b) `x = 2 % 2 + 2 * 2 - 2 / 2;`
  ANS: `%` is first, `*` is second, `/` is third, `+` is fourth, `-` is fifth. Value of `x` is 3.
  c) `x = (3 * 9 * (3 + (9 * 3 / (3))));`
  ANS: 5   6   4   2   3   1. Value of `x` is 324.

1.23 Write a program that asks the user to enter two numbers, obtains the two numbers from the user, and prints the sum, product, difference, and quotient of the two numbers.

ANS:
```
// Exercise 1.23 Solution
#include <iostream.h>

main()
{
    int num1, num2;

    cout << "Enter two integers: ";
    cin >> num1 >> num2;

    cout << "The sum is " << num1 + num2 << endl
         << "The product is " << num1 * num2 << endl
         << "The difference is " << num1 - num2 << endl
         << "The quotient is " << num1 / num2 << endl;

    return 0;
}
```

```
Enter two integers: 15 6
The sum is 21
The product is 90
The difference is 9
The quotient is 2
```

1.24   Write a program that prints the numbers 1 to 4 on the same line with each pair of adjacent numbers separated by one space. Write the program using the following methods.

    a)   Using one output statement with one stream insertion operator.

    b)   Using one output statement with four stream insertion operators.

    c)   Using four output statements.

ANS:
```
// Exercise 1.24 Solution
#include <iostream.h>

main()
{
    // Part A
    cout << "1 2 3 4" << endl;

    // Part B
    cout << "1 " << "2 " << "3 " << "4" << endl;

    // Part C
    cout << "1 ";
    cout << "2 ";
    cout << "3 ";
    cout << "4" << endl;

    return 0;
}
```

```
1 2 3 4
1 2 3 4
1 2 3 4
```

1.25   Write a program that asks the user to enter two integers, obtains the numbers from the user, and then prints the larger number followed by the words "**is larger**." If the numbers are equal, print the message "**These numbers are equal**."

ANS:
```cpp
// Exercise 1.25 Solution
#include <iostream.h>

main()
{
    int num1, num2;

    cout << "Enter two integers: ";
    cin >> num1 >> num2;

    if (num1 == num2)
        cout << "These numbers are equal." << endl;

    if (num1 > num2)
        cout << num1 << " is larger." << endl;

    if (num2 > num1)
        cout << num2 << " is larger." << endl;

    return 0;
}
```

```
Enter two integers: 73 2
73 is larger.
```

```
Enter two integers: 2 73
73 is larger.
```

1.26 Write a program that inputs three integers from the keyboard, and prints the sum, average, product, smallest, and largest of these numbers. The screen dialogue should appear as follows:

```
Input three different integers: 13 27 14
Sum is 54
Average is 18
Product is 4914
Smallest is 13
Largest is 27
```

ANS:
```cpp
// Exercise 1.26 Solution
#include <iostream.h>

main()
{
    int num1, num2, num3, smallest, largest;

    cout << "Input three different integers: ";
    cin >> num1 >> num2 >> num3;

    largest = num1;

    if (num2 > largest)
        largest = num2;

    if (num3 > largest)
        largest = num3;

    smallest = num1;
```

```
      if (num2 < smallest)
         smallest = num2;

      if (num3 < smallest)
         smallest = num3;

      cout << "Sum is " << num1 + num2 + num3 << endl
           << "Average is " << (num1 + num2 + num3) / 3 << endl
           << "Product is " << num1 * num2 * num3 << endl
           << "Smallest is " << smallest << endl
           << "Largest is " << largest << endl;

      return 0;
   }
```

1.27   Write a program that reads in the radius of a circle and prints the circle's diameter, circumference, and area. Use the constant value 3.14159 for π. Do these calculations in output statements. (Note: In this chapter, we have discussed only integer constants and variables. In Chapter 3 we will discuss floating point numbers, i.e., values that can have decimal points.)

ANS:
```
// Exercise 1.27 Solution
#include <iostream.h>

main()
{
   int radius;

   cout << "Enter the circle radius: ";
   cin >> radius;

   cout << "Diameter is " << radius * 2 << endl
        << "Circumference is " << 2 * 3.14159 * radius << endl
        << "Area is " << 3.14159 * radius * radius << endl;

   return 0;
}
```

```
Enter the circle radius: 1
Diameter is 2
Circumference is 6.28318
Area is 3.14159
```

1.28   Write a program that prints a box, an oval, an arrow, and a diamond as follows:

```
********         ***            *              *
*      *        *   *          ***            * *
*      *       *     *        *****          *    *
*      *       *     *          *           *      *
*      *       *     *          *          *        *
*      *       *     *          *          *        *
*      *       *     *          *           *      *
*      *        *   *           *            * *
********         ***            *              *
```

ANS:
```
// Exercise 1.28 Solution
#include <iostream.h>

main()
{
    cout << "*********        ***         *          *       " << endl
         << "*        *     *        *          ***         * *      " << endl
         << "*        *     *         *        *****       *     *     " << endl
         << "*        *     *        *          *          *       * " << endl
         << "*        *     *        *          *        *         *" << endl
         << "*        *     *        *          *         *       *  " << endl
         << "*        *     *        *          *           *   *    " << endl
         << "*        *      *     *        *          *            * *     " << endl
         << "*********        ***         *          *       " << endl;
    return 0;
}
```

1.29   What does the following code print?

```
cout << "*\n**\n***\n****\n*****\n";
```

ANS:

```
*
**
***
****
*****
```

1.30   Write a program that reads in five integers and determines and prints the largest and the smallest integers in the group. Use only the programming techniques you learned in this chapter.

ANS:
```
// Exercise 1.30 Solution
#include <iostream.h>

main()
{
    int num1, num2, num3, num4, num5, largest, smallest;

    cout << "Enter five integers: ";
    cin >> num1 >> num2 >> num3 >> num4 >> num5;

    largest = num1;

    if (num1 > largest)
        largest = num1;

    if (num2 > largest)
        largest = num2;

    if (num3 > largest)
        largest = num3;

    if (num4 > largest)
        largest = num4;

    if (num5 > largest)
        largest = num5;

    if (num1 < smallest)
        smallest = num1;
```

```
if (num2 < smallest)
   smallest = num2;

if (num3 < smallest)
   smallest = num3;

if (num4 < smallest)
   smallest = num4;

if (num5 < smallest)
   smallest = num5;

cout << "Largest is " << largest << endl
     << "Smallest is " << smallest << endl;

return 0;
}
```

```
Enter five integers: 5 17 -4 8 5
Largest is 17
Smallest is -4
```

1.31   Write a program that reads an integer and determines and prints whether it is odd or even. (Hint: Use the modulus operator. An even number is a multiple of two. Any multiple of two leaves a remainder of zero when divided by 2.)

ANS:
```
// Exercise 1.31 Solution
#include <iostream.h>

main()
{
   int num;

   cout << "Enter a number: ";
   cin >> num;

   if (num % 2 == 0)
      cout << "The number " << num << " is even." << endl;

   if (num % 2 != 0)
      cout << "The number " << num << " is odd." << endl;

   return 0;
}
```

```
Enter a number: 30
The number 30 is even.
```

```
Enter a number: 31
The number 31 is odd.
```

1.32   Write a program that reads in two integers and determines and prints if the first is a multiple of the second. (Hint: Use the modulus operator.)

```
ANS:
// Exercise 1.32 Solution
#include <iostream.h>

main()
{
   int num1, num2;

   cout << "Enter two integers: ";
   cin >> num1 >> num2;

   if (num1 % num2 == 0)
      cout << num1 << " is a multiple of " << num2 << endl;

   if (num1 % num2 != 0)
      cout << num1 << " is not a multiple of " << num2 << endl;

   return 0;
}
```

```
Enter two integers: 55 11
55 is a multiple of 11
```

```
Enter two integers: 11 55
11 is not a multiple of 55
```

1.33 Display a checkerboard pattern with eight output statements, and then display the same pattern with as few output statements as possible.

```
* * * * * * * *
 * * * * * * * *
* * * * * * * *
 * * * * * * * *
* * * * * * * *
 * * * * * * * *
* * * * * * * *
 * * * * * * * *
```

```
ANS:
// Exercise 1.33 Solution
#include <iostream.h>

main()
{
   // Eight output statements
   cout << "* * * * * * * * " << endl;
   cout << " * * * * * * * *" << endl;
   cout << "* * * * * * * * " << endl;
   cout << " * * * * * * * *" << endl;
   cout << "* * * * * * * * " << endl;
   cout << " * * * * * * * *" << endl;
   cout << "* * * * * * * * " << endl;
   cout << " * * * * * * * *" << endl << endl;

   // One output statement; 3 parts
   cout << "* * * * * * * * \n * * * * * * * *\n* * * * * * * * \n"
        << " * * * * * * * *\n* * * * * * * * \n * * * * * * * *\n"
        << "* * * * * * * * \n * * * * * * * *" << endl;
   return 0;
}
```

1.34   Distinguish between the terms fatal error and nonfatal error. Why might you prefer to experience a fatal error rather than a nonfatal error?

> **ANS:** A fatal error causes the program to terminate prematurely. A nonfatal error occurs when the logic of the program is incorrect, and the program does not work properly. A fatal error is preferred for debugging purposes. A fatal error immediately lets you know there is a problem with the program, whereas a nonfatal error can be subtle and possibly go undetected.

1.35   Here's a peek ahead. In this chapter you learned about integers and the type **int**. C++ can also represent uppercase letters, lowercase letters, and a considerable variety of special symbols. C++ uses small integers internally to represent each different character. The set of characters a computer uses and the corresponding integer representations for those characters is called that computer's character set. You can print a character by simply enclosing that character in single quotes as with

```
cout << 'A';
```

You can print the integer equivalent of a character by preceding that character with **(int)**—this is called a cast (we will say more about casts in Chapter 2).

```
cout << (int) 'A';
```

When the preceding statement executes, it prints the value 65 (on systems that use the so-called ASCII character set). Write a program that prints the integer equivalents of some uppercase letters, lowercase letters, digits and special symbols. At a minimum, determine the integer equivalents of the following: **A B C a b c 0 1 2 $ * + /** and the blank character.

> **ANS:**
```
// Exercise 1.35 Solution
#include <iostream.h>

main()
{
   char symbol;

   cout << "Enter a character: ";
   cin >> symbol;

   // output integer equivalents
   cout << "The integer equivalent of " << symbol << " is "
        << (int) symbol << endl;

   return 0;
}
```

```
Enter a character: r
The integer equivalent of r is 114
```

```
Enter a character: %
The integer equivalent of % is 37
```

1.36   Write a program that inputs a five-digit number, separates the number into its individual digits and prints the digits separated from one another by three spaces each. For example, if the user types in **42339** the program should print

```
4   2   3   3   9
```

```
ANS:
// Exercise 1.36 Solution
#include <iostream.h>

main()
{
   int num;

   cout << "Enter a five-digit number: ";
   cin >> num;

   cout << num / 10000 << "   ";
   num = num % 10000;
   cout << num / 1000 << "   ";
   num = num % 1000;
   cout << num / 100 << "   ";
   num = num % 100;
   cout << num / 10 << "   ";
   num = num % 10;
   cout << num << endl;

   return 0;
}
```

```
Enter a five-digit number: 12345
1   2   3   4   5
```

1.37   Using only the techniques you learned in this chapter, write a program that calculates the squares and cubes of the numbers from 0 to 10 and uses tabs to print the following table of values:

```
number   square   cube
0        0        0
1        1        1
2        4        8
3        9        27
4        16       64
5        25       125
6        36       216
7        49       343
8        64       512
9        81       729
10       100      1000
```

ANS:
```
// Exercise 1.37 Solution
#include <iostream.h>

main()
{
   int num = 0;

   cout << endl << "number\tsquare\tcube" << endl
        << num << '\t' << num * num << '\t' << num * num * num << endl;

   num = num + 1;
   cout << num << '\t' << num * num << '\t' << num * num * num << endl;

   num = num + 1;
   cout << num << '\t' << num * num << '\t' << num * num * num << endl;
```

```
num = num + 1;
cout << num << '\t' << num * num << '\t' << num * num * num << endl;

num = num + 1;
cout << num << '\t' << num * num << '\t' << num * num * num << endl;

num = num + 1;
cout << num << '\t' << num * num << '\t' << num * num * num << endl;

num = num + 1;
cout << num << '\t' << num * num << '\t' << num * num * num << endl;

num = num + 1;
cout << num << '\t' << num * num << '\t' << num * num * num << endl;

num = num + 1;
cout << num << '\t' << num * num << '\t' << num * num * num << endl;

num = num + 1;
cout << num << '\t' << num * num << '\t' << num * num * num << endl;

num = num + 1;
cout << num << '\t' << num * num << '\t' << num * num * num << endl;

   return 0;
}
```

1.38   Give a brief answer to each of the following "object think" questions:
a)   Why does this text choose to discuss structured programming in detail before proceeding with an in-depth treatment of object-oriented programming?
ANS: Objects are composed in part by structured program pieces.
b)   What are the typical steps (mentioned in the text) of an object-oriented design process?
ANS: (1) Determine which objects are needed to implement the system. (2) Determine each object's attributes. (3) Determine each object's behaviors. (4) Determine the interaction between the objects.
c)   How is multiple inheritance exhibited by human beings?
ANS: Children. A child receives genes from both parents.
d)   What kinds of messages do people send to one another?
ANS: People send messages to one another through gestures, expressions, writings, speech, etc.
e)   Objects send messages to one another across well-defined interfaces. What interfaces does a car radio (object) present to its user (a person object)?
ANS: Dials and buttons that allow the user to: tune into various frequencies, set the volume, adjust the bass, adjust the treble, etc.

1.39   You are probably wearing on your wrist one of the world's most common types of objects—a watch. Discuss how each of the following terms and concepts applies to the notion of a watch: object, attributes, behaviors, class, inheritance (consider, for example, an alarm clock), abstraction, modeling, messages, encapsulation, interface, information hiding, data members, and member functions.
ANS: The entire watch is an object that is composed of many other objects (such as the moving parts, the band, the face, etc.) Attributes of the watch are time, color, band, style (digital or analog), etc. The behaviors of the watch include setting the time and getting the time. A watch can be considered a specific type of clock (as can an alarm clock). With that in mind, it is possible that a class called Clock could exist from which other classes such as watch and alarm clock can inherit the basic features of a clock. The watch is an abstraction of the mechanics needed to keep track of the time. The user of the watch does not need to know the details of the mechanics; the user simply needs to know that the watch keeps the proper time. In this sense, the mechanics of the watch are encapsulated (hidden) inside the watch. The interface to the watch (its face and controls for setting the time) allows the user to set and get the time. The user is not allowed to directly touch the internal mechanics of the watch. All interaction with the internal mechanics is controlled by the interface to the watch. The data members stored in the watch are hidden inside the watch and the member functions (looking at the face to get the time and setting the time) provide the interface to the data.

2
Control Structures: Solutions

Exercises

Exercises 2.14 through 2.38 correspond to Sections 2.1 through 2.12.
Exercises 2.39 through 2.66 correspond to Sections 2.13 through 2.21.

2.14 Identify and correct the errors in each of the following (Note: there may be more than one error in each piece of code):

a)
```cpp
if (age >= 65);
    cout << "Age is greater than or equal to 65" << endl;
else
    cout << "Age is less than 65 << endl";
```
ANS: The semicolon at the end of the `if` condition should be removed.
```cpp
if (age >= 65)
    cout << "Age is greater than or equal to 65" << endl;
else
    cout << "Age is less than 65" << endl;
```

b)
```cpp
int x = 1, total;

while (x <= 10) {
    total += x;
    ++x;
}
```
ANS: `total` should be initialized to zero before being used.
```cpp
int x = 1, total = 0;

while (x <= 10) {
    total += x;
    ++x;
}
```

c)
```cpp
While (x <= 100)
    total += x;
    ++x;
```
ANS: The `W` in `While` should be lowercase and curly braces are needed to include the two statements in the body.
```cpp
while (x <= 100) {
    total += x;
    ++x;
}
```

d)
```cpp
while (y > 0) {
    cout << y << endl;
    ++y;
}
```
ANS:
```cpp
while (y > 0) {
    cout << y << endl;
    --y;
}
```

2.15 What does the following program print?

```cpp
#include <iostream.h>

main()
{
   int y, x = 1, total = 0;

   while (x <= 10) {
      y = x * x;
      cout << y << endl;
      total += y;
      ++x;
   }

   cout << "Total is " << total << endl;
   return 0;
}
```

ANS:

```
1
4
9
16
25
36
49
64
81
100
Total is 385
```

For Exercises 2.16 to 2.19 perform each of these steps:
1. Read the problem statement.
2. Formulate the algorithm using pseudocode and top-down, stepwise refinement.
3. Write a C++ program.
4. Test, debug, and execute the C++ program.

2.16 Because of the high price of gasoline, drivers are concerned with the mileage obtained by their automobiles. One driver has kept track of several tankfuls of gasoline by recording miles driven and gallons used for each tankful. Develop a C++ program that will input the miles driven and gallons used for each tankful. The program should calculate and display the miles per gallon obtained for each tankful. After processing all input information, the program should calculate and print the combined miles per gallon obtained for all tankfuls.

```
Enter the gallons used (-1 to end): 12.8
Enter the miles driven: 287
The miles / gallon for this tank was 22.4219

Enter the gallons used (-1 to end): 10.3
Enter the miles driven: 200
The miles / gallon for this tank was 19.4175

Enter the gallons used (-1 to end): 5
Enter the miles driven: 120
The miles / gallon for this tank was 24

Enter the gallons used (-1 to end): -1

The overall average miles/gallon was 21.6014
```

ANS:

2)   ***Top:***
        Determine the average miles/gallon for each tank of gas, and the overall miles/gallon for an arbitrary number of tanks of gas.

        First refinement:
        Initialize variables

        Input the gallons used and the miles driven, and calculate and print the miles/gallon for each tank of gas. Keep track of the total miles and the total gallons.

        Calculate and print the overall average miles/gallon.

        Second refinement:
        Initialize totalGallons to zero.
        Initialize totalMiles to zero.

        Input the gallons used for the first tank.

        While the sentinel value (-1) has not been entered for the gallons
                Add gallons to the running total in totalGallons
                Input the miles driven for the current tank
                Add miles to the running total in totalMiles
                Calculate and print the miles/gallon
                Input the gallons used for the next tank

        Set totalAverage to totalMiles divided by totalGallons.
        Print the average miles/gallon.

3)

```
// Exercise 2.16 Solution
#include <iostream.h>

main()
{
   float gallons, miles, totalGallons = 0.0, totalMiles = 0.0, average;

   cout << "Enter the gallons used (-1 to end): ";
   cin >> gallons;

   while (gallons != -1.0) {
      totalGallons += gallons;

      cout << "Enter the miles driven: ";
      cin >> miles;
      totalMiles += miles;

      cout << "The Miles / Gallon for this tank was "
           << miles / gallons << endl
           << endl << "Enter the gallons used (-1 to end): ";
      cin >> gallons;
   }

   average = totalMiles / totalGallons;
   cout << endl << "The overall average Miles/Gallon was "
        << average << endl;

   return 0;
}
```

```
Enter the gallons used (-1 to end): 12.4
Enter the miles driven: 220
The Miles / Gallon for this tank was 17.741936
Enter the gallons used (-1 to end): 14.9
Enter the miles driven: 275
The Miles / Gallon for this tank was 18.456377
Enter the gallons used (-1 to end): -1
The overall average Miles/Gallon was 18.131868
```

2.17   Develop a C++ program that will determine if a department store customer has exceeded the credit limit on a charge account. For each customer, the following facts are available:

1. Account number (an integer)
2. Balance at the beginning of the month
3. Total of all items charged by this customer this month
4. Total of all credits applied to this customer's account this month
5. Allowed credit limit

The program should input each of these facts, calculate the new balance (= beginning balance + charges - credits), and determine if the new balance exceeds the customer's credit limit. For those customers whose credit limit is exceeded, the program should display the customer's account number, credit limit, new balance, and the message "Credit limit exceeded."

```
Enter account number (-1 to end): 100
Enter beginning balance: 5394.78
Enter total charges: 1000.00
Enter total credits: 500.00
Enter credit limit: 5500.00
Account:      100
Credit limit: 5500.00
Balance:      5894.78
Credit Limit Exceeded.

Enter account number (-1 to end): 200
Enter beginning balance: 1000.00
Enter total charges: 123.45
Enter total credits: 321.00
Enter credit limit: 1500.00

Enter account number (-1 to end): 300
Enter beginning balance: 500.00
Enter total charges: 274.73
Enter total credits: 100.00
Enter credit limit: 800.00

Enter account number (-1 to end): -1
```

ANS:

2)   Top:
Determine if each of an arbitrary number of department store customers has exceeded the credit limit on a charge account.

First refinement:
Input the account number, beginning balance, total charges, total credits, and credit limit for a customer, calculate the customer's new balance and determine if the balance exceeds the credit limit. The process the next customer.

Second refinement:
Input the first customer's account number.

While the sentinel value (-1) has not been entered for the account number
    Input the customer's beginning balance
    Input the customer's total charges
    Input the customer's total credits
    Input the customer's credit limit
    Calculate the customers new balance

    If the balance exceeds the credit limit
        Print the account number
        Print the credit limit
        Print the balance
        Print "Credit Limit Exceeded"
        Input the next customer's account number.

```
3)
// Exercise 2.17 Solution
#include <iostream.h>
#include <iomanip.h>

main()
{
   int accountNumber;
   float balance, charges, credits, limit;

   cout << "Enter account number (-1 to end): ";
   cin >> accountNumber;

   while (accountNumber != -1) {
      cout << "Enter beginning balance: ";
      cin >> balance;
      cout << "Enter total charges: ";
      cin >> charges;
      cout << "Enter total credits: ";
      cin >> credits;
      cout << "Enter credit limit: ";
      cin >> limit;
      balance += charges - credits;
      cout.setf(ios::fixed | ios::showpoint);

      if (balance > limit)
         cout << "Account:        " << accountNumber << endl
              << "Credit limit: " << setprecision(2) << limit << endl
              << "Balance:        " << setprecision(2) << balance << endl
              << "Credit Limit Exceeded." << endl;

      cout << endl << "Enter account number (-1 to end): ";
      cin >> accountNumber;
   }

   return 0;
}
```

2.18   One large chemical company pays its salespeople on a commission basis. The salespeople receive $200 per week plus 9 percent of their gross sales for that week. For example, a salesperson who sells $5000 worth of chemicals in a week receives $200 plus 9 percent of $5000, or a total of $650. Develop a C++ program that will input each salesperson's gross sales for last week and will calculate and display that salesperson's earnings. Process one salesperson's figures at a time.

```
Enter sales in dollars (-1 to end): 5000.00
Salary is: $650.00

Enter sales in dollars (-1 to end): 1234.56
Salary is: $311.11

Enter sales in dollars (-1 to end): 1088.89
Salary is: $298.00

Enter sales in dollars (-1 to end): -1
```

ANS:

2) *Top:*
    For an arbitrary number of salespeople, determine each salesperson's earnings for the last week.

    First refinement:
    Input the salesperson's sales for the week, calculate and print the salesperson's wages for the week, then
        process the next salesperson.

    Second refinement:
    Input the first salesperson's sales in dollars.

    While the sentinel value (-1) has not been entered for the sales
        Calculate the salesperson's wages for the week
        Print the salesperson's wages for the week
        Input the next salesperson's sales in dollars

3)
```cpp
// Exercise 2.18 Solution
#include <iostream.h>
#include <iomanip.h>

main()
{
   float sales, wage;

   cout << "Enter sales in dollars (-1 to end): ";
   cin >> sales;

   cout.setf(ios::fixed | ios::showpoint);

   while (sales != -1.0) {
      wage = 200.0 + 0.09 * sales;
      cout << "Salary is: $" << setprecision(2) << wage << endl
           << endl << "Enter sales in dollars (-1 to end): ";
      cin >> sales;
   }

   return 0;
}
```

2.19   Develop a C++ program that will determine the gross pay for each of several employees. The company pays "straight-time" for the first 40 hours worked by each employee and pays "time-and-a-half" for all hours worked in excess of 40 hours. You are given a list of the employees of the company, the number of hours each employee worked last week, and the hourly rate of each employee. Your program should input this information for each employee, and should determine and display the employee's gross pay.

```
Enter hours worked (-1 to end): 39
Enter hourly rate of the worker ($00.00): 10.00
Salary is $390.00

Enter hours worked (-1 to end): 40
Enter hourly rate of the worker ($00.00): 10.00
Salary is $400.00

Enter hours worked (-1 to end): 41
Enter hourly rate of the worker ($00.00): 10.00
Salary is $415.00

Enter hours worked (-1 to end): -1
```

ANS:
2) Top:

For an arbitrary number of loans, determine the simple interest for each loan.

First refinement:
Input the principal of the loan, the interest rate, and the term of the loan, calculate and print the simple interest for the loan, and process the next loan.

Second refinement:
Input the first loan principal in dollars.

While the sentinel value (-1) has not been entered for the loan principal
> *Input the interest rate*
> *Input the term of the loan in days*
> *Calculate the simple interest for the loan*
> *Print the simple interest for the loan*
> *Input the loan principal for the next loan*

3)
```cpp
// Exercise 2.19 Solution
#include <iostream.h>
#include <iomanip.h>

main()
{
   float hours, rate, salary;

   cout << "Enter hours worked (-1 to end): ";
   cin >> hours;
   cout.setf(ios::fixed | ios::showpoint);

   while (hours != -1.0) {
      cout << "Enter hourly rate of the worker ($00.00): ";
      cin >> rate;

      if (hours <= 40)
         salary = hours * rate;
      else
         salary = 40.0 * rate + (hours - 40.0) * rate * 1.5;

      cout << "Salary is $" << setprecision(2) << salary << endl
           << endl << "Enter hours worked (-1 to end): ";
      cin >> hours;
   }

   return 0;
}
```

2.20   The process of finding the largest number (i.e., the maximum of a group of numbers) is used frequently in computer applications. For example, a program that determines the winner of a sales contest would input the number of units sold by each salesperson. The salesperson who sells the most units wins the contest. Write a pseudocode program and then a C++ program that inputs a series of 10 numbers, and determines and prints the largest of the numbers. Hint: Your program should use three variables as follows:

`counter:`   A counter to count to 10 (i.e., to keep track of how many numbers have been input, and to determine when all 10 numbers have been processed).

`number:`   The current number input to the program.

`largest:`   The largest number found so far.

ANS:

Input the first number directly into the variable largest
Increment counter to 2

While counter is less than or equal to 10
        input a new variable into the variable number

                If number is greater than largest
                        replace largest with number

        Increment counter

Print the value of largest (while condition false when counter is 11)
End program

```
// Exercise 2.20 Solution
#include <iostream.h>

main()
{
   int counter = 0, number, largest;

   cout << "Enter the first number: ";
   cin >> largest;

   while (++counter < 10) {
      cout << "Enter the next number : ";
      cin >> number;

      if (number > largest)
         largest = number;
   }

   cout << "Largest is " << largest << endl;
   return 0;
}
```

```
Enter the first number: 12
Enter the next number : 6
Enter the next number : 99
Enter the next number : 34
Enter the next number : 88
Enter the next number : 29
Enter the next number : 1
Enter the next number : 0
Enter the next number : 98
Enter the next number : 65
Largest is 99
```

2.21   Write a C++ program that utilizes looping and the tab escape sequence \t to print the following table of values:

```
N          10*N      100*N      1000*N

1          10        100        1000
2          20        200        2000
3          30        300        3000
4          40        400        4000
5          50        500        5000
```

ANS:
```cpp
// Exercise 2.21 Solution

#include <iostream.h>

main()
{
   int n = 0;

   cout << "N\t10 * N\t100 * N\t1000 * N" << endl << endl;

   while (++n <= 5)
      cout << n << '\t' << 10 * n<< '\t' << 100 * n
           << '\t' << 1000 * n << endl;

   return 0;
}
```

2.22   Using an approach similar to Exercise 2.20, find the *two* largest values of the 10 numbers. Note: You may input each number only once.

ANS:
```cpp
// Exercise 2.22 Solution

#include <iostream.h>

main()
{
   int counter = 0, number, largest, secondLargest = 0;

   cout << "Enter the first number: ";
   cin >> largest;

   while (++counter < 10) {
      cout << "Enter next number: ";
      cin >> number;

      if (number > largest) {
         secondLargest = largest;
         largest = number;
      }
      else if (number > secondLargest)
         secondLargest = number;
   }

   cout << endl << "Largest is " <<  largest << endl
        << "Second largest is " << secondLargest << endl;

   return 0;
}
```

```
Enter the first number: 67
Enter next number: 34
Enter next number: 54
Enter next number: 90
Enter next number: 121
Enter next number: 43
Enter next number: 99
Enter next number: 101
Enter next number: 65
Enter next number: 3

Largest is 121
Second largest is 101
```

2.23   Modify the program in Fig. 2.11 to validate its inputs. On any input, if the value entered is other than 1 or 2, keep looping until the user enters a correct value.

ANS:

```cpp
// Exercise 2.23 Solution
#include <iostream.h>

main()
{
    int passes = 0, failures = 0, student = 0, result;

    while (++student <= 10) {
        cout << "Enter result (1=pass, 2=fail): ";
        cin >> result;

        while (result != 1 && result != 2) {
            cout << "Invalid result" << endl
                 << "Enter result (1=pass, 2=fail): ";
            cin >> result;
        }

        if (result == 1)
            ++passes;
        else
            ++failures;
    }

    cout << "Passed: " << passes << endl
         << "Failed: " << failures << endl;

    if (passes >= 8)
        cout << "Raise tuition" << endl;

    return 0;
}
```

```
Enter result (1=pass, 2=fail): 1
Enter result (1=pass, 2=fail): 1
Enter result (1=pass, 2=fail): 2
Enter result (1=pass, 2=fail): 1
Enter result (1=pass, 2=fail): 3
Invalid result
Enter result (1=pass, 2=fail): 2
Enter result (1=pass, 2=fail): 2
Enter result (1=pass, 2=fail): 1
Enter result (1=pass, 2=fail): 2
Enter result (1=pass, 2=fail): 1
Enter result (1=pass, 2=fail): 1
Passed: 6
Failed: 4
```

2.24   What does the following program print?

```
#include <iostream.h>

main()
{
   int count = 1;

   while (count <= 10) {
      cout << (count % 2 ? "****" : "++++++++")
           << endl;
      ++count;
   }

   return 0;
}
```
ANS:
```
****
++++++++
****
++++++++
****
++++++++
****
++++++++
****
++++++++
```

2.25   What does the following program print?

```
#include <iostream.h>

main()
{
   int row = 10, column;

   while (row >= 1) {
      column = 1;

      while (column <= 10) {
         cout << (row % 2 ? "<" : ">");
         ++column;
      }

      --row;
      cout << endl;
   }

   return 0;
}
```
ANS:
```
>>>>>>>>>>
<<<<<<<<<<
>>>>>>>>>>
<<<<<<<<<<
>>>>>>>>>>
>>>>>>>>>>
<<<<<<<<<<
>>>>>>>>>>
<<<<<<<<<<
>>>>>>>>>>
```

2.26   *(Dangling Else Problem)* Determine the output for each of the following when **x** is **9** and **y** is **11** and when **x** is **11** and **y** is **9**. Note that the compiler ignores the indentation in a C++ program. Also, the C++ compiler always associates an **else** with the previous **if** unless told to do otherwise by the placement of braces **{ }**. Because, on first glance, the programmer may not be sure which **if** an **else** matches, this is referred to as the "dangling else" problem. We have eliminated the indentation from the following code to make the problem more challenging. (Hint: Apply indentation conventions you have learned.)

a)
```
if (x < 10)
if (y > 10)
cout << "*****" << endl;
else
cout << "#####" << endl;
cout << "$$$$$" << endl;
```

ANS:

$x = 9, y = 11$

```
*****
$$$$$
```

$x = 11, y = 9$

```
$$$$$
```

b)
```
if (x < 10) {
if (y > 10)
cout << "*****" << endl;
}
else {
cout << "#####" << endl;
cout << "$$$$$" << endl;
}
```

ANS:

$x = 9, y = 11$

```
*****
```

$x = 11, y = 9$

```
#####
$$$$$
```

2.27   *(Another Dangling Else Problem)* Modify the following code to produce the output shown. Use proper indentation techniques. You may not make any changes other than inserting braces. The compiler ignores indentation in a C++ program. We have eliminated the indentation from the following code to make the problem more challenging. Note: It is possible that no modification is necessary.

```
if (y == 8)
if (x == 5)
cout << "@@@@@" << endl;
else
cout << "#####" << endl;
cout << "$$$$$" << endl;
cout << "&&&&&" << endl;
```

a) Assuming **x = 5** and **y = 8**, the following output is produced.

```
@@@@@
$$$$$
&&&&&
```

ANS:
```
if (y == 8) {

   if (x == 5)
      printf("@@@@@\n");
   else
      printf("#####\n");

   printf("$$$$$\n");
   printf("&&&&&\n");
}
```

b) Assuming **x = 5** and **y = 8**, the following output is produced.

```
@@@@@
```

ANS:
```
if (y == 8)
   if (x == 5)
      printf("@@@@@\n");
   else {
      printf("#####\n");
      printf("$$$$$\n");
      printf("&&&&&\n");
   }
```

c) Assuming **x = 5** and **y = 8**. the following output is produced.

```
@@@@@
&&&&&
```

ANS:
```
if (y == 8)
   if (x == 5)
      printf("@@@@@\n");
   else {
      printf("#####\n");
      printf("$$$$$\n");
   }

printf("&&&&&\n");
```

d) Assuming **x = 5** and **y = 7**, the following output is produced. Note: The last three output statements after the **else** are all part of a compound statement.

```
#####
$$$$$
&&&&&
```

ANS:
```
if (y == 8) {
   if (x == 5)
      printf("@@@@@\n");
}
else {
   printf("#####\n");
   printf("$$$$$\n");
   printf("&&&&&\n");
}
```

2.28   Write a program that reads in the size of the side of a square and then prints a hollow square of that size out of asterisks and blanks. Your program should work for squares of all side sizes between 1 and 20. For example, if your program reads a size of 5, it should print

```
*****
*   *
*   *
*   *
*****
```

ANS:
```
// Exercise 2.28 Solution
#include <iostream.h>

main()
{
   int side, rowPosition, size;

   cout << "Enter the square side: ";
   cin >> side;

   size = side;

   while (side > 0) {
      rowPosition = size;

      while (rowPosition > 0) {

         if (size == side || side == 1 || rowPosition == 1 ||
                                          rowPosition == size)
            cout << '*';
         else
            cout << ' ';

         --rowPosition;
      }

      cout << endl;
      --side;
   }

   return 0;
}
```

2.29   A palindrome is a number or a text phrase that reads the same backwards as forwards. For example, each of the following five-digit integers are palindromes: 12321, 55555, 45554 and 11611. Write a program that reads in a five-digit integer and determines whether or not it is a palindrome. (Hint: Use the division and modulus operators to separate the number into its individual digits.)

ANS:
```cpp
// Exercise 2.29 Solution
#include <iostream.h>

main()
{
    int number, firstDigit, secondDigit, fourthDigit, fifthDigit;

    cout << "Enter a five-digit number: ";
    cin >> number;

    firstDigit = number / 10000;
    secondDigit = number % 10000 / 1000;
    fourthDigit = number % 10000 % 1000 % 100 / 10;
    fifthDigit = number % 10000 % 1000 % 10;

    if (firstDigit == fifthDigit && secondDigit == fourthDigit)
        cout << number << " is a palindrome" << endl;
    else
        cout << number << " is not a palindrome" << endl;

    return 0;
}
```

```
Enter a five-digit number: 12321
12321 is a palindrome
```

```
Enter a five-digit number: 23456
23456 is not a palindrome
```

2.30   Input an integer containing only 0s and 1s (i.e., a "binary" integer) and print its decimal equivalent. (Hint: Use the modulus and division operators to pick off the "binary" number's digits one at a time from right to left. Just as in the decimal number system where the rightmost digit has a positional value of 1, and the next digit left has a positional value of 10, then 100, then 1000, etc., in the binary number system the rightmost digit has a positional value of 1, the next digit left has a positional value of 2, then 4, then 8, etc. Thus the decimal number 234 can be interpreted as 4 * 1 + 3 * 10 + 2 * 100. The decimal equivalent of binary 1101 is 1 * 1 + 0 * 2 + 1 * 4 + 1 * 8 or 1 + 0 + 4 + 8 or 13.)

ANS:
```cpp
// Exercise 2.30 Solution
#include <iostream.h>

main()
{
    int binary, number, decimal = 0, highBit = 16, factor = 10000;

    cout << "Enter a binary number (5 digits maximum): ";
    cin >> binary;

    number = binary;

    while (highBit >= 1) {
        decimal += binary / factor * highBit;
        highBit /= 2;
        binary %= factor;
        factor /= 10;
    }

    cout << "The decimal equivalent of "
         << number << " is " << decimal << endl;
    return 0;
}
```

```
Enter a binary number (5 digits maximum): 11111
The decimal equivalent of 11111 is 31
```

```
Enter a binary number (5 digits maximum): 10101
The decimal equivalent of 10101 is 21
```

2.31   Write a program that displays the following checkerboard pattern

```
* * * * * * * *
 * * * * * * * *
* * * * * * * *
 * * * * * * * *
* * * * * * * *
 * * * * * * * *
* * * * * * * *
 * * * * * * * *
```

Your program may use only three output statements, one of the form

```
cout << "* ";
```

one of the form

```
cout << ' ';
```

and one of the form

```
cout << endl;
```


ANS:
```
// Exercise 2.31 Solution
#include <iostream.h>

main()
{
   int side = 8, row;

   while (side-- > 0) {
      row = 8;

      // output a space if needed
      if (side % 2 == 0)
         cout << ' ';

      // output asterisk and space
      while (row-- > 0)
         cout << "* ";

      cout << endl;
   }

   return 0;
}
```

2.32   Write a program that keeps printing the multiples of the integer 2, namely 2, 4, 8, 16, 32, 64, etc. Your loop should not terminate (i.e., you should create an infinite loop). What happens when you run this program?

ANS:

```
// Exercise 2.32 Solution
#include <iostream.h>

main()
{
   int multiple = 1;

   while (multiple *= 2)
      cout << multiple << endl;

   return 0;
}
```

```
2
4
8
16
32
64
128
256
512
1024
2048
4096
8192
16384
-32768
```

2.33   Write a program that reads the radius of a circle (as a **float** value) and computes and prints the diameter, the circumference, and the area. Use the value 3.14159 for π.

ANS:

```
// Exercise 2.33 Solution
#include <iostream.h>

main()
{
   float radius, pi = 3.14159;

   cout << "Enter the radius: ";
   cin >> radius;

   cout << "The diameter is " << radius * 2.0 << endl
        << "The circumference is " << 2.0 * pi * radius << endl
        << "The area is " << pi * radius * radius << endl;

   return 0;
}
```

```
Enter the radius: 10
The diameter is 20
The circumference is 62.831802
The area is 314.158997
```

2.34   What's wrong with the following statement? Provide the correct statement to accomplish what the programmer was probably trying to do.

```
cout << ++(x + y);
```

ANS: The `++` operator cannot be applied to the result of an arithmetic expression. It must be applied to a variable that can be modified.

```
cout << 1 + x + y;
```

2.35   Write a program that reads three nonzero `float` values and determines and prints if they could represent the sides of a triangle.

ANS:

```
// Exercise 2.35 Solution
#include <iostream.h>

main()
{
   float a, b, c;

   cout << "Enter three floating point numbers: ";
   cin >> a >> b >> c;

   if (c * c == a * a + b * b)
      cout << "The three numbers could"
           << " be sides of a right triangle" << endl;
   else
      cout << "The three numbers probably"
           << " are not the sides of a right triangle" << endl;

   return 0;
}
```

```
Enter three floating point numbers: 3.0 4.0 5.0
The three numbers could be sides of a right triangle
```

2.36   Write a program that reads three nonzero integers and determines and prints if they could be the sides of a right triangle.

ANS:

```
// Exercise 2.36 Solution
#include <iostream.h>

main()
{
  int a, b, c;

  do {
     cout << "Enter three integers: ";
     cin >> a >> b >> c;
  } while (a <= 0 || b <= 0 || c <= 0);

  if (c * c == a * a + b * b)
     cout << "The three integers are the"
          << " sides of a right triangle" << endl;
  else
     cout << "The three integers are not the"
          << " sides of a right triangle" << endl;

  return 0;
}
```

```
Enter three integers: 3 4 5
The three integers are the sides of a right triangle
```

2.37   A company wants to transmit data over the telephone, but they are concerned that their phones may be tapped. All of their data is transmitted as four-digit integers. They have asked you to write a program that will encrypt their data so that it may be transmitted more securely. Your program should read a four-digit integer and encrypt it as follows: Replace each digit by *(the sum of that digit plus 7) modulus 10*. Then, swap the first digit with the third, and swap the second digit with the fourth. Then print the encrypted integer. Write a separate program that inputs an encrypted four-digit integer, and decrypts it to form the original number.

ANS:

```
// Exercise 2.37 Part A Solution
#include <iostream.h>

main()
{
    int first, second, third, fourth, digit, temp;
    int encryptedNumber;

    cout << "Enter a four digit number to be encrypted: ";
    cin >> digit;

    first = (digit / 1000 + 7) % 10;
    second = (digit % 1000 / 100 + 7) % 10;
    third = (digit % 1000 % 100 / 10 + 7) % 10;
    fourth = (digit % 1000 % 100 % 10 + 7) % 10;

    temp = first;
    first = third * 1000;
    third = temp * 10;

    temp = second;
    second = fourth * 100;
    fourth = temp * 1;

    encryptedNumber = first + second + third + fourth;
    cout << "Encrypted number is " << encryptedNumber << endl;

    return 0;
}
```

```
Enter a four digit number to be encrypted: 8769
Encrypted number is 3654
```

```
// Exercise 2.37 Part B Solution
#include <iostream.h>

main()
{
    int first, second, third, fourth, decrypted, temp, num;

    cout << "Enter a four digit encrypted number: ";
    cin >> num;

    first = num / 1000;
    second = num % 1000 / 100;
    third = num % 1000 % 100 / 10;
    fourth = num % 1000 % 100 % 10;

    temp = (first + 3) % 10;
    first = (third + 3) % 10;
    third = temp;

    temp = (second + 3) % 10;
    second = (fourth + 3) % 10;
    fourth = temp;
```

```
    decrypted = first * 1000 + second * 100 + third * 10 + fourth;
    cout << "Decrypted number is " << decrypted << endl;
    return 0;
}
```

```
Enter a four digit encrypted number: 3654
Decrypted number is 8769
```

2.38   The factorial of a nonnegative integer n is written $n!$ (pronounced "n factorial") and is defined as follows:

$n! = n \cdot (n - 1) \cdot (n - 2) \cdot \ldots \cdot 1$ (for values of n greater than or equal to 1)

and

$n! = 1$ (for $n = 0$).

For example, $5! = 5 \cdot 4 \cdot 3 \cdot 2 \cdot 1$ which is 120.

a) Write a program that reads a nonnegative integer and computes and prints its factorial.

ANS:

```
// Exercise 2.38 Part A Solution
#include <iostream.h>

main()
{
    int n = 0, number;
    unsigned factorial = 1;

    do {
        cout << "Enter an positive integer: ";
        cin >> number;
    } while (number < 0);

    while (n++ < number)
        factorial *= n == 0 ? 1 : n;

    cout << number << "! is " << factorial << endl;
    return 0;
}
```

```
Enter an positive integer: 8
8! is 40320
```

b) Write a program that estimates the value of the mathematical constant e by using the formula:

$$e = 1 + \frac{1}{1!} + \frac{1}{2!} + \frac{1}{3!} + \ldots$$

ANS:

```
// Exercise 2.38 Part B Solution
#include <iostream.h>

main()
{
    int n = 0, fact = 1, accuracy = 10;
    float e = 1;

    while(++n < accuracy) {
        fact *= n == 0 ? 1 : n;
        e += 1.0 / fact;
    }

    cout << "e is " << e << endl;
    return 0;
}
```

```
e is 2.718182
```

c) Write a program that computes the value of e^x by using the formula

$$e^x = 1 + \frac{x}{1!} + \frac{x^2}{2!} + \frac{x^3}{3!} + ...$$

ANS:
```
// Exercise 2.38 Part C Solution
#include <iostream.h>
#include <iomanip.h>

main()
{
    int n = 0, accuracy = 15, x = 3.0, times = 0, count;
    float e = 1.0, exp = 0.0, fact = 1.0;

    while (n++ <= accuracy) {
        count = n;
        fact *= n == 0 ? 1.0 : n;

        while (times < count) {

            if (times == 0)
                exp = 1.0;

            exp *= x;
            ++times;
        }

        e += exp / fact;
    }

    cout.setf(ios::fixed | ios::showpoint);
    cout << "e raised to the " << x << " power is "
         << setprecision(4) << e << endl;

    return 0;
}
```

```
e raised to the 3 power is 20.0855
```

2.39   Find the error in each of the following (Note: there may be more than one error):
a) ```For (x = 100, x >= 1, x++)
       cout << x << endl;```

ANS:
```
for (x = 100; x >= 1; x--)
    cout << x << endl;
```

b) The following code should print whether integer **value** is odd or even:
```
switch (value % 2) {
    case 0:
        cout << "Even integer" << endl;
    case 1:
        cout << "Odd integer" << endl;
}
```

ANS:
```
switch (value % 2) {
   case 0:
      cout << "Even integer" << endl;
      break;
   case 1:
      cout << "Odd integer" << endl;
      break;    // not required in this particular case
}
```

c) The following code should output the odd integers from 19 to 1:
```
for (x = 19; x >= 1; x += 2)
   cout << x << endl;
```

ANS:
```
for (x = 19; x >= 1; x -= 2)
   cout << x << endl;
```

d) The following code should output the even integers from 2 to 100:
```
counter = 2;
do {
   cout << counter << endl;
   counter += 2;
} While (counter < 100);
```

ANS:
```
counter = 2;

do {
   cout << counter << endl;
   counter += 2;
} while (counter <= 100);
```

2.40   Write a program that sums a sequence of integers. Assume that the first integer read specifies the number of values remaining to be entered. Your program should read only one value per input statement. A typical input sequence might be

```
5 100 200 300 400 500
```

where the **5** indicates that the subsequent **5** values are to be summed.

ANS:
```
// Exercise 2.40 Solution
#include <iostream.h>

main()
{
   int sum = 0, number, value;

   cout << "Enter the number of values to be processed: ";
   cin >> number;

   for (int i = 1; i <= number; i++) {
      cout << "Enter a value: ";
      cin >> value;
      sum += value;
   }

   cout << "Sum of the " << number << " values is " << sum << endl;

   return 0;
}
```

```
Enter the number of values to be processed: 5
Enter a value: 1
Enter a value: 2
Enter a value: 3
Enter a value: 4
Enter a value: 5
Sum of the 5 values is 15
```

2.41 Write a program that calculates and prints the average of several integers. Assume the last value read is the sentinel **9999**. A typical input sequence might be

        10 8 11 7 9 9999

indicating that the average of all the values preceding **9999** is to be calculated.

ANS:
```
// Exercise 2.41 Solution

#include <iostream.h>

main()
{
   int value, count = 0, total = 0;

   cout << "Enter an integer (9999 to end): ";
   cin >> value;

   while (value != 9999) {
      total += value;
      ++count;
      cout << "Enter next integer (9999 to end): ";
      cin >> value;
   }

   if (count != 0)
      cout << endl << "The average is: "
           << (float) total / count << endl;
   else
      cout << endl << "No values were entered." << endl;

   return 0;
}
```

```
Enter an integer (9999 to end): 5
Enter next integer (9999 to end): 8
Enter next integer (9999 to end): 3
Enter next integer (9999 to end): 2
Enter next integer (9999 to end): 1
Enter next integer (9999 to end): 8
Enter next integer (9999 to end): 7
Enter next integer (9999 to end): 9
Enter next integer (9999 to end): 9999
The average is: 5.375
```

2.42   What does the following program do?

```
#include <iostream.h>

main()
{
   int x, y;

   cout << "Enter two integers in the range 1-20: ";
   cin >> x >> y;

   for (int i = 1; i <= y; i++) {

      for (int j = 1; j <= x; j++)
         cout << '@';

      cout << endl;
   }

   return 0;
}
```

ANS:

```
Enter two integers in the range 1-20: 3 4
@@@
@@@
@@@
@@@
```

2.43   Write a program that finds the smallest of several integers. Assume that the first value read specifies the number of values remaining.

ANS:

```
// Exercise 2.43 Solution
#include <iostream.h>

main()
{
   int number, value, smallest;

   cout << "Enter the number of integers to be processed: ";
   cin >> number;

   cout << "Enter an integer: ";
   cin >> smallest;

   for (int i = 2; i <= number; i++) {
      cout << "Enter next integer: ";
      cin >> value;

      if (value < smallest)
         smallest = value;
   }

   cout << endl << "The smallest integer is: " << smallest << endl;

   return 0;
}
```

```
Enter the number of integers to be processed: 6
Enter an integer: 8
Enter next integer: 27
Enter next integer: 81
Enter next integer: 2
Enter next integer: 3
Enter next integer: 11
The smallest integer is: 2
```

2.44 Write a program that calculates and prints the product of the odd integers from 1 to 15.
ANS:

```
// Exercise 2.44 Solution
#include <iostream.h>

main()
{
   long product = 1;

   for (long i = 3; i <= 15; i += 2)
      product *= i;

   cout << "Product of the odd integers from 1 to 15 is: "
        << product << endl;

   return 0;
}
```

```
Product of the odd integers from 1 to 15 is: 2027025
```

2.45 The *factorial* function is used frequently in probability problems. The factorial of a positive integer *n* (written *n!* and pronounced "n factorial") is equal to the product of the positive integers from 1 to *n*. Write a program that evaluates the factorials of the integers from 1 to 5. Print the results in tabular format. What difficulty might prevent you from calculating the factorial of 20?

ANS:

```
// Exercise 2.45 Solution
#include <iostream.h>

main()
{
   int factorial;

   cout << "X\tFactorial of X\n";

   for (int i = 1; i <= 5; i++) {
      factorial = 1;

      for (int j = 1; j <= i; j++)
         factorial *= j;

      cout << i << '\t' << factorial << endl;
   }

   return 0;
}
```

```
X    Factorial of X
1    1
2    2
3    6
4    24
5    120
```

2.46   Modify the compound interest program of Section 2.15 to repeat its steps for interest rates of 5 percent, 6 percent, 7 percent, 8 percent, 9 percent, and 10 percent. Use a **for** loop to vary the interest rate.

ANS:

```cpp
// Exercise 2.46 Solution
#include <iostream.h>
#include <iomanip.h>
#include <math.h>

main()
{
   double amount, principal = 1000.0;

   cout.setf(ios::fixed | ios::showpoint);

   for (int rate = 5; rate <= 10; rate++) {
      cout << "Interest Rate: " << setprecision(2) << rate / 100.0
           << endl << "Year\tAmount on deposit" << endl;

      for (int year = 1; year <= 10; year++) {
         amount = principal * pow(1 + (rate / 100.0), year);
         cout << year << '\t' << setprecision(2) << amount << endl;
      }

      cout << endl;
   }

   return 0;
}
```

```
Interest Rate: 0.05
Year   Amount on deposit
1    1050.00
2    1102.50
3    1157.63
...
10 1628.89

Interest Rate: 0.06
Year   Amount on deposit
1    1060.00
2    1123.60
3    1191.02
...
Interest Rate: 0.10
Year   Amount on deposit
1    1100.00
2    1210.00
3    1331.00
...
9    2357.95
10 2593.74
```

2.47   Write a program that prints the following patterns separately one below the other. Use **for** loops to generate the patterns. All asterisks (*) should be printed by a single statement of the form **cout << '*';** (this causes the asterisks to print side by side). Hint: The last two patterns require that each line begin with an appropriate number of blanks. Extra credit: Combine your code from the four separate problems into a single program that prints all four patterns side by side making clever use of nested **for** loops.

```
(A)             (B)              (C)              (D)
*               *********        **********               *
**              ********         *********                **
***             *******          ********                ***
****            ******           *******                ****
*****           *****            ******                *****
******          ****             *****                ******
*******         ***              ****                *******
********         **               ***               ********
*********         *               **               *********
**********                        *              **********
```

ANS:
```cpp
// Exercise 2.47 Solution
#include <iostream.h>

main()
{
   // Pattern A
   for (int row = 1; row <= 10; row++) {

      for (int col = 1; col <= row; col++)
         cout << '*';

      cout << endl;
   }

   cout << endl;

   // Pattern B
   for (row = 10; row >= 1; row--) {

      for (int col = 1; col <= row; col++)
         cout << '*';

      cout << endl;
   }

   cout << endl;

   // Pattern C
   for (row = 10; row >= 1; row--) {

      for (int space = 1; space <= 10 - row; space++)
         cout << ' ';

      for (int col = 1; col <= row; col++)
         cout << '*';

      cout << endl;
   }

   cout << endl;
```

```
                    // Pattern D
                    for (row = 1; row <= 10; row++) {

                        for (int space = 1; space <= 10 - row; space++)
                            cout << ' ';

                        for (int col = 1; col <= row; col++)
                            cout << '*';

                        cout << endl;
                    }

                    cout << endl;
                    return 0;
                }
```

2.48 One interesting application of computers is drawing graphs and bar charts (sometimes called "histograms"). Write a program that reads five numbers (each between 1 and 30). For each number read, your program should print a line containing that number of adjacent asterisks. For example, if your program reads the number seven, it should print *******.

ANS:
```
// Exercise 2.48 Solution
#include <iostream.h>

main()
{
    int number;

    cout << "Enter 5 numbers between 1 and 30: ";

    for (int i = 1; i <= 5; i++) {
        cin >> number;

        for (int j = 1; j <= number; j++)
            cout << '*';

        cout << endl;
    }

    return 0;
}
```

```
Enter 5 numbers between 1 and 30: 7 4 6 2 15
*******
****
******
**
***************
```

2.49 A mail order house sells five different products whose retail prices are product 1 — $2.98, product 2—$4.50, product 3—$9.98, product 4—$4.49, and product 5—$6.87. Write a program that reads a series of pairs of numbers as follows:

    1. Product number

    2. Quantity sold for one day

Your program should use a **switch** statement to help determine the retail price for each product. Your program should calculate and display the total retail value of all products sold last week.

ANS:

```cpp
// Exercise 2.49 Solution
#include <iostream.h>
#include <iomanip.h>

main()
{
    int product, quantity;
    float total = 0.0;

    cout << "Enter pairs of item numbers and quantities." << endl
         << "Enter -1 for the item number to end input: ";
    cin >> product;

    while (product != -1) {
        cin >> quantity;

        switch (product) {
            case 1:
                total += quantity * 2.98;
                break;
            case 2:
                total += quantity * 4.50;
                break;
            case 3:
                total += quantity * 9.98;
                break;
            case 4:
                total += quantity * 4.49;
                break;
            case 5:
                total += quantity * 6.87;
                break;
            default:
                cout << "Invalid product code: " << product << endl
                     << "               Quantity: " << quantity << endl;
                break;
        }

        cout << "Enter pairs of item numbers and quantities." << endl
             << "Enter -1 for the item number to end input: ";
        cin >> product;
    }

    cout.setf(ios::fixed | ios::showpoint);
    cout << "The total retail value was: " << setprecision(2)
         << total << endl;

    return 0;
}
```

```
Enter pairs of item numbers and quantities.
Enter -1 for the item number to end input: 2 4
Enter pairs of item numbers and quantities.
Enter -1 for the item number to end input: 1 5
Enter pairs of item numbers and quantities.
Enter -1 for the item number to end input: 3 7
Enter pairs of item numbers and quantities.
Enter -1 for the item number to end input: 4 8
Enter pairs of item numbers and quantities.
Enter -1 for the item number to end input: -1
The total retail value was: 138.68
```

2.50   Modify the program of Fig. 2.22 so that it calculates the grade point average for the class. A grade of 'A' is worth 4 points, 'B' is worth 3 points, etc.

ANS:

```
// Exercise 2.50 Solution

#include <iostream.h>
#include <iomanip.h>

main()
{
   int grade, gradeTotal = 0, gradeCount, aCount = 0,
      bCount = 0, cCount = 0, dCount = 0, fCount = 0;

   cout << "Enter the letter grades." << endl
      << "Enter the EOF character to end input." << endl;

   while ( ( grade = cin.get() ) != EOF ) {

      switch (grade) {
         case 'A': case 'a':
            gradeTotal += 4;
            ++aCount;
            break;
         case 'B': case 'b':
            gradeTotal += 3;
            ++bCount;
            break;
         case 'C': case 'c':
            gradeTotal += 2;
            ++cCount;
            break;
         case 'D': case 'd':
            gradeTotal += 1;
            ++dCount;
            break;
         case 'F': case 'f':
            ++fCount;
            break;
         case ' ': case '\n':
            break;
         default:
            cout << "Incorrect letter grade entered."
               << " Enter a new grade." << endl;
            break;
      }
   }

   gradeCount = aCount + bCount + cCount + dCount + fCount;
   cout.setf(ios::fixed | ios::showpoint);


   // check that at least one grade was entered
   if (gradeCount != 0)
      cout << endl << "The class average is: " << setprecision(1)
         << (float) gradeTotal / gradeCount << endl;


   return 0;
}
```

```
Enter the letter grades.
Enter the EOF character to end input.
a
v
Incorrect letter grade entered. Enter a new grade.
b
c
d
f
^Z
The class average is: 2.0
```

2.51   Modify the program in Fig. 2.21 so that it uses only integers to calculate the compound interest. (Hint: Treat all monetary amounts as integral numbers of pennies. Then "break" the result into its dollar portion and cents portion by using the division and modulus operations respectively. Insert a period.)

ANS:
```
// Exercise 2.51 Solution
#include <iostream.h>
#include <iomanip.h>
#include <math.h>

main()
{
   int amount, principal = 1000, dollars, cents;
   double rate = .05;

   cout << "Year" << setw(24) << "Amount on deposit" << endl;

   for (int year = 1; year <= 10; year++) {
      amount = principal * pow(1.0 + rate, year);
      cents = amount % 100;
      dollars = amount;  // assignment truncates decimal places
      cout << setw(4) << year << setw(21) << dollars << '.';

      if (cents < 10)
         cout << '0' << cents << endl;
      else
         cout << cents << endl;
   }

   return 0;
}
```

```
Year          Amount on deposit
   1                  1050.50
   2                  1102.02
   3                  1157.57
   4                  1215.15
   5                  1276.76
   6                  1340.40
   7                  1407.07
   8                  1477.77
   9                  1551.51
  10                  1628.28
```

2.52   Assume i = 1, j = 2, k = 3, and m = 2. What does each of the following statements print? Are the parentheses necessary in each case?

a) `cout << (i == 1) << endl;`
ANS: 1

b) cout << (j == 3) << endl;
ANS: 0
c) cout << (i >= 1 && j < 4) << endl;
ANS: 1
d) cout << (m <= 99 && k < m) << endl;
ANS: 0
e) cout << (j >= i || k == m) << endl;
ANS: 1
f) cout << (k + m < j || 3 - j >= k) << endl;
ANS: 0
g) cout << (!m) << endl;
ANS: 0
h) cout << (!(j - m)) << endl;
ANS: 1
i) cout << (!(k > m)) << endl;
ANS: 0

2.53   Write a program that prints a table of the binary, octal, and hexadecimal equivalents of the decimal numbers in the range 1 through 256. If you are not familiar with these number systems, read Appendix E first.
ANS:

```cpp
// Exercise 2.53 Solution
// The oct, hex, and dec identifiers are stream manipulators
// like endl that are defined in Chapter 11. The manipulator
// oct causes integers to be output in octal, the manipulator
// hex causes integers to be output in hexadecimal, and the manipulator
// dec causes integers to be output in decimal.
#include <iostream.h>

main()
{
    int number, temp;

    cout << "Decimal\t\tBinary\t\t\tOctal\tHexadecimal" << endl;

    for (int loop = 1; loop <= 256; loop++) {
        cout << dec << loop << "\t\t";

        // Output binary number
        number = loop;
        cout << (number == 256 ? '1' : '0');

        cout << (number < 256 && number >= 128 ? '1' : '0');
        number %= 128;

        cout << (number < 128 && number >= 64 ? '1' : '0');
        number %= 64;

        cout << (number < 64 && number >= 32 ? '1' : '0');
        number %= 32;

        cout << (number < 32 && number >= 16 ? '1' : '0');
        number %= 16;

        cout << (number < 16 && number >= 8 ? '1' : '0');
        number %= 8;

        cout << (number < 8 && number >= 4 ? '1' : '0');
        number %= 4;

        cout << (number < 4 && number >= 2 ? '1' : '0');
        number %= 2;

        cout << (number == 1 ? '1' : '0') << '\t';
```

```
        // Output octal and hexadecimal numbers
        cout << '\t' << oct << loop << '\t' << hex << loop << endl;
    }

    return 0;
}
```

```
Decimal    Binary                    Octal    Hexadecimal
1          000000001                 1        1
2          000000010                 2        2
3          000000011                 3        3
4          000000100                 4        4
5          000000101                 5        5
6          000000110                 6        6
7          000000111                 7        7
8          000001000                 10       8
9          000001001                 11       9
10         000001010                 12       a
11         000001011                 13       b
12         000001100                 14       c
13         000001101                 15       d
14         000001110                 16       e
15         000001111                 17       f
16         000010000                 20       10
...
249        011111001                 371      f9
250        011111010                 372      fa
251        011111011                 373      fb
252        011111100                 374      fc
253        011111101                 375      fd
254        011111110                 376      fe
255        011111111                 377      ff
256        100000000                 400      100
```

2.54   Calculate the value of _ from the infinite series

$$\pi = 4 - \frac{4}{3} + \frac{4}{5} - \frac{4}{7} + \frac{4}{9} - \frac{4}{11} + \dots$$

Print a table that shows the value of π approximated by 1 term of this series, by two terms, by three terms, etc. How many terms of this series do you have to use before you first get 3.14? 3.141? 3.1415? 3.14159?

ANS:
```
// Exercise 2.54 Solution

#include <iostream.h>
#include <iomanip.h>

main()
{
    long double pi = 0.0, num = 4.0, denom = 1.0;
    long accuracy = 400000;    // set decimal accuracy

    cout.setf(ios::fixed | ios::showpoint);
    cout << "Accuracy set at: " << accuracy << endl
        << "term\t\t  pi" << endl;

    for (long loop = 1; loop <= accuracy; loop++) {

        if (loop % 2 != 0)
            pi += num / denom;
        else
            pi -= num / denom;
```

```
            cout << loop << "\t\t" << setprecision(8) << pi << endl;
            denom += 2.0;
        }

        return 0;
    }
```

```
Accuracy set at: 400000
term      pi
1         4.00000000
2         2.66666667
3         3.46666667
4         2.89523810
5         3.33968254
6         2.97604618
7         3.28373848
8         3.01707182
9         3.25236593
10        3.04183962
11        3.23231581
12        3.05840277
...
376138    3.14158999
376139    3.14159531
376140    3.14159000
376141    3.14159531
376142    3.14159000
376143    3.14159531
376144    3.14159000
...
```

2.55   *(Pythagorean Triples)* A right triangle can have sides that are all integers. The set of three integer values for the sides of a right triangle is called a Pythagorean triple. These three sides must satisfy the relationship that the sum of the squares of two of the sides is equal to the square of the hypotenuse. Find all Pythagorean triples for **side1**, **side2**, and the **hypotenuse** all no larger than 500. Use a triple-nested **for**-loop that tries all possibilities. This is an example of "brute force" computing. You will learn in more advanced computer science courses that there are large numbers of interesting problems for which there is no known algorithmic approach other than using sheer brute force.

ANS:

```
// Exercise 2.55 Solution
#include<iostream.h>

main()
{
    int count = 0;
    long int hyptSquared, sidesSquared;

    for (long side1 = 1; side1 <= 500; side1++) {

        for (long side2 = 1; side2 <= 500; side2++) {

            for (long hypt = 1; hypt <= 500; hypt++) {
                hyptSquared = hypt * hypt;
                sidesSquared = side1 * side1 + side2 * side2;

                if (hyptSquared == sidesSquared) {
                    cout << side1 << '\t' << side2 << '\t'
                        << hypt << endl;
                    ++count;
                }
            }
        }
    }
}
```

```
    cout << "A total of " << count << " triples were found." << endl;
    return 0;
}
```

```
3       4       5
4       3       5
5       12      13
6       8       10
7       24      25
8       6       10
8       15      17
9       12      15
...
475     132     493
476     93      485
480     31      481
480     88      488
480     108     492
480     140     500
483     44      485
A total of 772 triples were found.
```

2.56   A company pays its employees as managers (who receive a fixed weekly salary), hourly workers (who receive a fixed hourly wage for up to the first 40 hours they work and "time-and-a-half," i.e., 1.5 times their hourly wage, for overtime hours worked), commission workers (who receive a $250 plus 5.7% of their gross weekly sales), or pieceworkers (who receive a fixed amount of money per item for each of the items they produce—each pieceworker in this company works on only one type of item). Write a program to compute the weekly pay for each employee. You do not know the number of employees in advance. Each type of employee has its own pay code: Managers have paycode 1, hourly workers have code 2, commission workers have code 3 and pieceworkers have code 4. Use a **switch** to compute each employee's pay based on that employee's paycode. Within the **switch**, prompt the user (i.e., the payroll clerk) to enter the appropriate facts your program needs to calculate each employee's pay based on that employee's paycode.

ANS:

```
// Exercise 2.56 Solution
#include<iostream.h>
#include<iomanip.h>

main()
{
    int payCode, managers = 0, hWorkers = 0, cWorkers = 0;
    int pWorkers = 0, pieces;
    float mSalary, hSalary, cSalary, pSalary, hours;
    float otPay, otHours, pay;

    cout << "Enter paycode (-1 to end): ";
    cin >> payCode;

    cout.setf(ios::fixed | ios::showpoint);

    while (payCode != -1) {

        switch (payCode) {

            case 1:
                cout << "Manager selected." << endl
                     << "Enter weekly salary: ";
                cin >> mSalary;
                cout << "The manager's pay is $ "
                     << setprecision(2) << mSalary;
                ++managers;
                break;
```

```
            case 2:
                cout << "Hourly worker selected." << endl
                     << "Enter the hourly salary: ";
                cin >> hSalary;
                cout << "Enter the total hours worked: ";
                cin >> hours;

                pay = hours > 40.0 ? (hours - 40) * 1.5 * hSalary + hSalary *
                                          40.0 : hSalary * hours;

                cout << "Worker's pay is $ " << setprecision(2) << pay << endl;
                ++hWorkers;
                break;
            case 3:
                cout << "Commission worker selected." << endl
                     << "Enter gross weekly sales: ";
                cin >> cSalary;
                pay = 250.0 + 0.057 * cSalary;
                cout << "Commission Worker's pay is $ " << setprecision(2)
                     << pay << endl;
                ++cWorkers;
                break;
            case 4:
                cout << "Piece worker selected." << endl
                     << "Enter number of pieces: ";
                cin >> pieces;
                cout << "Enter wage per piece: ";
                cin >> pSalary;
                pay = pieces * pSalary;
                cout << "Piece Worker's pay is $ " << setprecision(2)
                     << pay << endl;
                ++pWorkers;
                break;
            default:
                cout << "Invalid pay code." << endl;
                break;
        }

        cout << "\nEnter paycode (-1 to end): ";
        cin >> payCode;
    }

    cout << "\n\nTotal number of managers paid        : "
         << managers
         << "\nTotal number of hourly workers paid   : "
         << hWorkers
         << "\nTotal number of commission workers paid: "
         << cWorkers
         << "\nTotal number of piece workers paid    : "
         << pWorkers << endl;

    return 0;
}
```

```
Enter paycode (-1 to end): 1
Manager selected.
Enter weekly salary: 5000
The manager's pay is $ 5000

Enter paycode (-1 to end): 2
Hourly worker selected.
```
continued

```
                                                              continued

    Enter the hourly salary: 8
    Enter the total hours worked: 40
    Worker's pay is $ 320.00

    Enter paycode (-1 to end): 3
    Commission worker selected.
    Enter gross weekly sales: 6000
    Commission Worker's pay is $ 592.00

    Enter paycode (-1 to end): 4
    Piece worker selected.
    Enter number of pieces: 500
    Enter wage per piece: 2
    Piece Worker's pay is $ 1000.00

    Enter paycode (-1 to end): -1

    Total number of managers paid          : 1
    Total number of hourly workers paid    : 1
    Total number of commission workers paid: 1
    Total number of piece workers paid     : 1
```

2.57   *(De Morgan's Laws)* In this chapter, we discussed the logical operators **&&**, **||**, and **!**. De Morgan's Laws can sometimes make it more convenient for us to express a logical expression. These laws state that the expression **!** (*condition1* **&&** *condition2*) is logically equivalent to the expression (**!***condition1* **||** **!***condition2*). Also, the expression **!** (*condition1* **||** *condition2*) is logically equivalent to the expression (**!***condition1* **&&** **!***condition2*). Use De Morgan's Laws to write equivalent expressions for each of the following, and then write a program to show that both the original expression and the new expression in each case are equivalent:

   a) !(x < 5) && !(y >= 7)
   b) !(a == b) || !(g != 5)
   c) !((x <= 8) && (y > 4))
   d) !((i > 4) || (j <= 6))

ANS:
```cpp
// Exercise 2.57 Solution
#include<iostream.h>

main()
{
   int x = 10, y = 1, a = 3, b = 3,
      g = 5, Y = 1, i = 2, j = 9;

   cout << "current variable values are:" << endl
        << "x = " << x << ", y = " << y << ", a = " << a
        << ", b = " << b << endl << "g = " << g << ", Y = "
        << Y << ", i = " << i << ", j = " << j << endl << endl;

   if ((!(x < 5) && !(y >= 7)) && (!((x < 5) || (y >= 7))))
      cout << "!(x < 5) && !(y >= 7) is equivalent to"
           << " !((x < 5) || (y >= 7))" << endl;
   else
      cout << "!(x < 5) && !(y >= 7) is not equivalent to"
           << " !((x < 5) || (y >= 7))" << endl;

   if ((!(a == b) || !(g != 5)) && (!((a == b) && (g != 5))))
      cout << "!(a == b) || !(g != 5) is equivalent to"
           << " !((a == b) && (g != 5))" << endl;
   else
      cout << "!(a == b) || !(g != 5) is not equivalent to"
           << " !((a == b) && (g != 5))" << endl;
```

```
if (!((x <= 8) && (Y > 4)) && (!((x <= 8) || (Y > 4))))
   cout << "!((x <= 8) && (Y > 4)) is equivalent to"
        << " !((x <= 8) || (Y > 4))" << endl;
else
   cout << "!((x <= 8) && (Y > 4)) is not equivalent to"
        << " !((x <= 8) || (Y > 4))" << endl;

if (!((i > 4) || (j <= 6)) && !((i > 4) && (j <= 6)))
   cout << "!((i > 4) || (j <= 6)) is equivalent to"
        << " !((i > 4) && (j <= 6))" << endl;
else
   cout << "!((i > 4) || (j <= 6)) is not equivalent to"
        << " !((i > 4) && (j <= 6))" << endl;

   return 0;
}
```

```
current variable values are:
x = 10, y = 1, a = 3, b = 3
g = 5, Y = 1, i = 2, j = 9

!(x < 5) && !(y >= 7) is equivalent to !((x < 5) || (y >= 7))
!(a == b) || !(g != 5) is equivalent to !((a == b) && (g != 5))
!((x <= 8) && (Y > 4)) is equivalent to !((x <= 8) || (Y > 4))
!((i > 4) || (j <= 6)) is equivalent to !((i > 4) && (j <= 6))
```

2.58 Write a program that prints the following diamond shape. You may use output statements that print either a single asterisk (*) or a single blank. Maximize your use of repetition (with nested **for** structures) and minimize the number of output statements.

```
    *
   ***
  *****
 *******
*********
 *******
  *****
   ***
    *
```

ANS:
```
// Exercise 2.58 Solution
#include <iostream.h>

main()
{
   // top half
   for (int row = 1; row <= 5; row++) {

      for (int space = 1; space <= 5 - row; space++)
         cout << ' ';

      for (int asterisk = 1; asterisk <= 2 * row - 1; asterisk++)
         cout << '*';

      cout << endl;
   }
```

```
      // bottom half
      for (row = 4; row >= 1; row--) {

         for (int space = 1; space <= 5 - row; space++)
            cout << ' ';

         for (int asterisk = 1; asterisk <= 2 * row - 1; asterisk++)
            cout << '*';

         cout << endl;
      }

      return 0;
}
```

2.59   Modify the program you wrote in Exercise 2.58 to read an odd number in the range 1 to 19 to specify the number of rows in the diamond. Your program should then display a diamond of the appropriate size.

ANS:
```
// Exercise 2.59 Solution
#include <iostream.h>

main()
{
   int size;

   cout << "Enter an odd number for the diamond size (1-19): " << endl;
   cin >> size;

   // top half
   for (int rows = 1; rows <= size -  2; rows += 2) {

      for (int space = (size - rows) / 2; space > 0; space--)
         cout << ' ';

      for (int asterisk = 1; asterisk <= rows; asterisk++)
         cout << '*';

      cout << endl;
   }

   // bottom half
   for (rows = size; rows >= 0; rows -= 2) {

      for (int space = (size - rows) / 2; space > 0; space--)
         cout << ' ';

      for (int asterisk = 1; asterisk <= rows; asterisk++)
         cout << '*';

      cout << endl;
   }

   return 0;
}
```

```
Enter an odd number for the diamond size (1-19): 13
            *
           ***
          *****
         *******
        *********
       ***********
      *************
       ***********
        *********
         *******
          *****
           ***
            *
```

2.60 A criticism of the **break** statement and the **continue** statement is that each is unstructured. Actually **break** statements and **continue** statements can always be replaced by structured statements, although doing so can be awkward. Describe in general how you would remove any **break** statement from a loop in a program and replace that statement with some structured equivalent. (Hint: The **break** statement leaves a loop from within the body of the loop. The other way to leave is by failing the loop-continuation test. Consider using in the loop-continuation test a second test that indicates "early exit because of a 'break' condition.") Use the technique you developed here to remove the break statement from the program of Fig. 2.26.

ANS:

```cpp
// Exercise 2.60 Solution
#include <iostream.h>

main()
{
   int breakOut = 1;

   for (int x = 1; x <= 10 && breakOut == 1; x++) {

      if (x == 4)
         breakOut = -1;

      cout << x << ' ';
   }

   cout << endl << "Broke out of loop at x = " << x << endl;
   return 0;
}
```

```
1 2 3 4
Broke out of loop at x = 5
```

2.61 What does the following program segment do?

```cpp
for (i = 1; i <= 5; i++) {

   for (j = 1; j <= 3; j++) {

      for (k = 1, k <= 4; k++)
         cout << '*';

      cout << endl;
   }

   cout << endl;
}
```

ANS:

```
    ****
    ****
    ****

    ****
    ****
    ****

    ****
    ****
    ****

    ****
    ****
    ****

    ****
    ****
    ****
```

2.62   Describe in general how you would remove any **continue** statement from a loop in a program and replace that statement with some structured equivalent. Use the technique you developed here to remove the **continue** statement from the program of Fig. 2.27.

ANS:

```
// Exercise 2.62 Solution
#include <iostream.h>

main()
{
   for (int x = 1; x <= 10; x++) {

      if (x == 5)
         ++x;

      cout << x << ' ';
   }

   cout << endl << "Used ++x to skip printing the value 5" << endl;

   return 0;
}
```

```
 1 2 3 4 6 7 8 9 10
Used ++x to skip printing the value 5
```

2.63   *("The Twelve Days of Christmas" Song)* Write a program that uses repetition and **switch** structures to print the song "The Twelve Days of Christmas." One **switch** structure should be used to print the day (i.e., "First," "Second," etc.). A separate **switch** structure should be used to print the remainder of each verse.

ANS:

```
// Exercise 2.63 Solution

#include <iostream.h>

main()
{
   for (int day = 1; day < 13; day++) {
      cout << "On the ";
```

```
switch (day) {         // switch for current day
   case 1:
      cout << "first";
      break;
   case 2:
      cout << "second";
      break;
   case 3:
      cout << "third";
      break;
   case 4:
      cout << "fourth";
      break;
   case 5:
      cout << "fifth";
      break;
   case 6:
      cout << "sixth";
      break;
   case 7:
      cout << "seventh";
      break;
   case 8:
      cout << "eighth";
      break;
   case 9:
      cout << "ninth";
      break;
   case 10:
      cout << "tenth";
      break;
   case 11:
      cout << "eleventh";
      break;
   case 12:
      cout << "twelfth";
      break;
}

cout << " day of Christmas,\nMy true love sent to me:" << endl;

switch (day) {      // switch for gifts
   case 12:
      cout << "\tTwelve drummers drumming," << endl;
   case 11:
      cout << "\tEleven pipers piping," << endl;
   case 10:
      cout << "\tTen lords a-leaping," << endl;
   case 9:
      cout << "\tNine ladies dancing," << endl;
   case 8:
      cout << "\tEight maids a-milking," << endl;
   case 7:
      cout << "\tSeven swans a-swimming," << endl;
   case 6:
      cout << "\tSix geese a-laying," << endl;
   case 5:
      cout << "\tFive golden rings," << endl;
   case 4:
      cout << "\tFour calling birds," << endl;
   case 3:
      cout << "\tThree French hens," << endl;
   case 2:
      cout << "\tTwo turtle doves, and" << endl;
```

```
            case 1:
               cout << "A partridge in a pear tree." << endl << endl
                       << endl;
         }
      }

      return 0;
}
```

```
On the first day of Christmas,
My true love sent to me:
A partridge in a pear tree.


On the second day of Christmas,
My true love sent to me:
    Two turtle doves, and
A partridge in a pear tree.


On the third day of Christmas,
My true love sent to me:
    Three French hens,
    Two turtle doves, and
A partridge in a pear tree.
...
On the twelfth day of Christmas,
My true love sent to me:
    Twelve drummers drumming,
    Eleven pipers piping,
    Ten lords a-leaping,
    Nine ladies dancing,
    Eight maids a-milking,
    Seven swans a-swimming,
    Six geese a-laying,
    Five golden rings,
    Four calling birds,
    Three French hens,
    Two turtle doves, and
A partridge in a pear tree.
```

Exercise 2.64 corresponds to Section 2.22, "Thinking About Objects."

2.64   Describe in 200 words or less what an automobile is and does. List the nouns and verbs separately. In the text, we stated that each noun may correspond to an object that will need to be built to implement a system, in this case a car. Pick five of the objects you listed and for each list several attributes and several behaviors. Describe briefly how these objects interact with one another and other objects in your description. You have just performed several of the key steps in a typical object-oriented design.

ANS:

A specific type of vehicle containing: 4 wheels, doors, seats, windows, steering wheel, brakes, radio, engine, exhaust system, etc.

A car can accelerate, decelerate, turn, move forward, move backward, stop, etc.

Wheels:
Attributes: size, type.
Behaviors: rotate forward, rotate backward.

Doors:
Attributes: type (passenger, trunk), open or closed.
Behaviors: open, close.

Steering wheel:
Attributes: adjustable.
Behaviors: turn left, turn right, adjust up, adjust down.

Brakes:
Attributes: pressed or not pressed, how hard are they pressed.
Behaviors: press, antilock.

Engine:
Attributes: cylinders, radiator, timing belts, spark plugs, etc.
Behaviors: accelerate, decelerate, turn on, turn off.

Interactions:
Person turns the steering wheel which causes the wheels to turn in the appropriate direction.
Person depresses the accelerator pedal which causes the engine revolutions per minute to increase which causes the wheels to rotate faster.
Person opens door. Person closes door.
Person releases accelerator pedal which causes engine RPMs to decrease which causes wheels to rotate slower.
Person presses brake pedal which causes brakes to be applied to wheels which slows rotation of the wheels.

3

Functions: Solutions

Exercises

3.11 Show the value of x after each of the following statements is performed:

a) `x = fabs(7.5)`
ANS: 7.5

b) `x = floor(7.5)`
ANS: 7.0

c) `x = fabs(0.0)`
ANS: 0.0

d) `x = ceil(0.0)`
ANS: 0.0

e) `x = fabs(-6.4)`
ANS: 6.4

f) `x = ceil(-6.4)`
ANS: -6.0

g) `x = ceil(-fabs(-8 + floor(-5.5)))`
ANS: -14.0

3.12 A parking garage charges a $2.00 minimum fee to park for up to three hours. The garage charges an additional $0.50 per hour for each hour *or part thereof* in excess of three hours. The maximum charge for any given 24-hour period is $10.00. Assume that no car parks for longer than 24 hours at a time. Write a program that will calculate and print the parking charges for each of 3 customers who parked their cars in this garage yesterday. You should enter the hours parked for each customer. Your program should print the results in a neat tabular format, and should calculate and print the total of yesterday's receipts. The program should use the function `calculateCharges` to determine the charge for each customer. Your outputs should appear in the following format:

Car	Hours	Charge
1	1.5	2.00
2	4.0	2.50
3	24.0	10.00
TOTAL	29.5	14.50

ANS:
```
// Exercise 3.12 Solution
#include <iostream.h>
#include <iomanip.h>
#include <math.h>

float calculateCharges(float);

main()
{
    float hour, currentCharge, totalCharges = 0.0, totalHours = 0.0;
    int first = 1;
```

```
     cout << "Enter the hours parked for 3 cars: ";

  for (int i = 1; i <= 3; i++) {
     cin >> hour;
     totalHours += hour;

     if (first) {
        cout << setw(5) << "Car" << setw(15) << "Hours"
             << setw(15) << "Charge" << endl;
        first = 0;    // prevents this from printing again
     }

     totalCharges += (currentCharge = calculateCharges(hour));
     cout.setf(ios::fixed | ios::showpoint);
     cout << setw(3) << i << setw(17) << setprecision(1) << hour
          << setw(15) << setprecision(2) << currentCharge << endl;
  }

  cout << setw(7) << "TOTAL" << setw(13) << setprecision(1)
       << totalHours << setw(15) << setprecision(2)
       << totalCharges << endl;

  return 0;
}


float calculateCharges(float hours)
{
   float charge;

   if (hours < 3.0)
      charge = 2.0;
   else if (hours < 19.0)
      charge = 2.0 + .5 * ceil(hours - 3.0);
   else
      charge = 10.0;

   return charge;
}
```

```
Enter the hours parked for 3 cars: 14 5 7
   Car          Hours          Charge
   1            14.0           7.50
   2            5.0            3.00
   3            7.0            4.00
   TOTAL        26.0           14.50
```

3.13   An application of function `floor` is rounding a value to the nearest integer. The statement

```
y = floor(x + .5);
```

will round the number **x** to the nearest integer and assign the result to **y**. Write a program that reads several numbers and uses the preceding statement to round each of these numbers to the nearest integer. For each number processed, print both the original number and the rounded number.

    ANS:

```
// Exercise 3.13 Solution
#include <iostream.h>
#include <iomanip.h>
#include <math.h>

void roundToIntegers(void);
```

```
main()
{
   roundToIntegers();
   return 0;
}

void roundToIntegers(void)
{
   double x, y;

   cout.setf(ios::fixed | ios::showpoint);

   for (int loop = 1; loop <= 5; loop++) {
      cout << "Enter a floating point value: ";
      cin >> x;
      y = floor(x + .5);
      cout << x << " rounded is " << setprecision(1) << y << endl;
   }
}
```

```
Enter a floating point value: 5.5
5.5 rounded is 6.0
Enter a floating point value: -6.2
-6.2 rounded is -6.0
Enter a floating point value: 3.8
3.8 rounded is 4.0
Enter a floating point value: 2.2
2.2 rounded is 2.0
Enter a floating point value: -3.3
-3.3 rounded is -3.0
```

3.14   Function `floor` may be used to round a number to a specific decimal place. The statement

```
y = floor(x * 10 + .5) / 10;
```

rounds **x** to the tenths position (the first position to the right of the decimal point). The statement

```
y = floor(x * 100 + .5) / 100;
```

rounds **x** to the hundredths position (i.e., the second position to the right of the decimal point). Write a program that defines four functions to round a number **x** in various ways:

a) `roundToInteger(number)`
b) `roundToTenths(number)`
c) `roundToHundredths(number)`
d) `roundToThousandths(number)`

For each value read, your program should print the original value, the number rounded to the nearest integer, the number rounded to the nearest tenth, the number rounded to the nearest hundredth, and the number rounded to the nearest thousandth.

ANS:
```
// Exercise 3.14 Solution
#include <iostream.h>
#include <iomanip.h>
#include <math.h>

double roundToInteger(double);
double roundToTenths(double);
double roundToHundreths(double);
double roundToThousandths(double);
```

```
main()
{
    int count;
    double number;
    cout << "How many numbers do you want to process? ";
    cin >> count;

    for (int i = 0; i < count; i++) {
        cout << endl << "Enter number: ";
        cin >> number;
        cout.setf(ios::fixed | ios::showpoint);
        cout << number << " rounded to the nearest integer is:    "
             << setprecision(0) << roundToInteger(number) << endl
             << number << " rounded to the nearest tenth is:      "
             << roundToTenths(number) << endl
             << number << " rounded to the nearest hundredth is:  "
             << roundToHundreths(number) << endl
             << number << " rounded to the nearest thousandth is: "
             << roundToThousandths(number) << endl;
    }

    return 0;
}



double roundToInteger(double n)
{
    return floor(n + .5);
}



double roundToTenths(double n)
{
    return floor(n * 10 + .5) / 10;
}



double roundToHundreths(double n)
{
    return floor(n * 100 + .5) / 100;
}



double roundToThousandths(double n)
{
    return floor(n * 1000 + .5) / 1000;
}
```

```
How many numbers do you want to process? 2

Enter number: 5.6
5.600000 rounded to the nearest integer is:    6.000000
5.600000 rounded to the nearest tenth is:      5.600000
5.600000 rounded to the nearest hundredth is:  5.600000
5.600000 rounded to the nearest thousandth is: 5.600000

Enter number: -2.321343
-2.321343 rounded to the nearest integer is:    -2.000000
-2.321343 rounded to the nearest tenth is:      -2.300000
-2.321343 rounded to the nearest hundredth is:  -2.320000
-2.321343 rounded to the nearest thousandth is: -2.321000
```

3.15   Answer each of the following questions.

  a) What does it mean to choose numbers "at random?"

  ANS: Every number has an equal chance of being chosen at any time.

  b) Why is the **rand** function useful for simulating games of chance?

  ANS: Because it produces a sequence of pseudo random numbers that when scaled appear to be random.

  c) Why would you randomize a program by using **srand**? Under what circumstances is it desirable not to randomize?

  ANS: Using **srand** enables the sequence of pseudo random numbers produced by **rand** to change each time the program is executed. The program should not be randomized while in the debugging stages because repetition is helpful in debugging.

  d) Why is it often necessary to scale and/or shift the values produced by **rand**?

  ANS: To produce random values in a specific range.

  e) Why is computerized simulation of real-world situations a useful technique?

  ANS: It enables more accurate predictions of random events such as cars arriving at toll booths and people arriving in lines at a supermarket. The results of a simulation can help determine how many toll booths to have open or how many cashiers to have open at specified times.

3.16   Write statements that assign random integers to the variable n in the following ranges:

  a) $1 \le n \le 2$

  ANS: n = 1 + rand() % 2;

  b) $1 \le n \le 100$

  ANS: n = 1 + rand() % 100;

  c) $0 \le n \le 9$

  ANS: n = rand() % 10;

  d) $1000 \le n \le 1112$

  ANS: n = 1000 + rand() % 113;

  e) $-1 \le n \le 1$

  ANS: n = -1 + rand() % 3;

  f) $-3 \le n \le 11$

  ANS: n = -3 + rand() % 15;

3.17   For each of the following sets of integers, write a single statement that will print a number at random from the set.

  a) 2, 4, 6, 8, 10.

  ANS: cout << 2 * (1 + rand() % 5)) << endl;

  b) 3, 5, 7, 9, 11.

  ANS: cout << 1 + 2 * (1 + rand() % 5)) << endl;

  c) 6, 10, 14, 18, 22.

  ANS: cout << 6 + 4 * (rand() % 5)) << endl;

3.18   Write a function **integerPower(base, exponent)** that returns the value of

  $$base^{\,exponent}$$

For example, **integerPower(3,4)** = 3 * 3 * 3 * 3. Assume that **exponent** is a positive, nonzero integer, and **base** is an integer. The function **integerPower** should use **for** or **while** to control the calculation. Do not use any math library functions.

  ANS:

```
// Exercise 3.18 Solution
#include <iostream.h>

int integerPower(int, int);

main()
{
   int exp, base;

   cout << "Enter base and exponent: ";
   cin >> base >> exp;

   cout << base << " to the power " << exp << " is: "
        << integerPower(base, exp) << endl;

   return 0;
}
```

```
int integerPower(int b, int e)
{
    int product = 1;

    for (int i = 1; i <= e; i++)
        product *= b;

    return product;
}
```

```
Enter base and exponent: 4 5
4 to the power 5 is 1024
```

3.19 Define a function `hypotenuse` that calculates the length of the hypotenuse of a right triangle when the other two sides are given. Use this function in a program to determine the length of the hypotenuse for each of the following triangles. The function should take two arguments of type **double** and return the hypotenuse as a **double**.

Triangle	Side 1	Side 2
1	3.0	4.0
2	5.0	12.0
3	8.0	15.0

ANS:
```
// Exercise 3.19 Solution
#include <iostream.h>
#include <iomanip.h>
#include <math.h>

double hypotenuse(double, double);

main()
{
    double side1, side2;

    for (int i = 1; i <= 3; i++) {
        cout << endl << "Enter 2 sides of right triangle: ";
        cin >> side1 >> side2;
        cout.setf(ios::fixed | ios::showpoint);
        cout << "Hypotenuse:   " << setprecision(1)
             << hypotenuse(side1, side2) << endl;
    }

    return 0;
}

double hypotenuse(double s1, double s2)
{
    return sqrt(s1 * s1 + s2 * s2);
}
```

```
Enter 2 sides of right triangle: 3 4
Hypotenuse:   5.0

Enter 2 sides of right triangle: 5 12
Hypotenuse:   13.0

Enter 2 sides of right triangle: 8 15
Hypotenuse:   17.0
```

3.20   Write a function `multiple` that determines for a pair of integers whether the second integer is a multiple of the first. The function should take two integer arguments and return **1** (true) if the second is a multiple of the first, and **0** (false) otherwise. Use this function in a program that inputs a series of pairs of integers.

ANS:

```
// Exercise 3.20 Solution
#include <iostream.h>

int multiple(int, int);

main()
{
   int x, y;

   for (int i = 1; i <= 3; i++) {
      cout << "Enter two integers: ";
      cin >> x >> y;

      if (multiple(x, y))
         cout << y << " is a multiple of " << x << endl << endl;
      else
         cout << y << " is not a multiple of " << x << endl << endl;
   }

   return 0;
}

int multiple(int a, int b)
{
   return !(b % a);
}
```

```
Enter two integers: 5 2
2 is not a multiple of 5
```

```
Enter two integers: 25 5
25 is a multiple of 5
```

3.21   Write a program that inputs a series of integers and passes them one at a time to function **even** which uses the modulus operator to determine if an integer is even. The function should take an integer argument and return **1** if the integer is even and **0** otherwise.

ANS:

```
// Exercise 3.21 Solution
#include <iostream.h>

int even(int);

main()
{
   int x;

   for (int i = 1; i <= 3; i++) {
      cout << "Enter an integer: ";
      cin >> x;

      if (even(x))
         cout << x << " is an even integer\n" << endl;
      else
         cout << x << " is an odd integer\n" << endl;
   }

   return 0;
}
```

```
int even(int a)
{
   return !(a % 2);
}
```

```
Enter an integer: 17
17 is an odd integer

Enter an integer: 5
5 is an odd integer

Enter an integer: 100
100 is an even integer
```

3.22 Write a function that displays at the left margin of the screen a solid square of asterisks whose side is specified in integer parameter **side**. For example, if **side** is **4**, the function displays

```
****
****
****
****
```

ANS:
```
// Exercise 3.22 Solution
#include <iostream.h>

void square(int);

main()
{
   int side;

   cout << "Enter side: ";
   cin >> side;
   cout << endl;
   square(side);

   return 0;
}

void square(int s)
{
   for (int row = 1; row <= s; row++) {

      for (int col = 1; col <= s; col++)
         cout << '*';

      cout << endl;
   }
}
```

3.23 Modify the function created in Exercise 3.22 to form the square out of whatever character is contained in character parameter **fillCharacter**. Thus if **side** is **5** and **fillCharacter** is "#" then this function should print

```
#####
#####
#####
#####
#####
```

ANS:
```cpp
// Exercise 3.23 Solution
#include <iostream.h>

void square(int, char);

main()
{
    int s;
    char c;

    cout << "Enter a character and the side length: ";
    cin >> c >> s;
    cout << endl;
    square(s, c);
    return 0;
}

void square(int side, char fillCharacter)
{
    for (int row = 1; row <= side; row++) {

        for (int col = 1; col <= side; col++)
            cout << fillCharacter;

        cout << endl;
    }
}
```

3.24   Use techniques similar to those developed in Exercises 3.22 and 3.23 to produce a program that graphs a wide range of shapes.

3.25   Write program segments that accomplish each of the following:
a) Calculate the integer part of the quotient when integer **a** is divided by integer **b**.
b) Calculate the integer remainder when integer **a** is divided by integer **b**.
c) Use the program pieces developed in a) and b) to write a function that inputs an integer between **1** and **32767** and prints it as a series of digits, each pair of which is separated by two spaces. For example, the integer **4562** should be printed as

```
    4   5   6   2
```

ANS:
```cpp
// Exercise 3.25 Solution
#include <iostream.h>
#include <iomanip.h>

int quotient(int, int);
int remainder(int, int);

main()
{
    int number, divisor = 10000;

    cout << "Enter an integer between 1 and 32767: ";
    cin >> number;
    cout << "The digits in the number are:" << endl;

    while (number >= 1) {
        if (number >= divisor) {
            cout << setw(3) << quotient(number, divisor);
            number = remainder(number, divisor);
            divisor = quotient(divisor, 10);
        }
        else
            divisor = quotient(divisor, 10);
    }

    return 0;
}
```

```
// Part A: determine quotient using integer division
int quotient(int a, int b)
{
   return a / b;
}

// Part B: determine remainder using the modulus operator
int remainder(int a, int b)
{
   return a % b;
}
```

```
Enter an integer between 1 and 32767: 32767
The digits in the number are:
3 2 7 6 7
```

3.26   Write a function that takes the time as three integer arguments (for hours, minutes, and seconds), and returns the number of seconds since the last time the clock "struck 12." Use this function to calculate the amount of time in seconds between two times, both of which are within one 12-hour cycle of the clock.

ANS:

```
// Exercise 3.26 Solution
#include <iostream.h>

unsigned seconds(unsigned, unsigned, unsigned);

main()
{
   unsigned hours, minutes, secs, temp;

   cout << "Enter the first time as three integers: ";
   cin >> hours >> minutes >> secs;

   temp = seconds(hours, minutes, secs);

   cout << "Enter the second time as three integers: ";
   cin >> hours >> minutes >> secs;

   cout << "The difference between the times is "
        << seconds(hours, minutes, secs) - temp << " seconds" << endl;

   return 0;
}

unsigned seconds(unsigned h, unsigned m, unsigned s)
{
   return 3600 * (h >= 12 ? h - 12 : h) + 60 * m + s;
}
```

```
Enter the first time as three integers: 1 30 30
Enter the second time as three integers: 2 30 30
The difference between the times is 3600
```

3.27   Implement the following integer functions:
   a) Function **celsius** returns the Celsius equivalent of a Fahrenheit temperature.
   b) Function **fahrenheit** returns the Fahrenheit equivalent of a Celsius temperature.
   c) Use these functions to write a program that prints charts showing the Fahrenheit equivalents of all Celsius temperatures from 0 to 100 degrees, and the Celsius equivalents of all Fahrenheit temperatures from 32 to 212 degrees. Print the outputs in a neat tabular format that minimizes the number of lines of output while remaining readable.

```
ANS:
// Exercise 3.27 Solution
#include <iostream.h>

int celsius(int);
int fahrenheit(int);

main()
{
   cout << "Fahrenheit equivalents of Celsius temperatures:" << endl
        << "Celsius\t\tFahrenheit" << endl;

   for (int i = 0; i <= 100; i++)
      cout << i << "\t\t" << fahrenheit(i) << endl;

   cout << endl << "Celsius equivalents of Fahrenheit temperatures:"
        << endl << "Fahrenheit\tCelsius" << endl;

   for (i = 32; i <= 212; i++)
      cout << i << "\t\t" << celsius(i) << endl;

   return 0;
}

int celsius(int fTemp)
{
   return (int) (5.0 / 9.0 * (fTemp - 32));
}

int fahrenheit(int cTemp)
{
   return (int) (9.0 / 5.0 * cTemp + 32);
}
```

```
Fahrenheit equivalents of Celsius temperatures:
Celsius     Fahrenheit
0           32
1           33
2           35
3           37
4           39
5           41
6           42
7           44
8           46
.
.
.
Celsius equivalents of Fahrenheit temperatures:
Fahrenheit Celsius
32          0
33          0
34          1
35          1
36          2
37          2
38          3
39          3
40          4
...
```

3.28   Write a function that returns the smallest of three floating-point numbers.

ANS:

```
// Exercise 3.28 Solution
#include <iostream.h>
#include <iomanip.h>

float smallest3(float, float, float);

main()
{
    float x, y, z;

    cout << "Enter three floating point values: ";
    cin >> x >> y >> z;
    cout << "The smallest value is " << smallest3(x, y, z) << endl;
    return 0;
}

float smallest3(float smallest, float b, float c)
{
    if (b < smallest && c > smallest)
        return b;
    else if (c < smallest)
        return c;
    else
        return smallest;
}
```

```
Enter three floating point values: 1.1 2.2 3.3
The smallest value is 1.1
```

```
Enter three floating point values: 2.2 1.1 3.3
The smallest value is 1.1
```

```
Enter three floating point values: 3.3 2.2 1.1
The smallest value is 1.1
```

3.29   An integer number is said to be a *perfect number* if its factors, including 1 (but not the number itself), sum to the number. For example, 6 is a perfect number because $6 = 1 + 2 + 3$. Write a function **perfect** that determines if parameter **number** is a perfect number. Use this function in a program that determines and prints all the perfect numbers between 1 and 1000. Print the factors of each perfect number to confirm that the number is indeed perfect. Challenge the power of your computer by testing numbers much larger than 1000.

ANS:

```
// Exercise 3.29 Solution
#include <iostream.h>

int perfect(int);

main()
{
    cout << "For the integers from 1 to 1000:" << endl;

    for (int j = 2; j <= 1000; j++)
        if (perfect(j))
            cout << j << " is perfect" << endl;

    return 0;
}
```

```
int perfect(int value)
{
   int factorSum = 1;

   for (int i = 2; i <= value / 2; i++)
      if (value % i == 0)
         factorSum += i;

   return factorSum == value ? 1 : 0;
}
```

```
For the integers from 1 to 1000:
6 is perfect
28 is perfect
496 is perfect
```

3.30   An integer is said to be *prime* if it is divisible only by 1 and itself. For example, 2, 3, 5, and 7 are prime, but 4, 6, 8, and 9 are not.

a) Write a function that determines if a number is prime.

b) Use this function in a program that determines and prints all the prime numbers between 1 and 10,000. How many of these 10,000 numbers do you really have to test before being sure that you have found all the primes?

ANS:

```
// Exercise 3.30 Solution
#include <iostream.h>
#include <iomanip.h>

int prime(int);

main()
{
   int number, count = 0;

   cout << "The prime numbers from 1 to 10000 are:" << endl;

   for (int loop = 1; loop <= 10000; loop++)
      if (prime(loop)) {
         ++count;
         cout << setw(6) << loop;

         if (count % 10 == 0)
            cout << endl;
      }

   return 0;
}

int prime(int n)
{
   for (int loop2 = 2; loop2 <= n / 2; loop2++)
      if (n % loop2 == 0)
         return 0;

   return 1;
}
```

```
The prime numbers from 1 to 10000 are:
     1     2     3     5     7    11    13    17    19    23
    29    31    37    41    43    47    53    59    61    67
    71    73    79    83    89    97   101   103   107   109
   113   127   131   137   139   149   151   157   163   167
   173   179   181   191   193   197   199   211   223   227
   ...
  9631  9643  9649  9661  9677  9679  9689  9697  9719  9721
  9733  9739  9743  9749  9767  9769  9781  9787  9791  9803
  9811  9817  9829  9833  9839  9851  9857  9859  9871  9883
  9887  9901  9907  9923  9929  9931  9941  9949  9967  9973
```

c) Initially you might think that *n*/2 is the upper limit for which you must test to see if a number is prime, but you need only go as high as the square root of *n*. Why? Rewrite the program, and run it both ways. Estimate the performance improvement.

ANS:

```
// Exercise 3.30 Part C Solution
#include <iostream.h>
#include <iomanip.h>
#include <math.h>

int prime(int n);

main()
{
    int number, count = 0;

    cout << "The prime numbers from 1 to 10000 are:" << endl;

    for (int j = 1; j <= 10000; j++)
        if (prime(j)) {
            ++count;
            cout << setw(5) << j;

            if (count % 10 == 0)
                cout << endl;
        }

    return 0;
}

int prime(int n)
{
    for (int i = 2; i <= (int) sqrt(n); i++)
        if (n % i == 0)
            return 0;

    return 1;
}
```

```
The prime numbers from 1 to 10000 are:
    1     2     3     5     7    11    13    17    19    23
   29    31    37    41    43    47    53    59    61    67
   71    73    79    83    89    97   101   103   107   109
  113   127   131   137   139   149   151   157   163   167
  173   179   181   191   193   197   199   211   223   227

 9631  9643  9649  9661  9677  9679  9689  9697  9719  9721
 9733  9739  9743  9749  9767  9769  9781  9787  9791  9803
 9811  9817  9829  9833  9839  9851  9857  9859  9871  9883
 9887  9901  9907  9923  9929  9931  9941  9949  9967  9973
```

3.31   Write a function that takes an integer value and returns the number with its digits reversed. For example, given the number 7631, the function should return 1367.

ANS:

```
// Exercise 3.31 Solution
#include <iostream.h>
#include <iomanip.h>

int reverseDigits(int);
int width(int);
```

```
    main()
    {
       int number;

       cout << "Enter a number between 1 and 9999: ";
       cin >> number;

       cout << "The number with its digits reversed is: "
            << setw((width(number))) << setfill('0') << reverseDigits(number)
            << endl;

       return 0;
    }

    int reverseDigits(int n)
    {
       int reverse = 0, divisor = 1000, multiplier = 1;

       while (n > 10) {

          if (n >= divisor) {
             reverse += n / divisor * multiplier;
             n %= divisor;
             divisor /= 10;
             multiplier *= 10;
          }
          else
             divisor /= 10;
       }

       reverse += n * multiplier;
       return reverse;
    }

    int width(int n)
    {
       if (n /= 1000)
          return 4;
       else if (n /= 100)
          return 3;
       else if (n /= 10)
          return 2;
       else
          return 1;
    }
```

```
Enter a number between 1 and 9999: 7631
The number with its digits reversed is: 1367
```

```
Enter a number between 1 and 9999: 8000
The number with its digits reversed is: 0008
```

```
Enter a number between 1 and 9999: 41
The number with its digits reversed is: 14
```

3.32   The *greatest common divisor (GCD)* of two integers is the largest integer that evenly divides each of the two numbers. Write a function **gcd** that returns the greatest common divisor of two integers.

ANS:
```
// Exercise 3.32 Solution
#include <iostream.h>

int gcd(int, int);

main()
{
   int a, b;

   for (int j = 1; j <= 5; j++) {
      cout << "Enter two integers: ";
      cin >> a >> b;

      cout << "The greatest common divisor of " << a << " and "
           << b << " is " << gcd(a, b) << endl << endl;
   }

   return 0;
}

int gcd(int x, int y)
{
   int greatest = 1;

   for (int i = 2; i <= ((x < y) ? x : y); i++)

      if (x % i == 0 && y % i == 0)
         greatest = i;

   return greatest;
}
```

```
Enter two integers: 5555 33
The greatest common divisor of 5555 and 33 is 11

Enter two integers: 12678 56
The greatest common divisor of 12678 and 56 is 2

Enter two integers: 225 125
The greatest common divisor of 225 and 125 is 25

Enter two integers: 64 8
The greatest common divisor of 64 and 8 is 8

Enter two integers: 6433 7
The greatest common divisor of 6433 and 7 is 7
```

3.33   Write a function **qualityPoints** that inputs a student's average and returns 4 if a student's average is 90-100, 3 if the average is 80-89, 2 if the average is 70-79, 1 if the average is 60-69, and 0 if the average is lower than 60.

ANS:
```
// Exercise 3.33 Solution
#include <iostream.h>

int qualityPoints(int);
```

```
main()
{
   int average;

   for (int loop = 1; loop <= 5; loop++) {

      cout << endl << "Enter the student's average: ";
      cin >> average;

      cout << average << " on a 4 point scale is "
           << qualityPoints(average) << endl;
   }

   return 0;
}

int qualityPoints(int average)
{
   if (average >= 90)
      return 4;
   else if (average >= 80)
      return 3;
   else if (average >= 70)
      return 2;
   else if (average >= 60)
      return 1;
   else
      return 0;
}
```

```
Enter the student's average: 99
99 on a 4 point scale is 4

Enter the student's average: 56
56 on a 4 point scale is 0

Enter the student's average: 78
78 on a 4 point scale is 2

Enter the student's average: 82
82 on a 4 point scale is 3

Enter the student's average: 93
93 on a 4 point scale is 4
```

3.34 Write a program that simulates coin tossing. For each toss of the coin the program should print **Heads** or **Tails**. Let the program toss the coin 100 times, and count the number of times each side of the coin appears. Print the results. The program should call a separate function **flip** that takes no arguments and returns **0** for tails and **1** for heads. *Note:* If the program realistically simulates the coin tossing, then each side of the coin should appear approximately half the time.

ANS:
```
// Exercise 3.34 Solution
#include <iostream.h>
#include <stdlib.h>
#include <time.h>

int flip(void);
```

```
main()
{
    int headCount = 0, tailCount = 0;

    srand(time(NULL));

    for (int loop = 1; loop <= 100; loop++) {
        if (flip() == 0) {
            tailCount++;
            cout << "Tails ";
        }
        else {
            headCount++;
            cout << "Heads ";
        }

        if (loop % 10 == 0)
            cout << endl;
    }

    cout << endl << "The total number of Heads was "
         << headCount << endl << "The total number of Tails was "
         << tailCount << endl;

    return 0;
}

int flip(void)
{
    return rand() % 2;
}
```

```
Heads Heads Tails Heads Tails Heads Heads Heads Tails Heads
Heads Heads Tails Tails Tails Heads Tails Tails Tails Tails
Tails Heads Heads Tails Heads Tails Tails Tails Heads Tails
Tails Heads Heads Heads Heads Heads Tails Heads Tails Heads
Tails Heads Heads Heads Tails Heads Heads Tails Tails Tails
Tails Tails Heads Heads Tails Tails Heads Tails Tails Tails
Heads Heads Heads Heads Tails Tails Heads Heads Heads Tails
Tails Tails Tails Tails Tails Tails Heads Tails Heads Tails
Heads Tails Heads Heads Tails Tails Heads Tails Tails Tails
Heads Heads Tails Tails Heads Heads Tails Tails Heads Tails

The total number of Heads was 47
The total number of Tails was 53
```

3.35   Computers are playing an increasing role in education. Write a program that will help an elementary school student learn multiplication. Use **rand** to produce two positive one-digit integers. It should then type a question such as:

```
How much is 6 times 7?
```

The student then types the answer. Your program checks the student's answer. If it is correct, print **"Very good!"** and then ask another multiplication question. If the answer is wrong, print **"No. Please try again."** and then let the student try the same question again repeatedly until the student finally gets it right.

ANS:
```
// Exercise 3.35 Solution
#include <iostream.h>
#include <stdlib.h>
#include <time.h>

void multiplication(void);
```

```
main()
{
   srand(time(NULL));
   multiplication();
   return 0;
}

void multiplication(void)
{
   int x, y, response = 0;

   cout << "Enter -1 to End." << endl;

   while (response != -1) {
      x = rand() % 10;
      y = rand() % 10;

      cout << "How much is " << x << " times " << y << " (-1 to End)? ";
      cin >> response;

      while (response != -1 && response != x * y) {
         cout << "No. Please try again." << endl << "? ";
         cin >> response;
      }

      if (response != -1)
         cout << "Very good!" << endl << endl;
   }

   cout << "That's all for now. Bye." << endl;
}
```

```
Enter -1 to End.
How much is 8 times 8 (-1 to End)? 64
Very Good!

How much is 2 times 7 (-1 to End)? 14
Very Good!

How much is 5 times 5 (-1 to End)? 23
No. Please try again.
? 25
Very Good!

How much is 9 times 4 (-1 to End)? -1
That's all for now. Bye.
```

3.36   The use of computers in education is referred to as *computer-assisted instruction* (CAI). One problem that develops in CAI environments is student fatigue. This can be eliminated by varying the computer's dialogue to hold the student's attention. Modify the program of Exercise 3.35 so the various comments are printed for each correct answer and each incorrect answer as follows:

Responses to a correct answer

```
Very good!
Excellent!
Nice work!
Keep up the good work!
```

Responses to an incorrect answer

```
No. Please try again.
Wrong. Try once more.
Don't give up!
No. Keep trying.
```

Use the random number generator to choose a number from 1 to 4 to select an appropriate response to each answer. Use a **switch** structure to issue the responses.

ANS:
```cpp
// Exercise 3.36 Solution
#include <iostream.h>
#include <stdlib.h>
#include <time.h>

void correctMessage(void);
void incorrectMessage(void);
void multiplication(void);

main()
{
    srand(time(NULL));
    multiplication();

    return 0;
}

void correctMessage(void)
{
    switch (rand() % 4) {
        case 0:
            cout << "Very good!";
            break;
        case 1:
            cout << "Excellent!";
            break;
        case 2:
            cout << "Nice work!";
            break;
        case 3:
            cout << "Keep up the good work!";
            break;
    }

    cout << endl << endl;
}

void incorrectMessage(void)
{
    switch (rand() % 4) {
        case 0:
            cout << "No. Please try again.";
            break;
        case 1:
            cout << "Wrong. Try once more.";
            break;
        case 2:
            cout << "Don't give up!";
            break;
        case 3:
            cout << "No. Keep trying.";
            break;
    }

    cout << endl << "? ";
}
```

```
void multiplication(void)
{
    int x, y, response = 0;

    while (response != -1) {

        x = rand() % 10;
        y = rand() % 10;

        cout << "How much is " << x << " times " << y
             << " (-1 to End)? ";
        cin >> response;

        while (response != -1 && response != x * y) {
            incorrectMessage();
            cin >> response;
        }

        if (response != -1) {
            correctMessage();
        }
    }

    cout << "That's all for now. Bye." << endl;

}
```

```
Enter -1 to End.
How much is 4 times 8 (-1 to End)? 32
Keep up the good work!

How much is 1 times 5 (-1 to End)? 5
Very Good!

How much is 7 times 5 (-1 to End)? 32
No. Please try again.
? 33
No. Keep trying.
? 34
Wrong. Try once more.
? 35
Very Good!

How much is 6 times 6 (-1 to End)? -1
That's all for now. Bye.
```

3.37 More sophisticated computer-aided instructions systems monitor the student's performance over a period of time. The decision to begin a new topic is often based on the student's success with previous topics. Modify the program of Exercise 3.36 to count the number of correct and incorrect responses typed by the student. After the student types 10 answers, your program should calculate the percentage of correct responses. If the percentage is lower than 75 percent, your program should print **"Please ask your instructor for extra help"** and then terminate.

ANS:
```
// Exercise 3.37 Solution
#include <iostream.h>
#include <stdlib.h>
#include <time.h>

void multiplication(void);
void correctMessage(void);
void incorrectMessage(void);
```

```cpp
main()
{
    srand(time(NULL));
    multiplication();
    return 0;
}
void multiplication(void)
{
    int x, y, response, right = 0, wrong = 0;
    for (int i = 1; i <= 10; i++) {
        x = rand() % 10;
        y = rand() % 10;
        cout << "How much is " << x << " times " << y << "? ";
        cin >> response;
        while (response != x * y) {
            ++wrong;
            incorrectMessage();
            cin >> response;
        }
        ++right;
        correctMessage();
    }
    if ((float) right / (right + wrong) < .75)
        cout << "Please ask your instructor for extra help." << endl;
    cout << "That's all for now. Bye." << endl;
}
void correctMessage(void)
{
    switch (rand() % 4) {
        case 0:
            cout << "Very good!";
            break;
        case 1:
            cout << "Excellent!" ;
            break;
        case 2:
            cout << "Nice work!";
            break;
        case 3:
            cout << "Keep up the good work!";
            break;
    }
    cout << endl << endl;
}
void incorrectMessage(void)
{
    switch (rand() % 4) {
        case 0:
            cout << "No. Please try again.";
            break;
        case 1:
            cout << "Wrong. Try once more.";
            break;
        case 2:
            cout << "Don't give up!";
            break;
        case 3:
            cout << "No. Keep trying.";
            break;
    }
    cout << endl << "? ";
}
```

```
How much is 9 times 3? 20
No. Please try again.
? 21
No. Please try again.
? 22
Wrong. Try once more.
? 23
No. Please try again.
? 24
No. Keep trying.
? 25
No. Keep trying.
? 26
Wrong. Try once more.
? 27
Very good!

How much is 8 times 6? 48
Very good!
...
How much is 0 times 8? 0
Excellent!

How much is 3 times 6? 18
Nice work!

How much is 8 times 9? 72
Nice work!

Please ask your instructor for extra help.
That's all for now. Bye.
```

3.38   Write a program that plays the game of "guess the number" as follows: Your program chooses the number to be guessed by selecting an integer at random in the range 1 to 1000. The program then types:

```
I have a number between 1 and 1000.
Can you guess my number?
Please type your first guess.
```

The player then types a first guess. The program responds with one of the following:

```
1. Excellent! You guessed the number!
   Would you like to play again (y or n)?
2. Too low. Try again.
3. Too high. Try again.
```

If the player's guess is incorrect, your program should loop until the player finally gets the number right. Your program should keep telling the player **Too high** or **Too low** to help the player "zero in" on the correct answer. Note: The searching technique employed in this problem is called *binary search*. We will say more about this in the next problem.

ANS:
```
// Exercise 3.38 Solution
#include <iostream.h>
#include <stdlib.h>
#include <time.h>

void guessGame(void);
```

```
main()
{
   srand(time(NULL));
   guessGame();
   return 0;
}

void guessGame(void)
{
   int x, guess, response;

   do {
      x = 1 + rand() % 1000;
      cout << endl << "I have a number between 1 and 1000." << endl
           << "Can you guess my number?" << endl
           << "Please type your first guess." << endl << "? ";
      cin >> guess;

      while (guess != x) {
         if (guess < x)
            cout << "Too low. Try again." << endl << "? ";
         else
            cout << "Too high. Try again." << endl << "? ";

         cin >> guess;
      }

      cout << endl << "Excellent! You guessed the number!" << endl
           << "Would you like to play again?" << endl
           << "Please type (1 = yes, 2 = no)? ";
      cin >> response;

   } while (response == 1);
}
```

```
I have a number between 1 and 1000.
Can you guess my number?
Please type your first guess.
? 500
Too low. Try again.
? 750
Too low. Try again.
? 875
Too high. Try again.
? 812
Too high. Try again.
? 781
Too high. Try again.
? 765
Too high. Try again.
? 757
Too high. Try again.
? 753
Too low. Try again.
? 755
Too low. Try again.
? 756

Excellent! You guessed the number!
Would you like to play again?
Please type (1=yes, 2=no)? 2
```

3.39 Modify the program of Exercise 3.38 to count the number of guesses the player makes. If the number is 10 or fewer, print **Either you know the secret or you got lucky!** If the player guesses the number in 10 tries, then print **Ahah! You know the secret!** If the player makes more than 10 guesses, then print **You should be able to do better!** Why should it take no more than 10 guesses? Well with each "good guess" the player should be able to eliminate half of the numbers. Now show why any number 1 to 1000 can be guessed in 10 or fewer tries.

ANS:

```cpp
// Exercise 3.39 Solution
#include <iostream.h>
#include <stdlib.h>
#include <time.h>

void guessGame(void);

main()
{
    srand(time(NULL));
    guessGame();
    return 0;
}

void guessGame(void)
{
    int x, guess, total = 1, response;

    do {
        x = 1 + rand() % 1000;
        cout << "I have a number between 1 and 1000." << endl
             << "Can you guess my number?" << endl << "Please type"
             << " your first guess." << endl << "? ";
        cin >> guess;

        while (guess != x) {

            if (guess < x)
                cout << "Too low. Try again." << endl << "? ";
            else
                cout << "Too high. Try again." << endl << "? ";

            cin >> guess;
            ++total;
        }

        cout << endl << "Excellent! You guessed the number!" << endl;

        if (total < 10)
            cout << "Either you know the secret or you got lucky!" << endl;
        else if (total == 10)
            cout << "Ahah! You know the secret!" << endl;
        else
            cout << "You should be able to do better!" << endl << endl;

        cout << "Would you like to play again?" << endl
             << "Please type (1 = yes, 2 = no)? ";
        cin >> response;

    } while (response == 1);
}
```

```
I have a number between 1 and 1000,
Can you guess my number?
Please type your first guess.
? 500
```
continued

```
                                                                    continued
Too high.  Try again.
? 250
Too high.  Try again.
? 125
Too low.  Try again.
? 187
Too low.  Try again.
? 156
Too low.  Try again.
? 172
Too high.  Try again.
? 164
Too low.  Try again.
? 168
Too high.  Try again.
? 166
Too high.  Try again.

Excellent! You guessed the number!
Ahah! You know the secret!
Would you like to play again?
Please type (1=yes, 2=no)? 2
```

3.40   Write a recursive function **power (base, exponent)** that when invoked returns

$$base^{exponent}$$

For example, **power(3, 4)** = 3 * 3 * 3 * 3. Assume that **exponent** is an integer greater than or equal to 1. *Hint:* The recursion step would use the relationship

$$base^{exponent} = base \cdot base^{exponent - 1}$$

and the terminating condition occurs when **exponent** is equal to **1** because

$$base^1 = base$$

ANS:
```cpp
// Exercise 3.40 Solution
#include <iostream.h>

long power(long, long);

main()
{
   long b, e;

   cout << "Enter a base and an exponent: ";
   cin >> b >> e;
   cout << b << " raised to the " << e << " is "
        << power(b, e) << endl;

   return 0;
}

long power(long base, long exponent)
{
   return exponent == 1 ? base : base * power(base, exponent - 1);
}
```

```
Enter a base and an exponent: 2 5
2 raised to the 5 is 32
```

3.41   The Fibonacci series

0, 1, 1, 2, 3, 5, 8, 13, 21, ...

begins with the terms 0 and 1 and has the property that each succeeding term is the sum of the two preceding terms. a) Write a *nonrecursive* function `fibonacci(n)` that calculates the *n*th Fibonacci number. b) Determine the largest Fibonacci number that can be printed on your system. Modify the program of part a) to use **double** instead of **int** to calculate and return Fibonacci numbers, and use this modified program to repeat part b).

ANS:

```
// Exercise 3.41 Part A Solution
#include <iostream.h>

const int MAX = 23;     // the maximum number for which the
                        // fibonacci value can be calculated
                        // on 2-byte integer systems

int fibonacci(int);

main()
{
    for (int loop = 0; loop <= MAX; loop++)
        cout << "fibonacci(" << loop << ") = " << fibonacci(loop) << endl;

    return 0;
}

int fibonacci(int n)
{
    int fib[MAX];

    fib[0] = 0;
    fib[1] = 1;

    for (int j = 2; j <= n; j++)
        fib[j] = fib[j - 1] + fib[j - 2];

    return fib[n];
}
```

```
fibonacci(0)  = 0
fibonacci(1)  = 1
fibonacci(2)  = 1
fibonacci(3)  = 2
fibonacci(4)  = 3
fibonacci(5)  = 5
fibonacci(6)  = 8
fibonacci(7)  = 13
fibonacci(8)  = 21
fibonacci(9)  = 34
fibonacci(10) = 55
fibonacci(11) = 89
fibonacci(12) = 144
fibonacci(13) = 233
fibonacci(14) = 377
fibonacci(15) = 610
fibonacci(16) = 987
fibonacci(17) = 1597
fibonacci(18) = 2584
fibonacci(19) = 4181
fibonacci(20) = 6765
fibonacci(21) = 10946
fibonacci(22) = 17711
fibonacci(23) = 28657
```

```
// Exercise 3.41 Part B Solution
#include <iostream.h>
#include <iomanip.h>

const int SIZE = 100;

double fibonacci(int);

main()
{
    cout.setf(ios::fixed | ios::showpoint);

    for (int loop = 0; loop < SIZE; loop++)
        cout << setprecision(1) << "fibonacci(" << loop << ") = "
             << fibonacci(loop) << endl;

    return 0;
}

double fibonacci(int n)
{
    double fib[SIZE];

    fib[0] = 0.0;
    fib[1] = 1.0;

    for (int j = 2; j <= n; j++)
        fib[j] = fib[j - 1] + fib[j - 2];

    return fib[n];
}
```

```
fibonacci(0)  = 0.0
fibonacci(1)  = 1.0
fibonacci(2)  = 1.0
fibonacci(3)  = 2.0
fibonacci(4)  = 3.0
fibonacci(5)  = 5.0
fibonacci(6)  = 8.0
fibonacci(7)  = 13.0
fibonacci(8)  = 21.0
fibonacci(9)  = 34.0
fibonacci(10) = 55.0
fibonacci(11) = 89.0
fibonacci(12) = 144.0
fibonacci(13) = 233.0
fibonacci(14) = 377.0
fibonacci(15) = 610.0
fibonacci(16) = 987.0
fibonacci(17) = 1597.0
fibonacci(18) = 2584.0
fibonacci(19) = 4181.0
fibonacci(20) = 6765.0
    .
    .
    .
```

3.42   *(Towers of Hanoi)* Every budding computer scientist must grapple with certain classic problems, and the Towers of Hanoi is one of the most famous of these. Legend has it that in a temple in the Far East, priests are attempting to move a stack of disks from one peg to another. The initial stack had 64 disks threaded onto one peg and arranged from bottom to top by decreasing size. The priests are attempting to move the stack from this peg to a second peg under the constraints that exactly one disk is moved at a time, and at no time may a larger disk be placed above a smaller disk. A third peg is available for temporarily holding disks. Supposedly the world will end when the priests complete their task, so there is little incentive for us to facilitate their efforts.

Let us assume that the priests are attempting to move the disks from peg 1 to peg 3. We wish to develop an algorithm that will print the precise sequence of peg-to-peg disk transfers.

If we were to approach this problem with conventional methods, we would rapidly find ourselves hopelessly knotted up in managing the disks. Instead, if we attack the problem with recursion in mind, it immediately becomes tractable. Moving n disks can be viewed in terms of moving only $n - 1$ disks (and hence the recursion) as follows:

1. Move $n - 1$ disks from peg 1 to peg 2, using peg 3 as a temporary holding area.
2. Move the last disk (the largest) from peg 1 to peg 3.
3. Move the $n - 1$ disks from peg 2 to peg 3, using peg 1 as a temporary holding area.

The process ends when the last task involves moving $n = 1$ disk, i.e., the base case. This is accomplished by trivially moving the disk without the need for a temporary holding area.

Write a program to solve the Towers of Hanoi problem. Use a recursive function with four parameters:

1. The number of disks to be moved
2. The peg on which these disks are initially threaded
3. The peg to which this stack of disks is to be moved
4. The peg to be used as a temporary holding area

Your program should print the precise instructions it will take to move the disks from the starting peg to the destination peg. For example, to move a stack of three disks from peg 1 to peg 3, your program should print the following series of moves:

$1 \rightarrow 3$ (This means move one disk from peg 1 to peg 3.)
$1 \rightarrow 2$
$3 \rightarrow 2$
$1 \rightarrow 3$
$2 \rightarrow 1$
$2 \rightarrow 3$
$1 \rightarrow 3$

ANS:

```
// Exercise 3.42 Solution
#include <iostream.h>

void towers(int, int, int, int);

main()
{
    int nDisks;

    cout << "Enter the starting number of disks: ";
    cin >> nDisks;
    towers(nDisks, 1, 3, 2);
    return 0;
}

void towers(int disks, int start, int end, int temp)
{
    if (disks == 1) {
        cout << start << " --> " << end << endl;
        return;
    }

    // move disks - 1 disks from start to temp
    towers(disks - 1, start, temp, end);

    // move last disk from start to end
    cout << start << " --> " << end << endl;

    // move disks - 1 disks from temp to end
    towers(disks - 1, temp, end, start);
}
```

```
Enter starting number of disks: 4
1 --> 2
1 --> 3
2 --> 3
1 --> 2
3 --> 1
3 --> 2
1 --> 2
1 --> 3
2 --> 3
2 --> 1
3 --> 1
2 --> 3
1 --> 2
1 --> 3
2 --> 3
```

3.43   Any program that can be implemented recursively can be implemented iteratively, although sometimes with more difficulty and less clarity. Try writing an iterative version of the Towers of Hanoi. If you succeed, compare your iterative version with the recursive version you developed in Exercise 3.42. Investigate issues of performance, clarity, and your ability to demonstrate the correctness of the programs.

3.44   (Visualizing Recursion) It is interesting to watch recursion "in action." Modify the factorial function of Fig. 3.14 to print its local variable and recursive call parameter. For each recursive call, display the outputs on a separate line and add a level of indentation. Do your utmost to make the outputs clear, interesting, and meaningful. Your goal here is to design and implement an output format that helps a person understand recursion better. You may want to add such display capabilities to the many other recursion examples and exercises throughout the text.

ANS:
```cpp
// Exercise 3.44 Solution
#include <iostream.h>
#include <iomanip.h>

long factorial(long);
void printRecursion(int);

main()
{
   for (int i = 0; i <= 10; i++)
      cout << setw(3) << i << "! = " << factorial(i) << endl;

   return 0;
}

long factorial(long number)
{
   if (number <= 1)
      return 1;
   else {
      printRecursion(number);
      return (number * factorial(number - 1));
   }
}

void printRecursion(int n)
{
   cout << "number =" << setw(n) << n << endl;
}
```

```
   0! = 1
   1! = 1
 number = 2
   2! = 2
 number =   3
 number = 2
   3! = 6
 number =     4
 number =   3
 number = 2
   4! = 24
 number =       5
 number =     4
 number =   3
 number = 2
   5! = 120
 ...
 number =           9
 number =         8
 number =       7
 number =     6
 number =   5
 number =     4
 number =   3
 number = 2
   9! = 362880
 number =           10
 number =         9
 number =       8
 number =     7
 number =   6
 number =   5
 number =     4
 number =   3
 number = 2
  10! = 3628800
```

3.45   The greatest common divisor of integers **x** and **y** is the largest integer that evenly divides both **x** and **y**. Write a recursive function **gcd** that returns the greatest common divisor of **x** and **y**. The **gcd** of **x** and **y** is defined recursively as follows: If **y** is equal to 0, then **gcd(x, y)** is **x**; otherwise **gcd(x, y)** is **gcd(y, x % y)** where % is the modulus operator.

ANS:
```cpp
// Exercise 3.45 Solution
#include <iostream.h>

unsigned int gcd(unsigned int, unsigned int);

main()
{
   unsigned int x, y, gcDiv;

   cout << "Enter two integers: ";
   cin >> x >> y;

   gcDiv = gcd(x, y);
   cout << "Greatest common divisor of " << x << " and "
        << y << " is " << gcDiv << endl;

   return 0;
}
```

```
unsigned int gcd(unsigned int xMatch, unsigned int yMatch)
{
   return yMatch == 0 ? xMatch : gcd(yMatch, xMatch % yMatch);
}
```

```
Enter two integers: 4096 128
Greatest common divisor of 4096 and 128 is 128
```

3.46   Can **main** be called recursively? Write a program containing a function **main**. Include **static** local variable **count** initialized to 1. Postincrement and print the value of **count** each time **main** is called. Run your program. What happens?

   ANS: main cannot be called recursively. Attempts to recursively call **main** result in compilation errors.

```
// Exercise 3.46 Solution
#include <iostream.h>

main()
{
   static int count = 1;

   count++;
   cout << count << endl;
   main();   // ERROR cannot recursively call main() in C++

   return 0;
}
```

3.47   Exercises 3.35 through 3.37 developed a computer-assisted instruction program to teach an elementary school student multiplication. This exercise suggests enhancements to that program.

   a) Modify the program to allow the user to enter a grade-level capability. A grade level of 1 means to use only single-digit numbers in the problems, a grade level of two means to use numbers as large as two-digits, etc.

   ANS:

```
// Exercise 3.47 Part A Solution
#include <iostream.h>
#include <stdlib.h>
#include <time.h>

int randValue(int);
void multiplication(void);
void correctMessage(void);
void incorrectMessage(void);

main()
{
   srand(time(NULL));
   multiplication();
   return 0;
}

int randValue(int level)
{
   switch (level) {
      case 1:
         return rand() % 10;
      case 2:
         return rand() % 100;
      case 3:
         return rand() % 1000;
      default:
         return rand() % 10;
   }
}
```

```
void multiplication(void)
{
    int x, y, gradeLevel, right = 0, wrong = 0;
    unsigned int response;

    cout << "Enter the grade-level (1 to 3): ";
    cin >> gradeLevel;

    for (int i = 1; i <= 10; i++) {
        x = randValue(gradeLevel);
        y = randValue(gradeLevel);

        cout << "How much is " << x << " times " << y << "? ";
        cin >> response;

        while (response != x * y) {
            ++wrong;
            incorrectMessage();
            cin >> response;
        }

        ++right;
        correctMessage();
    }

    if ((float) right / (right + wrong) < .75)
        cout << "Please ask your instructor for extra help." << endl;

    cout << "That's all for now. Bye." << endl;
}
void correctMessage(void)
{
    switch (rand() % 4) {
        case 0:
            cout << "Very good!";
            break;
        case 1:
            cout << "Excellent!";
            break;
        case 2:
            cout << "Nice work!";
            break;
        case 3:
            cout << "Keep up the good work!";
            break;
    }
    cout << endl << endl;
}
void incorrectMessage(void)
{
    switch (rand() % 4) {
        case 0:
            cout << "No. Please try again.";
            break;
        case 1:
            cout << "Wrong. Try once more.";
            break;
        case 2:
            cout << "Don't give up!";
            break;
        case 3:
            cout << "No. Keep trying.";
            break;
    }
    cout << endl << "? ";
}
```

```
Enter the grade-level (1 to 3): 1
How much is 6 times 5? 30
Very good!

How much is 2 times 2? 8
Don't give up!
? 4
Nice work!
...
```

```
Enter the grade-level (1 to 3): 2
How much is 6 times 53? 318
Excellent!

How much is 45 times 80? 200
Wrong try once more.
? 3600
Excellent!
...
```

```
Enter the grade-level (1 to 3): 3
How much is 260 times 123? 31980
Keep up the good work!

How much is 776 times 21? 16299
No. Keep trying.
? 16296
Very Good!
...
```

b) Modify the program to allow the user to pick the type of arithmetic problems he or she wishes to study. An option of 1 means addition problems only, 2 means subtraction problems only, 3 means multiplication problems only, 4 means division problems only, and 5 means to randomly intermix problems of all these types.

ANS:
```cpp
// Exercise 3.47 Part B Solution
#include <iostream.h>
#include <stdlib.h>
#include <time.h>

int menu(void);
void arithmetic(void);
void correctMessage(void);
void incorrectMessage(void);

main()
{
   srand(time(NULL));
   arithmetic();

   return 0;
}
```

```
int menu(void)
{
   int choice;

   do {
      cout << "Choose type of problem to study." << endl
           << "Enter: 1 for addition, 2 for subtraction" << endl
           << "Enter: 3 for multiplication, 4 for division" << endl
           << "Enter: 5 for a combination of 1 through 4" << endl << "? ";
      cin >> choice;
   } while (choice < 1 || choice > 5);

   return choice;
}
void incorrectMessage(void)
{
   switch (rand() % 4) {
      case 0:
         cout << "No. Please try again.";
         break;
      case 1:
         cout << "Wrong. Try once more.";
         break;
      case 2:
         cout << "Don't give up!";
         break;
      case 3:
         cout << "No. Keep trying.";
         break;
   }

   cout << endl << "? ";
}

void correctMessage(void)
{
   switch (rand() % 4) {
      case 0:
         cout << "Very good!";
         break;
      case 1:
         cout << "Excellent!";
         break;
      case 2:
         cout << "Nice work!";
         break;
      case 3:
         cout << "Keep up the good work!";
         break;
   }

   cout << endl << endl;
}


void arithmetic(void)
{
   int x, y, response, answer, selection, right = 0, wrong = 0;
   int type, problemMix;
   char op;

   selection = menu();
   type = selection;

   for (int i = 1; i <= 10; i++) {
      x = rand() % 10;
      y = rand() % 10;
```

```
            if (selection == 5) {
                problemMix = 1 + rand() % 4;
                type = problemMix;
            }

            switch (type) {
                case 1:
                    op = '+';
                    answer = x + y;
                    break;
                case 2:                    // note negative answers can exist
                    op = '-';
                    answer = x - y;
                    break;
                case 3:
                    op = '*';
                    answer = x * y;
                    break;
                case 4:                    // note this is integer division
                    op = '/';

                    if (y == 0) {
                        y = 1;             // eliminate divide by zero error
                        answer = x / y;
                    }
                    else {
                        x *= y;            // create "nice" division
                        answer = x / y;
                    }

                    break;
            }

            cout << "How much is " << x << " " << op << " " << y << "? ";
            cin >> response;

            while (response != answer) {
                ++wrong;
                incorrectMessage();
                cin >> response;
            }

            ++right;
            correctMessage();
        }

    if ((float) right / (right + wrong) < .75)
        cout << "Please ask your instructor for extra help." << endl;

    cout << "That's all for now. Bye." << endl;
}
```

```
Choose type of problem to study.
Enter: 1 for addition, 2 for subtraction
Enter: 3 for multiplication, 4 for division
Enter: 5 for a combination of 1 through 4
? 5
How much is 6 / 6? 1
Very good!

How much is 4 * 9? 36
Excellent!
                                                          continued
```

```
                                                              continued

How much is 3 * 9? 27
Excellent!

How much is 3 + 9? 7
Wrong. Try once more.
? 12
Keep up the good work!

How much is 4 / 2? 2
Excellent!

How much is 7 - 7? 0
Very good!
...
```

3.48   Write function `distance` that calculates the distance between two points (x1, y1) and (x2, y2). All numbers and return values should be of type `float`.

ANS:

```cpp
// Exercise 3.48 Solution
#include <iostream.h>
#include <iomanip.h>
#include <math.h>

float distance(float, float, float, float);

main()
{
   float x1, y1, x2, y2, dist;

   cout << "Enter the first point: ";
   cin >> x1 >> y1;

   cout << "Enter the second point: ";
   cin >> x2 >> y2;

   dist = distance(x1, y1, x2, y2);

   cout.setf(ios::fixed | ios::showpoint);
   cout << "Distance between (" << setprecision(1) << x1 << ", "
        << y1 << ") and (" << x2 << ", " << y2 << ") is " << dist << endl;
   return 0;
}

float distance(float xOne, float yOne, float xTwo, float yTwo)
{
   return sqrt(pow(xOne - xTwo, 2) + pow(yOne - yTwo, 2));
}
```

```
Enter the first point: 3 4
Enter the second point: 0 0
Distance between (3.00, 4.00) and (0.00, 0.00) is 5.00
```

3.49   What does the following program do?

```cpp
#include <iostream.h>

main()
{
   int c;

   if ( ( c = cin.get() ) != EOF) {
      main();
      cout << c;
   }

   return 0;
}
```

ANS: Nothing. Attempting to recursively call **main** is a compilation error.

3.50   What does the following program do?

```cpp
#include <iostream.h>

int mystery(int, int);

main()
{
   int x, y;

   cout << "Enter two integers: ";
   cin >> x >> y;
   cout << "The result is " << mystery(x, y) << endl;
   return 0;
}

// Parameter b must be a positive
// integer to prevent infinite recursion
int mystery(int a, int b)
{
   if (b == 1)
      return a;
   else
      return a + mystery(a, b - 1);
}
```

ANS: Calculates x times y.

3.51   After you determine what the program of Exercise 3.50 does, modify the program to function properly after removing the restriction of the second argument being nonnegative.

ANS:
```cpp
// Exercise 3.51 Solution
#include <iostream.h>

int mystery(int, int);

main()
{
   int x, y;

   cout << "Enter two integers: ";
   cin >> x >> y;

   cout << "The result is " << mystery(x, y) << endl;
   return 0;
}

int mystery(int a, int b)
{
   if (( a < 0 && b < 0) || b < 0) {
      a *= -1;
      b *= -1;
   }

   return b == 1 ? a : a + mystery(a, b - 1);
}
```

```
Enter two integers: -87 6
The result is -522
```

```
Enter two integers: 87 -6
The result is -522
```

```
Enter two integers: -87 -6
The result is 522
```

3.52   Write a program that tests as many of the math library functions in Fig. 3.2 as you can. Exercise each of these functions by having your program print out tables of return values for a diversity of argument values.
ANS:

```
// Exercise 3.52 Solution
#include <iostream.h>
#include <iomanip.h>
#include <math.h>

main()
{
   cout << "function";        // header

   for (int loop = 1; loop < 6; loop++)
      cout << setw(12) << loop << ' ';

   cout.setf(ios::fixed | ios::showpoint);
   cout << endl << endl << "sqrt()   ";

   for (loop = 1; loop < 6; loop++)
      cout << setw(12) << setprecision(2) << sqrt(loop) << ' ';

   cout << endl << "exp()    ";

   for (loop = 1; loop < 6; loop++)
      cout << setw(12) << setprecision(2) << exp(loop) << ' ';

   cout << endl << "log()    ";

   for (loop = 1; loop < 6; loop++)
      cout << setw(12) << setprecision(2) << log(loop) << ' ';

   cout << endl << "log10() ";

   for (loop = 1; loop < 6; loop++)
      cout << setw(12) << setprecision(2) << log10(loop) << ' ';
   cout << endl << "pow(2,x)";

   for (loop = 1; loop < 6; loop++)
      cout << setw(12) << setprecision(2) << pow(2, loop) << ' ';

   cout << endl << endl << endl << "function";        // header

   for (float loop2 = -1.5; loop2 < 3.0; loop2 += 1.1)
      cout << setw(12) << setprecision(2) << loop2 << ' ';

   cout << endl << endl << "fabs()   ";

   for (loop2 = -1.5; loop2 < 3.0; loop2 += 1.1)
      cout << setw(12) << setprecision(2) << fabs(loop2) << ' ';

   cout << endl << "ceil()   ";

   for (loop2 = -1.5; loop2 < 3.0; loop2 += 1.1)
      cout << setw(12) << setprecision(2) << ceil(loop2) << ' ';

   cout << endl << "floor() ";

   for (loop2 = -1.5; loop2 < 3.0; loop2 += 1.1)
      cout << setw(12) << setprecision(2) << floor(loop2) << ' ';
```

```
        cout << endl << "sin()    ";

    for (loop2 = -1.5; loop2 < 3.0; loop2 += 1.1)
       cout << setw(12) << setprecision(2) << sin(loop2) << ' ';

    cout << endl << "cos()    ";

    for (loop2 = -1.5; loop2 < 3.0; loop2 += 1.1)
       cout << setw(12) << setprecision(2) << cos(loop2) << ' ';

    cout << endl << "tan()    ";

    for (loop2 = -1.5; loop2 < 3.0; loop2 += 1.1)
       cout << setw(12) << setprecision(2) << tan(loop2) << ' ';

    cout << endl;

    return 0;
}
```

function	1	2	3	4	5
sqrt()	1.00	1.41	1.73	2.00	2.24
exp()	2.72	7.39	20.09	54.60	148.41
log()	0.00	0.69	1.10	1.39	1.61
log10()	0.00	0.30	0.48	0.60	0.70
pow(2,x)	2.00	4.00	8.00	16.00	32.00
function	-1.50	-0.40	0.70	1.80	2.90
fabs()	1.50	0.40	0.70	1.80	2.90
ceil()	-1.00	0.00	1.00	2.00	3.00
floor()	-2.00	-1.00	0.00	1.00	2.00
sin()	-1.00	-0.39	0.64	0.97	0.24
cos()	0.07	0.92	0.76	-0.23	-0.97
tan()	-14.10	-0.42	0.84	-4.29	-0.25

3.53 Find the error in each of the following program segments and explain how to correct it:

a)
```
float cube(float);    /* function prototype */
    ...
cube(float number)    /* function definition */
{
    return number * number * number;
}
```
ANS: Function definition header is missing **float** return type.

b) `register auto int x = 7;`
ANS: Too many storage class specifiers. The **auto** specifier can be removed.

c) `int randomNumber = srand();`
ANS: Improper use of **srand()**. The **rand()** function should be used instead.

d)
```
float y = 123.45678;
int x;

x = y;
cout << (float) x << endl;
```
ANS: Assignment of a **float** to an **int** truncates decimal places. Type-casting the **int** back to a **float** is useless, because the original decimal places are lost.

e)
```
double square(double number)
{
    double number;
    return number * number;
}
```
ANS: **number** is declared twice. The declaration inside function body should be removed.

```
f) int sum(int n)
   {
      if (n == 0)
         return 0;
      else
         return n + sum(n);
   }
```
ANS: Infinite recursion. The **else** portion should be **return n + sum(n - 1);**.

3.54   Modify the craps program of Fig. 3.10 to allow wagering. Package as a function the portion of the program
that runs one game of craps. Initialize variable **bankBalance** to 1000 dollars. Prompt the player to enter a **wager**.
Use a **while** loop to check that **wager** is less than or equal to **bankBalance** and if not prompt the user to reenter
wager until a valid **wager** is entered. After a correct **wager** is entered, run one game of craps. If the player wins,
increase **bankBalance** by **wager** and print the new **bankBalance**. If the player loses, decrease **bankBalance**
by **wager**, print the new **bankBalance**, check if **bankBalance** has become zero, and if so print the message
"Sorry. You busted!" As the game progresses, print various messages to create some "chatter" such as **"Oh,
you're going for broke, huh?"**, or **"Aw cmon, take a chance!"**, or **"You're up big. Now's the
time to cash in your chips!"**.

ANS:
```
// Exercise 3.54 Solution
#include <iostream.h>
#include <stdlib.h>
#include <time.h>

enum Status { CONTINUE, WON, LOST };

int rollDice(void);
int craps(void);
void chatter(void);

main()
{
   int result, wager = 0, bankBalance = 1000;

   srand(time(NULL));

   cout << "You have $" << bankBalance << " in the bank." << endl
        << "Place your wager: ";
   cin >> wager;

   while (wager <= 0 || wager > 1000) {
      cout << "Please bet a valid amount." << endl;
      cin >> wager;
   }

   result = craps();

   if (result == LOST) {
      bankBalance -= wager;
      cout << "Your new bank balance is $" << bankBalance << endl;

      if (bankBalance == 0)
         cout << "Sorry. You Busted! Thank You For Playing." << endl;
   }
   else {
      bankBalance += wager;
      cout << "Your new bank balance is $" << bankBalance << endl;
   }

   return 0;
}
```

```
int rollDice(void)
{
    int die1, die2, workSum;

    die1 = 1 + rand() % 6;
    die2 = 1 + rand() % 6;
    workSum = die1 + die2;
    cout << "Player rolled " << die1 << " + " << die2 << " = "
        << workSum << endl;

    return workSum;
}

int craps(void)
{
    int gameStatus, sum, myPoint;

    sum = rollDice();

    switch (sum) {
        case 7: case 11:
            gameStatus = WON;
            chatter();
            break;
        case 2: case 3: case 12:
            gameStatus = LOST;
            chatter();
            break;
        default:
            gameStatus = CONTINUE;
            myPoint = sum;
            cout << "Point is " << myPoint << endl;
            chatter();
            break;
    }

    while (gameStatus == CONTINUE) {
        chatter();
        sum = rollDice();
        if (sum == myPoint)
            gameStatus = WON;
        else if (sum == 7)
            gameStatus = LOST;
    }

    if (gameStatus == WON) {
        cout << "Player wins" << endl;
        return WON;
    }
    else {
        cout << "Player loses" << endl;
        return LOST;
    }
}

void chatter(void)
{
    switch (1 + rand() % 8) {
        case 1:
            cout << "Oh, you're going for broke, huh?";
            break;
        case 2:
            cout << "Aw cmon, take a chance!";
            break;
```

```
            case 3:
               cout << "Hey, I think this guy is going to break the bank!!";
               break;
            case 4:
               cout << "You're up big. Now's the time to cash in your chips!";
               break;
            case 5:
               cout << "Way too lucky! Those dice have to be loaded!";
               break;
            case 6:
               cout << "Bet it all! Bet it all!";
               break;
            case 7:
               cout << "Roll a seven, and goto heaven!";
               break;
            case 8:
               cout << "Let's try our luck at another table.";
            default:
               break;
      }

      cout << endl;
}
```

```
You have $1000 in the bank.
Place your wager: 500
Player rolled 5 + 4 = 9
Point is 9
You're up big. Now's the time to cash in your chips!
Bet it all! Bet it all!
Player rolled 5 + 1 = 6
Way too lucky! Those dice have to be loaded!
Player rolled 3 + 4 = 7
Player loses
Your new bank balance is $500
```

3.55   Write a C++ program that uses an **inline** function **circleArea** to prompt the user for the radius of a circle, and to calculate and print the area of that circle.

ANS:

```
// Exercise 3.55 Solution
#include <iostream.h>

const float PI = 3.14159;

inline float circleArea(float r) { return PI * r * r; }

main()
{
    float radius;

    cout << "Enter the radius of the circle: ";
    cin >> radius;
    cout << "The area of the circle is " << circleArea(radius);

    return 0;
}
```

```
Enter the radius of the circle: 1
The area of the circle is 3.14159
```

3.56   Write a complete C++ program with the two alternate functions specified below that each simply triple the variable **count** defined in **main**. Then compare and contrast the two approaches. These two functions are
   a) Function **tripleCallByValue** that passes a copy of **count** call-by-value, triples the copy, and returns the new value.
   b) Function **tripleByReference** that passes **count** with true call-by-reference via a reference parameter, and triples the original copy of **count** through its alias (i.e., the reference parameter).

ANS:
```
// Exercise 3.56 Solution
#include <iostream.h>

int tripleCallByValue(int);
void tripleByReference(int &);

main()
{
    int value, &valueRef = value;

    cout << "Enter an integer: ";
    cin >> value;

    cout << endl << "Value before call to tripleCallByValue() is: "
        << value << endl << "Value returned from tripleCallByValue() is: "
        << tripleCallByValue(value) << endl
        << "Value (in main) after tripleCallByValue() is: " << value
        << endl << endl << "Value before call to tripleByReference() is: "
        << value << endl;

    tripleByReference(valueRef);

    cout << "Value (in main) after call to tripleByReference() is: "
        << value << endl;

    return 0;
}

int tripleCallByValue(int valueCopy)
{
    return valueCopy *= 3;
}

void tripleByReference(int &aliasRef)
{
    aliasRef *= 3;
}
```

```
Enter an integer: 7
Value before call to tripleCallByValue() is: 7
Value returned from tripleCallByValue() is: 21
Value (in main) after tripleCallByValue() is: 7

Value before call to tripleByReference() is: 7
Value (in main) after call to tripleByReference() is: 21
```

3.57   What is the purpose of the unary scope resolution operator?
   ANS: C++ provides the unary scope resolution operator to access a global variable when a local variable of the same name is in scope.

3.58   Write a program that uses a function template called **min** to determine the smaller of two arguments. Test the program using integer, character, and floating-point number pairs.

ANS:
```
// Exercise 3.58 Solution
#include <iostream.h>

template <class T>
void min(T value1, T value2)   // find the smallest value
{
   if (value1 > value2)
      cout << value2 << " is smaller than " << value1 << endl;
   else
      cout << value1 << " is smaller than " << value2 << endl;
}

main()
{
   min(7, 54);        // integers
   min(4.35, 8.46);  // floats
   min('g', 'T');    // characters
   return 0;
}
```

```
7 is smaller than 54
4.35 is smaller than 8.46
T is smaller than g
```

3.59 Write a program that uses a function template called **max** to determine the larger of three arguments. Test the program using integer, character, and floating-point number pairs.

ANS:
```
// Exercise 3.59 Solution
#include <iostream.h>

template <class T>
void max(T value1, T value2, T value3)  // find the largest value
{
   if (value1 > value2 && value1 > value3)
      cout << value1 << " is greater than " << value2
           << " and " << value3 << endl;
   else if (value2 > value1 && value2 > value3)
      cout << value2 << " is greater than " << value1
           << " and " << value3 << endl;
   else
      cout << value3 << " is greater than " << value1
           << " and " << value2 << endl;
}

main()
{
   max(7, 5, 2);              // integers
   max(9.35, 8.461, 94.3);   // floats
   max('!', 'T', '$');       // characters

   return 0;
}
```

```
7 is greater than 5 and 2
94.3 is greater than 9.35 and 8.461
T is greater than ! and $
```

3.60 Determine if the following program segments contain errors. For each error, explain how it can be corrected. Note: For a particular program segment, it is possible that no errors are present in the segment.

a)
```
template <class A>
int sum(int num1, int num2, int num3)
{
    return num1 + num2 + num3;
}
```
ANS: The return type for the function definition should be **A**.

b)
```
void printResults(int x, int y)
{
    cout << "The sum is " << x + y << '\n';
    return x + y;
}
```
ANS: The function attempts to return a value, when the return type specified is **void**. The return statement should be removed from the function body.

c)
```
template <A>
A product(A num1, A num2, A num3)
{
    return num1 * num2 * num3;
}
```
ANS: **class** is needed in template definition. (**template < class A>**)

d)
```
double cube(int);
int cube(int);
```
ANS: The signatures (i.e., the name and parameters) of multiple functions must be unique. Changing the first prototype to **double cube(double);** would be one way of creating a unique signature.

4

Arrays:
Solutions

Exercises

4.6 Fill in the blanks in each of the following:

a) C++ stores lists of values in _____.

ANS: arrays.

b) The elements of an array are related by the fact that they _____.

ANS: have the same name and type.

c) When referring to an array element, the position number contained within parentheses is called a _____.

ANS: subscript.

d) The names of the four elements of array **p** are _____, _____, _____, and _____.

ANS: p[0], p[1], p[2], and p[3].

e) Naming an array, stating its type, and specifying the number of elements in the array is called _____ the array.

ANS: declaring.

f) The process of placing the elements of an array into either ascending or descending order is called _____.

ANS: sorting.

g) In a double-subscripted array, the first subscript (by convention) identifies the _____ of an element, and the second subscript (by convention) identifies the _____ of an element.

ANS: row, column.

h) An m-by-n array contains _____ rows, _____ columns, and _____ elements.

ANS: m, n, m * n.

i) The name of the element in row 3 and column 5 of array **d** is _____.

ANS: d[3] [5].

4.7 State which of the following are true and which are false; for those that are false, explain why they are false.

a) To refer to a particular location or element within an array, we specify the name of the array and the value of the particular element.

ANS: False. The name of the array and the subscript are specified.

b) An array declaration reserves space for the array.

ANS: True.

c) To indicate that 100 locations should be reserved for integer array **p**, the programmer writes the declaration

```
p[100];
```

ANS: False. The type must be specified. A correct declaration would be **int p[100];**

d) A C++ program that initializes the elements of a 15-element array to zero must contain at least one **for** statement.

ANS: False. The array can be initialized in the declaration.

e) A C++ program that totals the elements of a double-subscripted array must contain nested **for** statements.

ANS: False. It is possible to total the elements of a double-subscripted array by enumerating all the elements in an assignment statement.

4.8   Write C++ statements to accomplish each of the following:
a) Display the value of the seventh element of character array **f**.
ANS: `cout << f[6];`
b) Input a value into element 4 of single-subscripted floating-point array **b**.
ANS: `cin >> b[3];`
c) Initialize each of the 5 elements of single-subscripted integer array **g** to **8**.
ANS:
```
for (int j = 0; j < 5; j++)
        g[j] = 8;
```
d) Total and print the elements of floating-point array **c** of 100 elements.
ANS:
```
for (int x = 0; x < 100; x++) {
        total += c[x];   // assume total was initialized to zero
        cout << c[x];
    }
```
e) Copy array **a** into the first portion of array **b**. Assume `float a[11], b[34];`
ANS:
```
for (int i = 0; i < 11; i++)
        b[i] = a[i];
```
f) Determine and print the smallest and largest values contained in 99-element floating-point array **w**.
ANS:
```
// assume variables smallest and largest have been declared
    for (int z = 0; z < 99; z++) {
        if (w[z] < smallest)
            smallest = w[z];
        else if (w[z] > largest)
            largest = w[z];

        cout << smallest << ' ' << largest;
    }
```

4.9   Consider a 2-by-3 integer array **t**.
a) Write a declaration for **t**.
ANS: `int t[2][3];`
b) How many rows does **t** have?
ANS: 2
c) How many columns does **t** have?
ANS: 3
d) How many elements does **t** have?
ANS: 6
e) Write the names of all the elements in the second row of **t**.
ANS: `t[1][0];`, `t[1][1];`, `t[1][2];`
f) Write the names of all the elements in the third column of **t**.
ANS: `t[0][2];`, `t[1][2];`, `t[2][2];`
g) Write a single statement that sets the element of **t** in row 1 and column 2 to zero.
ANS: `t[0][1] = 0;`
h) Write a series of statements that initializes each element of **t** to zero. Do not use a repetition structure.
ANS:
```
t[0][0] = 0;
    t[0][1] = 0;
    t[0][2] = 0;
    t[1][0] = 0;
    t[1][1] = 0;
    t[1][2] = 0;
```
i) Write a nested **for** structure that initializes each element of **t** to zero.
ANS:
```
for (int r = 0; r < 2; r++)
        for (int c = 0; c < 3; c++)
            t[r][c] = 0;
```
j) Write a statement that inputs the values for the elements of **t** from the terminal.
ANS:
```
for (int r = 0; r < 2; r++)
        for (int c = 0; c < 3; c++)
            cin >> t[r][c];
```

k) Write a series of statements that determines and prints the smallest value in array **t**.

ANS:
```
int smallest = 0;
    for (int r = 0; r < 2; r++)
        for (int c = 0; c < 3; c++)
            if (t[r][c] < smallest)
                smallest = t[r][c];
    cout << smallest;
```

l) Write a statement that displays the elements of the first row of **t**.

ANS: `cout << t[0][0] << t[0][1] << t[0][2];`

m) Write a statement that totals the elements of the fourth column of **t**.

ANS: **t** does not have a fourth column.

n) Write a series of statements that prints the array **t** in neat, tabular format. List the column subscripts as headings across the top and list the row subscripts at the left of each row.

ANS:
```
cout << "    0      1      2      3" << endl;
    for (int i = 0; i < 2; i++) {
        cout << i << ' ';

        for (int j = 0 ; j < 3; j++)
            cout << t[i][j] << "      ";

        cout << endl;
    }
```

4.10 Use a single-subscripted array to solve the following problem. A company pays its salespeople on a commission basis. The salespeople receive $200 per week plus 9 percent of their gross sales for that week. For example, a salesperson who grosses $5000 in sales in a week receives $200 plus 9 percent of $5000, or a total of $650. Write a program (using an array of counters) that determines how many of the salespeople earned salaries in each of the following ranges (assume that each salesperson's salary is truncated to an integer amount):

1. $200–$299
2. $300–$399
3. $400–$499
4. $500–$599
5. $600–$699
6. $700–$799
7. $800–$899
8. $900–$999
9. $1000 and over

ANS:
```
// Exercise 4.10 Solution
#include <iostream.h>
#include <iomanip.h>

main()
{
    int salaries[11] = {0}, sales;
    float salary, i = 0.09;

    cout << "Enter employee gross sales (-1 to end): ";
    cin >> sales;
    cout.setf(ios::fixed | ios::showpoint);

    while (sales != -1) {
        salary = 200.0 + sales * i;
        cout << setprecision(2) << "Employee Commission is $"
             << salary << endl;

        if (salary >= 200 && salary < 1000)
            ++salaries[(int) salary / 100];
        else if (salary >= 1000)
            ++salaries[10];

        cout << endl << "Enter employee gross sales (-1 to end): ";
        cin >> sales;
```

```
cout << "Employees in the range:" << endl
     << "$200-$299 : " << salaries[2] << endl
     << "$300-$399 : " << salaries[3] << endl
     << "$400-$499 : " << salaries[4] << endl
     << "$500-$599 : " << salaries[5] << endl
     << "$600-$699 : " << salaries[6] << endl
     << "$700-$799 : " << salaries[7] << endl
     << "$800-$899 : " << salaries[8] << endl
     << "$900-$999 : " << salaries[9] << endl
     << "Over $1000: " << salaries[10] << endl;

   return 0;
}
```

```
Enter employee gross sales (-1 to end): 10000
Employee Commission is $1100.00

Enter employee gross sales (-1 to end): 4235
Employee Commission is $581.15

Enter employee gross sales (-1 to end): 600
Employee Commission is $254.00

Enter employee gross sales (-1 to end): 12500
Employee Commission is $1325.00

Enter employee gross sales (-1 to end): -1
Employees in the range:
$200-$299 : 1
$300-$399 : 0
$400-$499 : 0
$500-$599 : 1
$600-$699 : 0
$700-$799 : 0
$800-$899 : 0
$900-$999 : 0
Over $1000: 2
```

4.11   The bubble sort presented in Fig. 4.16 is inefficient for large arrays. Make the following simple modifications to improve the performance of the bubble sort.

a) After the first pass, the largest number is guaranteed to be in the highest-numbered element of the array; after the second pass, the two highest numbers are "in place," and so on. Instead of making nine comparisons on every pass, modify the bubble sort to make eight comparisons on the second pass, seven on the third pass, and so on.

ANS:
```
// Exercise 4.11 Part A Solution
#include <iostream.h>
#include <iomanip.h>

main()
{
   const int SIZE = 10;
   int a[SIZE] = {2, 6, 4, 8, 10, 12, 89, 68, 45, 37};
   int hold, numberOfComp = 0;

   cout << "Data items in original order" << endl;

   for (int i = 0; i < SIZE; i++)
      cout << setw(4) << a[i];
```

```
         cout << endl << endl;

      for (int pass = 1; pass < SIZE; pass++) {
         cout << "After pass " << pass - 1 << ": ";

         for (i = 0; i < SIZE - pass; i++) {
            ++numberOfComp;

            if (a[i] > a[i + 1]) {
               hold = a[i];
               a[i] = a[i + 1];
               a[i + 1] = hold;
            }

            cout << setw(3) << a[i];
         }

         cout << setw(3) << a[i] << endl;    // print last array value
      }

      cout << endl << "Data items in ascending order" << endl;

      for (i = 0; i < SIZE; i++)
         cout << setw(4) << a[i];

      cout << endl << "Number of comparisons = " << numberOfComp << endl;
      return 0;
   }
```

```
Data items in original order
   2    6    4    8   10   12   89   68   45   37

After pass 0:    2    4    6    8 10 12 68 45 37 89
After pass 1:    2    4    6    8 10 12 45 37 68
After pass 2:    2    4    6    8 10 12 37 45
After pass 3:    2    4    6    8 10 12 37
After pass 4:    2    4    6    8 10 12
After pass 5:    2    4    6    8 10
After pass 6:    2    4    6    8
After pass 7:    2    4    6
After pass 8:    2    4

Data items in ascending order
   2    4    6    8   10   12   37   45   68   89
Number of comparisons = 45
```

b) The data in the array may already be in the proper order or near-proper order, so why make nine passes if fewer will suffice? Modify the sort to check at the end of each pass if any swaps have been made. If none has been made, then the data must already be in the proper order, so the program should terminate. If swaps have been made, then at least one more pass is needed.

ANS:
```
// Exercise 4.11 Part B Solution
#include <iostream.h>
#include <iomanip.h>

main()
{
   enum Boolean { FALSE, TRUE };
   const int SIZE = 10;
   int a[SIZE] = {6, 4, 2, 8, 10, 12, 37, 45, 68, 89};
   int hold, numberOfComp = 0;
   Boolean swapCheck = TRUE;
```

```
         cout << "Data items in original order" << endl;

         for (int i = 0; i < SIZE; i++)
            cout << setw(4) << a[i];

         cout << endl << endl;

         for (int pass = 1; pass < SIZE - 1 && swapCheck == TRUE; pass++) {
            cout << "After pass " << pass - 1 << ": ";
            swapCheck = FALSE;   // assume no swaps will be made

            for (i = 0; i < SIZE - pass; i++) {
               ++numberOfComp;

               if (a[i] > a[i + 1]) {
                  hold = a[i];
                  a[i] = a[i + 1];
                  a[i + 1] = hold;
                  swapCheck = TRUE;   // a swap has been made
               }

               cout << setw(3) << a[i];
            }

            cout << setw(3) << a[i] << endl;   // print last array value
         }

         cout << endl << "Data items in ascending order" << endl;

         for (i = 0; i < SIZE; i++)
            cout << setw(4) << a[i];

         cout << endl << "Number of comparisons = " << numberOfComp << endl;
         return 0;
      }
```

```
    Data items in original order
        6    4    2    8   10   12   37   45   68   89

    After pass 0:    4   2   6   8 10 12 37 45 68 89
    After pass 1:    2   4   6   8 10 12 37 45 68
    After pass 2:    2   4   6   8 10 12 37 45

    Data items in ascending order
        2    4    6    8   10   12   37   45   68   89
    Number of comparisons = 24
```

4.12 Write single statements that perform the following single-subscripted array operations:

a) Initialize the 10 elements of integer array **counts** to zeros.

ANS:
```
for (int s = 0; s < 10; s++)
   counts[s] = 0;
```

b) Add 1 to each of the 15 elements of integer array **bonus**.

ANS:
```
for (int y = 0; y < 15; y++)
   ++bonus[y];
```

c) Read 12 values for **float** array **monthlyTemperatures** from the keyboard.

ANS:
```
for (int m = 0; m < 12; m++) {
   cout << "Enter a temperature: ";
   cin >> monthlyTemperatures[m];
}
```

d) Print the 5 values of integer array **bestScores** in column format.

ANS: `for (int k = 0; k < 5; k++)`
        `cout << bestScores[k] << '\t';`

4.13 Find the error(s) in each of the following statements:

a) Assume: `char str[5];`

  `cin >> str;`   `// User types hello`

ANS: **str** is too small. A minimum size of six is needed, the extra space is for the null character.

b) Assume: `int a[3];`

  `cout << a[1] << " " << a[2] << " " << a[3] << endl;`

ANS: Garbage values are being output, and subscripts are off by one (i.e. subscript of 3 is not a valid subscript)

c) `float f[3] = {1.1, 10.01, 100.001, 1000.0001};`

ANS: Too many member initializers.

d) Assume: `double d[2][10];`

  `d[1, 9] = 2.345;`

ANS: Brackets are needed in the assignment, not a comma. Should be `d[1][9] = 2.345;`

4.14 Modify the program of Fig. 4.17 so function **mode** is capable of handling a tie for the mode value. Also modify function **median** so the two middle elements are averaged in an array with an even number of elements.

ANS:
```
// Exercise 4.14 Solution
#include <iostream.h>
#include <iomanip.h>

const int SIZE = 100, MAXFREQUENCY = 10;

void mean(int [], int);
void median(int [], int);
void mode(int [], int [], int, int);

main()
{
    int response[SIZE] = {6, 7, 8, 9, 8, 7, 8, 9, 8, 9,
                          7, 8, 9, 5, 9, 8, 7, 8, 7, 1,
                          6, 7, 8, 9, 3, 9, 8, 7, 1, 7,
                          7, 8, 9, 8, 9, 8, 9, 7, 1, 9,
                          6, 7, 8, 7, 8, 7, 9, 8, 9, 2,
                          7, 8, 9, 8, 9, 8, 9, 7, 5, 3,
                          5, 6, 7, 2, 5, 3, 9, 4, 6, 4,
                          7, 8, 9, 6, 8, 7, 8, 9, 7, 1,
                          7, 4, 4, 2, 5, 3, 8, 7, 5, 6,
                          4, 5, 6, 1, 6, 5, 7, 8, 7, 9};

    int frequency[MAXFREQUENCY] = {0}, n;

    mean(response, SIZE);
    median(response, SIZE);
    mode(frequency, response, SIZE, MAXFREQUENCY);

    return 0;
}


void mean(int answer[], int size)        // mean
{
    int total = 0;

    cout << "******" << endl << " Mean" << endl << "******" << endl;

    for (int j = 0; j < size; j++)
        total += answer[j];
```

```
        cout.setf(ios::fixed | ios::showpoint);

        cout << "The mean is the average value of the data items." << endl
             << "The mean is equal to the total of all the data" << endl
             << "items divided by the number of data items (" << size << ")."
             << endl << "The mean value for this run is: " << total
             << " / " << size << " = " << setprecision(2)
             << (float) total / size << endl << endl;
}

void median(int answer[], int size)                        // median
{
    int hold;

    cout << endl << "******" << endl << "Median" << endl << "******" << endl
         << "The unsorted array of responses is" << endl;

    for (int loop = 0, firstRow = 1; loop < size; loop++) {
        if (loop % 20 == 0 && !firstRow)
            cout << endl;

        cout << setw(2) << answer[loop];
        firstRow = 0;
    }

    cout << endl << endl;

    for (int pass = 0; pass <= size - 2; pass++)
        for (loop = 0; loop <= size - 2; loop++)
            if (answer[loop] > answer[loop + 1]) {
                hold = answer[loop];
                answer[loop] = answer[loop + 1];
                answer[loop + 1] = hold;
            }

    cout << "The sorted array is" << endl;

    for (loop = 0, firstRow = 1; loop < size; loop++) {
        if (loop % 20 == 0 && !firstRow)
            cout << endl;

        cout << setw(2) << answer[loop];
        firstRow = 0;
    }

    cout << endl << endl;

    if (size % 2 == 0)        // even number of elements
        cout << "The median is the average of elements " << (size + 1) / 2
             << " and " << 1 + (size + 1) / 2 << " of the sorted "
             << size << " element array." << endl
             << "For this run the median" << " is " << setprecision(1)
             << (float)(answer[(size + 1) / 2] +
                         answer[(size + 1) / 2 + 1]) / 2 << endl << endl;
    else // odd number of elements
        cout << "The median is element " << (size + 1) / 2  << " of "
             << "the sorted " << size << " element array." << endl
             << "For this run the median is " << answer[(size + 1) / 2 - 1]
             << endl << endl;
}

void mode(int freq[], int answer[], int aSize, int fSize)
{
    const int SIZE2 = 10;
    int largest = 0, array[SIZE2] = {0}, count = 0;

    cout << endl << "******" << endl << " Mode" << endl << "******" << endl;
```

```
for (int rating = 1; rating < fSize; rating++)
   freq[rating] = 0;

for (int loop = 0; loop < aSize; loop++)
   ++freq[answer[loop]];

cout << setw(13) << "Response" << setw(11) << "Frequency" << setw(19)
     << "Histogram" << endl << endl << setw(54) << "1    1    2    2"
     << endl << setw(54) << "5    0    5    0    5" << endl << endl;

for (rating = 1; rating < fSize; rating++) {
   cout << setw(8) << rating << setw(11) << freq[rating] << "            ";

   if (freq[rating] > largest) {
      largest = freq[rating];

      for (loop = 0; loop < SIZE2; loop++)
         array[loop] = 0;

      array[rating] = largest;
      ++count;
   }
   else if (freq[rating] == largest) {
      array[rating] = largest;
      ++count;
   }

   for (loop = 1; loop <= freq[rating]; loop++)
      cout << '*';

   cout << endl;
}

cout << endl << (count > 1 ? "The modes are:   " : "The mode is: ");

for (loop = 1; loop < SIZE2; loop++)
   if (array[loop] != 0)
      cout << loop << " with a frequency of " << array[loop] << endl
           << "\t\t";

cout << endl;
}
```

```
******
 Mean
******
The mean is the average value of the data items.
The mean is equal to the total of all the data
items divided by the number of data items (100).
The mean value for this run is: 662 / 100 = 6.62

******
Median
******
The unsorted array of responses is
 6 7 8 9 8 7 8 9 8 9 7 8 9 5 9 8 7 8 7 1
 6 7 8 9 3 9 8 7 1 7 7 8 9 8 9 8 9 7 1 9
 6 7 8 7 8 7 9 8 9 2 7 8 9 8 9 8 9 7 5 3
 5 6 7 2 5 3 9 4 6 4 7 8 9 6 8 7 8 9 7 1
 7 4 4 2 5 3 8 7 5 6 4 5 6 1 6 5 7 8 7 9
```

continued

continued

```
The sorted array is
1 1 1 1 1 2 2 2 3 3 3 3 4 4 4 4 4 5 5 5
5 5 5 5 5 6 6 6 6 6 6 6 6 6 7 7 7 7 7 7
7 7 7 7 7 7 7 7 7 7 7 7 7 7 7 7 7 7 8 8 8
8 8 8 8 8 8 8 8 8 8 8 8 8 8 8 8 8 8 8 8 8
9 9 9 9 9 9 9 9 9 9 9 9 9 9 9 9 9 9 9 9

The median is the average of elements 50 and 51 of the sorted 100
element array.
For this run the median is 7.0


******
 Mode
******
     Response   Frequency          Histogram

                                  1   1   2   2
                              5   0   5   0   5

        1          5        *****
        2          3        ***
        3          4        ****
        4          5        *****
        5          8        ********
        6          9        *********
        7         23        ***********************
        8         23        ***********************
        9         20        ********************

The modes are:  7 with a frequency of 23
                8 with a frequency of 23
```

4.15   Use a single-subscripted array to solve the following problem. Read in 20 numbers, each of which is between 10 and 100, inclusive. As each number is read, print it only if it is not a duplicate of a number already read. Provide for the "worst case" in which all 20 numbers are different. Use the smallest possible array to solve this problem.

ANS:

```cpp
// Exercise 4.15 Solution
#include <iostream.h>
#include <iomanip.h>

main()
{
   const int SIZE = 20;
   int a[SIZE] = {0}, subscript = 0, duplicate, value;

   cout << "Enter 20 integers between 10 and 100: " << endl;

   for (int i = 0; i < SIZE; i++) {

      duplicate = 0;
      cin >> value;

      for (int j = 0; j < subscript; j++)
         if (value == a[j]) {
            duplicate = 1;
            break;
         }

      if (!duplicate)
         a[subscript++] = value;
   }
```

```
    cout << endl << "The nonduplicate values are: " << endl;

    for (i = 0; a[i] != 0; i++)
        cout << setw(4) << a[i];

    cout << endl;
    return 0;
}
```

```
Enter 20 integers between 10 and 100:
100 42 68 32 24 72 6 32 12 72 16 99 4 68 42 100 42 19 97 75

The nonduplicate values are:
 100  42  68  32  24  72   6  12  16  99   4  19  97  75
```

4.16   Label the elements of 3-by-5 double-subscripted array **sales** to indicate the order in which they are set to zero by the following program segment:

```
for (row = 0; row < 3; row++)
    for (column = 0; column < 5; column++)
        sales[row][column] = 0;
```

ANS: sales[0][0], sales[0][1], sales[0][2], sales[0][3], sales[0][4],
     sales[1][0], sales[1][1], sales[1][2], sales[1][3], sales[1][4],
     sales[2][0], sales[2][1], sales[2][2], sales[2][3], sales[2][4].

4.17   Write a program that simulates the rolling of two dice. The program should use **rand** to roll the first die, and should use **rand** again to roll the second die. The sum of the two values should then be calculated. *Note:* Since each die can show an integer value from 1 to 6, then the sum of the two values will vary from 2 to 12 with 7 being the most frequent sum and 2 and 12 being the least frequent sums. Figure 4.24 shows the 36 possible combinations of the two dice. Your program should roll the two dice 36,000 times. Use a single-subscripted array to tally the numbers of times each possible sum appears. Print the results in a tabular format. Also, determine if the totals are reasonable, i.e., there are six ways to roll a 7, so approximately one sixth of all the rolls should be 7.

```
ANS:
// Exercise 4.17 Solution
#include <iostream.h>
#include <iomanip.h>
#include <stdlib.h>
#include <time.h>

main()
{
    const long ROLLS = 36000;
    const int SIZE = 13;

    // array expected contains counts for the expected
    // number of times each sum occurs in 36 rolls of the dice
    int expected[SIZE] = {0, 0, 1, 2, 3, 4, 5, 6, 5, 4, 3, 2, 1};
    int x, y, sum[SIZE] = {0};

    srand(time(NULL));

    for (long i = 1; i <= ROLLS; i++) {
        x = 1 + rand() % 6;
        y = 1 + rand() % 6;
        ++sum[x + y];
    }

    cout << setw(10) << "Sum" << setw(10) << "Total" << setw(10)
         << "Expected" << setw(10) << "Actual" << endl;
```

```
cout.setf(ios::fixed | ios::showpoint);

for (int j = 2; j < SIZE; j++)
   cout << setw(10) << j << setw(10) << sum[j] << setprecision(3)
        << setw(9) << 100.0 * expected[j] / 36 << "%" << setprecision(3)
        << setw(9) << 100.0 * sum[j] / 36000 << "%" << endl;

return 0;
}
```

Sum	Total	Expected	Actual
2	990	2.778%	2.750%
3	1959	5.556%	5.442%
4	3027	8.333%	8.408%
5	4054	11.111%	11.261%
6	4949	13.889%	13.747%
7	6074	16.667%	16.872%
8	4952	13.889%	13.756%
9	3959	11.111%	10.997%
10	3013	8.333%	8.369%
11	1992	5.556%	5.533%
12	1031	2.778%	2.864%

4.18   What does the following program do?

```
#include <iostream.h>

int whatIsThis(int [], int);

main()
{
   const int arraySize = 10;
   int a[arraySize] = {1, 2, 3, 4, 5, 6, 7, 8, 9, 10};

   int result = whatIsThis(a, arraySize);

   cout << "Result is " << result << endl;
   return 0;
}

int whatIsThis(int b[], int size)
{
   if (size == 1)
      return b[0];
   else
      return b[size - 1] + whatIsThis(b, size - 1);
}
```

ANS: Function whatIsThis recursively sums the elements in a.

```
Result is 55
```

4.19   Write a program that runs 1000 games of craps and answers the following questions:
   a) How many games are won on the first roll, second roll, ..., twentieth roll, and after the twentieth roll?
   b) How many games are lost on the first roll, second roll, ..., twentieth roll, and after the twentieth roll?
   c) What are the chances of winning at craps? (*Note:* You should discover that craps is one of the fairest casino games. What do you suppose this means?)
   d) What is the average length of a game of craps?
   e) Do the chances of winning improve with the length of the game?

```
ANS:
// Exercise 4.19 Solution
#include <iostream.h>
#include <iomanip.h>
#include <stdlib.h>
#include <time.h>

int rollDice(void);

main()
{
   enum Outcome { CONTINUE, WIN, LOSE };
   const int SIZE = 22, ROLLS = 1000;
   int gameStatus, sum, myPoint, roll, length = 0, wins[SIZE] = {0},
       losses[SIZE] = {0}, winSum = 0, loseSum = 0;
   Outcome result;

   srand(time(NULL));

   for (int i = 1; i <= ROLLS; i++) {

      sum = rollDice();
      roll = 1;

      switch (sum) {
         case 7: case 11:
            gameStatus = WIN;
            break;
         case 2: case 3: case 12:
            gameStatus = LOSE;
            break;
         default:
            gameStatus = CONTINUE;
            myPoint = sum;
            break;
      }

      while (gameStatus == CONTINUE) {
         sum = rollDice();
         ++roll;

         if (sum == myPoint)
            gameStatus = WIN;
         else if (sum == 7)
            gameStatus = LOSE;
      }

      if (roll > 21)
         roll = 21;

      if (gameStatus == WIN) {
         ++wins[roll];
         ++winSum;
      }
      else {
         ++losses[roll];
         ++loseSum;
      }
   }

   cout << "Games won or lost after the 20th roll" << endl
        << "are displayed as the 21st roll." << endl << endl;

   for (i = 1; i <= 21; i++)
      cout << setw(3) << wins[i] << " games won and " << setw(3)
           << losses[i] << " games lost on roll " << i << endl;
```

```
      // calculate chances of winning
      cout.setf(ios::fixed | ios::showpoint);
      cout << endl << "The chances of winning are " << winSum << " / "
          << winSum + loseSum << " = " << setprecision(2)
          << 100.0 * winSum / (winSum + loseSum) << "%" << endl;

      // calculate average length of game
      for (i = 1; i <= 21; i++)
         length += wins[i] * i + losses[i] * i;

      cout << "The average game length is " << setprecision(2)
          << length / 1000.0 << " rolls." << endl;

      return 0;
   }

int rollDice(void)
{
   int die1, die2, workSum;

   die1 = 1 + rand() % 6;
   die2 = 1 + rand() % 6;
   workSum = die1 + die2;

   return workSum;
}
```

```
Games won or lost after the 20th roll
are displayed as the 21st roll.

233 games won and 104 games lost on roll 1
 79 games won and 113 games lost on roll 2
 71 games won and  66 games lost on roll 3
 31 games won and  57 games lost on roll 4
 26 games won and  44 games lost on roll 5
 19 games won and  26 games lost on roll 6
 17 games won and  19 games lost on roll 7
  7 games won and  19 games lost on roll 8
 12 games won and  14 games lost on roll 9
  5 games won and  14 games lost on roll 10
  3 games won and   4 games lost on roll 11
  2 games won and   0 games lost on roll 12
  3 games won and   3 games lost on roll 13
  2 games won and   1 games lost on roll 14
  0 games won and   2 games lost on roll 15
  0 games won and   0 games lost on roll 16
  0 games won and   0 games lost on roll 17
  0 games won and   0 games lost on roll 18
  1 games won and   0 games lost on roll 19
  0 games won and   1 games lost on roll 20
  1 games won and   1 games lost on roll 21

The chances of winning are 512 / 1000 = 51.20%
The average game length is 3.32 rolls.
```

4.20 (*Airline Reservations System*) A small airline has just purchased a computer for its new automated reservations system. You have been asked to program the new system. You are to write a program to assign seats on each flight of the airline's only plane (capacity: 10 seats).

Your program should display the following menu of alternatives:

```
Please type 1 for "smoking"
Please type 2 for "nonsmoking"
```

If the person types 1, then your program should assign a seat in the smoking section (seats 1-5). If the person types 2, then your program should assign a seat in the nonsmoking section (seats 6-10). Your program should then print a boarding pass indicating the person's seat number and whether it is in the smoking or nonsmoking section of the plane.

Use a single-subscripted array to represent the seating chart of the plane. Initialize all the elements of the array to 0 to indicate that all seats are empty. As each seat is assigned, set the corresponding elements of the array to 1 to indicate that the seat is no longer available.

Your program should, of course, never assign a seat that has already been assigned. When the smoking section is full, your program should ask the person if it is acceptable to be placed in the nonsmoking section (and vice versa). If yes, then make the appropriate seat assignment. If no, then print the message **"Next flight leaves in 3 hours."**

ANS:
```cpp
// Exercise 4.20 Solution
#include <iostream.h>
#include <ctype.h>

main()
{
    const int SEATS = 11;
    int plane[SEATS] = {0}, people = 0, nonSmoking = 1, smoking = 6, choice;
    char response[2];

    while (people < 10) {
        cout << endl << "Please type 1 for \"smoking\"" << endl
             << "Please type 2 for \"non-smoking\"" << endl;
        cin >> choice;

        if (choice == 1) {

            if (!plane[smoking] && smoking <= 10) {
                cout << "Your seat assignment is " << smoking << endl;
                plane[smoking++] = 1;
                ++people;
            }
            else if (smoking > 10 && nonSmoking <= 5) {
                cout << "The smoking section is full." << endl
                     << "Would you like to sit in the non-smoking"
                     << " section (Y or N)? ";
                cin >> response;

                if (toupper(response[0]) == 'Y') {
                    cout << "Your seat assignment is " << nonSmoking << endl;
                    plane[nonSmoking++] = 1;
                    ++people;
                }
                else
                    cout << "Next flight leaves in 3 hours." << endl;
            }
            else
                cout << "Next flight leaves in 3 hours." << endl;
        }
        else {
            if (!plane[nonSmoking] && nonSmoking <= 5) {
                cout << "Your seat assignment is " << nonSmoking << endl;
                plane[nonSmoking++] = 1;
                ++people;
            }
            else if (nonSmoking > 5 && smoking <= 10) {
                cout << "The non-smoking section is full." << endl
                     << "Would you like to sit in the smoking"
                     << " section (Y or N)? ";
                cin >> response;
```

```
                if (toupper(response[0]) == 'Y') {
                    cout << "Your seat assignment is " << smoking << endl;
                    plane[smoking++] = 1;
                    ++people;
                }
                else
                    cout << "Next flight leaves in 3 hours." << endl;
            }
            else
                cout << "Next flight leaves in 3 hours." << endl;
        }
    }

    cout << "All seats for this flight are sold." << endl;
    return 0;
}
```

```
Please type 1 for "smoking"
Please type 2 for "nonsmoking"
? 2
Your seat assignment is 1

Please type 1 for "smoking"
Please type 2 for "nonsmoking"
? 1
Your seat assignment is 6

Please type 1 for "smoking"
Please type 2 for "nonsmoking"
? 2
Your seat assignment is 2

Please type 1 for "smoking"
Please type 2 for "nonsmoking"
? 1
Your seat assignment is 7

Please type 1 for "smoking"
Please type 2 for "nonsmoking"
? 2
Your seat assignment is 3

Please type 1 for "smoking"
Please type 2 for "nonsmoking"
? 2
Your seat assignment is 4

Please type 1 for "smoking"
Please type 2 for "nonsmoking"
? 2
Your seat assignment is 5

Please type 1 for "smoking"
Please type 2 for "nonsmoking"
? 2
The nonsmoking section is full.
Would you like to sit in the smoking section (Y or N)? y
Your seat assignment is 8

Please type 1 for "smoking"
Please type 2 for "nonsmoking"
? 2
```
continued

```
                                                                continued
The nonsmoking section is full.
Would you like to sit in the smoking section (Y or N)? n
Next flight leaves in 3 hours.

Please type 1 for "smoking"
Please type 2 for "nonsmoking"
? 1
Your seat assignment is 9

Please type 1 for "smoking"
Please type 2 for "nonsmoking"
? 1
Your seat assignment is 10

All seats for this flight are sold.
```

4.21   What does the following program do?

```cpp
#include <iostream.h>

void someFunction(int [], int);

main()
{
   const int arraySize = 10;
   int a[arraySize] = {32, 27, 64, 18, 95, 14, 90, 70, 60, 37};

   cout << "The values in the array are:" << endl;
   someFunction(a, arraySize);
   cout << endl;
   return 0;
}

void someFunction(int b[], int size)
{
   if (size > 0) {
      someFunction(&b[1], size - 1);
      cout << b[0] << "   ";
   }
}
```

ANS: Function **someFunction** recursively outputs an array in reverse order.

```
The values in the array are:
37   60   70   90   14   95   18   64   27   32
```

4.22   Use a double-subscripted array to solve the following problem. A company has four salespeople (1 to 4) who sell five different products (1 to 5). Once a day, each salesperson passes in a slip for each different type of product sold. Each slip contains:

1. The salesperson number
2. The product number
3. The total dollar value of that product sold that day

Thus, each salesperson passes in between 0 and 5 sales slips per day. Assume that the information from all of the slips for last month is available. Write a program that will read all this information for last month's sales, and summarize the total sales by salesperson by product. All totals should be stored in the double-subscripted array **sales**. After processing all the information for last month, print the results in tabular format with each of the columns representing a particular salesperson and each of the rows representing a particular product. Cross total each row to get the total sales of each product for last month; cross total each column to get the total sales by salesperson for last month. Your tabular printout should include these cross totals to the right of the totaled rows and to the bottom of the totaled columns.

ANS:

```cpp
// Exercise 4.22 Solution
#include <iostream.h>
#include <iomanip.h>

main()
{
    const int PEOPLE = 5, PRODUCTS = 6;
    float sales[PEOPLE][PRODUCTS] = {0.0}, value, totalSales,
          productSales[PRODUCTS] = {0.0};
    int salesPerson, product;

    cout << "Enter the salesperson (1 - 4), product number (1 - 5), "
         << "and total sales." << endl << "Enter -1 for the salesperson"
         << " to end input." << endl;
    cin >> salesPerson;

    while (salesPerson != -1) {
        cin >> product >> value;
        sales[salesPerson][product] = value;
        cin >> salesPerson;
    }

    cout << endl << "The total sales for each salesperson are displayed"
         << " at the end of each row," << endl << "and the total sales for"
         << " each product are displayed at the bottom of each" << endl
         << "column." << endl << " " << setw(12) << 1 << setw(12) << 2
         << setw(12) << 3 << setw(12) << 4 << setw(12) << 5 << setw(13)
         << "Total" << endl;

    cout.setf(ios::fixed | ios::showpoint);

    for (int i = 1; i < PEOPLE; i++) {
        totalSales = 0.0;
        cout << i;

        for (int j = 1; j < PRODUCTS; j++) {
            totalSales += sales[i][j];
            cout << setw(12) << setprecision(2) << sales[i][j];
            productSales[j] += sales[i][j];
        }

        cout << setw(12) << setprecision(2) << totalSales << endl;
    }

    cout << endl << "Total" << setw(8) << setprecision(2) << productSales[1];

    for (int j = 2; j < PRODUCTS; j++)
        cout << setw(12) << setprecision(2) << productSales[j];

    cout << endl;
    return 0;
}
```

```
Enter the salesperson (1 - 4), product number (1 - 5), and total sales.
Enter -1 for the salesperson to end input.
1 1 4.55
2 2 6.88
4 3 12.00
3 4 5.00
3 5 9.99
1 3 5.99
```

continued

```
                                                          continued
      The total sales for each salesperson are displayed at the end of
      each row, and the total sales for each product are displayed at
      the bottom of each column.
                    1         2         3         4         5      Total
      1           4.55      0.00      5.99      0.00      0.00     10.54
      2           0.00      6.88      0.00      0.00      0.00      6.88
      3           0.00      0.00      0.00      5.00      9.99     14.99
      4           0.00      0.00     12.00      0.00      0.00     12.00

      Total       4.55      6.88     17.99      5.00      9.99
```

4.23 (*Turtle Graphics*) The Logo language, which is particularly popular among personal computer users, made the concept of *turtle graphics* famous. Imagine a mechanical turtle that walks around the room under the control of a C++ program. The turtle holds a pen in one of two positions, up or down. While the pen is down, the turtle traces out shapes as it moves; while the pen is up, the turtle moves about freely without writing anything. In this problem you will simulate the operation of the turtle and create a computerized sketchpad as well.

Use a 20-by-20 array **floor** which is initialized to zeros. Read commands from an array that contains them. Keep track of the current position of the turtle at all times and whether the pen is currently up or down. Assume that the turtle always starts at position 0,0 of the floor with its pen up. The set of turtle commands your program must process are as follows:

Command	Meaning
1	Pen up
2	Pen down
3	Turn right
4	Turn left
5,10	Move forward 10 spaces (or a number other than 10)
6	Print the 20-by-20 array
9	End of data (sentinel)

Suppose that the turtle is somewhere near the center of the floor. The following "program" would draw and print a 12-by 12-square leaving the pen in the up position:

```
2
5,12
3
5,12
3
5,12
3
5,12
1
6
9
```

As the turtle moves with the pen down, set the appropriate elements of array **floor** to 1s. When the **6** command (print) is given, wherever there is a 1 in the array, display an asterisk, or some other character you choose. Wherever there is a zero display a blank. Write a program to implement the turtle graphics capabilities discussed here. Write several turtle graphics programs to draw interesting shapes. Add other commands to increase the power of your turtle graphics language.

```
ANS:
// Exercise 4.23 Solution
#include <iostream.h>
const int MAXCOMMANDS = 100, SIZE = 20;
int turnRight(int);
int turnLeft(int);
void getCommands(int [][2]);
void movePen(int, int [][SIZE], int, int);
void printArray(const int [][SIZE]);
main()
{
    enum Boolean { FALSE, TRUE };
    int floor[SIZE][SIZE] = {0}, command, direction = 0,
        commandArray[MAXCOMMANDS][2] = {0}, distance, count = 0;
    Boolean penDown = FALSE;

    getCommands(commandArray);
    command = commandArray[count][0];

    while (command != 9) {
        switch (command) {
            case 1:
                penDown = FALSE;
                break;
            case 2:
                penDown = TRUE;
                break;
            case 3:
                direction = turnRight(direction);
                break;
            case 4:
                direction = turnLeft(direction);
                break;
            case 5:
                distance = commandArray[count][1];
                movePen(penDown, floor, direction, distance);
                break;
            case 6:
                cout << endl << "The drawing is:" << endl << endl;
                printArray(floor);
                break;
        }
        command = commandArray[++count][0];
    }
    return 0;
}

void getCommands(int commands[][2])
{
    int tempCommand;
    cout << "Enter command (9 to end input): ";
    cin >> tempCommand;
    for (int i = 0; tempCommand != 9 && i < MAXCOMMANDS; i++) {
        commands[i][0] = tempCommand;

        if (tempCommand == 5) {
            cin.ignore();    // skip comma
            cin >> commands[i][1];
        }
        cout << "Enter command (9 to end input): ";
        cin >> tempCommand;
    }
    commands[i][0] = 9;   // last command
}
```

```
int turnRight(int d)
{
   return ++d > 3 ? 0 : d;
}

int turnLeft(int d)
{
   return --d < 0 ? 3 : d;
}

void movePen(int down, int a[][SIZE], int dir, int dist)
{
   static int xPos = 0, yPos = 0;

   switch (dir) {
      case 0:    // move to the right
         for (int j = 1; j <= dist && yPos + j < SIZE; j++)
            if (down)
               a[xPos][yPos + j] = 1;

         yPos += j - 1;
         break;
      case 1:    // move down
         for (int i = 1; i <= dist && xPos + i < SIZE; i++)
            if (down)
               a[xPos + i][yPos] = 1;

         xPos += i - 1;
         break;
      case 2:    // move to the left
         for (j = 1; j <= dist && yPos - j >= 0; j++)
            if (down)
               a[xPos][yPos - j] = 1;

         yPos -= j - 1;
         break;
      case 3:    // move up
         for (i = 1; i <= dist && xPos - i >= 0; i++)
            if (down)
               a[xPos - i][yPos] = 1;

         xPos -= i - 1;
         break;
   }
}

void printArray(const int a[][SIZE])
{
   for (int i = 0; i < SIZE; i++) {
      for (int j = 0; j < SIZE; j++)
         cout << (a[i][j] ? '*' : ' ');

      cout << endl;
   }
}
```

```
Enter command (9 to end input): 2
Enter command (9 to end input): 5, 12
Enter command (9 to end input): 3
Enter command (9 to end input): 5, 12
Enter command (9 to end input): 3
Enter command (9 to end input): 5, 12
                                              continued
```

```
                                                                    continued

Enter command (9 to end input): 3
Enter command (9 to end input): 5, 12
Enter command (9 to end input): 1
Enter command (9 to end input): 6
Enter command (9 to end input): 9

The drawing is:

* * * * * * * * * * * *
*                     *
*                     *
*                     *
*                     *
*                     *
*                     *
*                     *
*                     *
*                     *
*                     *
*                     *
* * * * * * * * * * * *
```

4.24   (*Knight's Tour*) One of the more interesting puzzlers for chess buffs is the Knight's Tour problem, originally proposed by the mathematician Euler. The question is this: Can the chess piece called the knight move around an empty chessboard and touch each of the 64 squares once and only once? We study this intriguing problem in depth here.

The knight makes L-shaped moves (over two in one direction and then over one in a perpendicular direction). Thus, from a square in the middle of an empty chessboard, the knight can make eight different moves (numbered 0 through 7) as shown in Fig. 4.25.

a) Draw an 8-by-8 chessboard on a sheet of paper and attempt a Knight's Tour by hand. Put a **1** in the first square you move to, a **2** in the second square, a **3** in the third, etc. Before starting the tour, estimate how far you think you will get, remembering that a full tour consists of 64 moves. How far did you get? Was this close to your estimate?

b) Now let us develop a program that will move the knight around a chessboard. The board is represented by an 8-by-8 double-subscripted array **board**. Each of the squares is initialized to zero. We describe each of the eight possible moves in terms of both their horizontal and vertical components. For example, a move of type 0 as shown in Fig. 4.25 consists of moving two squares horizontally to the right and one square vertically upward. Move 2 consists of moving one square horizontally to the left and two squares vertically upward. Horizontal moves to the left and vertical moves upward are indicated with negative numbers. The eight moves may be described by two single-subscripted arrays, **horizontal** and **vertical**, as follows:

```
horizontal[0] = 2
horizontal[1] = 1
horizontal[2] = -1
horizontal[3] = -2
horizontal[4] = -2
horizontal[5] = -1
horizontal[6] = 1
horizontal[7] = 2
vertical[0] = -1
vertical[1] = -2
vertical[2] = -2
vertical[3] = -1
vertical[4] = 1
vertical[5] = 2
vertical[6] = 2
vertical[7] = 1
```

Let the variables **currentRow** and **currentColumn** indicate the row and column of the knight's current position. To make a move of type **moveNumber**, where **moveNumber** is between 0 and 7, your program uses the statements

```
currentRow += vertical[moveNumber];
currentColumn += horizontal[moveNumber];
```

Keep a counter that varies from **1** to **64**. Record the latest count in each square the knight moves to. Remember to test each potential move to see if the knight has already visited that square. And, of course, test every potential move to make sure that the knight does not land off the chessboard. Now write a program to move the knight around the chessboard. Run the program. How many moves did the knight make?

c) After attempting to write and run a Knight's Tour program, you have probably developed some valuable insights. We will use these to develop a *heuristic* (or strategy) for moving the knight. Heuristics do not guarantee success, but a carefully developed heuristic greatly improves the chance of success. You may have observed that the outer squares are more troublesome than the squares nearer the center of the board. In fact, the most troublesome, or inaccessible, squares are the four corners.

Intuition may suggest that you should attempt to move the knight to the most troublesome squares first and leave open those that are easiest to get to so when the board gets congested near the end of the tour there will be a greater chance of success.

We may develop an "accessibility heuristic" by classifying each of the squares according to how accessible they are, and then always moving the knight to the square (within the knight's L-shaped moves, of course) that is most inaccessible. We label a double-subscripted array **accessibility** with numbers indicating from how many squares each particular square is accessible. On a blank chessboard, each center square is rated as **8**, each corner square is rated as **2**, and the other squares have accessibility numbers of **3**, **4**, or **6** as follows:

```
2  3  4  4  4  4  3  2
3  4  6  6  6  6  4  3
4  6  8  8  8  8  6  4
4  6  8  8  8  8  6  4
4  6  8  8  8  8  6  4
4  6  8  8  8  8  6  4
3  4  6  6  6  6  4  3
2  3  4  4  4  4  3  2
```

Now write a version of the Knight's Tour program using the accessibility heuristic. At any time, the knight should move to the square with the lowest accessibility number. In case of a tie, the knight may move to any of the tied squares. Therefore, the tour may begin in any of the four corners. (*Note:* As the knight moves around the chessboard, your program should reduce the accessibility numbers as more and more squares become occupied. In this way, at any given time during the tour, each available square's accessibility number will remain equal to precisely the number of squares from which that square may be reached.) Run this version of your program. Did you get a full tour? Now modify the program to run 64 tours, one starting from each square of the chessboard. How many full tours did you get?

ANS:
```
// Exercise 4.24 Part C Solution
// Knight's Tour - access version
// runs one tour

#include <iostream.h>
#include <iomanip.h>
#include <stdlib.h>
#include <time.h>

const int SIZE = 8;

void clearBoard(int [][SIZE]);
void printBoard(const int [][SIZE]);
int validMove(int, int, const int [][SIZE]);
```

```
main()
{
   enum Boolean { FALSE, TRUE };
   int board[SIZE][SIZE], currentRow, currentColumn, moveNumber = 0,
      access[SIZE][SIZE] = {2, 3, 4, 4, 4, 4, 3, 2,
                            3, 4, 6, 6, 6, 6, 4, 3,
                            4, 6, 8, 8, 8, 8, 6, 4,
                            4, 6, 8, 8, 8, 8, 6, 4,
                            4, 6, 8, 8, 8, 8, 6, 4,
                            4, 6, 8, 8, 8, 8, 6, 4,
                            3, 4, 6, 6, 6, 6, 4, 3,
                            2, 3, 4, 4, 4, 4, 3, 2},

      testRow, testColumn, count, minRow, minColumn,
      minAccess = 9, accessNumber,
      horizontal[SIZE] = {2, 1, -1, -2, -2, -1, 1, 2},
      vertical[SIZE] = {-1, -2, -2, -1, 1, 2, 2, 1};
   Boolean done;

   srand(time(NULL));

   clearBoard(board);    // initialize array board
   currentRow = rand() % 8;
   currentColumn = rand() % 8;
   board[currentRow][currentColumn] = ++moveNumber;
   done = FALSE;

   while (!done) {
      accessNumber = minAccess;

      for (int moveType = 0; moveType < SIZE; moveType++) {
         testRow = currentRow + vertical[moveType];
         testColumn = currentColumn + horizontal[moveType];

         if (validMove(testRow, testColumn, board)) {

            if (access[testRow][testColumn] < accessNumber) {
               accessNumber = access[testRow][testColumn];
               minRow = testRow;
               minColumn = testColumn;
            }

            --access[testRow][testColumn];
         }
      }

      if (accessNumber == minAccess)
         done = TRUE;
      else {
         currentRow = minRow;
         currentColumn = minColumn;
         board[currentRow][currentColumn] = ++moveNumber;
      }
   }

   cout << "The tour ended with " << moveNumber << " moves." << endl;

   if (moveNumber == 64)
      cout << "This was a full tour!" << endl << endl;
   else
      cout << "This was not a full tour." << endl << endl;

   cout << "The board for this test is:" << endl << endl;
   printBoard(board);

   return 0;
}
```

```
void clearBoard(int workBoard[][SIZE])
{
   for (int row = 0; row < SIZE; row++)
      for (int col = 0; col < SIZE; col++)
         workBoard[row][col] = 0;
}


void printBoard(const int workBoard[][SIZE])
{
   cout << "   0  1  2  3  4  5  6  7" << endl;

   for (int row = 0; row < SIZE; row++) {
      cout << row;

      for (int col = 0; col < SIZE; col++)
         cout << setw(3) << workBoard[row][col];

      cout << endl;
   }

   cout << endl;
}


int validMove(int row, int column, const int workBoard[][SIZE])
{
   // NOTE: This test stops as soon as it becomes false
   return (row >= 0 && row < SIZE && column >= 0 && column < SIZE
          && workBoard[row][column] == 0);
}
```

```
The tour ended with 64 moves.
This was a full tour!

The board for this test is:

   0  1  2  3  4  5  6  7
0  7  4  9 24 31  2 19 22
1 10 25  6  3 20 23 34  1
2  5  8 27 30 35 32 21 18
3 26 11 56 49 28 41 36 33
4 57 50 29 42 61 54 17 40
5 12 43 60 55 48 39 64 37
6 51 58 45 14 53 62 47 16
7 44 13 52 59 46 15 38 63
```

d) Write a version of the Knight's Tour program which, when encountering a tie between two or more squares, decides what square to choose by looking ahead to those squares reachable from the "tied" squares. Your program should move to the square for which the next move would arrive at a square with the lowest accessibility number.

4.25 (*Knight's Tour: Brute Force Approaches*) In Exercise 4.24 we developed a solution to the Knight's Tour problem. The approach used, called the "accessibility heuristic," generates many solutions and executes efficiently.

As computers continue increasing in power, we will be able to solve more problems with sheer computer power and relatively unsophisticated algorithms, Let us call this approach "brute force" problem solving.

a) Use random number generation to enable the knight to walk around the chess board (in its legitimate L-shaped moves, of course) at random. Your program should run one tour and print the final chessboard. How far did the knight get?

```
ANS:
// Exercise 4.25 Part A Solution
#include <iostream.h>
#include <iomanip.h>
#include <stdlib.h>
#include <time.h>

const int SIZE = 8;
int validMove(int, int, const int [][SIZE]);
void printBoard(const int [][SIZE]);

main()
{
    enum Answer { NO, YES };
    int currentRow, currentColumn, moveType, moveNumber = 0,
        testRow, testColumn, goodMove, board[SIZE][SIZE] = {0},
        horizontal[SIZE] = {2, 1, -1, -2, -2, -1, 1, 2},
        vertical[SIZE] = {-1, -2, -2, -1, 1, 2, 2, 1};
    Answer done;

    srand(time(NULL));

    currentRow = rand() % SIZE;
    currentColumn = rand() % SIZE;
    board[currentRow][currentColumn] = ++moveNumber;
    done = NO;

    while (!done) {
        moveType = rand() % SIZE;
        testRow = currentRow + vertical[moveType];
        testColumn = currentColumn + horizontal[moveType];
        goodMove = validMove(testRow, testColumn, board);

        if (goodMove) {
            currentRow = testRow;
            currentColumn = testColumn;
            board[currentRow][currentColumn] = ++moveNumber;
        }
        else {
            for (int count = 0; count < SIZE - 1 && !goodMove; count++) {
                moveType = ++moveType % SIZE;
                testRow = currentRow + vertical[moveType];
                testColumn = currentColumn + horizontal[moveType];
                goodMove = validMove(testRow, testColumn, board);

                if (goodMove) {
                    currentRow = testRow;
                    currentColumn = testColumn;
                    board[currentRow][currentColumn] = ++moveNumber;
                }
            }

            if (!goodMove)
                done = YES;
        }

        if (moveNumber == 64)
            done = YES;
    }

    cout << "The tour has ended with " << moveNumber << " moves." << endl;

    if (moveNumber == 64)
        cout << "This was a full tour!" << endl;
    else
        cout << "This was not a full tour." << endl;

    cout << "The board for this random test was:" << endl << endl;
    printBoard(board);
    return 0;
}
```

```
int validMove(int row, int column, const int workBoard[][SIZE])
{
   // NOTE: This test stops as soon as it becomes false
   return (row >= 0 && row < SIZE && column >= 0 && column < SIZE
           && workBoard[row][column] == 0);
}

void printBoard(const int board[][SIZE])
{
   cout << "    0  1  2  3  4  5  6  7" << endl;

   for (int row = 0; row < SIZE; row++) {
      cout << row;

      for (int col = 0; col < SIZE; col++)
         cout << setw(3) << board[row][col];

      cout << endl;
   }

   cout << endl;
}
```

```
The tour has ended with 49 moves.
This was not a full tour.
The board for this random test was:

    0  1  2  3  4  5  6  7
0   0 46  0 28 25 34 49 36
1   0 29 26 33 48 37 24  0
2  45  0 47  0 27 40 35 38
3  30  1 44 17 32 19  0 23
4  43 16 31 20 41 14 39 10
5   2  5 42 15 18 11 22 13
6   0  0  7  4 21  0  9  0
7   6  3  0  0  8  0 12  0
```

b) Most likely, the preceding program produced a relatively short tour. Now modify your program to attempt 1000 tours. Use a single-subscripted array to keep track of the number of tours of each length. When your program finishes attempting the 1000 tours, it should print this information in neat tabular format. What was the best result?

ANS:
```
// Exercise 4.25 Part B Solution

#include <iostream.h>
#include <iomanip.h>
#include <stdlib.h>
#include <time.h>

const int SIZE = 8, TOURS = 1000, MAXMOVES = 65;
enum Answer { NO, YES };

int validMove(int, int, int, const int [][SIZE]);

main()
{
   int currentRow, currentColumn, moveType, moveNumber, testRow, testColumn,
       moveTotal[MAXMOVES] = {0}, goodMove, board[SIZE][SIZE],
       horizontal[SIZE] = {2, 1, -1, -2, -2, -1, 1, 2},
       vertical[SIZE] = {-1, -2, -2, -1, 1, 2, 2, 1};
```

```
        Answer done;
        srand(time(NULL));
        for (int i = 0; i < TOURS; i++) {
            for (int row = 0; row < SIZE; row++)
                for (int col = 0; col < SIZE; col++)
                    board[row][col] = 0;

            moveNumber = 0;
            currentRow = rand() % SIZE;
            currentColumn = rand() % SIZE;
            board[currentRow][currentColumn] = ++moveNumber;
            done = NO;

            while (!done) {
                moveType = rand() % SIZE;
                testRow = currentRow + vertical[moveType];
                testColumn = currentColumn + horizontal[moveType];
                goodMove = validMove(testRow, testColumn, moveType, board);

                if (goodMove) {
                    currentRow = testRow;
                    currentColumn = testColumn;
                    board[currentRow][currentColumn] = ++moveNumber;
                }
                else {
                    for (int count = 0; count < SIZE - 1 && !goodMove; count++) {
                        moveType = ++moveType % SIZE;
                        testRow = currentRow + vertical[moveType];
                        testColumn = currentColumn + horizontal[moveType];
                        goodMove = validMove(testRow, testColumn, moveType, board);

                        if (goodMove) {
                            currentRow = testRow;
                            currentColumn = testColumn;
                            board[currentRow][currentColumn] = ++moveNumber;
                        }
                    }

                    if (!goodMove)
                        done = YES;
                }

                if (moveNumber == 64)
                    done = YES;
            }

            ++moveTotal[moveNumber];
        }

        for (i = 1; i < MAXMOVES; i++)
            if (moveTotal[i])
                cout << "There were " << moveTotal[i] << " tours of " << i
                    << " moves." << endl;

        return 0;
    }

    int validMove(int testRow, int testColumn, int moveType,
                  const int board[][SIZE])
    {
        if (testRow >= 0 && testRow < SIZE && testColumn >= 0 &&
                                                testColumn < SIZE)
            return board[testRow][testColumn] != 0 ? NO : YES;
        else
            return NO;
    }
```

```
There were 1 tours of 5 moves.
There were 1 tours of 7 moves.
There were 1 tours of 8 moves.
There were 1 tours of 9 moves.
There were 5 tours of 10 moves.
There were 3 tours of 11 moves.
There were 5 tours of 12 moves.
There were 6 tours of 13 moves.
There were 6 tours of 14 moves.
There were 5 tours of 15 moves.
There were 11 tours of 16 moves.
There were 9 tours of 17 moves.
There were 7 tours of 18 moves.
There were 14 tours of 19 moves.
There were 16 tours of 20 moves.
There were 12 tours of 21 moves.
There were 19 tours of 22 moves.
There were 20 tours of 23 moves.
There were 12 tours of 24 moves.
There were 13 tours of 25 moves.
There were 17 tours of 26 moves.
There were 20 tours of 27 moves.
There were 29 tours of 28 moves.
There were 16 tours of 29 moves.
There were 26 tours of 30 moves.
There were 20 tours of 31 moves.
There were 30 tours of 32 moves.
There were 21 tours of 33 moves.
There were 37 tours of 34 moves.
There were 25 tours of 35 moves.
There were 30 tours of 36 moves.
There were 35 tours of 37 moves.
There were 34 tours of 38 moves.
There were 40 tours of 39 moves.
There were 43 tours of 40 moves.
There were 40 tours of 41 moves.
There were 31 tours of 42 moves.
There were 23 tours of 43 moves.
There were 38 tours of 44 moves.
There were 29 tours of 45 moves.
There were 32 tours of 46 moves.
There were 35 tours of 47 moves.
There were 36 tours of 48 moves.
There were 22 tours of 49 moves.
There were 25 tours of 50 moves.
There were 17 tours of 51 moves.
There were 23 tours of 52 moves.
There were 11 tours of 53 moves.
There were 13 tours of 54 moves.
There were 14 tours of 55 moves.
There were 8 tours of 56 moves.
There were 5 tours of 57 moves.
There were 4 tours of 58 moves.
There were 1 tours of 59 moves.
There were 2 tours of 60 moves.
There were 1 tours of 61 moves.
```

c) Most likely, the preceding program gave you some "respectable" tours but no full tours. Now "pull all the stops out" and simply let your program run until it produces a full tour. (*Caution:* This version of the program could run for hours on a powerful computer.) Once again, keep a table of the number of tours of each length, and print this table when the first full tour is found. How many tours did your program attempt before producing a full tour? How much time did it take?

    d) Compare the brute force version of the Knight's Tour with the accessibility heuristic version. Which required a more careful study of the problem? Which algorithm was more difficult to develop? Which required more computer power? Could we be certain (in advance) of obtaining a full tour with the accessibility heuristic approach? Could we be certain (in advance) of obtaining a full tour with the brute force approach? Argue the pros and cons of brute force problem solving in general.

4.26 (*Eight Queens*) Another puzzler for chess buffs is the Eight Queens problem. Simply stated: Is it possible to place eight queens on an empty chessboard so that no queen is "attacking" any other, i.e., no two queens are in the same row, the same column, or along the same diagonal? Use the thinking developed in Exercise 4.24 to formulate a heuristic for solving the Eight Queens problem. Run your program. (*Hint:* It is possible to assign a value to each square of the chessboard indicating how many squares of an empty chessboard are "eliminated" if a queen is placed in that square. Each of the corners would be assigned the value 22, as in Fig. 4.26.) Once these "elimination numbers" are placed in all 64 squares, an appropriate heuristic might be: Place the next queen in the square with the smallest elimination number. Why is this strategy intuitively appealing?

4.27 (*Eight Queens: Brute Force Approaches*) In this exercise you will develop several brute force approaches to solving the Eight Queens problem introduced in Exercise 4.26.

    a) Solve the Eight Queens exercise, using the random brute force technique developed in Exercise 4.25.
    ANS:

```cpp
// Exercise 4.27 Part A Solution
#include <iostream.h>
#include <iomanip.h>
#include <time.h>
#include <stdlib.h>

enum Answer { NO, YES };

int queenCheck(const char [][8], int, int);
void placeQueens(char [][8]);
void printBoard(const char [][8]);
void xConflictSquares(char [][8], int, int);
void xDiagonals(char [][8], int, int);
Answer availableSquare(const char [][8]);

inline int validMove(const char board[][8], int row, int col)
   { return (row >= 0 && row < 8 && col >= 0 && col < 8); }

main()
{
   char board [8][8] = {'\0'};

   srand(time(NULL));

   placeQueens(board);
   printBoard(board);

   return 0;
}

Answer availableSquare(const char board[][8])
{
   for (int row = 0; row < 8; row++)
      for (int col = 0; col < 8; col++)
         if (board[row][col] == '\0')
            return NO;  // at least one open square is available

   return YES;  // no available squares
}

void placeQueens(char board[][8])
{
   const char QUEEN = 'Q';
   int rowMove, colMove, queens = 0;
   Answer done = NO;
```

```
      while (queens < 8 && done == NO) {
         rowMove = rand() % 8;
         colMove = rand() % 8;

         if (queenCheck(board, rowMove, colMove)) {
            board[rowMove][colMove] = QUEEN;
            xConflictSquares(board, rowMove, colMove);
            ++queens;
         }

         done = availableSquare(board);
      }
}

void xConflictSquares(char board[][8], int row, int col)
{
    for (int loop = 0; loop < 8; loop++) {
       // place an '*' in the row occupied by the queen
       if (board[row][loop] == '\0')
          board[row][loop] = '*';

       // place an '*' in the col occupied by the queen
       if (board[loop][col] == '\0')
          board[loop][col] = '*';
    }

    // place an '*' in the diagonals occupied by the queen
    xDiagonals(board, row, col);
}

int queenCheck(const char board[][8], int row, int col)
{
   int r = row, c = col;

   // check row and column for a queen
   for (int d = 0; d < 8; d++)
      if (board[row][d] == 'Q' || board[d][col] == 'Q')
         return NO;

   // check upper left diagonal for a queen
   for (d = 0; d < 8 && validMove(board, --r, --c); d++)
      if (board[r][c] == 'Q')
         return NO;

   r = row;
   c = col;
   // check upper right diagonal for a queen
   for (d = 0; d < 8 && validMove(board, --r, ++c); d++)
      if (board[r][c] == 'Q')
         return NO;

   r = row;
   c = col;
   // check lower left diagonal for a queen
   for (d = 0; d < 8 && validMove(board, ++r, --c); d++)
      if (board[r][c] == 'Q')
         return NO;

   r = row;
   c = col;
   // check lower right diagonal for a queen
   for (d = 0; d < 8 && validMove(board, ++r, ++c); d++)
      if (board[r][c] == 'Q')
         return NO;

   return YES;  // no queen in conflict
}
```

```cpp
void xDiagonals(char board[][8], int row, int col)
{
    int r = row, c = col;

    // upper left diagonal
    for (int d = 0; d < 8 && validMove(board, --r, --c); d++)
        board[r][c] = '*';

    r = row;
    c = col;
    // upper right diagonal
    for (d = 0; d < 8 && validMove(board, --r, ++c); d++)
        board[r][c] = '*';

    r = row;
    c = col;
    // lower left diagonal
    for (d = 0; d < 8 && validMove(board, ++r, --c); d++)
        board[r][c] = '*';

    r = row;
    c = col;
    // lower right diagonal
    for (d = 0; d < 8 && validMove(board, ++r, ++c); d++)
        board[r][c] = '*';
}

void printBoard(const char board[][8])
{
    int queens = 0;

    // header for columns
    cout << "   0 1 2 3 4 5 6 7" << endl;
    for (int r = 0; r < 8; r++) {
        cout << setw(2) << r << ' ';

        for (int c = 0; c < 8; c++) {
            cout << board[r][c] << ' ';

            if (board[r][c] == 'Q')
                ++queens;
        }

        cout << endl;
    }

    if (queens == 8)
        cout << endl << "Eight Queens were placed on the board!" << endl;
    else
        cout << endl << queens << " Queens were placed on the board."
             << endl;
}
```

```
   0 1 2 3 4 5 6 7
0  * * * * Q * * *
1  * * * * * * * *
2  * Q * * * * * *
3  * * * * * Q * *
4  * * Q * * * * *
5  Q * * * * * * *
6  * * * * * * Q *
7  * * * Q * * * *

7 Queens were placed on the board.
```

```
      0 1 2 3 4 5 6 7
   0  * * * Q * * * *
   1  * Q * * * * * *
   2  * * * * * * Q *
   3  * * Q * * * * *
   4  * * * * * Q * *
   5  * * * * * * * Q
   6  Q * * * * * * *
   7  * * * * Q * * *

   Eight Queens were placed on the board!
```

b) Use an exhaustive technique, i.e., try all possible combinations of eight queens on the chessboard.

c) Why do you suppose the exhaustive brute force approach may not be appropriate for solving the Knight's Tour problem?

d) Compare and contrast the random brute force and exhaustive brute force approaches in general.

4.28 (*Knight's Tour: Closed Tour Test*) In the Knight's Tour, a full tour occurs when the knight makes 64 moves touching each square of the chess board once and only once. A closed tour occurs when the 64th move is one move away from the location in which the knight started the tour. Modify the Knight's Tour program you wrote in Exercise 4.24 to test for a closed tour if a full tour has occurred.

ANS:

```cpp
// Exercise 4.28 Solution
#include <iostream.h>
#include <iomanip.h>
#include <stdlib.h>
#include <time.h>

const int SIZE = 8;

void clearBoard(int [][SIZE]);
void printBoard(const int [][SIZE]);
int validMove(int, int, const int [][SIZE]);

main()
{
    enum Answer { NO, YES };
    int board[SIZE][SIZE], firstMoveRow, firstMoveCol,
        access[SIZE][SIZE] = {2, 3, 4, 4, 4, 4, 3, 2,
                              3, 4, 6, 6, 6, 6, 4, 3,
                              4, 6, 8, 8, 8, 8, 6, 4,
                              4, 6, 8, 8, 8, 8, 6, 4,
                              4, 6, 8, 8, 8, 8, 6, 4,
                              4, 6, 8, 8, 8, 8, 6, 4,
                              3, 4, 6, 6, 6, 6, 4, 3,
                              2, 3, 4, 4, 4, 4, 3, 2},
        currentRow, currentColumn, moveNumber = 0, testRow, testColumn,
        minRow, minColumn, minAccess = 9, accessNumber,
        horizontal[SIZE] = {2, 1, -1, -2, -2, -1, 1, 2},
        vertical[SIZE] = {-1, -2, -2, -1, 1, 2, 2, 1};

    Answer done, closedTour = NO;

    srand(time(NULL));

    clearBoard(board);   // initialize array board
    currentRow = rand() % SIZE;
    currentColumn = rand() % SIZE;
    firstMoveRow = currentRow;       // store first moves row
    firstMoveCol = currentColumn;    // store first moves col

    board[currentRow][currentColumn] = ++moveNumber;
    done = NO;
```

```
        while (!done) {
            accessNumber = minAccess;

            for (int moveType = 0; moveType < SIZE; moveType++) {
                testRow = currentRow + vertical[moveType];
                testColumn = currentColumn + horizontal[moveType];

                if (validMove(testRow, testColumn, board)) {

                    if (access[testRow][testColumn] < accessNumber) {
                        accessNumber = access[testRow][testColumn];
                        minRow = testRow;
                        minColumn = testColumn;
                    }

                    --access[testRow][testColumn];
                }
            }

            if (accessNumber == minAccess)
                done = YES;
            else {
                currentRow = minRow;
                currentColumn = minColumn;
                board[currentRow][currentColumn] = ++moveNumber;

                // check for closed tour
                if (moveNumber == 64)
                    for (moveType = 0; moveType < SIZE; moveType++) {
                        testRow = currentRow + vertical[moveType];
                        testColumn = currentColumn + horizontal[moveType];

                        if (testRow == firstMoveRow && testColumn == firstMoveCol)
                            closedTour = YES;
                    }
            }
        }

        cout << "The tour ended with " << moveNumber << " moves." << endl;

        if (moveNumber == 64 && closedTour == YES)
            cout << "This was a CLOSED tour!" << endl << endl;
        else if (moveNumber == 64)
            cout << "This was a full tour!" << endl << endl;
        else
            cout << "This was not a full tour." << endl << endl;

        cout << "The board for this test is:" << endl << endl;

        printBoard(board);

        return 0;
}

void clearBoard(int workBoard[][SIZE])
{
    for (int row = 0; row < SIZE; row++)
        for (int col = 0; col < SIZE; col++)
            workBoard[row][col] = 0;
}
```

```
void printBoard(const int workBoard[][SIZE])
{
   cout << "   0  1  2  3  4  5  6  7" << endl;

   for (int row = 0; row < SIZE; row++) {
      cout << row;

      for (int col = 0; col < SIZE; col++)
         cout << setw(3) << workBoard[row][col];

      cout << endl;
   }

   cout << endl;
}


int validMove(int row, int column, const int workBoard[][SIZE])
{
   // NOTE: This test stops as soon as it becomes false
   return (row >= 0 && row < SIZE && column >= 0 && column < SIZE
           && workBoard[row][column] == 0);
}
```

```
The tour ended with 64 moves.
This was a CLOSED tour!

The board for this test is:

   0  1  2  3  4  5  6  7
0  4 23 38 49  6 21 28 61
1 39 48  5 22 37 60  7 20
2 24  3 50 45 52 27 62 29
3 47 40 53 26 59 36 19  8
4  2 25 46 51 44 63 30 35
5 41 54 13 64 33 58  9 18
6 14  1 56 43 16 11 34 31
7 55 42 15 12 57 32 17 10
```

4.29   (*The Sieve of Eratosthenes*) A prime integer is any integer that is evenly divisible only by itself and 1. The Sieve of Eratosthenes is a method of finding prime numbers. It operates as follows:

   1) Create an array with all elements initialized to 1 (true). Array elements with prime subscripts will remain 1. All other array elements will eventually be set to zero.

   2) Starting with array subscript 2 (subscript 1 must be prime), every time an array element is found whose value is 1, loop through the remainder of the array and set to zero every element whose subscript is a multiple of the subscript for the element with value 1. For array subscript 2, all elements beyond 2 in the array that are multiples of 2 will be set to zero (subscripts 4, 6, 8, 10, etc.); for array subscript 3, all elements beyond 3 in the array that are multiples of 3 will be set to zero (subscripts 6, 9, 12, 15, etc.); and so on.

When this process is complete, the array elements that are still set to one indicate that the subscript is a prime number. These subscripts can then be printed. Write a program that uses an array of 1000 elements to determine and print the prime numbers between 1 and 999. Ignore element 0 of the array.

```
ANS:
// Exercise 4.29 Solution
#include <iostream.h>
#include <iomanip.h>

main()
{
   const int SIZE = 1000;
   int array[SIZE], count = 0;

   for (int loop = 0; loop < SIZE; loop++)
      array[loop] = 1;

   for (loop = 1; loop < SIZE; loop++)
      if (array[loop] == 1 && loop != 1)
         for (int loop2 = loop; loop2 <= SIZE; loop2++)
            if (loop2 % loop == 0 && loop2 != loop)
               array[loop2] = 0;

   // range 2 - 197
   for (loop = 2; loop < SIZE; loop++)
      if (array[loop] == 1) {
         cout << setw(3) << loop << " is a prime number." << endl;
         ++count;
      }

   cout << "A total of " << count << " prime numbers were found." << endl;

   return 0;
}
```

```
  2 is a prime number.
  3 is a prime number.
  5 is a prime number.
  7 is a prime number.
 11 is a prime number.
 13 is a prime number.
 17 is a prime number.
 19 is a prime number.
 23 is a prime number.
 29 is a prime number.
...
941 is a prime number.
947 is a prime number.
953 is a prime number.
967 is a prime number.
971 is a prime number.
977 is a prime number.
983 is a prime number.
991 is a prime number.
997 is a prime number.
```

4.30   (*Bucket Sort*) A bucket sort begins with a single-subscripted array of positive integers to be sorted, and a double-subscripted array of integers with rows subscripted from 0 to 9 and columns subscripted from 0 to $n - 1$ where n is the number of values in the array to be sorted. Each row of the double-subscripted array is referred to as a bucket. Write a function `bucketSort` that takes an integer array and the array size as arguments and performs as follows:

1) Place each value of the single-subscripted array into a row of the bucket array based on the value's ones digit. For example, 97 is placed in row 7, 3 is placed in row 3, and 100 is placed in row 0. This is called a "distribution pass."

2) Loop through the bucket array row-by-row and copy the values back to the original array. This is called a "gathering pass." The new order of the preceding values in the single-subscripted array is 100, 3, and 97.

3) Repeat this process for each subsequent digit position (tens, hundreds, thousands, etc.).

On the second pass, 100 is placed in row 0, 3 is placed in row 0 (because 3 has no tens digit), and 97 is placed in row 9. After the gathering pass, the order of the values in the single-subscripted array is 100, 3, and 97. On the third pass, 100 is placed in row 1, 3 is placed in row zero and 97 is placed in row zero (after the 3). After the last gathering pass, the original array is now in sorted order.

Note that the double-subscripted array of buckets is ten times the size of the integer array being sorted. This sorting technique provides better performance than a bubble sort, but requires much more memory. The bubble sort requires space for only one additional element of data. This is an example of the space-time tradeoff: The bucket sort uses more memory than the bubble sort, but performs better. This version of the bucket sort requires copying all the data back to the original array on each pass. Another possibility is to create a second double-subscripted bucket array and repeatedly swap the data between the two bucket arrays.

ANS:

```cpp
// Exercise 4.30 Solution
#include <iostream.h>
#include <iomanip.h>

// constant size must be defined as the array size for bucketSort to work
const int SIZE = 12;

void bucketSort(int []);
void distributeElements(int [], int [][SIZE], int);
void collectElements(int [], int [][SIZE]);
int numberOfDigits(int [], int);
void zeroBucket(int [][SIZE]);

main()
{
    int array[SIZE] = {19, 13, 5, 27, 1, 26, 31, 16, 2, 9, 11, 21};

    cout << "Array elements in original order:" << endl;

    for (int i = 0; i < SIZE; i++)
        cout << setw(3) << array[i];

    cout << endl;
    bucketSort(array);

    cout << endl << "Array elements in sorted order:" << endl;

    for (i = 0; i < SIZE; i++)
        cout << setw(3) << array[i];

    cout << endl;
    return 0;
}

// Perform the bucket sort algorithm
void bucketSort(int a[])
{
    int totalDigits, bucket[10][SIZE] = {0};

    totalDigits = numberOfDigits(a, SIZE);

    for (int i = 1; i <= totalDigits; i++) {
        distributeElements(a, bucket, i);
        collectElements(a, bucket);

        if (i != totalDigits)
            zeroBucket(bucket);  // set all bucket contents to zero
    }
}
```

```
// Determine the number of digits in the largest number
int numberOfDigits(int b[], int arraySize)
{
   int largest = b[0], digits = 0;

   for (int i = 1; i < arraySize; i++)
      if (b[i] > largest)
         largest = b[i];

   while (largest != 0) {
      ++digits;
      largest /= 10;
   }

   return digits;
}

// Distribute elements into buckets based on specified digit
void distributeElements(int a[], int buckets[][SIZE], int digit)
{
   int divisor = 10, bucketNumber, elementNumber;

   for (int i = 1; i < digit; i++)    // determine the divisor
      divisor *= 10;                  // used to get specific digit
   for (i = 0; i < SIZE; i++) {
      // bucketNumber example for hundreds digit:
      // (1234 % 1000 - 1234 % 100) / 100 --> 2
      bucketNumber = (a[i] % divisor - a[i] % (divisor / 10)) /
                                                (divisor / 10);

      // retrieve value in buckets[bucketNumber][0] to determine
      // which element of the row to store a[i] in.
      elementNumber = ++buckets[bucketNumber][0];
      buckets[bucketNumber][elementNumber] = a[i];
   }
}

// Return elements to original array
void collectElements(int a[], int buckets[][SIZE])
{
   int subscript = 0;

   for (int i = 0; i < 10; i++)
      for (int j = 1; j <= buckets[i][0]; j++)
         a[subscript++] = buckets[i][j];
}

// Set all buckets to zero
void zeroBucket(int buckets[][SIZE])
{
   for (int i = 0; i < 10; i++)
      for (int j = 0; j < SIZE; j++)
         buckets[i][j] = 0;
}
```

```
Array elements in original order:
  19 13   5 27   1 26 31 16   2   9 11 21

Array elements in sorted order:
   1   2   5   9 11 13 16 19 21 26 27 31
```

Recursion Exercises

4.31   (*Selection Sort*) A selection sort searches an array looking for the smallest element in the array. Then, the smallest element is swapped with the first element of the array. The process is repeated for the subarray beginning with the second element of the array. Each pass of the array results in one element being placed in its proper location. This sort performs comparably to the bubble sort—for an array of n elements, $n - 1$ passes must be made, and for each subarray, $n - 1$ comparisons must be made to find the smallest value. When the subarray being processed contains one element, the array is sorted. Write recursive function **selectionSort** to perform this algorithm.

ANS:

```
// Exercise 4.31 Solution

#include <iostream.h>
#include <iomanip.h>
#include <stdlib.h>
#include <time.h>

void selectionSort(int [], int);

main()
{
    const int SIZE = 10, MAXRANGE = 1000;
    int sortThisArray[SIZE] = {0};

    srand(time(NULL));

    for (int loop = 0; loop < SIZE; loop++)
        sortThisArray[loop] = 1 + rand() % MAXRANGE;

    cout << endl << "Unsorted array is:" << endl;
    for (loop = 0; loop < SIZE; loop++)
        cout << ' ' << sortThisArray[loop] << ' ';

    selectionSort(sortThisArray, SIZE);

    cout << endl << endl << "Sorted array is:" << endl;
    for (loop = 0; loop < SIZE; loop++)
        cout << ' ' << sortThisArray[loop] << ' ';

    cout << endl << endl;
    return 0;
}

void selectionSort(int array[], int size)
{
    int temp;

    if (size >= 1) {

        for (int loop = 0; loop < size; loop++)
            if (array[loop] < array[0]) {
                temp = array[loop];
                array[loop] = array[0];
                array[0] = temp;
            }

        selectionSort(&array[1], size - 1);
    }
}
```

```
Unsorted array is:
 725  394  408  377  45  527  244  555  312  542

Sorted array is:
 45  244  312  377  394  408  527  542  555  725
```

4.32   (*Palindromes*) A palindrome is a string that is spelled the same way forwards and backwards. Some examples of palindromes are: "radar," "able was i ere i saw elba," and (if blanks are ignored) "a man a plan a canal panama." Write a recursive function **testPalindrome** that returns 1 if the string stored in the array is a palindrome, and 0 otherwise. The function should ignore spaces and punctuation in the string.

ANS:

```
// Exercise 4.32 Solution
#include <iostream.h>

int testPalindrome(const char [], int, int);

main()
{
    const int SIZE = 80;
    char c, string[SIZE], copy[SIZE];
    int count = 0;

    cout << "Enter a sentence:" << endl;

    while ( ( c = cin.get() ) != '\n' && count < SIZE)
        string[count++] = c;

    string[count] = '\0';    // terminate string

    // make a copy of string without spaces
    for (int copyCount = 0, i = 0; string[i] != '\0'; i++)
        if (string[i] != ' ')
            copy[copyCount++] = string[i];

    if (testPalindrome(copy, 0, copyCount - 1))
        cout << '\"' << string << "\" is a palindrome" << endl;
    else
        cout << '\"' << string << "\" is not a palindrome" << endl;

    return 0;
}

int testPalindrome(const char array[], int left, int right)
{
    if (left == right || left > right)
        return 1;
    else if (array[left] != array[right])
        return 0;
    else
        return testPalindrome(array, left + 1, right - 1);
}
```

```
Enter a sentence:
"no gorf was a saw frog on" is a palindrome
```

```
Enter a sentence:
"no gorf was a frog saw on" is not a palindrome
```

4.33   (*Linear Search*) Modify Fig. 4.19 to use recursive function **linearSearch** to perform a linear search of the array. The function should receive an integer array and the size of the array as arguments. If the search key is found, return the array subscript; otherwise, return −1.

ANS:
```
// Exercise 4.33 Solution
#include <iostream.h>

int linearSearch(const int [], int, int, int);

main()
{
   const int SIZE = 100;
   int array[SIZE], searchKey, element;

   for (int loop = 0; loop < SIZE; loop++)
      array[loop] = 2 * loop;

   cout << "Enter the integer search key: ";
   cin >> searchKey;

   element = linearSearch(array, searchKey, 0, SIZE - 1);

   if (element != -1)
      cout << "Found value in element " << element << endl;
   else
      cout << "Value not found" << endl;

   return 0;
}

int linearSearch(const int array[], int key, int low, int high)
{
   if (array[low] == key)
      return low;
   else if (low == high)
      return -1;
   else
      return linearSearch(array, key, low + 1, high);
}
```

```
Enter the integer search key: 6
Found value in element 3
```

```
Enter the integer search key: 7
Value not found
```

4.34   (*Binary Search*) Modify the program of Fig. 4.20 to use a recursive function **binarySearch** to perform the binary search of the array. The function should receive an integer array and the starting subscript and ending subscript as arguments. If the search key is found, return the array subscript; otherwise, return –1.

ANS:
```
// Exercise 4.34 Solution
#include <iostream.h>
#include <iomanip.h>

const int SIZE = 15;

int binarySearch(const int [], int, int, int);
void printRow(const int [], int, int, int);
void printHeader(void);
```

```
main()
{
   int a[SIZE], key, result;

   for (int i = 0; i < SIZE; i++)
      a[i] = 2 * i;

   cout << "Enter a number between 0 and 28: ";
   cin >> key;

   printHeader();
   result = binarySearch(a, key, 0, SIZE - 1);

   if (result != -1)
      cout << endl << key << " found in array element " << result << endl;
   else
      cout << endl << key << " not found" << endl;

   return 0;
}

int binarySearch(const int b[], int searchKey, int low, int high)
{
   int middle;

   if (low <= high) {
      middle = (low + high) / 2;
      printRow(b, low, middle, high);

      if (searchKey == b[middle])
         return middle;
      else if (searchKey < b[middle])
         return binarySearch(b, searchKey, low, middle - 1);
      else
         return binarySearch(b, searchKey, middle + 1, high);
   }

   return -1;   // searchKey not found
}

// Print a header for the output
void printHeader(void)
{
   cout << "Subscripts:" << endl;

   for (int i = 0; i < SIZE; i++)
      cout << setw(3) << i << ' ';

   cout << endl;

   for (i = 1; i <= 4 * SIZE; i++)
      cout << '-';

   cout << endl;
}


// print one row of output showing the current
// part of the array being processed.
void printRow(const int b[], int low, int mid, int high)
{
   for (int i = 0; i < SIZE; i++)
      if (i < low || i > high)
         cout << "    ";
      else if (i == mid)
         cout << setw(3) << b[i] << '*';     // mark middle value
      else
         cout << setw(3) << b[i] << ' ';

   cout << endl;
}
```

```
Enter a number between 0 and 28: Subscripts:
   0   1   2   3   4   5   6   7   8   9  10  11  12  13  14
---------------------------------------------------------------
   0   2   4   6   8  10  12  14* 16  18  20  22  24  26  28
   0   2   4   6*  8  10  12
   0   2*  4
           4*

3 not found
```

```
Enter a number between 0 and 28: Subscripts:
   0   1   2   3   4   5   6   7   8   9  10  11  12  13  14
---------------------------------------------------------------
   0   2   4   6   8  10  12  14* 16  18  20  22  24  26  28
                                  16  18  20  22* 24  26  28
                                  16  18* 20

18 found in array element 9
```

4.35 (*Eight Queens*) Modify the Eight Queens program you created in Exercise 4.26 to solve the problem recursively.

4.36 (*Print an array*) Write a recursive function `printArray` that takes an array and the size of the array as arguments and returns nothing. The function should stop processing and return when it receives an array of size zero.

ANS:

```cpp
// Exercise 4.36 Solution
#include <iostream.h>
#include <iomanip.h>
#include <stdlib.h>
#include <time.h>

void printArray(const int [], int, int);

main()
{
   const int SIZE = 10, MAXNUMBER = 500;
   int array[SIZE];

   srand(time(NULL));

   for (int loop = 0; loop < SIZE; loop++)
      array[loop] = 1 + rand() % MAXNUMBER;

   cout << "Array values printed in main:" << endl;

   for (loop = 0; loop < SIZE; loop++)
      cout << setw(5) << array[loop];

   cout << endl << endl << "Array values printed in printArray:" << endl;
   printArray(array, 0, SIZE - 1);
   cout << endl;
   return 0;
}

void printArray(const int array[], int low, int high)
{
   cout << setw(5) << array[low];

   if (low == high)
      return;
   else
      printArray(array, low + 1, high);
}
```

```
Array values printed in main:
  299   185   444   302    21    91   419   110    63   100

Array values printed in printArray:
  299   185   444   302    21    91   419   110    63   100
```

4.37   (*Print a string backwards*) Write a recursive function **stringReverse** that takes a character array containing a string as an argument, prints the string backwards, and returns nothing. The function should stop processing and return when the terminating null character is encountered.

ANS:

```cpp
// Exercise 4.37 Solution
#include <iostream.h>

void stringReverse(char []);

main()
{
    const int SIZE = 30;
    char strArray[SIZE] = "Print this string backwards.";

    for (int loop = 0; loop < SIZE; loop++)
        cout << strArray[loop];

    cout << endl;
    stringReverse(strArray);
    cout << endl;

    return 0;
}

void stringReverse(char strArray[])
{
    if (strArray[0] == '\0')
        return;

    stringReverse(&strArray[1]);
    cout << strArray[0];
}
```

```
Print this string backwards.
.sdrawkcab gnirts siht tnirP
```

4.38   · (*Find the minimum value in an array*) Write a recursive function **recursiveMinimum** that takes an integer array and the array size as arguments and returns the smallest element of the array. The function should stop processing and return when it receives an array of 1 element.

ANS:

```cpp
// Exercise 4.38 Solution
#include <iostream.h>
#include <iomanip.h>
#include <stdlib.h>
#include <time.h>

const int MAXRANGE = 1000;
int recursiveMinimum(const int [], int, int);

main()
{
    const int SIZE = 10;
    int array[SIZE], smallest;
```

```
   srand(time(NULL));

   for (int loop = 0; loop < SIZE; loop++)
      array[loop] = 1 + rand() % MAXRANGE;

   cout << "Array members are:" << endl;
   for (loop = 0; loop < SIZE; loop++)
      cout << setw(5) << array[loop];

   cout << endl;
   smallest = recursiveMinimum(array, 0, SIZE - 1);
   cout << endl << "Smallest element is: " << smallest << endl;
   return 0;
}

int recursiveMinimum(const int array[], int low, int high)
{
   static int smallest = MAXRANGE;

   if (array[low] < smallest)
      smallest = array[low];

   return low == high ? smallest : recursiveMinimum(array, low + 1, high);
}
```

```
Array members are:
  466    75   495   107   647   293   429   460   140   192

Smallest element is: 75
```

5

Pointers and Strings:
Solutions

Exercises

5.8 State whether the following are true or false. If false, explain why.

a) Two pointers that point to different arrays cannot be compared meaningfully.

ANS: True. It is not possible to know where these arrays will be stored in advance.

b) Because the name of an array is a pointer to the first element of the array, array names may be manipulated in precisely the same manner as pointers.

ANS: False. Array names cannot be modified to point to another location in memory.

5.9 Answer each of the following. Assume that unsigned integers are stored in 2 bytes, and that the starting address of the array is at location 1002500 in memory.

a) Declare an array of type **unsigned int** called **values** with 5 elements, and initialize the elements to the even integers from 2 to 10. Assume the symbolic constant **SIZE** has been defined as **5**.

ANS: `unsigned int values[SIZE] = {2, 4, 6, 8, 10};`

b) Declare a pointer **vPtr** that points to an object of type **unsigned int**.

ANS: `unsigned int *vPtr;`

c) Print the elements of array **values** using array subscript notation. Use a **for** structure and assume integer control variable **i** has been declared.

ANS:
```
for (i = 0; i < SIZE ; i++)
     cout << values[i];
```

d) Give two separate statements that assign the starting address of array **values** to pointer variable **vPtr**.

ANS:
```
vPtr = values;
     vPtr = &values[0];
```

e) Print the elements of array **values** using pointer/offset notation.

ANS:
```
for (offset = 0; offset < SIZE; offset++)
     cout << *(vPtr + offset);
```

f) Print the elements of array **values** using pointer/offset notation with the array name as the pointer.

ANS:
```
for (offset = 0; offset < SIZE; offset++)
     cout << *(values + offset);
```

g) Print the elements of array **values** by subscripting the pointer to the array.

ANS:
```
for (subscript = 0; subscript < SIZE; subscript++)
     cout << vPtr[subscript];
```

h) Refer to element 5 of array **values** using array subscript notation, pointer/offset notation with the array name as the pointer, pointer subscript notation, and pointer/offset notation.

ANS: `values[5];, *(values + 5);, vPtr[5];, *(vPtr + 5);`

i) What address is referenced by **vPtr + 3**? What value is stored at that location?

ANS: 100256, 6.

j) Assuming **vPtr** points to **values[4]**, what address is referenced by **vPtr -= 4**. What value is stored at that location?

ANS: 100250, 2.

5.10 For each of the following, write a single statement that performs the indicated task. Assume that long integer variables **value1** and **value2** have been declared, and that **value1** has been initialized to **200000**.

a) Declare the variable **lPtr** to be a pointer to an object of type **long**.

ANS: `long *lPtr;`

b) Assign the address of variable **value1** to pointer variable **lPtr**.

ANS: lPtr = &value1;

c) Print the value of the object pointed to by **lPtr**.

ANS: cout << *lPtr;

d) Assign the value of the object pointed to by **lPtr** to variable **value2**.

ANS: value2 = *lPtr;

e) Print the value of **value2**.

ANS: cout << value2;

f) Print the address of **value1**.

ANS: cout << &value1;

g) Print the address stored in **lPtr**. Is the value printed the same as the address of **value1**?

ANS: cout << lPtr; , yes.

5.11   Do each of the following.

a) Write the function header for function **zero** which takes a long integer array parameter **bigIntegers** and does not return a value.

ANS: void zero(long int *bigIntegers)

b) Write the function prototype for the function in part **(a)**.

ANS: void zero(long int *);

c) Write the function header for function **add1AndSum** which takes an integer array parameter **one-TooSmall** and returns an integer.

ANS: int add1AndSum(int *oneTooSmall)

d) Write the function prototype for the function described in part **(c)**.

ANS: int add1AndSum(int *);

Note: Exercises 5.12 through 5.15 are reasonably challenging. Once you have done these problems, you ought to be able to implement most popular card games easily.

5.12   Modify the program in Fig. 5.24 so that the card dealing function deals a five-card poker hand. Then write the following additional functions:

a) Determine if the hand contains a pair.

b) Determine if the hand contains two pairs.

c) Determine if the hand contains three of a kind (e.g., three jacks).

d) Determine if the hand contains four of a kind (e.g., four aces).

e) Determine if the hand contains a flush (i.e., all five cards of the same suit).

f) Determine if the hand contains a straight (i.e., five cards of consecutive face values).

ANS:

```
// Exercise 5.12 Solution
#include <iostream.h>
#include <iomanip.h>
#include <stdlib.h>
#include <time.h>

void shuffle(int [] [13]);
void deal(const int [] [13], const char *[], const char *[], int [] [2]);
void pair(const int [] [13], const int [] [2], const char *[]);
void threeOfKind(const int [] [13], const int [] [2], const char *[]);
void fourOfKind(const int [] [13], const int [] [2], const char *[]);
void flushHand(const int [] [13], const int [] [2], const char *[]);
void straightHand(const int [] [13], const int [] [2], const char *[],
                  const char *[]);

main()
{
   char *suit[] = {"Hearts", "Diamonds", "Clubs", "Spades"};
   char *face[] = {"Ace", "Deuce", "Three", "Four", "Five", "Six","Seven"
                   "Eight", "Nine", "Ten", "Jack", "Queen", "King"};
   int deck[4] [13] = {0}, hand[5] [2] = {0};
```

```cpp
   srand(time(NULL));

   shuffle(deck);
   deal(deck, face, suit, hand);
   pair(deck, hand, face);
   threeOfKind(deck, hand, face);
   fourOfKind(deck, hand, face);
   flushHand(deck, hand, suit);
   straightHand(deck, hand, suit, face);

   return 0;
}

void shuffle(int wDeck[][13])
{
   int row, column;

   for (int card = 1; card <= 52; card++) {
      do {
         row = rand() % 4;
         column = rand() % 13;
      } while (wDeck[row][column] != 0);

      wDeck[row][column] = card;
   }
}

// deal a five card poker hand
void deal(const int wDeck[][13], const char *wFace[],
          const char *wSuit[], int wHand[][2])
{
   int r = 0;

   cout << "The hand is: " << endl;

   for (int card = 1; card < 6; card++)
      for (int row = 0; row <= 3; row++)
         for (int column = 0; column <= 12; column++)
            if (wDeck[row][column] == card) {
               wHand[r][0] = row;
               wHand[r][1] = column;
               cout << setw(5) << setiosflags(ios::right) << wFace[column]
                    << " of " << setw(8) << setiosflags(ios::left)
                    << wSuit[row] << (card % 2 == 0 ? '\n' : '\t');
               ++r;
            }

   cout << endl;
}


// pair determines if the hand contains one or two pair
void pair(const int wDeck[][13], const int wHand[][2], const char *wFace[])
{
   int counter[13] = {0};

   for (int r = 0; r < 5; r++)
      ++counter[wHand[r][1]];

   cout << endl;

   for (int p = 0; p < 13; p++)
      if (counter[p] == 2)
         cout << "The hand contains a pair of " << wFace[p] << "'s." << endl;
}
```

```
void threeOfKind(const int wDeck[][13], const int wHand[][2],
                 const char *wFace[])
{
   int counter[13] = {0};

   for (int r = 0; r < 5; r++)
      ++counter[wHand[r][1]];

   for (int t = 0; t < 13; t++)
      if (counter[t] == 3)
         cout << "The hand contains three " << wFace[t]
              << "'s." << endl;
}




void fourOfKind(const int wDeck[][13], const int wHand[][2],
                const char *wFace[])
{
   int counter[13] = {0};

   for (int r = 0; r < 5; r++)
      ++counter[wHand[r][1]];

   for (int k = 0; k < 13; k++)
      if (counter[k] == 4)
         cout << "The hand contains four " << wFace[k] << "'s." << endl;
}




void flushHand(const int wDeck[][13], const int wHand[][2],
               const char *wSuit[])
{
   int count[4] = {0};

   for (int r = 0; r < 5; r++)
      ++count[wHand[r][0]];

   for (int f = 0; f < 4; f++)
      if (count[f] == 5)
         cout << "The hand contains a flush of " << wSuit[f]
              << "'s." << endl;
}




void straightHand(const int wDeck[][13], const int wHand[][2],
                  const char *wSuit[], const char *wFace[])
{
   int s[5] = {0}, temp;

   // copy column locations to sort
   for (int r = 0; r < 5; r++)
      s[r] = wHand[r][1];

   // bubble sort column locations
   for (int pass = 1; pass < 5; pass++)
      for (int comp = 0; comp < 4; comp++)
         if (s[comp] > s[comp + 1]) {
            temp = s[comp];
            s[comp] = s[comp + 1];
            s[comp + 1] = temp;
         }
```

```
            // check if sorted columns are a straight
            if (s[4] - 1 == s[3] && s[3] - 1 == s[2] && s[2] - 1 == s[1] &&
                s[1] - 1 == s[0])
               cout << "The hand contains a straight consisting of "
                    << wFace[wHand[0][1]] << " of " << wSuit[wHand[0][0]]
                    << ", " << wFace[wHand[1][1]] << " of " << wSuit[wHand[1][0]]
                    << ", " << wFace[wHand[2][1]] << " of " << wSuit[wHand[2][0]]
                    << ", " << wFace[wHand[3][1]] << " of " << wSuit[wHand[3][0]]
                    << ", " << wFace[wHand[4][1]] << " of " << wSuit[wHand[4][0]]
                    << endl;
}
```

```
The hand is:
Three of Diamonds        Five of Hearts
Deuce of Diamonds        Ace of Clubs
 Four of Diamonds

The hand contains a straight consisting of Three of Diamonds,
Five of Hearts, Deuce of Diamonds, Ace of Clubs, Four of Diamonds
```

```
The hand is:
 Ace of Clubs           Jack of Diamonds
 Four of Spades         Ace of Hearts
Three of Hearts

The hand contains a pair of Ace's.
```

```
The hand is:
Eight of Spades         Queen of Clubs
Queen of Hearts         Queen of Diamonds
Deuce of Hearts

The hand contains three Queen's.
```

5.13 Use the functions developed in Exercise 5.12 to write a program that deals two five-card poker hands, evaluates each hand, and determines which is the better hand.

5.14 Modify the program developed in Exercise 5.13 so that it can simulate the dealer. The dealer's five-card hand is dealt "face down" so the player cannot see it. The program should then evaluate the dealer's hand and, based on the quality of the hand, the dealer should draw one, two, or three more cards to replace the corresponding number of unneeded cards in the original hand. The program should then reevaluate the dealer's hand. (*Caution:* This is a difficult problem!)

5.15 Modify the program developed in Exercise 5.14 so that it can handle the dealer's hand automatically, but the player is allowed to decide which cards of the player's hand to replace. The program should then evaluate both hands and determine who wins. Now use this new program to play 20 games against the computer. Who wins more games, you or the computer? Have one of your friends play 20 games against the computer. Who wins more games? Based on the results of these games, make appropriate modifications to refine your poker playing program (this, too, is a difficult problem). Play 20 more games. Does your modified program play a better game?

5.16 In the card shuffling and dealing program of Fig. 5.24, we intentionally used an inefficient shuffling algorithm that introduced the possibility of indefinite postponement. In this problem, you will create a high-performance shuffling algorithm that avoids indefinite postponement.

Modify the program of Fig. 5.24 as follows. Begin by initializing the **deck** array as shown in Fig. 5.35. Modify the **shuffle** function to loop row-by-row and column-by-column through the array touching every element once. Each element should be swapped with a randomly selected element of the array.

Print the resulting array to determine if the deck is satisfactorily shuffled (as in Fig. 5.36, for example). You may want your program to call the **shuffle** function several times to ensure a satisfactory shuffle.

	0	1	2	3	4	5	6	7	8	9	10	11	12
0	1	2	3	4	5	6	7	8	9	10	11	12	13
1	14	15	16	17	18	19	20	21	22	23	24	25	26
2	27	28	29	30	31	32	33	34	35	36	37	38	39
3	40	41	42	43	44	45	46	47	48	49	50	51	52

Fig. 5.35   Unshuffled `deck` array.

	0	1	2	3	4	5	6	7	8	9	10	11	12
0	19	40	27	25	36	46	10	34	35	41	18	2	44
1	13	28	14	16	21	30	8	11	31	17	24	7	1
2	12	33	15	42	43	23	45	3	29	32	4	47	26
3	50	38	52	39	48	51	9	5	37	49	22	6	20

Fig. 5.36   Sample shuffled `deck` array.

Note that although the approach in this problem improves the shuffling algorithm, the dealing algorithm still requires searching the `deck` array for card 1, then card 2, then card 3, and so on. Worse yet, even after the dealing algorithm locates and deals the card, the algorithm continues searching through the remainder of the deck. Modify the program of Fig. 5.24 so that once a card is dealt, no further attempts are made to match that card number, and the program immediately proceeds with dealing the next card. In Chapter 16, we develop a dealing algorithm that requires only one operation per card.

ANS:

```
// Exercise 5.16 Solution
#include <iostream.h>
#include <iomanip.h>
#include <stdlib.h>
#include <time.h>

void shuffle(int [] [13]);
void deal(int [] [13], char *[], char *[]);

main()
{
   int card = 1, deck[4] [13];
   char *suit[4] = {"Hearts", "Diamonds", "Clubs", "Spades"};
   char *face[13] = {"Ace", "Deuce", "Three", "Four", "Five", "Six",
                     "Seven", "Eight", "Nine", "Ten", "Jack", "Queen",
                     "King"};

   srand(time(NULL));

   // initialize deck
   for (int row = 0; row <= 3; row++)
      for (int column = 0; column <= 12; column++)
         deck[row] [column] = card++;

   shuffle(deck);
   deal(deck, face, suit);
   return 0;
}

void shuffle(int workDeck[] [13])
{
   int temp, randRow, randColumn;

   for (int row = 0; row <= 3; row++)
      for (int column = 0; column <= 12; column++) {
         randRow = rand() % 4;
         randColumn = rand() % 13;
         temp = workDeck[row] [column];
         workDeck[row] [column] = workDeck[randRow] [randColumn];
         workDeck[randRow] [randColumn] = temp;
      }
}
```

```
void deal(int workDeck2[][13], char *workFace[], char *workSuit[])
{
    for (int card = 1; card <= 52; card++)
        for (int row = 0; row <= 3; row++)
            for (int column = 0; column <= 12; column++)
                if (workDeck2[row][column] == card) {
                    cout << setw(8) << workFace[column] << " of "
                        << setw(-8) << workSuit[row];
                    card % 2 == 0 ? cout << endl : cout << '\t';
                    break;
                }
}
```

```
      King of Spades       Seven of Hearts
     Queen of Clubs      Seven of Diamonds
      Four of Diamonds      Nine of Hearts
       Six of Diamonds      Jack of Spades
     Eight of Hearts        Six of Spades
       Ten of Hearts       King of Diamonds
     Three of Diamonds      Nine of Clubs
       Ace of Diamonds      Five of Diamonds
      Nine of Diamonds       Ace of Hearts
      Five of Hearts       King of Hearts
      Jack of Hearts      Seven of Clubs
      Jack of Clubs      Eight of Diamonds
      Nine of Spades        Six of Clubs
     Three of Spades      Queen of Hearts
     Eight of Spades      Deuce of Diamonds
      Four of Spades        Six of Hearts
     Eight of Clubs        Ten of Clubs
      Four of Hearts        Ten of Diamonds
     Queen of Spades      Queen of Diamonds
     Three of Hearts      Three of Clubs
     Deuce of Clubs       Five of Spades
      King of Clubs       Four of Clubs
       Ace of Spades       Jack of Diamonds
       Ace of Clubs      Seven of Spades
     Deuce of Spades        Ten of Spades
     Deuce of Hearts       Five of Clubs
```

5.17   (*Simulation: The Tortoise and the Hare*) In this problem you will recreate one of the truly great moments in history, namely the classic race of the tortoise and the hare. You will use random number generation to develop a simulation of this memorable event.

Our contenders begin the race at "square 1" of 70 squares. Each square represents a possible position along the race course. The finish line is at square 70. The first contender to reach or pass square 70 is rewarded with a pail of fresh carrots and lettuce. The course weaves its way up the side of a slippery mountain, so occasionally the contenders lose ground. There is a clock that ticks once per second. With each tick of the clock, your program should adjust the position of the animals according to the following rules:

Animal	Move type	Percentage of the time	Actual move
Tortoise	Fast plod	50%	3 squares to the right
	Slip	20%	6 squares to the left
	Slow plod	30%	1 square to the right
Hare	Sleep	20%	No move at all
	Big hop	20%	9 squares to the right
	Big slip	10%	12 squares to the left
	Small hop	30%	1 square to the right
	Small slip	20%	2 squares to the left

Use variables to keep track of the positions of the animals (i.e., position numbers are 1-70). Start each animal at position 1 (i.e., the "starting gate"). If an animal slips left before square 1, move the animal back to square 1.

Generate the percentages in the preceding table by producing a random integer, i, in the range $1 \leq i \leq 10$. For the tortoise, perform a "fast plod" when $1 \leq i \leq 5$, a "slip" when $6 \leq i \leq 7$, or a "slow plod" when $8 \leq i \leq 10$. Use a similar technique to move the hare.

Begin the race by printing

```
BANG !!!!!
AND THEY'RE OFF !!!!!
```

Then, for each tick of the clock (i.e., each repetition of a loop), print a 70-position line showing the letter **T** in the position of the tortoise and the letter **H** in the position of the hare. Occasionally, the contenders will land on the same square. In this case, the tortoise bites the hare and your program should print **OUCH!!!** beginning at that position. All print positions other than the **T**, the **H**, or the **OUCH!!!** (in case of a tie) should be blank.

After each line is printed, test if either animal has reached or passed square 70. If so, then print the winner and terminate the simulation. If the tortoise wins, print **TORTOISE WINS!!! YAY!!!** If the hare wins, print **Hare wins. Yuch.** If both animals win on the same tick of the clock, you may want to favor the turtle (the "underdog"), or you may want to print **It's a tie**. If neither animal wins, perform the loop again to simulate the next tick of the clock. When you are ready to run your program, assemble a group of fans to watch the race. You'll be amazed at how involved your audience gets!

ANS:
```cpp
// Exercise 5.17 Solution
#include <iostream.h>
#include <stdlib.h>
#include <time.h>

const int RACE_END = 70;

void moveTortoise(int *);
void moveHare(int *);
void printCurrentPositions(int *, int *);

main()
{
   int tortoise = 1, hare = 1, timer = 0;

   srand(time(NULL));

   cout << "ON YOUR MARK, GET SET" << endl << "BANG            !!!!"
        << endl << "AND THEY'RE OFF    !!!!" << endl;

   while (tortoise != RACE_END && hare != RACE_END) {
      moveTortoise(&tortoise);
      moveHare(&hare);
      printCurrentPositions(&tortoise, &hare);
      ++timer;
   }

   if (tortoise >= hare)
      cout << endl << "TORTOISE WINS!!! YAY!!!" << endl;
   else
      cout << "Hare wins. Yuch." << endl;

   cout << "TIME ELAPSED = " << timer << " seconds" << endl;

   return 0;
}
```

```cpp
void moveTortoise(int *turtlePtr)
{
   int x = 1 + rand() % 10;

   if (x >= 1 && x <= 5)        // fast plod
      *turtlePtr += 3;
   else if (x == 6 || x == 7)   // slip
      *turtlePtr -= 6;
   else                         // slow plod
      ++(*turtlePtr);

   if (*turtlePtr < 1)
      *turtlePtr = 1;
   else if (*turtlePtr > RACE_END)
      *turtlePtr = RACE_END;
}

void moveHare(int *rabbitPtr)
{
   int y = 1 + rand() % 10;

   if (y == 3 || y == 4)        // big hop
      *rabbitPtr += 9;
   else if (y == 5)             // big slip
      *rabbitPtr -= 12;
   else if (y >= 6 && y <= 8)   // small hop
      ++(*rabbitPtr);
   else if (y == 9 || y == 10)  // small slip
      *rabbitPtr -= 2;

   if (*rabbitPtr < 1)
      *rabbitPtr = 1;
   else if (*rabbitPtr > RACE_END)
      *rabbitPtr = RACE_END;
}

void printCurrentPositions(int *snapperPtr, int *bunnyPtr)
{
   for (int count = 1; count <= RACE_END; count++)

      if (count == *snapperPtr && count == *bunnyPtr)
         cout << "OUCH!!!";
      else if (count == *bunnyPtr)
         cout << 'H';
      else if (count == *snapperPtr)
         cout << 'T';
      else
         cout << ' ';

   cout << endl;
}
```

```
ON YOUR MARK, GET SET
BANG                !!!!
AND THEY'RE OFF     !!!!
 H T
T          H
   T       H
      T          H
         T        H
          T               H
            T                H
```
continued

```
                                                                continued
      T                         H
        T                      H
          T                   H
            T                H
              T                    H
                T                 H
                  T               H
                    T                    H
                      T                   H
                    T                    H
                  T                          H
                T                           H
              T                            H
            T                             H
          T                        H
        T                           H
      T                              H
        T                             H
          T              H
             OUCH!!!
             HT
               HT
                 T            H
                   T           H
                 T              H
                              H
               T                 H
             T                      H
               T                      H
                 T                 H
                 T                  H
                   T                    H
                     T    H               H
                          TH
                            T          H
                              T H
                               TH
                              H    T
                                T        T H
                                   T       H
                                      T     H
                                       T    H
                                       T    H
                                       HT
                                        H  T
                                  T              H
                                    T             H
                                      T            H
                                        T          H
                                      H        T
                                      H          T
                                                  T
                          H                        T
                          H                         T
                          H                          T
                          H                          T
                          H                           T

TORTOISE WINS!!! YAY!!!
TIME ELAPSED = 59 seconds
```

Special Section: Building Your Own Computer

In the next several problems, we take a temporary diversion away from the world of high-level language programming. We "peel open" a computer and look at its internal structure. We introduce machine language programming and write several machine language programs. To make this an especially valuable experience, we then build a computer (through the technique of software-based *simulation)* on which you can execute your machine language programs!

5.18   (*Machine Language Programming*) Let us create a computer we will call the Simpletron. As its name implies, it is a simple machine, but, as we will soon see, a powerful one as well. The Simpletron runs programs written in the only language it directly understands, that is, Simpletron Machine Language, or SML for short.

The Simpletron contains an *accumulator*—a "special register" in which information is put before the Simpletron uses that information in calculations or examines it in various ways. All information in the Simpletron is handled in terms of *words*. A word is a signed four-digit decimal number such as **+3364**, **-1293**, **+0007**, **-0001**, etc. The Simpletron is equipped with a 100-word memory, and these words are referenced by their location numbers **00**, **01**,..., **99**.

Before running an SML program, we must *load* or place the program into memory. The first instruction (or statement) of every SML program is always placed in location **00**. The simulator will start executing at this location.

Each instruction written in SML occupies one word of the Simpletron's memory (and hence instructions are signed four-digit decimal numbers). We shall assume that the sign of an SML instruction is always plus, but the sign of a data word may be either plus or minus. Each location in the Simpletron's memory may contain either an instruction, a data value used by a program, or an unused (and hence undefined) area of memory. The first two digits of each SML instruction are the *operation code,* which specifies the operation to be performed. SML operation codes are summarized in Fig. 5.37.

Operation code	Meaning
Input/output operations:	
#define READ 10	Read a word from the terminal into a specific location in memory.
#define WRITE 11	Write a word from a specific location in memory to the terminal.
Load/store operations:	
#define LOAD 20	Load a word from a specific location in memory into the accumulator.
#define STORE 21	Store a word from the accumulator into a specific location in memory.
Arithmetic operations:	
#define ADD 30	Add a word from a specific location in memory to the word in the accumulator (leave result in accumulator).
#define SUBTRACT 31	Subtract a word from a specific location in memory from the word in the accumulator (leave result in accumulator).
#define DIVIDE 32	Divide a word from a specific location in memory into the word in the accumulator (leave result in accumulator).
#define MULTIPLY 33	Multiply a word from a specific location in memory by the word in the accumulator (leave result in accumulator).

Fig. 5.37   Simpletron Machine Language (SML) operation codes (part 1 of 2).

Operation code	Meaning
Transfer of control operations:	
`#define BRANCH 40`	Branch to a specific location in memory.
`#define BRANCHNEG 41`	Branch to a specific location in memory if the accumulator is negative.
`#define BRANCHZERO 42`	Branch to a specific location in memory if the accumulator is zero.
`#define HALT 43`	Halt, i.e., the program has completed its task.

Fig. 5.37   Simpletron Machine Language (SML) operation codes (part 2 of 2).

The last two digits of an SML instruction are the *operand,* which is the address of the memory location containing the word to which the operation applies. Now let us consider several simple SML programs.

The first SML program (Example 1) reads two numbers from the keyboard and computes and prints their sum. The instruction `+1007` reads the first number from the keyboard and places it into location `07` (which has been initialized to zero). Then instruction `+1008` reads the next number into location `08`. The *load* instruction, `+2007`, puts the first number into the accumulator, and the *add* instruction, `+3008`, adds the second number to the number in the accumulator. *All SML arithmetic instructions leave their results in the accumulator.* The *store* instruction, `+2109`, places the result back into memory location `09` from which the *write* instruction, `+1109`, takes the number and prints it (as a signed four-digit decimal number). The *halt* instruction, `+4300`, terminates execution.

Example 1

Location	Number	Instruction
00	+1007	(Read A)
01	+1008	(Read B)
02	+2007	(Load A)
03	+3008	(Add B)
04	+2109	(Store C)
05	+1109	(Write C)
06	+4300	(Halt)
07	+0000	(Variable A)
08	+0000	(Variable B)
09	+0000	(Result C)

Example 2

Location	Number	Instruction
00	+1009	(Read A)
01	+1010	(Read B)
02	+2009	(Load A)
03	+3110	(Subtract B)
04	+4107	(Branch negative to 07)
05	+1109	(Write A)
06	+4300	(Halt)
07	+1110	(Write B)
08	+4300	(Halt)
09	+0000	(Variable A)
10	+0000	(Variable B)

This SML program reads two numbers from the keyboard and determines and prints the larger value. Note the use of the instruction `+4107` as a conditional transfer of control, much the same as C++'s `if` statement. Now write SML programs to accomplish each of the following tasks.

a) Use a sentinel-controlled loop to read 10 positive numbers and compute and print their sum.
ANS:

```
00      +1009      (Read Value)
01      +2009      (Load Value)
02      +4106      (Branch negative to 06)
03      +3008      (Add Sum)
04      +2108      (Store Sum)
05      +4000      (Branch 00)
06      +1108      (Write Sum)
07      +4300      (Halt)
08      +0000      (Variable Sum)
09      +0000      (Variable Value)
```

b) Use a counter-controlled loop to read seven numbers, some positive and some negative, and compute and print their average.
ANS:

```
00      +2018      (Load Counter)
01      +3121      (Subtract Termination)
02      +4211      (Branch zero to 11)
03      +2018      (Load Counter)
04      +3019      (Add Increment)
05      +2118      (Store Counter)
06      +1017      (Read Value)
07      +2016      (Load Sum)
08      +3017      (Add Value)
09      +2116      (Store Sum)
10      +4000      (Branch 00)
11      +2016      (Load Sum)
12      +3218      (Divide Counter)
13      +2120      (Store Result)
14      +1120      (Write Result)
15      +4300      (Halt)
16      +0000      (Variable Sum)
17      +0000      (Variable Value)
18      +0000      (Variable Counter)
19      +0001      (Variable Increment)
20      +0000      (Variable Result)
21      +0007      (Variable Termination)
```

c) Read a series of numbers and determine and print the largest number. The first number read indicates how many numbers should be processed.

ANS:

```
00      +1017      (Read Endvalue)
01      +2018      (Load Counter)
02      +3117      (Subtract Endvalue)
03      +4215      (Branch zero to 15)
04      +2018      (Load Counter)
05      +3021      (Add Increment)
06      +2118      (Store Counter)
07      +1019      (Read Value)
08      +2020      (Load Largest)
09      +3119      (Subtract Value)
10      +4112      (Branch negative to 12)
11      +4001      (Branch 01)
12      +2019      (Load Value)
13      +2120      (Store Largest)
14      +4001      (Branch 01)
15      +1120      (Write Largest)
16      +4300      (Halt)
17      +0000      (Variable Endvalue)
18      +0000      (Variable Counter)
19      +0000      (Variable Value)
20      +0000      (Variable Largest)
21      +0001      (Variable Increment)
```

5.19   (*A Computer Simulator*) It may at first seem outrageous, but in this problem you are going to build your own computer. No, you will not be soldering components together. Rather, you will use the powerful technique of *software-based simulation* to create a *software model* of the Simpletron. You will not be disappointed. Your Simpletron simulator will turn the computer you are using into a Simpletron, and you will actually be able to run, test, and debug the SML programs you wrote in Exercise 5.18.

When you run your Simpletron simulator, it should begin by printing:

```
*** Welcome to Simpletron! ***

*** Please enter your program one instruction ***
*** (or data word) at a time. I will type the ***
*** location number and a question mark (?).  ***
*** You then type the word for that location. ***
*** Type the sentinel -99999 to stop entering ***
*** your program. ***
```

Simulate the memory of the Simpletron with a single-subscripted array **memory** that has 100 elements. Now assume that the simulator is running, and let us examine the dialog as we enter the program of Example 2 of Exercise 5.18:

```
00 ? +1009
01 ? +1010
02 ? +2009
03 ? +3110
04 ? +4107
05 ? +1109
06 ? +4300
07 ? +1110
08 ? +4300
09 ? +0000
10 ? +0000
11 ? -99999

*** Program loading completed ***
*** Program execution begins  ***
```

The SML program has now been placed (or loaded) in array **memory**. Now the Simpletron executes your SML program. Execution begins with the instruction in location **00** and, like C++, continues sequentially, unless directed to some other part of the program by a transfer of control.

Use the variable **accumulator** to represent the accumulator register. Use the variable **instruction-Counter** to keep track of the location in memory that contains the instruction being performed. Use the variable **operationCode** to indicate the operation currently being performed, i.e., the left two digits of the instruction word. Use the variable **operand** to indicate the memory location on which the current instruction operates. Thus, **operand** is the rightmost two digits of the instruction currently being performed. Do not execute instructions directly from memory. Rather, transfer the next instruction to be performed from memory to a variable called **instructionRegister**. Then "pick off" the left two digits and place them in **operationCode**, and "pick off" the right two digits and place them in **operand**.

When Simpletron begins execution, the special registers are initialized as follows:

```
accumulator              +0000
instructionCounter          00
instructionRegister      +0000
operationCode            00
operand                     00
```

Now let us "walk through" the execution of the first SML instruction, **+1009** in memory location **00**. This is called an *instruction execution cycle.*

The **instructionCounter** tells us the location of the next instruction to be performed. We *fetch* the contents of that location from **memory** by using the C++ statement

```
instructionRegister = memory[instructionCounter];
```

The operation code and the operand are extracted from the instruction register by the statements

```
operationCode = instructionRegister / 100;
operand = instructionRegister % 100;
```

Now the Simpletron must determine that the operation code is actually a *read* (versus a *write*, a *load*, etc.). A **switch** differentiates among the twelve operations of SML.

In the **switch** structure, the behavior of various SML instructions is simulated as follows (we leave the others to the reader):

read: `cin >> memory[operand];`

load: `accumulator = memory[operand];`

add:`accumulator += memory[operand];`

Various branch instructions: We'll discuss these shortly.

*halt:***This instruction prints the message**

        `*** Simpletron execution terminated ***`

and then prints the name and contents of each register as well as the complete contents of memory. Such a printout is often called a *computer dump* (and, no, a computer dump is not a place where old computers go). To help you program your dump function, a sample dump format is shown in Fig. 5.38. Note that a dump after executing a Simpletron program would show the actual values of instructions and data values at the moment execution terminated.

Let us proceed with the execution of our program's first instruction, namely the **+1009** in location **00**. As we have indicated, the **switch** statement simulates this by performing the C++ statement

    `cin >> memory[operand];`

A question mark (**?**) should be displayed on the screen before the **cin** is executed to prompt the user for input. The Simpletron waits for the user to type a value and then press the *Return key.* The value is then read into location **09**.

At this point, simulation of the first instruction is completed. All that remains is to prepare the Simpletron to execute the next instruction. Since the instruction just performed was not a transfer of control, we need merely increment the instruction counter register as follows:

    `++instructionCounter;`

This completes the simulated execution of the first instruction. The entire process (i.e., the instruction execution cycle) begins anew with the fetch of the next instruction to be executed.

Now let us consider how the branching instructions—the transfers of control—are simulated. All we need to do is adjust the value in the instruction counter appropriately. Therefore, the unconditional branch instruction (**40**) is simulated within the **switch** as

    `instructionCounter = operand;`

The conditional "branch if accumulator is zero" instruction is simulated as

    `if (accumulator == 0)`
        `instructionCounter = operand;`

At this point you should implement your Simpletron simulator and run each of the SML programs you wrote in Exercise 5.18. You may embellish SML with additional features and provide for these in your simulator.

```
REGISTERS:
accumulator         +0000
instructionCounter     00
instructionRegister +0000
operationCode          00
operand                00

MEMORY:
        0      1      2      3      4      5      6      7      8      9
 0  +0000  +0000  +0000  +0000  +0000  +0000  +0000  +0000  +0000  +0000
10  +0000  +0000  +0000  +0000  +0000  +0000  +0000  +0000  +0000  +0000
20  +0000  +0000  +0000  +0000  +0000  +0000  +0000  +0000  +0000  +0000
30  +0000  +0000  +0000  +0000  +0000  +0000  +0000  +0000  +0000  +0000
40  +0000  +0000  +0000  +0000  +0000  +0000  +0000  +0000  +0000  +0000
50  +0000  +0000  +0000  +0000  +0000  +0000  +0000  +0000  +0000  +0000
60  +0000  +0000  +0000  +0000  +0000  +0000  +0000  +0000  +0000  +0000
70  +0000  +0000  +0000  +0000  +0000  +0000  +0000  +0000  +0000  +0000
80  +0000  +0000  +0000  +0000  +0000  +0000  +0000  +0000  +0000  +0000
90  +0000  +0000  +0000  +0000  +0000  +0000  +0000  +0000  +0000  +0000
```

Fig. 5.38   A sample dump.

Your simulator should check for various types of errors. During the program loading phase, for example, each number the user types into the Simpletron's **memory** must be in the range **-9999** to **+9999**. Your simulator should use a **while** loop to test that each number entered is in this range, and, if not, keep prompting the user to reenter the number until the user enters a correct number.

During the execution phase, your simulator should check for various serious errors, such as attempts to divide by zero, attempts to execute invalid operation codes, accumulator overflows (i.e., arithmetic operations resulting in values larger than **+9999** or smaller than **-9999**), and the like. Such serious errors are called *fatal errors*. When a fatal error is detected, your simulator should print an error message such as:

```
*** Attempt to divide by zero ***
*** Simpletron execution abnormally terminated ***
```

and should print a full computer dump in the format we have discussed previously. This will help the user locate the error in the program.

ANS:

```cpp
// Exercise 5.19 Solution
#include <iostream.h>
#include <iomanip.h>

const int SIZE = 100, MAX_WORD = 9999, MIN_WORD = -9999;
const long SENTINEL = -99999;
enum Boolean { FALSE, TRUE };
enum Commands { READ = 10, WRITE, LOAD = 20, STORE, ADD = 30, SUBTRACT,
                DIVIDE, MULTIPLY, BRANCH = 40, BRANCHNEG, BRANCHZERO,
                HALT };

void load(int *);
void execute(int *, int * , int *, int *, int *, int *);
void dump(const int *, int, int, int, int, int);
int validWord(int);

main()
{
    int memory[SIZE] = {0}, accumulator = 0, instructionCounter = 0,
        opCode = 0, operand = 0, instructionRegister = 0;

    load(memory);
    execute(memory, &accumulator, &instructionCounter, &instructionRegister,
            &opCode, &operand);
    dump(memory, accumulator, instructionCounter, instructionRegister,
         opCode, operand);
    return 0;
}

void load(int *loadMemory)
{
    long int instruction;
    int i = 0;

    cout << "***            Welcome to Simpletron            ***" << endl
         << "*** Please enter your program one instruction ***" << endl
         << "*** (or data word) at a time. I will type the ***" << endl
         << "*** location number and a question mark (?).  ***" << endl
         << "*** You then type the word for that location. ***" << endl
         << "*** Type the sentinel -99999 to stop entering ***" << endl
         << "*** your program.                             ***" << endl
         << "00 ? ";
    cin >> instruction;
    while (instruction != SENTINEL) {
        if (!validWord(instruction))
            cout << "Number out of range. Please enter again." << endl;
        else
            loadMemory[i++] = instruction;
        cout << setw(2) << setfill('0') << i << " ? ";
        cin >> instruction;
    }
}
```

```
void execute(int *memory, int *acPtr, int *icPtr, int *irPtr,
             int *opCodePtr, int *opPtr)
{
   int fatal = FALSE, temp;
   cout << endl << "***********START SIMPLETRON EXECUTION************"
        << endl << endl;
   *irPtr = memory[*icPtr];
   *opCodePtr = *irPtr / 100;
   *opPtr = *irPtr % 100;

   while (*opCodePtr != HALT && !fatal) {
      switch (*opCodePtr) {
         case READ:
            cout << "Enter an integer: ";
            cin >> temp;
            while (!validWord(temp)) {
               cout << "Number out of range. Please enter again: ";
               cin >> temp;
            }
            memory[*opPtr] = temp;
            ++(*icPtr);
            break;
         case WRITE:
            cout << "Contents of " << setw(2) << setfill('0') << *opPtr
                 << ": " << memory[*opPtr] << endl;
            ++(*icPtr);
            break;
         case LOAD:
            *acPtr = memory[*opPtr];
            ++(*icPtr);
            break;
         case STORE:
            memory[*opPtr] = *acPtr;
            ++(*icPtr);
            break;
         case ADD:
            temp = *acPtr + memory[*opPtr];
            if (!validWord(temp)) {
               cout << "*** FATAL ERROR: Accumulator overflow         ***"
                    << endl << "*** Simpletron execution abnormally "
                    << "terminated ***" << endl;
               fatal = TRUE;
            }
            else {
               *acPtr = temp;
               ++(*icPtr);
            }
            break;
         case SUBTRACT:
            temp = *acPtr - memory[*opPtr];
            if (!validWord(temp)) {
               cout << "*** FATAL ERROR: Accumulator overflow         ***"
                    << endl << "*** Simpletron execution abnormally "
                    << "terminated ***" << endl;
               fatal = TRUE;
            }
            else {
               *acPtr = temp;
               ++(*icPtr);
            }

            break;
```

```
                  case DIVIDE:
                     if (memory[*opPtr] == 0) {
                        cout << "*** FATAL ERROR: Attempt to divide by zero   ***"
                             << endl << "*** Simpletron execution abnormally "
                             << "terminated ***" << endl;
                        fatal = TRUE;
                     }
                     else {
                        *acPtr /= memory[*opPtr];
                        ++(*icPtr);
                     }
                     break;
                  case MULTIPLY:
                     temp = *acPtr * memory[*opPtr];
                     if (!validWord(temp)) {
                        cout << "*** FATAL ERROR: Accumulator overflow      ***"
                             << endl << "*** Simpletron execution abnormally "
                             << "terminated ***" << endl;
                        fatal = TRUE;
                     }
                     else {
                        *acPtr = temp;
                        ++(*icPtr);
                     }
                     break;
                  case BRANCH:
                     *icPtr = *opPtr;
                     break;
                  case BRANCHNEG:
                     *acPtr < 0 ? *icPtr = *opPtr : ++(*icPtr);
                     break;
                  case BRANCHZERO:
                     *acPtr == 0 ? *icPtr = *opPtr : ++(*icPtr);
                     break;
                  default:
                     cout << "*** FATAL ERROR: Invalid opcode detected      ***"
                          << endl << "*** Simpletron execution abnormally "
                          << "terminated ***" << endl;
                     fatal = TRUE;
                     break;
               }
            *irPtr = memory[*icPtr];
            *opCodePtr = *irPtr / 100;
            *opPtr = *irPtr % 100;
         }
      cout << endl << "*************END SIMPLETRON EXECUTION*************"
           << endl;
   }
   void dump(const int *memory, int accumulator, int instructionCounter,
             int instructionRegister, int operationCode, int operand)
   {
      cout << endl << "REGISTERS:" << endl << "accumulator          "
           << setw(5) << setiosflags(ios::internal | ios::showpos)
           << setfill('0') << accumulator << endl
           << "instructionCounter     " << setw(2) << setfill('0')
           << resetiosflags(ios::internal | ios::showpos)
           << instructionCounter << endl << "instructionRegister " << setw(4)
           << setiosflags(ios::internal | ios::showpos) << setfill('0')
           << instructionRegister << endl
           << resetiosflags(ios::internal | ios::showpos)
           << "operationCode          " << setw(2) << setfill('0')
           << operationCode << endl << "operand                 "
           << setw(2) << setfill('0') << operand << endl << endl << "MEMORY:"
           << endl << resetiosflags(ios::internal | ios::showpos);
```

```cpp
   // print header
   for (int i = 0; i <= 9; i++)
      cout << setw(5) << setfill(' ') << i << ' ';


   for (i = 0; i < SIZE; i++) {
      if (i % 10 == 0)
         cout << endl << setw(2) << i << ' ';

      cout << (memory[i] >= 0 ? "+" : "") << setw(4) << setfill('0')
           << setiosflags(ios::internal)
           << memory[i] << ' ' << resetiosflags(ios::internal);
   }

   cout << endl;
}



int validWord(int word)
{
   return word >= MIN_WORD && word <= MAX_WORD;
}
```

```
   ***              Welcome to Simpletron          ***
   *** Please enter your program one instruction ***
   *** (or data word) at a time. I will type the ***
   *** location number and a question mark (?).   ***
   *** You then type the word for that location. ***
   *** Type the sentinel -99999 to stop entering ***
   *** your program.                              ***
   00 ? 1099
   01 ? 1098
   02 ? 2099
   03 ? 3098
   04 ? 2195
   05 ? 1199
   06 ? 1198
   07 ? 1195
   08 ? 4300
   09 ? -99999

   ************START SIMPLETRON EXECUTION************

   Enter an integer: 8
   Enter an integer: 12

   Contents of 99: 8
   Contents of 98: 12
   Contents of 95: 20

   ************END SIMPLETRON EXECUTION************

   REGISTERS:
   accumulator          +0020
   instructionCounter      08
   instructionRegister  +4300
   operationCode           43
   operand                 00

                                        continued
```

```
                                                                          continued
   MEMORY:
          0      1      2      3      4      5      6      7      8      9
    0  +1099  +1098  +2099  +3098  +2195  +1199  +1198  +1195  +4300  +0000
   10  +0000  +0000  +0000  +0000  +0000  +0000  +0000  +0000  +0000  +0000
   20  +0000  +0000  +0000  +0000  +0000  +0000  +0000  +0000  +0000  +0000
   30  +0000  +0000  +0000  +0000  +0000  +0000  +0000  +0000  +0000  +0000
   40  +0000  +0000  +0000  +0000  +0000  +0000  +0000  +0000  +0000  +0000
   50  +0000  +0000  +0000  +0000  +0000  +0000  +0000  +0000  +0000  +0000
   60  +0000  +0000  +0000  +0000  +0000  +0000  +0000  +0000  +0000  +0000
   70  +0000  +0000  +0000  +0000  +0000  +0000  +0000  +0000  +0000  +0000
   80  +0000  +0000  +0000  +0000  +0000  +0000  +0000  +0000  +0000  +0000
   90  +0000  +0000  +0000  +0000  +0000  +0020  +0000  +0000  +0012  +0008
```

More Pointer Exercises

5.20   Modify the card shuffling and dealing program of Fig. 5.24 so the shuffling and dealing operations are performed by the same function (shuffleAndDeal). The function should contain one nested looping structure that is similar to function shuffle in Fig. 5.24.

ANS:

```cpp
// Exercise 5.20 Solution
#include <iostream.h>
#include <iomanip.h>
#include <stdlib.h>
#include <time.h>

void shuffleAndDeal(int [][13], char *[], char *[]);

main()
{
   char *suit[4] = {"Hearts", "Diamonds", "Clubs", "Spades"};
   char *face[13] = {"Ace", "Deuce", "Three", "Four", "Five", "Six",
                     "Seven", "Eight", "Nine", "Ten", "Jack", "Queen",
                     "King"};
   int deck[4][13] = {0};

   srand(time(NULL));
   shuffleAndDeal(deck, face, suit);

   return 0;
}

void shuffleAndDeal(int workdeck[][13], char *workface[], char *worksuit[])
{
   int row, column;

   for (int card = 1; card <= 52; card++) {

      do {
         row = rand() % 4;
         column = rand() % 13;
      } while(workdeck[row][column] != 0);

      workdeck[row][column] = card;
      cout << setw(8) << workface[column] << " of " << setw(-8)
           << worksuit[row];
      card % 2 == 0 ? cout << endl : cout << '\t';
   }
}
```

```
        Four of Clubs       Ten of Spades
       Three of Clubs     Seven of Spades
         Six of Clubs       Six of Spades
        Four of Diamonds     Nine of Spades
        Four of Hearts      Three of Diamonds
       Deuce of Hearts        Ten of Diamonds
        Five of Spades      Five of Clubs
         Ace of Hearts      Jack of Hearts
        Nine of Diamonds    Five of Hearts
       Queen of Spades        Ace of Spades
       Seven of Clubs       King of Diamonds
         Ten of Clubs       King of Hearts
       Three of Hearts      Eight of Clubs
         Ten of Hearts      Queen of Hearts
        King of Clubs      Deuce of Spades
       Seven of Hearts      Deuce of Diamonds
       Queen of Diamonds      Six of Hearts
       Queen of Clubs        Six of Diamonds
       Eight of Spades      Eight of Diamonds
       Eight of Hearts      Seven of Diamonds
        Four of Spades       Jack of Diamonds
        Nine of Hearts       King of Spades
        Jack of Spades      Three of Spades
        Nine of Clubs        Ace of Clubs
         Ace of Diamonds    Deuce of Clubs
        Jack of Clubs       Five of Diamonds
```

5.21   What does this program do?

```cpp
#include <iostream.h>

void mystery1(char *, const char *);

main()
{
    char string1[80], string2[80];

    cout << "Enter two strings: ";
    cin >> string1 >> string2;
    mystery1(string1, string2);
    cout << string1 << endl;

    return 0;
}

void mystery1(char *s1, const char *s2)
{
    while (*s1 != '\0')
        ++s1;

    for ( ; *s1 = *s2; s1++, s2++)
        ;    // empty statement
}
```

ANS: The function mystery concatenates string2 to string1.

```
Enter a two strings: computer science
computerscience
```

5.22   What does this program do?

```cpp
#include <iostream.h>

int mystery2(const char *);

main()
{
   char string[80];

   cout << "Enter a string: ";
   cin >> string;
   cout << mystery2(string) << endl;

   return 0;
}

int mystery2(const char *s)
{
   for (int x = 0; *s != '\0'; s++)
      ++x;

   return x;
}
```

ANS: Function **mystery2** determines the length of a string.

```
Enter a string: length
6
```

5.23   Find the error in each of the following program segments. If the error can be corrected, explain how.

a) `int *number;`
   `cout << number << endl;`

ANS: The uninitialized address value of **number** is printed. As a good programming practice, **number** should be named **numberPtr**.

b) `float *realPtr;`
   `long *integerPtr;`
   `integerPtr = realPtr;`

ANS: Pointers must be assigned to the same pointer data type or to **void ***. Type-casting **realPtr** to **long *** is one possible solution.

c) `int * x, y;`
   `x = y;`

ANS: **y** is not a pointer. **y** must either be declared as a pointer or **x** must be assigned the address of **y**.

d) `char s[] = "this is a character array";`
   `for ( ; *s != '\0'; s++)`
   `   cout << *s << ' ';`

ANS: **s** cannot be incremented; it is the name of an array (i.e., a contant pointer to the first element of the array).

e) `short *numPtr, result;`
   `void *genericPtr = numPtr;`
   `result = *genericPtr + 7;`

ANS: A **void *** pointer may not be dereferenced. **numPtr** should be used instead of **genericPtr**.

f) `float x = 19.34;`
   `float xPtr = &x;`
   `cout << xPtr << endl;`

ANS: The address contained in **xPtr** is printed. **xPtr** should be dereferenced using the dereferincing operator *****.

g) `char *s;`
   `cout << s << endl;`

ANS: **s** is not pointing to a character string yet, so garbage will most likely be printed. **s** should be **NULL**, **0**, or a valid address of a string.

5.24 (*Quicksort*) In the examples and exercises of Chapter 4, we discussed the sorting techniques of bubble sort, bucket sort, and selection sort. We now present the recursive sorting technique called Quicksort. The basic algorithm for a single-subscripted array of values is as follows:

1) *Partitioning Step:* Take the first element of the unsorted array and determine its final location in the sorted array. This occurs when all values to the left of the element in the array are less than the element, and all values to the right of the element in the array are greater than the element. We now have one element in its proper location and two unsorted subarrays.
2) *Recursive Step:* Perform step 1 on each unsorted subarray.

Each time step 1 is performed on a subarray, another element is placed in its final location of the sorted array, and two unsorted subarrays are created. When a subarray consists of one element, it must be sorted, therefore that element is in its final location.

The basic algorithm seems simple enough, but how do we determine the final position of the first element of each subarray. As an example, consider the following set of values (the element in bold is the partitioning element—it will be placed in its final location in the sorted array):

37   2   6   4   89   8   10   12   68   45

1) Starting from the rightmost element of the array, compare each element to **37** until an element less than **37** is found, then swap **37** and that element. The first element less than **37** is 12, so **37** and 12 are swapped. The new array is:

12   2   6   4   89   8   10   **37**   68   45

Element 12 is in italic to indicate that it was just swapped with **37**.
2) Starting from the left of the array, but beginning with the element after 12, compare each element to **37** until an element greater than **37** is found, then swap **37** and that element. The first element greater than **37** is 89, so **37** and 89 are swapped. The new array is:

12   2   6   4   **37**   8   10   *89*   68   45

3) Starting from the right, but beginning with the element before 89, compare each element to **37** until an element less than **37** is found, then swap **37** and that element. The first element less than **37** is 10, so **37** and 10 are swapped. The new array is:

12   2   6   4   *10*   8   **37**   89   68   45

4) Starting from the left, but beginning with the element after 10, compare each element to **37** until an element greater than **37** is found, then swap **37** and that element. There are no more elements greater than **37**, so when we compare **37** to itself we know that **37** has been placed in its final location of the sorted array.

Once the partition has been applied on the above array, there are two unsorted subarrays. The subarray with values less than 37 contains 12, 2, 6, 4, 10, and 8. The subarray with values greater than 37 contains 89, 68, and 45. The sort continues with both subarrays being partitioned in the same manner as the original array.

Based on the preceding discussion, write recursive function **quickSort** to sort a single-subscripted integer array. The function should receive as arguments an integer array, a starting subscript, and an ending subscript. Function **partition** should be called by **quickSort** to perform the partitioning step.

ANS:

```
// Exercise 5.24 Solution

#include <iostream.h>
#include <iomanip.h>
#include <stdlib.h>
#include <time.h>

const int SIZE = 10, MAX_NUMBER = 1000;

int partition(int *, int, int);
void quicksort(int *, int, int);
void swap(int *, int *);
```

```cpp
main()
{
    int arrayToBeSorted[SIZE] = {0};

    srand(time(NULL));

    for (int loop = 0; loop < SIZE; loop++)
        arrayToBeSorted[loop] = rand() % MAX_NUMBER;

    cout << "Initial array values are: " << endl;

    for (loop = 0; loop < SIZE; loop++)
        cout << setw(4) << arrayToBeSorted[loop];

    cout << endl << endl;

    if (SIZE == 1)
        cout << "Array is sorted: " << arrayToBeSorted[0] << endl;
    else {
        quicksort(arrayToBeSorted, 0, SIZE - 1);
        cout << "The sorted array values are:" << endl;

        for (loop = 0; loop < SIZE; loop++)
            cout << setw(4) << arrayToBeSorted[loop];

        cout << endl;
    }

    return 0;
}

void quicksort(int array[], int first, int last)
{
    int currentLocation;

    if (first >= last)
        return;

    currentLocation = partition(array, first, last);   // place an element
    quicksort(array, first, currentLocation - 1);      // sort left side
    quicksort(array, currentLocation + 1, last);       // sort right side
}

int partition(int array[], int left, int right)
{
    int position = left;

    while (1) {
        while (array[position] <= array[right] && position != right)
            --right;

        if (position == right)
            return position;

        if (array[position] > array[right]) {
            swap(&array[position ], &array[right]);
            position = right;
        }

        while (array[left] <= array[position] && left != position )
            ++left;

        if (position == left)
            return position;

        if (array[left] > array[position]) {
            swap(&array[position], &array[left]);
            position = left;
        }
    }
}
```

```
void swap(int *ptr1, int *ptr2)
{
   int temp;

   temp = *ptr1;
   *ptr1 = *ptr2;
   *ptr2 = temp;
}
```

```
Initial array values are:
 460 144 290 273 273 395 392 452 420 120

The sorted array values are:
 120 144 273 273 290 392 395 420 452 460
```

5.25 (*Maze Traversal*) The following grid of #s and dots (.) is a double-subscripted array representation of a maze.

```
# # # # # # # # # # # #
# . . . # . . . . . . #
. . # . # . # # # # . #
# # # . # . . . . # . #
# . . . . # # # . # . .
# # # # . # . # . # . #
# . . # . # . # . # . #
# # . # . # . # . # . #
# . . . . . . . . # . #
# # # # # . # # # . # #
# . . . . . . # . . . #
# # # # # # # # # # # #
```

In the preceding double-subscripted array, the #s represent the walls of the maze and the dots represent squares in the possible paths through the maze. Moves can only be made to a location in the array that contains a dot.

There is a simple algorithm for walking through a maze that guarantees finding the exit (assuming there is an exit). If there is not an exit, you will arrive at the starting location again. Place your right hand on the wall to your right and begin walking forward. Never remove your hand from the wall. If the maze turns to the right, you follow the wall to the right. As long as you do not remove your hand from the wall, eventually you will arrive at the exit of the maze. There may be a shorter path than the one you have taken, but you are guaranteed to get out of the maze if you follow the algorithm.

Write recursive function **mazeTraverse** to walk through the maze. The function should receive as arguments a 12-by-12 character array representing the maze, and the starting location of the maze. As **mazeTraverse** attempts to locate the exit from the maze, it should place the character **X** in each square in the path. The function should display the maze after each move so the user can watch as the maze is solved.

ANS:

```
// Exercise 5.25 Solution
// This solution assumes that there is only one
// entrance and one exit for a given maze, and
// these are the only two zeroes on the border.
#include <iostream.h>
#include <stdlib.h>

enum Direction { DOWN, RIGHT, UP, LEFT };
const int X_START = 2, Y_START = 0;   // starting coordinate for maze

void mazeTraversal(char [][12], int, int, int);
void printMaze(const char[][12]);
int validMove(const char [][12], int, int);
int coordsAreEdge(int, int);
```

```
main()
{
    char maze[12][12] =
            {{'#', '#', '#', '#', '#', '#', '#', '#', '#', '#', '#', '#'},
             {'#', '.', '.', '.', '#', '.', '.', '.', '.', '.', '.', '#'},
             {'.', '.', '#', '.', '#', '.', '#', '#', '#', '#', '.', '#'},
             {'#', '#', '#', '.', '#', '.', '.', '.', '.', '#', '.', '#'},
             {'#', '.', '.', '.', '.', '#', '#', '#', '.', '#', '.', '.'},
             {'#', '#', '#', '#', '.', '#', '.', '#', '.', '#', '.', '#'},
             {'#', '.', '.', '#', '.', '#', '.', '#', '.', '#', '.', '#'},
             {'#', '#', '.', '#', '.', '#', '.', '#', '.', '#', '.', '#'},
             {'#', '.', '.', '.', '.', '.', '.', '.', '.', '#', '.', '#'},
             {'#', '#', '#', '#', '#', '#', '.', '#', '#', '#', '.', '#'},
             {'#', '.', '.', '.', '.', '.', '.', '#', '.', '.', '.', '#'},
             {'#', '#', '#', '#', '#', '#', '#', '#', '#', '#', '#', '#'}};
    mazeTraversal(maze, X_START, Y_START, RIGHT);
    return 0;
}
void mazeTraversal(char maze[][12], int xCoord, int yCoord, int direction)
{
    static int flag = 0;

    maze[xCoord][yCoord] = 'x';
    printMaze(maze);
    if (coordsAreEdge(xCoord,yCoord) && xCoord != X_START &&
                                          yCoord != Y_START) {
        cout << endl << "Maze successfully exited!" << endl << endl;
        return;    // maze is complete
    }
    else if (xCoord == X_START && yCoord == X_START && flag == 1) {
        cout << endl<< "Arrived back at the starting location."<< endl<< endl;
        return;
    }
    else {
        flag = 1;
        for (int move=direction, count=0; count<4; ++count, ++move,move%=4)
            switch(move) {
                case DOWN:
                    if (validMove(maze, xCoord + 1, yCoord)) { // move down
                        mazeTraversal(maze, xCoord + 1, yCoord, LEFT);
                        return;
                    }
                    break;
                case RIGHT:
                    if (validMove(maze, xCoord, yCoord + 1)) { // move right
                        mazeTraversal(maze, xCoord, yCoord + 1, DOWN);
                        return;
                    }
                    break;
                case UP:
                    if (validMove(maze, xCoord - 1, yCoord)) { // move up
                        mazeTraversal(maze, xCoord - 1, yCoord, RIGHT);
                        return;
                    }
                    break;
                case LEFT:
                    if (validMove(maze, xCoord, yCoord - 1)) { // move left
                        mazeTraversal(maze, xCoord, yCoord - 1, UP);
                        return;
                    }
                    break;
            }
    }
}
```

```
int validMove(const char maze[][12], int r, int c)
{
    return (r >= 0 && r <= 11 && c >= 0 && c <= 11 && maze[r][c] != '#');
}

int coordsAreEdge(int x, int y)
{
    if ((x == 0 || x == 11) && (y >= 0 && y <= 11))
        return 1;
    else if ((y == 0 || y == 11) && (x >= 0 && x <= 11))
        return 1;
    else
        return 0;
}

void printMaze(const char maze[][12])
{
    for (int x = 0; x < 12; x++) {

        for (int y = 0; y < 12; y++)
            cout << maze[x][y] << ' ';

        cout << endl;
    }

    cout << endl << "Hit return to see next move" << endl;
    cin.get();
}
```

```
# # # # # # # # # # # #
# . . . # . . . . . . #
x . # . # . # # # # . #
# # # . # . . . . # . #
# . . . . # # # . # . .
# # # # . # . # . # . #
# . . # . # . # . # . #
# # . # . # . # . # . #
# . . . . . . . . # . #
# # # # # . # # # . #
# . . . . . # . . . #
# # # # # # # # # # # #

Hit return to see next move
...

# # # # # # # # # # # #
# x x x # x x x x x x #
x x # x # x # # # # x #
# # # x # x x x x # x #
# x x x x # # # x # x .
# # # # x # . # x # x #
# x x # x # . # x # x #
# # x # x # . # x # x #
# x x x x x x x # x #
# # # # # # x # # # x #
# x x x x x x # x x x #
# # # # # # # # # # # #

Hit return to see next move
```

                                                                continued

```
                                                                  continued
   # # # # # # # # # # # #
   # x x x # x x x x x x #
   x x # x # x # # # # x #
   # # # x # x x x x x x #
   # x x x x # # # x # x .
   # # # # x # . # x # x #
   # x x # x # . # x # x #
   # # x # x # . # x # x #
   # x x x x x x x x # x #
   # # # # # # x # # # x #
   # x x x x x x # x x x #
   # # # # # # # # # # # #

   Hit return to see next move

   # # # # # # # # # # # #
   # x x x # x x x x x x #
   x x # x # x # # # # x #
   # # # x # x x x x x # x #
   # x x x x # # # x # x x
   # # # # x # . # x # x #
   # x x # x # . # x # x #
   # # x # x # . # x # x #
   # x x x x x x x x # x #
   # # # # # # x # # # x #
   # x x x x x x # x x x #
   # # # # # # # # # # # #

   Hit return to see next move

   Maze successfully exited!
```

5.26   (*Generating Mazes Randomly*) Write a function **mazeGenerator** that takes as an argument a double-subscripted 12-by-12 character array and randomly produces a maze. The function should also provide the starting and ending locations of the maze. Try your function **mazeTraverse** from Exercise 5.25 using several randomly generated mazes.

ANS:

```
// Exercise 5.26 Solution
#include <iostream.h>
#include <stdlib.h>
#include <time.h>

enum Direction { DOWN, RIGHT, UP, LEFT };
const int MAX_DOTS = 100;  // maximum possible dots for maze

void mazeTraversal(char [][12], const int, const int, int, int, int);
void mazeGenerator(char [][12], int *, int *);
void printMaze(const char[][12]);
int validMove(const char [][12], int, int);
int coordsAreEdge(int, int);

main()
{
   char maze[12][12];
   int xStart, yStart, x, y;

   srand(time(NULL));

   for (int loop = 0; loop < 12; loop++)
      for (int loop2 = 0; loop2 < 12; loop2++)
         maze[loop][loop2] = '#';
```

```
        mazeGenerator(maze, &xStart, &yStart);

        x = xStart;   // starting row
        y = yStart;   // starting col

        mazeTraversal(maze, xStart, yStart, x, y, RIGHT);

        return 0;
}

// Assume that there is exactly 1 entrance and exactly 1 exit to the maze.
void mazeTraversal(char maze[][12], const int xCoord, const int yCoord,
                   int row, int col, int direction)
{
    static int flag = 0;    // starting position flag

    maze[row][col] = 'x';   // insert X at current location
    printMaze(maze);

    if (coordsAreEdge(row, col) && row != xCoord && col != yCoord) {
        cout << "Maze successfully exited!" << endl << endl;
        return;    // maze is complete
    }
    else if (row == xCoord && col == yCoord && flag == 1) {
        cout << "Arrived back at the starting location." << endl << endl;
        return;
    }
    else {
        flag = 1;

        for (int move = direction, count = 0; count < 4; ++count, ++move,
                                                        move %= 4)

            switch(move) {
                case DOWN:
                    if (validMove(maze, row + 1, col)) { // move down
                        mazeTraversal(maze, xCoord, yCoord, row + 1, col, LEFT);
                        return;
                    }

                    break;
                case RIGHT:
                    if (validMove(maze, row, col + 1)) { // move right
                        mazeTraversal(maze, xCoord, yCoord, row, col + 1, DOWN);
                        return;
                    }

                    break;
                case UP:
                    if (validMove(maze, row - 1, col)) { // move up
                        mazeTraversal(maze, xCoord, yCoord, row - 1, col, RIGHT);
                        return;
                    }

                    break;
                case LEFT:
                    if (validMove(maze, row, col - 1)) { // move left
                        mazeTraversal(maze, xCoord, yCoord, row, col - 1, UP);
                        return;
                    }

                    break;
            }
    }
}
```

```
int validMove(const char maze[][12], int r, int c)
{
    return (r >= 0 && r <= 11 && c >= 0 && c <= 11 && maze[r][c] != '#');
}

int coordsAreEdge(int x, int y)
{
    if ((x == 0 || x == 11) && (y >= 0 && y <= 11))
        return 1;
    else if ((y == 0 || y == 11) && (x >= 0 && x <= 11))
        return 1;
    else
        return 0;
}

void printMaze(const char maze[][12])
{
    for (int x = 0; x < 12; x++) {
        for (int y = 0; y < 12; y++)
            cout << maze[x][y] << ' ';

        cout << endl;
    }

    cout << "Hit return to see next move";
    cin.get();
}

void mazeGenerator(char maze[][12], int *xPtr, int *yPtr)
{
    int a, x, y, entry, exit;

    do {
        entry = rand() % 4;
        exit = rand() % 4;
    } while (entry == exit);

    // Determine entry position
    if (entry == 0) {
        *xPtr = 1 + rand() % 10;      // avoid corners
        *yPtr = 0;
        maze[*xPtr][0] = '.';
    }
    else if (entry == 1) {
        *xPtr = 0;
        *yPtr = 1 + rand() % 10;
        maze[0][*yPtr] = '.';
    }
    else if (entry == 2) {
        *xPtr = 1 + rand() % 10;
        *yPtr = 11;
        maze[*xPtr][11] = '.';
    }
    else {
        *xPtr = 11;
        *yPtr = 1 + rand() % 10;
        maze[11][*yPtr] = '.';
    }

    // Determine exit location
    if (exit == 0) {
        a = 1 + rand() % 10;
        maze[a][0] = '.';
    }
```

```
        else if (exit == 1) {
           a = 1 + rand() % 10;
           maze[0][a] = '.';
        }
        else if (exit == 2) {
           a = 1 + rand() % 10;
           maze[a][11] = '.';
        }
        else {
           a = 1 + rand() % 10;
           maze[11][a] = '.';
        }
        for (int loop = 1; loop < MAX_DOTS; loop++) {    // add dots randomly
           x = 1 + rand() % 10;
           y = 1 + rand() % 10;
           maze[x][y] = '.';
        }
}
```

```
# # # # # # # # # # # #
# . # . # . . . # # . #
# . # # # # . # # # #
# . . # # # . . # # # #
# . . . # # . . . # . #
# . . . . # . . . # . #
# . . . . . . . . . . #
# . . . . # . . # # . #
x . . . . . . . . . . #
# . . . . # # . . # . #
# . . # . . # . . # . #
# # . # # # # # # # # #
Hit return to see next move
...
# # # # # # # # # # # #
# . # . # . . . # # . #
# . # # # # . # # # #
# . . # # # . . # # # #
# . . . # # . . . # . #
# . . . . # . . . # . #
# . . . . . . . . . . #
# . . . . # . . # # . #
x x . . . . . . . . . #
# x . . . # # . . # . #
# x x # . . # . . # . #
# # . # # # # # # # # #

Hit return to see next move
# # # # # # # # # # # #
# . # . # . . . # # . #
# . # # # # . # # # #
# . . # # # . . # # # #
# . . . # # . . . # . #
# . . . . # . . . # . #
# . . . . . . . . . . #
# . . . . # . . # # . #
x x . . . . . . . . . #
# x . . . # # . . # . #
# x x # . . # . . # . #
# # x # # # # # # # # #
Hit return to see next move
Maze successfully exited!
```

5.27   (*Mazes of Any Size*) Generalize functions **mazeTraverse** and **mazeGenerator** of Exercises 5.25 and 5.26 to process mazes of any width and height.

ANS:

```cpp
// Exercise 5.27 Solution
#include <iostream.h>
#include <stdlib.h>
#include <time.h>

enum Direction { DOWN, RIGHT, UP, LEFT };
const int ROWS = 15, COLS = 30;

void mazeTraversal(char [][COLS], const int, const int, int, int, int);
void mazeGenerator(char [][COLS], int *, int *);
void printMaze(const char[][COLS]);
int validMove(const char [][COLS], int, int);
int coordsAreEdge(int, int);

main()
{
   char maze[ROWS][COLS];
   int xStart, yStart, x, y;

   srand(time(NULL));

   for (int loop = 0; loop < ROWS; loop++)
      for (int loop2 = 0; loop2 < COLS; loop2++)
         maze[loop][loop2] = '#';

   mazeGenerator(maze, &xStart, &yStart);

   x = xStart;   // starting row
   y = yStart;   // starting col

   mazeTraversal(maze, xStart, yStart, x, y, RIGHT);
   return 0;
}

// Assume that there is exactly 1 entrance and exactly 1 exit to the maze.
void mazeTraversal(char maze[][COLS], const int xCoord, const int yCoord,
                   int row, int col, int direction)
{
   static int flag = 0;    // starting position flag

   maze[row][col] = 'x';   // insert x at current location
   printMaze(maze);

   if (coordsAreEdge(row, col) && row != xCoord && col != yCoord) {
      cout << endl << "Maze successfully exited!" << endl << endl;
      return;    // maze is complete
   }
   else if (row == xCoord && col == yCoord && flag == 1) {
      cout << endl << "Arrived back at the starting location."
           << endl << endl;

      return;
   }
   else {
      flag = 1;

      for (int move = direction, count = 0; count < 4;
                                     ++count, ++move, move %= 4)
         switch(move) {
            case DOWN:
               if (validMove(maze, row + 1, col)) { // move down
                  mazeTraversal(maze, xCoord, yCoord, row + 1, col, LEFT);
                  return;
               }

               break;
```

```
            case RIGHT:
               if (validMove(maze, row, col + 1)) { // move right
                  mazeTraversal(maze, xCoord, yCoord, row, col + 1, DOWN);
                  return;
               }

               break;
            case UP:
               if (validMove(maze, row - 1, col)) { // move up
                  mazeTraversal(maze, xCoord, yCoord, row - 1, col, RIGHT);
                  return;
               }

               break;
            case LEFT:
               if (validMove(maze, row, col - 1)) { // move left
                  mazeTraversal(maze, xCoord, yCoord, row, col - 1, UP);
                  return;
               }

               break;
         }
      }
}

int validMove(const char maze[][COLS], int r, int c)
{
   return (r >= 0 && r <= ROWS - 1 && c >= 0 && c <= COLS - 1 &&
           maze[r][c] != '#');  // a valid move
}


int coordsAreEdge(int x, int y)
{
   if ((x == 0 || x == ROWS - 1) && (y >= 0 && y <= COLS - 1))
      return 1;
   else if ((y == 0 || y == COLS - 1) && (x >= 0 && x <= ROWS - 1))
      return 1;
   else
      return 0;
}


void printMaze(const char maze[][COLS])
{
   for (int x = 0; x < ROWS; x++) {

      for (int y = 0; y < COLS; y++)
         cout << maze[x][y] << ' ';

      cout << endl;
   }

   cout << endl << "Hit return to see next move";
   cin.get();
}

void mazeGenerator(char maze[][COLS], int *xPtr, int *yPtr)
{
   int a, x, y, entry, exit;

   do {
      entry = rand() % 4;
      exit = rand() % 4;
   } while (entry == exit);
```

```
     // Determine entry position
     if (entry == 0) {
        *xPtr = 1 + rand() % (ROWS - 2);     // avoid corners
        *yPtr = 0;
        maze[*xPtr][*yPtr] = '.';
     }
     else if (entry == 1) {
        *xPtr = 0;
        *yPtr = 1 + rand() % (COLS - 2);
        maze[*xPtr][*yPtr] = '.';
     }
     else if (entry == 2) {
        *xPtr = 1 + rand() % (ROWS - 2);
        *yPtr = COLS - 1;
        maze[*xPtr][*yPtr] = '.';
     }
     else {
        *xPtr = ROWS - 1;
        *yPtr = 1 + rand() % (COLS - 2);
        maze[*xPtr][*yPtr] = '.';
     }

     // Determine exit location
     if (exit == 0) {
        a = 1 + rand() % (ROWS - 2);
        maze[a][0] = '.';
     }
     else if (exit == 1) {
        a = 1 + rand() % (COLS - 2);
        maze[0][a] = '.';
     }
     else if (exit == 2) {
        a = 1 + rand() % (ROWS - 2);
        maze[a][COLS - 1] = '.';
     }
     else {
        a = 1 + rand() % (COLS - 2);
        maze[ROWS - 1][a] = '.';
     }
     for (int loop = 1; loop < (ROWS - 2) * (COLS - 2); loop++) {
        x = 1 + rand() % (ROWS - 2);     // add dots to maze
        y = 1 + rand() % (COLS - 2);
        maze[x][y] = '.';
     }
}
```

```
# # # # # # # # # # # # # # # . # # # # # # # # # # # # # #
# . . # . . . . # . . # . . # . # . . # . . . . . # . . # . #
# # . . . # # . # . . . # . . . . . # # # . . . . . . . . #
# . . # . # . . . . # . . # # . . . . # # # # # . . . . # . #
# # # . . . . . # . . # . . # # . # . . # . # . . . # . # #
# # # . . . . # . . # . . . . . # # . . # . # . # # # . #
# . . # # # # . # . . . . # . . . . . # # . . . # . . . #
# . # . . . # . # # # # . # . . # . # . . # . . . # . # . #
# . . . . # . # . . . . # . . . . . . # # . . # . . #
# . . # . # . # . . # # # . # # . . . # . . # . # # . # #
# # . # . # # # # . . # . # # . . # . . . . . . . # # . #
# . . . . # # # . # # # . # . # . . # . . # # . # . . . . #
# . . . # . . # # . . . . # . # # . . # . . . . # . . . #
# # . # . # . . . # . . # # . . . . . . # . # . # # # . . #
# # # # # # # # # # # # # # # # # x # # # # # # # # # # # #
...
```

continued

```
                                                              continued
# # # # # # # # # # # # # x # # # # # # # # # # # # #
# . . # . . . . # . . # . . # x x # . . . . . # . . . # . #
# # . . . . # # . # . . . # . . . . x x # # # . . . . . . . . # . #
# . . # . # . . . . # . . # # . . x x x # # # # . . # . . . . # . #
# # # . . . . . # . . # . . # # x # x x # . # . . . . # . # #
# # # . . . . # . . # . . . . . x # # x x # x # . # # # x #
# . . # # # # . # . . . # . . . x x x # # x x x # x x x x #
# . # . . . # . # # # # . . # . . # x x # x x x # x # x x #
# . . . . # . # . . . . . . # . . . . x x x # # x x # x x #
# . . # . # . # . . # # # . # # . . . # . x x # x # # x # #
# # . # . # # # # . . # . # # . . # . . x x x x x x # # x #
# . . . . # # # . # # # . # . . # x x # # x x # x x x x #
# . . . # . . # # . # . . . # . . # # . x # x x x x # x x x #
# # . # . # . . # . . # # . . . x x x # x # x # # # x x #
# # # # # # # # # # # # # # # # # # x # # # # # # # # # # #

Hit return to see next move
Maze successfully exited!
```

5.28 (*Arrays of Pointers to Functions*) Rewrite the program of Fig. 4.23 to use a menu-driven interface. The program should offer the user 4 options as follows (these should be displayed on the screen):

```
Enter a choice:
   0   Print the array of grades
   1   Find the minimum grade
   2   Find the maximum grade
   3   Print the average on all tests for each student
   4   End program
```

One restriction on using arrays of pointers to functions is that all the pointers must have the same type. The pointers must be to functions of the same return type that receive arguments of the same type. For this reason, the functions in Fig. 4.23 must be modified so they each return the same type and take the same parameters. Modify functions **minimum** and **maximum** to print the minimum or maximum value and return nothing. For option 3, modify function **average** of Fig. 4.23 to output the average for each student (not a specific student). Function **average** should return nothing and take the same parameters as **printArray**, **minimum**, and **maximum**. Store the pointers to the functions in array **processGrades** and use the choice made by the user as the subscript into the array for calling each function.

ANS:
```cpp
// Exercise 5.28 Solution
#include <iostream.h>
#include <iomanip.h>

const int STUDENTS = 3, EXAMS = 4;

void minimum(int [][EXAMS], int, int);
void maximum(int [][EXAMS], int, int);
void average(int [][EXAMS], int, int);
void printArray(int [][EXAMS], int, int);
void printMenu(void);

main()
{
   void (*processGrades[4])(int [][EXAMS], int, int)
                       = {printArray, minimum, maximum, average};

   int student, choice = 0,
       studentGrades[STUDENTS][EXAMS] = {{77, 68, 86, 73},
                                         {96, 87, 89, 78},
                                         {70, 90, 86, 81}};
```

```cpp
    while (choice != 4) {

        do {
            printMenu();
            cin >> choice;
        } while (choice < 0 || choice > 4);

        if (choice != 4)
            (*processGrades[choice])(studentGrades, STUDENTS, EXAMS);
        else
            cout << "Program Ended." << endl;
    }

    return 0;
}

void minimum(int grades[][EXAMS], int pupils, int tests)
{
    int lowGrade = 100;

    for (int i = 0; i < pupils; i++)
        for (int j = 0; j < tests; j++)
            if (grades[i][j] < lowGrade)
                lowGrade = grades[i][j];

    cout << endl << "\tThe lowest grade is " << lowGrade << endl;
}

void maximum(int grades[][EXAMS], int pupils, int tests)
{
    int highGrade = 0;

    for (int i = 0; i < pupils; i++)
        for (int j = 0; j < tests; j++)
            if (grades[i][j] > highGrade)
                highGrade = grades[i][j];

    cout << endl << "\tThe highest grade is " << highGrade << endl;
}

void average(int grades[][EXAMS], int pupils, int tests)
{
    int total;

    cout.setf(ios::showpoint);
    cout << endl;

    for (int i = 0; i < pupils; i++) {
        total = 0;  // reset total

        for (int j = 0; j < tests; j++)
            total += grades[i][j];

        cout << "\tThe average for student " << pupils + 1 << " is "
             << setprecision(1) << (float) total / tests << endl;
    }
}

void printArray(int grades[][EXAMS], int pupils, int tests)
{
    cout << endl << "\t                        [0]   [1]   [2]   [3]";

    for (int i = 0; i < pupils; i++) {
        cout << endl << "\tstudentGrades[" << i << ']';

        for (int j = 0; j < tests; j++)
            cout << setw(5) << grades[i][j];
    }

    cout << endl;
}
```

```
void printMenu(void)
{
   cout << endl << "\tEnter a choice:" << endl
        << "\t  0   Print the array of grades" << endl
        << "\t  1   Find the minimum grade" << endl
        << "\t  2   Find the maximum grade" << endl
        << "\t  3   Print the average on all tests for each student" << endl
        << "\t  4   End program" << endl << "\t? ";
}
```

```
Enter a choice:
   0  Print the array of grades
   1  Find the minimum grade
   2  Find the maximum grade
   3  Print the average on all tests for each student
   4  End program
? 0

                   [0]   [1]   [2]   [3]
studentGrades[0]   77    68    86    73
studentGrades[1]   96    87    89    78
studentGrades[2]   70    90    86    81

Enter a choice:
   0  Print the array of grades
   1  Find the minimum grade
   2  Find the maximum grade
   3  Print the average on all tests for each student
   4  End program
? 1
The lowest grade is 68

Enter a choice:
   0  Print the array of grades
   1  Find the minimum grade
   2  Find the maximum grade
   3  Print the average on all tests for each student
   4  End program
? 2
The highest grade is 96

Enter a choice:
   0  Print the array of grades
   1  Find the minimum grade
   2  Find the maximum grade
   3  Print the average on all tests for each student
   4  End program
? 3
The average for student 4 is 76.0
The average for student 4 is 87.5
The average for student 4 is 81.8

Enter a choice:
   0  Print the array of grades
   1  Find the minimum grade
   2  Find the maximum grade
   3  Print the average on all tests for each student
   4  End program
? 4

Program Ended.
```

5.29   (*Modifications to the Simpletron Simulator*) In Exercise 5.19, you wrote a software simulation of a computer that executes programs written in Simpletron Machine Language (SML). In this exercise, we propose several modifications and enhancements to the Simpletron Simulator. In Exercises 15.26 and 15.27, we propose building a compiler that converts programs written in a high-level programming language (a variation of BASIC) to Simpletron Machine Language. Some of the following modifications and enhancements may be required to execute the programs produced by the compiler.

a) Extend the Simpletron Simulator's memory to contain 1000 memory locations to enable the Simpletron to handle larger programs.

b) Allow the simulator to perform modulus calculations. This requires an additional Simpletron Machine Language instruction.

c) Allow the simulator to perform exponentiation calculations. This requires an additional Simpletron Machine Language instruction.

d) Modify the simulator to use hexadecimal values rather than integer values to represent Simpletron Machine Language instructions.

e) Modify the simulator to allow output of a newline. This requires an additional Simpletron Machine Language instruction.

f) Modify the simulator to process floating-point values in addition to integer values.

g) Modify the simulator to handle string input. Hint: Each Simpletron word can be divided into two groups, each holding a two-digit integer. Each two-digit integer represents the ASCII decimal equivalent of a character. Add a machine language instruction that will input a string and store the string beginning at a specific Simpletron memory location. The first half of the word at that location will be a count of the number of characters in the string (i.e., the length of the string). Each succeeding half-word contains one ASCII character expressed as two decimal digits. The machine language instruction converts each character into its ASCII equivalent and assigns it to a half-word.

h) Modify the simulator to handle output of strings stored in the format of part (g). Hint: Add a machine language instruction that will print a string beginning at a certain Simpletron memory location. The first half of the word at that location is a count of the number of characters in the string (i.e., the length of the string). Each succeeding half-word contains one ASCII character expressed as two decimal digits. The machine language instruction checks the length and prints the string by translating each two-digit number into its equivalent character.

5.30   What does this program do?

```
#include <iostream.h>

int mystery3(const char *, const char *);

main()
{
   char string1[80], string2[80];

   cout << "Enter two strings: ";
   cin >> string1 >> string2;
   cout << "The result is "
        << mystery3(string1, string2) << endl;

   return 0;
}

int mystery3(const char *s1, const char *s2)
{
   for ( ; *s1 != '\0' && *s2 != '\0'; s1++, s2++)
      if (*s1 != *s2)
         return 0;

   return 1;
}
```

ANS: The function **mystery3** compares two strings for equality.

```
Enter two strings: string1 string2
The result is 0
```

```
Enter two strings: string2 string2
The result is 1
```

String Manipulation Exercises

5.31   Write a program that uses function **strcmp** to compare two strings input by the user. The program should state whether the first string is less than, equal to, or greater than the second string.

ANS:
```cpp
// Exercise 5.31 Solution
#include <iostream.h>
#include <string.h>

const int SIZE = 20;

main()
{
    char string1[SIZE], string2[SIZE];
    int result;

    cout << "Enter two strings: ";
    cin >> string1 >> string2;
    result = strcmp(string1, string2);

    if (result > 0)
        cout << '\"' << string1 << '\"' << " is greater than \""
             << string2 << '\"' << endl;
    else if (result == 0)
        cout << '\"' << string1 << '\"' << " is equal to \"" << string2
             << '\"' << endl;
    else
        cout << '\"' << string1 << '\"' << " is less than \"" << string2
             << '\"' << endl;

    return 0;
}
```

```
Enter two strings: marlin shark
"marlin" is less than "shark"
```

```
Enter two strings: marlin marlin
"marlin" is equal to "marlin"
```

```
Enter two strings: marlin dolphin
"marlin" is greater than "dolphin"
```

5.32   Write a program that uses function **strncmp** to compare two strings input by the user. The program should input the number of characters to be compared. The program should state whether the first string is less than, equal to, or greater than the second string.

ANS:

```
// Exercise 5.32 Solution
#include <iostream.h>
#include <string.h>

const int SIZE = 20;

main()
{
    char string1[SIZE], string2[SIZE];
    int result, compareCount;

    cout << "Enter two strings: ";
    cin >> string1 >> string2;
    cout << "How many characters should be compared: ";
    cin >> compareCount;
      result = strncmp(string1, string2, compareCount);

    if (result > 0)
       cout << '\"' << string1 << "\" is greater than \"" << string2
            << "\" up to " << compareCount << " characters" << endl;
    else if (result == 0)
       cout << '\"' << string1 << "\" is equal to \"" << string2
            << "\" up to " << compareCount << " characters" << endl;
    else
       cout << '\"' << string1 << "\" is less than \"" << string2
            << "\" up to " << compareCount << " characters" << endl;

    return 0;
}
```

```
Enter two strings: ape apex
How many characters should be compared: 3
"ape" is equal to "apex" upto 3 characters
```

```
Enter two strings: ape apex
How many characters should be compared: 4
"ape" is less than "apex" upto 4 characters
```

5.33   Write a program that uses random number generation to create sentences. The program should use four arrays of pointers to `char` called `article`, `noun`, `verb`, and `preposition`. The program should create a sentence by selecting a word at random from each array in the following order: `article`, `noun`, `verb`, `preposition`, `article`, and `noun`. As each word is picked, it should be concatenated to the previous words in an array which is large enough to hold the entire sentence. The words should be separated by spaces. When the final sentence is output, it should start with a capital letter and end with a period. The program should generate 20 such sentences.

The arrays should be filled as follows: the `article` array should contain the articles `"the"`, `"a"`, `"one"`, `"some"`, and `"any"`; the `noun` array should contain the nouns `"boy"`, `"girl"`, `"dog"`, `"town"`, and `"car"`; the `verb` array should contain the verbs `"drove"`, `"jumped"`, `"ran"`, `"walked"`, and `"skipped"`; the `preposition` array should contain the prepositions `"to"`, `"from"`, `"over"`, `"under"`, and `"on"`.

After the preceding program is written and working, modify the program to produce a short story consisting of several of these sentences. (How about the possibility of a random term paper writer!)

ANS:

```
// Exercise 5.33 Solution
#include <iostream.h>
#include <stdlib.h>
#include <time.h>
#include <string.h>
#include <ctype.h>
```

```
const int SIZE = 100;

main()
{
    char *article[] = {"the", "a", "one", "some", "any"},
         *noun[] = {"boy", "girl", "dog", "town", "car"},
         *verb[] = {"drove", "jumped", "ran", "walked", "skipped"},
         *preposition[] = {"to", "from", "over", "under", "on"},
         sentence[SIZE] = "";

    for (int i = 1; i <= 20; i++) {
        strcat(sentence, article[rand() % 5]);
        strcat(sentence, " ");
        strcat(sentence, noun[rand() % 5]);
        strcat(sentence, " ");
        strcat(sentence, verb[rand() % 5]);
        strcat(sentence, " ");
        strcat(sentence, preposition[rand() % 5]);
        strcat(sentence, " ");
        strcat(sentence, article[rand() % 5]);
        strcat(sentence, " ");
        strcat(sentence, noun[rand() % 5]);
        cout << (char) toupper(sentence[0]) << &sentence[1] << '.' << endl;
        sentence[0] = '\0';
    }

    return 0;
}
```

```
A boy ran to a dog.
The boy walked from any town.
A car ran to one girl.
Some dog skipped from the boy.
Any car ran from any girl.
A girl drove under any boy.
Any boy jumped over any town.
A car ran under a car.
Any girl ran to the dog.
Some girl ran over any car.
Any town jumped from the town.
The car drove under some car.
The dog walked over a town.
The town jumped to one dog.
One boy jumped under a car.
Some car jumped over the girl.
The boy drove from one boy.
Some dog ran from some town.
Any town jumped under a boy.
Any car jumped on a boy.
```

5.34   *(Limericks)* A limerick is a humorous five-line verse in which the first and second lines rhyme with the fifth, and the third line rhymes with the fourth. Using techniques similar to those developed in Exercise 5.33, write a C++ program that produces random limericks. Polishing this program to produce good limericks is a challenging problem, but the result will be worth the effort!

5.35   Write a program that encodes English language phrases into pig Latin. Pig Latin is a form of coded language often used for amusement. Many variations exist in the methods used to form pig Latin phrases. For simplicity, use the following algorithm:

To form a pig Latin phrase from an English language phrase, tokenize the phrase into words with function **strtok**. To translate each English word into a pig Latin word, place the first letter of the English word at the end of the English word, and add the letters "**ay**." Thus the word "**jump**" becomes "**umpjay**," the word "**the**" becomes "**hetay**," and the word "**computer**" becomes "**omputercay**." Blanks between words remain as blanks. Assume the following: The English phrase consists of words separated by blanks, there are no punctuation marks, and all words have two or more letters. Function **printLatinWord** should display each word. Hint: Each time a token is found in a call to **strtok**, pass the token pointer to function **printLatinWord**, and print the pig Latin word.

ANS:

```
// Exercise 5.35 Solution
#include <iostream.h>
#include <string.h>

const int SIZE = 80;
void printLatinWord(char *);

main()
{
   char sentence[SIZE], *tokenPtr;

   cout << "Enter a sentence:" << endl;
   cin.getline(sentence, SIZE);
   cout << endl << "The sentence in Pig Latin is:" << endl;
   tokenPtr = strtok(sentence, " .,;");

   while (tokenPtr) {
      printLatinWord(tokenPtr);
      tokenPtr = strtok(NULL, " .,;");

      if (tokenPtr)
         cout << ' ';
   }

   cout << '.';

   return 0;
}

void printLatinWord(char *word)
{
   for (int i = 1; i < strlen(word); i++)
      cout << word[i];

   cout << word[0] << "ay";
}
```

```
Enter a sentence:
The house was large.

The sentence in Pig Latin is:
heTay ousehay asway argelay.
```

5.36   Write a program that inputs a telephone number as a string in the form **(555) 555-5555**. The program should use function **strtok** to extract the area code as a token, the first three digits of the phone number as a token, and the last four digits of the phone number as a token. The seven digits of the phone number should be concatenated into one string. The program should convert the area code string to **int** and convert the phone number string to **long**. Both the area code and the phone number should be printed.

ANS:

```
// Exercise 5.36 Solution
#include <iostream.h>
#include <string.h>
#include <stdlib.h>
```

```
main()
{
    const int SIZE1 = 20, SIZE2 = 10;
    char p[SIZE1], b[SIZE2], c[SIZE2], phoneNumber[SIZE2] = {'\0'},
        *tokenPtr;
    int  areaCode;
    long phone;

    cout << "Enter a phone number in the form (555) 555-5555: " << endl;
    cin.getline(p, SIZE1);
    areaCode = atoi(strtok(p, "()"));
    tokenPtr = strtok(0, "-");
    strcpy(phoneNumber, tokenPtr);
    tokenPtr = strtok(0, "");
    strcat(phoneNumber, tokenPtr);
    phone = atol(phoneNumber);
    cout << endl << "The integer area code is " << areaCode << endl
        << "The long integer phone number is " << phone << endl;
    return 0;
}
```

```
Enter a phone number in the form (555) 555-5555:
(555) 349-7371

The integer area code is 555
The long integer phone number is 3497371
```

5.37   Write a program that inputs a line of text, tokenizes the line with function **strtok**, and outputs the tokens in reverse order.

ANS:
```
// Exercise 5.37 Solution
#include <iostream.h>
#include <string.h>

void reverseTokens(char *);

main()
{
    const int SIZE = 80;
    char text[SIZE];

    cout << "Enter a line of text:" << endl;
    cin.getline(text, SIZE);
    reverseTokens(text);
    return 0;
}

void reverseTokens(char *sentence)
{
    char *pointers[50], *temp;
    int count = 0;

    temp = strtok(sentence, " ");

    while (temp) {
        pointers[count++] = temp;
        temp = strtok(NULL, " ");
    }

    cout << endl << "The tokens in reverse order are:" << endl;

    for (int i = count - 1; i >= 0; i--)
        cout << pointers[i] << ' ';
}
```

```
Enter a line of text:
string processing at its best

The tokens in reverse order are:
best its at processing string
```

5.38   Use the string comparison functions discussed in Section 5.12.2 and the techniques for sorting arrays developed in Chapter 4 to write a program that alphabetizes a list of strings. Use the names of 10 or 15 towns in your area as data for your program.

ANS:

```cpp
// Exercise 5.38 Solution
#include <iostream.h>
#include <string.h>

const int SIZE = 50;
void bubbleSort(char [][SIZE]);

main()
{
    char array[10][SIZE];

    for (int i = 0; i < 10; i++) {
        cout << "Enter a string: ";
        cin >> &array[i][0];
    }

    bubbleSort(array);
    cout << endl << "The strings in sorted order are:" << endl;

    for (i = 0; i < 10; i++)
        cout << &array[i][0] << endl;

    return 0;
}

void bubbleSort(char a[][SIZE])
{
    char temp[SIZE];

    for (int i = 0; i <= 8; i++)
        for (int j = 0; j <= 8; j++)
            if (strcmp(&a[j][0], &a[j + 1][0]) > 0) {
                strcpy(temp, &a[j][0]);
                strcpy(&a[j][0], &a[j + 1][0]);
                strcpy(&a[j + 1][0], temp);
            }
}
```

```
Enter a string: Warren
Enter a string: Pittsford
Enter a string: Killington
Enter a string: Marlboro
Enter a string: Middlebury
Enter a string: Grafton
Enter a string: Barre
Enter a string: Montpelier
Enter a string: Wolcott
Enter a string: Windsor
```

continued

```
                                                                    continued
    The strings in sorted order are:
    Barre
    Grafton
    Killington
    Marlboro
    Middlebury
    Montpelier
    Pittsford
    Warren
    Windsor
    Wolcott
```

5.39   Write two versions of each of the string copy and string concatenation functions in Fig. 5.29. The first version should use array subscripting, and the second version should use pointers and pointer arithmetic.

ANS:

```cpp
// Exercise 5.39 Solution
#include <iostream.h>

char *stringCopy1(char *, const char *);
char *stringCopy2(char *, const char *);
char *stringNCopy1(char *, const char *, unsigned);
char *stringNCopy2(char *, const char *, unsigned);
char *stringCat1(char *, const char *);
char *stringCat2(char *, const char *);
char *stringNCat1(char *, const char *, unsigned);
char *stringNCat2(char *, const char *, unsigned);

main()
{
    int n = 4;
    char string1[100], string2[100];

    cout << "Enter a string: ";
    cin >> string2;

    cout << "Copied string returned from stringCopy1 is "
         << stringCopy1(string1, string2) << endl
         << "Copied string returned from stringCopy2 is "
         << stringCopy2(string1, string2) << endl;
    cout << "Copied " << n << " elements returned from stringNCopy1 is "
         << stringNCopy1(string1, string2, n) << endl;
    cout << "Copied " << n << " elements returned from stringNCopy2 is "
         << stringNCopy2(string1, string2, n) << endl;
    cout << "Concatenated string returned from stringCat1 is "
         << stringCat1(string1, string2) << endl;
    cout << "Concatenated string returned from stringCat2 is "
         << stringCat2(string1, string2) << endl;
    cout << "Concatenated string returned from stringNCat1 is "
         << stringNCat1(string1, string2, n) << endl;
    cout << "Concatenated string returned from stringNCat2 is "
         << stringNCat2(string1, string2, n) << endl;

    return 0;
}

char *stringCopy1(char *s1, const char *s2)
{
    for (int sub = 0; s1[sub] = s2[sub]; sub++)
        ; // empty body

    return s1;
}
```

```
char *stringCopy2(char *s1, const char *s2)
{
   char *ptr = s1;

   for ( ; *s1 = *s2; s1++, s2++)
      ; // empty body

   return ptr;
}

char *stringNCopy1(char *s1, const char *s2, unsigned n)
{
   for (unsigned c = 0; c < n && (s1[c] = s2[c]); c++)
      ; // empty body

   s1[c] = '\0';
   return s1;
}

char *stringNCopy2(char *s1, const char *s2, unsigned n)
{
   char *ptr = s1;

   for (unsigned c = 0; c < n; c++, s1++, s2++)
      *s1 = *s2;

   *s1 = '\0';
   return ptr;
}

char *stringCat1(char *s1, const char *s2)
{
   for (int x = 0; s1[x] != '\0'; x++)
      ; // empty body

   for (int y = 0; s1[x] = s2[y]; x++, y++)
      ; // empty body

   return s1;
}

char *stringCat2(char *s1, const char *s2)
{
   char *ptr = s1;

   for ( ; *s1 != '\0'; s1++)
      ; // empty body

   for ( ; *s1 = *s2; s1++, s2++)
      ; // empty body

   return ptr;
}

char *stringNCat1(char *s1, const char *s2, unsigned n)
{
   for (int x = 0; s1[x] != '\0'; x++)
      ; // empty body

   for (unsigned y = 0; y < n && (s1[x] = s2[y]); x++, y++)
      ; // empty body

   s1[x] = '\0';

   return s1;
}
```

```cpp
char *stringNCat2(char *s1, const char *s2, unsigned n)
{
   char *ptr = s1;

   for ( ; *s1 != '\0'; s1++)
      ; // empty body

   for (unsigned c = 0 ; c < n && (*s1 = *s2); s1++, s2++)
      ; // empty body

   *s1 = '\0';

   return ptr;
}
```

```
Enter a string: clock
Copied string returned from stringCopy1 is clock
Copied string returned from stringCopy2 is clock
Copied 4 elements returned from stringNCopy1 is cloc
Copied 4 elements returned from stringNCopy2 is cloc
Concatenated string returned from stringCat1 is clocclock
Concatenated string returned from stringCat2 is clocclockclock
Concatenated string returned from stringNCat1 is clocclockclockcloc
Concatenated string returned from stringNCat2 is clocclockclockclocclock
```

5.40   Write two versions of each string comparison function in Fig. 5.29. The first version should use array subscripting, and the second version should use pointers and pointer arithmetic.

ANS:

```cpp
// Exercise 5.40 Solution
#include <iostream.h>

int stringCompare1(const char *, const char *);
int stringCompare2(const char *, const char *);
int stringNCompare1(const char *, const char *, unsigned);
int stringNCompare2(const char *, const char *, unsigned);

main()
{
   char string1[100], string2[100];
   unsigned n = 3;   // number of characters to be compared

   cout << "Enter two strings: ";
   cin >> string1 >> string2;

   cout << "The value returned from stringCompare1(\"" << string1
        << "\", \"" << string2 << "\") is "
        << stringCompare1(string1, string2) << endl
        << "The value returned from stringCompare2(\"" << string1
        << "\", \"" << string2 << "\") is "
        << stringCompare2(string1, string2) << endl;

   cout << endl << "The value returned from stringNCompare1(\"" << string1
        << "\", \"" << string2 << "\", " << n << ") is "
        << stringNCompare1(string1, string2, n) << endl
        << "The value returned from stringNCompare2(\"" << string1
        << "\", \"" << string2 << "\", " << n << ") is "
        << stringNCompare2(string1, string2, n) << endl;

   return 0;
}
```

```cpp
int stringCompare1(const char *s1, const char *s2)
{
   // array subscript notation
   for (int sub = 0; s1[sub] == s2[sub]; sub++)
      ; // empty statement

   --sub;

   if (s1[sub] == '\0' && s2[sub] == '\0')
      return 0;
   else if (s1[sub] < s2[sub])
      return -1;
   else
      return 1;
}

int stringCompare2(const char *s1, const char *s2)
{
   // pointer notation
   for ( ; *s1 == *s2; s1++, s2++)
      ; // empty statement

   --s1;
   --s2;

   if (*s1 == '\0' && *s2 == '\0')
      return 0;
   else if (*s1 < *s2)
      return -1;
   else
      return 1;
}

int stringNCompare1(const char *s1, const char *s2, unsigned n)
{
   // array subscript notation
   for (unsigned sub = 0; sub < n && (s1[sub] == s2[sub]); sub++)
      ; // empty body

   --sub;

   if (s1[sub] == s2[sub])
      return 0;
   else if (s1[sub] < s2[sub])
      return -1;
   else
      return 1;
}

int stringNCompare2(const char *s1, const char *s2, unsigned n)
{
   for (unsigned c = 0; c < n && (*s1 == *s2); c++, s1++, s2++)
      ; // empty statement

   --s1;
   --s2;

   if (*s1 == *s2)
      return 0;
   else if (*s1 < *s2)
      return -1;
   else
      return 1;
}
```

```
Enter two strings: juice juice
The value returned from stringCompare1("juice", "juice") is 0
The value returned from stringCompare2("juice", "juice") is 0

The value returned from stringNCompare1("juice", "juice", 3) is 0
The value returned from stringNCompare2("juice", "juice", 3) is 0
```

```
Enter two strings: tomato tommy
The value returned from stringCompare1("tomato", "tommy") is 1
The value returned from stringCompare2("tomato", "tommy") is 1

The value returned from stringNCompare1("tomato", "tommy", 3) is 0
The value returned from stringNCompare2("tomato", "tommy", 3) is 0
```

```
Enter two strings: texas montana
The value returned from stringCompare1("texas", "montana") is 1
The value returned from stringCompare2("texas", "montana") is 1

The value returned from stringNCompare1("texas", "montana", 3) is 1
The value returned from stringNCompare2("texas", "montana", 3) is 1
```

5.41   Write two versions of function **strlen** in Fig. 5.29. The first version should use array subscripting, and the second version should use pointers and pointer arithmetic.

ANS:
```cpp
// Exercise 5.41 Solution
#include <iostream.h>

unsigned long stringLength1(const char *);
unsigned long stringLength2(const char *);

main()
{
   char string[100];

   cout << "Enter a string: ";
   cin >> string;

   cout << endl << "According to stringLength1 the string length is: "
        << stringLength1(string) << endl
        << "According to stringLength2 the string length is: "
        << stringLength2(string) << endl;

   return 0;
}

unsigned long stringLength1(const char *s)
{
   // array subscript notation
   for (int length = 0; s[length] != '\0'; length++)
     ; // empty body

   return length;
}
```

```
unsigned long stringLength2(const char *s)
{
   // pointer notation
   for (int length = 0; *s != '\0'; s++, length++)
      ; // empty body

   return length;
}
```

```
Enter a string: howlongcouldthisstringpossiblybe?

According to stringLength1 the string length is: 33
According to stringLength2 the string length is: 33
```

Special Section: Advanced String Manipulation Exercises

The preceding exercises are keyed to the text and designed to test the reader's understanding of fundamental string manipulation concepts. This section includes a collection of intermediate and advanced string manipulation exercises. The reader should find these problems challenging yet enjoyable. The problems vary considerably in difficulty. Some require an hour or two of program writing and implementation. Others are useful for lab assignments that might require two or three weeks of study and implementation. Some are challenging term projects.

5.42   *(Text Analysis)* The availability of computers with string manipulation capabilities has resulted in some rather interesting approaches to analyzing the writings of great authors. Much attention has been focused on whether William Shakespeare ever lived. Some scholars believe there is substantial evidence indicating that Christopher Marlowe or other authors actually penned the masterpieces attributed to Shakespeare. Researchers have used computers to find similarities in the writings of these two authors. This exercise examines three methods for analyzing texts with a computer.

a) Write a program that reads several lines of text from the keyboard and prints a table indicating the number of occurrences of each letter of the alphabet in the text. For example, the phrase

```
      To be, or not to be: that is the question:
```

contains one "a," two "b's," no "c's," etc.

ANS:

```
// Exercise 5.42 Part A Solution
#include <iostream.h>
#include <iomanip.h>
#include <ctype.h>

const int SIZE = 80;

main()
{
   char letters[26] = {0}, text[3][SIZE];

   cout << "Enter three lines of text:" << endl;
      for (int i = 0; i <= 2; i++)
      cin.getline(&text[i][0], SIZE);

   for (i = 0; i <= 2; i++)
      for (int j = 0; text[i][j] != '\0'; j++)
         if (isalpha(text[i][j]))
            ++letters[tolower(text[i][j]) - 'a'];

   cout << endl << "Total letter counts:" << endl;
      for (i = 0; i <= 25; i++)
      cout << setw(3) << (char) ('a' + i) << ':' << setw(3)
           << (int) letters[i] << endl;

   return 0;
}
```

```
Enter three lines of text:
pointers are a powerful feature of C++
pointer offset notation
pointer subscript notation

Total letter counts:
  a:  5
  b:  1
  c:  2
  d:  0
  e:  8
  f:  4
  g:  0
  h:  0
  i:  6
  j:  0
  k:  0
  l:  1
  m:  0
  n:  7
  o:  9
  p:  5
  q:  0
  r:  7
  s:  4
  t: 10
  u:  3
  v:  0
  w:  1
  x:  0
  y:  0
  z:  0
```

b) Write a program that reads several lines of text and prints a table indicating the number of one-letter words, two-letter words, three-letter words, etc. appearing in the text. For example, the phrase

Whether 'tis nobler in the mind to suffer

contains

Word length	Occurrences
1	0
2	2
3	2
4	2 (including 'tis)
5	0
6	2
7	1

ANS:
```
// Exercise 5.42 Part B Solution
#include <iostream.h>
#include <string.h>
```

```
main()
{
   const int SIZE = 80;
   char text[3][SIZE], *temp;
   int lengths[20] = {0};

   cout << "Enter three lines of text:" << endl;

   for (int i = 0; i <= 2; i++)
      cin.getline(&text[i][0], SIZE);

   for (i = 0; i <= 2; i++) {
      temp = strtok(&text[i][0], ". \n");

      while (temp) {
         ++lengths[strlen(temp)];
         temp = strtok(NULL, ". \n");
      }
   }

   cout.put('\n');

   for (i = 1; i <= 19; i++)
      if (lengths[i])
         cout << lengths[i] << " word(s) " << " of length " << i << endl;

   return 0;
}
```

```
Enter three lines of text:
first line of text entered
second line of text entered
the third line of text entered

3 word(s)   of length 2
1 word(s)   of length 3
6 word(s)   of length 4
2 word(s)   of length 5
1 word(s)   of length 6
3 word(s)   of length 7
```

c) Write a program that reads several lines of text and prints a table indicating the number of occurrences of each different word in the text. The first version of your program should include the words in the table in the same order in which they appear in the text. For example, the lines

```
To be, or not to be: that is the question:
Whether 'tis nobler in the mind to suffer
```

contain the words "to" three times, the word "be" two times, the word "or" once, etc. A more interesting (and useful) printout should then be attempted in which the words are sorted alphabetically.

ANS:
```
// Exercise 5.42 Part C Solution
#include <iostream.h>
#include <string.h>

const int SIZE = 80;

main()
{
   char text[3][SIZE], *temp, words[100][20] = {""};
```

```cpp
        int count[100] = {0};

        cout << "Enter three lines of text:" << endl;

        for (int i = 0; i <= 2; i++)
           cin.getline(&text[i][0], SIZE);

        for (i = 0; i <= 2; i++) {
           temp = strtok(&text[i][0], ". \n");

           while (temp) {
              for (int j = 0; words[j][0] && strcmp(temp, &words[j][0]) != 0; j++)
                 ;  // empty body

              ++count[j];

              if (!words[j][0])
                 strcpy(&words[j][0], temp);

              temp = strtok(NULL, ". \n");
           }
        }

        cout.put('\n');

        for (int j = 0; words[j][0] != '\0' && j <= 99; j++)
           cout << "\"" << &words[j][0] << "\" appeared " << count[j]
                << " time(s)" << endl;

        return 0;
     }
```

```
     Enter three lines of text:
     the city of dallas has three teams
     one of the teams is the cowboys
     another team is the stars and
     the other team is the mavericks

     "the" appeared 6 time(s)
     "city" appeared 1 time(s)
     "of" appeared 2 time(s)
     "dallas" appeared 1 time(s)
     "has" appeared 1 time(s)
     "three" appeared 1 time(s)
     "teams" appeared 2 time(s)
     "one" appeared 1 time(s)
     "is" appeared 3 time(s)
     "cowboys" appeared 1 time(s)
     "another" appeared 1 time(s)
     "team" appeared 2 time(s)
     "stars" appeared 1 time(s)
     "and" appeared 1 time(s)
     "other" appeared 1 time(s)
     "mavericks" appeared 1 time(s)
```

5.43   *(Word Processing)* One important function in word processing systems is *type-justification*—the alignment of words to both the left and right margins of a page. This generates a professional-looking document that gives the appearance of being set in type rather than prepared on a typewriter. Type-justification can be accomplished on computer systems by inserting blank characters between each of the words in a line so that the rightmost word aligns with the right margin.

Write a program that reads several lines of text and prints this text in type-justified format. Assume that the text is to be printed on 8 1/2-inch-wide paper, and that one-inch margins are to be allowed on both the left and right sides of the printed page. Assume that the computer prints 10 characters to the horizontal inch. Therefore, your program should print 6 1/2 inches of text or 65 characters per line.

5.44   *(Printing Dates in Various Formats)* Dates are commonly printed in several different formats in business correspondence. Two of the more common formats are:

> **07/21/55 and July 21, 1955**

Write a program that reads a date in the first format and prints that date in the second format.

> **ANS:**
> ```
> // Exercise 5.44 Solution
> #include <iostream.h>
>
> main()
> {
>     char *months[13] = {"", "January", "February", "March", "April", "May",
>                         "June", "July", "August", "September", "October",
>                         "November", "December"};
>     int m, d, y;
>
>     cout << "Enter a date in the form mm/dd/yy: " << endl;
>     cin >> m;
>     cin.ignore();
>     cin >> d;
>     cin.ignore();
>     cin >> y;
>
>     cout << "The date is: " << months[m] << ' ' << d << ' '
>          << 1900 + y << endl;
>
>     return 0;
> }
> ```

> ```
> Enter a date in the form mm/dd/yy:
> 8/1/93
> The date is: August 1 1993
> ```

5.45   *(Check Protection)* Computers are frequently employed in check-writing systems such as payroll and accounts payable applications. Many strange stories circulate regarding weekly paychecks being printed (by mistake) for amounts in excess of $1 million. Weird amounts are printed by computerized check-writing systems because of human error and/or machine failure. Systems designers build controls into their systems to prevent such erroneous checks from being issued.

Another serious problem is the intentional alteration of a check amount by someone who intends to cash a check fraudulently. To prevent a dollar amount from being altered, most computerized check-writing systems employ a technique called *check protection*.

Checks designed for imprinting by computer contain a fixed number of spaces in which the computer may print an amount. Suppose a paycheck contains eight blank spaces in which the computer is supposed to print the amount of a weekly paycheck. If the amount is large, then all eight of those spaces will be filled, for example:

> ```
> 1,230.60 (check amount)
> --------
> 12345678  (position numbers)
> ```

On the other hand, if the amount is less than $1000, then several of the spaces would ordinarily be left blank. For example,

```
       99.87
    --------
    12345678
```

contains three blank spaces. If a check is printed with blank spaces, it is easier for someone to alter the amount of the check. To prevent a check from being altered, many check-writing systems insert *leading asterisks* to protect the amount as follows:

```
    ***99.87
    --------
    12345678
```

Write a program that inputs a dollar amount to be printed on a check, and then prints the amount in check-protected format with leading asterisks if necessary. Assume that nine spaces are available for printing an amount.

ANS:
```
// Exercise 5.45 Solution
#include <iostream.h>
#include <iomanip.h>

main()
{
    double amount, base = 100000.0;

    cout << "Enter check amount: ";
    cin >> amount;
    cout << "The protected amount is $";

    for (int i = 0; amount < base; i++)
       base /= 10;

    for (int j = 1; j <= i; j++)
       cout.put('*');

    cout.setf(ios::showpoint);
    cout << setw(9 - i) << setfill('*') << setprecision(2) << amount << endl;

    return 0;
}
```

```
Enter check amount: 76.78
The protected amount is $****76.78
```

5.46   *(Writing the Word Equivalent of a Check Amount)* Continuing the discussion of the previous example, we reiterate the importance of designing check-writing systems to prevent alteration of check amounts. One common security method requires that the check amount be written both in numbers, and "spelled out" in words as well. Even if someone is able to alter the numerical amount of the check, it is extremely difficult to change the amount in words.

Many computerized check-writing systems do not print the amount of the check in words. Perhaps the main reason for this omission is the fact that most high-level languages used in commercial applications do not contain adequate string manipulation features. Another reason is that the logic for writing word equivalents of check amounts is somewhat involved.

Write a C++ program that inputs a numeric check amount and writes the word equivalent of the amount. For example, the amount 112.43 should be written as

ONE HUNDRED TWELVE and 43/100

ANS:
```
// Exercise 5.46 Solution
// NOTE: THAT THIS PROGRAM ONLY HANDLES VALUES UP TO $99.99
// The program is easily modified to process larger values
#include <iostream.h>
```

```
main()
{
    char *digits[10] = {"", "ONE", "TWO", "THREE", "FOUR", "FIVE", "SIX",
                        "SEVEN", "EIGHT", "NINE"};
    char *teens[10] = {"TEN", "ELEVEN", "TWELVE", "THIRTEEN", "FOURTEEN",
                       "FIFTEEN", "SIXTEEN", "SEVENTEEN", "EIGHTEEN",
                       "NINETEEN"};
    char *tens[10] = {"", "TEN", "TWENTY", "THIRTY", "FORTY", "FIFTY",
                      "SIXTY", "SEVENTY", "EIGHTY", "NINETY"};
    int dollars, cents, digit1, digit2;

    cout << "Enter the check amount (0.00 to 99.99): ";
    cin >> dollars;
    cin.ignore();

    cin >> cents;
    cout << "The check amount in words is:" << endl;

    if (dollars < 10)
        cout << digits[dollars] << ' ';
    else if (dollars < 20)
        cout << teens[dollars - 10] << ' ';
    else {
        digit1 = dollars / 10;
        digit2 = dollars % 10;

        if (digit2 == 0)
            cout << tens[digit1] << ' ';
        else
            cout << tens[digit1] << "-" << digits[digit2] << ' ';
    }

    cout << "Dollars and " << cents << "/100" << endl;

    return 0;
}
```

```
Enter the check amount (0.00 to 99.99): 76.78

The check amount in words is:
SEVENTY-SIX Dollars and 78/100
```

5.47   *(Morse Code)* Perhaps the most famous of all coding schemes is the Morse code, developed by Samuel Morse in 1832 for use with the telegraph system. The Morse code assigns a series of dots and dashes to each letter of the alphabet, each digit, and a few special characters (such as period, comma, colon, and semicolon). In sound-oriented systems, the dot represents a short sound and the dash represents a long sound. Other representations of dots and dashes are used with light-oriented systems and signal-flag systems.

Separation between words is indicated by a space, or, quite simply, the absence of a dot or dash. In a sound-oriented system, a space is indicated by a short period of time during which no sound is transmitted. The international version of the Morse code appears in Fig. 5.39.

Write a program that reads an English language phrase and encodes the phrase into Morse code. Also write a program that reads a phrase in Morse code and converts the phrase into the English language equivalent. Use one blank between each Morse-coded letter and three blanks between each Morse-coded word.

5.48   *(A Metric Conversion Program)* Write a program that will assist the user with metric conversions. Your program should allow the user to specify the names of the units as strings (i.e., centimeters, liters, grams, etc. for the metric system and inches, quarts, pounds, etc. for the English system) and should respond to simple questions such as

Character	Code	Character	Code
A	. -	T	-
B	- . . .	U	. . -
C	- . - .	V	. . . -
D	- . .	W	. - -
E	.	X	- . . -
F	. . - .	Y	- . - -
G	- - .	Z	- - . .
H	. . . .		
I	. .	**Digits**	
J	. - - -	1	. - - - -
K	- . -	2	. . - - -
L	. - . .	3	. . . - -
M	- -	4	. . . . -
N	- .	5	. . . . .
O	- - -	6	- . . . .
P	. - - .	7	- - . . .
Q	- - . -	8	- - - . .
R	. - .	9	- - - - .
S	. . .	0	- - - - -

Fig. 5.39   The letters of the alphabet as expressed in international Morse code.

```
"How many inches are in 2 meters?"
"How many liters are in 10 quarts?"
```
Your program should recognize invalid conversions. For example, the question
```
"How many feet in 5 kilograms?"
```
is not meaningful because **"feet"** are units of length while **"kilograms"** are units of weight.

A challenging string manipulation project

5.49   (*A Crossword Puzzle Generator*) Most people have worked a crossword puzzle, but few have ever attempted to generate one. Generating a crossword puzzle is a difficult problem. It is suggested here as a string manipulation project requiring substantial sophistication and effort. There are many issues the programmer must resolve to get even the simplest crossword puzzle generator program working. For example, how does one represent the grid of a crossword puzzle inside the computer? Should one use a series of strings, or should double-subscripted arrays be used? The programmer needs a source of words (i.e., a computerized dictionary) that can be directly referenced by the program. In what form should these words be stored to facilitate the complex manipulations required by the program? The really ambitious reader will want to generate the "clues" portion of the puzzle in which the brief hints for each "across" word and each "down" word are printed for the puzzle worker. Merely printing a version of the blank puzzle itself is not a simple problem.

6
Classes and Data Abstraction: Solutions

Exercises

6.3 What is the purpose of the scope resolution operator?

ANS: The scope resolution operator is used to specify the class to which a function belongs. It also resolves the ambiguity caused by multiple classes having member functions of the same name.

6.4 Compare and contrast the notions of **struct** and **class** in C++.

ANS: In C++, the keywords **struct** and **class** can be used to define types containing data members and member functions. The differences occur in the default access privileges for each. The default access for members of a **class** is **private**, the default access for members of a **struct** is **public**. The access privileges for **class** and **struct** can be specified explicitly.

6.5 Provide a constructor that is capable of using the current time from the **time()** function—declared in the C Standard Library header **time.h**—to initialize an object of the **Time** class.

ANS:
```
// P6_5.H
#ifndef P6_5_H
#define P6_5_H

#include <iostream.h>
#include <time.h>

class Time {
public:
   Time();
   void setHour(int h) { hour = (h >= 0 && h < 24) ? h : 0; }
   void setMinute(int m) { minute = (m >= 0 && m < 60) ? m : 0; }
   void setSecond(int s) { second = (s >= 0 && s < 60) ? s : 0; }
   int getHour(void) { return hour; }
   int getMinute(void) { return minute; }
   int getSecond(void) { return second; }
   void printStandard(void);
private:
   int hour;
   int minute;
   int second;
};

#endif
```

```cpp
// p6_5M.cpp
// member function definitions for p6_5.cpp
#include <iostream.h>
#include <time.h>
#include "p6_5.h"
Time::Time()
{
   long int totalTime;           // time in seconds since 1970
   int currentYear = 1994 - 1970; // current years elapsed
   double totalYear;             // current time in years
   double totalDay;              // days since beginning of year
   double day;                   // current time in days
   long double divisor;          // conversion divisor
   int timeShift = 7;            // time returned by time() is
                                 // given as the number of seconds
                                 //  elapsed since 1/1/70 GMT.
                                 // Depending on the time zone
                                 // you are in, you must shift
                                 // the time by a certain
                                 // number of hours. For this
                                 // problem, 7 hours is the
                                 // current shift for EST.


   totalTime = time(NULL);
   divisor = (60.0 * 60.0 * 24.0 * 365.0);
   totalYear = totalTime / divisor - currentYear;
   totalDay = 365 * totalYear;      // leap years ignored
   day = totalDay - (int) totalDay;

   setHour(day * 24 + timeShift);
   setMinute((day * 24 - (int)(day * 24)) * 60);
   setSecond((minute * 60 - (int)(minute * 60)) * 60);
}

void Time::printStandard()
{
   cout << ((hour % 12 == 0) ? 12 : hour % 12) << ':'
        << (minute < 10 ? "0" : "") << minute << ':'
        << (second < 10 ? "0" : "") << second
        << (hour < 12 ? " AM" : " PM");
}
```

```cpp
// driver for p6_5.cpp
#include <iostream.h>
#include "p6_5.h"

main()
{
   Time t;

   t.printStandard();
   return 0;
}
```

```
2:33:35 AM
```

6.6   Create a class called **Complex** for performing arithmetic with complex numbers. Write a driver program to test your class.

Complex numbers have the form

```
realPart + imaginaryPart * i
```

where *i* is

$$\sqrt{-1}$$

Use floating-point variables to represent the private data of the class. Provide a constructor function that enables an object of this class to be initialized when it is declared. The constructor should contain default values in case no initializers are provided. Provide public member functions for each of the following:

a) Addition of two **Complex** numbers: The real parts are added together and the imaginary parts are added together.

b) Subtraction of two **Complex** numbers: The real part of the right operand is subtracted from the real part of the left operand and the imaginary part of the right operand is subtracted from the imaginary part of the left operand.

c) Printing **Complex** numbers in the form **(a, b)** where **a** is the real part and **b** is the imaginary part.

ANS:

```cpp
// P6_6.H
#ifndef p6_6_H
#define p6_6_H
#include <iostream.h>

class Complex {
public:
   Complex(float = 0.0, float = 0.0); // default constructor
   void addition(const Complex &);
   void subtraction(const Complex &);
   void printComplex(void);
   void setComplexNumber(float, float);
private:
   float realPart;
   float imaginaryPart;
};

#endif
```

```cpp
// p6_6M.cpp
// member function definitions for p6_6.cpp
#include <iostream.h>
#include "p6_6.h"

Complex::Complex(float real, float imaginary)
   { setComplexNumber(real, imaginary); }

void Complex::addition(const Complex &a)
{
   realPart += a.realPart;
   imaginaryPart += a.imaginaryPart;
}

void Complex::subtraction(const Complex &s)
{
   realPart -= s.realPart;
   imaginaryPart -= s.imaginaryPart;
}

void Complex::printComplex(void)
   { cout << '(' << realPart << ", " << imaginaryPart << ')'; }
```

```cpp
void Complex::setComplexNumber(float rp, float ip)
{
   realPart = rp;
   imaginaryPart = ip;
}
```

```cpp
// driver for p6_6.cpp
#include <iostream.h>
#include "p6_6.h"

main()
{
   Complex b(1, 7), c(9, 2);

   b.printComplex();
   cout << " + ";
   c.printComplex();
   cout << " = ";
   b.addition(c);
   b.printComplex();

   cout << endl;
   b.setComplexNumber(10,1);    // reset realPart and imaginaryPart
   c.setComplexNumber(11,5);
   b.printComplex();
   cout << " - ";
   c.printComplex();
   cout << " = ";
   b.subtraction(c);
   b.printComplex();
   cout << endl;

   return 0;
}
```

```
(1, 7) + (9, 2) = (10, 9)
(10, 1) - (11, 5) = (-1, -4)
```

6.7   Create a class called **Rational** for performing arithmetic with fractions. Write a driver program to test your class.

· Use integer variables to represent the private data of the class—the numerator and the denominator. Provide a constructor function that enables an object of this class to be initialized when it is declared. The constructor should contain default values in case no initializers are provided and should store the fraction in reduced form (i.e., the fraction

$$\frac{2}{4}$$

would be stored in the object as 1 in the numerator and 2 in the denominator). Provide public member functions for each of the following:

a)   Addition of two **Rational** numbers. The result should be stored in reduced form.
b)   Subtraction of two **Rational** numbers. The result should be stored in reduced form.
c)   Multiplication of two **Rational** numbers. The result should be stored in reduced form.
d)   Division of two **Rational** numbers. The result should be stored in reduced form.
e)   Printing **Rational** numbers in the form **a/b** where **a** is the numerator and **b** is the denominator.
f)   Printing **Rational** numbers in floating point format.

ANS:

```
// P6_7.H
#ifndef P6_7_H
#define P6_7_H
#include <iostream.h>

class Rational {
public:
   Rational(int = 0, int = 1);  // default constructor
   Rational addition(const Rational &);
   Rational subtraction(const Rational &);
   Rational multiplication(const Rational &);
   Rational division(Rational &);
   void printRational(void);
   void printRationalAsFloating(void);
private:
   int numerator;
   int denominator;
   void reduction(void);    // utility function
};

#endif
```

```
// P6_7M.cpp
// member function definitions for p6_7.cpp
#include <iostream.h>
#include "p6_7.h"

Rational::Rational(int n, int d)
{
   numerator = n;
   denominator = d;
}

Rational Rational::addition(const Rational &a)
{
   Rational t;

   t.numerator = a.numerator * denominator + a.denominator * numerator;
   t.denominator = a.denominator * denominator;
   t.reduction();
   return t;
}

Rational Rational::subtraction(const Rational &s)
{
   Rational t;

   t.numerator = s.denominator * numerator - denominator * s.numerator;
   t.denominator = s.denominator * denominator;
   t.reduction();
   return t;
}

Rational Rational::multiplication(const Rational &m)
{
   Rational t;

   t.numerator = m.numerator * numerator;
   t.denominator = m.denominator * denominator;
   t.reduction();
   return t;
}
```

```cpp
Rational Rational::division(Rational &v)
{
   Rational t;

   t.numerator = v.denominator * numerator;
   t.denominator = denominator * v.numerator;
   t.reduction();

   return t;
}

void Rational::printRational(void)
{
   if (denominator == 0)
      cout << "\nDIVIDE BY ZERO ERROR!!!" << endl;
   else if (numerator == 0)
      cout << 0;
   else
      cout << numerator << '/' << denominator;
}

void Rational::printRationalAsFloating(void)
   {  cout << (float) numerator / denominator; }


void Rational::reduction(void)
{
   int largest = numerator > denominator ? numerator : denominator;

   int gcd = 0;   // greatest common divisor

   for (int loop = 2; loop <= largest; loop++)
      if (numerator % loop == 0 && denominator % loop == 0)
         gcd = loop;

   if (gcd != 0) {
      numerator /= gcd;
      denominator /= gcd;
   }
}
```

```cpp
// driver for P6_7.cpp
#include <iostream.h>
#include "p6_7.h"

main()
{
   Rational c(1,3), d(7,8), x;

   c.printRational();
   cout << " + ";
   d.printRational();
   x = c.addition(d);
   cout << " = ";
   x.printRational();
   cout << endl;
   x.printRational();
   cout << " = ";
   x.printRationalAsFloating();
   cout << endl << endl;
```

```
            c.printRational();
            cout << " - ";
            d.printRational();
            x = c.subtraction(d);
            cout << " = ";
            x.printRational();
            cout << endl;
            x.printRational();
            cout << " = ";
            x.printRationalAsFloating();
            cout << endl << endl;

            c.printRational();
            cout << " x ";
            d.printRational();
            x = c.multiplication(d);
            cout << " = ";
            x.printRational();
            cout << endl;
            x.printRational();
            cout << " = ";
            x.printRationalAsFloating();
            cout << endl << endl;

            c.printRational();
            cout << " / ";
            d.printRational();
            x = c.division(d);
            cout << " = ";
            x.printRational();
            cout << endl;
            x.printRational();
            cout << " = ";
            x.printRationalAsFloating();
            cout << endl;

            return 0;
         }
```

```
1/3 + 7/8 = 29/24
29/24 = 1.208333

1/3 - 7/8 = -13/24
-13/24 = -0.541667

1/3 x 7/8 = 7/24
7/24 = 0.291667

1/3 / 7/8 = 8/21
8/21 = 0.380952
```

6.8   Modify the **Time** class of Fig. 6.10 to include a **tick** member function that increments the time stored in a **Time** object by one second. The **Time** object should always remain in a consistent state. Write a driver program that tests the **tick** member function in a loop that prints the time in standard format during each iteration of the loop to illustrate that the **tick** member function works correctly. Be sure to test the following cases:

a) Incrementing into the next minute.
b) Incrementing into the next hour.
c) Incrementing into the next day (i.e., 11:59:59 PM to 12:00:00 AM).

ANS:

```cpp
// P6_8.H
#ifndef p6_8_H
#define p6_8_H
#include <iostream.h>

class Time {
public:
   Time(int = 0, int = 0, int = 0);
   void setTime(int, int, int);
   void setHour(int);
   void setMinute(int);
   void setSecond(int);
   int getHour(void);
   int getMinute(void);
   int getSecond(void);
   void printStandard(void);
   void tick(void);
private:
   int hour;
   int minute;
   int second;
};

#endif
```

```cpp
// P6_8M.cpp
// member function definitions for p6_8.cpp
#include <iostream.h>
#include "p6_8.h"

Time::Time(int hr, int min, int sec) { setTime(hr, min, sec); }

void Time::setTime(int h, int m, int s)
{
   setHour(h);
   setMinute(m);
   setSecond(s);
}

void Time::setHour(int h) { hour = (h >= 0 && h < 24) ? h : 0; }

void Time::setMinute(int m) { minute = (m >= 0 && m < 60) ? m : 0; }

void Time::setSecond(int s) { second = (s >= 0 && s < 60) ? s : 0; }

int Time::getHour(void) { return hour; }

int Time::getMinute(void) { return minute; }

int Time::getSecond(void) { return second; }

void Time::printStandard(void)
{
   cout << ((hour % 12 == 0) ? 12 : hour % 12) << ':'
        << (minute < 10 ? "0" : "") << minute << ':'
        << (second < 10 ? "0" : "") << second
        << (hour < 12 ? " AM" : " PM");
}
```

```
void Time::tick(void)
{
   setSecond( second + 1 );

   if ( second == 0 ) {
      setMinute( minute + 1 );

      if ( minute == 0 )
         setHour( hour + 1 );
   }
}
```

```
// driver for p6_8.cpp
#include <iostream.h>
#include "p6_8.h"

const int MAX_TICKS = 3000;

main()
{
   Time t;

   t.setTime(23, 59, 57);

   for (int ticks = 1; ticks < MAX_TICKS; ticks++) {
      t.printStandard();
      cout << endl;
      t.tick();
   }

   return 0;
}
```

```
11:59:57 PM
11:59:58 PM
11:59:59 PM
12:00:00 AM
12:00:01 AM
12:00:02 AM
 .
 .
 .
```

6.9   Modify the Date class of Fig. 6.12 to perform error checking on the initializer values for data members **month**, **day**, and **year**. Also, provide a member function **nextDay** to increment the day by one. The **Date** object should always remain in a consistent state. Write a driver program that tests the **nextDay** function in a loop that prints the date during each iteration of the loop to illustrate that the **nextDay** function works correctly. Be sure to test the following cases:

a) Incrementing into the next month.
b) Incrementing into the next year.

ANS:

```cpp
// P6_9.H
#ifndef p6_9_H
#define p6_9_H

#include <iostream.h>

class Date {
public:
   Date(int = 1, int = 1, int = 1900);  // default constructor
   void print(void);
   void setDate(int, int, int);
   void setMonth(int);
   void setDay(int);
   void setYear(int);
   int getMonth(void);
   int getDay(void);
   int getYear(void);
   int leapYear(void);
   int monthDays(void);
   void nextDay(void);
private:
   int month;
   int day;
   int year;
};

#endif
```

```cpp
// p6_9M.cpp
// member function definitions for p6_9.cpp
#include <iostream.h>
#include "p6_9.h"

Date::Date(int m, int d, int y) { setDate(m, d, y);}

int Date::getDay() { return day;}

int Date::getMonth() { return month;}

int Date::getYear() { return year;}

void Date::setDay(int d)
{
   if (month == 2 && leapYear())
      day = (d <= 29 && d >= 1) ? d : 1;
   else
      day = (d <= monthDays() && d >= 1) ? d : 1;
}

void Date::setMonth(int m) { month = m <= 12 && m >= 1 ? m : 1;}

void Date::setYear(int y) { year = y <= 2000 && y >= 1900 ? y : 1900;}

void Date::setDate(int mo, int dy, int yr)
{
   setMonth(mo);
   setDay(dy);
   setYear(yr);
}

void Date::print()
   { cout << month << '-' << day << '-' << year << "\n"; }
```

```
void Date::nextDay()
{
   setDay( day + 1 );

   if ( day == 1 ) {
      setMonth( month + 1 );

      if ( month == 1 )
         setYear(year + 1);
   }
}

int Date::leapYear(void)
{
   if (year % 400 == 0 || (year % 4 == 0 && year % 100 != 0))
       return 1;
   else
       return 0;    // not a leap year
}

int Date::monthDays(void)
{
   const int days[12] = {31, 28, 31, 30, 31, 30, 31, 31, 30, 31, 30, 31};

   return month == 2 && leapYear() ? 29 : days[month - 1];
}
```

```
// driver for p6_9.cpp
#include <iostream.h>
#include "p6_9.h"

main()
{
   const int MAXDAYS = 160;
   Date d(7, 28, 1994);

   for (int loop = 1; loop <= MAXDAYS; loop++) {
      d.print();
      d.nextDay();
   }

   cout << endl;
   return 0;
}
```

```
7-28-1994
...
12-30-1994
12-31-1995
1-1-1995
1-2-1995
1-3-1995
```

6.10   Combine the modified **Time** class of Exercise 6.8 and the modified **Date** class of Exercise 6.9 into one class called **DateAndTime** (in Chapter 9 we will discuss inheritance which will enable us to accomplish this task quickly without modifying the existing class definitions). Modify the **tick** function to call the **nextDay** function if the time is incremented into the next day. Modify function **printStandard** and **PrintMilitary** to output the date in addition to the time. Write a driver program to test the new class **DateAndTime**. Specifically test incrementing the time into the next day.

```
ANS:
// P6_10.H
#ifndef p6_10_H
#define p6_10_H
#include <iostream.h>

class DateAndTime {
public:
   DateAndTime(int = 1, int = 1, int = 1900, int = 0, int = 0, int = 0);
   void setDate(int, int, int);
   void setMonth(int);
   void setDay(int);
   void setYear(int);
   int getMonth(void);
   int getDay(void);
   int getYear(void);
   void nextDay(void);
   void setTime(int, int, int);
   void setHour(int);
   void setMinute(int);
   void setSecond(int);
   int getHour(void);
   int getMinute(void);
   int getSecond(void);
   void printStandard(void);
   void printMilitary(void);
   int monthDays(void);
   void tick(void);
   int leapYear(void);
private:
   int month;
   int day;
   int year;
   int hour;
   int minute;
   int second;
};

#endif
```

```
// P6_10M.cpp
// member function definitions for p6_10.cpp
#include <iostream.h>
#include "p6_10.h"

DateAndTime::DateAndTime(int m, int d, int y, int hr, int min, int sec)
{
   setDate(m, d, y);
   setTime(hr, min, sec);
}

int DateAndTime::getDay(void) { return day;}

int DateAndTime::getMonth(void) { return month;}

int DateAndTime::getYear(void) { return year;}

void DateAndTime::setDay(int d)
{
   if (month == 2 && leapYear())
      day = (d <= 29 && d >= 1) ? d : 1;
   else
      day = (d <= monthDays() && d >= 1) ? d : 1;
}
```

```cpp
void DateAndTime::setMonth(int m) { month = m <= 12 && m >= 1 ? m : 1;}

void DateAndTime::setYear(int y)
   { year = y <= 2000 && y >= 1900 ? y : 1900;}

void DateAndTime::setDate(int mo, int dy, int yr)
{
   setDay(dy);
   setMonth(mo);
   setYear(yr);
}


void DateAndTime::nextDay(void)
{
   setDay( day + 1 );

   if ( day == 1 ) {
      setMonth( month + 1 );

      if ( month == 1 )
         setYear(year + 1);
   }
}

void DateAndTime::setTime(int hr, int min, int sec)
{
   setHour(hr);
   setMinute(min);
   setSecond(sec);
}

void DateAndTime::setHour(int h) { hour = (h >= 0 && h < 24) ? h : 0; }

void DateAndTime::setMinute(int m)
   { minute = (m >= 0 && m < 60) ? m : 0; }

void DateAndTime::setSecond(int s)
   { second = (s >= 0 && s < 60) ? s : 0; }

int DateAndTime::getHour(void) { return hour; }

int DateAndTime::getMinute(void) { return minute; }

int DateAndTime::getSecond(void) { return second; }

void DateAndTime::printStandard(void)
{
   cout << ((hour % 12 == 0) ? 12 : hour % 12) << ':'
        << (minute < 10 ? "0" : "") << minute << ':'
        << (second < 10 ? "0" : "") << second
        << (hour < 12 ? " AM " : " PM ")
        << month << '-' << day << '-' << year << endl;
}

void DateAndTime::printMilitary(void)
{
   cout << (hour < 10 ? "0" : "") << hour << ':'
        << (minute < 10 ? "0" : "") << minute << ':'
        << (second < 10 ? "0" : "") << second << "      "
        << month << '-' << day << '-' << year << endl;
}
```

```
void DateAndTime::tick(void)
{
    setSecond( second + 1 );

    if ( second == 0 ) {
        setMinute( minute + 1 );

        if ( minute == 0 ) {
            setHour( hour + 1 );

            if ( hour == 0 )
                nextDay();
        }
    }
}

int DateAndTime::leapYear(void)
{
    if (year % 400 == 0 || (year % 4 == 0 && year % 100 != 0))
        return 1;
    else
        return 0;    // not a leap year
}

int DateAndTime::monthDays(void)
{
    const int days[12] = {31, 28, 31, 30, 31, 30, 31, 31, 30, 31, 30, 31};
    return month == 2 && leapYear() ? 29 : days[month - 1];
}
```

```
// driver for p6_10.cpp
#include <iostream.h>
#include "p6_10.h"

main()
{
    const int MAXTICKS = 3000;
    DateAndTime d(7, 22, 1994, 23, 50, 0);

    for (int ticks = 1; ticks <= MAXTICKS; ticks++) {
        cout << "Military time: ";
        d.printMilitary();
        cout << "Standard time: ";
        d.printStandard();
        d.tick();
    }

    cout << endl;
    return 0;
}
```

```
...
Military time: 23:59:58    7-1-1994
Standard time: 11:59:58 PM 7-1-1994
Military time: 23:59:59    7-1-1994
Standard time: 11:59:59 PM 7-1-1994
Military time: 00:00:00    7-2-1994
Standard time: 12:00:00 AM 7-2-1994
Military time: 00:00:01    7-2-1994
Standard time: 12:00:01 AM 7-2-1994
Military time: 00:00:02    7-2-1994
Standard time: 12:00:02 AM 7-2-1994
Military time: 00:00:03    7-2-1994
Standard time: 12:00:03 AM 7-2-1994
...
```

6.11　Modify the set functions in the program of Fig. 6.10 to return appropriate error values if an attempt is made to set a data member of an object of class **Time** to an invalid value.

ANS:

```
// P6_11.H
#ifndef P6_11_H
#define P6_11_H
class Time {
public:
   Time(int = 0, int = 0, int = 0);
   void setTime(int, int, int);
   void setHour(int);
   void setMinute(int);
   void setSecond(int);
   void setInvalidTime(int t) { invalidTime = t; }
   int getHour(void) { return hour; }
   int getMinute(void) { return minute; }
   int getSecond(void) { return second; }
   int getInvalidTime(void) { return invalidTime; }
   void printMilitary(void);
   void printStandard(void);
private:
   int hour;
   int minute;
   int second;
   int invalidTime;    // set if an invalid time is attempted
};

#endif
```

```
// P6_11M.cpp
// member function definitions for p6_11.cpp
#include <iostream.h>
#include "p6_11.h"
Time::Time(int hr, int min, int sec) { setTime(hr, min, sec); }

void Time::setTime(int h, int m, int s)
{
   setHour(h);
   setMinute(m);
   setSecond(s);
}
void Time::setHour(int hr)
{
   if (hr >= 0 && hr < 24) {
      hour = hr;
      setInvalidTime(1);   // hour is valid
   }
   else {
      hour = 0;
      setInvalidTime(0);   // hour is invalid
   }
}
void Time::setMinute(int min)
{
   if (min >= 0 && min < 60) {
      minute = min;
      setInvalidTime(1);   // minute is valid
   }
   else {
      minute = 0;
      setInvalidTime(0);   // minute is invalid
   }
}
```

```
void Time::setSecond(int sec)
{
    if (sec >= 0 && sec < 60) {
        second = sec;
        setInvalidTime(1);   // second is valid
    }
    else {
        second = 0;
        setInvalidTime(0);   // second is invalid
    }
}

void Time::printMilitary(void)
{
    cout << (hour < 10 ? "0" : "") << hour << ':'
         << (minute < 10 ? "0" : "") << minute << ':'
         << (second < 10 ? "0" : "") << second;
}

void Time::printStandard(void)
{
    cout << ((hour % 12 == 0) ? 12 : hour % 12) << ':'
         << (minute < 10 ? "0": "") << minute << ':'
         << (second < 10 ? "0": "") << second
         << (hour < 12 ? " AM" : " PM");
}
```

```
// driver for p6_11.cpp
#include <iostream.h>
#include "p6_11.h"

main()
{
    Time t1(17, 34, 25), t2(99, 345, -897);

    // all t1 object's times are valid
    if (t1.getInvalidTime() == 0)
       cout << "Error: invalid time setting(s) attempted." << endl
            << "Invalid setting(s) changed to zero." << endl;

    t1.printStandard();

    // object t2 has invalid time settings
    if (t2.getInvalidTime() == 0)
       cout << endl << "Error: invalid time setting(s) attempted."
            << endl << "Invalid setting(s) changed to zero." << endl;

    t2.printMilitary();
    return 0;
}
```

```
5:34:25 PM
Error: invalid time setting(s) attempted.
Invalid setting(s) changed to zero.
00:00:00
```

6.12   Create a class Rectangle. The class has attributes length and width, each of which defaults to 1. It has member functions that calculate the perimeter and the area of the rectangle. It has set and get functions for both length and width. The set functions should verify that length and width are each floating point numbers larger than 0.0 and less than 20.0.

```
ANS:
// P6_12.H
#ifndef P6_12_H
#define P6_12_H
#include <iostream.h>

class Rectangle {
   public:
      Rectangle(double = 1.0, double = 1.0);
      double perimeter(void);
      double area(void);
      void setWidth(double w);
      void setLength(double l);
      double getWidth(void);
      double getLength(void);
   private:
      double length;
      double width;
};

#endif
```

```
// P6_12M.cpp
// member function definitions for p6_12.cpp
#include <iostream.h>
#include "p6_12.h"

Rectangle::Rectangle(double w, double l)
{
   setWidth(w);
   setLength(l);
}

double Rectangle::perimeter(void) { return 2 * (width + length); }

double Rectangle::area(void) { return width * length; }

void Rectangle::setWidth(double w)
   { width = w > 0 && w < 20.0 ? w : 1.0; }

void Rectangle::setLength(double l)
   { length = l > 0 && l < 20.0 ? l : 1.0; }

double Rectangle::getWidth(void) { return width; }

double Rectangle::getLength(void) { return length; }
```

```
// driver for p6_12.cpp
#include <iostream.h>
#include <iomanip.h>
#include "p6_12.h"

main()
{
   Rectangle a, b(4.0, 5.0), c(67.0, 888.0);

   cout.setf(ios::fixed | ios::showpoint);
   cout << setprecision(1);

   // output Rectangle a
   cout << "a: length = " << a.getLength() << "; width = " << a.getWidth()
        << "; perimeter = " << a.perimeter() << "; area = "
        << a.area() << endl;
```

```
        // output Rectangle b
        cout << "b: length = " << b.getLength() << "; width = "
             << b.getWidth() << "; perimeter = " << b.perimeter()
             << "; area = " << b.area() << endl;

        // output Rectangle c; bad values attempted
        cout << "c: length = " << c.getLength() << "; width = "
             << c.getWidth() << "; perimeter = " << c.perimeter()
             << "; area = " << c.area() << endl;

        return 0;
}
```

```
    a: length = 1.0; width = 1.0; perimeter = 4.0; area = 1.0
    b: length = 5.0; width = 4.0; perimeter = 18.0; area = 20.0
    c: length = 1.0; width = 1.0; perimeter = 4.0; area = 1.0
```

6.13   Create a more sophisticated **Rectangle** class than the one you created in Exercise 6.12. This class stores only the Cartesian coordinates of the four corners of the rectangle. The constructor calls a set function that accepts four sets of coordinates and verifies that each of these is in the first quadrant with no single x or y coordinate larger than 20.0. The set function also verifies that the supplied coordinates do, in fact, specify a rectangle. Member functions calculate the **length**, **width**, **perimeter**, and **area**. The length is the larger of the two dimensions. Include a predicate function **square** which determines if the rectangle is a square.

```
ANS:
// P6_13.H
#ifndef P6_13_H
#define P6_13_H

class Rectangle {
   public:
      Rectangle(double [], double [], double [], double []);
      void setCoord(double [], double [], double [], double []);
      void perimeter(void);
      void area(void);
      void square(void);
   private:
      double point1[2];
      double point2[2];
      double point3[2];
      double point4[2];
};


#endif
```

```
// P6_13M.cpp
// member function definitions for p6_13.cpp
#include <iostream.h>
#include <iomanip.h>
#include <math.h>
#include "p6_13.h"


Rectangle::Rectangle(double a[], double b[], double c[], double d[])
   { setCoord(a, b, c, d); }
```

```cpp
void Rectangle::setCoord(double p1[], double p2[], double p3[],
                         double p4[])
{
   // Arrangement of points
   // p4........p3
   //  .         .
   //  .         .
   // p1........p2

   const int x = 0, y = 1;  // added for clarity

   // validate all points
   point1[x] = p1[x] > 20.0 || p1[x] < 0.0 ? 0.0 : p1[x];
   point1[y] = p1[y] > 20.0 || p1[y] < 0.0 ? 0.0 : p1[y];
   point2[x] = p2[x] > 20.0 || p2[x] < 0.0 ? 0.0 : p2[x];
   point2[y] = p2[y] > 20.0 || p2[y] < 0.0 ? 0.0 : p2[y];
   point3[x] = p3[x] > 20.0 || p3[x] < 0.0 ? 0.0 : p3[x];
   point3[y] = p3[y] > 20.0 || p3[y] < 0.0 ? 0.0 : p3[y];
   point4[x] = p4[x] > 20.0 || p4[x] < 0.0 ? 0.0 : p4[x];
   point4[y] = p4[y] > 20.0 || p4[y] < 0.0 ? 0.0 : p4[y];

   // verify that points form a rectangle
   if (p1[y] == p2[y] && p1[x] == p4[x] && p2[x] == p3[x] &&
       p3[y] == p4[y]) {

      perimeter();
      area();
      square();
   }
   else
      cout << "Coordinates do not form a rectangle!" << endl;
}

void Rectangle::perimeter(void)
{
   double l = fabs(point4[1] - point1[1]),
          w = fabs(point2[0] - point1[0]);

   cout.setf(ios::fixed | ios::showpoint);
   cout << setprecision(1) << "length = " << (l > w ? l : w)
        << '\t' << "width = " << (l > w ? w : l)
        << "  The perimeter is: " << 2 * (w + l) << '\t';
}

void Rectangle::area(void)
{
   double l = fabs(point4[1] - point1[1]),
          w = fabs(point2[0] - point1[0]);

   cout.setf(ios::fixed | ios::showpoint);
   cout << setprecision(1) << "The area is: " << w * l << endl;
}

void Rectangle::square(void)
{
   const int x = 0, y = 1;   // added for clarity

   if (fabs(point4[y] - point1[y]) == fabs(point2[x] - point1[x]))
      cout << "The rectangle is a square." << endl << endl;
}
```

```
// driver for p6_13.cpp
#include <iostream.h>
#include "p6_13.h"

main()
{
    double w[2] = {1.0, 1.0}, x[2] = {5.0, 1.0}, y[2] = {5.0, 3.0},
           z[2] = {1.0, 3.0}, j[2] = {0.0, 0.0}, k[2] = {1.0, 0.0},
           m[2] = {1.0, 1.0}, n[2] = {0.0, 1.0}, v[2] = {99.0, -2.3};
    Rectangle a(z, y, x, w), b(j, k, m, n), c(w, x, m, n), d(v, x, y, z);

    return 0;
}
```

```
length = 4.0   width = 2.0   The perimeter is: 12.0   The area is: 8.0
length = 1.0   width = 1.0   The perimeter is: 4.0    The area is: 1.0
The rectangle is a square.

Coordinates do not form a rectangle!
Coordinates do not form a rectangle!
```

6.14   Modify the `Rectangle` class of Exercise 6.13 to include a **draw** function that displays the rectangle inside a 25-by-25 box enclosing the portion of the first quadrant in which the rectangle resides. Include a **setFillCharacter** function to specify the character out of which the body of the rectangle will be drawn. Include a **setPerimeterCharacter** function to specify the character that will be used to draw the border of the rectangle. If you feel ambitious you might include functions to scale the size of the rectangle, rotate it, and move it around within the designated portion of the first quadrant.

ANS:
```
// P6_14.H
#ifndef P6_14_H
#define P6_14_H

class Rectangle {
public:
    Rectangle(double [], double [], double [], double [], char, char);
    void setCoord(double [], double [], double [], double []);
    void perimeter(void);
    void area(void);
    void draw(void);
    void square(void);
    void setFillCharacter(char c) { fillChar = c; }
    void setPerimeterCharacter(char c) { periChar = c;}
    int getValid(void) { return valid; }
    void setValid(int v) { valid = v; }
private:
    double point1[2];
    double point2[2];
    double point3[2];
    double point4[2];
    char fillChar;
    char periChar;
    int valid;
};

#endif
```

```cpp
// P6_14M.cpp
// member function definitions for p6_14.cpp
#include <iostream.h>
#include <iomanip.h>
#include <math.h>
#include "p6_14.h"


Rectangle::Rectangle(double a[], double b[], double c[], double d[],
                     char x, char y)
{
   setCoord(a, b, c, d);
   setFillCharacter(x);
   setPerimeterCharacter(y);
}


void Rectangle::setCoord(double p1[], double p2[], double p3[],
                         double p4[])
{
   // Arrangement of points
   // p4........p3
   // .          .
   // .          .
   // p1........p2

   const int x = 0, y = 1;   // added for clarity

   // validate all points
   point1[x] = p1[x] > 20.0 || p1[x] < 0.0 ? 0.0 : p1[x];
   point1[y] = p1[y] > 20.0 || p1[y] < 0.0 ? 0.0 : p1[y];
   point2[x] = p2[x] > 20.0 || p2[x] < 0.0 ? 0.0 : p2[x];
   point2[y] = p2[y] > 20.0 || p2[y] < 0.0 ? 0.0 : p2[y];
   point3[x] = p3[x] > 20.0 || p3[x] < 0.0 ? 0.0 : p3[x];
   point3[y] = p3[y] > 20.0 || p3[y] < 0.0 ? 0.0 : p3[y];
   point4[x] = p4[x] > 20.0 || p4[x] < 0.0 ? 0.0 : p4[x];
   point4[y] = p4[y] > 20.0 || p4[y] < 0.0 ? 0.0 : p4[y];

   // verify that points form a rectangle
   if (point1[y] == point2[y] && point1[x] == point4[x] &&
       point2[x] == point3[x] && point3[y] == point4[y]) {

      perimeter();
      area();
      square();
      setValid(1);    // valid set of points
   }
   else {
      cout << "Coordinates do not form a rectangle!" << endl;
      setValid(0);    // invalid set of points
   }
}


void Rectangle::perimeter(void)
{
   double l = fabs(point4[1] - point1[1]),
          w = fabs(point2[0] - point1[0]);

   cout.setf(ios::fixed | ios::showpoint);
   cout << setprecision(1) << "length = " << (l > w ? l : w)
        << '\t' << "width = " << (l > w ? w : l)
        << "  The perimeter is: " << 2 * (w + l) << '\t';
}
```

```cpp
void Rectangle::area(void)
{
   double l = fabs(point4[1] - point1[1]),
          w = fabs(point2[0] - point1[0]);

   cout.setf(ios::fixed | ios::showpoint);
   cout << setprecision(1) << "The area is: " << w * l << endl;
}



void Rectangle::square(void)
{
   const int x = 0, y = 1;   // added for clarity

   if (fabs(point4[y] - point1[y]) == fabs(point2[x] - point1[x]))
      cout << "The rectangle is a square." << endl << endl;
}



void Rectangle::draw(void)
{
   for (double y = 25.0; y >= 0.0; y--) {

      for (double x = 0.0; x <= 25.0; x++) {
         if ((point1[0] == x && point1[1] == y) ||
             (point4[0] == x && point4[1] == y)) {

            // print horizontal perimeter of rectangle
            while (x <= point2[0]) {
               cout << periChar;
               ++x;
            }

            // print remainder of quadrant
            cout << '.';
         }
         // prints vertical perimeter of rectangle
         else if (((x <= point4[0] && x >= point1[0])) &&
                    point4[1] >= y && point1[1] <= y) {
            cout << periChar;

            // fill inside of rectangle
            for (x++ ; x < point2[0]; ) {
               cout << fillChar;
               ++x;
            }

            cout << periChar;
         }
         else
            cout << '.';   // print quadrant background
      }

      cout << '\n';
   }
}
```

```
// driver for p6_14.cpp
#include <iostream.h>
#include "p6_14.h"

main()
{
    double xy1[2] = {12.0, 12.0}, xy2[2] = {18.0, 12.0},
           xy3[2] = {18.0, 20.0}, xy4[2] = {12.0, 20.0};
    Rectangle a(xy1, xy2, xy3, xy4, '?', '*');

    if (a.getValid())
        a.draw();

    return 0;
}
```

```
length = 8.0   width = 6.0   The perimeter is: 28.0    The area is: 48.0
.........................
.........................
.........................
.........................
.........................
.........................
..............*******......
..............*?????*......
..............*?????*......
..............*?????*......
..............*?????*......
..............*?????*......
..............*?????*......
..............*?????*......
..............*******......
.........................
.........................
.........................
.........................
.........................
.........................
.........................
.........................
.........................
.........................
.........................
.........................
.........................
.........................
```

6.15   Create a class **HugeInteger** which uses a 40-element array of digits to store integers as large as 40-digits each. Provide member functions **inputHugeInteger, outputHugeInteger, addHugeIntegers**, and **substractHugeIntegers**. For comparing **HugeInteger** objects provide functions **isEqualTo, isNotEqualTo, isGreaterThan, isLessThan, IsGreaterThanOrEqualTo**, and **isLessThanOrEqualTo**— each of these is a "predicate" function that simply returns **1** (true) if the relationship holds between the two huge integers and returns 0 (false) if the relationship does not hold. Provide a predicate function **isZero**. If you feel ambitious, also provide member functions **multiplyHugeIntegers, divideHugeIntegers**, and **modulusHugeIntegers**.

6.16   Create a class **TicTacToe** that will enable you to write a complete program to play the game of tic-tac-toe. The class contains as private data a 3-by-3 double array of integers. The constructor should initialize the empty board to all zeros. Allow two human players. Wherever the first player moves, place a 1 in the specified square; place a 2 wherever the second player moves. Each move must be to an empty square. After each move determine if the game has been won, or if the game is a draw. If you feel ambitious, modify your program so that the computer makes the moves for one of the players automatically. Also, allow the player to specify whether he or she wants to go first or second. If you feel exceptionally ambitious, develop a program that will play three-dimensional tic-tac-toe on a 4-by-4-by-4 board (Caution: This is an extremely challenging project that could take many weeks of effort!).

ANS:
```
// p6.16_H
#ifndef P6_16_H
#define P6_16_H

class TicTacToe {
public:
   TicTacToe();
   void makeMove(void);
   void printBoard(void);
   int validMove(int, int);
   int gameStatus(void);
private:
   int board[3][3];
};

#endif
```

```
// P6_16M.cpp
// member function definitions for p6_16.cpp
#include <iostream.h>
#include <iomanip.h>
#include "p6_16.h"

TicTacToe::TicTacToe()
{
   for (int j = 0; j < 3; j++)      // initialize board
      for (int k = 0; k < 3; k++)
         board[j][k] = 0;
}

int TicTacToe::validMove(int r, int c)
{ return r >= 0 && r < 3 && c >= 0 && c < 3 && board[r][c] == 0; }

int TicTacToe::gameStatus(void)
{
   const int win = 1, draw = 2, unfinished = 0;   // added for clarity

   // check for a win on diagonals
   if (board[0][0] != 0 && board[0][0] == board[1][1] &&
       board[0][0] == board[2][2])
      return win;
   else if (board[2][0] != 0 && board[2][0] == board[1][1] &&
            board[2][0] == board[0][2])
      return win;
   // check for win in rows
   else if (board[0][0] != 0 && board[0][0] == board[0][1] &&
            board[0][0] == board[0][2])
      return win;
   else if (board[1][0] != 0 && board[1][0] == board[1][1] &&
            board[1][0] == board[1][2])
      return win;
   else if (board[2][0] != 0 && board[2][0] == board[2][1] &&
            board[2][0] == board[2][2])
      return win;
   // check for win in columns
   else if (board[0][0] != 0 && board[0][0] == board[1][0] &&
            board[0][0] == board[2][0])
      return win;
   else if (board[0][1] != 0 && board[0][1] == board[1][1] &&
            board[0][1] == board[2][1])
      return win;
```

```
      else if (board[0][2] != 0 && board[0][2] == board[1][2] &&
               board[0][2] == board[2][2])
         return win;

      // check for a completed game
      for (int r = 0; r < 3; r++)
         for (int c = 0; c < 3; c++)
            if (board[r][c] == 0)
               return unfinished; // game is not finished

      return draw; // game is a draw
}


void TicTacToe::printBoard(void)
{
      cout << "    0    1    2" << endl << endl;

      for (int r = 0; r < 3; r++) {

         cout << r;

         for (int c = 0; c < 3; c++) {
            cout << setw(3) << board[r][c];

            if (c != 2)
               cout << " |";
         }

         if (r != 2)
            cout << endl << "    ___|___|___"
                 << endl << "       |   |   " << endl;
      }

      cout << endl << endl;
}


void TicTacToe::makeMove(void)
{
      int x, y, status;

      printBoard();
      status = gameStatus();

      while (status == 0) {

         do {
            cout << "Player 1 enter move: ";
            cin >> x >> y;
            cout << endl;
         } while (!validMove(x, y));

         board[x][y] = 1;
         printBoard();

         status = gameStatus();

         if (status == 1)
            cout << "Player 1 wins!" << endl;
         else if (status == 2) {
               cout << "Game is a draw." << endl;
               status = 1;  // end game
         }
```

```
        else {
            do {
               cout << "Player 2 enter move: ";
               cin >> x >> y;
               cout << endl;
            } while (!validMove(x, y));

            board[x][y] = 2;
            printBoard();
            status = gameStatus();

            if (status == 1)
               cout << "Player 2 wins!" << endl;
        }
    }
}
```

```
// driver for p6_16.cpp
#include "p6_16.h"

main()
{
   TicTacToe g;
   g.makeMove();
   return 0;
}
```

```
        0     1     2

0    0  |  0  |  0
    ____|____|____
        |     |
1    0  |  0  |  0
    ____|____|____
        |     |
2    0  |  0  |  0

Player 1 enter move: 1 1

        0     1     2

0    0  |  0  |  0
    ____|____|____
        |     |
1    0  |  1  |  0
    ____|____|____
        |     |
2    0  |  0  |  0

Player 2 enter move: 0 2

        0     1     2

0    0  |  0  |  2
    ____|____|____
        |     |
1    0  |  1  |  0
    ____|____|____
        |     |
2    0  |  0  |  0
```

                                                            continued

continued

```
Player 1 enter move: 2 2

      0     1     2

0  0  |  0  |  2
   ___ | ___ | ___
      |     |
1  0  |  1  |  0
   ___ | ___ | ___
      |     |
2  0  |  0  |  1

Player 2 enter move: 0 1

      0     1     2

0  0  |  2  |  2
   ___ | ___ | ___
      |     |
1  0  |  1  |  0
   ___ | ___ | ___
      |     |
2  0  |  0  |  1

Player 1 enter move: 0 0

      0     1     2

0  1  |  2  |  2
   ___ | ___ | ___
      |     |
1  0  |  1  |  0
   ___ | ___ | ___
      |     |
2  0  |  0  |  1

Player 1 wins!
```

7
Classes: Part II
Solutions

Exercises

7.3 Compare and contrast dynamic memory allocation with the C++ operators **new** and **delete**, with dynamic memory allocation with the C Standard Library functions **malloc** and **free**.

> **ANS:** In C, dynamic memory allocation and deallocation requires function calls to **malloc** and **free**, as well as reference to the **sizeof** operator in **malloc**. C++ accomplishes dynamic memory allocation with the built-in operators **new** and **delete**. **new** determines the size of an object automatically and returns a pointer of the appropriate type. Since the operations are now performed by operators, they are faster than in C, and they are less complicated.

7.4 Explain the notion of friendship in C++. Explain the negative aspects of friendship as described in the text.

> **ANS:** A **friend** function or **friend** class of a particular class is able to access the **private** and **protected** members of that class. Some people in the object-oriented programming community feel that friendship corrupts the information hiding concept and weakens the value of an object-oriented design approach.

7.5 Can a correct **Time** class definition include both of the following constructors?
```
Time (int h = 0, int m = 0, int s = 0);
Time ();
```
ANS: No, ambiguous case can exist due to the default value of **h**.

7.6 What happens when a return type, even **void**, is specified for a constructor or destructor?

> **ANS:** An error occurs, no return type of any kind can be specified.

7.7 Create a **Date** class with the following capabilities:

a) Output the date in multiple formats such as
```
DDD YYYY
MM/DD/YY
June 14, 1992
```
b) Use overloaded constructors to create **Date** objects initialized with dates of the formats in part (a).
c) Create a **Date** constructor that reads the system date using the standard library functions of the **time.h** header and sets the **Date** members.

In Chapter 8, we will be able to create operators for testing the equality of two dates and for comparing dates to determine if one date is prior to or after another.

```
ANS:
// P7_7.H
#ifndef p7_7_H
#define p7_7_H

#include <iostream.h>
#include <time.h>
#include <string.h>

class Date {
public:
   Date();
   Date(int, int);
   Date(int, int, int);
   Date(char *, int, int);
   void setMonth(int);
   void setDay(int);
   void setYear(int);
   void printDateSlash(void) const;
   void printDateMonth(void) const;
   void printDateDay(void);
   const char* monthName(void) const;
   int leapYear(void) const;
   int daysOfMonth(void) const;
   void convert1(int);
   int convert2(void);
   void convert3(char *);
   const char* monthList(int) const;
   int days(int) const;
private:
   int day;
   int month;
   int year;
};

#endif
```

```
// P7_7M.cpp
// member function definitions for p7_7.cpp
#include <iostream.h>
#include <string.h>
#include <time.h>
#include "p7_7.h"

// Date constructor that uses functions from time.h
Date::Date()
{
   struct tm *ptr;            // pointer of type struct tm
                              // which holds calendar time components
   time_t *timePtr;           // pointer of an arithmetic type
                              // capable of representing time

   time(timePtr);             // determine the current calendar time
                              // which is assigned to timePtr

   ptr = localtime(timePtr);  // convert the current calendar time
                              // pointed to by timePtr into
                              // broken down time and assign it to ptr

   day = ptr->tm_mday;        // broken down day of month
   month = 1 + ptr->tm_mon;   // broken down month since January
   year = ptr->tm_year + 1900; // broken down year since 1900
}
```

```cpp
// Date constructor that uses day of year and year
Date::Date(int ddd, int yyyy)
{
   setYear(yyyy);
   convert1(ddd);   // convert to month and day
}

// Date constructor that uses month, day and year
Date::Date(int mm, int dd, int yy)
{
   setYear(yy + 1900);
   setMonth(mm);
   setDay(dd);
}

// Date constructor that uses month name, day and year
Date::Date(char *m, int dd, int yyyy)
{
   setYear(yyyy);
   setDay(dd);
   convert3(m);
}

// Set the day
void Date::setDay(int d)
   { day = d >= 1 && d <= daysOfMonth() ? d : 1; }

// Set the month
void Date::setMonth(int m) { month = m >= 1 && m <= 12 ? m : 1; }

// Set the year
void Date::setYear(int y) { year = y >= 1900 && y <= 1999 ? y : 1900; }

// Print Date in the form: mm/dd/yyyy
void Date::printDateSlash(void) const
   { cout << month << '/' << day << '/' << year << endl; }

// Print Date in the form: monthname dd, yyyy
void Date::printDateMonth(void) const
   { cout << monthName() << ' ' << day << ", " << year << endl; }

// Print Date in the form: ddd yyyy
void Date::printDateDay(void)
{
   int ddd;

   ddd = convert2();
   cout << ddd << ' ' << year << endl;
}

// Return the month name
const char* Date::monthName(void) const { return monthList(month - 1); }

// Return the number of days in the month
int Date::daysOfMonth(void) const
  { return leapYear() && month == 2 ? 29 : days(month); }

// Test for a leap year
int Date::leapYear(void) const
{
   if (year % 400 == 0 || (year % 4 == 0 && year % 100 != 0))
      return 1;
   else
      return 0;
}
```

```cpp
// Convert ddd to mm and dd
void Date::convert1(int ddd)   // convert to mm / dd / yyyy
{
    int dayTotal = 0;

    if (ddd < 1 || ddd > 366)  // check for invalid day
        ddd = 1;

    setMonth(1);

    for (int m = 1; m < 13 && (dayTotal + daysOfMonth()) < ddd; m++) {
        dayTotal += daysOfMonth();
        setMonth(m + 1);
    }

    setDay(ddd - dayTotal);
    setMonth(m);
}

// Convert mm and dd to ddd
int Date::convert2(void)      // convert to a ddd yyyy format
{
    int ddd = 0;

    for (int m = 1; m != month; m++)
        ddd += days(m);

    ddd += day;
    return ddd;
}

// Convert from month name to month number
void Date::convert3(char *m)    // convert to mm / dd / yyyy
{
    int flag = 0; // unset

    for (int subscript = 0; subscript < 12; subscript++)
        if (strcmp(m, monthList(subscript)) == 0) {
            setMonth(subscript + 1);
            flag = 1; // set flag
            break;     // stop checking for month
        }

    if (flag != 1)
        setMonth(1); // invalid month default is january
}

// Return the name of the month
const char* Date::monthList(int mm) const
{
    char *months[] = {"January", "February", "March", "April", "May",
                      "June", "July", "August", "September", "October",
                      "November", "December"};

    return months[mm];
}

// Return the days in the month
int Date::days(int m) const
{
    const int monthDays[] = {31, 28, 31, 30, 31, 30, 31, 31, 30, 31, 30, 31};

    return monthDays[m - 1];
}
```

```cpp
// driver for p7_7.cpp
#include <iostream.h>
#include "p7_7.h"

main()
{
    Date d1(7, 4, 93), d2(86, 1992), d3, d4("September", 1, 1993);

    d1.printDateSlash();    // format m / dd / yy
    d2.printDateSlash();
    d3.printDateSlash();
    d4.printDateSlash();
    cout << endl;

    d1.printDateDay();      // format ddd yyyy
    d2.printDateDay();
    d3.printDateDay();
    d4.printDateDay();
    cout << endl;

    d1.printDateMonth();    // format "month" d, yyyy
    d2.printDateMonth();
    d3.printDateMonth();
    d4.printDateMonth();

    return 0;
}
```

```
7/4/1993
3/26/1992
3/27/1994
9/1/1993

185 1993
85 1992
86 1994
244 1993

July 4, 1993
March 26, 1992
March 27, 1994
September 1, 1993
```

7.8   Create a `SavingsAccount` class. Use a static data member to contain the `annualInterestRate` for each of the savers. Each member of the class contains a private data member `savingsBalance` indicating the amount the saver currently has on deposit. Provide a `calculateMonthlyInterest` member function that calculates the monthly interest by multiplying the `balance` by `annualInterestRate` divided by 12; this interest should be added to `savingsBalance`. Provide a static member function `modifyInterestRate` that sets the static `annualInterestRate` to a new value. Write a driver program to test class `SavingsAccount`. Instantiate two different `savingsAccount` objects, `saver1` and `saver2`, with balances of $2000.00 and $3000.00, respectively. Set `annualInterestRate` to 3%, then calculate the monthly interest and print the new balances for each of the savers. Then set the `annualInterestRate` to 4% and calculate the next month's interest and print the new balances for each of the savers.

ANS:

```
// P7_8.H
#ifndef P7_8_H
#define P7_8_H

class SavingsAccount {
public:
    SavingsAccount(double b) { savingsBalance = b >= 0 ? b : 0; }
    void calculateMonthlyInterest(void);
    static void modifyInterestRate(double);
    void printBalance(void);
private:
    double savingsBalance;
    static double annualInterestRate;
};

#endif
```

```
// P7.8M.cpp
// Member function definitions for p7_8.cpp
#include "p7_8.h"
#include <iostream.h>
#include <iomanip.h>

// initialize static data member
double SavingsAccount::annualInterestRate = 0.0;

void SavingsAccount::calculateMonthlyInterest(void)
    { savingsBalance += savingsBalance * (annualInterestRate / 12.0); }

void SavingsAccount::modifyInterestRate(double i)
    { annualInterestRate = (i >= 0 && i <= 1.0) ? i : .03; }

void SavingsAccount::printBalance(void)
{
    cout.setf(ios::fixed | ios::showpoint);
    cout << '$' << setprecision(2) << savingsBalance;
}
```

```
// driver for p7_8.cpp
#include <iostream.h>
#include <iomanip.h>
#include "p7_8.h"

main()
{
    SavingsAccount saver1(2000.0), saver2(3000.0);

    SavingsAccount::modifyInterestRate(.03);

    cout << endl << "Output monthly balances for one year at .03" << endl
         << "Balances: Saver 1 ";
    saver1.printBalance();
    cout << "\tSaver 2 ";
    saver2.printBalance();

    for (int month = 1; month <= 12; month++) {
        saver1.calculateMonthlyInterest();
        saver2.calculateMonthlyInterest();

        cout << endl << "Month" << setw(3) << month << ": Saver 1 ";
        saver1.printBalance();
        cout << "\tSaver 2 ";
        saver2.printBalance();
    }
```

```
SavingsAccount::modifyInterestRate(.04);
  saver1.calculateMonthlyInterest();
  saver2.calculateMonthlyInterest();
  cout << endl << "After setting interest rate to .04" << endl
       << "Balances: Saver 1 ";
  saver1.printBalance();
  cout << "\tSaver 2 ";
  saver2.printBalance();

  return 0;
}
```

```
Output monthly balances for one year at .03
Balances: Saver 1 $2000.00      Saver 2 $3000.00
Month  1: Saver 1 $2005.00      Saver 2 $3007.50
Month  2: Saver 1 $2010.01      Saver 2 $3015.02
Month  3: Saver 1 $2015.04      Saver 2 $3022.56
Month  4: Saver 1 $2020.08      Saver 2 $3030.11
Month  5: Saver 1 $2025.13      Saver 2 $3037.69
Month  6: Saver 1 $2030.19      Saver 2 $3045.28
Month  7: Saver 1 $2035.26      Saver 2 $3052.90
Month  8: Saver 1 $2040.35      Saver 2 $3060.53
Month  9: Saver 1 $2045.45      Saver 2 $3068.18
Month 10: Saver 1 $2050.57      Saver 2 $3075.85
Month 11: Saver 1 $2055.69      Saver 2 $3083.54
Month 12: Saver 1 $2060.83      Saver 2 $3091.25
After setting interest rate to .04
Balances: Saver 1 $2067.70      Saver 2 $3101.55
```

7.9   Create a class **IntegerSet**. Each object of the class can hold integers in the range 0 through 100. A set is represented internally as an array of ones and zeros. Array element **a[i]** is 1 if integer i is in the set. Array element **a[j]** is 0 if integer j is not in the set. The default constructor initializes a set to the so-called "empty set," i.e., a set whose array representation contains all zeros.

Provide member functions for the common set operations. For example, provide a **unionOfIntegerSets** member function that creates a third set which is the set-theoretic union of two existing sets (i.e., an element of the third set's array is set to 1 if that element is 1 in either or both of the existing sets, and an element of the third set's array is set to 0 if that element is 0 in each of the existing sets).

Provide an **intersectionOfIntegerSets** member function that creates a third set which is the set-theoretic intersection of two existing sets i.e., an element of the third set's array is set to 0 if that element is 0 in either or both of the existing sets, and an element of the third set's array is set to 1 if that element is 1 in each of the existing sets).

Provide an **insertElement** member function that inserts a new integer k into a set (by setting **a[k]** to 1). Provide a **deleteElement** member function that deletes integer m (by setting **a[m]** to 0).

Provide a **setPrint** member function that prints a set as a list of numbers separated by spaces. Print only those elements that are present in the set. Print - - - for an empty set.

Provide an **isEqualTo** member function that determines if two sets are equal.

Provide an additional constructor to take five integer arguments which can be used to initialize a set object. If you want to provide fewer than five elements in the set, use default arguments of -1 for the others.

Now write a driver program to test your **IntegerSet** class. Instantiate several **IntegerSet** objects. Test that all your member functions work properly.

ANS:

```
// P7_9.H
#ifndef P7_9_H
#define P7_9_H


class IntegerSet {
public:
    IntegerSet() { emptySet(); }
    IntegerSet(int, int = -1, int = -1, int = -1, int = -1);
    IntegerSet unionOfIntegerSets(const IntegerSet&);
    IntegerSet intersectionOfIntegerSets(const IntegerSet&);
    void emptySet(void);
    void inputSet(void);
    void insertElement(int);
    void deleteElement(int);
    void setPrint(void) const;
    int isEqualTo(const IntegerSet&) const;

private:
    int set[101];  // range of 0 - 100
    int validEntry(int x) const { return x >= 0 && x <= 100;}
};


#endif
```

```
//P7_9M.cpp
//Member function definitions for p7_9.cpp

#include <iostream.h>
#include <iomanip.h>
#include "p7_9.h"


IntegerSet::IntegerSet(int a, int b, int c, int d, int e)
{
    emptySet();

    if (validEntry(a))
        insertElement(a);

    if (validEntry(b))
        insertElement(b);

    if (validEntry(c))
        insertElement(c);

    if (validEntry(d))
        insertElement(d);

    if (validEntry(e))
        insertElement(e);
}


void IntegerSet::emptySet(void)
{
    for (int y = 0; y < 101; y++)
        set[y] = 0;
}
```

```
void IntegerSet::inputSet(void)
{
    int number;

    do {
        cout << "Enter an element (-1 to end): ";
        cin >> number;

        if (validEntry(number))
            set[number] = 1;
        else if (number != -1)
            cerr << "Invalid Element" << endl;

    } while (number != -1);

    cout << "Entry complete" << endl;
}

void IntegerSet::setPrint(void) const
{
    int x, empty = 1;  // assume set is empty
    cout << '{';

    for (int u = 0; u < 101; u++)
        if (set[u]) {
            cout << setw(4) << u << (x % 10 == 0 ? "\n" : "");
            empty = 0; // set is not empty
            ++x;
        }

    if (empty)
        cout << setw(4) << "---";  // display an empty set

    cout << setw(2) << '}' << endl;
}

IntegerSet IntegerSet::unionOfIntegerSets(const IntegerSet &r)
{
    IntegerSet temp;

    for (int n = 0; n < 101; n++)
        if (set[n] == 1 || r.set[n] == 1)
            temp.set[n] = 1;

    return temp;
}

IntegerSet IntegerSet::intersectionOfIntegerSets(const IntegerSet &r)
{
    IntegerSet temp;

    for (int w = 0; w < 101; w++)
        if (set[w] == 1 && r.set[w] == 1)
            temp.set[w] = 1;

    return temp;
}

void IntegerSet::insertElement(int k)
{
    if (validEntry(k))
        set[k] = 1;
    else
        cerr << "Invalid insert attempted!" << endl;
}
```

```
void IntegerSet::deleteElement(int m)
{
   if (validEntry(m))
      set[m] = 0;
   else
      cerr << "Invalid delete attempted!" << endl;
}


int IntegerSet::isEqualTo(const IntegerSet &r) const
{
   for (int v = 0; v < 101; v++)
      if (set[v] != r.set[v])
         return 0;    // sets are not-equal

   return 1;    // sets are equal
}
```

```
// driver for p7_9.cpp
#include <iostream.h>
#include "p7_9.h"

main()
{

   IntegerSet a, b, c, d, e(8, 5, 7);

   cout << "Enter set A:" << endl;
   a.inputSet();
   cout << endl << "Enter set B:" << endl;
   b.inputSet();
   c = a.unionOfIntegerSets(b);
   d = a.intersectionOfIntegerSets(b);
   cout << endl << "Union of A and B is:" << endl;
   c.setPrint();
   cout << "Intersection of A and B is:" << endl;
   d.setPrint();

   if (a.isEqualTo(b))
      cout << "Set A is equal to set B" << endl;
   else
      cout << "Set A is not equal to set B" << endl;

   cout << endl << "Inserting 77 into set A..." << endl;
   a.insertElement(77);
   cout << "Set A is now:" << endl;
   a.setPrint();

   cout << endl << "Deleting 77 from set A..." << endl;
   a.deleteElement(77);
   cout << "Set A is now:" << endl;
   a.setPrint();

   cout << endl << "Set e is: " << endl;
   e.setPrint();

   cout << endl;

   return 0;
}
```

```
Enter set A:
Enter an element (-1 to end): 1
Enter an element (-1 to end): 2
Enter an element (-1 to end): 3
Enter an element (-1 to end): 4
Enter an element (-1 to end): -1
Entry complete

Enter set B:
Enter an element (-1 to end): 3
Enter an element (-1 to end): 4
Enter an element (-1 to end): 5
Enter an element (-1 to end): -1
Entry complete

Union of A and B is:
{   1    2    3    4    5 }
Intersection of A and B is:
{   3    4 }
Set A is not equal to set B

Inserting 77 into set A...
Set A is now:
{   1    2    3    4    77 }

Deleting 77 from set A...
Set A is now:
{   1    2    3    4}

Set e is:
{   5    7    8 }
```

8
Operator Overloading: Solutions

Exercises

8.6   Give as many examples as you can of operator overloading implicit in C. Give as many examples as you can of operator overloading implicit in C++. Give a reasonable example of a situation in which you might want to overload an operator explicitly in C++.

> **ANS:** In C, the operators **+, - , *, &** are overloaded. The context of these operators determines how they are used. It can be argued that the arithmetic operators are all overloaded, because they can be used to perform operations on more than one type of data. In C++, the same operators as C are overloaded, as well as the left shift and right shift operators (**<<** and **>>**).

8.7   The C++ operators that cannot be overloaded are _____, _____, _____, _____, and _____.

> **ANS: sizeof** operator, structure member operator (**.**), conditional operator (**?:**), class member dereferencing operator (**.***), scope resolution operator (**::**).

8.8   String concatenation requires two operands—the two strings that are to be concatenated. In the text we showed how to implement an overloaded concatenation operator that concatenates the second **String** object to the right of the first **String** object, thus modifying the first **String** object. In some applications, it is desirable to produce a concatenated **String** object without modifying the two **String** arguments. Implement **operator+** to allow operations such as

```
string1 = string2 + string3;
```

ANS:

```
// P8_8.H
#ifndef p8_8_H
#define p8_8_H

#include <iostream.h>
#include <string.h>
#include <assert.h>

class String {
    friend ostream &operator<<(ostream &, const String &);
public:
    String(const char * = ""); // conversion constructor
    String(const String &);    // copy constructor
    ~String();                 // destructor
    const String &operator=(const String &);
    String operator+(const String &);
private:
    char *sPtr;
    int length;
};

#endif
```

```cpp
// P8_8M.cpp
// member function definitions for p8_8.cpp
// class String
#include <iostream.h>
#include <string.h>
#include "p8_8.h"

// Conversion constructor: Convert a char * to String
String::String(const char *s)
{
   length = strlen(s);          // compute length
   sPtr = new char[length + 1]; // allocate storage
   assert(sPtr != 0);  // terminate if memory not allocated
   strcpy(sPtr, s);             // copy literal to object
}

// Copy constructor
String::String(const String &copy)
{
   length = copy.length;        // copy length
   sPtr = new char[length + 1]; // allocate storage
   assert(sPtr != 0);           // ensure memory allocated
   strcpy(sPtr, copy.sPtr);     // copy string
}

// Destructor
String::~String() { delete [] sPtr; }  // reclaim string

// Overloaded = operator; avoids self assignment
const String &String::operator=(const String &right)
{
   if (&right != this) {             // avoid self assignment
      delete [] sPtr;                // prevents memory leak
      length = right.length;         // new String length
      sPtr = new char[length + 1];   // allocate memory
      assert(sPtr != 0);             // ensure memory allocated
      strcpy(sPtr, right.sPtr);      // copy string
   }
   else
      cout << "Attempted assignment of a String to itself\n";

   return *this;    // enables concatenated assignments
}

// Concatenate right operand and this object and
// store in temp object.
String String::operator+(const String &right)
{
   String temp;

   temp.length = length + right.length;
   temp.sPtr = new char[temp.length + 1]; // create space
   assert(sPtr != 0);    // terminate if memory not allocated
   strcpy(temp.sPtr, sPtr);        // left part of new String
   strcat(temp.sPtr, right.sPtr); // right part of new String
   return temp;                    // enables concatenated calls
}

// Overloaded output operator
ostream &operator<<(ostream &output, const String &s)
{
   output << s.sPtr;
   return output;    // enables concatenation
}
```

```
// driver for p8_8.cpp
#include <iostream.h>
#include "p8_8.h"

main()
{
    String string1, string2("The date is");
    String string3(" August 1, 1993");

    cout << "string1 = string2 + string3" << endl;
    string1 = string2 + string3;
    cout << string1 << " = " << string2 << " + "
         << string3 << endl;

    return 0;
}
```

```
string1 = string2 + string3
The date is August 1, 1993 = The date is + August 1, 1993
```

8.9 *(Ultimate operator overloading exercise)* To appreciate the care that should go into selecting operators for overloading, list each of C++'s overloadable operators and for each list a possible meaning (or several, if appropriate) for each of several classes you have studied in this course. We suggest you try:

    a) Array
    b) Stack
    c) String

After doing this, comment on which operators seem to have meaning for a wide variety of classes. Which operators seem to be of little value for overloading? What operators seem ambiguous?

8.10 Now work the process described in the previous problem in reverse. List each of C++'s overloadable operators. For each, list what you feel is perhaps the "ultimate operation" the operator should be used to represent. If there are several excellent operations, list them all.

8.11 *(Project)* C++ is an evolving language, and new languages are always being developed. What additional operators would you recommend adding to C++ or to a future language like C++ that would support both procedural programming and object-oriented programming? Write a careful justification. You might consider sending your suggestions to the ANSI C++ Committee.

8.12 One nice example of overloading the function call operator `()` is to allow the more common form of double array subscripting. Instead of saying

       `chessBoard[row][column]`

for an array of objects, overload the function call operator to allow the alternate form

       `chessBoard(row, column)`

ANS:
```
// P8_12.H
#ifndef P8_12_H
#define P8_12_H
#include <iostream.h>

class CallOperator {
public:
    CallOperator();
    int operator()(int, int); // overloaded function call operator
private:
    int chessBoard[8][8];
};

#endif
```

```
// P8_12M.CPP
// member function definitions for p8_12.cpp
#include "p8_12.h"

CallOperator::CallOperator()
{
   for (int loop = 0; loop < 8; loop++)
      for (int loop2 = 0; loop2 < 8; loop2++)
         chessBoard[loop][loop2] = loop2;
}

int CallOperator::operator()(int r, int c) { return chessBoard[r][c]; }
```

```
// driver for p8_12.cpp
#include <iostream.h>
#include "p8_12.h"

main()
{
   CallOperator board;

   cout << "board[2][5] is " << board(2, 5) << endl;

   return 0;
}
```

```
board[2][5] is 5
```

8.13 Overload the subscript operator to return a given member of a linked list.
      NOTE: This problem belongs in Chapter 15 and was accidently misplaced during publication.
      ANS:

```
// P8_13L.H
#ifndef p8_13_H
#define p8_13_H

#include <iostream.h>
#include <stdlib.h>
#include "p8_13ln.h"

class ListNode;    // forward declaration

class List {
public:
   List();
   void insertItem(const char);
   char deleteItem(const char);
   void printList(void) const;
   int isEmpty(void) const;
   char operator[](int);
private:
   ListNode *startPtr;
};

#endif
```

```
// P8_13LN.H
#ifndef p8_13LN_H
#define p8_13LN_H
#include <iostream.h>

class ListNode {
friend class List;
public:
   ListNode(char d)
   {
      data = d;
      nextPtr = 0;
   }
private:
   char data;
   ListNode *nextPtr;
};


#endif
```

```
// P8_13LM.cpp
// member function definitions p8_13.cpp
// class List
#include <iostream.h>
#include "p8_131.h"
#include "p8_131n.h"

List::List() { startPtr = 0; }

int List::isEmpty(void) const { return startPtr == 0; }

void List::printList(void) const
{
   ListNode *currentPtr;

   currentPtr = startPtr;

   if (currentPtr == 0)
      cout << "List is empty.\n\n";
   else {
      cout << "The list is:\n";

      while (currentPtr != 0) {
         cout << currentPtr->data << " --> ";
         currentPtr = currentPtr->nextPtr;
      }

      cout << "NULL\n\n";
   }
}

void List::insertItem(const char value)
{
   ListNode *newPtr, *previousPtr, *currentPtr;

   newPtr = new ListNode(value);

   if (newPtr != 0) {        //is space available
      previousPtr = 0;
      currentPtr = startPtr;
```

```
        while (currentPtr != 0 && value > currentPtr->data) {
            previousPtr = currentPtr;            // walk to ...
            currentPtr = currentPtr->nextPtr;  // ... next node
        }

        if (previousPtr == 0) {
            newPtr->nextPtr = startPtr;
            startPtr = newPtr;
        }
        else {
            previousPtr->nextPtr = newPtr;
            newPtr->nextPtr = currentPtr;
        }

    }
    else
        cout << value << " not inserted. No memory available.\n";
}

char List::deleteItem(const char value)
{
    ListNode *previousPtr, *currentPtr, *tempPtr;

    if (value == startPtr->data) {
        tempPtr = startPtr;
        startPtr = startPtr->nextPtr;  // de-thread the node
        delete tempPtr;                // free the de-threaded node

        return value;
    }
    else {
        previousPtr = startPtr;
        currentPtr = startPtr->nextPtr;

        while (currentPtr != 0 && currentPtr->data != value) {
            previousPtr = currentPtr;            // walk to ...
            currentPtr = currentPtr->nextPtr;  // ... next node
        }

        if (currentPtr != 0) {
            tempPtr = currentPtr;
            previousPtr->nextPtr = currentPtr->nextPtr;
            delete tempPtr;
            return value;
        }
    }

    return '\0';
}

char List::operator[](int loc)
{
    ListNode *currentPtr;

    currentPtr = startPtr;

    for (int loop = 1; currentPtr != 0 && loop < loc; loop++)
        currentPtr = currentPtr->nextPtr;

    return loop == loc ? currentPtr->data : '\0';
}
```

```cpp
// p8_13.cpp
#include <iostream.h>
#include <stdlib.h>
#include "p8_131.h"
#include "p8_131n.h"

void instructions(void);
void runMenu(List&);

main()
{
    List l;
    int location;

    runMenu(l);
    cout << "\nEnter location to find value for: \n";
    cin >> location;
    cout << "Value at location " << location << " is " << l[location]
         << endl;

    return 0;
}

void instructions(void)
{
    cout << "Enter your choice:\n"
         << "    1 to insert an element into the list.\n"
         << "    2 to delete an element from the list.\n"
         << "    3 to end.\n";
}

void runMenu(List& list)
{
    int choice;
    char item;

    instructions();
    cout << "? ";
    cin >> choice;

    while (choice != 3) {

        switch (choice) {
            case 1:
                cout << "Enter a character: ";
                cin >> item;
                list.insertItem(item);
                list.printList();
                break;
            case 2:
                if (!list.isEmpty()) {
                    cout << "Enter character to be deleted: ";
                    cin >> item;

                    if (list.deleteItem(item)) {
                        cout << item << " was deleted\n";
                        list.printList();
                    }
                    else
                        cout << item << " not found.\n\n";
                }
                else
                    cout << "List is empty.\n\n";

                break;
```

```
        default:
            cout << "Invalid choice.\n\n";
            instructions();
            break;
    }

    cout << "? ";
    cin >> choice;
}

cout << "End of run." << endl;
}
```

```
Enter your choice:
    1 to insert an element into the list.
    2 to delete an element from the list.
    3 to end.
? 1
Enter a character: r
The list is:
r --> NULL

? 1
Enter a character: o
The list is:
o --> r --> NULL

? 1
Enter a character: x
The list is:
o --> r --> x --> NULL

? 1
Enter a character: z
The list is:
o --> r --> x --> z --> NULL

? 1
Enter a character: b
The list is:
b --> o --> r --> x --> z --> NULL

? 1
Enter a character: m
The list is:
b --> m --> o --> r --> x --> z --> NULL

? 1
Enter a character: k
The list is:
b --> k --> m --> o --> r --> x --> z --> NULL

? 1
Enter a character: d
The list is:
b --> d --> k --> m --> o --> r --> x --> z --> NULL

? 1
Enter a character: j
The list is:
b --> d --> j --> k --> m --> o --> r --> x --> z --> NULL
```

continued

```
                                                                    continued
? 3
End of run.

Enter location to find value for: 8
Value at location 8 is x
```

8.14   Overload the subscript operator to return the largest element of a collection, the second largest, the third largest, etc.

NOTE: This problem belongs in Chapter 15 and was accidently misplaced during publication.

ANS:

```
// P8_14L.H
#ifndef p8_14L_H
#define p8_14L_H
#include <iostream.h>

class ListNode;    // forward declaration

class List {
public:
    List();
    void insertItem(const char);
    char deleteItem(const char);
    void printList(void) const;
    int isEmpty(void) const;
    char operator[](const int);   // overloaded subscript operator
    void setListLength(int);
private:
    ListNode *startPtr;
    int listLength;
};


#endif
```

```
// P8_14LN.H
#ifndef p8_14LN_H
#define p8_14LN_H
#include <iostream.h>

class ListNode {
friend class List;
public:
    ListNode(char d)
    {
        data = d;
        nextPtr = 0;
    }
private:
    char data;
    ListNode *nextPtr;
};


#endif
```

```cpp
//  P8_14LM.cpp
// member function definitions for p8_14.cpp
// class List
#include <iostream.h>
#include "p8_14l.h"
#include "p8_14ln.h"

List::List()
{
   startPtr = 0;
   listLength = 0;
}

int List::isEmpty(void) const { return startPtr == 0; }

void List::printList(void) const
{
   ListNode *currentPtr;

   currentPtr = startPtr;

   if (currentPtr == 0)
      cout << "List is empty.\n\n";
   else {
      cout << "The list is:\n";

      while (currentPtr != 0) {
         cout << currentPtr->data << " --> ";
         currentPtr = currentPtr->nextPtr;
      }

      cout << "NULL\n\n";
   }
}

void List::setListLength(int length) { listLength += length; }

void List::insertItem(const char value)
{
   ListNode *newPtr, *previousPtr, *currentPtr;

   newPtr = new ListNode(value);

   if (newPtr != 0) {       //is space available
      previousPtr = 0;
      currentPtr = startPtr;

      while (currentPtr != 0 && value > currentPtr->data) {
         previousPtr = currentPtr;           // walk to ...
         currentPtr = currentPtr->nextPtr;   // ... next node
      }

      if (previousPtr == 0) {
         newPtr->nextPtr = startPtr;
         startPtr = newPtr;
      }
      else {
         previousPtr->nextPtr = newPtr;
         newPtr->nextPtr = currentPtr;
      }

      setListLength(1);
   }
   else
      cout << value << " not inserted. No memory available.\n";
}
```

```cpp
char List::deleteItem(const char value)
{
    ListNode *previousPtr, *currentPtr, *tempPtr;

    if (value == startPtr->data) {
        tempPtr = startPtr;
        startPtr = startPtr->nextPtr;   // de-thread the node
        delete tempPtr;                 // free the de-threaded node
        setListLength(-1);
        return value;
    }
    else {
        previousPtr = startPtr;
        currentPtr = startPtr->nextPtr;

        while (currentPtr != 0 && currentPtr->data != value) {
            previousPtr = currentPtr;          // walk to ...
            currentPtr = currentPtr->nextPtr;  // ... next node
        }

        if (currentPtr != 0) {
            tempPtr = currentPtr;
            previousPtr->nextPtr = currentPtr->nextPtr;
            delete tempPtr;
            setListLength(-1);
            return value;
        }
    }

    return '\0';
}


char List::operator[](const int magnitude)
{
    ListNode *currentPtr;

    currentPtr = startPtr;

    if (magnitude < listLength && magnitude > 0)
        for (int loop = 1; loop <= listLength - magnitude; loop++)
            currentPtr = currentPtr->nextPtr;

    else {
        cout << "\nMagnitude out of Range!" << endl;
        return '\0';
    }

    return currentPtr->data;
}
```

```cpp
// p8_14.cpp
#include <iostream.h>
#include "p8_141.h"
#include "p8_141n.h"

void instructions(void);
void runMenu(List&);
```

```
main()
{
    List l;
    int largest;

    runMenu(l);
    cout << "Select the magnitude (1 = largest, 2 = next largest, etc.)"
        << endl << "for the value: ";
    cin >> largest;
    cout << "value selected is: " << l[largest] << endl;
    return 0;
}

void instructions(void)
{
    cout << "Enter your choice:\n"
        << "   1 to insert an element into the list.\n"
        << "   2 to delete an element from the list.\n"
        << "   3 to end." << endl;
}

void runMenu(List& list)
{
    int choice;
    char item;

    instructions();
    cout << "? ";
    cin >> choice;

    while (choice != 3) {

        switch (choice) {
            case 1:
                cout << "Enter a character: ";
                cin >> item;
                list.insertItem(item);
                list.printList();
                break;
            case 2:
                if (!list.isEmpty()) {
                    cout << "Enter character to be deleted: ";
                    cin >> item;

                    if (list.deleteItem(item)) {
                        cout << item << " was deleted\n";
                        list.printList();
                    }
                    else
                        cout << item << " not found.\n\n";
                }
                else
                    cout << "List is empty.\n\n";

                break;
            default:
                cout << "Invalid choice.\n\n";
                instructions();
                break;
        }

        cout << "? ";
        cin >> choice;
    }

    cout << "End of run.\n";
}
```

```
Enter your choice:
   1 to insert an element into the list.
   2 to delete an element from the list.
   3 to end.
? 1
Enter a character: e
The list is:
e --> NULL

? 1
Enter a character: i
The list is:
e --> i --> NULL

? 1
Enter a character: 4
The list is:
4 --> e --> i --> NULL

? 1
Enter a character: &
The list is:
& --> 4 --> e --> i --> NULL

? 1
Enter a character: f
The list is:
& --> 4 --> e --> f --> i --> NULL

? 1
Enter a character: n
The list is:
& --> 4 --> e --> f --> i --> n --> NULL

? 1
Enter a character: c
The list is:
& --> 4 --> c --> e --> f --> i --> n --> NULL

? 1
Enter a character: x
The list is:
& --> 4 --> c --> e --> f --> i --> n --> x --> NULL

? 3
End of run.
Select the magnitude ( 1 = largest, 2 = next largest, etc.): 4
value selected is: f
```

8.15   Consider class **Complex** shown in Fig. 8.7. The class enables operations on so-called *complex numbers*. These are numbers of the form **realPart + imaginaryPart** * *i* where *i* has the value:

$$\sqrt{-1}$$

a) Modify the class to enable input and output of complex numbers through the overloaded **>>** and **<<** operators, respectively (you should remove the print function from the class).
b) Overload the multiplication operator to enable multiplication of two complex numbers as in algebra.
c) Overload the **==** and **!=** operators to allow comparisons of complex numbers.

ANS:

```
// P8_15.H
#ifndef P8_15.H
#define P8_15.H
#include <iostream.h>

class Complex {
    friend ostream &operator<<(ostream &, const Complex &);
    friend istream &operator>>(istream &, Complex &);
public:
    Complex(double = 0.0, double = 0.0);      // constructor
    Complex operator+(const Complex&) const; // addition
    Complex operator-(const Complex&) const; // subtraction
    Complex operator*(const Complex&) const; // multiplication
    Complex& operator=(const Complex&);       // assignment
    int operator==(const Complex&) const;
    int operator!=(const Complex&) const;
private:
    double real;        // real part
    double imaginary;   // imaginary part
};

#endif
```

```
// P8_15M.cpp
// member function definitions for p8_15.cpp
#include "p8_15.h"

// Constructor
Complex::Complex(double r, double i)
{
    real = r;
    imaginary = i;
}

// Overloaded addition operator
Complex Complex::operator+(const Complex &operand2) const
{
    Complex sum;
    sum.real = real + operand2.real;
    sum.imaginary = imaginary + operand2.imaginary;
    return sum;
}

// Overloaded subtraction operator
Complex Complex::operator-(const Complex &operand2) const
{
    Complex diff;
    diff.real = real - operand2.real;
    diff.imaginary = imaginary - operand2.imaginary;
    return diff;
}

// Overloaded multiplication operator
Complex Complex::operator*(const Complex &operand2) const
{
    Complex times;
    times.real = real * operand2.real + imaginary * operand2.imaginary;
    times.imaginary = real * operand2.imaginary + imaginary * operand2.real;
    return times;
}
```

```
// Overloaded = operator
Complex& Complex::operator=(const Complex &right)
{
   real = right.real;
   imaginary = right.imaginary;
   return *this;    // enables concatenation
}

int Complex::operator==(const Complex &right) const
   { return right.real == real && right.imaginary == imaginary ? 1 : 0; }

int Complex::operator!=(const Complex &right) const
   { return !(*this == right); }

ostream& operator<<(ostream &output, const Complex &complex)
{
   output << complex.real << " + " << complex.imaginary << "i";
   return output;
}

istream& operator>>(istream &input, Complex &complex)
{
   input >> complex.real;
   input.ignore(3);          //skip spaces and +
   input >> complex.imaginary;
   input.ignore(2);
   return input;
}
```

```
// driver for p8_15.cpp
#include "p8_15.h"

main()
{
   Complex x, y(4.3, 8.2), z(3.3, 1.1), k;

   cout << "Enter a complex number in the form: a + bi\n? ";
   cin >> k;

   cout << "x: " << x << "\ny: " << y << "\nz: " << z << "\nk: "
        << k << endl;

   x = y + z;
   cout << "\nx = y + z:\n" << x << " = " << y << " + " << z << endl;

   x = y - z;
   cout << "\nx = y - z:\n" << x << " = " << y << " - " << z << endl;

   x = y * z;
   cout << "\nx = y * z:\n" << x << " = " << y << " * " << z << endl
        << endl;

   if (x != k)
      cout << x << " != " << k << endl;

   cout << endl;
   x = k;

   if (x == k)
      cout << x << " == " << k << endl;

   return 0;
}
```

```
Enter a complex number in the form: a + bi
? 22 + 8i
x: 0 + 0i
y: 4.3 + 8.2i
z: 3.3 + 1.1i
k: 22 + 8i

x = y + z:
7.6 + 9.3i = 4.3 + 8.2i + 3.3 + 1.1i

x = y - z:
1 + 7.1i = 4.3 + 8.2i - 3.3 + 1.1i

x = y * z:
23.21 + 31.79i = 4.3 + 8.2i * 3.3 + 1.1i

23.21 + 31.79i != 22 + 8i

22 + 8i == 22 + 8i
```

8.16   A machine with 32-bit integers can represent integers in the range of approximately −2 billion to +2 billion. This fixed-size restriction is rarely troublesome. But there are many applications in which we would like to be able to use a much wider range of integers. This is what C++ was built to do, namely create powerful new data types. Consider class **HugeInt** of Fig. 8.8. Study the class carefully, then

 a) Describe precisely how it operates.
 b) What restrictions does the class have?
 c) Modify the class to process arbitrarily large integers. (Hint: Use a linked list to represent a **HugeInt**.)
 d) Overload the * multiplication operator.
 e) Overload the / division operator.
 f) Overload all the relational and equality operators.

8.17   Create a class **rationalNumber** (fractions) with the following capabilities:

 a) Create a constructor that prevents a 0 denominator, reduces fractions, and avoids negative denominators.
 b) Overload the addition, subtraction, multiplication and division operators for this class.
 c) Overload the relational and equality operators for this class.

ANS:

```
// P8_17.H
#ifndef P8_17.H
#define P8_17.H
#include <iostream.h>

class RationalNumber {
public:
   RationalNumber(int = 0, int = 1); // default constructor
   RationalNumber operator+(const RationalNumber&);
   RationalNumber operator-(const RationalNumber&);
   RationalNumber operator*(const RationalNumber&);
   RationalNumber operator/(RationalNumber&);
   int operator>(const RationalNumber&) const;
   int operator<(const RationalNumber&) const;
   int operator>=(const RationalNumber&) const;
   int operator<=(const RationalNumber&) const;
   int operator==(const RationalNumber&) const;
   int operator!=(const RationalNumber&) const;
   void printRational(void) const;
private:
   int numerator;
   int denominator;
   void reduction(void);
};

#endif
```

```cpp
// P8_17M.cpp
// member function definitions for p8_17.cpp
#include <stdlib.h>
#include "p8_17.h"

RationalNumber::RationalNumber(int n, int d)
{
   numerator = n;
   denominator = d;
   reduction();
}

RationalNumber RationalNumber::operator+(const RationalNumber &a)
{
   RationalNumber sum;

   sum.numerator = numerator * a.denominator + denominator * a.numerator;
   sum.denominator = denominator * a.denominator;
   sum.reduction();
   return sum;
}

RationalNumber RationalNumber::operator-(const RationalNumber &s)
{
   RationalNumber sub;

   sub.numerator = numerator * s.denominator - denominator * s.numerator;
   sub.denominator = denominator * s.denominator;
   sub.reduction();
   return sub;
}

RationalNumber RationalNumber::operator*(const RationalNumber &m)
{
   RationalNumber multiply;

   multiply.numerator = numerator * m.numerator;
   multiply.denominator = denominator * m.denominator;
   multiply.reduction();
   return multiply;
}

RationalNumber RationalNumber::operator/(RationalNumber &d)
{
   RationalNumber divide;

   if (d.numerator != 0) {    // check for a zero in numerator
      divide.numerator = numerator * d.denominator;
      divide.denominator = denominator * d.numerator;
      divide.reduction();
   }
   else {
      cout << "Divide by zero error: terminating program" << endl;
      exit(1);
   }

   return divide;
}

int RationalNumber::operator>(const RationalNumber &gr) const
{
   if ((float)numerator / denominator > (float)gr.numerator / gr.denominator)
      return 1;
   else
      return 0;
}
```

```cpp
int RationalNumber::operator<(const RationalNumber &lr) const
{
    if ((float)numerator / denominator < (float)lr.numerator / lr.denominator)
        return 1;
    else
        return 0;
}

int RationalNumber::operator>=(const RationalNumber &ger) const
    { return *this == ger || *this > ger; }

int RationalNumber::operator<=(const RationalNumber &ler) const
    { return *this == ler || *this < ler; }

int RationalNumber::operator==(const RationalNumber &er) const
{
    if (numerator == er.numerator && denominator == er.denominator)
        return 1;
    else
        return 0;
}

int RationalNumber::operator!=(const RationalNumber &ner) const
    { return !(*this == ner); }

void RationalNumber::printRational(void) const
{
    if (numerator == 0)              // print fraction as zero
        cout << numerator;
    else if (denominator == 1)   // print fraction as integer
        cout << numerator;
    else
        cout << numerator << "/" << denominator;
}

void RationalNumber::reduction(void)
{
    int largest, gcd = 1;   // greatest common divisor;

    largest = (numerator > denominator) ? numerator: denominator;

    for (int loop = 2; loop <= largest; loop++)
        if (numerator % loop == 0 && denominator % loop == 0)
            gcd = loop;

    numerator /= gcd;
    denominator /= gcd;
}
```

```cpp
// driver for p8_17.cpp
#include "p8_17.h"

main()
{
    RationalNumber c(7,3), d(3,9), x;

    c.printRational();
    cout << " + " ;
    d.printRational();
    cout << " = ";
    x = c + d;
    x.printRational();
```

```
            cout << "\n";
            c.printRational();
            cout << " - " ;
            d.printRational();
            cout << " = ";
            x = c - d;
            x.printRational();

            cout << "\n";
            c.printRational();
            cout << " * " ;
            d.printRational();
            cout << " = ";
            x = c * d;
            x.printRational();

            cout << "\n";
            c.printRational();
            cout << " / " ;
            d.printRational();
            cout << " = ";
            x = c / d;
            x.printRational();

            cout << "\n";
            c.printRational();
            cout << " is:\n";

            cout << ((c > d) ? "  > " : "  <= ");
            d.printRational();
            cout << " according to the overloaded > operator\n";

            cout << ((c < d) ? "  < " : "  >= ");
            d.printRational();
            cout << " according to the overloaded < operator\n";

            cout << ((c >= d) ? "  >= " : "  < ");
            d.printRational();
            cout << " according to the overloaded >= operator\n";

            cout << ((c <= d) ? "  <= " : "  > ");
            d.printRational();
            cout << " according to the overloaded <= operator\n";

            cout << ((c == d) ? "  == " : "  != ");
            d.printRational();
            cout << " according to the overloaded == operator\n";

            cout << ((c != d) ? "  != " : "  == ");
            d.printRational();
            cout << " according to the overloaded != operator" << endl;
            return 0;
}
```

```
7/3 + 1/3 = 8/3
7/3 - 1/3 = 2
7/3 * 1/3 = 7/9
7/3 / 1/3 = 7
7/3 is:
    > 1/3 according to the overloaded > operator
    >= 1/3 according to the overloaded < operator
    >= 1/3 according to the overloaded >= operator
    > 1/3 according to the overloaded <= operator
    != 1/3 according to the overloaded == operator
    != 1/3 according to the overloaded != operator
```

8.18   Study the C string handling library functions and implement each of the functions as part of the **String** class. Then, use these functions to perform text manipulations.

8.19   Develop class **Polynomial**. The internal representation of a **Polynomial** is an array of terms. Each term contains a coefficient and an exponent. The term

$$2x^4$$

has a coefficient of 2 and an exponent of 4. Develop a full class containing proper constructor and destructor functions as well as *set* and *get* functions. The class should also provide the following overloaded operator capabilities:

   a) Overload the addition operator (**+**) to add two **Polynomials**.
   b) Overload the subtraction operator (**-**) to subtract two **Polynomials**.
   c) Overload the assignment operator to assign one **Polynomial** to another.
   d) Overload the multiplication operator (*****) to multiply two **Polynomials**.
   e) Overload the addition assignment operator (**+=**), the subtraction assignment operator (**-=**), the multiplication assignment operator (***=**).

NOTE: The description calls for set and get functions as well as a destructor. As implemented, no destructor function is necessary. Set and get functions have not been provided.

```
ANS:
// P8_19P.H
#ifndef P8_19P.H
#define P8_19P.H

#include <iostream.h>

class Polynomial {
public:
    Polynomial();
    Polynomial operator+(const Polynomial&) const;
    Polynomial operator-(const Polynomial&) const;
    Polynomial operator*(const Polynomial&);
    Polynomial& operator+=(const Polynomial&);
    Polynomial& operator-=(const Polynomial&);
    Polynomial& operator*=(const Polynomial&);
    void enterTerms(void);
    void printPolynomial(void) const;
private:
    int exponents[100];
    int coefficients[100];
    void polynomialCombine(Polynomial&);   // combine common terms
};


#endif
```

```
// P8_19M.cpp
// member function definitions for p8_19.cpp
// NOTE: The assignment operator does not need to be overloaded,
// because default member-wise copy can be used
#include <iomanip.h>
#include "p8_19p.h"

Polynomial::Polynomial()
{
    for (int t = 0; t < 100; t++) {
        coefficients[t] = 0;
        exponents[t] = 0;
    }
}
```

```cpp
void Polynomial::printPolynomial(void) const
{
   int start, zero = 0;

   if (coefficients[0]) {            // output constants
      cout << coefficients[0];
      start = 1;
      zero = 1;      // at least one term exists
   }
   else {

      if (coefficients[1]) {
         cout << coefficients[1] << 'x';   // constant does not exist
                                           // so output first term
                                           // without a sign
         if ((exponents[1] != 0) && (exponents[1] != 1))
            cout << '^' << exponents[1];

         zero = 1;   // at least one term exists
      }

      start = 2;
   }

   // output remaining polynomial terms
   for (int x = start; x < 100; x++) {
      if (coefficients[x] != 0) {
         cout << setiosflags(ios::showpos) << coefficients[x]
              << resetiosflags(ios::showpos) << 'x';

         if ((exponents[x] != 0) && (exponents[x] != 1))
            cout << '^' << exponents[x];

         zero = 1;   // at least one term exists
      }
   }

   if (zero == 0)    // no terms exist in the polynomial
      cout << '0';

   cout << endl;
}


Polynomial Polynomial::operator+(const Polynomial& r) const
{
   Polynomial temp;
   int exponentExists;

   // process element with a zero exponent
   temp.coefficients[0] = coefficients[0] + r.coefficients[0];

   // copy right arrays into temp object s will be used to keep
   // track of first open coefficient element
   for (int s = 1; (s < 100) && (r.exponents[s] != 0); s++) {
      temp.coefficients[s] = r.coefficients[s];
      temp.exponents[s] = r.exponents[s];
   }

   for (int x = 1; x < 100; x++) {
      exponentExists = 0; // assume exponent will not be found

      for (int t = 1; (t < 100) && (exponentExists == 0); t++)
         if (exponents[x] == temp.exponents[t]) {
            temp.coefficients[t] += coefficients[x];
            exponentExists = 1;   // exponent found
         }
```

```cpp
         // exponent was not found, insert into temp
         if (exponentExists == 0) {
            temp.exponents[s] = exponents[x];
            temp.coefficients[s] += coefficients[x];
            ++s;
         }
      }
   }

   return temp;
}


Polynomial &Polynomial::operator+=(const Polynomial &r)
{
   *this = *this + r;
   return *this;
}


Polynomial Polynomial::operator-(const Polynomial& r) const
{
   Polynomial temp;
   int exponentExists;

   // process element with a zero exponent
   // zero exponents evaluate to one
   temp.coefficients[0] = coefficients[0] - r.coefficients[0];

   // copy left arrays into temp object s will be used to keep
   // track of first open coefficient element
   for (int s = 1; (s < 100) && (exponents[s] != 0); s++) {
      temp.coefficients[s] = coefficients[s];
      temp.exponents[s] = exponents[s];
   }

   for (int x = 1; x < 100; x++) {
      exponentExists = 0; // assume exponent will not be found

      for (int t = 1; (t < 100) && (exponentExists == 0); t++)
         if (r.exponents[x] == temp.exponents[t]) {
            temp.coefficients[t] -= r.coefficients[x];
            exponentExists = 1;  // exponent found
         }

      // exponent was not found, insert into temp
      if (exponentExists == 0) {
         temp.exponents[s] = r.exponents[x];
         temp.coefficients[s] -= r.coefficients[x];
         ++s;
      }
   }

   return temp;
}


Polynomial &Polynomial::operator-=(const Polynomial& r)
{
   *this = *this - r;
   return *this;
}
```

```cpp
Polynomial Polynomial::operator*(const Polynomial& r)
{
    Polynomial temp;
    int s = 1;    // subscript location for temp coefficients and exponents

    for (int x = 0; (x < 100) && (x == 0 || coefficients[x] != 0); x++)

        for (int y = 0; (y < 100) && (y == 0 || r.coefficients[y] != 0); y++)

            if (coefficients[x] * r.coefficients[y])

                if ((exponents[x] == 0) && (r.exponents[y] == 0))
                    temp.coefficients[0] += coefficients[x] * r.coefficients[y];
                else {
                    temp.coefficients[s] = coefficients[x] * r.coefficients[y];
                    temp.exponents[s] = exponents[x] + r.exponents[y];
                    ++s;
                }

    polynomialCombine(temp);   // combine common terms

    return temp;
}


void Polynomial::polynomialCombine(Polynomial& w)
{
    Polynomial temp = w;
    int exp;

    // zero out elements of w
    for (int x = 0; x < 100; x++) {
        w.coefficients[x] = 0;
        w.exponents[x] = 0;
    }

    for (x = 1; x < 100; x++) {
        exp = temp.exponents[x];

        for (int y = x + 1; y < 100; y++)
            if (exp == temp.exponents[y]) {
                temp.coefficients[x] += temp.coefficients[y];
                temp.exponents[y] = 0;
                temp.coefficients[y] = 0;
            }
    }

    w = temp;
}


Polynomial &Polynomial::operator*=(const Polynomial& r)
{
    *this = *this * r;
    return *this;
}


void Polynomial::enterTerms(void)
{
    int found = 0, numberOfTerms, c, e;

    cout << endl << "Enter number of polynomial terms: ";
    cin >> numberOfTerms;
```

```cpp
   for (int n = 1; n <= numberOfTerms; n++) {
      cout << endl << "Enter coefficient: ";
      cin >> c;
      cout << "Enter exponent: ";
      cin >> e;

      if (c != 0) {
         // exponents of zero are forced into first element
         if (e == 0) {
            coefficients[0] += c;
            continue;
         }

         for (int term = 1; (term < 100) && (coefficients[term] != 0); term++)
            if (e == exponents[term]) {
               coefficients[term] += c;
               exponents[term] = e;
               found = 1;  // existing exponent updated
            }

         if (found == 0) {                    // add term
            coefficients[term] += c;
            exponents[term] = e;
         }
      }
   }
}
```

```cpp
// driver for p8_19.cpp
#include "p8_19p.h"

main()
{
   Polynomial a, b, c, t;

   a.enterTerms();
   b.enterTerms();
   cout << "First polynomial is: " << endl;
   a.printPolynomial();
   cout << "Second polynomial is: " << endl;
   b.printPolynomial();
   cout << endl << "Adding the polynomials yields: " << endl;
   c = a + b;
   c.printPolynomial();
   cout << endl << "+= the polynomials yields: " << endl;
   t = a;  // save value of a
   a += b;
   a.printPolynomial();
   cout << endl << "Subtracting the polynomials yields: " << endl;
   a = t;  // reset a to original value
   c = a - b;
   c.printPolynomial();
   cout << endl << "-= the polynomials yields: " << endl;
   a -= b;
   a.printPolynomial();
   cout << endl << "Multiplying the polynomials yields: " << endl;
   a = t;  // reset a to original value
   c = a * b;
   c.printPolynomial();
   cout << endl << "*= the polynomials yields: " << endl;
   a *= b;
   a.printPolynomial();
   cout << endl;
   return 0;
}
```

```
Enter number of polynomial terms: 3

Enter coefficient: 1
Enter exponent: 2

Enter coefficient: -2
Enter exponent: 3

Enter coefficient: 3
Enter exponent: 4

Enter number of polynomial terms: 2

Enter coefficient: 1
Enter exponent: 3

Enter coefficient: 1
Enter exponent: 4

First polynomial is:
1x^2-2x^3+3x^4
Second polynomial is:
1x^3+1x^4

Adding the polynomials yields:
-1x^3+4x^4+1x^2

+= the polynomials yields:
-1x^3+4x^4+1x^2

Subtracting the polynomials yields:
1x^2-3x^3+2x^4

-= the polynomials yields:
1x^2-3x^3+2x^4

Multiplying the polynomials yields:
1x^5-1x^6+1x^7+3x^8

*= the polynomials yields:
1x^5-1x^6+1x^7+3x^8
```

9
Inheritance: Solutions

Exercises

9.2 Consider the class **bicycle**. Given your knowledge of some common components of bicycles, show a class hierarchy in which the class **bicycle** inherits from other classes, which, in turn, inherit from yet other classes. Discuss the instantiation of various objects of class **bicycle**. Discuss inheritance from class **bicycle** for other closely related derived classes.

> **ANS:** Possible classes are displayed in bold.
>
> **Bicycle** composed of:
>   **handle bars**
>   **seat**
>   **frame**
>   **wheels** composed of:
>   **tires**
>   **rims**
>   **spokes**
>   **pedals**
>   **chain** composed of:
>   **links**
>   **brakes** composed of:
>   **wires**
>   **brake pads**
>   **brake handles**

Classes that may be derivable from **Bicycle** are **Unicycle**, **Motorcycle**, **Moped**, and **Tricycle**.

9.3 Briefly define each of the following terms: inheritance, multiple inheritance, base class, and derived class.

> **ANS:**
> - Inheritance is the process by which a class incorporates the attributes and behaviors of a previously defined class.
> - Multiple inheritance is the process by which a class incorporates the attributes and behaviors of more than one previously defined class.
> - A base class is a class from which other classes inherit attributes and behaviors..
> - A derived class is a class that has inherited attributes and behaviors from one or more base classes.

9.4 Discuss why converting a base-class pointer to a derived-class pointer is considered dangerous by the compiler.

> **ANS:** The pointer must point to the object of the derived class, before being dereferenced. When the compiler looks at an object through a derived-class pointer, it expects to see all the pieces of the derived class. However, if the base-class pointer originally pointed to a base-class object, the additional pieces added by the derived class do not exist.

9.5 Distinguish between single inheritance and multiple inheritance.

> **ANS:** Single inheritance inherits from one class only. Multiple inheritance inherits from two or more classes.

9.6 (True/False) A derived class is often called a subclass because it represents a subset of its base class, i.e., a derived class is generally smaller than its base class.

> **ANS:** False. Derived classes are often larger than their base classes, because they need specific features in addition to those inherited from the base class. The term subclass means that the derived class is a more specific version of its base class. For example, a car is a specific type of vehicle.

9.7 (True/False) A derived-class object is also an object of that derived class's base class.

> **ANS:** True.

9.8   Some programmers prefer not to use **protected** access because it breaks the encapsulation of the base class. Discuss the relative merits of using **protected** access vs. insisting on using **private** access in base classes.

> ANS: Inherited **private** data is hidden in the derived class and is accessible only through the **public** or **protected** members functions of the base class. Using **protected** access enables the derived class to manipulate the **protected** members without using the access functions of the base class. If the base class members are **private**, the member functions of the base class must be used to access the data. This may result in a decrease in performance due to the extra function calls.

9.9   Many programs written with inheritance could be solved with composition instead, and vice versa. Discuss the relative merits of these approaches in the context of the **Point, Circle, Cylinder** class hierarchy in this chapter. Rewrite the program of Fig. 9.10 (and the supporting classes) to use composition rather than inheritance. After you do this, reassess the relative merits of the two approaches both for the **Point, Circle, Cylinder** problem and for object-oriented programs in general.

> ANS:

```
// P9_9.H
#ifndef P9_9_H
#define P9_9_H

class Point {
    friend ostream &operator<<(ostream &, const Point &);
public:
    Point(float a = 0, float b = 0) { setPoint(a, b); }
    void setPoint(float, float);
    void print(void) const;
    float getX(void) const { return x; }
    float getY(void) const { return y; }
private:
    float x, y;
};


#endif
```

```
// P9_9PM.cpp
// Member functions for class Point
#include <iostream.h>
#include "p9_9.h"

void Point::setPoint(float a, float b)
{
    x = a;
    y = b;
}


ostream &operator<<(ostream &output, const Point &p)
{
    p.print();
    return output;
}


void Point::print(void) const
    { cout << '[' << getX() << ", " << getY() << ']'; }
```

```
// P9_9C.H
#ifndef P9_9C_H
#define P9_9C_H
#include "p9_9.h"

class Circle {
   friend ostream &operator<<(ostream &, const Circle &);
public:
   Circle(float = 0.0, float = 0.0, float = 0.0);
   void setRadius(float r) { radius = r; }
   float getRadius(void) const { return radius; }
   float area(void) const;
   void print(void) const;
private:
   float radius;
   Point pointObject;
};

#endif
```

```
// P9_9CM.cpp
// Member function definitions for class Circle
#include <iostream.h>
#include <iomanip.h>
#include "p9_9c.h"

Circle::Circle(float r, float a, float b) : pointObject(a, b)
   { setRadius(r); }

float Circle::area(void) const
   { return 3.14159 * getRadius() * getRadius(); }

ostream &operator<<(ostream &output, const Circle &c)
{
   c.print();
   return output;
}

void Circle::print(void) const
{
   cout << "Center = ";
   pointObject.print();
   cout << "; Radius = " << setiosflags(ios::showpoint)
        << setprecision(2) << getRadius();
}
```

```
// P9_9CY.H
#ifndef P9_9CY_H
#define P9_9CY_H
#include "p9_9.h"
#include "p9_9c.h"

class Cylinder {
   friend ostream& operator<<(ostream&, const Cylinder&);
public:
   Cylinder(float = 0.0, float = 0.0, float = 0.0, float = 0.0);
   void setHeight(float h) { height = h; }
   float getHeight(void) const { return height; }
   void print(void) const;
   float area(void) const;
   float volume(void) const;
private:
   float height;
   Circle circleObject;
};

#endif
```

```cpp
// P9_9CYM.cpp
// Member function definitions for class Cylinder.
#include <iostream.h>
#include <iomanip.h>
#include "p9_9cy.h"

Cylinder::Cylinder(float h, float r, float x, float y)
    : circleObject(r, x, y) { height = h; }

float Cylinder::area(void) const
    { return 2 * circleObject.area() + 2 * 3.14159 *
      circleObject.getRadius() * getHeight(); }

ostream& operator<<(ostream &output, const Cylinder& c)
{
    c.print();

    return output;
}

float Cylinder::volume(void) const
    { return circleObject.area() * getHeight(); }

void Cylinder::print(void) const
{
    circleObject.print();
    cout << "; Height = " << getHeight() << endl;
}
```

```cpp
// P9_9.cpp
#include <iostream.h>
#include <iomanip.h>
#include "p9_9.h"
#include "p9_9c.h"
#include "p9_9cy.h"

main()
{
    Point p(1.1, 8.5);
    Circle c(2.0, 6.4, 9.8);
    Cylinder cyl(5.7, 2.5, 1.2, 2.3);

    cout << "Point: " << p << endl << "Circle: " << c << endl
         << "Cylinder: " << cyl << endl;

    return 0;
}
```

```
Point: [1.1, 8.5]
Circle: Center = [6.4, 9.8]; Radius = 2
Cylinder: Center = [1.2, 2.3]; Radius = 2.5; Height = 5.7
```

9.10   Rewrite the **Point, Circle, Cylinder** program of Fig. 9.10 as a **Point, Square, Cube** program. Do this two ways—once with inheritance and once with composition.

```
ANS:
// Inheritance Solution
// P9_10.H
#ifndef P9_10_H
#define P9_10_H

class Point {
    friend ostream &operator<<(ostream&, const Point&);
public:
    Point(float = 0, float = 0, float = 0);
    void setPoint(float, float, float);
    float getX(void) const { return x; }
    float getY(void) const { return y; }
    float getZ(void) const { return z; }
private:
    float x, y, z;
};

#endif
```

```
//P9_10MP.cpp
// member function definitions for class Point
#include <iostream.h>
#include <iomanip.h>
#include "p9_10.h"

Point::Point(float a, float b, float c) { setPoint(a, b, c); }

void Point::setPoint(float a, float b, float c)
{
    x = a;
    y = b;
    z = c;
}

ostream &operator<<(ostream &output, const Point &p)
{
    output << setiosflags(ios::fixed | ios::showpoint)
           << "The point is: [" << setprecision(2) << p.x
           << ", " << setprecision(2) << p.y << setprecision(2)
           << ", " << p.z << ']' << endl;
    return output;
}
```

```
//P9_10S.H
#ifndef P9_10S_H
#define P9_10S_H
#include "p9_10.h"

class Square : public Point {
    friend ostream &operator<<(ostream &, const Square &);
public:
    Square(float = 0, float = 0, float = 0, float = 1.0);
    void setSide(float s) { side = s > 0 && s <= 20.0 ? s : 1.0; }
    float area(void) const { return side * side; }
    float getSide(void) const { return side; }
protected:
    float side;
};

#endif
```

```cpp
//P9_10MS.cpp
//member functions for class Square
#include <iostream.h>
#include <iomanip.h>
#include "p9_10s.h"

Square::Square(float x, float y, float z, float s) : Point(x, y, z)
   { setSide(s); }

ostream &operator<<(ostream &output, const Square &s)
{
    output << setiosflags(ios::fixed | ios::showpoint)
           << "The lower left coordinate of the square is: ["
           << setprecision(2) << s.getX() << ", " << setprecision(2)
           << s.getY() << ", " << setprecision(2) << s.getZ() << ']'
           << endl << "The square side is: " << setprecision(2) << s.side
           << endl << "The area of the square is: " << setprecision(2)
           << s.area() << endl;
    return output;
}
```

```cpp
// P9_10C.H
#ifndef P9_10C_H
#define P9_10C_H
#include "p9_10s.h"

class Cube : public Square {
    friend ostream &operator<<(ostream&, const Cube&);
public:
    Cube(float = 0, float = 0, float = 0, float = 1.0);
    float area(void) const { return 6 * Square::area(); }
    float volume(void) const { return Square::area() * getSide(); }
};

#endif
```

```cpp
//P9_10MC.cpp
//member function definitions for class Cube
#include <iostream.h>
#include <iomanip.h>
#include "p9_10c.h"

Cube::Cube(float j, float k, float m, float s) : Square(j, k, m, s) { }

ostream &operator<<(ostream &output, const Cube &c)
{
    output << setiosflags(ios::fixed | ios::showpoint)
           << "The lower left coordinate of the cube is: ["
           << setprecision(2) << c.getX() << ", " << setprecision(2)
           << c.getY() << ", " << setprecision(2) << c.getZ() << ']' << endl
           << "The cube side is: " << setprecision(2) << c.side << endl
           << "The surface area of the cube is: " << setprecision(2)
           << c.area() << endl << "The volume of the cube is: "
           << setprecision(2) << c.volume() << endl;

    return output;
}
```

```
// driver for p9_10.cpp
#include <iostream.h>
#include <iomanip.h>
#include "p9_10.h"
#include "p9_10s.h"
#include "p9_10c.h"

main()
{
    Point p(7.9, 12.5, 8.8);
    Square s(0.0, 0.0, 0.0, 5.0);
    Cube c(0.5, 8.3, 12.0, 2.0);

    cout << p << endl << s << endl << c;
    return 0;
}
```

```
The point is: [7.90, 12.50, 8.80]

The lower left coordinate of the square is: [0.00, 0.00, 0.00]
The square side is: 5.00
The area of the square is: 25.00

The lower left coordinate of the cube is: [0.50, 8.30, 12.00]
The cube side is: 2.00
The surface area of the cube is: 24.00
The volume of the cube is: 8.00
```

```
// Composition solution
// P9_10B.H
#ifndef P9_10B_H
#define P9_10B_H

class Point {
    friend ostream &operator<<(ostream&, const Point&);
public:
    Point(float = 0, float = 0, float = 0);
    void setPoint(float, float, float);
    void print(void) const;
    float getX(void) const { return x; }
    float getY(void) const { return y; }
    float getZ(void) const { return z; }
private:
    float x, y, z;
};

#endif
```

```
//P9_10BMP.cpp
// member function definitions for class Point
#include <iostream.h>
#include <iomanip.h>
#include "p9_10b.h"

Point::Point(float a, float b, float c) { setPoint(a, b, c); }

void Point::setPoint(float a, float b, float c)
{
    x = a;
    y = b;
    z = c;
}
```

```
ostream &operator<<(ostream &output, const Point &p)
{
   output << "The point is: ";
   p.print();
   return output;
}

void Point::print(void) const
{
   cout << setiosflags(ios::fixed | ios::showpoint)
        << '[' << setprecision(2) << getX()
        << ", " << setprecision(2) << getY() << setprecision(2)
        << ", " << getZ() << ']' << endl;
}
```

```
//P9_10BS.H
#ifndef P9_10BS_H
#define P9_10BS_H
#include "p9_10B.h"

class Square {
   friend ostream &operator<<(ostream &, const Square &);
public:
   Square(float = 0, float = 0, float = 0, float = 1.0);
   void setSide(float s) { side = s > 0 && s <= 20.0 ? s : 1.0; }
   void print(void) const;
   float getXCoord() const { return pointObject.getX(); }
   float getYCoord() const { return pointObject.getY(); }
   float getZCoord() const { return pointObject.getZ(); }
   float area(void) const { return side * side; }
   float getSide(void) const { return side; }
protected:
   float side;
   Point pointObject;
};

#endif
```

```
//P9_10BMS.cpp
//member functions for class Square
#include <iostream.h>
#include <iomanip.h>
#include "p9_10bs.h"

Square::Square(float x, float y, float z, float s) : pointObject(x, y, z)
   { setSide(s); }

ostream &operator<<(ostream &output, const Square &s)
{
   s.print();
   return output;
}

void Square::print(void) const
{
   cout << setiosflags(ios::fixed | ios::showpoint)
        << "The lower left coordinate of the square is: ";
   pointObject.print();
   cout << "The square side is: " << setprecision(2) << getSide()
        << endl << "The area of the square is: " << setprecision(2)
        << area() << endl;
}
```

```cpp
// P9_10BC.H
#ifndef P9_10BC_H
#define P9_10BC_H
#include "p9_10bs.h"

class Cube {
   friend ostream &operator<<(ostream&, const Cube&);
public:
   Cube(float = 0, float = 0, float = 0, float = 1.0);
   void print(void) const;
   float area(void) const;
   float volume(void) const;
private:
   Square squareObject;
};

#endif
```

```cpp
//P9_10BMC.cpp
//member function definitions for class Cube
#include <iostream.h>
#include <iomanip.h>
#include "p9_10bc.h"

Cube::Cube(float j, float k, float m, float s)
   : squareObject(j, k, m, s) { }

ostream &operator<<(ostream &output, const Cube &c)
{
   c.print();
   return output;
}

void Cube::print(void) const
{
   cout << setiosflags(ios::fixed | ios::showpoint)
        << "The lower left coordinate of the cube is: ["
        << setprecision(2) << squareObject.getXCoord() << ", "
        << setprecision(2) << squareObject.getYCoord() << ", "
        << setprecision(2) << squareObject.getZCoord() << ']' << endl
        << "The cube side is: " << setprecision(2) << squareObject.getSide()
        << endl << "The surface area of the cube is: " << setprecision(2)
        << area() << endl << "The volume of the cube is: "
        << setprecision(2) << volume() << endl;
}

float Cube::area(void) const
   { return 6 * squareObject.area(); }

float Cube::volume(void) const
   { return squareObject.area() * squareObject.getSide(); }
```

```cpp
// driver for p9_10b.cpp
#include <iostream.h>
#include <iomanip.h>
#include "p9_10b.h"
#include "p9_10bs.h"
#include "p9_10bc.h"
```

```
main()
{
    Point p(7.9, 12.5, 8.8);
    Square s(0.0, 0.0, 0.0, 5.0);
    Cube c(0.5, 8.3, 12.0, 2.0);

    cout << p << endl << s << endl << c << endl;
    return 0;
}
```

```
The point is: [7.90, 12.50, 8.80]

The lower left coordinate of the square is: [0.00, 0.00, 0.00]
The square side is: 5.00
The area of the square is: 25.00

The lower left coordinate of the cube is: [0.50, 8.30, 12.00]
The cube side is: 2.00
The surface area of the cube is: 24.00
The volume of the cube is: 8.00
```

9.11   In the chapter, we stated "When a base-class member is inappropriate for a derived class, that member can be redefined in the derived class with an appropriate implementation." If this is done, does the derived-class-is-a-base-class-object relationship still hold? Explain your answer.

   ANS: No the "derived-class-is-a-base-class-object relationship" does not hold any longer. This relationship assumes that everything that belongs to a base class object belongs to the derived class object also and that all functionality of a base class object is present in the derived class object as well.

9.12   Study the inheritance hierarchy of Fig. 9.2. For each class, indicate some common attributes and behaviors consistent with the hierarchy. Add some other classes (i.e., **UndergraduateStudent**, **GraduateStudent**, **Freshman**, **Sophomore**, **Junior**, **Senior**, etc. to enrich the hierarchy.

   ANS:

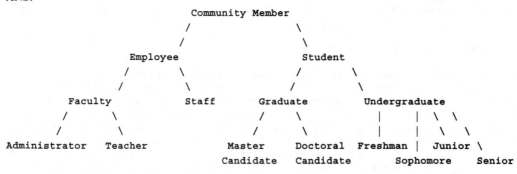

9.13   Write an inheritance hierarchy for class **Quadrilateral**, **Trapezoid**, **Parallelogram**, **Rectangle**, and **Square**. Use **Quadrilateral** as the base class of the hierarchy. Make the hierarchy as deep (i.e., as many levels) as possible. The private data of **Quadrilateral** should be the *(x, y)* coordinate pairs for the four endpoints of the **Quadrilateral**. Write a driver program that instantiates and displays objects of each of these classes.

   ANS:

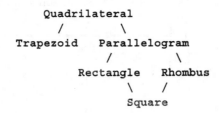

```
// P9_13.H
#ifndef P9_13_H
#define P9_13_H
#include <iostream.h>

class Point {
    friend ostream &operator<<(ostream&, const Point&);
public:
    Point(float = 0, float = 0);
    void setPoint(float, float);
    void print(void) const;
    float getX(void) const { return x; }
    float getY(void) const { return y; }
private:
    float x, y;
};

#endif
```

```
//P9_13PM.cpp
// member function definitions for class Point
#include <iostream.h>
#include <iomanip.h>
#include "p9_13.h"

Point::Point(float a, float b) { setPoint(a, b); }

void Point::setPoint(float a, float b)
{
    x = a;
    y = b;
}

ostream &operator<<(ostream &output, const Point &p)
{
    output << "The point is: ";
    p.print();
    return output;
}

void Point::print(void) const
{
    cout << setiosflags(ios::fixed | ios::showpoint)
         << '[' << setprecision(2) << getX()
         << ", " << setprecision(2) << getY() << ']' << endl;
}
```

```
// P9_13Q.H
#ifndef P9_13Q_H
#define P9_13Q_H
#include "p9_13.h"

class Quadrilateral {
    friend ostream &operator<<(ostream&, Quadrilateral&);
public:
    Quadrilateral(float = 0, float = 0, float = 0, float = 0, float = 0,
                  float = 0, float = 0, float = 0);
    void print(void) const;
protected:
    Point p1;
    Point p2;
    Point p3;
    Point p4;
};

#endif
```

```cpp
// P9_13QM.cpp
// member functions for class Quadrilateral
#include "p9_13q.h"

Quadrilateral::Quadrilateral(float x1, float y1, float x2, float y2,
                             float x3, float y3, float x4, float y4)
   : p1(x1, y1), p2(x2, y2), p3(x3, y3), p4(x4, y4)   { }

ostream &operator<<(ostream& output, Quadrilateral& q)
{
   output << "Coordinates of Quadrilateral are: " << endl;
   q.print();
   output << endl;
   return output;
}

void Quadrilateral::print(void) const
{
   cout << '(' << p1.getX()
        << ", " << p1.getY() << ") , (" << p2.getX() << ", " << p2.getY()
        << ") , (" << p3.getX() << ", " << p3.getY() << ") , ("
        << p4.getX() << ", " << p4.getY() << ')' << endl;
}
```

```cpp
// P9_13T.H
#ifndef P9_13T_H
#define P9_13T_H
#include "p9_13q.h"

class Trapazoid : public Quadrilateral {
   friend ostream& operator<<(ostream&, Trapazoid&);
public:
   Trapazoid(float = 0, float = 0, float = 0, float = 0, float = 0,
             float = 0, float = 0, float = 0, float = 0);
   void print(void) const;
   void setHeight(float h) { height = h; }
   float getHeight(void) const { return height; }
private:
   float height;
};


#endif
```

```cpp
// P9_13TM.cpp
// member function definitions for class Trapazoid
#include "p9_13t.h"

Trapazoid::Trapazoid(float h, float x1, float y1, float x2, float y2,
                     float x3, float y3, float x4, float y4)
         : Quadrilateral(x1, y1, x2, y2, x3, y3, x4, y4)
{ setHeight(h); }

ostream& operator<<(ostream& out, Trapazoid& t)
{
   out << "The Coordinates of the Trapazoid are: " << endl;
   t.print();
   return out;
}
```

```
void Trapazoid::print(void) const
{
   Quadrilateral::print();
   cout << "Height is : " << getHeight() << endl << endl;
}
```

```
// P9_13PA_H
#ifndef P9_13PA_H
#define P9_13PA_H
#include "p9_13q.h"

class Parallelogram : public Quadrilateral {
   friend ostream& operator<<(ostream&, Parallelogram&);
public:
   Parallelogram(float = 0, float = 0, float = 0, float = 0,
                 float = 0, float = 0, float = 0, float = 0);
   void print(void) const;
private:
   // no private data members
};

#endif
```

```
// P9_13PAM.cpp
#include "p9_13q.h"
#include "p9_13pa.h"

Parallelogram::Parallelogram(float x1, float y1, float x2, float y2,
                             float x3, float y3, float x4, float y4)
   : Quadrilateral(x1, y1, x2, y2, x3, y3, x4, y4) { }

ostream& operator<<(ostream& out, Parallelogram& pa)
{
   out << "The coordinates of the Parallelogram are: " << endl;
   pa.print();
   return out;
}

void Parallelogram::print(void) const
   {   Quadrilateral::print(); }
```

```
// P9_13R.H
#ifndef P9_13R_H
#define P9_13R_H
#include "p9_13pa.h"

class Rectangle : public Parallelogram {
   friend ostream& operator<<(ostream&, Rectangle&);
public:
   Rectangle(float = 0, float = 0, float = 0, float = 0,
             float = 0, float = 0, float = 0, float = 0);
   void print(void) const;
private:
   // no private data members
};

#endif
```

```cpp
// P9_13RM.cpp
#include "p9_13r.h"
#include "p9_13pa.h"
Rectangle::Rectangle(float x1, float y1, float x2, float y2,
                     float x3, float y3, float x4, float y4)
   : Parallelogram(x1, y1, x2, y2, x3, y3, x4, y4) { }

ostream& operator<<(ostream& out, Rectangle& r)
{
   out << endl << "The coordinates of the Rectangle are: " << endl;
   r.print();
   return out;
}

void Rectangle::print(void) const { Parallelogram::print(); }
```

```cpp
// P9_13RH.H
#ifndef P9_13RH_H
#define P9_13RH_H
#include "p9_13pa.h"

class Rhombus : public Parallelogram {
   friend ostream& operator<<(ostream&, Rhombus&);
public:
   Rhombus(float = 0, float = 0, float = 0, float = 0, float = 0,
           float = 0, float = 0, float = 0);
   void print(void) const { Parallelogram::print(); }
private:
   // no private data members
};

#endif
```

```cpp
//P9_13HM.cpp
#include "p9_13rh.h"
#include "p9_13pa.h"

Rhombus::Rhombus(float x1, float y1, float x2, float y2, float x3, float y3,
                 float x4, float y4)
   : Parallelogram(x1, y1, x2, y2, x3, y3, x4, y4) { }

ostream& operator<<(ostream& out, Rhombus& r)
{
   out << endl << "The coordinates of the Rhombus are: " << endl;
   r.print();
   return out;
}
```

```cpp
// P9_13S.H
#ifndef P9_13S_H
#define P9_13S_H
#include "p9_13pa.h"

class Square : public Parallelogram {
   friend ostream& operator<<(ostream&, Square&);
public:
   Square(float = 0, float = 0, float = 0, float = 0,
          float = 0, float = 0, float = 0, float = 0);
   void print(void) const { Parallelogram::print(); }
private:
   // no private data members
};

#endif
```

```
// P9_13SM.cpp
#include "p9_13s.h"
#include "p9_13pa.h"

Square::Square(float x1, float y1, float x2, float y2,
               float x3, float y3, float x4, float y4)
   : Parallelogram(x1, y1, x2, y2, x3, y3, x4, y4) { }

ostream& operator<<(ostream& out, Square& s)
{
   out << endl << "The coordinates of the Square are: " << endl;
   s.print();
   return out;
}
```

```
// P9_13.cpp
#include "p9_13.h"
#include "p9_13q.h"
#include "p9_13t.h"
#include "p9_13pa.h"
#include "p9_13rh.h"
#include "p9_13r.h"
#include "p9_13s.h"

main()
{
   // NOTE: All coordinates are assumed to form the proper shapes

   // A quadrilateral is a four-sided polygon
   Quadrilateral q(1.1, 1.2, 6.6, 2.8, 6.2, 9.9, 2.2, 7.4);
   // A trapezoid is a quadrilateral having two and only two parallel sides
   Trapezoid t(5.0, 0.0, 0.0, 10.0, 0.0, 8.0, 5.0, 3.3, 5.0);
   // A parallelogram is a quadrilateral whose opposite sides are parallel
   Parallelogram p(5.0, 5.0, 11.0, 5.0, 12.0, 20.0, 6.0, 20.0);
   // A rhombus is an equilateral parallelogram
   Rhombus rh(0.0, 0.0, 5.0, 0.0, 8.5, 3.5, 3.5, 3.5);
   // A rectangle is an equiangular parallelogram
   Rectangle r(17.0, 14.0, 30.0, 14.0, 30.0, 28.0, 17.0, 28.0);
   // A square is an equiangular and equilateral parallelogram
   Square s(4.0, 0.0, 8.0, 0.0, 8.0, 4.0, 4.0, 4.0);

   cout << q << t << p << rh << r << s << endl;
   return 0;
}
```

```
Coordinates of Quadrilateral are:
(1.1, 1.2) , (6.6, 2.8) , (6.2, 9.9) , (2.2, 7.4)

The Coordinates of the Trapazoid are:
(0, 0) , (10, 0) , (8, 5) , (3.3, 5)
Height is : 5

The coordinates of the Parallelogram are:
(5, 5) , (11, 5) , (12, 20) , (6, 20)

The coordinates of the Rhombus are:
(0, 0) , (5, 0) , (8.5, 3.5) , (3.5, 3.5)

The coordinates of the Rectangle are:
(17, 14) , (30, 14) , (30, 28) , (17, 28)

The coordinates of the Square are:
(4, 0) , (8, 0) , (8, 4) , (4, 4)
```

9.14   Write down all the shapes you can think of—both two-dimensional and three-dimensional—and form those shapes into a shape hierarchy. Your hierarchy should have base class **Shape** from which class **TwoDimensional-Shape** and class **ThreeDimensionalShape** are derived. Once you have developed the hierarchy, define each of the classes in the hierarchy. We will use this hierarchy in the exercises of Chapter 10 to process all shapes as objects of base-class **Shape**. This is a technique called polymorphism.

ANS:
```
Shape
   TwoDimensional
      Quadrilateral
            Parallelogram
                  Rectangle
                        Square
                  Rhombus
            Trapezoid
      Ellipse
            Circle
      Triangle
      etc...
   ThreeDimensional
      Ellipsoid
            Sphere
      Prism
      Cylinder
      Cone
      Cube
      Tetrahedron
   etc...
```

10
Virtual Functions and Polymorphism: Solutions

Exercises

10.2 What are virtual functions? Describe a circumstance in which virtual functions would be appropriate.

ANS: Virtual functions are functions with the same function prototype that are defined throughout a class hierarchy. At least the base class occurrence of the function is preceded by the keyword virtual. Virtual functions are used to enable generic processing of an entire class hierarchy of objects through a base class pointer. For example, in a shape hierarchy, all shapes can be printed. If all shapes are derived from a base class **Shape** and all shape classes have a virtual print function, then generic processing of the hierarchy can be performed.

10.3 Given that constructors cannot be virtual, describe a scheme for how you might achieve a similar effect.

ANS: Create a virtual function called **initialize** that is called from the constructor function.

10.4 How is it that polymorphism enables you to program "in the general" rather than "in the specific." Discuss the key advantages of programming "in the general."

ANS: Polymorphism enables the programmer to concentrate on the processing of common operations that are applied to all data types in the system without going into the individual details of each data type. The general processing capabilities are separated from the internal details of each type.

10.5 Discuss the problems of programming with **switch** logic. Explain why polymorphism is an effective alternative to using **switch** logic.

ANS: The main problem with programming using the **switch** structure is the extensibility and maintainability of the program. A program containing many **switch** structures is difficult to modify. All the structures must be modified to handle the processing of an additional type or of one less type.

10.6 Distinguish between static binding and dynamic binding. Explain the use of virtual functions and the vtable in dynamic binding.

ANS: Static binding is performed at compile-time when a function is called via a specific object or via a pointer to a specific object. Dynamic binding is performed at run-time when a virtual function is called via a base-class pointer to a derived-class object (the object can be of any of the types derived from the base class). The virtual function table (vtable) is used at run-time to enable the proper function to be called for the object to which the base-class pointer points. Each class containing virtual functions has its own vtable that specifies where the virtual functions that are specific to that class are located. Every object of a class with virtual functions contains a hidden pointer to the class's vtable. When a virtual function is called via a base-class pointer, the hidden pointer is dereferenced to locate the vtable, then the vtable is searched for the proper function to call.

10.7 Distinguish between inheriting interface and inheriting implementation. How do inheritance hierarchies designed for inheriting interface differ from those designed for inheriting implementation?

ANS: When a class inherits implementation, it inherits previously defined functionality from another class. When a class inherits interface, it inherits the definition of what the interface to the new class type should be. The implementation is then provided by the programmer defining the new class type.

Inheritance hierarchies designed for inheriting implementation are used to reduce the amount of new code that is being written. Such hierarchies are commonly used to facilitate software reusability.

Inheritance hierarchies designed for inheriting interface are used to write programs the perform generic processing of many class types. Such hierarchies are commonly used to facilitate software extensibility (i.e., new types can be added to the hierarchy without changing the generic processing capabilities of the program).

10.8   Distinguish between virtual functions and pure virtual functions.

ANS: A virtual function must have a definition in the class in which it is declared.

Pure virtual functions are used to create abstract base classes. Definitions are not provided for pure virtual functions. Classes derived directly from an abstract base class must provide a definition of the pure virtual function; otherwise, such classes also become abstract base classes.

10.9   (True/False) All virtual functions in an abstract base class must be declared as pure virtual functions.

ANS: False.

10.10   Suggest one or more levels of abstract base classes for the **Shape** hierarchy discussed in this chapter (the first level is **Shape** and the second level consists of the classes **TwoDimensionalShape** and **ThreeDimensionalShape**).

10.11   How does polymorphism promote extensibility?

ANS: Polymorphism makes programs more extensible by making all function calls generic. When a new class type with the appropriate virtual functions is added to the hierarchy, no changes need to be made to the generic function calls.

10.12   You have been asked to develop a flight simulator that will have elaborate graphical outputs. Explain why polymorphic programming would be especially effective for a problem of this nature.

10.13   Develop a basic graphics package. Use the **Shape** class inheritance hierarchy from Chapter 9. Limit yourself to two-dimensional shapes such as squares, rectangles, triangles, and circles. Interact with the user. Let the user specify the position, size, shape, and fill characters to be used in drawing each shape. The user can specify many items of the same shape. As you create each shape, place a **Shape *** pointer to each new **Shape** object into an array. Each class has its own **draw** member function. Write a polymorphic screen manager that walks through the array (preferably using an iterator) sending **draw** messages to each object in the array to form a screen image. Redraw the screen image each time the user specifies an additional shape.

10.14   Modify the payroll system of Fig. 10.1 to add private data members **birthDate** (a **Date** object) and **departmentCode** (an **int**) to class **Employee**. Assume this payroll is processed once per month. Then, as your program calculates the payroll for each **Employee** (polymorphically), add a $100.00 bonus to the person's payroll amount if this is the month in which the **Employee**'s birthday occurs.

ANS:
```
// BOSS.H
// Boss class derived from Employee
#ifndef BOSS_H
#define BOSS_H
#include "employ.h"

class Boss : public Employee {
public:
   Boss(const char *, const char *, int, int, int, float = 0.0, int = 0);
   void setWeeklySalary(float);
   virtual float earnings() const;
   virtual void print() const;
private:
   float weeklySalary;
};


#endif
```

```
// BOSS.CPP
// Member function definitions for class Boss
#include <iostream.h>
#include "boss.h"

// Constructor function for class Boss
Boss::Boss(const char *first, const char *last, int mn, int dy,
          int yr, float s, int dept)
   : Employee(first, last, mn, dy, yr, dept)
{ weeklySalary = s > 0 ? s : 0; }

void Boss::setWeeklySalary(float s)
   { weeklySalary = s > 0 ? s : 0; }

// Get the Boss's pay
float Boss::earnings() const { return weeklySalary; }

// Print the Boss's name
void Boss::print() const
{
   cout << endl << "              Boss: " << getFirstName()
        << ' ' << getLastName();
}
```

```
// COMMIS.H
// CommissionWorker class derived from Employee
#ifndef COMMIS_H
#define COMMIS_H
#include "employ.h"

class CommissionWorker : public Employee {
public:
   CommissionWorker(const char *, const char *, int, int, int,
                    float = 0.0, float = 0.0, unsigned = 0, int = 0);
   void setSalary(float);
   void setCommission(float);
   void setQuantity(unsigned);
   virtual float earnings() const;
   virtual void print() const;
private:
   float salary;       // base salary per week
   float commission;   // amount per item sold
   unsigned quantity;  // total items sold for week
};

#endif
```

```
// COMMIS.CPP
// Member function definitions for class CommissionWorker
#include <iostream.h>
#include "commis.h"

// Constructor for class CommissionWorker
CommissionWorker::CommissionWorker(const char *first,
       const char *last, int mn, int dy, int yr,
       float s, float c, unsigned q, int dept)
   : Employee(first, last, mn, dy, yr, dept)
{
   salary = s > 0 ? s : 0;
   commission = c > 0 ? c : 0;
   quantity = q > 0 ? q : 0;
}
```

```cpp
// Set CommissionWorker's weekly base salary
void CommissionWorker::setSalary(float s)
   { salary = s > 0 ? s : 0; }

// Set CommissionWorker's commission
void CommissionWorker::setCommission(float c)
   { commission = c > 0 ? c : 0; }

// Set CommissionWorker's quantity sold
void CommissionWorker::setQuantity(unsigned q)
   { quantity = q > 0 ? q : 0; }

// Determine CommissionWorker's earnings
float CommissionWorker::earnings() const
   { return salary + commission * quantity; }

// Print the CommissionWorker's name
void CommissionWorker::print() const
{
   cout << endl << "Commission worker: " << getFirstName()
        << ' ' << getLastName();
}
```

```cpp
// DATE.H
// Declaration of the Date class.
// Member functions defined in DATE1.CPP
#ifndef DATE_H
#define DATE_H

class Date {
public:
   Date(int = 1, int = 1, int = 1900);  // default constructor
   int getMonth() const; // return the month
   int getDay() const;   // return the day
   int getYear()const;   // return the year
   void print() const;    // print date in month/day/year format
private:
   int month;  // 1-12
   int day;    // 1-31 based on month
   int year;   // any year

   // utility function to test proper day for month and year
   int checkDay(int);
};

#endif
```

```cpp
// DATE.CPP
// Member function definitions for Date class.
#include <iostream.h>
#include "date.h"

// Constructor: Confirm proper value for month;
// call utility function checkDay to confirm proper value for day.
Date::Date(int mn, int dy, int yr)
{
   if (mn > 0 && mn <= 12)            // validate the month
      month = mn;
   else {
      month = 1;
      cout << "Month " << mn << " invalid. Set to month 1." << endl;
   }
   year = yr >= 1900 && yr <= 2100 ? yr : 1990;
   day = checkDay(dy);                // validate the day
}
```

```cpp
// Utility function to confirm proper day value based on month and year.
int Date::checkDay(int testDay)
{
    int daysPerMonth[13] = {0, 31, 28, 31, 30, 31, 30,
                            31, 31, 30, 31, 30, 31};

    if (testDay > 0 && testDay <= daysPerMonth[month])
        return testDay;

    if (month == 2 &&        // February: Check for possible leap year
        testDay == 29 &&
        (year % 400 == 0 || (year % 4 == 0 && year % 100 != 0)))
        return testDay;

    cout << "Day " << testDay << " invalid. Set to day 1." << endl;

    return 1;   // leave object in consistent state if bad value
}

// Return the month
int Date::getMonth() const { return month; }

// Return the day
int Date::getDay() const { return day; }

// Return the year
int Date::getYear() const { return year; }

// Print Date object in form  month/day/year
void Date::print() const
    { cout << month << '/' << day << '/' << year; }
```

```cpp
// EMPLOY.H
// Abstract base class Employee
#ifndef EMPLOY_H
#define EMPLOY_H

#include "date.h"

class Employee {
public:
    Employee(const char *, const char *, int, int, int, int);
    ~Employee();
    const char *getFirstName() const;
    const char *getLastName() const;
    Date getBirthDate() const;
    int getDepartmentCode() const;

    // Pure virtual functions make Employee abstract base class.
    virtual float earnings() const = 0; // pure virtual
    virtual void print() const = 0;     // pure virtual
private:
    char *firstName;
    char *lastName;
    Date birthDate;
    int departmentCode;
};


#endif
```

```
// EMPLOY.CPP
// Member function definitions for
// abstract base class Employee.
//
// Note: No definitions given for pure virtual functions.
#include <iostream.h>
#include <string.h>
#include <assert.h>
#include "employ.h"


// Constructor dynamically allocates space for the
// first and last name and uses strcpy to copy
// the first and last names into the object.
Employee::Employee(const char *first, const char *last,
                     int mn, int dy, int yr, int dept)
   : birthDate(mn, dy, yr), departmentCode(dept)
{
   firstName = new char[ strlen(first) + 1 ];
   assert(firstName != 0);     // test that new worked
   strcpy(firstName, first);

   lastName = new char[ strlen(last) + 1 ];
   assert(lastName != 0);      // test that new worked
   strcpy(lastName, last);
}


// Destructor deallocates dynamically allocated memory
Employee::~Employee()
{
   delete [] firstName;
   delete [] lastName;
}

// Return a pointer to the first name
const char *Employee::getFirstName() const
{
   // Const prevents caller from modifying private data.
   // Caller should copy returned string before destructor
   // deletes dynamic storage to prevent undefined pointer.

   return firstName;   // caller must delete memory
}


// Return a pointer to the last name
const char *Employee::getLastName() const
{
   // Const prevents caller from modifying private data.
   // Caller should copy returned string before destructor
   // deletes dynamic storage to prevent undefined pointer.

   return lastName;    // caller must delete memory
}

// Return the employee's birth date
Date Employee::getBirthDate() const { return birthDate; }

// Return the employee's department code
int Employee::getDepartmentCode() const { return departmentCode; }
```

```
// HOURLY.H
// Definition of class HourlyWorker
#ifndef HOURLY_H
#define HOURLY_H
#include "employ.h"

class HourlyWorker : public Employee {
public:
   HourlyWorker(const char *, const char *, int, int, int,
                float = 0.0, float = 0.0, int = 0);
   void setWage(float);
   void setHours(float);
   virtual float earnings() const;
   virtual void print() const;
private:
   float wage;    // wage per hour
   float hours;   // hours worked for week
};

#endif
```

```
// HOURLY.CPP
// Member function definitions for class HourlyWorker
#include <iostream.h>
#include "hourly.h"

// Constructor for class HourlyWorker
HourlyWorker::HourlyWorker(const char *first, const char *last, int mn,
                           int dy, int yr, float w, float h, int dept)
   : Employee(first, last, mn, dy, yr, dept)
{
   wage = w > 0 ? w : 0;
   hours = h >= 0 && h < 168 ? h : 0;
}

// Set the wage
void HourlyWorker::setWage(float w) { wage = w > 0 ? w : 0; }

// Set the hours worked
void HourlyWorker::setHours(float h)
   { hours = h >= 0 && h < 168 ? h : 0; }

// Get the HourlyWorker's pay
float HourlyWorker::earnings() const { return wage * hours; }

// Print the HourlyWorker's name
void HourlyWorker::print() const
{
   cout << endl << "    Hourly worker: " << getFirstName()
        << ' ' << getLastName();
}
```

```
// Exercise 10.14 solution
// Driver for Employee hierarchy
#include <iostream.h>
#include <iomanip.h>
#include <time.h>
#include <stdlib.h>
#include "employ.h"
#include "boss.h"
#include "commis.h"
#include "piece.h"
#include "hourly.h"
```

```cpp
int determineMonth();

main()
{
    // set output formatting
    cout << setiosflags(ios::fixed | ios::showpoint) << setprecision(2);

    Boss b("John", "Smith", 6, 15, 44, 800.00, 1);
    CommissionWorker c("Sue", "Jones", 9, 8, 54, 200.0, 3.0, 150, 1);
    PieceWorker p("Bob", "Lewis", 4, 11, 65, 2.5, 200, 1);
    HourlyWorker h("Karen", "Price", 6, 29, 60, 13.75, 40, 1);

    Employee *ptr[4] = {&b, &c, &p, &h};  // base-class array of pointers

    int month = determineMonth();

    cout << "The month is " << month << endl << "The payroll is:" << endl;

    for (int x = 0; x < 4; x++) {
        ptr[x]->print();
        cout << " of department " << ptr[x]->getDepartmentCode()
             << endl << " whose birthday is ";
        ptr[x]->getBirthDate().print();
        cout << " earned ";

        if (ptr[x]->getBirthDate().getMonth() == month)
            cout << ptr[x]->earnings() + 100.0 << " HAPPY BIRTHDAY!" << endl;
        else
            cout << ptr[x]->earnings() << endl;
    }

    return 0;
}

// Determine the current month using standard library functions
// of time.h.
int determineMonth()
{
    time_t currentTime;
    char monthString[3];

    time(&currentTime);
    strftime(monthString, 3, "%m", localtime(&currentTime));
    return atoi(monthString);
}
```

```
The month is 6
The payroll is:

          Boss: John Smith of department 1
 whose birthday is 6/15/1990 earned 900.00 HAPPY BIRTHDAY!

Commission worker: Sue Jones of department 1
 whose birthday is 9/8/1990 earned 650.00

    Piece worker: Bob Lewis of department 1
 whose birthday is 4/11/1990 earned 500.00

    Hourly worker: Karen Price of department 1
 whose birthday is 6/29/1990 earned 650.00 HAPPY BIRTHDAY!
```

10.15   In Exercise 9.14, you developed a **Shape** class hierarchy and defined the classes in the hierarchy. Modify the hierarchy so that class **Shape** is an abstract base class containing the interface to the hierarchy. Derive **TwoDimensionalShape** and **ThreeDimensionalShape** from class **Shape**—these classes should also be abstract. Use a virtual **print** function to output the type and dimensions of each class. Also include virtual **area** and **volume** functions so these calculations can be performed for objects of each concrete class in the hierarchy. Write a driver program that tests the **Shape** class hierarchy.

ANS:

```
// CIRCLE.H
// Definition of class Circle
#ifndef CIRCLE_H
#define CIRCLE_H

#include "twodim.h"

class Circle : public TwoDimensionalShape {
public:
   Circle(double = 0.0, double = 0, double = 0);
   double getRadius() const;
   double area() const;
   void print() const;
private:
   double radius;
};

#endif
```

```
// CIRCLE.CPP
// Member function definitions for Circle
#include "circle.h"

Circle::Circle(double r, double x, double y)
   : TwoDimensionalShape(x, y) { radius = r > 0 ? r : 0; }

double Circle::getRadius() const { return radius; }

double Circle::area() const { return 3.14159 * radius * radius; }

void Circle::print() const
{
   cout << "Circle with radius " << radius << "; center at ("
        << xCenter << ", " << yCenter << "); " << endl
        << " area of " << area() << endl;
}
```

```
// CUBE.H
// Definition of class Cube
#ifndef CUBE.H
#define CUBE.H

#include "threedim.h"

class Cube : public ThreeDimensionalShape {
public:
   Cube(double = 0, double = 0, double = 0);
   double area() const;
   double volume() const;
   double getSideLength() const;
   void print() const;
private:
   double sideLength;
};

#endif
```

```cpp
// CUBE.CPP
// Member function definitions for Cube
#include "cube.h"

Cube::Cube(double s, double x, double y)
   : ThreeDimensionalShape(x, y) { sideLength = s > 0 ? s : 0; }

double Cube::area() const { return sideLength * sideLength; }

double Cube::volume() const
   { return sideLength * sideLength * sideLength; }

double Cube::getSideLength() const { return sideLength; }

void Cube::print() const
{
   cout << "Cube with side length " << sideLength << "; center at ("
        << xCenter << ", " << yCenter << "); " << endl << " area of "
        << area() << "; volume of " << volume() << endl;
}
```

```cpp
// SHAPE.H
// Definition of base-class Shape
#ifndef SHAPE_H
#define SHAPE_H

#include <iostream.h>

class Shape {
   friend ostream & operator<<(ostream &, Shape &);
public:
   Shape(double = 0, double = 0);
   double getCenterX() const;
   double getCenterY() const;
   virtual void print() const = 0;
protected:
   double xCenter;
   double yCenter;
};

#endif
```

```cpp
// SHAPE.CPP
// Member and friend definitions for Shape
#include "shape.h"

Shape::Shape(double x, double y)
{
   xCenter = x;
   yCenter = y;
}

double Shape::getCenterX() const { return xCenter; }

double Shape::getCenterY() const { return yCenter; }

ostream & operator<<(ostream &out, Shape &s)
{
   s.print();
   return out;
}
```

```cpp
// SPHERE.H
// Definition of class Sphere
#ifndef SPHERE_H
#define SPHERE_H

#include "threedim.h"

class Sphere : public ThreeDimensionalShape {
public:
   Sphere(double = 0, double = 0, double = 0);
   double area() const;
   double volume() const;
   double getRadius() const;
   void print() const;
private:
   double radius;
};

#endif
```

```cpp
// SPHERE.CPP
// Member function definitions for Sphere
#include "sphere.h"

Sphere::Sphere(double r, double x, double y)
   : ThreeDimensionalShape(x, y) { radius = r > 0 ? r : 0; }

double Sphere::area() const
   { return 4.0 * 3.14159 * radius * radius; }

double Sphere::volume() const
   { return 4.0/3.0 * 3.14159 * radius * radius * radius; }

double Sphere::getRadius() const { return radius; }

void Sphere::print() const
{
   cout << "Sphere with radius " << radius << "; center at ("
        << xCenter << ", " << yCenter << "); " << endl << " area of "
        << area() << "; volume of " << volume() << endl;
}
```

```cpp
// SQUARE.H
// Definition of class Square
#ifndef SQUARE_H
#define SQUARE_H

#include "twodim.h"

class Square : public TwoDimensionalShape {
public:
   Square(double = 0, double = 0, double = 0);
   double getSideLength() const;
   double area() const;
   void print() const;
private:
   double sideLength;
};

#endif
```

```cpp
// SQUARE.CPP
// Member function definitions for Square
#include "square.h"

Square::Square(double s, double x, double y)
   : TwoDimensionalShape(x, y) { sideLength = s > 0 ? s : 0; }

double Square::getSideLength() const { return sideLength; }

double Square::area() const { return sideLength * sideLength; }

void Square::print() const
{
   cout << "Square with side length " << sideLength << "; center at ("
        << xCenter << ", " << yCenter << "); " << endl
        << " area of " << area() << endl;
}
```

```cpp
// THREEDIM.H
// Definition of class ThreeDimensionalShape
#ifndef THREEDIM_H
#define THREEDIM_H

#include "shape.h"

class ThreeDimensionalShape : public Shape {
public:
   ThreeDimensionalShape(double x, double y) : Shape(x, y) { }
   virtual double area() const = 0;
   virtual double volume() const = 0;
};

#endif
```

```cpp
// TWODIM.H
// Definition of class TwoDimensionalShape
#ifndef TWODIM_H
#define TWODIM_H

#include "shape.h"

class TwoDimensionalShape : public Shape {
public:
   TwoDimensionalShape(double x, double y) : Shape(x, y) { }
   virtual double area() const = 0;
};

#endif
```

```cpp
// Exercise 10.15 solution
// Driver to test Shape hierarchy
#include <iostream.h>
#include "circle.h"
#include "square.h"
#include "sphere.h"
#include "cube.h"
```

```
main()
{
    Circle cir(3.5, 6, 9);
    Square sqr(12, 2, 2);
    Sphere sph(5, 1.5, 4.5);
    Cube cub(2.2);
    Shape *ptr[4] = {&cir, &sqr, &sph, &cub};

    for (int x = 0; x < 4; x++)
        cout << *(ptr[x]) << endl;

    return 0;
}
```

```
Circle with radius 3.5; center at (6, 9);
 area of 38.4845

Square with side length 12; center at (2, 2);
 area of 144

Sphere with radius 5; center at (1.5, 4.5);
 area of 314.159; volume of 523.598

Cube with side length 2.2; center at (0, 0);
 area of 4.84; volume of 10.648
```

11
C++ Stream
Input/Output: Solutions

Exercises

11.6 Write a statement for each of the following:

a) Print integer **40000** left-justified in a **15**-digit field.

ANS: cout << setiosflags(ios::left) << setw(15) << 40000 << endl;

b) Read a string into character array variable **state**.

ANS: cin >> state;

c) Print **200** with and without a sign.

ANS: cout << 200 << setw(4) << setiosflags(ios::showpos) << 200 << endl;

d) Print the decimal value **100** in hexadecimal form preceded by **0x**.

ANS: cout << setiosflags(ios::showbase) << hex << 100 << endl;

e) Read characters into array **s** until the character **'p'** is encountered up to a limit of 10 characters (including the terminating null character). Extract the delimiter from the input stream and discard it.

ANS: cin.getline(s, 10, 'p');

f) Print **1.234** in a **9**-digit field with preceding zeros.

ANS:
```
cout << setiosflags(ios::fixed | ios::showpoint) << setw(9)
     << setfill('0') << setiosflags(ios::internal) << 1.234 << endl;
```

g) Read a string of the form **"characters"** from the standard input. Store the string in character array **s**. Eliminate the quotation marks from the input stream. Read a maximum of 50 characters (including the terminating null character).

11.7 Write a program to test inputting integer values in decimal, octal, and hexadecimal format. Output each integer read by the program in all three formats. Test the program with the following input data: 10, 010, 0x10.

ANS:
```
// Exercise 11.7 Solution
#include <iostream.h>
#include <iomanip.h>

main()
{
    int integer;

    cout << "Enter an integer: ";
    cin >> integer;

    cout << setiosflags(ios::showbase) << "As a decimal number "  << dec
         << integer << endl << "As an octal number " << oct << integer
         << endl << "As a hexadecimal number " << hex << integer << endl;

    return 0;
}
```

```
Enter an integer: 10
As a decimal number 10
As an octal number 012
As a hexadecimal number 0xa
```

```
Enter an integer: 010
As a decimal number 8
As an octal number 010
As a hexadecimal number 0x8
```

```
Enter an integer: 0x10
As a decimal number 16
As an octal number 020
As a hexadecimal number 0x10
```

11.8   Write a program that prints pointer values using casts to all the integer data types. Which ones print strange values? Which ones cause errors?

ANS:
```
// Exercise 11.8 Solution
#include <iostream.h>

main()
{
    char *string = "test";

    cout << "Value of string is             : " << string << endl
         << "Value of (void *)string is     : " << (void *)string << endl
         << "Value of (char)string is       : " << (char)string << endl
         << "Value of (int)string is        : " << (int)string << endl
         << "Value of (long)string is       : " << (long)string << endl
         << "Value of (short)string is      : " << (short)string << endl
         << "Value of (unsigned)string is   : " << (unsigned)string << endl;

    return 0;
}
```

```
Value of string is             : test
Value of (void *)string is     : 0x00aa
Value of (char)string is       : ª
Value of (int)string is        : 170
Value of (long)string is       : 519176362
Value of (short)string is      : 170
Value of (unsigned)string is   : 170
```

11.9   Write a program to test the results of printing the integer value **12345** and the floating-point value **1.2345** in various size fields. What happens when the values are printed in fields containing fewer digits than the values?

ANS:
```
// Exercise 11.9 Solution
#include <iostream.h>
#include <iomanip.h>

main()
{
   int x = 12345;
   double y = 1.2345;

   for (int loop = 0; loop <= 10; loop ++)
      cout << x << "  printed in a field of size " << loop << " is "
           << setw(loop) << x << endl << y << " printed in a field "
           << "of size " << loop << " is " << setw(loop) << y << endl;

   return 0;
}
```

```
12345  printed in a field of size 0 is 12345
1.2345 printed in a field of size 0 is 1.2345
12345  printed in a field of size 1 is 12345
1.2345 printed in a field of size 1 is 1.2345
12345  printed in a field of size 2 is 12345
1.2345 printed in a field of size 2 is 1.2345
12345  printed in a field of size 3 is 12345
1.2345 printed in a field of size 3 is 1.2345
12345  printed in a field of size 4 is 12345
1.2345 printed in a field of size 4 is 1.2345
12345  printed in a field of size 5 is 12345
1.2345 printed in a field of size 5 is 1.2345
12345  printed in a field of size 6 is  12345
1.2345 printed in a field of size 6 is 1.2345
12345  printed in a field of size 7 is   12345
1.2345 printed in a field of size 7 is  1.2345
12345  printed in a field of size 8 is    12345
1.2345 printed in a field of size 8 is   1.2345
12345  printed in a field of size 9 is     12345
1.2345 printed in a field of size 9 is    1.2345
12345  printed in a field of size 10 is      12345
1.2345 printed in a field of size 10 is     1.2345
```

11.10 Write a program that prints the value **100.453627** rounded to the nearest digit, tenth, hundredth, thousandth, and ten thousandth.

ANS:
```
// Exercise 11.10 Solution
#include <iostream.h>
#include <iomanip.h>

main()
{
   double x = 100.453627;

   for (int loop = 0; loop <= 5; loop++)
      cout << setprecision(loop) << "Rounded to " << loop << " digit(s) is "
           << x << endl;

   return 0;
}
```

```
Rounded to 0 digit(s) is 100.453627
Rounded to 1 digit(s) is 100.5
Rounded to 2 digit(s) is 100.45
Rounded to 3 digit(s) is 100.454
Rounded to 4 digit(s) is 100.4536
Rounded to 5 digit(s) is 100.45363
```

11.11   Write a program that inputs a string from the keyboard and determines the length of the string. Print the string using twice the length as the field width.

ANS:

```cpp
// Exercise 11.11 Solution
#include <iostream.h>
#include <iomanip.h>
#include <string.h>

const int SIZE = 80;

main()
{
    char string[SIZE];
    int stringLength;

    cout << "Enter a string: ";
    cin >> string;

    stringLength = strlen(string);

    // print string using twice the length as field with
    cout << setw(2 * stringLength) << string << endl;

    return 0;
}
```

```
Enter a string: computer
        computer
```

11.12   Write a program that converts integer Fahrenheit temperatures from 0 to 212 degrees to floating-point Celsius temperatures with 3 digits of precision. Use the formula

```
celsius = 5.0/9.0 * (fahrenheit - 32);
```

to perform the calculation. The output should be printed in two right-justified columns, and the Celsius temperatures should be preceded by a sign for both positive and negative values.

ANS:

```cpp
// Exercise 11.12 Solution
#include <iostream.h>
#include <iomanip.h>

main()
{
    double celsius;

    cout << setw(20) << "Fahrenheit " << setw(20) << "Celsius" << endl
         << setiosflags(ios::fixed | ios::showpoint);

    for (int fahrenheit = 0; fahrenheit <= 212; fahrenheit++) {
        celsius = 5.0 / 9.0 * (fahrenheit - 32);
        cout << setw(15) << resetiosflags(ios::showpos) << fahrenheit
             << setw(23) << setprecision(3) << setiosflags(ios::showpos)
             << celsius << endl;
    }

    return 0;
}
```

Fahrenheit	Celsius
0	-17.778
1	-17.222
2	-16.667
3	-16.111
4	-15.556
5	-15.000
6	-14.444
7	-13.889
8	-13.333
9	-12.778
10	-12.222
...	...
210	+98.889
211	+99.444
212	+100.000

11.13 In some programming languages, strings are entered surrounded by either single or double quotation marks. Write a program that reads the three strings **suzy**, **"suzy"**, and **'suzy'**. Are the single and double quotes ignored or read as part of the string?

ANS:

```
// Exercise 11.13 Solution
#include <iostream.h>

const int SIZE = 80;

main()
{
   char string[SIZE];

   cout << "Enter a string: ";
   cin >> string;

   cout << "String is " << string << endl;

   return 0;
}
```

```
Enter a string: suzy
String is suzy
```

```
Enter a string: "suzy"
String is "suzy"
```

```
Enter a string: 'suzy'
String is 'suzy'
```

11.14 In Fig. 11.30, the stream-extraction and -insertion operators were overloaded for input and output of objects of the **PhoneNumber** class. Rewrite the stream-extraction operator to perform the following error checking on input. The **operator>>** function will need to be entirely recoded.

   a) Input the entire phone number into an array. Test that the proper number of characters have been entered. There should be a total of 14 characters read for a phone number of the form **(800) 555-1212**. Use the stream member function **clear** to set **ios::failbit** for improper input.

b) The area code and exchange do not begin with **0** or **1**. Test the first digit of the area code and exchange portions of the phone number to be sure that neither begins with **0** or **1**. Use stream member function **clear** to set **ios::failbit** for improper input.

c) The middle digit of an area code is always **0** or **1**. Test the middle digit for a value of **0** or **1**. Use the stream member function **clear** to set **ios::failbit** for improper input. If none of the above operations results in **ios::failbit** being set for improper input, copy the three parts of the telephone number into the **areaCode**, **exchange**, and **line** members of the **PhoneNumber** object In the main program, if **ios::failbit** has been set on the input, have the program print an error message and end rather than print the phone number.

ANS:

```cpp
// P11_14.H
#ifndef P11_14.H
#define P11_14.H

#include <iostream.h>
#include <iomanip.h>
#include <string.h>
#include <stdlib.h>

class PhoneNumber {
    friend ostream& operator<<(ostream&, PhoneNumber&);
    friend istream& operator>>(istream&, PhoneNumber&);
public:
    PhoneNumber();
private:
    char phone[15];
    char areaCode[4];
    char exchange[4];
    char line[5];
};

#endif
```

```cpp
// P11_14M.cpp
// member function definition for p11_14.cpp
#include "p11_14.h"

PhoneNumber::PhoneNumber()
{
    phone[0] = '\0';
    areaCode[0] = '\0';
    exchange[0] = '\0';
    line[0] = '\0';
}

ostream &operator<<(ostream &output, PhoneNumber &number)
{
    output << "(" << number.areaCode << ") " << number.exchange
           << '-' << number.line << endl;

    return output;
}

istream &operator>>(istream &input, PhoneNumber &number)
{
    cin.getline(number.phone, 15);

    if (strlen(number.phone) != 14)
        cin.clear(ios::failbit);

    if (number.phone[1] == '0' || number.phone[6] == '0' ||
        number.phone[1] == '1' || number.phone[6] == '1')
        cin.clear(ios::failbit);
```

```
        if (number.phone[2] != '0' && number.phone[2] != '1')
           cin.clear(ios::failbit);

        if (cin.fail() == 0) {
           for (int loop = 0; loop <= 2; loop++) {
              number.areaCode[loop] = number.phone[loop + 1];
              number.exchange[loop] = number.phone[loop + 6];
           }

           number.areaCode[loop] = number.exchange[loop] = '\0';

           for (loop = 0; loop <= 3; loop++)
              number.line[loop] = number.phone[loop + 10];

           number.line[loop] = '\0';
        }
        else {
           cout << "Invalid phone number entered." << endl;
           exit(1);
        }

        return input;
   }
```

```
   // driver for p11_14.cpp
   #include "p11_14.h"

   main()
   {
        PhoneNumber telephone;

        cout << "Enter a phone number in the form (123) 456-7890:" << endl;
        cin >> telephone;

        cout << "The phone number entered was:  " << telephone << endl;

        return 0;
   }
```

```
   Enter a phone number in the form (123) 456-7890:
   (800) 899-0987
   The phone number entered was:   (800) 899-0987
```

```
   Enter a phone number in the form (123) 456-7890:
   8894kkyd
   Invalid phone number entered.
```

11.15   Write a program that accomplishes each of the following:
   a) Create the user-defined class **Point** that contains the private integer data members **xCoordinate** and **yCoordinate**, and declares stream-insertion and stream-extraction overloaded operator functions as **friend**s of the class.
   b) Define the stream-insertion and stream-extraction operator functions. The stream-extraction operator function should determine if the data entered is valid data, and if not, it should set the **ios::failbit** to indicate improper input. The stream-insertion operator should not be able to display the point after an input error occurred.
   c) Write a **main** function that tests input and output of user-defined class **Point** using the overloaded stream-extraction and stream-insertion operators.

```
ANS:
// P11_15.H
#ifndef P11_15.H
#define P11_15.H
#include <iostream.h>

class Point {
    friend ostream &operator<<(ostream&, Point&);
    friend istream &operator>>(istream&, Point&);
private:
    int xCoordinate;
    int yCoordinate;
};

#endif
```

```
// P11_15M.cpp
// member function definitions for p11_15.cpp
#include "p11_15.h"

ostream& operator<<(ostream& out, Point& p)
{
    if (cin.fail() == 0)
        cout << '(' << p.xCoordinate << ", " << p.yCoordinate << ')' << endl;
    else
        cout << endl << "Invalid data" << endl;

    return out;
}

istream& operator>>(istream& i, Point& p)
{
    if (cin.peek() != '(')
        cin.clear(ios::failbit);
    else
        i.ignore();  // skip (

    cin >> p.xCoordinate;

    if (cin.peek() != ',')
        cin.clear(ios::failbit);
    else {
        i.ignore(); // skip ,

        if (cin.peek() == ' ')
            i.ignore(); // skip space
        else
            cin.clear(ios::failbit);
    }

    cin >> p.yCoordinate;

    if (cin.peek() == ')')
        i.ignore();  // skip )
    else
        cin.clear(ios::failbit);

    return i;
}
```

```
// driver for p11_15.cpp
#include "p11_15.h"

main()
{
    Point pt;

    cout << "Enter a point in the form (x, y):\n";
    cin >> pt;

    cout << "Point entered was: " << pt << endl;
    return 0;
}
```

```
Enter a point in the form (x, y):
(99, 99)
Point entered was: (99, 99)
```

```
Enter a point in the form (x, y):
(i, y)
Point entered was:
Invalid data
```

11.16   Write a program that accomplishes each of the following:

   a)   Create the user-defined class **Complex** that contains the private integer data members **real** and **imaginary**, and declares stream-insertion and stream-extraction overloaded operator functions as **friend**s of the class.

   b)   Define the stream-insertion and -extraction operator functions. The stream-extraction operator function should determine if the data entered is valid, and if not, it should set **ios::failbit** to indicate improper input. The input should be of the form:

$$3 + 8i$$

       The values can be negative or positive, and it is possible that one of the two values is not provided. If a value is not provided, the appropriate data member should be set to **0**. The stream-insertion operator should not be able to display the point if an input error occurred. The output format should be identical to the input format shown above. For negative imaginary values, a minus sign should be printed rather than a plus sign.

   c)   Write a **main** function that tests input and output of user-defined class **Complex** using the overloaded stream-extraction and stream-insertion operators.

ANS:

```
// P11_16.H
#ifndef P11_16.H
#define P11_16.H
#include <iostream.h>
#include <iomanip.h>

class Complex {
    friend ostream &operator<<(ostream&, Complex&);
    friend istream &operator>>(istream&, Complex&);
public:
    Complex(void);    // constructor
private:
    int real;
    int imaginary;
};


#endif
```

```
// P11_16M.cpp
// member function definitions for p11_16.cpp
#include "p11_16.h"

Complex::Complex(void)
{
   real = 0;
   imaginary = 0;
}

ostream &operator<<(ostream &output, Complex &c)
{
   if (cin.fail() == 0)
      output << c.real << " + " << c.imaginary << 'i' << endl;
   else
      output << "Invalid Data Entered" << endl;

   return output;
}

istream &operator>>(istream &input, Complex &c)
{
   int number;
   char temp;

   input >> number;

   if (cin.peek() == ' ') {                    // case a + bi
      c.real = number;
      cin >> temp;

      if (cin.peek() != ' ')
         cin.clear(ios::failbit);              // set bad bit
      else {

         if (cin.peek() == ' ') {
            input >> c.imaginary;
            cin >> temp;
            if (cin.peek() != '\n')
               cin.clear(ios::failbit); // set bad bit
         }
         else
            cin.clear(ios::failbit);     // set bad bit
      }
   }
   else if (cin.peek() == 'i') {               // case bi
         cin >> temp;

         if (cin.peek() == '\n') {
            c.real = 0;
            c.imaginary = number;
         }
         else
            cin.clear(ios::failbit);     // set bad bit
   }

   else if (cin.peek() == '\n') {              // case a
      c.real = number;
      c.imaginary = 0;
   }
   else
      cin.clear(ios::failbit);                 // set bad bit

   return input;
}
```

```
// driver for p11_16.cpp
#include "p11_16.h"

main()
{
   Complex complex;

   cout << "Input a complex number in the form A + Bi:\n";
   cin >> complex;

   cout << "Complex number entered was:\n" << complex << endl;
   return 0;
}
```

```
Input a complex number in the form A + Bi:
45
Complex number entered was:
45 + 0i
```

```
Input a complex number in the form A + Bi:
9i
Complex number entered was:
0 + 9i
```

```
Input a complex number in the form A + Bi:
4 + 105i
Complex number entered was:
4 + 105i
```

```
Input a complex number in the form A + Bi:
67fi.y
Complex number entered was:
Invalid Data
```

11.17   Write a program that uses a **for** structure to print a table of ASCII values for the characters in the ASCII character set from **33** to **126**. The program should print the decimal value, octal value, hexadecimal value, and character value for each character. Use the stream manipulators **dec**, **oct**, and **hex** to print the integer values.

ANS:

```
// Exercise 11.17 Solution
#include <iostream.h>
#include <iomanip.h>

main()
{
   cout << setw(7) << "Decimal" << setw(9) << "Octal " << setw(15)
        << "Hexadecimal " << setw(13) << "Character"
        << setiosflags(ios::showbase) << endl;

   for (int loop = 33; loop <= 126; loop++)
      cout << setw(7) << dec << loop << setw(9) << oct << loop
           << setw(15) << hex << loop << setw(13) << (char) loop << endl;

   return 0;
}
```

Decimal	Octal	Hexadecimal	Character
33	041	0x21	!
34	042	0x22	"
35	043	0x23	#
36	044	0x24	$
37	045	0x25	%
38	046	0x26	&
39	047	0x27	'
40	050	0x28	(
41	051	0x29	)
42	052	0x2a	*
...			
118	0166	0x76	v
119	0167	0x77	w
120	0170	0x78	x
121	0171	0x79	y
122	0172	0x7a	z
123	0173	0x7b	{
124	0174	0x7c		
125	0175	0x7d	}
126	0176	0x7e	~

11.18 Write a program to show that the `getline` and three-argument `get` istream member functions each end the input string with a string terminating null character. Also show that `get` leaves the delimiter character on the input stream while `getline` extracts the delimiter character and discards it. What happens to the unread characters in the stream?

ANS:

```
// Exercise 11.18 Solution
#include <iostream.h>
#include <ctype.h>

const int SIZE = 80;

main()
{
   char array[SIZE], array2[SIZE], c;

   cout << "Enter a sentence to test getline() and get(): " << endl;
   cin.getline(array, SIZE, '*');
   cout << array << endl;

   cin >> c;  // read next character in input
   cout << "The next character in the input is: " << c << endl;

   cin.get(array2, SIZE, '*');
   cout << array2 << endl;

   cin >> c;  // read next character in input
   cout << "The next character in the input is: " << c << endl;

   return 0;
}
```

```
Enter a sentence to test getline() and get():
happy*birthday*to*you
happy
The next character in the input is: b
irthday
The next character in the input is: *
```

11.19   Write a program that creates the user-defined manipulator **skipwhite** to skip leading whitespace characters in the input stream. The manipulator should use the **isspace** function from the **ctype.h** library to test if the character is a whitespace character. Each character should be input using the **istream** member function **get**. When a non-whitespace character is encountered, the **skipwhite** manipulator finishes its job by placing the character back on the input stream and returning an **istream** reference.

Test the manipulator by creating a **main** function in which the **ios::skipws** flag is unset so that the stream-extraction operator does not automatically skip whitespace. Then test the manipulator on the input stream by entering a character preceded by whitespace as input. Print the character that was input to confirm that a whitespace character was not input.

12
Templates: Solutions

Exercises

12.3   Write a function template `bubbleSort` based on the sort program of Fig. 5.15. Write a driver program that inputs, sorts, and outputs an `int` array and a `float` array.

ANS:

```
// Exercise 12.3 solution
// This program puts values into an array, sorts the values into
// ascending order, and prints the resulting array.
#include <iostream.h>
#include <iomanip.h>


// Function template for bubbleSort
template <class T>
void bubbleSort(T *array, int size)
{
    void swap(T *, T *);

    for (int pass = 1; pass < size; pass++)
        for (int j = 0; j < size - pass; j++)
            if (array[j] > array[j + 1])
                swap(&array[j], &array[j + 1]);
}


template <class T>
void swap(T *element1Ptr, T *element2Ptr)
{
    T temp = *element1Ptr;
    *element1Ptr = *element2Ptr;
    *element2Ptr = temp;
}


main()
{
    const int arraySize = 10;
    int a[arraySize] = {10, 9, 8, 7, 6, 5, 4, 3, 2, 1};

    // Process an array of integers
    cout << "Integer data items in original order" << endl;

    for (int i = 0; i < arraySize; i++)
        cout << setw(6) << a[i];

    bubbleSort(a, arraySize);               // sort the array
    cout << endl << "Integer data items in ascending order" << endl;

    for (i = 0; i < arraySize; i++)
        cout << setw(6) << a[i];
```

```
      cout << endl << endl;

      // Process an array of floating point values
      float b[arraySize] = {10.1, 9.9, 8.8, 7.7, 6.6, 5.5,
                            4.4, 3.3, 2.2, 1.1};

      cout << "Floating point data items in original order" << endl;

      for (i = 0; i < arraySize; i++)
         cout << setw(6) << b[i];

      bubbleSort(b, arraySize);            // sort the array
      cout << endl << "Floating point data items in ascending order" << endl;

      for (i = 0; i < arraySize; i++)
         cout << setw(6) << b[i];

      cout << endl;

      return 0;
   }
```

```
   Integer data items in original order
       10       9       8       7       6       5       4       3       2       1
   Integer data items in ascending order
        1       2       3       4       5       6       7       8       9      10

   Floating point data items in original order
     10.1     9.9     8.8     7.7     6.6     5.5     4.4     3.3     2.2     1.1
   Floating point data items in ascending order
      1.1     2.2     3.3     4.4     5.5     6.6     7.7     8.8     9.9    10.1
```

12.4 Overload function template `printArray` of Fig. 12.2 so that it takes two-additional integer arguments, namely `int lowSubscript` and `int highSubscript`. A call to this function will print only the designated portion of the array. Validate `lowSubscript` and `highSubscript`; if either is out-of-range or if `highSub-script` is less than or equal to `lowSubscript` the overloaded `printArray` function should return 0; otherwise, `printArray` should return the number of elements printed. Then modify `main` to exercise both versions of `printArray` on arrays a, b, and c. Be sure to test all capabilities of both versions of `printArray`.

ANS:

```
// Exercise 12.4 solution
// Using template functions
#include <iostream.h>

template<class T>
int printArray(T *array, int size, int lowSubscript, int highSubscript)
{
   if (size < 0 || lowSubscript < 0 || highSubscript >= size)
      return 0;   // negative size or subscript out of range

   for (int i = lowSubscript, count = 0; i <= highSubscript; i++) {
      ++count;
      cout << array[i] << " ";
   }

   cout << endl;

   return count;  // number or elements output
}
```

```
main()
{
    const int aCount = 5, bCount = 7, cCount = 6;
    int a[aCount] = {1, 2, 3, 4, 5};
    float b[bCount] = {1.1, 2.2, 3.3, 4.4, 5.5, 6.6, 7.7};
    char c[cCount] = "HELLO";   // 6th position for null

    cout << "Array a contains:" << endl;
    cout << printArray(a, aCount, 0, aCount - 1)
         << " elements were output" << endl;

    cout << "Array a from 1 to 3 is:" << endl;
    cout << printArray(a, aCount, 1, 3)
         << " elements were output" << endl;

    cout << "Array a output with invalid subscripts:" << endl;
    cout << printArray(a, aCount, -1, 10)
         << " elements were output" << endl << endl;

    cout << "Array b contains:" << endl;
    cout << printArray(b, bCount, 0, bCount - 1)
         << " elements were output" << endl;

    cout << "Array b from 1 to 5 is:" << endl;
    cout << printArray(b, bCount, 1, 3)
         << " elements were output" << endl;

    cout << "Array b output with invalid subscripts:" << endl;
    cout << printArray(b, bCount, -1, 10)
         << " elements were output" << endl << endl;

    cout << "Array c contains:" << endl;
    cout << printArray(c, cCount, 0, cCount - 1)
         << " elements were output" << endl;

    cout << "Array c from 1 to 4 is:" << endl;
    cout << printArray(c, cCount, 1, 3)
         << " elements were output" << endl;

    cout << "Array c output with invalid subscripts:" << endl;
    cout << printArray(c, cCount, -1, 10)
         << " elements were output" << endl;

    return 0;
}
```

```
Array a contains:
1 2 3 4 5
5 elements were output
Array a from 1 to 3 is:
2 3 4
3 elements were output
Array a output with invalid subscripts:
0 elements were output

Array b contains:
1.1 2.2 3.3 4.4 5.5 6.6 7.7
7 elements were output
Array b from 1 to 5 is:
2.2 3.3 4.4
3 elements were output
Array b output with invalid subscripts:
0 elements were output
                                        continued
```

```
                                                              continued
  Array c contains:
  H E L L O _
  6 elements were output
  Array c from 1 to 4 is:
  E L L
  3 elements were output
  Array c output with invalid subscripts:
  0 elements were output
```

12.5   Overload function template **printArray** of Fig. 12.2 with a non-template version that specifically prints an array of character strings in neat, tabular, column format.

ANS:

```cpp
// Exercise 12.5 solution
// Using template functions
#include <iostream.h>
#include <iomanip.h>

template<class T>
void printArray(T *array, int size)
{
    for (int i = 0; i < size; i++)
      cout << array[i] << " ";

    cout << endl;
}

void printArray(char *stringArray[], int size)
{
    for (int i = 0; i < size; i++) {
        cout << setw(10) << stringArray[i];

        if ((i + 1) % 4 == 0)
            cout << endl;
    }

    cout << endl;
}

main()
{
    const int aCount = 5, bCount = 7, cCount = 6, sCount = 8;
    int a[aCount] = {1, 2, 3, 4, 5};
    float b[bCount] = {1.1, 2.2, 3.3, 4.4, 5.5, 6.6, 7.7};
    char c[cCount] = "HELLO";   // 6th position for null
    char *strings[sCount] = {"one", "two", "three", "four",
                             "five", "six", "seven", "eight"};


    cout << "Array a contains:" << endl;
    printArray(a, aCount);  // integer template function

    cout << endl << "Array b contains:" << endl;
    printArray(b, bCount);  // float template function

    cout << endl << "Array c contains:" << endl;
    printArray(c, cCount);  // character template function

    cout << endl << "Array strings contains:" << endl;
    printArray(strings, sCount);  // function specific to string arrays

    return 0;
}
```

```
Array a contains:
1 2 3 4 5

Array b contains:
1.1 2.2 3.3 4.4 5.5 6.6 7.7

Array c contains:
H E L L O

Array strings contains:
        one         two         three       four
        five        six         seven       eight
```

12.6   Write a simple function template for predicate function **isEqualTo** that compares its two arguments with the equality operator (**==**) and returns 1 if they are equal and 0 if they are not equal. Use this function template in a program that calls **isEqualTo** only with a variety of built-in types. Now write a separate version of the program that calls **isEqualTo** with a user-defined class type, but does not overload the equality operator. What happens when you attempt to run this program? Now overload the equality operator (with operator function **operator==**). Now what happens when you attempt to run this program?

ANS:
```cpp
// Exercise 12.6 solution
// Combined solution to entire problem
#include <iostream.h>

template <class T>
int isEqualTo(T &arg1, T &arg2) { return arg1 == arg2; }

class SomeClass {
    friend ostream &operator<<(ostream &, SomeClass &);
public:
    SomeClass(int s, float t)
    {
        x = s;
        y = t;
    }

    // Overloaded equality operator. If this is not provided, the
    // program will not compile.
    int operator==(SomeClass &right) const
        { return x == right.x && y == right.y; }

private:
    int x;
    float y;
};

ostream &operator<<(ostream &out, SomeClass &obj)
{
    out << '(' << obj.x << ", " << obj.y << ')';
    return out;
}

main()
{
    int a, b;

    cout << "Enter two integer values: ";
    cin >> a >> b;
    cout << a << " and " << b << " are "
         << (isEqualTo(a, b) ? "equal" : "not equal") << endl;
```

```
    char c, d;

    cout << endl << "Enter two character values: ";
    cin >> c >> d;
    cout << c << " and " << d << " are "
         << (isEqualTo(c, d) ? "equal" : "not equal") << endl;

    float e, f;

    cout << endl << "Enter two floating point values: ";
    cin >> e >> f;
    cout << e << " and " << f << " are "
         << (isEqualTo(e, f) ? "equal" : "not equal") << endl;

    SomeClass g(1, 1.1), h(1, 1.1);

    cout << endl << "The class objects " << g << " and " << h << " are "
         << (isEqualTo(g, h) ? "equal" : "not equal") << endl;
    return 0;
}
```

```
Enter two integer values: 7 7
7 and 7 are equal

Enter two character values: A B
A and B are not equal

Enter two floating point values: 2.345 6.789
2.345 and 6.789 are not equal

The class objects (1, 1.1) and (1, 1.1) are equal
```

12.7   Use a non-type parameter numberOfElements and a type parameter elementType to help create a template for the Array class we developed in Chapter 8, "Overloading." This template will enable Array objects to be instantiated with a specified number of elements of a specified element type at compile time.

ANS:
```
#ifndef ARRAY1_H
#define ARRAY1_H

#include <iostream.h>
#include <stdlib.h>
#include <assert.h>


template <class elementType, int numberOfElements>
class Array {
public:
   Array();                                 // default constructor
   ~Array();                                // destructor
   int getSize() const;                     // return size
   int operator==(const Array &) const;     // compare equal
   int operator!=(const Array &) const;     // compare !equal
   elementType &operator[](int);            // subscript operator
   static int getArrayCount();              // Return count of
                                            // arrays instantiated.
   void inputArray();                       // input the array elements
   void outputArray() const;                // output the array elements
private:
   elementType ptr[numberOfElements]; // pointer to first array element
   int size; // size of the array
   static int arrayCount;  // # of Arrays instantiated
};
```

```cpp
// Initialize static data member at file scope
template <class elementType, int numberOfElements>
int Array<elementType, numberOfElements>::arrayCount = 0; // no objects

// Default constructor for class Array
template <class elementType, int numberOfElements>
Array<elementType, numberOfElements>::Array()
{
   ++arrayCount;                   // count one more object
   size = numberOfElements;

   for (int i = 0; i < size; i++)
      ptr[i] = 0;                  // initialize array
}

// Destructor for class Array
template <class elementType, int numberOfElements>
Array<elementType, numberOfElements>::~Array() { --arrayCount; }

// Get the size of the array
template <class elementType, int numberOfElements>
int Array<elementType, numberOfElements>::getSize() const
   { return size; }

// Determine if two arrays are equal and
// return 1 if true, 0 if false.
template <class elementType, int numberOfElements>
int Array<elementType, numberOfElements>::
                                  operator==(const Array &right) const
{
   if (size != right.size)
      return 0;     // arrays of different sizes

   for (int i = 0; i < size; i++)
      if (ptr[i] != right.ptr[i])
         return 0; // arrays are not equal

   return 1;        // arrays are equal
}

// Determine if two arrays are not equal and
// return 1 if true, 0 if false.
template <class elementType, int numberOfElements>
int Array<elementType, numberOfElements>::
                                  operator!=(const Array &right) const
{
   if (size != right.size)
      return 1;          // arrays of different sizes

   for (int i = 0; i < size; i++)
      if (ptr[i] != right.ptr[i])
         return 1;        // arrays are not equal

   return 0;              // arrays are equal
}

// Overloaded subscript operator
template <class elementType, int numberOfElements>
elementType &Array<elementType, numberOfElements>::
                                           operator[](int subscript)
{
   // check for subscript out of range error
   assert(0 <= subscript && subscript < size);

   return ptr[subscript];   // reference return creates lvalue
}
```

```cpp
// Return the number of Array objects instantiated
template <class elementType, int numberOfElements>
int Array<elementType, numberOfElements>::getArrayCount()
   { return arrayCount; }

// Input values for entire array.
template <class elementType, int numberOfElements>
void Array<elementType, numberOfElements>::inputArray()
{
   for (int i = 0; i < size; i++)
      cin >> ptr[i];
}

// Output the array values
template <class elementType, int numberOfElements>
void Array<elementType, numberOfElements>::outputArray() const
{
   for (int i = 0; i < size; i++) {
      cout << ptr[i] << ' ';

      if ((i + 1) % 10 == 0)
         cout << endl;
   }

   if (i % 10 != 0)
      cout << endl;
}

#endif
```

```cpp
// Exercise 12.7 solution
#include <iostream.h>
#include "arraytmp.h"

main()
{
   Array<int, 5> intArray;

   cout << "Enter " << intArray.getSize() << " integer values:" << endl;
   intArray.inputArray();

   cout << endl << "The values in intArray are:" << endl;
   intArray.outputArray();

   Array<float, 5> floatArray;

   cout << endl << "Enter " << floatArray.getSize()
        << " floating point values:" << endl;
   floatArray.inputArray();

   cout << endl << "The values in floatArray are:" << endl;
   floatArray.outputArray();
   return 0;
}
```

```
Enter 5 integer values:
1 2 3 4 5

The values in intArray are:
1 2 3 4 5

Enter 5 floating point values:
1.1 2.2 3.3 4.4 5.5

The values in floatArray are:
1.1 2.2 3.3 4.4 5.5
```

12.8   Write a program with class template **Array**. The template can instantiate an **Array** of any element type. Override the template with a specific definition for an **Array** of **float** elements (**class Array<float>**). The driver should demonstrate the instantiation of an **Array** of **int** through the template, and should show that an attempt to instantiate an **Array** of **float** uses the definition provided in **class Array<float>**.

12.9   Distinguish between the terms function template and template function.
   ANS: A function template is used to instantiate template functions.

12.10   Which is more like a stencil—a class template or a template class? Explain your answer.
   ANS: A class template can be viewed as a stencil from which a template class can be created. A template class can be viewed as a stencil from which objects of that class can be created. So, in a way, both can be viewed as stencils.

12.11   What is the relationship between function templates and overloading?
   ANS: Function templates create overloaded versions of a function. The main difference between function templates and function overloading is that, at compile time, the compiler automatically creates the code for the template functions from the function template rather than the programmer creating the code.

12.12   Why might you choose to use a function template instead of a macro?
   ANS: A macro is simply a text substitution done by the preprocessor. A function template provides real function definitions with all the type checking capabilities of the compiler available to ensure that the function is called correctly.

12.13   What performance problem can result from using function templates and class templates?
   ANS: There can be a tremendous proliferation of code in the program due to the many copies of the code that are generated by the compiler.

12.14   The compiler performs a matching process to determine the template function to call when a function is invoked. Under what circumstances does an attempt to make a match result in a compile error?
   ANS: If the compiler cannot match the function call made to a template or if the matching process results in multiple matches at compile time, the compiler generates an error message.

12.15   Why is it appropriate to call a class template a parameterized type?
   ANS: When creating template classes from a class template, it is necessary to provide a type (or possibly several types) to complete the definition of the new type being declared. For example, when creating an "Array of integers" from an Array class template, the type int is provided to the class template to complete the definition of an array of integers.

12.16   Explain why you might use the statement

```
Array<Employee> workerList(100);
```

in a C++ program with template classes.
   ANS: This statement declares an Array object to store Employee objects and passes 100 to the constructor function (probably as the size of the array).

12.17   Review your answer to Exercise 12.16. Now, why you might use the statement

```
Array<Employee> workerList;
```

in a C++ program with template classes?
   ANS: This statement also declares an Array object to store Employee objects. However, it uses the default constructor for the Array class.

12.18   Explain the use of the following notation in a C++ program with template classes:

```
template<class T> Array<T>::Array(int s)
```

   ANS: This notation is used to begin the definition of the Array(int) constructor function for the class template Array.

12.19   Why might you typically use a non-type parameter with a class template for a container such as an array or stack?
   ANS: To specify at compile time the size of the container class object being declared.

12.20   Describe how to provide a class for a specific type to override the class template for that type.

12.21   Describe the relationship between class templates and inheritance.

12.22 Suppose a class template has the header

```
template<class T1> class C1
```

Describe the friendship relationships established by placing each of the following friendship declarations inside this class template header. Identifiers beginning with "**f**" are functions, identifiers beginning with "**C**" are classes, and identifiers beginning with "**T**" can represent any type (i.e., built-in types or class types).

    a) `friend void f1();`
    b) `friend void f2(C1<T1> &);`
    c) `friend void C2::f4();`
    d) `friend void C3<T1>::f5(C1<T1> &);`
    e) `friend class C5;`
    f) `friend class C6<T1>;`

ANS:
    a) Function **f1** is a friend of all template classes instantiated from class template **C1**.
    b) Function **f2** for a specific type **T1** is a friend of the template class of type **T1**. For example, if **T1** is **int**, the function with the prototype

$$\texttt{void f2(C1<int> \&);}$$

    is a friend of the class **C1<int>**.
    c) Function **f4** of class **C2** is a friend of all template classes instantiated from class template **C1**.
    d) Function **f5** of class **C3** for a specific type **T1** is a friend of the template class of type **T1**. For example, if **T1** is **int**, the function with the prototype

$$\texttt{void c3<int>::f5(C1<int> \&);}$$

    is a friend of the class **C1<int>**.
    e) Makes every member function of class **C5** a friend of all template classes instantiated from the class template **C1**.
    f) For a specific type **T1**, makes every member function of the class **C6<T1>** a friend of the class **C1<T1>**. For example if **T1** is **int**, every member function of class **C6<int>** is a friend of class **C1<int>**.

12.23 Suppose class template **Employee** has a **static** data member **count**. Suppose three template classes are instantiated from the class template. How many copies of the **static** data member will exist? How will the use of each be constrained (if at all)?

    ANS: For static members of a class template, each template class instantiated receives its own copy of all the static members. Then, all objects instantiated for a given template class access that particular template class's static members.

13
Exception Handling: Solutions

Exercises

13.20 List the various exceptional conditions which have occurred in programs throughout this text. List as many additional exceptional conditions as you can. For each of these, describe briefly how a program would typically handle the exception using the exception handling techniques discussed in this chapter. Some typical exceptions are: Division by zero, arithmetic overflow, array subscript out of bounds, exhaustion of the free store, etc.

13.21 Under what circumstances would the programmer not provide a parameter name when defining the type of the object that will be caught by a handler?

ANS: If there is no information in the object that is required in the handler, a parameter name is not required in the handler.

13.22 A program contains the statement

```
throw;
```

Where would you normally expect to find such a statement? What if that statement appeared in a different part of a program?

ANS: The preceding statement would be found inside an exception handler to rethrow the exception. If any **throw** expression occurs outside a **try** block, the function **unexpected** is called.

13.23 Under what circumstances would you use the following statement?

```
catch(...) { throw; }
```

ANS: The preceding statement is used to catch any exception and rethrow it for handling by an exception handler in a previous function call.

13.24 Compare and contrast exception handling with the various error-processing schemes discussed in the text.

ANS: Exception handling enables the programmer to build more robust classes with built-in error processing capabilities. Once created, such classes allow clients of the classes to concentrate on using the classes rather than defining what should happen if an error occurs while using the class. Exception handling offers the possibility that an error can be processed and that the program can continue execution. Other forms of error checking such as **assert** exit the program immediately without any further processing.

13.25 List the benefits of exception handling over conventional means of error-processing.

13.26 Give several reasons why exceptions should not be used as an alternate form of program control.

ANS: Exceptions were designed for "exceptional cases." Exceptions do not follow conventional forms of program control. Therefore, using exceptions for anything other than error processing will not be easily recognized by others reading the code. This may make the program difficult to modify and maintain.

13.27 Describe a technique for handling related exceptions.

ANS: Create a base class for all the related exceptions. In this class, place all information and functionality that is common to the related exceptions. From this class, derive all the related exception classes. Once the exception class hierarchy is created, exceptions from the hierarchy can be caught as the base class exception type or as one of the derived class exception types.

13.28 Until this chapter, we have found that dealing with errors detected by constructors is a bit awkward. Exceptions gives us a much better means of dealing with such errors. Consider a constructor for a **String** class. The constructor uses **new** to obtain space from the free store. Suppose **new** fails. Show how you would deal with this without exception handling. Discuss the key issues. Show how you would deal with such memory exhaustion with exception handling. Explain why the exception handling method is superior.

```
ANS:
// str_err.h
// String exception class definitions
#ifndef str_err_h
#define str_err_h

// Base class for all String class exceptions
class StringError {
public:
    StringError(char *messageString, char *file, short line)
        : message(messageString), fileName(file), lineNumber(line) { }
    void print() const
        { cout << '\a' << message << endl << "in file " << fileName
                << " at line " << lineNumber << endl; }
private:
    const char *message;
    const char *fileName;
    const short lineNumber;
};


// Out of memory error class
class StringOutOfMemoryError : public StringError {
public:
    StringOutOfMemoryError(char *nameOfFile, short lineNum)
        : StringError("Operator new unable to allocate memory",
                        nameOfFile, lineNum) { }
};


// Subscript out of range error class
class StringOutOfRangeError : public StringError {
public:
    StringOutOfRangeError(char *nameOfFile, short lineNum)
        : StringError("String subscript out of range",
                        nameOfFile, lineNum) { }
};


// Negative substring length error class
class StringNegativeSubLengthError : public StringError {
public:
    StringNegativeSubLengthError(char *nameOfFile, short lineNum)
        : StringError("Substring length must be positive",
                        nameOfFile, lineNum) { }
};

#endif
```

```
// STRING3.H
// Definition of a String class
#ifndef STRING1_H
#define STRING1_H

#include <iostream.h>
#include "str_err.h"
```

```
class String {
   friend ostream &operator<<(ostream &, const String &);
   friend istream &operator>>(istream &, String &);

public:
   String(const char * = "");  // conversion constructor
   String(const String &);     // copy constructor
   ~String();                  // destructor
   const String &operator=(const String &);  // assignment
   String &operator+=(const String &);    // concatenation
   int operator!() const;                 // is String empty?
   int operator==(const String &) const;  // test s1 == s2
   int operator!=(const String &) const;  // test s1 != s2
   int operator<(const String &)  const;  // test s1 < s2
   int operator>(const String &)  const;  // test s1 > s2
   int operator>=(const String &) const;  // test s1 >= s2
   int operator<=(const String &) const;  // test s1 <= s2
   char &operator[](int);      // return char reference
   String &operator()(int, int); // return a substring
   int getLength() const;      // return string length

private:
   char *sPtr;                 // pointer to start of string
   int length;                 // string length
};

#endif
```

```cpp
// STRING3.CPP
// Member function definitions for class String
#include <iostream.h>
#include <iomanip.h>
#include <string.h>
#include "string3.h"
#include <except.h>


// Conversion constructor: Convert char * to String
String::String(const char *s)
{
   length = strlen(s);          // compute length

   try {
      sPtr = new char[length + 1]; // allocate storage
   }
   catch(xalloc){    // xalloc is an exception type defined in except.h
      throw StringOutOfMemoryError(__FILE__, __LINE__);
   }

   strcpy(sPtr, s);             // copy literal to object
}


// Copy constructor
String::String(const String &copy)
{
   length = copy.length;        // copy length

   try {
      sPtr = new char[length + 1]; // allocate storage
   }
```

```
      catch(xalloc){
         throw StringOutOfMemoryError(__FILE__, __LINE__);
      }

   strcpy(sPtr, copy.sPtr);       // copy string
}


// Destructor
String::~String() { delete [] sPtr; }    // reclaim string


// Overloaded = operator; avoids self assignment
const String &String::operator=(const String &right)
{
   if (&right != this) {          // avoid self assignment
      delete [] sPtr;             // prevents memory leak
      length = right.length;      // new String length

      try {
         sPtr = new char[length + 1]; // allocate storage
      }
      catch(xalloc){
         throw StringOutOfMemoryError(__FILE__, __LINE__);
      }

      strcpy(sPtr, right.sPtr);     // copy string
   }
   else
      cout << "Attempted assignment of a String to itself" << endl;

   return *this;   // enables concatenated assignments
}


// Concatenate right operand to this object and
// store in this object.
String &String::operator+=(const String &right)
{
   char *tempPtr = sPtr;          // hold to be able to delete
   length += right.length;        // new String length

   try {
      sPtr = new char[length + 1]; // allocate storage
   }
   catch(xalloc){
      throw StringOutOfMemoryError(__FILE__, __LINE__);
   }

   strcpy(sPtr, tempPtr);         // left part of new String
   strcat(sPtr, right.sPtr);      // right part of new String
   delete [] tempPtr;             // reclaim old space

   return *this;                  // enables concatenated calls
}


// Is this String empty?
int String::operator!() const { return length == 0; }


// Is this String equal to right String?
int String::operator==(const String &right) const
   { return strcmp(sPtr, right.sPtr) == 0; }
```

```cpp
// Is this String not equal to right String?
int String::operator!=(const String &right) const
   { return strcmp(sPtr, right.sPtr) != 0; }

// Is this String less than right String?
int String::operator<(const String &right) const
   { return strcmp(sPtr, right.sPtr) < 0; }

// Is this String greater than right String?
int String::operator>(const String &right) const
   { return strcmp(sPtr, right.sPtr) > 0; }

// Is this String greater than or equal to right String?
int String::operator>=(const String &right) const
   { return strcmp(sPtr, right.sPtr) >= 0; }

// Is this String less than or equal to right String?
int String::operator<=(const String &right) const
   { return strcmp(sPtr, right.sPtr) <= 0; }

// Return a reference to a character in a String.
char &String::operator[](int subscript)
{
   // First test for subscript out of range
   if (0 > subscript || subscript > length)
      throw StringOutOfRangeError(__FILE__, __LINE__);

   return sPtr[subscript];   // creates lvalue
}

// Return a substring beginning at index and
// of length subLength as a reference to a String object.
String &String::operator()(int index, int subLength)
{
   // ensure index is in range and substring length >= 0
   if (index < 0 || index >= length)
      throw StringOutOfRangeError(__FILE__, __LINE__);

   if (subLength < 0)
      throw StringNegativeSubLengthError(__FILE__, __LINE__);

   try {
      String *subPtr = new String;   // empty String

      // determine length of substring
      if ((subLength == 0) || (index + subLength > length))
         subPtr->length = length - index + 1;
      else
         subPtr->length = subLength + 1;

      delete subPtr->sPtr;       // delete character from object

      // allocate memory for substring
      subPtr->sPtr = new char[subPtr->length];

      // copy substring into new String
      strncpy(subPtr->sPtr, &sPtr[index], subPtr->length);
      subPtr->sPtr[subPtr->length] = '\0'; // terminate new String
      return *subPtr;                // return new String
   }
   catch(xalloc){
      throw StringOutOfMemoryError(__FILE__, __LINE__);
   }
}
```

```cpp
// Return string length
int String::getLength() const { return length; }

// Overloaded output operator
ostream &operator<<(ostream &output, const String &s)
{
   output << s.sPtr;
   return output;    // enables concatenation
}

// Overloaded input operator
istream &operator>>(istream &input, String &s)
{
   char temp[100];   // buffer to store input

   input >> setw(100) >> temp;
   s = temp;         // use String class assignment operator
   return input;     // enables concatenation
}
```

```cpp
// Exercise 13.28 solution
// String class example using exception handling for
// failures to allocate memory with operator new.

#include <iostream.h>
#include "string3.h"

main()
{
   try {
      String s("Welcome to C++ Exception Handling!");

      cout << "The string is: " << s << endl;
   }
   catch(StringError &sError) {
      sError.print();
      cout << endl << "Terminating Program Execution" << endl;
   }

   return 0;
}
```

```cpp
// driver.cpp
// String class example using exception handling for
// failures to allocate memory with operator new.

#include <iostream.h>
#include "string3.h"

main()
{
   try {
      String s("Welcome to C++ Exception Handling!");

      cout << "The string is: " << s << endl;
   }
   catch(StringError &sError) {
      sError.print();
      cout << endl << "Terminating Program Execution" << endl;
   }

   return 0;
}
```

13.29   Suppose a program throws an exception and the appropriate exception handler begins executing. Now suppose that the exception handler itself throws the same exception. Does this create an infinite recursion? Write a C++ program to check your observation.

ANS:
```
// Exercise 13.29 solution
#include <iostream.h>

class TestException {
public:
    TestException(char *mPtr) : message(mPtr) {}
    void print() const { cout << message << endl; }
private:
    char *message;
};

main()
{
    try {
        throw TestException("This is a test");
    }
    catch (TestException &t) {
        t.print();
        throw TestException("This is another test");
    }
}
```

```
This is a test
Abnormal program termination
```

13.30   Use inheritance to create a base exception class and various derived exception classes. Then show that the `catch` handler specifying the base class catches derived class exceptions.

13.31   Throwing exceptions with a conditional expression can be tricky. Show a conditional expression that returns either a **double** or an **int**. Provide an **int catch** handler and a **double catch** handler. Show that only the **double catch** handler executes regardless of whether the **int** or the **double** is returned.

ANS:
```
// Exercise 13.31 solution
#include <iostream.h>

main()
{
    try {
        int a = 7;
        double b = 9.9;

        throw a < b ? a : b;
    }
    catch (int x) {
        cout << "The int value " << x << " was thrown" << endl;
    }
    catch (double y) {
        cout << "The double value " << y << " was thrown" << endl;
    }

    return 0;
}
```

```
The double value 7 was thrown
```

13.32 Write a C++ program designed to generate and handle a memory exhaustion error. Your program should loop on a request to create dynamic storage through operator **new**.

13.33 Write a C++ program which shows that all destructors for objects constructed in a block are called before an exception is thrown from that block.

ANS:
```
// Exercise 13.33 Solution
#include <iostream.h>

class Object {
public:
    Object(int val) : value(val)
        { cout << "Object " << value << " constructor" << endl; }
    ~Object()
        { cout << "Object " << value << " destructor" << endl; }
private:
    int value;
};

class Error {
public:
    Error(char *s) : string(s) {}
    void print() const { cout << endl << string << endl; }
private:
    char *string;
};

main()
{
    try {
        Object a(1), b(2), c(3);
        cout << endl;
        throw Error("This is a test exception");
    }
    catch (Error &e) {
        e.print();
    }

    return 0;
}
```

```
Object 1 constructor
Object 2 constructor
Object 3 constructor

Object 3 destructor
Object 2 destructor
Object 1 destructor

This is a test exception
```

13.34 Write a C++ program which shows that member object destructors are called for only those member objects that were constructed before an exception occurred.

ANS:

```cpp
// Exercise 13_34 solution
#include <iostream.h>


// A sample exception class
class ExceptionClass {
public:
    ExceptionClass() : message("An exception was thrown") {}
    void print() const { cout << endl << message << endl; }

private:
    char *message;
};


// A class from which to build member objects
class Member {
public:
    Member(int val) : value(val)
    {
        cout << "Member object " << value << " constructor called" << endl;

        // If value is 3, throw an exception for demonstration purposes.
        if (value == 3)
            throw ExceptionClass();
    }

    ~Member()
        {cout << "Member object " << value << " destructor called" << endl;}

private:
    int value;
};


// A class to encapsulate objects of class Member
class Encapsulate {
public:
    Encapsulate() : m1(1), m2(2), m3(3), m4(4), m5(5) {}
private:
    Member m1, m2, m3, m4, m5;
};


main()
{
    cout << "Constructing an object of class Encapsulate" << endl;

    try {
        Encapsulate e;
    }
    catch(ExceptionClass &except) {
        except.print();
    }

    return 0;
}
```

```
Constructing an object of class Encapsulate
Member object 1 constructor called
Member object 2 constructor called
Member object 3 constructor called
Member object 2 destructor called
Member object 1 destructor called

An exception was thrown
```

13.35 Write a C++ program that demonstrates how any exception is caught with `catch(...)`.

ANS:
```cpp
// Exercise 13.35 solution
#include <iostream.h>

// A sample exception class
class ExceptionClass {
public:
    ExceptionClass() : message("An exception was thrown") {}
    void print() const { cout << endl << message << endl; }

private:
    char *message;
};

void generateException();

main()
{
    try {
        generateException();
    }
    catch(...) {
        cout << "The \"catch all\" exception handler was invoked" << endl;
    }

    return 0;
}

void generateException()
{
    throw ExceptionClass();
}
```

```
The "catch all" exception handler was invoked
```

13.36 Write a C++ program which shows that the order of exception handlers is important. The first matching handler is the one that executes. Compile and run your program two different ways to show that two different handlers execute with two different effects.

```
ANS:
// str_err.h
// String exception class definitions

#ifndef str_err_h
#define str_err_h


// Base class for all String class exceptions
class StringError {
public:
    StringError(char *messageString, char *file, short line)
        : message(messageString), fileName(file), lineNumber(line) { }
    void print() const
        { cout << '\a' << message << endl << "in file " << fileName
               << " at line " << lineNumber << endl; }

private:
    const char *message;
    const char *fileName;
    const short lineNumber;
};


// Out of memory error class
class StringOutOfMemoryError : public StringError {
public:
    StringOutOfMemoryError(char *nameOfFile, short lineNum)
        : StringError("Operator new unable to allocate memory",
                      nameOfFile, lineNum) { }
};


// Subscript out of range error class
class StringOutOfRangeError : public StringError {
public:
    StringOutOfRangeError(char *nameOfFile, short lineNum)
        : StringError("String subscript out of range",
                      nameOfFile, lineNum) { }
};


// Negative substring length error class
class StringNegativeSubLengthError : public StringError {
public:
    StringNegativeSubLengthError(char *nameOfFile, short lineNum)
        : StringError("Substring length must be positive",
                      nameOfFile, lineNum) { }
};

#endif
```

```
// STRING3.H
// Definition of a String class
#ifndef STRING1_H
#define STRING1_H

#include <iostream.h>
#include "str_err.h"
```

```cpp
class String {
   friend ostream &operator<<(ostream &, const String &);
   friend istream &operator>>(istream &, String &);
public:
   String(const char * = ""); // conversion constructor
   String(const String &);    // copy constructor
   ~String();                 // destructor
   const String &operator=(const String &);  // assignment
   String &operator+=(const String &);    // concatenation
   int operator!() const;                 // is String empty?
   int operator==(const String &) const;  // test s1 == s2
   int operator!=(const String &) const;  // test s1 != s2
   int operator<(const String &)  const;  // test s1 < s2
   int operator>(const String &)  const;  // test s1 > s2
   int operator>=(const String &) const;  // test s1 >= s2
   int operator<=(const String &) const;  // test s1 <= s2
   char &operator[](int);      // return char reference
   String &operator()(int, int); // return a substring
   int getLength() const;      // return string length

private:
   char *sPtr;                 // pointer to start of string
   int length;                 // string length
};

#endif
```

```cpp
// STRING3.CPP
// Member function definitions for class String
#include <iostream.h>
#include <iomanip.h>
#include <string.h>
#include "string3.h"
#include <except.h>

// Conversion constructor: Convert char * to String
String::String(const char *s)
{
   length = strlen(s);          // compute length

   try {
      sPtr = new char[length + 1]; // allocate storage
   }
   catch(xalloc){    // xalloc is an exception type defined in except.h
      throw StringOutOfMemoryError(__FILE__, __LINE__);
   }

   strcpy(sPtr, s);             // copy literal to object
}

String::String(const String &copy)
{
   length = copy.length;        // copy length

   try {
      sPtr = new char[length + 1]; // allocate storage
   }
   catch(xalloc){
      throw StringOutOfMemoryError(__FILE__, __LINE__);
   }

   strcpy(sPtr, copy.sPtr);     // copy string
}
```

```
// Destructor
String::~String() { delete [] sPtr; }     // reclaim string


// Overloaded = operator; avoids self assignment
const String &String::operator=(const String &right)
{
   if (&right != this) {          // avoid self assignment
      delete [] sPtr;            // prevents memory leak
      length = right.length;     // new String length

      try {
         sPtr = new char[length + 1]; // allocate storage
      }
      catch(xalloc){
         throw StringOutOfMemoryError(__FILE__, __LINE__);
      }

      strcpy(sPtr, right.sPtr);    // copy string
   }
   else
      cout << "Attempted assignment of a String to itself" << endl;

   return *this;    // enables concatenated assignments
}


// Concatenate right operand to this object and
// store in this object.
String &String::operator+=(const String &right)
{
   char *tempPtr = sPtr;       // hold to be able to delete
   length += right.length;     // new String length

   try {
      sPtr = new char[length + 1]; // allocate storage
   }
   catch(xalloc){
      throw StringOutOfMemoryError(__FILE__, __LINE__);
   }

   strcpy(sPtr, tempPtr);      // left part of new String
   strcat(sPtr, right.sPtr);   // right part of new String
   delete [] tempPtr;          // reclaim old space
   return *this;               // enables concatenated calls
}


// Is this String empty?
int String::operator!() const { return length == 0; }


// Is this String equal to right String?
int String::operator==(const String &right) const
   { return strcmp(sPtr, right.sPtr) == 0; }


// Is this String not equal to right String?
int String::operator!=(const String &right) const
   { return strcmp(sPtr, right.sPtr) != 0; }

// Is this String less than right String?
int String::operator<(const String &right) const
   { return strcmp(sPtr, right.sPtr) < 0; }
```

```
// Is this String greater than right String?
int String::operator>(const String &right) const
   { return strcmp(sPtr, right.sPtr) > 0; }


// Is this String greater than or equal to right String?
int String::operator>=(const String &right) const
   { return strcmp(sPtr, right.sPtr) >= 0; }


// Is this String less than or equal to right String?
int String::operator<=(const String &right) const
   { return strcmp(sPtr, right.sPtr) <= 0; }


// Return a reference to a character in a String.
char &String::operator[](int subscript)
{
   // First test for subscript out of range
   if (0 > subscript || subscript > length)
      throw StringOutOfRangeError(__FILE__, __LINE__);

   return sPtr[subscript];  // creates lvalue
}


// Return a substring beginning at index and
// of length subLength as a reference to a String object.
String &String::operator()(int index, int subLength)
{
   // ensure index is in range and substring length >= 0
   if (index < 0 || index >= length)
      throw StringOutOfRangeError(__FILE__, __LINE__);

   if (subLength < 0)
      throw StringNegativeSubLengthError(__FILE__, __LINE__);

   try {
      String *subPtr = new String;   // empty String

      // determine length of substring
      if ((subLength == 0) || (index + subLength > length))
         subPtr->length = length - index + 1;
      else
         subPtr->length = subLength + 1;

      delete subPtr->sPtr;        // delete character from object

      // allocate memory for substring
      subPtr->sPtr = new char[subPtr->length];

      // copy substring into new String
      strncpy(subPtr->sPtr, &sPtr[index], subPtr->length);
      subPtr->sPtr[subPtr->length] = '\0'; // terminate new String

      return *subPtr;             // return new String
   }
   catch(xalloc){
      throw StringOutOfMemoryError(__FILE__, __LINE__);
   }
}
```

```cpp
// Return string length
int String::getLength() const { return length; }


// Overloaded output operator
ostream &operator<<(ostream &output, const String &s)
{
   output << s.sPtr;
   return output;    // enables concatenation
}


// Overloaded input operator
istream &operator>>(istream &input, String &s)
{
   char temp[100];    // buffer to store input

   input >> setw(100) >> temp;
   s = temp;          // use String class assignment operator

   return input;     // enables concatenation
}
```

```cpp
// Exercise 13.36a solution
#include <iostream.h>
#include "string3.h"

main()
{
   try {
      String s("Welcome to C++ Exception Handling!");

      cout << s[100] << endl;
   }

   // Base class handler will be invoked before derived handler
   // if base class handler is listed first.
   catch(StringError &sError) {
      cout << "Handler invoked for base class exception" << endl;
      sError.print();
      cout << endl << "Terminating Program Execution" << endl;
   }
   catch(StringOutOfRangeError &somError)
   {
      cout << "Handler invoked for derived class exception" << endl;
      somError.print();
      cout << endl << "Terminating Program Execution" << endl;
   }

   return 0;
}
```

```
NOTE: The compiler warns that the base class exception handler hides
the derived class exception handlers.

Handler invoked for base class exception
String subscript out of range
in file STRING3.CPP at line 116

Terminating Program Execution
```

```
// Exercise 13.36b solution
#include <iostream.h>
#include "string3.h"

main()
{
    try {
        String s("Welcome to C++ Exception Handling!");

        cout << s[100] << endl;
    }

    // Derived class handler will be invoked before base handler
    // if derived class handler is listed first.
    catch(StringOutOfRangeError &somError)
    {
        cout << "Handler invoked for derived class exception" << endl;
        somError.print();
        cout << endl << "Terminating Program Execution" << endl;
    }
    catch(StringError &sError) {
        cout << "Handler invoked for base class exception" << endl;
        sError.print();
        cout << endl << "Terminating Program Execution" << endl;
    }

    return 0;
}
```

```
Handler invoked for derived class exception
String subscript out of range
in file STRING3.CPP at line 116

Terminating Program Execution
```

13.37 Write a C++ program that shows a constructor passing information about constructor failure to an exception handler after a **try** block.

ANS:

```
// Exercise 13_37 solution
#include <iostream.h>

class InvalidIDNumberError {
public:
    InvalidIDNumberError(char *s) : errorMessage(s) {}
    void print() const { cout << errorMessage; }
private:
    char *errorMessage;
};

class TestInvalidIDNumberError {
public:
    TestInvalidIDNumberError(int id) : idNumber(id)
    {
        cout << "Constructor for object " << idNumber << endl;

        if (idNumber < 0)
            throw InvalidIDNumberError("ERROR: Negative ID number");
    }
private:
    int idNumber;
};
```

```
main()
{
   try {
      TestInvalidIDNumberError valid(10), invalid(-1);
   }
   catch (InvalidIDNumberError &error) {
      error.print();
      cout << endl;
   }

   return 0;
}
```

```
Constructor for object 10
Constructor for object -1
ERROR: Negative ID number
```

13.38 Write a C++ program that uses a multiple inheritance hierarchy of exception classes to create a situation in which the order of exception handlers matters.

13.39 Using **setjmp/longjmp**, a program can transfer control immediately to an error routine from a deeply nested function invocation. Unfortunately, as the stack is unwound, destructors are not called for the automatic objects that were created during the sequence of nested function calls. Write a C++ program which demonstrates that these destructors are, in fact, not called.

13.40 Write a C++ program that illustrates rethrowing an exception.
ANS:

```
// Exercise 13.40 solution
#include <iostream.h>

class TestException {
public:
   TestException(char *m) : message(m) {}
   void print() const { cout << message << endl; }
private:
   char *message;
};

void f() { throw TestException("Test exception thrown"); }

void g()
{
   try {
      f();
   }
   catch (...) {
      cout << "Exception caught in function g(); rethrowing..." << endl;
      throw;
   }
}

main()
{
   try {
      g();  // start function call chain
   }
   catch (...) {
      cout << "Exception caught in function main()" << endl;
   }

   return 0;
}
```

```
Exception caught in function g(); rethrowing...
Exception caught in function main()
```

13.41   Write a C++ program that uses **set_unexpected** to set a user-defined function for **unexpected**, uses **set_unexpected** again, and then resets **unexpected** back to its previous function. Write a similar program to test **set_terminate** and **terminate**.

ANS:
```
// Exercise 13.41 part 1 solution
#include <iostream.h>
#include <unexpected.h>

class TestException {
public:
   TestException(char *m) : message(m) {}
   void print() const { cout << message << endl; }
private:
   char *message;
};
void userUnexpected()
{
   cout << "User-defined function for unexpected" << endl
        << "exception called to terminate program" << endl;
}

main()
{
   void (*fPtr)();
   fPtr = set_unexpected(userUnexpected);
   throw TestException;
}
```

13.42   Write a C++ program which shows that a function with its own **try** block does not have to catch every possible error generated within the **try**. Some exceptions can slip through to, and be handled in, other scopes.

ANS:
```
// Exercise 13.42 solution
#include <iostream.h>

class TestException1 {
public:
   TestException1(char *m) : message(m) {}
   void print() const { cout << message << endl; }
private:
   char *message;
};

class TestException2 {
public:
   TestException2(char *m) : message(m) {}
   void print() const { cout << message << endl; }
private:
   char *message;
};

void f()
{
   throw TestException1("TestException1");
}
```

```cpp
void g()
{
    try {
        f();
    }
    catch (TestException2 &t2) {
        cout << "In g: Caught ";
        t2.print();
    }
}

main()
{
    try {
        g();
    }
    catch (TestException1 &t1) {
        cout << "In main: Caught ";
        t1.print();
    }

    return 0;
}
```

```
In main: Caught TestException1
```

13.43 Write a C++ program that throws an error from a deeply nested function call and still has the **catch** handler following the **try** block enclosing the call chain catch the exception.

ANS:
```cpp
// Exercise 13.43 solution
#include <iostream.h>

class TestException {
public:
    TestException(char *m) : message(m) {}
    void print() const { cout << message << endl; }
private:
    char *message;
};

void f() { throw TestException("TestException"); }

void g() { f(); }

void h() { g(); }

main()
{
    try {
        h();
    }
    catch (TestException &t) {
        cout << "In main: Caught ";
        t.print();
    }

    return 0;
}
```

```
In main: Caught TestException
```

14
File Processing and String Stream I/O: Solutions

Exercises

14.5 Fill in the blanks in each of the following:

a) Computers store large amounts of data on secondary storage devices as _____.
ANS: files.

b) A _____ is composed of several fields.
ANS: record.

c) A field that may contain only digits, letters, and blanks is called an_____ field.
ANS: alphanumeric.

d) To facilitate the retrieval of specific records from a file, one field in each record is chosen as a _____.
ANS: key.

e) The vast majority of information stored in computer systems is stored in _____ files.
ANS: sequential.

f) A group of related characters that conveys meaning is called a _____.
ANS: field.

g) The standard stream objects declared by header file `<iostream.h>` are_____ , _____ , _____ , and _____ .
ANS: `cin, cout, cerr, clog`.

h) The `ostream` member function _____ outputs a character to the specified stream.
ANS: `put`.

i) The `ostream` member function _____ is generally used to write data to a randomly accessed file.
ANS: `write`.

j) The `istream` member function _____ repositions the file position pointer in a file.
ANS: `seekg`.

14.6 State which of the following are true and which are false (and for those that are false, explain why):

a) The impressive functions performed by computers essentially involve the manipulation of zeros and ones.
ANS: True.

b) People prefer to manipulate bits instead of characters and fields because bits are more compact.
ANS: False. False. People prefer to manipulate characters and fields because they are less cumbersome and more understandable.

c) People specify programs and data items as characters; computers then manipulate and process these characters as groups of zeros and ones.
ANS: True.

d) A person's 5-digit zip code is an example of a numeric field.
ANS: True.

e) A person's street address is generally considered to be an alphabetic field in computer applications.
ANS: False. A street address is generally considered to be alphanumeric.

f) Data items represented in computers form a data hierarchy in which data items become larger and more complex as we progress from fields to characters to bits, etc.
ANS: False. Data items processed by a computer form a data hierarchy in which data items because larger and more complex as we progress from bits to characters to fields, etc.
g) A record key identifies a record as belonging to a particular field.
ANS: False. A record key identifies a record as belonging to a particular person or entity.
h) Most organizations store all their information in a single file to facilitate computer processing.
ANS: False. Most organizations have many files in which they store their information.
i) Each statement that processes a file in a C++ program explicitly refers to that file by name.
ANS: False. A pointer to each file is used to refer to the file.
j) When a program creates a file, the file is automatically retained by the computer for future reference.
ANS: True.

14.7   Exercise 14.3 asked the reader to write a series of single statements. Actually, these statements form the core of an important type of file processing program, namely, a file-matching program. In commercial data processing, it is common to have several files in each application system. In an accounts receivable system, for example, there is generally a master file containing detailed information about each customer such as the customer's name, address, telephone number, outstanding balance, credit limit, discount terms, contract arrangements, and possibly a condensed history of recent purchases and cash payments.

As transactions occur (i.e., sales are made and cash payments arrive in the mail), they are entered into a file. At the end of each business period (i.e., a month for some companies, a week for others, and a day in some cases) the file of transactions (called **"trans.dat"** in Exercise 14.3) is applied to the master file (called **"oldmast.dat"** in Exercise 14.3), thus updating each account's record of purchases and payments. During an updating run, the master file is rewritten as a new file (**"newmast.dat"**), which is then used at the end of the next business period to begin the updating process again.

File-matching programs must deal with certain problems that do not exist in single-file programs. For example, a match does not always occur. A customer on the master file may not have made any purchases or cash payments in the current business period, and therefore no record for this customer will appear on the transaction file. Similarly, a customer who did make some purchases or cash payments may have just moved to this community, and the company may not have had a chance to create a master record for this customer.

Use the statements written in Exercise 14.3 as a basis for writing a complete file-matching accounts receivable program. Use the account number on each file as the record key for matching purposes. Assume that each file is a sequential file with records stored in increasing account number order.

When a match occurs (i.e., records with the same account number appear on both the master file and the transaction file), add the dollar amount on the transaction file to the current balance on the master file, and write the **"newmast.dat"** record. (Assume that purchases are indicated by positive amounts on the transaction file, and that payments are indicated by negative amounts.) When there is a master record for a particular account but no corresponding transaction record, merely write the master record to **"newmast.dat"**. When there is a transaction record but no corresponding master record, print the message **"Unmatched transaction record for account number _"** (fill in the account number from the transaction record).
ANS:
```
// Exercise 14.7 Solution
#include <iostream.h>
#include <fstream.h>
#include <iomanip.h>
#include <stdlib.h>

const int SIZE = 20;

void printOutput(ofstream&, int, const char *, const char *, float);

main()
{
   int masterAccount, transactionAccount;
   float masterBalance, transactionBalance;
   char masterFirstName[SIZE], masterLastName[SIZE];

   ifstream inOldMaster("oldmast.dat", ios::in),
            inTransaction("trans.dat", ios::in);
   ofstream outNewMaster("newmast.dat", ios::out);
```

```cpp
   if (!inOldMaster) {
      cerr << "Unable to open oldmast.dat" << endl;
      exit(1);
   }

   if (!inTransaction) {
      cerr << "Unable to open trans.dat" << endl;
      exit(1);
   }

   if (!outNewMaster) {
      cerr << "Unable to open newmast.dat" << endl;
      exit(1);
   }

   cout << "Processing..." << endl;
   inTransaction >> transactionAccount >> transactionBalance;

   while (!inTransaction.eof()) {
      inOldMaster >> masterAccount >> masterFirstName
                  >> masterLastName >> masterBalance;

      while (masterAccount < transactionAccount && !inOldMaster.eof()) {
         printOutput(outNewMaster, masterAccount, masterFirstName,
                     masterLastName, masterBalance);

         inOldMaster >> masterAccount >> masterFirstName
                     >> masterLastName >> masterBalance;
      }

      if (masterAccount > transactionAccount) {
         cout << "Unmatched transaction record for account "
              << transactionAccount << endl;

         inTransaction >> transactionAccount >> transactionBalance;
      }

      if (masterAccount == transactionAccount) {
         masterBalance += transactionBalance;
         printOutput(outNewMaster, masterAccount, masterFirstName,
                     masterLastName, masterBalance);
      }

      inTransaction >> transactionAccount >> transactionBalance;
   }

   return 0;
}


void printOutput(ofstream &oRef, int mAccount, const char *mfName,
                 const char *mlName, float mBalance)
{
      cout.setf(ios::fixed | ios::showpoint);
      oRef.setf(ios::fixed | ios::showpoint);

      oRef << mAccount << ' ' << mfName << ' ' << mlName << ' '
           << setprecision(2) << mBalance << endl;
      cout << mAccount << ' ' << mfName << ' ' << mlName << ' '
           << setprecision(2) << mBalance << endl;
}
```

Contents of "oldmast.dat":

```
100 alan jones 348.17
300 mary smith 27.19
400 maggie kelly 421.78
500 sam sharp 0.00
700 suzy green -14.22
900 malise yzaga 50.00
```

Contents of "trans.dat":

```
100 134.17
300 627.19
400 1000.00
445 888.88
500 7.00
700 -78.22
900 100.00
```

Contents of "newmast.dat":

```
100 alan jones 482.34
300 mary smith 654.38
400 maggie kelly 1421.78
500 sam sharp 7.00
700 suzy green -92.44
900 malise yzaga 150.00
```

```
Processing...
100 alan jones 482.34
300 mary smith 654.38
400 maggie kelly 1421.78
Unmatched transaction record for account 445
500 sam sharp 7.00
700 suzy green -92.44
900 malise yzaga 150.00
```

14.8   After writing the program of Exercise 14.7, write a simple program to create some test data for checking out the program. Use the following sample account data:

Master file:

Account number	Name	Balance
100	Alan Jones	348.17
300	Mary Smith	27.19
500	Sam Sharp	0.00
700	Suzy Green	-14.22

Transaction file:

Account number	Dollar amount
100	27.14
300	62.11
400	100.56
900	82.17

ANS:

```
// Exercise 14.8 Solution
#include <iostream.h>
#include <iomanip.h>
#include <fstream.h>
#include <stdlib.h>
#include <time.h>

main()
{
   char *firstNames[] = {"Walter", "Alice", "Alan", "Mary", "Steve",
                         "Gina", "Tom", "Cindy", "Paul", "Pam"},
        *lastNames[] = {"Red", "Blue", "Yellow", "Orange", "Purple",
                         "Green", "Violet", "White", "Black", "Brown"};
   ofstream outOldMaster("oldMast.dat", ios::out),
            outTransaction("trans.dat", ios::out);

   srand(time(0));

   if (!outOldMaster) {
      cerr << "Unable to open oldmast.dat" << endl;
      exit(1);
   }

   if (!outTransaction) {
      cerr << "Unable to open trans.dat" << endl;
      exit(1);
   }

   cout.setf(ios::fixed | ios::showpoint);
   cout << "Contents of \"oldmast.dat\":" << endl;

   for (int z = 1; z < 11; z++) {
      int value = rand() % 10, value2 = rand() % 50;
      outOldMaster << z * 100 << ' ' << firstNames[z - 1] << ' '
                   << lastNames[value] << ' '
                   << setiosflags(ios::fixed | ios::showpoint)
                   << setprecision(2)
                   << (value * 100) / (value2 / 3 + 4.32) << endl;
      cout << z * 100 << ' ' << firstNames[z - 1] << ' '
           << lastNames[value] << ' ' << setprecision(2)
           << (value * 100) / (value2 / 3 + 4.32) << endl;
   }

   cout << endl << "Contents of \"trans.dat\":" << endl;
   for (z = 1; z < 11; z++) {
      int value = 25 - rand() % 50;
      outTransaction << z * 100 << ' '
                     << setiosflags(ios::fixed | ios::showpoint)
                     << setprecision(2)
                     << (value*100) / (2.667 * (1 + rand() % 10)) << endl;
      cout << z * 100 << ' ' << setprecision(2)
           << (value * 100) / (2.667 * (1 + rand() % 10)) << endl;
   }

   return 0;
}
```

Contents written to "oldmast.dat":

```
100 Walter Yellow 46.30
200 Alice White 40.42
300 Alan Green 28.87
400 Mary Yellow 46.30
500 Steve Brown 62.85
600 Gina White 95.63
700 Tom White 36.23
800 Cindy Brown 96.57
900 Paul White 36.23
1000 Pam Violet 31.06
```

Contents written to "trans.dat":

```
100 -299.96
200 82.49
300 -84.36
400 10.71
500 224.97
600 56.24
700 87.49
800 -179.98
900 -118.74
1000 -25.00
```

```
Contents of "oldmast.dat":
100 Walter Yellow 46.30
200 Alice White 40.42
300 Alan Green 28.87
400 Mary Yellow 46.30
500 Steve Brown 62.85
600 Gina White 95.63
700 Tom White 36.23
800 Cindy Brown 96.57
900 Paul White 36.23
1000 Pam Violet 31.06

Contents of "trans.dat":
100 -299.96
200 82.49
300 -84.36
400 10.71
500 224.97
600 56.24
700 87.49
800 -179.98
900 -118.74
1000 -25.00
```

14.9   Run the program of Exercise 14.7 using the files of test data created in Exercise 14.8. Print the new master file. Check that the accounts have been updated correctly.

ANS:

Contents of "newmast.dat":

```
100 Walter Yellow -253.66
200 Alice White 122.91
300 Alan Green -55.49
400 Mary Yellow 57.01
500 Steve Brown 287.82
600 Gina White 151.87
700 Tom White 123.72
800 Cindy Brown -83.41
900 Paul White -82.51
1000 Pam Violet 6.06
```

14.10 It is possible (actually common) to have several transaction records with the same record key. This occurs because a particular customer might make several purchases and cash payments during a business period. Rewrite your accounts receivable file-matching program of Exercise 14.7 to provide for the possibility of handling several transaction records with the same record key. Modify the test data of Exercise 14.8 to include the following additional transaction records:

Account number	Dollar amount
300	83.89
700	80.78
700	1.53

ANS:

```cpp
// Exercise 14.10 Solution
#include <iostream.h>
#include <fstream.h>
#include <iomanip.h>
#include <stdlib.h>

const int SIZE = 20;

void printOutput(ofstream&, int, const char *, const char *, float);

main()
{
   int masterAccount, transactionAccount;
   float masterBalance, transactionBalance;
   char masterFirstName[SIZE], masterLastName[SIZE];

   ifstream inOldmaster("oldmast.dat", ios::in),
            inTransaction("trans.dat", ios::in);
   ofstream outNewmaster("newmast.dat", ios::out);

   if (!inOldmaster) {
      cerr << "Unable to open oldmast.dat" << endl;
      exit(1);
   }

   if (!inTransaction) {
      cerr << "Unable to open trans.dat" << endl;
      exit(1);
   }

   if (!outNewmaster) {
      cerr << "Unable to open newmast.dat" << endl;
      exit(1);
   }
```

```
        cout << "Processing..." << endl;
        inTransaction >> transactionAccount >> transactionBalance;

        while (!inTransaction.eof()) {
           inOldmaster >> masterAccount >> masterFirstName >> masterLastName
                       >> masterBalance;

           while (masterAccount < transactionAccount && !inOldmaster.eof()) {
              printOutput(outNewmaster, masterAccount, masterFirstName,
                          masterLastName, masterBalance);
              inOldmaster >> masterAccount >> masterFirstName
                          >> masterLastName >> masterBalance;
           }

           if (masterAccount > transactionAccount) {
              cout << "Unmatched transaction record for account "
                   << transactionAccount << endl;
              inTransaction >> transactionAccount >> transactionBalance;
           }
           else if (masterAccount < transactionAccount) {
              cout << "Unmatched transaction record for account "
                   << transactionAccount << endl;
              inTransaction >> transactionAccount >> transactionBalance;
           }

           if (masterAccount == transactionAccount) {

              while (masterAccount == transactionAccount
                                            && !inTransaction.eof()) {
                 masterBalance += transactionBalance;
                 inTransaction >> transactionAccount >> transactionBalance;
              }

              printOutput(outNewmaster, masterAccount, masterFirstName,
                          masterLastName, masterBalance);
           }
        }

        return 0;
}


void printOutput(ofstream &oRef, int mAccount, const char *mfName,
                 const char *mlName, float mBalance)
{
        cout.setf(ios::showpoint);
        oRef << mAccount << ' ' << mfName << ' ' << mlName << ' '
             << setiosflags(ios::fixed | ios::showpoint) << setprecision(2)
             << mBalance << endl;
        cout << mAccount << ' ' << mfName << ' ' << mlName << ' '
             << setprecision(2) << mBalance << endl;
}
```

Contents of "trans.dat":

```
100  27.14
300  62.11
300  83.89
400  100.56
500  50.00
700  80.78
700  1.53
900  82.17
```

Contents of "oldmast.dat":

```
100 Alan Jones 348.17
300 Mary Smith 27.19
500 Sam Sharp 0.00
700 Suzy Green -14.22
```

Contents of "newmast.dat":

```
100 Alan Jones 375.31
300 Mary Smith 173.19
500 Sam Sharp 50.00
700 Suzy Green 68.09
```

```
Processing...
100 Alan Jones 375.31
300 Mary Smith 173.19
Unmatched transaction record for account 400
500 Sam Sharp 50.00
700 Suzy Green 68.09
Unmatched transaction record for account 900
```

14.11   Write a series of statements that accomplish each of the following. Assume the structure

```
struct person {
    char lastName[15];
    char firstName[15];
    char age[2];
};
```

has been defined, and that the random access file has been opened properly.

a)   Initialize the file **"nameage.dat"** with 100 records containing **lastName = "unassigned"**, **firstName = ""**, and **age = "0"**.

ANS:
```
// fstream object "fileObject" corresponds to file "nameage.dat"
person personInfo = {"unassigned", "", 0};

for (int record = 1; record <= 100; record++)
    fileObject.write((char *)&personInfo, sizeof(personInfo));
```
b)   Input 10 last names, first names, and ages, and write them to the file.

ANS:
```
fileObject.seekp(0);

for (int x = 1; x <= 10; x++) {
    cout << "Enter the last name, first name, and age:" << endl;
    cin >> personInfo.lastName >> personInfo.firstName >> personInfo.age;
    fileObject.write((char *)&person, sizeof(person));
}
```
c)   Update a record that has information in it, and if there is none tell the user **"No info"**

d)   Delete a record that has information by reinitializing that particular record.

14.12   You are the owner of a hardware store and need to keep an inventory that can tell you what different tools you have, how many of each you have on hand, and the cost of each one. Write a program that initializes the random access file **"hardware.dat"** to one hundred empty records, lets you input the data concerning each tool, enables you to list all your tools, lets you delete a record for a tool that you no longer have, and lets you update **any** information in the file. The tool identification number should be the record number. Use the following information to start your file:

Record #	Tool name	Quantity	Cost
3	Electric sander	7	57.98
17	Hammer	76	11.99
24	Jig saw	21	11.00
39	Lawn mower	3	79.50
56	Power saw	18	99.99
68	Screwdriver	106	6.99
77	Sledge hammer	11	21.50
83	Wrench	34	7.50

```
ANS:
// Exercise 14.12 Solution

#include <iostream.h>
#include <fstream.h>
#include <iomanip.h>
#include <string.h>
#include <ctype.h>
#include <stdlib.h>

const int SIZE = 30;

void initializeFile(fstream &);
void inputData(fstream &);
void listTools(fstream &);
void updateRecord(fstream &);
void insertRecord(fstream &);
void deleteRecord(fstream &);
int instructions(void);

struct Data {
   int partNumber;
   char toolName[SIZE];
   int inStock;
   float unitPrice;
};

main()
{
   int choice;
   char response[2];
   fstream file("hardware.dat", ios::in | ios::out);

   if (!file) {
      cerr << "File could not be opened.\n";
      exit(1);
   }

   cout << "Should the file be initialized (Y or N): ";
   cin >> response;

   while (toupper(response[0]) != 'Y' && toupper(response[0]) != 'N') {
      cout << "Invalid response. Enter Y or N: ";
      cin >> response;
   }
```

```cpp
   if (toupper(response[0]) == 'Y') {
      initializeFile(file);
      inputData(file);
   }

   while ( ( choice = instructions() ) != 5 ) {

      switch (choice) {
         case 1:
            listTools(file);
            break;
         case 2:
            updateRecord(file);
            break;
         case 3:
            insertRecord(file);
            break;
         case 4:
            deleteRecord(file);
            break;
         default:
            cerr << "Invalid choice." << endl;
            break;
      }

      file.clear();     // reset eof indicator
   }

   return 0;
}


void initializeFile(fstream &fRef)
{
   Data blankItem = {-1, "", 0, 0.0};

   for (int i = 0; i < 100; i++)
      fRef.write((char *)&blankItem, sizeof(Data));
}


void inputData(fstream &fRef)
{
   Data temp;

   cout << "Enter the part number (0 - 99, -1 to end input): ";
   cin >> temp.partNumber;

   while (temp.partNumber != -1) {
      cout << "Enter the tool name: " << endl;
      cin.ignore();  // ignore the newline on the input stream
      cin.getline(temp.toolName, SIZE);
      cout << "Enter quantity and price:" << endl;
      cin >> temp.inStock >> temp.unitPrice;
      fRef.seekp((temp.partNumber) * sizeof(Data));
      fRef.write((char *)&temp, sizeof(Data));

      cout << "Enter the partnumber (0 - 99, -1 to end input): ";
      cin >> temp.partNumber;
   }
}
```

```cpp
int instructions(void)
{
   int choice;

   cout << endl << "Enter a choice:" << endl << "1  List all tools."
        << endl << "2  Update record." << endl << "3  Insert record."
        << endl << "4  Delete record." << endl << "5  End program.\n";

   do {
      cout << "? ";
      cin >> choice;
   } while (choice < 1 || choice > 5);

   return choice;
}

void listTools(fstream &fRef)
{
   Data temp;

   cout << setw(7) << "Record#" << "    " << setiosflags(ios::left)
        << setw(30) << "Tool name" << resetiosflags(ios::left)
        << setw(13) << "Quantity" << setw(10) << "Cost" << endl;

   for (int count = 0; count < 100 && !fRef.eof(); count++) {
      fRef.seekg(count * sizeof(Data));
      fRef.read((char *)&temp, sizeof(Data));

      if (temp.partNumber >= 0 && temp.partNumber < 100) {
         cout.setf(ios::fixed | ios::showpoint);
         cout << setw(7) << temp.partNumber << "    "
              << setiosflags(ios::left) << setw(30) << temp.toolName
              << resetiosflags(ios::left) << setw(13) << temp.inStock
              << setprecision(2) << setw(10) << temp.unitPrice << endl;
      }
   }
}

void updateRecord(fstream &fRef)
{
   Data temp;
   int part;

   cout << "Enter the part number for update: ";
   cin >> part;
   fRef.seekg(part * sizeof(Data));
   fRef.read((char *)&temp, sizeof(Data));

   if (temp.partNumber != -1) {
      cout << setw(7) << "Record#" << "    " << setiosflags(ios::left)
           << setw(30) << "Tool name" << resetiosflags(ios::left)
           << setw(13) << "Quantity" << setw(10) << "Cost" << endl;
      cout.setf(ios::fixed | ios::showpoint);
      cout << setw(7) << temp.partNumber << "    "
           << setiosflags(ios::left) << setw(30) << temp.toolName
           << resetiosflags(ios::left) << setw(13) << temp.inStock
           << setprecision(2) << setw(10) << temp.unitPrice << endl;
      cout << "Enter the tool name: " << endl;
      cin.ignore();  // ignore the newline on the input stream
      cin.getline(temp.toolName, SIZE);
      cout << "Enter quantity and price:" << endl;
      cin >> temp.inStock >> temp.unitPrice;
      fRef.seekp((temp.partNumber) * sizeof(Data));
      fRef.write((char *)&temp, sizeof(Data));
   }
   else
      cerr << "Cannot update. The record is empty." << endl;
}
```

```
void insertRecord(fstream &fRef)
{
   Data temp;
   int part;

   cout << "Enter the partnumber for insertion: ";
   cin >> part;

   fRef.seekg((part) * sizeof(Data));
   fRef.read((char *)&temp, sizeof(Data));

   if (temp.partNumber == -1) {
      temp.partNumber = part;
      cout << "Enter the tool name: " << endl;
      cin.ignore();  // ignore the newline on the input stream
      cin.getline(temp.toolName, SIZE);
      cout << "Enter quantity and price:" << endl;
      cin >> temp.inStock >> temp.unitPrice;

      fRef.seekp((temp.partNumber) * sizeof(Data));
      fRef.write((char *)&temp, sizeof(Data));
   }
   else
      cerr << "Cannot insert. The record contains information." << endl;
}

void deleteRecord(fstream &fRef)
{
   Data blankItem = {-1, "", 0, 0.0}, temp;
   int part;

   cout << "Enter the partnumber for deletion: ";
   cin >> part;

   fRef.seekg(part * sizeof(Data));
   fRef.read((char *)&temp, sizeof(Data));

   if (temp.partNumber != -1) {
      fRef.seekp(part * sizeof(Data));
      fRef.write((char *)&blankItem, sizeof(Data));
      cout << "Record deleted." << endl;
   }
   else
      cerr << "Cannot delete. The record is empty." << endl;
}
```

```
Should the file be initialized (Y or N): y
Enter the partnumber (0 - 99, -1 to end input): 3
Enter the tool name:
Electric Sander
Enter quantity and price:
7 57.98
Enter the partnumber (0 - 99, -1 to end input): 17
Enter the tool name:
Hammer
Enter quantity and price:
76 11.99
Enter the partnumber (0 - 99, -1 to end input): 24
Enter the tool name:
Jig Saw
Enter quantity and price:
21 11.00
                                          continued
```

continued

```
Enter the partnumber (0 - 99, -1 to end input): 39
Enter the tool name:
Lawn Mower
Enter quantity and price:
3 79.50
Enter the partnumber (0 - 99, -1 to end input): 56
Enter the tool name:
Power Saw
Enter quantity and price:
18 99.99
Enter the partnumber (0 - 99, -1 to end input): -1

Enter a choice:
1  List all tools.
2  Update record.
3  Insert record.
4  Delete record.
5  End program.
? 1
Record#       Tool name                    Quantity        Cost
      3       Electric Sander                     7       57.98
     17       Hammer                             76       11.99
     24       Jig Saw                            21       11.00
     39       Lawn Mower                          3       79.50
     56       Power Saw                          18       99.99

Enter a choice:
1  List all tools.
2  Update record.
3  Insert record.
4  Delete record.
5  End program.
? 2
Enter the part number for update: 24
Record#       Tool name                    Quantity        Cost
     24       Jig Saw                            21       11.00
Enter the tool name:
Jig Saw
Enter quantity and price:
15 9.99

Enter a choice:
1  List all tools.
2  Update record.
3  Insert record.
4  Delete record.
5  End program.
? 3
Enter the partnumber for insertion: 33
Enter the tool name:
Wrench
Enter quantity and price:
100 12.99

Enter a choice:
1  List all tools.
2  Update record.
3  Insert record.
4  Delete record.
5  End program.
? 4
Enter the partnumber for deletion: 39
```

continued

```
                                                                 continued
   Record deleted.

   Enter a choice:
   1  List all tools.
   2  Update record.
   3  Insert record.
   4  Delete record.
   5  End program.
   ? 1
   Record#       Tool name                     Quantity       Cost
         3       Electric Sander                      7      57.98
        17       Hammer                              76      11.99
        24       Jig Saw                             15       9.99
        33       Wrench                             100      12.99
        56       Power Saw                           18      99.99

   Enter a choice:
   1  List all tools.
   2  Update record.
   3  Insert record.
   4  Delete record.
   5  End program.
   ? 5
```

14.13   Modify the telephone number word generating program you wrote in Chapter 4 so that it writes its output to a file. This allows you to read the file at your convenience. If you have a computerized dictionary available, modify your program to look up the thousands of seven-letter words in the dictionary. Some of the interesting seven-letter combinations created by this program may consist of two or more words. For example, the phone number 8432677 produces "THEBOSS." Modify your program to use the computerized dictionary to check each possible seven-letter word to see if it is a valid one-letter word followed by a valid six-letter word, a valid two-letter word followed by a valid five-letter word, etc.

ANS:

```cpp
// Exercise 14.13 Solution
#include <iostream.h>
#include <iomanip.h>
#include <fstream.h>
#include <stdlib.h>

void wordGenerator(int *);

main()
{
   int phoneNumber[7] = {0};

   cout << "Enter a phone number one digit at a time"
        << " using the digits 2 thru 9:" << endl;

   for (int loop = 0; loop < 7; loop++) {
      cout << "? ";
      cin >> phoneNumber[loop];

      while (phoneNumber[loop] < 2 || phoneNumber[loop] > 9) {
         cout << endl << "Invalid number entered. Please enter again: ";
         cin >> phoneNumber[loop];
      }
   }

   wordGenerator(phoneNumber);

   return 0;
}
```

```
void wordGenerator(int number[])
{
   ofstream outFile("phone.dat", ios::out);
   const char *phoneLetters[10] = {"", "", "ABC", "DEF", "GHI", "JKL",
                                    "MNO", "PRS", "TUV", "WXY"};

   if (!outFile) {
      cerr << "\"phone.dat\" could not be opened." << endl;
      exit(1);
   }

   // print all possible combinations
   for (int loop1 = 0; loop1 <= 2; loop1++)
      for (int loop2 = 0; loop2 <= 2; loop2++)
         for (int loop3 = 0; loop3 <= 2; loop3++)
            for (int loop4 = 0; loop4 <= 2; loop4++)
               for (int loop5 = 0; loop5 <= 2; loop5++)
                  for (int loop6 = 0; loop6 <= 2; loop6++)
                     for (int loop7 = 0; loop7 <= 2; loop7++)
                        outFile << phoneLetters[number[0]][loop1]
                                << phoneLetters[number[1]][loop2]
                                << phoneLetters[number[2]][loop3]
                                << phoneLetters[number[3]][loop4]
                                << phoneLetters[number[4]][loop5]
                                << phoneLetters[number[5]][loop6]
                                << phoneLetters[number[6]][loop7] << endl;

   outFile << endl << "Phone number is ";

   for (int loop = 0; loop < 7; loop++) {
      if (loop == 3)
         outFile << '-';

      outFile << number[loop];
   }
}
```

```
Enter a phone number one digit at a time using the digits 2 thru 9:
? 5
? 5
? 5
? 7
? 8
? 9
? 3
```

Contents written to "phone.dat":

```
PDDATGJ PDDATGK PDDATGL PDDATHJ PDDATHK PDDATHL PDDATIJ PDDATIK PDDATIL
PDDAUGJ PDDAUGK PDDAUGL PDDAUHJ PDDAUHK PDDAUHL PDDAUIJ PDDAUIK PDDAUIL
PDDAVGK PDDAVGK PDDAVGL PDDAVHJ PDDAVHK PDDAVHL PDDAVIJ PDDAVIK PDDAVIL
...
SFFCTGJ SFFCTGK SFFCTGL SFFCTHJ SFFCTHK SFFCTHL SFFCTIJ SFFCTIK SFFCTIL
SFFCUGJ SFFCUGK SFFCUGL SFFCUHJ SFFCUHK SFFCUHL SFFCUIJ SFFCUIK SFFCUIL
SFFCVGJ SFFCVGK SFFCVGL SFFCVHJ SFFCVHK SFFCVHL SFFCVIJ SFFCVIK SFFCVIL

Phone number is 733-2845
```

14.14 Write a program that uses the **sizeof** operator to determine the sizes in bytes of the various data types on your computer system. Write the results to the file **"datasize.dat"** so you may print the results later. The format for the results in the file should be:

```
Data type             Size
char                    1
unsigned char           1
short int               2
unsigned short int      2
int                     4
unsigned int            4
long int                4
unsigned long int       4
float                   4
double                  8
long double            16
```

Note: The sizes of the built-in data types on your computer may differ from those listed above.

ANS:

```cpp
// Exercise 14.14 Solution
#include <iostream.h>
#include <iomanip.h>
#include <fstream.h>
#include <stdlib.h>

main()
{
    ofstream outFile("datasize.dat", ios::out);

    if (!outFile) {
        cerr << "Unable to open \"datasize.dat\"." << endl;
        exit(1);
    }

    outFile << "Data type" << setw(16) << "Size" << endl
            << "char" << setw(21) << sizeof(char) << endl
            << "unsigned char" << setw(12) << sizeof(unsigned char)
            << endl << "short int" << setw(16) << sizeof(short int)
            << endl << "unsigned short int" << setw(7)
            << sizeof(unsigned short int) << endl << "int" << setw(22)
            << sizeof(int) << endl;
    outFile << "unsigned int" << setw(13) << sizeof(unsigned int) << endl
            << "long int" << setw(17) << sizeof(long int) << endl
            << "unsigned long int" << setw(8) << sizeof(unsigned long int)
            << endl << "float" << setw(20) << sizeof(float) << endl
            << "double" << setw(19) << sizeof(double) << endl
            << "long double" << setw(14) << sizeof(long double) << endl;
    return 0;
}
```

```
Data type             Size
char                    1
unsigned char           1
short int               2
unsigned short int      2
int                     2
unsigned int            2
long int                4
unsigned long int       4
float                   4
double                  8
long double            10
```

15
Data Structures: Solutions

Exercises

15.6 Write a program that concatenates two linked list objects of characters. The program should include function `concatenate` that takes references to both objects as arguments and concatenates the second list to the first list.

ANS:

```
// LIST.H
// Template List class definition
// Added copy constructor to member functions (not included in chapter).
#ifndef LIST_H
#define LIST_H

#include <iostream.h>
#include <assert.h>
#include "listnd.h"

template <class NODETYPE>
class List {
public:
   List();                             // default constructor
   List(const List<NODETYPE> &);  // copy constructor
   ~List();                            // destructor
   void insertAtFront(const NODETYPE &);
   void insertAtBack(const NODETYPE &);
   int removeFromFront(NODETYPE &);
   int removeFromBack(NODETYPE &);
   int isEmpty() const;
   void print() const;
private:
   ListNode<NODETYPE> *firstPtr;  // pointer to first node
   ListNode<NODETYPE> *lastPtr;   // pointer to last node

   // Utility function to allocate a new node
   ListNode<NODETYPE> *getNewNode(const NODETYPE &);
};

// Default constructor
template<class NODETYPE>
List<NODETYPE>::List() { firstPtr = lastPtr = 0; }

// Copy constructor
template<class NODETYPE>
List<NODETYPE>::List(const List<NODETYPE> &copy)
{
   firstPtr = lastPtr = 0;  // initialize pointers

   ListNode<NODETYPE> *currentPtr = copy.firstPtr;

   while (currentPtr != 0) {
      insertAtBack(currentPtr->data);
      currentPtr = currentPtr->nextPtr;
   }
}
```

```cpp
// Destructor
template<class NODETYPE>
List<NODETYPE>::~List()
{
   if (!isEmpty()) {     // List is not empty
      cout << "Destroying nodes ... " << endl;

      ListNode<NODETYPE> *currentPtr = firstPtr, *tempPtr;

      while (currentPtr != 0) {  // delete remaining nodes
         tempPtr = currentPtr;
         cout << tempPtr->data << ' ';
         currentPtr = currentPtr->nextPtr;
         delete tempPtr;
      }
   }

   cout << endl << "All nodes destroyed" << endl << endl;
}

// Insert a node at the front of the list
template<class NODETYPE>
void List<NODETYPE>::insertAtFront(const NODETYPE &value)
{
   ListNode<NODETYPE> *newPtr = getNewNode(value);

   if (isEmpty())  // List is empty
      firstPtr = lastPtr = newPtr;
   else {          // List is not empty
      newPtr->nextPtr = firstPtr;
      firstPtr = newPtr;
   }
}

// Insert a node at the back of the list
template<class NODETYPE>
void List<NODETYPE>::insertAtBack(const NODETYPE &value)
{
   ListNode<NODETYPE> *newPtr = getNewNode(value);

   if (isEmpty())  // List is empty
      firstPtr = lastPtr = newPtr;
   else {          // List is not empty
      lastPtr->nextPtr = newPtr;
      lastPtr = newPtr;
   }
}

// Delete a node from the front of the list
template<class NODETYPE>
int List<NODETYPE>::removeFromFront(NODETYPE &value)
{
   if (isEmpty())                // List is empty
      return 0;                  // delete unsuccessful
   else {
      ListNode<NODETYPE> *tempPtr = firstPtr;

      if (firstPtr == lastPtr)
         firstPtr = lastPtr = 0;
      else
         firstPtr = firstPtr->nextPtr;

      value = tempPtr->data;  // data being removed
      delete tempPtr;
      return 1;               // delete successful
   }
}
```

```cpp
// Delete a node from the back of the list
template<class NODETYPE>
int List<NODETYPE>::removeFromBack(NODETYPE &value)
{
   if (isEmpty())
      return 0;    // delete unsuccessful
   else {
      ListNode<NODETYPE> *tempPtr = lastPtr;

      if (firstPtr == lastPtr)
         firstPtr = lastPtr = 0;
      else {
         ListNode<NODETYPE> *currentPtr = firstPtr;

         while (currentPtr->nextPtr != lastPtr)
            currentPtr = currentPtr->nextPtr;

         lastPtr = currentPtr;
         currentPtr->nextPtr = 0;
      }

      value = tempPtr->data;
      delete tempPtr;

      return 1;    // delete successful
   }
}

// Is the List empty?
template<class NODETYPE>
int List<NODETYPE>::isEmpty() const { return firstPtr == 0; }

// Return a pointer to a newly allocated node
template<class NODETYPE>
ListNode<NODETYPE> *List<NODETYPE>::getNewNode(const NODETYPE &value)
{
   ListNode<NODETYPE> *ptr = new ListNode<NODETYPE>(value);
   assert(ptr != 0);

   return ptr;
}

// Display the contents of the List
template<class NODETYPE>
void List<NODETYPE>::print() const
{
   if (isEmpty()) {
      cout << "The list is empty" << endl << endl;
      return;
   }

   ListNode<NODETYPE> *currentPtr = firstPtr;

   cout << "The list is: ";

   while (currentPtr != 0) {
      cout << currentPtr->data << ' ';
      currentPtr = currentPtr->nextPtr;
   }

   cout << endl << endl;
}

#endif
```

```
// LISTND.H
// ListNode template definition
#ifndef LISTND_H
#define LISTND_H

template<class NODETYPE>
class ListNode {
   friend class List<NODETYPE>; // make List a friend
public:
   ListNode(const NODETYPE &);  // constructor
   NODETYPE getData() const;    // return the data in the node
private:
   NODETYPE data;               // data
   ListNode *nextPtr;           // next node in the list
};

// Constructor
template<class NODETYPE>
ListNode<NODETYPE>::ListNode(const NODETYPE &info)
{
   data = info;
   nextPtr = 0;
}

// Return a copy of the data in the node
template<class NODETYPE>
NODETYPE ListNode<NODETYPE>::getData() const { return data;}

#endif
```

```
// Exercise 15.6 solution
#include <iostream.h>
#include "list.h"

template<class T>
void concatenate(List<T> &first, List<T> &second)
{
   List<T> temp(second); // create a copy of second
   T value;              // variable to store removed item from temp

   while (!temp.isEmpty()) {
      temp.removeFromFront(value);  // remove value from temp list
      first.insertAtBack(value);    // insert at end of first list
   }
}

main()
{
   List<char> list1, list2;

   for (char c = 'a'; c <= 'e'; c++)
      list1.insertAtBack(c);

   list1.print();

   for (c = 'f'; c <= 'j'; c++)
      list2.insertAtBack(c);

   list2.print();

   concatenate(list1, list2);
   cout << "The new list1 after concatenation is:" << endl;
   list1.print();

   return 0;
}
```

```
The list is: a b c d e

The list is: f g h i j


All nodes destroyed

The new list1 after concatenation is:
The list is: a b c d e f g h i j

Destroying nodes ...
f g h i j
All nodes destroyed

Destroying nodes ...
a b c d e f g h i j
All nodes destroyed
```

15.7   Write a program that merges two ordered list objects of integers into a single ordered list object of integers. Function **merge** should receive references to each of the list objects to be merged, and should return a reference to the merged list object.

ANS:

```cpp
// LIST.H
// Template List class definition
// Added copy constructor to member functions (not included in chapter).

#ifndef LIST_H
#define LIST_H

#include <iostream.h>
#include <assert.h>
#include "listnd.h"

template<class NODETYPE>
class List {
public:
   List();                             // default constructor
   List(const List<NODETYPE> &);  // copy constructor
   ~List();                            // destructor
   void insertAtFront(const NODETYPE &);
   void insertAtBack(const NODETYPE &);
   int removeFromFront(NODETYPE &);
   int removeFromBack(NODETYPE &);
   int isEmpty() const;
   void print() const;

private:
   ListNode<NODETYPE> *firstPtr;  // pointer to first node
   ListNode<NODETYPE> *lastPtr;   // pointer to last node

   // Utility function to allocate a new node
   ListNode<NODETYPE> *getNewNode(const NODETYPE &);
};


// Default constructor
template<class NODETYPE>
List<NODETYPE>::List() { firstPtr = lastPtr = 0; }
```

```cpp
// Copy constructor
template<class NODETYPE>
List<NODETYPE>::List(const List<NODETYPE> &copy)
{
   firstPtr = lastPtr = 0;  // initialize pointers

   ListNode<NODETYPE> *currentPtr = copy.firstPtr;

   while (currentPtr != 0) {
      insertAtBack(currentPtr->data);
      currentPtr = currentPtr->nextPtr;
   }
}


// Destructor
template<class NODETYPE>
List<NODETYPE>::~List()
{
   if (!isEmpty()) {     // List is not empty
      cout << "Destroying nodes ... " << endl;

      ListNode<NODETYPE> *currentPtr = firstPtr, *tempPtr;

      while (currentPtr != 0) {  // delete remaining nodes
         tempPtr = currentPtr;
         cout << tempPtr->data << ' ';
         currentPtr = currentPtr->nextPtr;
         delete tempPtr;
      }
   }

   cout << endl << "All nodes destroyed" << endl << endl;
}


// Insert a node at the front of the list
template<class NODETYPE>
void List<NODETYPE>::insertAtFront(const NODETYPE &value)
{
   ListNode<NODETYPE> *newPtr = getNewNode(value);

   if (isEmpty())  // List is empty
      firstPtr = lastPtr = newPtr;
   else {          // List is not empty
      newPtr->nextPtr = firstPtr;
      firstPtr = newPtr;
   }
}


// Insert a node at the back of the list
template<class NODETYPE>
void List<NODETYPE>::insertAtBack(const NODETYPE &value)
{
   ListNode<NODETYPE> *newPtr = getNewNode(value);

   if (isEmpty())  // List is empty
      firstPtr = lastPtr = newPtr;
   else {          // List is not empty
      lastPtr->nextPtr = newPtr;
      lastPtr = newPtr;
   }
}
```

```cpp
// Delete a node from the front of the list
template<class NODETYPE>
int List<NODETYPE>::removeFromFront(NODETYPE &value)
{
   if (isEmpty())              // List is empty
      return 0;                // delete unsuccessful
   else {
      ListNode<NODETYPE> *tempPtr = firstPtr;

      if (firstPtr == lastPtr)
         firstPtr = lastPtr = 0;
      else
         firstPtr = firstPtr->nextPtr;

      value = tempPtr->data;   // data being removed
      delete tempPtr;

      return 1;                // delete successful
   }
}


// Delete a node from the back of the list
template<class NODETYPE>
int List<NODETYPE>::removeFromBack(NODETYPE &value)
{
   if (isEmpty())
      return 0;    // delete unsuccessful
   else {
      ListNode<NODETYPE> *tempPtr = lastPtr;

      if (firstPtr == lastPtr)
         firstPtr = lastPtr = 0;
      else {
         ListNode<NODETYPE> *currentPtr = firstPtr;

         while (currentPtr->nextPtr != lastPtr)
            currentPtr = currentPtr->nextPtr;

         lastPtr = currentPtr;
         currentPtr->nextPtr = 0;
      }

      value = tempPtr->data;
      delete tempPtr;

      return 1;    // delete successful
   }
}


// Is the List empty?
template<class NODETYPE>
int List<NODETYPE>::isEmpty() const { return firstPtr == 0; }


// Return a pointer to a newly allocated node
template<class NODETYPE>
ListNode<NODETYPE> *List<NODETYPE>::getNewNode(const NODETYPE &value)
{
   ListNode<NODETYPE> *ptr = new ListNode<NODETYPE>(value);
   assert(ptr != 0);
   return ptr;
}
```

```cpp
// Display the contents of the List
template<class NODETYPE>
void List<NODETYPE>::print() const
{
   if (isEmpty()) {
      cout << "The list is empty" << endl << endl;
      return;
   }

   ListNode<NODETYPE> *currentPtr = firstPtr;

   cout << "The list is: ";

   while (currentPtr != 0) {
      cout << currentPtr->data << ' ';
      currentPtr = currentPtr->nextPtr;
   }

   cout << endl << endl;
}

#endif
```

```cpp
// LISTND.H
// ListNode template definition
#ifndef LISTND_H
#define LISTND_H

template<class NODETYPE>
class ListNode {
   friend class List<NODETYPE>; // make List a friend
public:
   ListNode(const NODETYPE &);   // constructor
   NODETYPE getData() const;     // return the data in the node
private:
   NODETYPE data;                // data
   ListNode *nextPtr;            // next node in the list
};

// Constructor
template<class NODETYPE>
ListNode<NODETYPE>::ListNode(const NODETYPE &info)
{
   data = info;
   nextPtr = 0;
}

// Return a copy of the data in the node
template<class NODETYPE>
NODETYPE ListNode<NODETYPE>::getData() const { return data;}

#endif
```

```cpp
// Exercise 15.7 solution
#include <iostream.h>
#include "list.h"

template<class T>
List<T> &merge(List<T> &first, List<T> &second)
{
   // If both lists are empty, return an empty result
   if (first.isEmpty() && second.isEmpty()) {
      List<T> *ptr = new List<T>;        // dynamically allocated result
      return *ptr;
   }
```

```
   // If first list is empty, return result containing second list
   if (first.isEmpty()) {
      List<T> *ptr = new List<T>(second); // dynamically allocated
                                          // result object
      return *ptr;
   }

   // If second list is empty, return result containing first list
   if (second.isEmpty()) {
      List<T> *ptr = new List<T>(first); // dynamically allocated result
      return *ptr;
   }

   List<T> tempFirst(first),    // create a copy of first
           tempSecond(second);  // create a copy of second
   List<T> *ptr = new List<T>; // dynamically allocated result object
   T value1, value2;

   tempFirst.removeFromFront(value1);
   tempSecond.removeFromFront(value2);

   while (!tempFirst.isEmpty() && !tempSecond.isEmpty()) {
      if (value1 <= value2) {
         ptr->insertAtBack(value1);
         tempFirst.removeFromFront(value1);
      }
      else {
         ptr->insertAtBack(value2);
         tempSecond.removeFromFront(value2);
      }
   }

   // Insert the values currently in value1 and value2
   if (value1 < value2) {
      ptr->insertAtBack(value1);
      ptr->insertAtBack(value2);
   }
   else {
      ptr->insertAtBack(value2);
      ptr->insertAtBack(value1);
   }

   // Complete the insertion of the list that is not empty.
   // NOTE: Only one of the following 2 while structures will execute
   // because one of the lists must be empty to exit the preceding while.
   if (!tempFirst.isEmpty())  // Items left in tempFirst? Insert in result.
      do {
         tempFirst.removeFromFront(value1);
         ptr->insertAtBack(value2);
      } while (!tempFirst.isEmpty());
   else                       // Items left in tempSecond? Insert in result.
      do {
         tempSecond.removeFromFront(value2);
         ptr->insertAtBack(value2);
      } while (!tempSecond.isEmpty());

   return *ptr;
}

main()
{
   List<int> list1, list2;

   for (int i = 1; i <= 9; i += 2)
      list1.insertAtBack(i);
```

```
    list1.print();

    for (i = 2; i <= 10; i += 2)
      list2.insertAtBack(i);

    list2.print();

    List<int> &listRef = merge(list1, list2);

    cout << "The merged list is:" << endl;
    listRef.print();

    delete &listRef;    // delete the dynamically allocated list

    return 0;
}
```

```
The list is: 1 3 5 7 9

The list is: 2 4 6 8 10


All nodes destroyed


All nodes destroyed

The merged list is:
The list is: 1 2 3 4 5 6 7 8 9 10

Destroying nodes ...
1 2 3 4 5 6 7 8 9 10
All nodes destroyed

Destroying nodes ...
2 4 6 8 10
All nodes destroyed

Destroying nodes ...
1 3 5 7 9

All nodes destroyed
```

15.8   Write a program that inserts 25 random integers from 0 to 100 in order in a linked list object. The program should calculate the sum of the elements, and the floating-point average of the elements.

ANS:
```
// LIST.H
// Template List class definition
// Added copy constructor and insertInOrder to member functions
// (not included in chapter).
#ifndef LIST_H
#define LIST_H

#include <iostream.h>
#include <assert.h>
#include "listnd.h"

template<class NODETYPE>
class List {
public:
   List();                            // default constructor
   List(const List<NODETYPE> &);  // copy constructor
```

```
       ~List();                            // destructor
    void insertAtFront(const NODETYPE &);
    void insertAtBack(const NODETYPE &);
    void insertInOrder(const NODETYPE &);
    int removeFromFront(NODETYPE &);
    int removeFromBack(NODETYPE &);
    int isEmpty() const;
    void print() const;
private:
    ListNode<NODETYPE> *firstPtr;  // pointer to first node
    ListNode<NODETYPE> *lastPtr;   // pointer to last node

    // Utility function to allocate a new node
    ListNode<NODETYPE> *getNewNode(const NODETYPE &);
};

// Default constructor
template<class NODETYPE>
List<NODETYPE>::List() { firstPtr = lastPtr = 0; }

// Copy constructor
template<class NODETYPE>
List<NODETYPE>::List(const List<NODETYPE> &copy)
{
    firstPtr = lastPtr = 0;  // initialize pointers

    ListNode<NODETYPE> *currentPtr = copy.firstPtr;

    while (currentPtr != 0) {
        insertAtBack(currentPtr->data);
        currentPtr = currentPtr->nextPtr;
    }
}

// Destructor
template<class NODETYPE>
List<NODETYPE>::~List()
{
    if (!isEmpty()) {      // List is not empty
        cout << "Destroying nodes ... " << endl;

        ListNode<NODETYPE> *currentPtr = firstPtr, *tempPtr;

        while (currentPtr != 0) {  // delete remaining nodes
            tempPtr = currentPtr;
            cout << tempPtr->data << ' ';
            currentPtr = currentPtr->nextPtr;
            delete tempPtr;
        }
    }

    cout << endl << "All nodes destroyed" << endl << endl;
}

// Insert a node at the front of the list
template<class NODETYPE>
void List<NODETYPE>::insertAtFront(const NODETYPE &value)
{
    ListNode<NODETYPE> *newPtr = getNewNode(value);

    if (isEmpty())  // List is empty
        firstPtr = lastPtr = newPtr;
    else {          // List is not empty
        newPtr->nextPtr = firstPtr;
        firstPtr = newPtr;
    }
}
```

```
// Insert a node at the back of the list
template<class NODETYPE>
void List<NODETYPE>::insertAtBack(const NODETYPE &value)
{
   ListNode<NODETYPE> *newPtr = getNewNode(value);

   if (isEmpty())  // List is empty
      firstPtr = lastPtr = newPtr;
   else {          // List is not empty
      lastPtr->nextPtr = newPtr;
      lastPtr = newPtr;
   }
}


// Insert a node in order
template<class NODETYPE>
void List<NODETYPE>::insertInOrder(const NODETYPE &value)
{
   if (isEmpty()) { // List is empty
      ListNode<NODETYPE> *newPtr = getNewNode(value);
      firstPtr = lastPtr = newPtr;
   }
   else {                 // List is not empty
      if (firstPtr->data > value)
         insertAtFront(value);
      else if (lastPtr->data < value)
         insertAtBack(value);
      else {
         ListNode<NODETYPE> *currentPtr = firstPtr->nextPtr,
                            *previousPtr = firstPtr,
                            *newPtr = getNewNode(value);

         while (currentPtr != lastPtr && currentPtr->data < value) {
            previousPtr = currentPtr;
            currentPtr = currentPtr->nextPtr;
         }

         previousPtr->nextPtr = newPtr;
         newPtr->nextPtr = currentPtr;
      }
   }
}


// Delete a node from the front of the list
template<class NODETYPE>
int List<NODETYPE>::removeFromFront(NODETYPE &value)
{
   if (isEmpty())              // List is empty
      return 0;                // delete unsuccessful
   else {
      ListNode<NODETYPE> *tempPtr = firstPtr;

      if (firstPtr == lastPtr)
         firstPtr = lastPtr = 0;
      else
         firstPtr = firstPtr->nextPtr;

      value = tempPtr->data;   // data being removed
      delete tempPtr;

      return 1;                // delete successful
   }
}
```

```cpp
// Delete a node from the back of the list
template<class NODETYPE>
int List<NODETYPE>::removeFromBack(NODETYPE &value)
{
   if (isEmpty())
      return 0;    // delete unsuccessful
   else {
      ListNode<NODETYPE> *tempPtr = lastPtr;

      if (firstPtr == lastPtr)
         firstPtr = lastPtr = 0;
      else {
         ListNode<NODETYPE> *currentPtr = firstPtr;

         while (currentPtr->nextPtr != lastPtr)
            currentPtr = currentPtr->nextPtr;

         lastPtr = currentPtr;
         currentPtr->nextPtr = 0;
      }

      value = tempPtr->data;
      delete tempPtr;

      return 1;    // delete successful
   }
}


// Is the List empty?
template<class NODETYPE>
int List<NODETYPE>::isEmpty() const { return firstPtr == 0; }

// Return a pointer to a newly allocated node
template<class NODETYPE>
ListNode<NODETYPE> *List<NODETYPE>::getNewNode(const NODETYPE &value)
{
   ListNode<NODETYPE> *ptr = new ListNode<NODETYPE>(value);
   assert(ptr != 0);
   return ptr;
}


// Display the contents of the List
template<class NODETYPE>
void List<NODETYPE>::print() const
{
   if (isEmpty()) {
      cout << "The list is empty" << endl << endl;
      return;
   }

   ListNode<NODETYPE> *currentPtr = firstPtr;

   cout << "The list is: " << endl;

   while (currentPtr != 0) {
      cout << currentPtr->data << ' ';
      currentPtr = currentPtr->nextPtr;
   }

   cout << endl << endl;
}

#endif
```

```
// LISTND.H
// ListNode template definition
#ifndef LISTND_H
#define LISTND_H

template<class NODETYPE>
class ListNode {
   friend class List<NODETYPE>; // make List a friend
public:
   ListNode(const NODETYPE &);  // constructor
   NODETYPE getData() const;    // return the data in the node
private:
   NODETYPE data;               // data
   ListNode *nextPtr;           // next node in the list
};

// Constructor
template<class NODETYPE>
ListNode<NODETYPE>::ListNode(const NODETYPE &info)
{
   data = info;
   nextPtr = 0;
}

// Return a copy of the data in the node
template<class NODETYPE>
NODETYPE ListNode<NODETYPE>::getData() const { return data;}

#endif
```

```
// Exercise 15.8 solution
#include <iostream.h>
#include <stdlib.h>
#include <time.h>
#include "list.h"

// Integer specific list sum
int sumList(List<int> &listRef)
{
   List<int> temp(listRef);
   int sum = 0, value;

   while (!temp.isEmpty()) {
      temp.removeFromFront(value);
      sum += value;
   }

   return sum;
}

// Integer specific list average
double aveList(List<int> &listRef)
{
   List<int> temp(listRef);
   int sum = 0, value, count = 0;

   while (!temp.isEmpty()) {
      temp.removeFromFront(value);
      ++count;
      sum += value;
   }

   return (double) sum / count;
}
```

```
main()
{
    srand(time(NULL));   // randomize the random number generator

    List<int> intList;

    for (int i = 1; i <= 25; i++)
        intList.insertInOrder(rand() % 101);

    intList.print();

    cout << "The sum of the elements is: " << sumList(intList) << endl;
    cout << "The average of the elements is: " << aveList(intList) << endl;
    return 0;
}
```

```
The list is:
5 9 14 15 18 19 21 21 29 30 36 41 41 43 47 47 47 51 52 53 57
59 74 80 100


All nodes destroyed

The sum of the elements is: 1009

All nodes destroyed

The average of the elements is: 40.36
Destroying nodes ...
5 9 14 15 18 19 21 21 29 30 36 41 41 43 47 47 47 51 52 53 57
59 74 80 100

All nodes destroyed
```

15.9   Write a program that creates a linked list object of 10 characters, then creates a second list object containing a copy of the first list, but in reverse order.

ANS:

```
// LIST.H
// Template List class definition
// Added copy constructor to member functions (not included in chapter).
#ifndef LIST_H
#define LIST_H

#include <iostream.h>
#include <assert.h>
#include "listnd.h"

template<class NODETYPE>
class List {
public:
    List();                         // default constructor
    List(const List<NODETYPE> &);   // copy constructor
    ~List();                        // destructor
    void insertAtFront(const NODETYPE &);
    void insertAtBack(const NODETYPE &);
    int removeFromFront(NODETYPE &);
    int removeFromBack(NODETYPE &);
    int isEmpty() const;
    void print() const;

private:
    ListNode<NODETYPE> *firstPtr;   // pointer to first node
    ListNode<NODETYPE> *lastPtr;    // pointer to last node

    // Utility function to allocate a new node
    ListNode<NODETYPE> *getNewNode(const NODETYPE &);
};
```

```cpp
// Default constructor
template<class NODETYPE>
List<NODETYPE>::List() { firstPtr = lastPtr = 0; }

// Copy constructor
template<class NODETYPE>
List<NODETYPE>::List(const List<NODETYPE> &copy)
{
    firstPtr = lastPtr = 0;  // initialize pointers

    ListNode<NODETYPE> *currentPtr = copy.firstPtr;

    while (currentPtr != 0) {
        insertAtBack(currentPtr->data);
        currentPtr = currentPtr->nextPtr;
    }
}

// Destructor
template<class NODETYPE>
List<NODETYPE>::~List()
{
    if (!isEmpty()) {      // List is not empty
        cout << "Destroying nodes ... " << endl;

        ListNode<NODETYPE> *currentPtr = firstPtr, *tempPtr;

        while (currentPtr != 0) {  // delete remaining nodes
            tempPtr = currentPtr;
            cout << tempPtr->data << ' ';
            currentPtr = currentPtr->nextPtr;
            delete tempPtr;
        }
    }

    cout << endl << "All nodes destroyed" << endl << endl;
}

// Insert a node at the front of the list
template<class NODETYPE>
void List<NODETYPE>::insertAtFront(const NODETYPE &value)
{
    ListNode<NODETYPE> *newPtr = getNewNode(value);

    if (isEmpty())  // List is empty
        firstPtr = lastPtr = newPtr;
    else {          // List is not empty
        newPtr->nextPtr = firstPtr;
        firstPtr = newPtr;
    }
}

// Insert a node at the back of the list
template<class NODETYPE>
void List<NODETYPE>::insertAtBack(const NODETYPE &value)
{
    ListNode<NODETYPE> *newPtr = getNewNode(value);

    if (isEmpty())  // List is empty
        firstPtr = lastPtr = newPtr;
    else {          // List is not empty
        lastPtr->nextPtr = newPtr;
        lastPtr = newPtr;
    }
}
```

```cpp
// Delete a node from the front of the list
template<class NODETYPE>
int List<NODETYPE>::removeFromFront(NODETYPE &value)
{
   if (isEmpty())                // List is empty
      return 0;                  // delete unsuccessful
   else {
      ListNode<NODETYPE> *tempPtr = firstPtr;

      if (firstPtr == lastPtr)
         firstPtr = lastPtr = 0;
      else
         firstPtr = firstPtr->nextPtr;

      value = tempPtr->data;   // data being removed
      delete tempPtr;
      return 1;                 // delete successful
   }
}


// Delete a node from the back of the list
template<class NODETYPE>
int List<NODETYPE>::removeFromBack(NODETYPE &value)
{
   if (isEmpty())
      return 0;    // delete unsuccessful
   else {
      ListNode<NODETYPE> *tempPtr = lastPtr;

      if (firstPtr == lastPtr)
         firstPtr = lastPtr = 0;
      else {
         ListNode<NODETYPE> *currentPtr = firstPtr;

         while (currentPtr->nextPtr != lastPtr)
            currentPtr = currentPtr->nextPtr;

         lastPtr = currentPtr;
         currentPtr->nextPtr = 0;
      }

      value = tempPtr->data;
      delete tempPtr;
      return 1;    // delete successful
   }
}


// Is the List empty?
template<class NODETYPE>
int List<NODETYPE>::isEmpty() const { return firstPtr == 0; }


// Return a pointer to a newly allocated node
template<class NODETYPE>
ListNode<NODETYPE> *List<NODETYPE>::getNewNode(const NODETYPE &value)
{
   ListNode<NODETYPE> *ptr = new ListNode<NODETYPE>(value);
   assert(ptr != 0);
   return ptr;
}
```

```
// Display the contents of the List
template<class NODETYPE>
void List<NODETYPE>::print() const
{
   if (isEmpty()) {
      cout << "The list is empty" << endl << endl;
      return;
   }

   ListNode<NODETYPE> *currentPtr = firstPtr;

   cout << "The list is: ";

   while (currentPtr != 0) {
      cout << currentPtr->data << ' ';
      currentPtr = currentPtr->nextPtr;
   }

   cout << endl << endl;
}

#endif
```

```
// LISTND.H
// ListNode template definition
#ifndef LISTND_H
#define LISTND_H

template<class NODETYPE>
class ListNode {
   friend class List<NODETYPE>; // make List a friend

public:
   ListNode(const NODETYPE &);  // constructor
   NODETYPE getData() const;    // return the data in the node

private:
   NODETYPE data;               // data
   ListNode *nextPtr;           // next node in the list
};

// Constructor
template<class NODETYPE>
ListNode<NODETYPE>::ListNode(const NODETYPE &info)
{
   data = info;
   nextPtr = 0;
}

// Return a copy of the data in the node
template<class NODETYPE>
NODETYPE ListNode<NODETYPE>::getData() const { return data;}

#endif
```

```
// Exercise 15.9 solution
#include <iostream.h>
#include "list.h"

// Function template that takes two List objects as arguments
// and makes a copy of the second argument reversed in the first argument.
template<class T>
void reverseList(List<T> &first, List<T> &second)
{
    List<T> temp(second); // create a copy of second
    T value;              // variable to store removed item from temp

    while (!temp.isEmpty()) {
       temp.removeFromFront(value);  // remove value from temp list
       first.insertAtFront(value);   // insert at beginning of first list
    }
}

main()
{
    List<char> list1, list2;

    for (char c = 'a'; c <= 'g'; c++)
       list1.insertAtBack(c);

    list1.print();

    reverseList(list2, list1);
    cout << "After reversing:" << endl;
    list2.print();

    return 0;
}
```

```
The list is: a b c d e f g


All nodes destroyed

After reversing:
The list is: g f e d c b a

Destroying nodes ...
g f e d c b a
All nodes destroyed

Destroying nodes ...
a b c d e f g
All nodes destroyed
```

15.10   Write a program that inputs a line of text and uses a stack object to print the line reversed.
        ANS:
```
// STACK.H
// Definition of class Stack
// NOTE: This is not the Stack class used in Figure 15.9 or 15.11
// (both of which are based on the list class). This is a standalone
// Stack class template.

#ifndef STACK_H
#define STACK_H

#include <iostream.h>
#include <assert.h>
#include "stacknd.h"
```

```
template <class T>
class Stack {
public:
    Stack();                // default constructor
    ~Stack();               // destructor
    void push(T &);         // insert item in stack
    T pop();                // remove item from stack
    int isEmpty() const;    // is the stack empty?
    void print() const;     // output the stack
private:
    StackNode<T> *topPtr;    // pointer to fist StackNode
};


// Member function definitions for class Stack
template <class T>
Stack<T>::Stack() { topPtr = 0; }

template <class T>
Stack<T>::~Stack()
{
    StackNode<T> *tempPtr, *currentPtr = topPtr;

    while (currentPtr != 0) {
        tempPtr = currentPtr;
        currentPtr = currentPtr->nextPtr;
        delete tempPtr;
    }
}

template <class T>
void Stack<T>::push(T &d)
{
    StackNode<T> *newPtr = new StackNode<T>(d, topPtr);

    assert(newPtr != 0);   // was memory allocated?
    topPtr = newPtr;
}

template <class T>
T Stack<T>::pop()
{
    assert(!isEmpty());

    StackNode<T> *tempPtr = topPtr;

    topPtr = topPtr->nextPtr;
    T poppedValue = tempPtr->data;
    delete tempPtr;

    return poppedValue;
}

template <class T>
int Stack<T>::isEmpty() const { return topPtr == 0; }

template <class T>
void Stack<T>::print() const
{
    StackNode<T> *currentPtr = topPtr;

    if (isEmpty())              // Stack is empty
        cout << "Stack is empty" << endl;
    else {                      // Stack is not empty
        cout << "The stack is:" << endl;
```

```
        while (currentPtr != 0) {
           cout << currentPtr->data;
           currentPtr = currentPtr->nextPtr;
        }

        cout << endl;
    }
}

#endif
```

```
// STACKND.H
// Definition of template class StackNode
#ifndef STACKND_H
#define STACKND_H

template <class T>
class StackNode {
    friend class Stack<T>;
public:
    StackNode(const T & = 0, StackNode * = 0);
    T getData() const;
private:
    T data;
    StackNode *nextPtr;
};

// Member function definitions for class StackNode
template <class T>
StackNode<T>::StackNode(const T &d, StackNode<T> *ptr)
{
    data = d;
    nextPtr = ptr;
}

template <class T>
T StackNode<T>::getData() const { return data; }

#endif
```

```
// Exercise 15.10 solution
#include <iostream.h>
#include "stack.h"

main()
{
    Stack<char> charStack;
    char c;

    cout << "Enter a sentence:" << endl;

    while ( ( c = cin.get() ) != '\n')
       charStack.push(c);

    cout << endl << "The sentence in reverse is:" << endl;

    while (!charStack.isEmpty())
       cout << charStack.pop();

    cout << endl;

    return 0;
}
```

```
Enter a sentence:
welcome to c++

The sentence in reverse is:
++c ot emoclew
```

15.11   Write a program that uses a stack object to determine if a string is a palindrome (i.e., the string is spelled identically backwards and forwards). The program should ignore spaces and punctuation.

ANS:
```
// STACK.H
// Definition of class Stack
// NOTE: This is not the Stack class used in Figure 15.9 or 15.11
// (both of which are based on the list class). This is a standalone
// Stack class template.

#ifndef STACK_H
#define STACK_H

#include <iostream.h>
#include <assert.h>
#include "stacknd.h"

template <class T>
class Stack {
public:
    Stack();              // default constructor
    ~Stack();             // destructor
    void push(T &);       // insert item in stack
    T pop();              // remove item from stack
    int isEmpty() const;  // is the stack empty?
    void print() const;   // output the stack

private:
    StackNode<T> *topPtr;    // pointer to fist StackNode
};

// Member function definitions for class Stack
template <class T>
Stack<T>::Stack() { topPtr = 0; }

template <class T>
Stack<T>::~Stack()
{
    StackNode<T> *tempPtr, *currentPtr = topPtr;

    while (currentPtr != 0) {
       tempPtr = currentPtr;
       currentPtr = currentPtr->nextPtr;
       delete tempPtr;
    }
}

template <class T>
void Stack<T>::push(T &d)
{
    StackNode<T> *newPtr = new StackNode<T>(d, topPtr);

    assert(newPtr != 0);  // was memory allocated?
    topPtr = newPtr;
}
```

```cpp
template <class T>
T Stack<T>::pop()
{
   assert(!isEmpty());

   StackNode<T> *tempPtr = topPtr;

   topPtr = topPtr->nextPtr;
   T poppedValue = tempPtr->data;
   delete tempPtr;
   return poppedValue;
}

template <class T>
int Stack<T>::isEmpty() const { return topPtr == 0; }

template <class T>
void Stack<T>::print() const
{
   StackNode<T> *currentPtr = topPtr;

   if (isEmpty())                // Stack is empty
      cout << "Stack is empty" << endl;
   else {                        // Stack is not empty
      cout << "The stack is:" << endl;

      while (currentPtr != 0) {
         cout << currentPtr->data;
         currentPtr = currentPtr->nextPtr;
      }

      cout << endl;
   }
}

#endif
```

```cpp
// STACKND.H
// Definition of template class StackNode
#ifndef STACKND_H
#define STACKND_H

template <class T>
class StackNode {
   friend class Stack<T>;
public:
   StackNode(const T & = 0, StackNode * = 0);
   T getData() const;

private:
   T data;
   StackNode *nextPtr;
};

// Member function definitions for class StackNode
template <class T>
StackNode<T>::StackNode(const T &d, StackNode<T> *ptr)
{
   data = d;
   nextPtr = ptr;
}

template <class T>
T StackNode<T>::getData() const { return data; }

#endif
```

```
// Exercise 15.11 solution
#include <iostream.h>
#include <ctype.h>
#include <string.h>
#include "stack.h"

main()
{
    Stack<char> charStack;
    char c, string1[80], string2[80];
    int i = 0;

    cout << "Enter a sentence:" << endl;

    while ( ( c = cin.get() ) != '\n')
        if (isalpha(c)) {
            string1[i++] = c;
            charStack.push(c);
        }

    string1[i] = '\0';

    i = 0;

    while (!charStack.isEmpty())
        string2[i++] = charStack.pop();

    string2[i] = '\0';

    if (strcmp(string1, string2) == 0)
        cout << endl << "The sentence is a palindrome" << endl;
    else
        cout << endl << "The sentence is not a palindrome" << endl;

    return 0;
}
```

```
Enter a sentence:
a man a plan a canal panama

The sentence is a palindrome
```

15.12 Stacks are used by compilers to help in the process of evaluating expressions and generating machine language code. In this and the next exercise, we investigate how compilers evaluate arithmetic expressions consisting only of constants, operators, and parentheses.

Humans generally write expressions like 3 + 4 and 7 / 9 in which the operator (+ or / here) is written between its operands—this is called *infix notation*. Computers "prefer" *postfix notation* in which the operator is written to the right of its two operands. The preceding infix expressions would appear in postfix notation as 3 4 + and 7 9 /, respectively.

To evaluate a complex infix expression, a compiler would first convert the expression to postfix notation, and then evaluate the postfix version of the expression. Each of these algorithms requires only a single left-to-right pass of the expression. Each algorithm uses a stack object in support of its operation, and in each algorithm the stack is used for a different purpose.

In this exercise, you will write a C++ version of the infix-to-postfix conversion algorithm. In the next exercise, you will write a C++ version of the postfix expression evaluation algorithm. Later in the chapter, you will discover that code you write in this exercise can help you implement a complete working compiler.

Write a program that converts an ordinary infix arithmetic expression (assume a valid expression is entered) with single digit integers such as

(6 + 2) * 5 - 8 / 4

to a postfix expression. The postfix version of the preceding infix expression is

```
6  2  +  5  *  8  4  /  -
```

The program should read the expression into character array **infix**, and use modified versions of the stack functions implemented in this chapter to help create the postfix expression in character array **postfix**. The algorithm for creating a postfix expression is as follows:

1) Push a left parenthesis ' (' on the stack.
2) Append a right parenthesis ') ' to the end of **infix**.
3) While the stack is not empty, read **infix** from left to right and do the following:
   If the current character in **infix** is a digit, copy it to the next element of **postfix**.
   If the current character in **infix** is a left parenthesis, push it on the stack.
   If the current character in **infix** is an operator,
   Pop operators (if there are any) at the top of the stack while they have equal or higher precedence than the current operator, and insert the popped operators in **postfix**.
   Push the current character in **infix** on the stack.
   If the current character in **infix** is a right parenthesis
   Pop operators from the top of the stack and insert them in **postfix** until a left parenthesis is at the top of the stack.
   Pop (and discard) the left parenthesis from the stack.

The following arithmetic operations are allowed in an expression:

+	addition
-	subtraction
*	multiplication
/	division
^	exponentiation
%	modulus

The stack should be maintained with stack nodes that each contain a data member and a pointer to the next stack node. Some of the functional capabilities you may want to provide are:

a) Function **convertToPostfix** that converts the infix expression to postfix notation.
b) Function **isOperator** that determines if **c** is an operator.
c) Function **precedence** that determines if the precedence of **operator1** is less than, equal to, or greater than the precedence of **operator2**. The function returns -1, 0, and 1, respectively.
d) Function **push** that pushes a value on the stack.
e) Function **pop** that pops a value off the stack.
f) Function **stackTop** that returns the top value of the stack without popping the stack.
g) Function **isEmpty** that determines if the stack is empty.
h) Function **printStack** that prints the stack.

ANS: NOTE that the problem does not ask the student to use a **Stack** class object. This problem is solved using a **Stack** class template.

```
// STACK.H
// Definition of class Stack
// NOTE: This is not the Stack class used in Figure 15.9 or 15.11
// (both of which are based on the list class). This is a standalone
// Stack class template.
// Modified from previous exercises to include function stackTop.

#ifndef STACK_H
#define STACK_H

#include <iostream.h>
#include <assert.h>
#include "stacknd.h"
```

```cpp
template <class T>
class Stack {
public:
    Stack();              // default constructor
    ~Stack();             // destructor
    void push(T &);       // insert item in stack
    T pop();              // remove item from stack
    T stackTop() const;   // check the top value
    int isEmpty() const;  // is the stack empty?
    void print() const;   // output the stack
private:
    StackNode<T> *topPtr;    // pointer to fist StackNode
};

// Member function definitions for class Stack
template <class T>
Stack<T>::Stack() { topPtr = 0; }

template <class T>
Stack<T>::~Stack()
{
    StackNode<T> *tempPtr, *currentPtr = topPtr;

    while (currentPtr != 0) {
        tempPtr = currentPtr;
        currentPtr = currentPtr->nextPtr;
        delete tempPtr;
    }
}

template <class T>
void Stack<T>::push(T &d)
{
    StackNode<T> *newPtr = new StackNode<T>(d, topPtr);

    assert(newPtr != 0);  // was memory allocated?
    topPtr = newPtr;
}

template <class T>
T Stack<T>::pop()
{
    assert(!isEmpty());

    StackNode<T> *tempPtr = topPtr;

    topPtr = topPtr->nextPtr;
    T poppedValue = tempPtr->data;
    delete tempPtr;
    return poppedValue;
}

template <class T>
T Stack<T>::stackTop() const { return !isEmpty() ? topPtr->data : 0; }

template <class T>
int Stack<T>::isEmpty() const { return topPtr == 0; }

template <class T>
void Stack<T>::print() const
{
    StackNode<T> *currentPtr = topPtr;

    if (isEmpty())                // Stack is empty
        cout << "Stack is empty" << endl;
```

```
        else {                      // Stack is not empty
           cout << "The stack is:" << endl;

           while (currentPtr != 0) {
              cout << currentPtr->data << ' ';
              currentPtr = currentPtr->nextPtr;
           }

           cout << endl;
        }
     }

     #endif
```

```
     // STACKND.H
     // Definition of template class StackNode
     #ifndef STACKND_H
     #define STACKND_H

     template <class T>
     class StackNode {
        friend class Stack<T>;
     public:
        StackNode(const T & = 0, StackNode * = 0);
        T getData() const;

     private:
        T data;
        StackNode *nextPtr;
     };

     // Member function definitions for class StackNode
     template <class T>
     StackNode<T>::StackNode(const T &d, StackNode<T> *ptr)
     {
        data = d;
        nextPtr = ptr;
     }

     template <class T>
     T StackNode<T>::getData() const { return data; }

     #endif
```

```
     // Exercise 15.12 Solution
     // Infix to postfix conversion
     #include <iostream.h>
     #include <ctype.h>
     #include <string.h>
     #include "stack.h"

     void convertToPostfix(char *, char *);
     int isOperator(char);
     int precedence(char, char);

     main()
     {
        const int maxSize = 100;
        char c, inFix[maxSize], postFix[maxSize];
        int pos = 0;

        cout << "Enter the infix expression." << endl;
```

```cpp
        while ( ( c = cin.get() ) != '\n')
           if (c != ' ')
              inFix[pos++] = c;

     inFix[pos] = '\0';

     cout << "The original infix expression is:" << endl << inFix << endl;
     convertToPostfix(inFix, postFix);
     cout << "The expression in postfix notation is:" << endl
          << postFix << endl;

     return 0;
}


void convertToPostfix(char infix[], char postfix[])
{
     Stack<char> charStack;
     int infixCount, postfixCount, higher;
     char popValue, leftParen = '(';

     // push a left paren onto the stack and add a right paren to infix
     charStack.push(leftParen);
     charStack.print();
     strcat(infix, ")");

     // convert the infix expression to postfix
     for (infixCount = 0, postfixCount = 0; charStack.stackTop();
                                                       infixCount++) {
        if ( isdigit(infix[infixCount]) )
           postfix[postfixCount++] = infix[infixCount];
        else if ( infix[infixCount] == '(' ) {
           charStack.push(leftParen);
           charStack.print();
        }
        else if ( isOperator(infix[infixCount]) ) {
           higher = 1;   // used to store value of precedence test

           while (higher) {
              if ( isOperator(charStack.stackTop()) )
                 if ( precedence(charStack.stackTop(), infix[infixCount]) ) {
                    postfix[postfixCount++] = charStack.pop();
                    charStack.print();
                 }
                 else
                    higher = 0;   // false
              else
                 higher = 0;   // false
           }

           charStack.push(infix[infixCount]);
           charStack.print();
        }
        else if ( infix[infixCount] == ')' ) {
           while ( ( popValue = charStack.pop() ) != '(') {
              charStack.print();
              postfix[postfixCount++] = popValue;
           }

           charStack.print();
        }
     }

     postfix[postfixCount] = '\0';
}
```

```
// check if c is an operator
int isOperator(char c)
{
   if (c == '+' || c == '-' || c == '*' || c == '/' || c == '^')
      return 1;    // true
   else
      return 0;    // false
}

// If the precedence of operator1 is >= operator2,
// return 1 (true) else return 0 (false).
int precedence(char operator1, char operator2)
{
   if (operator1 == '^')
      return 1;
   else if (operator2 == '^')
      return 0;
   else if (operator1 == '*' || operator1 == '/')
      return 1;
   else if (operator1 == '+' || operator1 == '-')
      if (operator2 == '*' || operator2 == '/')
         return 0;
      else
         return 1;

   return 0;
}
```

```
Enter the infix expression.
(6 + 2) * 5 - 8 / 4
The original infix expression is:
(6+2)*5-8/4
The stack is:
(
The stack is:
( (
The stack is:
+ ( (
The stack is:
( (
The stack is:
(
The stack is:
* (
The stack is:
(
The stack is:
- (
The stack is:
/ - (
The stack is:
- (
The stack is:
(
Stack is empty
The expression in postfix notation is:
62+5*84/-
```

15.13   Write a program that evaluates a postfix expression (assume it is valid) such as

   6 2 + 5 * 8 4 / -

The program should read a postfix expression consisting of digits and operators into a character array. Using modified versions of the stack functions implemented earlier in this chapter, the program should scan the expression and evaluate it. The algorithm is as follows:

1) Append the null character (`'\0'`) to the end of the postfix expression. When the null character is encountered, no further processing is necessary.
2) While `'\0'` has not been encountered, read the expression from left to right.

    If the current character is a digit,

        Push its integer value on the stack (the integer value of a digit character is its value in the computer's character set minus the value of `'0'` in the computer's character set).

    Otherwise, if the current character is an *operator*,

        Pop the two top elements of the stack into variables **x** and **y**.

        Calculate **y** *operator* **x**.

        Push the result of the calculation onto the stack.
3) When the null character is encountered in the expression, pop the top value of the stack. This is the result of the postfix expression.

Note: In 2) above, if the operator is `'/'`, the top of the stack is **2**, and the next element in the stack is **8**, then pop **2** into **x**, pop **8** into **y**, evaluate **8 / 2**, and push the result, **4**, back on the stack. This note also applies to operator `'-'`. The arithmetic operations allowed in an expression are:

+	addition
–	subtraction
*	multiplication
/	division
^	exponentiation
%	modulus

The stack should be maintained with stack nodes that contain an **int** data member and a pointer to the next stack node. You may want to provide the following functional capabilities:

a) Function **evaluatePostfixExpression** that evaluates the postfix expression.
b) Function **calculate** that evaluates the expression **op1 operator op2**.
c) Function **push** that pushes a value on the stack.
d) Function **pop** that pops a value off the stack.
e) Function **isEmpty** that determines if the stack is empty.
f) Function **printStack** that prints the stack.

    ANS: NOTE that the problem does not ask the student to use a **Stack** class object. This problem is solved using a **Stack** class template.

```
// STACK.H
// Definition of class Stack
// NOTE: This is not the Stack class used in Figure 15.9 or 15.11
// (both of which are based on the list class). This is a standalone
// Stack class template.

#ifndef STACK_H
#define STACK_H

#include <iostream.h>
#include <assert.h>
#include "stacknd.h"

template <class T>
class Stack {
public:
    Stack();                // default constructor
    ~Stack();               // destructor
    void push(T &);         // insert item in stack
    T pop();                // remove item from stack
    int isEmpty() const;    // is the stack empty?
    void print() const;     // output the stack
private:
    StackNode<T> *topPtr;   // pointer to fist StackNode
};
```

```
// Member function definitions for class Stack
template <class T>
Stack<T>::Stack() { topPtr = 0; }


template <class T>
Stack<T>::~Stack()
{
   StackNode<T> *tempPtr, *currentPtr = topPtr;

   while (currentPtr != 0) {
      tempPtr = currentPtr;
      currentPtr = currentPtr->nextPtr;
      delete tempPtr;
   }
}


template <class T>
void Stack<T>::push(T &d)
{
   StackNode<T> *newPtr = new StackNode<T>(d, topPtr);

   assert(newPtr != 0);   // was memory allocated?
   topPtr = newPtr;
}


template <class T>
T Stack<T>::pop()
{
   assert(!isEmpty());

   StackNode<T> *tempPtr = topPtr;

   topPtr = topPtr->nextPtr;
   T poppedValue = tempPtr->data;
   delete tempPtr;
   return poppedValue;
}

template <class T>
int Stack<T>::isEmpty() const { return topPtr == 0; }

template <class T>
void Stack<T>::print() const
{
   StackNode<T> *currentPtr = topPtr;

   if (isEmpty())              // Stack is empty
      cout << "Stack is empty" << endl;
   else {                      // Stack is not empty
      cout << "The stack is:" << endl;

      while (currentPtr != 0) {
         cout << currentPtr->data << ' ';
         currentPtr = currentPtr->nextPtr;
      }

      cout << endl;
   }
}

#endif
```

```
// STACKND.H
// Definition of template class StackNode
#ifndef STACKND_H
#define STACKND_H


template <class T>
class StackNode {
   friend class Stack<T>;
public:
   StackNode(const T & = 0, StackNode * = 0);
   T getData() const;

private:
   T data;
   StackNode *nextPtr;
};


// Member function definitions for class StackNode
template <class T>
StackNode<T>::StackNode(const T &d, StackNode<T> *ptr)
{
   data = d;
   nextPtr = ptr;
}

template <class T>
T StackNode<T>::getData() const { return data; }

#endif
```

```
// Exercise 15.13 Solution
// Using a stack to evaluate an expression in postfix notation
#include <iostream.h>
#include <string.h>
#include <ctype.h>
#include <math.h>
#include "stack.h"

int evaluatePostfixExpression(char *);
int calculate(int, int, char);

main()
{
   char expression[100], c;
   int answer, i = 0;

   cout << "Enter a postfix expression:" << endl;

   while ( ( c = cin.get() ) != '\n')
      if (c != ' ')
         expression[i++] = c;

   expression[i] = '\0';

   answer = evaluatePostfixExpression(expression);
   cout << "The value of the expression is: " << answer << endl;

   return 0;
}
```

```
int evaluatePostfixExpression(char *expr)
{
    int i, popVal1, popVal2, pushVal;
    Stack<int> intStack;
    char c;

    strcat(expr, ")");

    for (i = 0; ( c = expr[i] ) != ')'; i++)
        if ( isdigit(expr[i]) ) {
            pushVal = c - '0';
            intStack.push(pushVal);
            intStack.print();
        }
        else {
            popVal2 = intStack.pop();
            intStack.print();
            popVal1 = intStack.pop();
            intStack.print();
            pushVal = calculate(popVal1, popVal2, expr[i]);
            intStack.push(pushVal);
            intStack.print();
        }

    return intStack.pop();
}

int calculate(int op1, int op2, char oper)
{
    switch(oper) {
        case '+':
            return op1 + op2;
        case '-':
            return op1 - op2;
        case '*':
            return op1 * op2;
        case '/':
            return op1 / op2;
        case '^':    // exponentiation
            return pow(op1, op2);
    }

    return 0;
}
```

```
Enter a postfix expression:
562+*84/-
The stack is:
5
The stack is:
6 5
The stack is:
2 6 5
The stack is:
6 5
The stack is:
5
The stack is:
8 5
The stack is:
5
Stack is empty
                                           continued
```

```
                                                           continued
The stack is:
40
The stack is:
8 40
The stack is:
4 8 40
The stack is:
8 40
The stack is:
40
The stack is:
2 40
The stack is:
40
Stack is empty
The stack is:
38
The value of the expression is: 38
```

15.14   Modify the postfix evaluator program of Exercise 15.13 so that it can process integer operands larger than 9.

15.15   *(Supermarket simulation)* Write a program that simulates a check-out line at a supermarket. The line is a queue object. Customers (i.e., customer objects) arrive in random integer intervals of 1 to 4 minutes. Also, each customer is serviced in random integer intervals of 1 to 4 minutes. Obviously, the rates need to be balanced. If the average arrival rate is larger than the average service rate, the queue will grow infinitely. Even with "balanced" rates, randomness can still cause long lines. Run the supermarket simulation for a 12-hour day (720 minutes) using the following algorithm:

1) Choose a random integer between 1 and 4 to determine the minute at which the first customer arrives.
2) At the first customer's arrival time:
   Determine customer's service time (random integer from 1 to 4);
   Begin servicing the customer;
   Schedule the arrival time of the next customer (random integer 1 to 4 added to the current time).
3) For each minute of the day:
   If the next customer arrives,
   Say so,
   Enqueue the customer;
   Schedule the arrival time of the next customer;
   If service was completed for the last customer;
   Say so
   Dequeue next customer to be serviced
      Determine customer's service completion time (random integer from 1 to 4 added to the current time).

Now run your simulation for 720 minutes and answer each of the following:
a) What is the maximum number of customers in the queue at any time?
b) What is the longest wait any one customer experiences?
c) What happens if the arrival interval is changed from 1-to-4 minutes to 1-to-3 minutes?

15.16   Modify the program of Fig. 15.16 to allow the binary tree object to contain duplicates.
ANS:

```
// TREE.H
// Definition of template class Tree
#ifndef TREE_H
#define TREE_H

#include <iostream.h>
#include <assert.h>
#include "treenode.h"
```

```
template<class NODETYPE>
class Tree {
public:
    Tree();
    void insertNode(const NODETYPE &);
    void preOrderTraversal() const;
    void inOrderTraversal() const;
    void postOrderTraversal() const;
private:
    TreeNode<NODETYPE> *rootPtr;

    // utility functions
    void insertNodeHelper(TreeNode<NODETYPE> **, const NODETYPE &);
    void preOrderHelper(TreeNode<NODETYPE> *) const;
    void inOrderHelper(TreeNode<NODETYPE> *) const;
    void postOrderHelper(TreeNode<NODETYPE> *) const;
};

template<class NODETYPE>
Tree<NODETYPE>::Tree() { rootPtr = 0; }

template<class NODETYPE>
void Tree<NODETYPE>::insertNode(const NODETYPE &value)
    { insertNodeHelper(&rootPtr, value); }

// This function receives a pointer to a pointer so the
// pointer can be modified.
// NOTE: THIS FUNCTION WAS MODIFIED TO ALLOW DUPLICATES.
template<class NODETYPE>
void Tree<NODETYPE>::insertNodeHelper(TreeNode<NODETYPE> **ptr,
                                      const NODETYPE &value)
{
    if (*ptr == 0) {                    // tree is empty
        *ptr = new TreeNode<NODETYPE>(value);
        assert(*ptr != 0);
    }
    else                                // tree is not empty
        if (value <= (*ptr)->data)
            insertNodeHelper( &((*ptr)->leftPtr), value);
        else
            insertNodeHelper(&((*ptr)->rightPtr), value);
}

template<class NODETYPE>
void Tree<NODETYPE>::preOrderTraversal() const { preOrderHelper(rootPtr); }

template<class NODETYPE>
void Tree<NODETYPE>::preOrderHelper(TreeNode<NODETYPE> *ptr) const
{
    if (ptr != 0) {
        cout << ptr->data << ' ';
        preOrderHelper(ptr->leftPtr);
        preOrderHelper(ptr->rightPtr);
    }
}

template<class NODETYPE>
void Tree<NODETYPE>::inOrderTraversal() const { inOrderHelper(rootPtr); }

template<class NODETYPE>
void Tree<NODETYPE>::inOrderHelper(TreeNode<NODETYPE> *ptr) const
{
    if (ptr != 0) {
        inOrderHelper(ptr->leftPtr);
        cout << ptr->data << ' ';
        inOrderHelper(ptr->rightPtr);
    }
}
```

```
template<class NODETYPE>
void Tree<NODETYPE>::postOrderTraversal() const { postOrderHelper(rootPtr); }

template<class NODETYPE>
void Tree<NODETYPE>::postOrderHelper(TreeNode<NODETYPE> *ptr) const
{
   if (ptr != 0) {
      postOrderHelper(ptr->leftPtr);
      postOrderHelper(ptr->rightPtr);
      cout << ptr->data << ' ';
   }
}

#endif
```

```
// TREENODE.H
// Definition of class TreeNode
#ifndef TREENODE_H
#define TREENODE_H

template<class NODETYPE>
class TreeNode {
   friend class Tree<NODETYPE>;
public:
   TreeNode(const NODETYPE &);  // constructor
   NODETYPE getData() const;    // return data
private:
   TreeNode *leftPtr;    // pointer to left subtree
   NODETYPE data;
   TreeNode *rightPtr;   // pointer to right subtree
};

// Constructor
template<class NODETYPE>
TreeNode<NODETYPE>::TreeNode(const NODETYPE &d)
{
   data = d;
   leftPtr = rightPtr = 0;
}

//Return a copy of the data value
template<class NODETYPE>
NODETYPE TreeNode<NODETYPE>::getData() const { return data; }

#endif
```

```
// Exercise 15.16 solution
// Driver to test class Tree
#include <iostream.h>
#include <iomanip.h>
#include "tree.h"

main()
{
   Tree<int> intTree;
   int intVal;

   cout << "Enter 10 integer values:" << endl;
   for(int i = 0; i < 10; i++) {
      cin >> intVal;
      intTree.insertNode(intVal);
   }
```

```
        cout << endl << "Preorder traversal" << endl;
        intTree.preOrderTraversal();

        cout << endl << "Inorder traversal" << endl;
        intTree.inOrderTraversal();

        cout << endl << "Postorder traversal" << endl;
        intTree.postOrderTraversal();

        Tree<float> floatTree;
        float floatVal;

        cout << endl << endl << endl << "Enter 10 float values:"
             << endl << setiosflags(ios::fixed | ios::showpoint)
             << setprecision(1);
        for(i = 0; i < 10; i++) {
           cin >> floatVal;
           floatTree.insertNode(floatVal);
        }

        cout << endl << "Preorder traversal" << endl;
        floatTree.preOrderTraversal();

        cout << endl << "Inorder traversal" << endl;
        floatTree.inOrderTraversal();

        cout << endl << "Postorder traversal" << endl;
        floatTree.postOrderTraversal();

        return 0;
}
```

```
Enter 10 integer values:
20 10 30 5 8 20 39 27 44 2

Preorder traversal
20 10 5 2 8 20 30 27 39 44
Inorder traversal
2 5 8 10 20 20 27 30 39 44
Postorder traversal
2 8 5 20 10 27 44 39 30 20


Enter 10 float values:
39.2 16.5 82.7 3.3 65.2 90.8 1.1 4.4 89.5 92.5

Preorder traversal
39.2 16.5 3.3 1.1 4.4 82.7 65.2 90.8 89.5 92.5
Inorder traversal
1.1 3.3 4.4 16.5 39.2 65.2 82.7 89.5 90.8 92.5
Postorder traversal
1.1 4.4 3.3 16.5 65.2 89.5 92.5 90.8 82.7 39.2
```

15.17   Write a program based on the program of Fig. 15.16 that inputs a line of text, tokenizes the sentence into separate words (you may want to use the **strtok** library function), inserts the words in a binary search tree, and prints the inorder, preorder, and postorder traversals of the tree. Use an OOP approach.

   ANS:

```
// TREE.H
// Definition of template class Tree
#ifndef TREE_H
#define TREE_H

#include <iostream.h>
#include <assert.h>
#include "treenode.h"
```

```
template<class NODETYPE>
class Tree {
public:
   Tree();
   void insertNode(const NODETYPE &);
   void preOrderTraversal() const;
   void inOrderTraversal() const;
   void postOrderTraversal() const;
private:
   TreeNode<NODETYPE> *rootPtr;

   // utility functions
   void insertNodeHelper(TreeNode<NODETYPE> **, const NODETYPE &);
   void preOrderHelper(TreeNode<NODETYPE> *) const;
   void inOrderHelper(TreeNode<NODETYPE> *) const;
   void postOrderHelper(TreeNode<NODETYPE> *) const;
};

template<class NODETYPE>
Tree<NODETYPE>::Tree() { rootPtr = 0; }

template<class NODETYPE>
void Tree<NODETYPE>::insertNode(const NODETYPE &value)
   { insertNodeHelper(&rootPtr, value); }

// This function receives a pointer to a pointer so the
// pointer can be modified.
// NOTE: THIS FUNCTION WAS MODIFIED TO ALLOW DUPLICATES.
template<class NODETYPE>
void Tree<NODETYPE>::insertNodeHelper(TreeNode<NODETYPE> **ptr,
                                      const NODETYPE &value)
{
   if (*ptr == 0) {                      // tree is empty
      *ptr = new TreeNode<NODETYPE>(value);
      assert(*ptr != 0);
   }
   else                                  // tree is not empty
      if (value <= (*ptr)->data)
         insertNodeHelper( &((*ptr)->leftPtr), value);
      else
         insertNodeHelper(&((*ptr)->rightPtr), value);
}

template<class NODETYPE>
void Tree<NODETYPE>::preOrderTraversal() const { preOrderHelper(rootPtr); }

template<class NODETYPE>
void Tree<NODETYPE>::preOrderHelper(TreeNode<NODETYPE> *ptr) const
{
   if (ptr != 0) {
      cout << ptr->data << ' ';
      preOrderHelper(ptr->leftPtr);
      preOrderHelper(ptr->rightPtr);
   }
}

template<class NODETYPE>
void Tree<NODETYPE>::inOrderTraversal() const { inOrderHelper(rootPtr); }

template<class NODETYPE>
void Tree<NODETYPE>::inOrderHelper(TreeNode<NODETYPE> *ptr) const
{
   if (ptr != 0) {
      inOrderHelper(ptr->leftPtr);
      cout << ptr->data << ' ';
      inOrderHelper(ptr->rightPtr);
   }
}
```

```
template<class NODETYPE>
void Tree<NODETYPE>::postOrderTraversal() const { postOrderHelper(rootPtr); }

template<class NODETYPE>
void Tree<NODETYPE>::postOrderHelper(TreeNode<NODETYPE> *ptr) const
{
   if (ptr != 0) {
      postOrderHelper(ptr->leftPtr);
      postOrderHelper(ptr->rightPtr);
      cout << ptr->data << ' ';
   }
}

#endif
```

```
// TREENODE.H
// Definition of class TreeNode
#ifndef TREENODE_H
#define TREENODE_H

template<class NODETYPE>
class TreeNode {
   friend class Tree<NODETYPE>;
public:
   TreeNode(const NODETYPE &);   // constructor
   NODETYPE getData() const;     // return data
private:
   TreeNode *leftPtr;    // pointer to left subtree
   NODETYPE data;
   TreeNode *rightPtr;   // pointer to right subtree
};

// Constructor
template<class NODETYPE>
TreeNode<NODETYPE>::TreeNode(const NODETYPE &d)
{
   data = d;
   leftPtr = rightPtr = 0;
}

//Return a copy of the data value
template<class NODETYPE>
NODETYPE TreeNode<NODETYPE>::getData() const { return data; }

#endif
```

```
// STRING2.H
// Definition of a String class
#ifndef STRING1_H
#define STRING1_H

#include <iostream.h>

class String {
   friend ostream &operator<<(ostream &, const String &);
   friend istream &operator>>(istream &, String &);

public:
   String(const char * = "");  // conversion constructor
   String(const String &);     // copy constructor
   ~String();                  // destructor
   const String &operator=(const String &);  // assignment
```

```
    String &operator+=(const String &);     // concatenation
    int operator!() const;                   // is String empty?
    int operator==(const String &) const;    // test s1 == s2
    int operator!=(const String &) const;    // test s1 != s2
    int operator<(const String &)  const;    // test s1 < s2
    int operator>(const String &)  const;    // test s1 > s2
    int operator>=(const String &) const;    // test s1 >= s2
    int operator<=(const String &) const;    // test s1 <= s2
    char &operator[](int);          // return char reference
    String &operator()(int, int);   // return a substring
    int getLength() const;          // return string length

private:
    char *sPtr;                     // pointer to start of string
    int length;                     // string length
};

#endif
```

```
// STRING2.CPP
// Member function definitions for class String.
// NOTE: The printing capabilities have been removed
// from the constructor and destructor functions.
#include <iostream.h>
#include <iomanip.h>
#include <string.h>
#include <assert.h>
#include "string2.h"

// Conversion constructor: Convert char * to String
String::String(const char *s)
{
    length = strlen(s);           // compute length
    sPtr = new char[length + 1];  // allocate storage
    assert(sPtr != 0);   // terminate if memory not allocated
    strcpy(sPtr, s);              // copy literal to object
}

// Copy constructor
String::String(const String &copy)
{
    length = copy.length;         // copy length
    sPtr = new char[length + 1];  // allocate storage
    assert(sPtr != 0);            // ensure memory allocated
    strcpy(sPtr, copy.sPtr);      // copy string
}

// Destructor
String::~String()
{
    delete [] sPtr;               // reclaim string
}

// Overloaded = operator; avoids self assignment
const String &String::operator=(const String &right)
{
    if (&right != this) {              // avoid self assignment
        delete [] sPtr;                // prevents memory leak
        length = right.length;         // new String length
        sPtr = new char[length + 1];   // allocate memory
        assert(sPtr != 0);             // ensure memory allocated
        strcpy(sPtr, right.sPtr);      // copy string
    }
```

```
      else
         cout << "Attempted assignment of a String to itself" << endl;

      return *this;    // enables concatenated assignments
}

// Concatenate right operand to this object and
// store in this object.
String &String::operator+=(const String &right)
{
   char *tempPtr = sPtr;         // hold to be able to delete
   length += right.length;       // new String length
   sPtr = new char[length + 1];  // create space
   assert(sPtr != 0);   // terminate if memory not allocated
   strcpy(sPtr, tempPtr);        // left part of new String
   strcat(sPtr, right.sPtr);     // right part of new String
   delete [] tempPtr;            // reclaim old space

   return *this;                 // enables concatenated calls
}

// Is this String empty?
int String::operator!() const { return length == 0; }

// Is this String equal to right String?
int String::operator==(const String &right) const
   { return strcmp(sPtr, right.sPtr) == 0; }

// Is this String not equal to right String?
int String::operator!=(const String &right) const
   { return strcmp(sPtr, right.sPtr) != 0; }

// Is this String less than right String?
int String::operator<(const String &right) const
   { return strcmp(sPtr, right.sPtr) < 0; }

// Is this String greater than right String?
int String::operator>(const String &right) const
   { return strcmp(sPtr, right.sPtr) > 0; }

// Is this String greater than or equal to right String?
int String::operator>=(const String &right) const
   { return strcmp(sPtr, right.sPtr) >= 0; }

// Is this String less than or equal to right String?
int String::operator<=(const String &right) const
   { return strcmp(sPtr, right.sPtr) <= 0; }

// Return a reference to a character in a String.
char &String::operator[](int subscript)
{
   // First test for subscript out of range
   assert(subscript >= 0 && subscript < length);

   return sPtr[subscript];  // creates lvalue
}

// Return a substring beginning at index and
// of length subLength as a reference to a String object.
String &String::operator()(int index, int subLength)
{
   // ensure index is in range and substring length >= 0
   assert(index >= 0 && index < length && subLength >= 0);

   String *subPtr = new String;  // empty String
   assert(subPtr != 0);        // ensure new String allocated
```

```
   // determine length of substring
   if ((subLength == 0) || (index + subLength > length))
      subPtr->length = length - index + 1;
   else
      subPtr->length = subLength + 1;

   // allocate memory for substring
   delete subPtr->sPtr;         // delete character from object
   subPtr->sPtr = new char[subPtr->length];
   assert(subPtr->sPtr != 0); // ensure space allocated

   // copy substring into new String
   strncpy(subPtr->sPtr, &sPtr[index], subPtr->length);
   subPtr->sPtr[subPtr->length] = '\0'; // terminate new String

   return *subPtr;             // return new String
}

// Return string length
int String::getLength() const { return length; }

// Overloaded output operator
ostream &operator<<(ostream &output, const String &s)
{
   output << s.sPtr;
   return output;    // enables concatenation
}

// Overloaded input operator
istream &operator>>(istream &input, String &s)
{
   char temp[100];    // buffer to store input

   input >> setw(100) >> temp;
   s = temp;          // use String class assignment operator
   return input;      // enables concatenation
}
```

```
// Exercise 15.17 solution
#include <iostream.h>
#include <iomanip.h>
#include <string.h>
#include "tree.h"
#include "string2.h"

main()
{
   Tree<String> stringTree;
   char sentence[80], *tokenPtr;

   cout << "Enter a sentence:" << endl;
   cin.getline(sentence, 80);

   tokenPtr = strtok(sentence, " ");

   while (tokenPtr != 0) {
      String *newString = new String(tokenPtr);
      stringTree.insertNode(*newString);
      tokenPtr = strtok(NULL, " ");
   }

   cout << endl << "Preorder traversal" << endl;
   stringTree.preOrderTraversal();
```

```
    cout << endl << "Inorder traversal" << endl;
    stringTree.inOrderTraversal();

    cout << endl << "Postorder traversal" << endl;
    stringTree.postOrderTraversal();

    return 0;
}
```

```
Enter a sentence:
welcome to the world of objects

Preorder traversal
welcome to the of objects world
Inorder traversal
objects of the to welcome world
Postorder traversal
objects of the to world welcome
```

15.18   In this chapter, we saw that duplicate elimination is straightforward when creating a binary search tree. Describe how you would perform duplicate elimination using only a single-subscripted array. Compare the performance of array-based duplicate elimination with the performance of binary-search-tree-based duplicate elimination.

15.19   Write a function **depth** that receives a binary tree and determines how many levels it has.

      ANS:

```
// TREE.H
// Definition of template class Tree
// Modified to include getDepth and determineDepth member functions.
#ifndef TREE_H
#define TREE_H

#include <iostream.h>
#include <assert.h>
#include "treenode.h"

template<class NODETYPE>
class Tree {
public:
    Tree();
    void insertNode(const NODETYPE &);
    void preOrderTraversal() const;
    void inOrderTraversal() const;
    void postOrderTraversal() const;
    int getDepth() const;

private:
    TreeNode<NODETYPE> *rootPtr;

    // utility functions
    void insertNodeHelper(TreeNode<NODETYPE> **, const NODETYPE &);
    void preOrderHelper(TreeNode<NODETYPE> *) const;
    void inOrderHelper(TreeNode<NODETYPE> *) const;
    void postOrderHelper(TreeNode<NODETYPE> *) const;
    void determineDepth(TreeNode<NODETYPE> *, int *, int *) const;
};

template<class NODETYPE>
Tree<NODETYPE>::Tree() { rootPtr = 0; }

template<class NODETYPE>
void Tree<NODETYPE>::insertNode(const NODETYPE &value)
    { insertNodeHelper(&rootPtr, value); }
```

```
// This function receives a pointer to a pointer so the
// pointer can be modified.
// NOTE: THIS FUNCTION WAS MODIFIED TO ALLOW DUPLICATES.
template<class NODETYPE>
void Tree<NODETYPE>::insertNodeHelper(TreeNode<NODETYPE> **ptr,
                                      const NODETYPE &value)
{
   if (*ptr == 0) {                        // tree is empty
      *ptr = new TreeNode<NODETYPE>(value);
      assert(*ptr != 0);
   }
   else                                    // tree is not empty
      if (value <= (*ptr)->data)
         insertNodeHelper( &((*ptr)->leftPtr), value);
      else
         insertNodeHelper(&((*ptr)->rightPtr), value);
}

template<class NODETYPE>
void Tree<NODETYPE>::preOrderTraversal() const { preOrderHelper(rootPtr); }

template<class NODETYPE>
void Tree<NODETYPE>::preOrderHelper(TreeNode<NODETYPE> *ptr) const
{
   if (ptr != 0) {
      cout << ptr->data << ' ';
      preOrderHelper(ptr->leftPtr);
      preOrderHelper(ptr->rightPtr);
   }
}

template<class NODETYPE>
void Tree<NODETYPE>::inOrderTraversal() const { inOrderHelper(rootPtr); }

template<class NODETYPE>
void Tree<NODETYPE>::inOrderHelper(TreeNode<NODETYPE> *ptr) const
{
   if (ptr != 0) {
      inOrderHelper(ptr->leftPtr);
      cout << ptr->data << ' ';
      inOrderHelper(ptr->rightPtr);
   }
}

template<class NODETYPE>
void Tree<NODETYPE>::postOrderTraversal() const { postOrderHelper(rootPtr); }

template<class NODETYPE>
void Tree<NODETYPE>::postOrderHelper(TreeNode<NODETYPE> *ptr) const
{
   if (ptr != 0) {
      postOrderHelper(ptr->leftPtr);
      postOrderHelper(ptr->rightPtr);
      cout << ptr->data << ' ';
   }
}

template<class NODETYPE>
int Tree<NODETYPE>::getDepth() const
{
   int totalDepth = 0, currentDepth = 0;

   determineDepth(rootPtr, &totalDepth, &currentDepth);

   return totalDepth;
}
```

```
template<class NODETYPE>
void Tree<NODETYPE>::determineDepth(TreeNode<NODETYPE> *ptr,
                                    int *totPtr, int *currPtr) const
{
   if (ptr != 0) {
      ++*currPtr;

      if (*currPtr > *totPtr)
         *totPtr = *currPtr;

      determineDepth(ptr->leftPtr, totPtr, currPtr);
      determineDepth(ptr->rightPtr, totPtr, currPtr);
      --*currPtr;
   }
}

#endif
```

```
// TREENODE.H
// Definition of class TreeNode
#ifndef TREENODE_H
#define TREENODE_H

template<class NODETYPE>
class TreeNode {
   friend class Tree<NODETYPE>;
public:
   TreeNode(const NODETYPE &);  // constructor
   NODETYPE getData() const;    // return data
private:
   TreeNode *leftPtr;   // pointer to left subtree
   NODETYPE data;
   TreeNode *rightPtr;  // pointer to right subtree
};

// Constructor
template<class NODETYPE>
TreeNode<NODETYPE>::TreeNode(const NODETYPE &d)
{
   data = d;
   leftPtr = rightPtr = 0;
}

//Return a copy of the data value
template<class NODETYPE>
NODETYPE TreeNode<NODETYPE>::getData() const { return data; }

#endif
```

```
// Exercise 15.19 solution
#include <iostream.h>
#include "tree.h"

main()
{
   Tree<int> intTree;
   int intVal;

   cout << "Enter 10 integer values:" << endl;

   for(int i = 0; i < 10; i++) {
      cin >> intVal;
      intTree.insertNode(intVal);
   }
```

```
        cout << endl << "Preorder traversal" << endl;
        intTree.preOrderTraversal();

        cout << endl << "Inorder traversal" << endl;
        intTree.inOrderTraversal();

        cout << endl << "Postorder traversal" << endl;
        intTree.postOrderTraversal();

        cout << endl << endl << "There are " << intTree.getDepth()
            << " levels in this binary tree" << endl;

        return 0;
    }
```

```
    Enter 10 integer values:
    49 28 83 18 40 71 69 99 11 44

    Preorder traversal
    49 28 18 11 40 44 83 71 69 99
    Inorder traversal
    11 18 28 40 44 49 69 71 83 99
    Postorder traversal
    11 18 44 40 28 69 71 99 83 49

    There are 4 levels in this binary tree
```

```
    Enter 10 integer values:
    11 18 28 32 40 49 69 71 72 83

    Preorder traversal
    11 18 28 32 40 49 69 71 72 83
    Inorder traversal
    11 18 28 32 40 49 69 71 72 83
    Postorder traversal
    83 72 71 69 49 40 32 28 18 11

    There are 10 levels in this binary tree
```

15.20   (*Recursively print a list backwards*) Write a member function **printListBackwards** that recursively outputs the items in a linked list object in reverse order. Write a test program that creates a sorted list of integers and prints the list in reverse order.

ANS:

```
// LIST.H
// Template List class definition
#ifndef LIST_H
#define LIST_H

#include <iostream.h>
#include <assert.h>
#include "listnd.h"

template<class NODETYPE>
class List {
public:
    List();        // constructor
    ~List();       // destructor
    void insertAtFront(const NODETYPE &);
    void insertAtBack(const NODETYPE &);
```

```cpp
      int removeFromFront(NODETYPE &);
      int removeFromBack(NODETYPE &);
      void recursivePrintReverse() const;
      int isEmpty() const;
      void print() const;

   private:
      ListNode<NODETYPE> *firstPtr;  // pointer to first node
      ListNode<NODETYPE> *lastPtr;   // pointer to last node

      // Utility functions
      ListNode<NODETYPE> *getNewNode(const NODETYPE &);
      void recursivePrintReverseHelper(ListNode<NODETYPE> *) const;
};

// Default constructor
template<class NODETYPE>
List<NODETYPE>::List() { firstPtr = lastPtr = 0; }

// Destructor
template<class NODETYPE>
List<NODETYPE>::~List()
{
   if (!isEmpty()) {     // List is not empty
      cout << "Destroying nodes ... " << endl;

      ListNode<NODETYPE> *currentPtr = firstPtr, *tempPtr;

      while (currentPtr != 0) {  // delete remaining nodes
         tempPtr = currentPtr;
         cout << tempPtr->data << endl;
         currentPtr = currentPtr->nextPtr;
         delete tempPtr;
      }
   }

   cout << "All nodes destroyed" << endl << endl;
}

// Insert a node at the front of the list
template<class NODETYPE>
void List<NODETYPE>::insertAtFront(const NODETYPE &value)
{
   ListNode<NODETYPE> *newPtr = getNewNode(value);

   if (isEmpty())  // List is empty
      firstPtr = lastPtr = newPtr;
   else {          // List is not empty
      newPtr->nextPtr = firstPtr;
      firstPtr = newPtr;
   }
}

// Insert a node at the back of the list
template<class NODETYPE>
void List<NODETYPE>::insertAtBack(const NODETYPE &value)
{
   ListNode<NODETYPE> *newPtr = getNewNode(value);

   if (isEmpty())  // List is empty
      firstPtr = lastPtr = newPtr;
   else {          // List is not empty
      lastPtr->nextPtr = newPtr;
      lastPtr = newPtr;
   }
}
```

```cpp
// Delete a node from the front of the list
template<class NODETYPE>
int List<NODETYPE>::removeFromFront(NODETYPE &value)
{
   if (isEmpty())              // List is empty
      return 0;                // delete unsuccessful
   else {
      ListNode<NODETYPE> *tempPtr = firstPtr;

      if (firstPtr == lastPtr)
         firstPtr = lastPtr = 0;
      else
         firstPtr = firstPtr->nextPtr;

      value = tempPtr->data;   // data being removed
      delete tempPtr;
      return 1;                // delete successful
   }
}

// Delete a node from the back of the list
template<class NODETYPE>
int List<NODETYPE>::removeFromBack(NODETYPE &value)
{
   if (isEmpty())
      return 0;    // delete unsuccessful
   else {
      ListNode<NODETYPE> *tempPtr = lastPtr;

      if (firstPtr == lastPtr)
         firstPtr = lastPtr = 0;
      else {
         ListNode<NODETYPE> *currentPtr = firstPtr;

         while (currentPtr->nextPtr != lastPtr)
            currentPtr = currentPtr->nextPtr;

         lastPtr = currentPtr;
         currentPtr->nextPtr = 0;
      }

      value = tempPtr->data;
      delete tempPtr;
      return 1;    // delete successful
   }
}

// Print a List backwards recursively.
template<class NODETYPE>
void List<NODETYPE>::recursivePrintReverse() const
{
   cout << "The list printed recursively backwards is:" << endl;
   recursivePrintReverseHelper(firstPtr);
   cout << endl;
}

// Helper for printing a list backwards recursively.
template<class NODETYPE>
void List<NODETYPE>::recursivePrintReverseHelper(ListNode<NODETYPE>
                                                  *currentPtr) const
{
   if (currentPtr == 0)
      return;

   recursivePrintReverseHelper(currentPtr->nextPtr);
   cout << currentPtr->data << ' ';
}
```

```cpp
// Is the List empty?
template<class NODETYPE>
int List<NODETYPE>::isEmpty() const { return firstPtr == 0; }

// Return a pointer to a newly allocated node
template<class NODETYPE>
ListNode<NODETYPE> *List<NODETYPE>::getNewNode(const NODETYPE &value)
{
   ListNode<NODETYPE> *ptr = new ListNode<NODETYPE>(value);
   assert(ptr != 0);
   return ptr;
}

// Display the contents of the List
template<class NODETYPE>
void List<NODETYPE>::print() const
{
   if (isEmpty()) {
      cout << "The list is empty" << endl << endl;
      return;
   }

   ListNode<NODETYPE> *currentPtr = firstPtr;

   cout << "The list is: ";

   while (currentPtr != 0) {
      cout << currentPtr->data << ' ';
      currentPtr = currentPtr->nextPtr;
   }

   cout << endl << endl;
}

#endif
```

```cpp
// LISTND.H
// ListNode template definition
#ifndef LISTND_H
#define LISTND_H

template<class NODETYPE>
class ListNode {
   friend class List<NODETYPE>; // make List a friend
public:
   ListNode(const NODETYPE &);  // constructor
   NODETYPE getData() const;    // return the data in the node

private:
   NODETYPE data;               // data
   ListNode *nextPtr;           // next node in the list
};

// Constructor
template<class NODETYPE>
ListNode<NODETYPE>::ListNode(const NODETYPE &info)
{
   data = info;
   nextPtr = 0;
}

// Return a copy of the data in the node
template<class NODETYPE>
NODETYPE ListNode<NODETYPE>::getData() const { return data;}

#endif
```

```
// Exercise 15.20 solution
#include <iostream.h>
#include "list.h"

main()
{
   List<int> intList;

   for (int i = 1; i <= 10; i++)
      intList.insertAtBack(i);

   intList.print();
   intList.recursivePrintReverse();

   return 0;
}
```

```
The list is: 1 2 3 4 5 6 7 8 9 10

The list printed recursively backwards is:
10 9 8 7 6 5 4 3 2 1
Destroying nodes ...
1
2
3
4
5
6
7
8
9
10
All nodes destroyed
```

15.21   (*Recursively search a list*) Write a member function **searchList** that recursively searches a linked list object for a specified value. The function should return a pointer to the value if it is found; otherwise, null should be returned. Use your function in a test program that creates a list of integers. The program should prompt the user for a value to locate in the list.

   ANS:

```
// LIST.H
// Template List class definition
#ifndef LIST_H
#define LIST_H

#include <iostream.h>
#include <assert.h>
#include "listnd.h"

template<class NODETYPE>
class List {
public:
   List();        // constructor
   ~List();       // destructor
   void insertAtFront(const NODETYPE &);
   void insertAtBack(const NODETYPE &);
   int removeFromFront(NODETYPE &);
   int removeFromBack(NODETYPE &);
   void recursivePrintReverse() const;
   NODETYPE *recursiveSearch(NODETYPE &) const;
   int isEmpty() const;
   void print() const;
```

```cpp
private:
   ListNode<NODETYPE> *firstPtr;   // pointer to first node
   ListNode<NODETYPE> *lastPtr;    // pointer to last node

   // Utility functions
   ListNode<NODETYPE> *getNewNode(const NODETYPE &);
   void recursivePrintReverseHelper(ListNode<NODETYPE> *) const;
   NODETYPE *recursiveSearchHelper(ListNode<NODETYPE> *, NODETYPE &) const;
};


// Default constructor
template<class NODETYPE>
List<NODETYPE>::List() { firstPtr = lastPtr = 0; }


// Destructor
template<class NODETYPE>
List<NODETYPE>::~List()
{
   if (!isEmpty()) {     // List is not empty
      cout << "Destroying nodes ... " << endl;

      ListNode<NODETYPE> *currentPtr = firstPtr, *tempPtr;

      while (currentPtr != 0) {  // delete remaining nodes
         tempPtr = currentPtr;
         cout << tempPtr->data << endl;
         currentPtr = currentPtr->nextPtr;
         delete tempPtr;
      }
   }

   cout << "All nodes destroyed" << endl << endl;
}


// Insert a node at the front of the list
template<class NODETYPE>
void List<NODETYPE>::insertAtFront(const NODETYPE &value)
{
   ListNode<NODETYPE> *newPtr = getNewNode(value);

   if (isEmpty())  // List is empty
      firstPtr = lastPtr = newPtr;
   else {          // List is not empty
      newPtr->nextPtr = firstPtr;
      firstPtr = newPtr;
   }
}


// Insert a node at the back of the list
template<class NODETYPE>
void List<NODETYPE>::insertAtBack(const NODETYPE &value)
{
   ListNode<NODETYPE> *newPtr = getNewNode(value);

   if (isEmpty())  // List is empty
      firstPtr = lastPtr = newPtr;
   else {          // List is not empty
      lastPtr->nextPtr = newPtr;
      lastPtr = newPtr;
   }
}
```

```cpp
// Delete a node from the front of the list
template<class NODETYPE>
int List<NODETYPE>::removeFromFront(NODETYPE &value)
{
   if (isEmpty())                 // List is empty
      return 0;                   // delete unsuccessful
   else {
      ListNode<NODETYPE> *tempPtr = firstPtr;

      if (firstPtr == lastPtr)
         firstPtr = lastPtr = 0;
      else
         firstPtr = firstPtr->nextPtr;

      value = tempPtr->data;   // data being removed
      delete tempPtr;
      return 1;                // delete successful
   }
}

// Delete a node from the back of the list
template<class NODETYPE>
int List<NODETYPE>::removeFromBack(NODETYPE &value)
{
   if (isEmpty())
      return 0;   // delete unsuccessful
   else {
      ListNode<NODETYPE> *tempPtr = lastPtr;

      if (firstPtr == lastPtr)
         firstPtr = lastPtr = 0;
      else {
         ListNode<NODETYPE> *currentPtr = firstPtr;

         while (currentPtr->nextPtr != lastPtr)
            currentPtr = currentPtr->nextPtr;

         lastPtr = currentPtr;
         currentPtr->nextPtr = 0;
      }

      value = tempPtr->data;
      delete tempPtr;

      return 1;   // delete successful
   }
}

// Print a List backwards recursively.
template<class NODETYPE>
void List<NODETYPE>::recursivePrintReverse() const
{
   cout << "The list printed recursively backwards is:" << endl;
   recursivePrintReverseHelper(firstPtr);
   cout << endl;
}

// Helper for printing a list backwards recursively.
template<class NODETYPE>
void List<NODETYPE>::recursivePrintReverseHelper(ListNode<NODETYPE>
                                                 *currentPtr) const
{
   if (currentPtr == 0)
      return;

   recursivePrintReverseHelper(currentPtr->nextPtr);
   cout << currentPtr->data << ' ';
}
```

```cpp
// Search a List recursively.
template<class NODETYPE>
NODETYPE *List<NODETYPE>::recursiveSearch(NODETYPE &val) const
   { return recursiveSearchHelper(firstPtr, val); }

// Helper for searching a list recursively.
template<class NODETYPE>
NODETYPE *List<NODETYPE>::recursiveSearchHelper(ListNode<NODETYPE>
                                     *currentPtr, NODETYPE &value) const
{
   if (currentPtr == 0)
      return 0;

   if (currentPtr->data == value)
      return &currentPtr->data;

   return recursiveSearchHelper(currentPtr->nextPtr, value);
}

// Is the List empty?
template<class NODETYPE>
int List<NODETYPE>::isEmpty() const { return firstPtr == 0; }

// Return a pointer to a newly allocated node
template<class NODETYPE>
ListNode<NODETYPE> *List<NODETYPE>::getNewNode(const NODETYPE &value)
{
   ListNode<NODETYPE> *ptr = new ListNode<NODETYPE>(value);
   assert(ptr != 0);
   return ptr;
}

// Display the contents of the List
template<class NODETYPE>
void List<NODETYPE>::print() const
{
   if (isEmpty()) {
      cout << "The list is empty" << endl << endl;
      return;
   }

   ListNode<NODETYPE> *currentPtr = firstPtr;

   cout << "The list is: ";

   while (currentPtr != 0) {
      cout << currentPtr->data << ' ';
      currentPtr = currentPtr->nextPtr;
   }

   cout << endl << endl;
}

#endif
```

```cpp
// LISTND.H
// ListNode template definition
#ifndef LISTND_H
#define LISTND_H

template<class NODETYPE>
class ListNode {
   friend class List<NODETYPE>; // make List a friend
```

```
public:
    ListNode(const NODETYPE &);    // constructor
    NODETYPE getData() const;      // return the data in the node
private:
    NODETYPE data;                 // data
    ListNode *nextPtr;             // next node in the list
};

// Constructor
template<class NODETYPE>
ListNode<NODETYPE>::ListNode(const NODETYPE &info)
{
    data = info;
    nextPtr = 0;
}

// Return a copy of the data in the node
template<class NODETYPE>
NODETYPE ListNode<NODETYPE>::getData() const { return data;}

#endif
```

```
// Exercise 15.21 solution
#include <iostream.h>
#include "list.h"

main()
{
    List<int> intList;

    for (int i = 2; i <= 20; i += 2)
        intList.insertAtBack(i);

    intList.print();

    int value, *ptr;

    cout << "Enter a value to search for: ";
    cin >> value;
    ptr = intList.recursiveSearch(value);

    if (ptr != 0)
        cout << *ptr << " was found" << endl;
    else
        cout << "Element not found" << endl;

    return 0;
}
```

```
The list is: 2 4 6 8 10 12 14 16 18 20

Enter a value to search for: 7
Element not found
Destroying nodes ...
2
4
6
8
10
12
14
16
18
20
All nodes destroyed
```

```
The list is: 2 4 6 8 10 12 14 16 18 20

Enter a value to search for: 14
14 was found
Destroying nodes ...
2
4
6
8
10
12
14
16
18
20
All nodes destroyed
```

15.22 (*Binary tree delete*) In this exercise, we discuss deleting items from binary search trees. The deletion algorithm is not as straightforward as the insertion algorithm. There are three cases that are encountered when deleting an item—the item is contained in a leaf node (i.e., it has no children), the item is contained in a node that has one child, or the item is contained in a node that has two children.

If the item to be deleted is contained in a leaf node, the node is deleted and the pointer in the parent node is set to null.

If the item to be deleted is contained in a node with one child, the pointer in the parent node is set to point to the child node and the node containing the data item is deleted. This causes the child node to take the place of the deleted node in the tree.

The last case is the most difficult. When a node with two children is deleted, another node in the tree must take its place. However, the pointer in the parent node cannot simply be assigned to point to one of the children of the node to be deleted. In most cases, the resulting binary search tree would not adhere to the following characteristic of binary search trees (with no duplicate values): *The values in any left subtree are less than the value in the parent node, and the values in any right subtree are greater than the value in the parent node.*

Which node is used as a *replacement node* to maintain this characteristic? Either the node containing the largest value in the tree less than the value in the node being deleted, or the node containing the smallest value in the tree greater than the value in the node being deleted. Let us consider the node with the smaller value. In a binary search tree, the largest value less than a parent's value is located in the left subtree of the parent node and is guaranteed to be contained in the rightmost node of the subtree. This node is located by walking down the left subtree to the right until the pointer to the right child of the current node is null. We are now pointing to the replacement node which is either a leaf node or a node with one child to its left. If the replacement node is a leaf node, the steps to perform the deletion are as follows:

1) Store the pointer to the node to be deleted in a temporary pointer variable (this pointer is used to delete the dynamically allocated memory)
2) Set the pointer in the parent of the node being deleted to point to the replacement node
3) Set the pointer in the parent of the replacement node to null
4) Set the pointer to the right subtree in the replacement node to point to the right subtree of the node to be deleted
5) Delete the node to which the temporary pointer variable points.

The deletion steps for a replacement node with a left child are similar to those for a replacement node with no children, but the algorithm also must move the child in to the replacement node's position in the tree. If the replacement node is a node with a left child, the steps to perform the deletion are as follows:

1) Store the pointer to the node to be deleted in a temporary pointer variable
2) Set the pointer in the parent of the node being deleted to point to the replacement node
3) Set the pointer in the parent of the replacement node to point to the left child of the replacement node
4) Set the pointer to the right subtree in the replacement node to point to the right subtree of the node to be deleted
5) Delete the node to which the temporary pointer variable points.

Write member function **deleteNode** which takes as its arguments a pointer to the root node of the tree object and the value to be deleted. The function should locate in the tree the node containing the value to be deleted and use the algorithms discussed here to delete the node. If the value is not found in the tree, the function should print a message that indicates whether or not the value is deleted. Modify the program of Fig. 15.16 to use this function. After deleting an item, call the **inOrder**, **preOrder**, and **postOrder** traversal functions to confirm that the delete operation was performed correctly.

15.23   (*Binary tree search*) Write member function **binaryTreeSearch** that attempts to locate a specified value in a binary search tree object. The function should take as arguments a pointer to the root node of the binary tree and a search key to be located. If the node containing the search key is found, the function should return a pointer to that node; otherwise, the function should return a null pointer.

```
ANS:
// TREE.H
// Definition of template class Tree
// Modified to include binarySearch and binarySearchHelper member functions.
#ifndef TREE_H
#define TREE_H

#include <iostream.h>
#include <assert.h>
#include "treenode.h"

template<class NODETYPE>
class Tree {
public:
   Tree();
   void insertNode(const NODETYPE &);
   void preOrderTraversal() const;
   void inOrderTraversal() const;
   void postOrderTraversal() const;
   TreeNode<NODETYPE> *binarySearch(int) const;
   int getDepth() const;

private:
   TreeNode<NODETYPE> *rootPtr;

   // utility functions
   void insertNodeHelper(TreeNode<NODETYPE> **, const NODETYPE &);
   void preOrderHelper(TreeNode<NODETYPE> *) const;
   void inOrderHelper(TreeNode<NODETYPE> *) const;
   void postOrderHelper(TreeNode<NODETYPE> *) const;
   TreeNode<NODETYPE> *binarySearchHelper(TreeNode<NODETYPE> *, int) const;
   void determineDepth(TreeNode<NODETYPE> *, int *, int *) const;
};

template<class NODETYPE>
Tree<NODETYPE>::Tree() { rootPtr = 0; }

template<class NODETYPE>
void Tree<NODETYPE>::insertNode(const NODETYPE &value)
   { insertNodeHelper(&rootPtr, value); }

// This function receives a pointer to a pointer so the
// pointer can be modified.
template<class NODETYPE>
void Tree<NODETYPE>::insertNodeHelper(TreeNode<NODETYPE> **ptr,
                                      const NODETYPE &value)
{
   if (*ptr == 0) {                         // tree is empty
      *ptr = new TreeNode<NODETYPE>(value);
      assert(*ptr != 0);
   }
```

```
      else                               // tree is not empty
         if (value < (*ptr)->data)
            insertNodeHelper(&((*ptr)->leftPtr), value);
         else if (value > (*ptr)->data)
            insertNodeHelper(&((*ptr)->rightPtr), value);
         else
            cout << "dup ";
}

template<class NODETYPE>
void Tree<NODETYPE>::preOrderTraversal() const
   { preOrderHelper(rootPtr); }

template<class NODETYPE>
void Tree<NODETYPE>::preOrderHelper(TreeNode<NODETYPE> *ptr) const
{
   if (ptr != 0) {
      cout << ptr->data << ' ';
      preOrderHelper(ptr->leftPtr);
      preOrderHelper(ptr->rightPtr);
   }
}

template<class NODETYPE>
void Tree<NODETYPE>::inOrderTraversal() const
   { inOrderHelper(rootPtr); }

template<class NODETYPE>
void Tree<NODETYPE>::inOrderHelper(TreeNode<NODETYPE> *ptr) const
{
   if (ptr != 0) {
      inOrderHelper(ptr->leftPtr);
      cout << ptr->data << ' ';
      inOrderHelper(ptr->rightPtr);
   }
}

template<class NODETYPE>
void Tree<NODETYPE>::postOrderTraversal() const
   { postOrderHelper(rootPtr); }

template<class NODETYPE>
void Tree<NODETYPE>::postOrderHelper(TreeNode<NODETYPE> *ptr) const
{
   if (ptr != 0) {
      postOrderHelper(ptr->leftPtr);
      postOrderHelper(ptr->rightPtr);
      cout << ptr->data << ' ';
   }
}

template<class NODETYPE>
TreeNode<NODETYPE> *Tree<NODETYPE>::binarySearch(int val) const
   { return binarySearchHelper(rootPtr, val); }

template<class NODETYPE>
TreeNode<NODETYPE> *Tree<NODETYPE>::binarySearchHelper(TreeNode<NODETYPE>
                                                *ptr, int value) const
{
   if (ptr == 0)
      return 0;

   cout << "Comparing " << value << " to " << ptr->data;
```

```
      if ( value == ptr->data) {     // match
         cout << "; search complete" << endl;
         return ptr;
      }
      else if (value < ptr->data) { // search val less than current data
         cout << "; smaller, walk left" << endl;
         return binarySearchHelper(ptr->leftPtr, value);
      }
      else {                        // search val greater than current data
         cout << "; larger, walk right" << endl;
         return binarySearchHelper(ptr->rightPtr, value);
      }
}

template<class NODETYPE>
int Tree<NODETYPE>::getDepth() const
{
   int totalDepth = 0, currentDepth = 0;

   determineDepth(rootPtr, &totalDepth, &currentDepth);

   return totalDepth;
}

template<class NODETYPE>
void Tree<NODETYPE>::determineDepth(TreeNode<NODETYPE> *ptr,
                                    int *totPtr, int *currPtr) const
{
   if (ptr != 0) {
      ++*currPtr;

      if (*currPtr > *totPtr)
         *totPtr = *currPtr;

      determineDepth(ptr->leftPtr, totPtr, currPtr);
      determineDepth(ptr->rightPtr, totPtr, currPtr);
      --*currPtr;
   }
}

#endif
```

```
// TREENODE.H
// Definition of class TreeNode

#ifndef TREENODE_H
#define TREENODE_H

template<class NODETYPE>
class TreeNode {
   friend class Tree<NODETYPE>;

public:
   TreeNode(const NODETYPE &);  // constructor
   NODETYPE getData() const;    // return data

private:
   TreeNode *leftPtr;  // pointer to left subtree
   NODETYPE data;
   TreeNode *rightPtr;  // pointer to right subtree
};
```

```cpp
// Constructor
template<class NODETYPE>
TreeNode<NODETYPE>::TreeNode(const NODETYPE &d)
{
   data = d;
   leftPtr = rightPtr = 0;
}

//Return a copy of the data value
template<class NODETYPE>
NODETYPE TreeNode<NODETYPE>::getData() const { return data; }

#endif
```

```cpp
// Exercise 15.23 solution

#include <iostream.h>
#include <stdlib.h>
#include <time.h>
#include "tree.h"

main()
{
   srand(time(NULL));   // randomize the random number generator

   Tree<int> intTree;
   int intVal;

   cout << "The values being placed in the tree are:" << endl;

   for (int i = 1; i <= 15; i++) {
      intVal = rand() % 100;
      cout << intVal << ' ';
      intTree.insertNode(intVal);
   }

   cout << endl << endl << "Enter a value to search for: ";
   cin >> intVal;

   TreeNode<int> *ptr = intTree.binarySearch(intVal);

   if (ptr != 0)
      cout << ptr->getData() << " was found" << endl;
   else
      cout << "Element was not found" << endl;

   return 0;
}
```

```
   The values being placed in the tree are:
   81 48 3 89 94 89 dup 68 37 65 72 12 29 64 33 12 dup

   Enter a value to search for: 12
   Comparing 12 to 81; smaller, walk left
   Comparing 12 to 48; smaller, walk left
   Comparing 12 to 3; larger, walk right
   Comparing 12 to 37; smaller, walk left
   Comparing 12 to 12; search complete
   12 was found
```

```
The values being placed in the tree are:
97 11 17 12 35 8 23 47 5 15 72 95 51 74 88

Enter a value to search for: 73
Comparing 73 to 97; smaller, walk left
Comparing 73 to 11; larger, walk right
Comparing 73 to 17; larger, walk right
Comparing 73 to 35; larger, walk right
Comparing 73 to 47; larger, walk right
Comparing 73 to 72; larger, walk right
Comparing 73 to 95; smaller, walk left
Comparing 73 to 74; smaller, walk left
Element was not found
```

15.24   (*Level-order binary tree traversal*) The program of Fig. 15.16 illustrated three recursive methods of traversing a binary tree—inorder, preorder, and postorder traversals. This exercise presents the *level-order traversal* of a binary tree in which the node values are printed level-by-level starting at the root node level. The nodes on each level are printed from left to right. The level-order traversal is not a recursive algorithm. It uses a queue object to control the output of the nodes. The algorithm is as follows:

1) Insert the root node in the queue
2) While there are nodes left in the queue,
    Get the next node in the queue
    Print the node's value
    If the pointer to the left child of the node is not null
        Insert the left child node in the queue
    If the pointer to the right child of the node is not null
        Insert the right child node in the queue.

Write member function **levelOrder** to perform a level-order traversal of a binary tree object. Modify the program of Fig 15.16 to use this function. (Note: You will also need to modify and incorporate the queue processing functions of Fig. 15.12 in this program.)

ANS:

```
// TREE.H
// Definition of template class Tree
// Modified to include levelOrderTraversal member function.
#ifndef TREE_H
#define TREE_H

#include <iostream.h>
#include <assert.h>
#include "treenode.h"
#include "queue.h"

template<class NODETYPE>
class Tree {
public:
   Tree();
   void insertNode(const NODETYPE &);
   void preOrderTraversal() const;
   void inOrderTraversal() const;
   void postOrderTraversal() const;
   void levelOrderTraversal() const;
   TreeNode<NODETYPE> *binarySearch(int) const;
   int getDepth() const;

private:
   TreeNode<NODETYPE> *rootPtr;

   // utility functions
   void insertNodeHelper(TreeNode<NODETYPE> **, const NODETYPE &);
   void preOrderHelper(TreeNode<NODETYPE> *) const;
   void inOrderHelper(TreeNode<NODETYPE> *) const;
```

```cpp
      void postOrderHelper(TreeNode<NODETYPE> *) const;
      TreeNode<NODETYPE> *binarySearchHelper(TreeNode<NODETYPE> *, int) const;
      void determineDepth(TreeNode<NODETYPE> *, int *, int *) const;
};

template<class NODETYPE>
Tree<NODETYPE>::Tree() { rootPtr = 0; }

template<class NODETYPE>
void Tree<NODETYPE>::insertNode(const NODETYPE &value)
   { insertNodeHelper(&rootPtr, value); }

// This function receives a pointer to a pointer so the
// pointer can be modified.
template<class NODETYPE>
void Tree<NODETYPE>::insertNodeHelper(TreeNode<NODETYPE> **ptr,
                                      const NODETYPE &value)
{
   if (*ptr == 0) {                     // tree is empty
      *ptr = new TreeNode<NODETYPE>(value);
      assert(*ptr != 0);
   }
   else                                 // tree is not empty
      if (value < (*ptr)->data)
         insertNodeHelper(&((*ptr)->leftPtr), value);
      else if (value > (*ptr)->data)
         insertNodeHelper(&((*ptr)->rightPtr), value);
      else
         cout << "dup ";
}


template<class NODETYPE>
void Tree<NODETYPE>::preOrderTraversal() const { preOrderHelper(rootPtr); }


template<class NODETYPE>
void Tree<NODETYPE>::preOrderHelper(TreeNode<NODETYPE> *ptr) const
{
   if (ptr != 0) {
      cout << ptr->data << ' ';
      preOrderHelper(ptr->leftPtr);
      preOrderHelper(ptr->rightPtr);
   }
}


template<class NODETYPE>
void Tree<NODETYPE>::inOrderTraversal() const { inOrderHelper(rootPtr); }


template<class NODETYPE>
void Tree<NODETYPE>::inOrderHelper(TreeNode<NODETYPE> *ptr) const
{
   if (ptr != 0) {
      inOrderHelper(ptr->leftPtr);
      cout << ptr->data << ' ';
      inOrderHelper(ptr->rightPtr);
   }
}


template<class NODETYPE>
void Tree<NODETYPE>::postOrderTraversal() const
   { postOrderHelper(rootPtr); }
```

```cpp
template<class NODETYPE>
void Tree<NODETYPE>::postOrderHelper(TreeNode<NODETYPE> *ptr) const
{
   if ( ptr != 0 ) {
      postOrderHelper(ptr->leftPtr);
      postOrderHelper(ptr->rightPtr);
      cout << ptr->data << ' ';
   }
}

template<class NODETYPE>
void Tree<NODETYPE>::levelOrderTraversal() const
{
   Queue< TreeNode<NODETYPE> *> queue;
   TreeNode<NODETYPE> *nodePtr;

   if ( rootPtr != 0 )
      queue.enqueue(rootPtr);

   while ( !queue.isEmpty() ) {
      nodePtr = queue.dequeue();
      cout << nodePtr->data << " ";

      if ( nodePtr->leftPtr != 0 )
         queue.enqueue(nodePtr->leftPtr);

      if ( nodePtr->rightPtr != 0 )
         queue.enqueue(nodePtr->rightPtr);
   }
}

template<class NODETYPE>
TreeNode<NODETYPE> *Tree<NODETYPE>::binarySearch(int val) const
   { return binarySearchHelper(rootPtr, val); }

template<class NODETYPE>
TreeNode<NODETYPE> *Tree<NODETYPE>::binarySearchHelper(TreeNode<NODETYPE>
                                                *ptr, int value) const
{
   if (ptr == 0)
      return 0;

   cout << "Comparing " << value << " to " << ptr->data;

   if ( value == ptr->data) {    // match
      cout << "; search complete" << endl;
      return ptr;
   }
   else if (value < ptr->data) { // search val less than current data
      cout << "; smaller, walk left" << endl;
      return binarySearchHelper(ptr->leftPtr, value);
   }
   else {                           // search val greater than current data
      cout << "; larger, walk right" << endl;
      return binarySearchHelper(ptr->rightPtr, value);
   }
}

template<class NODETYPE>
int Tree<NODETYPE>::getDepth() const
{
   int totalDepth = 0, currentDepth = 0;

   determineDepth(rootPtr, &totalDepth, &currentDepth);

   return totalDepth;
}
```

```cpp
template<class NODETYPE>
void Tree<NODETYPE>::determineDepth(TreeNode<NODETYPE> *ptr,
                                    int *totPtr, int *currPtr) const
{
   if (ptr != 0) {
      ++*currPtr;

      if (*currPtr > *totPtr)
         *totPtr = *currPtr;

      determineDepth(ptr->leftPtr, totPtr, currPtr);
      determineDepth(ptr->rightPtr, totPtr, currPtr);
      --*currPtr;
   }
}

#endif
```

```cpp
// TREENODE.H
// Definition of class TreeNode
#ifndef TREENODE_H
#define TREENODE_H

template<class NODETYPE>
class TreeNode {
   friend class Tree<NODETYPE>;
public:
   TreeNode(const NODETYPE &);  // constructor
   NODETYPE getData() const;    // return data
private:
   TreeNode *leftPtr;   // pointer to left subtree
   NODETYPE data;
   TreeNode *rightPtr;  // pointer to right subtree
};

// Constructor
template<class NODETYPE>
TreeNode<NODETYPE>::TreeNode(const NODETYPE &d)
{
   data = d;
   leftPtr = rightPtr = 0;
}

//Return a copy of the data value
template<class NODETYPE>
NODETYPE TreeNode<NODETYPE>::getData() const { return data; }

#endif
```

```cpp
// QUEUE.H
// Definition of class Queue
#ifndef QUEUE_H
#define QUEUE_H

#include <iostream.h>
#include <assert.h>
#include "queuend.h"
```

```
template <class T>
class Queue {
public:
   Queue();              // default constructor
   ~Queue();             // destructor
   void enqueue(T &);    // insert item in queue
   T dequeue();          // remove item from queue
   int isEmpty() const;  // is the queue empty?
   void print() const;   // output the queue

private:
   QueueNode<T> *headPtr;  // pointer to first QueueNode
   QueueNode<T> *tailPtr;  // pointer to last QueueNode
};

// Member function definitions for class Queue
template <class T>
Queue<T>::Queue() { headPtr = tailPtr = 0; }

template <class T>
Queue<T>::~Queue()
{
   QueueNode<T> *tempPtr, *currentPtr = headPtr;

   while (currentPtr != 0) {
      tempPtr = currentPtr;
      currentPtr = currentPtr->nextPtr;
      delete tempPtr;
   }
}

template <class T>
void Queue<T>::enqueue(T &d)
{
   QueueNode<T> *newPtr = new QueueNode<T>(d);
   assert(newPtr != 0);  // was memory allocated?

   if (isEmpty())
      headPtr = tailPtr = newPtr;
   else {
      tailPtr->nextPtr = newPtr;
      tailPtr = newPtr;
   }
}

template <class T>
T Queue<T>::dequeue()
{
   assert(!isEmpty());

   QueueNode<T> *tempPtr = headPtr;

   headPtr = headPtr->nextPtr;
   T value = tempPtr->data;
   delete tempPtr;

   if (headPtr == 0)
      tailPtr = 0;

   return value;
}

template <class T>
int Queue<T>::isEmpty() const { return headPtr == 0; }
```

```cpp
template <class T>
void Queue<T>::print() const
{
   QueueNode<T> *currentPtr = headPtr;

   if (isEmpty())             // Queue is empty
      cout << "Queue is empty" << endl;
   else {                     // Queue is not empty
      cout << "The queue is:" << endl;

      while (currentPtr != 0) {
         cout << currentPtr->data << ' ';
         currentPtr = currentPtr->nextPtr;
      }

      cout << endl;
   }
}

#endif
```

```cpp
// QUEUEND.H
// Definition of template class QueueNode
#ifndef QUEUEND_H
#define QUEUEND_H

template <class T>
class QueueNode {
   friend class Queue<T>;
public:
   QueueNode(const T & = 0);
   T getData() const;
private:
   T data;
   QueueNode *nextPtr;
};

// Member function definitions for class QueueNode
template <class T>
QueueNode<T>::QueueNode(const T &d)
{
   data = d;
   nextPtr = 0;
}

template <class T>
T QueueNode<T>::getData() const { return data; }

#endif
```

```cpp
// Exercise 15.24 solution
#include <iostream.h>
#include <stdlib.h>
#include <time.h>
#include "tree.h"

main()
{
   srand(time(NULL));   // randomize the random number generator

   Tree<int> intTree;
   int intVal;
```

```
    cout << "The values being placed in the tree are:" << endl;

    for (int i = 1; i <= 15; i++) {
       intVal = rand() % 100;
       cout << intVal << ' ';
       intTree.insertNode(intVal);
    }

    cout << endl << endl << "The level order traversal is:" << endl;
    intTree.levelOrderTraversal();

    return 0;
}
```

```
The values being placed in the tree are:
61 16 58 97 8 96 34 25 49 39 40 64 39 dup 1 19

The level order traversal is:
61 16 97 8 58 96 1 34 64 25 49 19 39 40
```

15.25   (*Printing trees*) Write a recursive member function **outputTree** to display a binary tree object on the screen. The function should output the tree row-by-row with the top of the tree at the left of the screen and the bottom of the tree toward the right of the screen. Each row is output vertically. For example, the binary tree illustrated in Fig. 15.19 is output as follows:

```
                      99
                 97
                      92
            83
                      72
                 71
                      69
      49
                      44
                 40
                      32
            28
                      19
                 18
                      11
```

Note the rightmost leaf node appears at the top of the output in the rightmost column and the root node appears at the left of the output. Each column of output starts five spaces to the right of the previous column. Function **outputTree** should receive an argument **totalSpaces** representing the number of spaces preceding the value to be output (this variable should start at zero so the root node is output at the left of the screen). The function uses a modified inorder traversal to output the tree—it starts at the rightmost node in the tree and works back to the left. The algorithm is as follows:

> While the pointer to the current node is not null
>> Recursively call **outputTree** with the right subtree of the current node and **totalSpaces** + 5
>> Use a **for** structure to count from 1 to **totalSpaces** and output spaces
>> Output the value in the current node
>> Set the pointer to the current node to point to the left subtree of the current node
>> Increment **totalSpaces** by 5.

ANS:
```
// TREE.H
// Definition of template class Tree
// Modified to include outputTree and outputTreeHelper member functions.
```

```
#ifndef TREE_H
#define TREE_H

#include <iostream.h>
#include <assert.h>
#include "treenode.h"


template<class NODETYPE>
class Tree {
public:
   Tree();
   void insertNode(const NODETYPE &);
   void preOrderTraversal() const;
   void inOrderTraversal() const;
   void postOrderTraversal() const;
   void outputTree() const;
   TreeNode<NODETYPE> *binarySearch(int) const;
   int getDepth() const;

private:
   TreeNode<NODETYPE> *rootPtr;

   // utility functions
   void insertNodeHelper(TreeNode<NODETYPE> **, const NODETYPE &);
   void preOrderHelper(TreeNode<NODETYPE> *) const;
   void inOrderHelper(TreeNode<NODETYPE> *) const;
   void postOrderHelper(TreeNode<NODETYPE> *) const;
   void outputTreeHelper(TreeNode<NODETYPE> *, int) const;
   TreeNode<NODETYPE> *binarySearchHelper(TreeNode<NODETYPE> *, int) const;
   void determineDepth(TreeNode<NODETYPE> *, int *, int *) const;
};


template<class NODETYPE>
Tree<NODETYPE>::Tree() { rootPtr = 0; }

template<class NODETYPE>
void Tree<NODETYPE>::insertNode(const NODETYPE &value)
   { insertNodeHelper(&rootPtr, value); }

// This function receives a pointer to a pointer so the
// pointer can be modified.
template<class NODETYPE>
void Tree<NODETYPE>::insertNodeHelper(TreeNode<NODETYPE> **ptr,
                                      const NODETYPE &value)
{
   if (*ptr == 0) {                    // tree is empty
      *ptr = new TreeNode<NODETYPE>(value);
      assert(*ptr != 0);
   }
   else                                // tree is not empty
      if (value < (*ptr)->data)
         insertNodeHelper(&((*ptr)->leftPtr), value);
      else if (value > (*ptr)->data)
         insertNodeHelper(&((*ptr)->rightPtr), value);
      else
         cout << "dup ";
}

template<class NODETYPE>
void Tree<NODETYPE>::preOrderTraversal() const
   { preOrderHelper(rootPtr); }
```

```cpp
template<class NODETYPE>
void Tree<NODETYPE>::preOrderHelper(TreeNode<NODETYPE> *ptr) const
{
   if (ptr != 0) {
      cout << ptr->data << ' ';
      preOrderHelper(ptr->leftPtr);
      preOrderHelper(ptr->rightPtr);
   }
}


template<class NODETYPE>
void Tree<NODETYPE>::inOrderTraversal() const { inOrderHelper(rootPtr); }


template<class NODETYPE>
void Tree<NODETYPE>::inOrderHelper(TreeNode<NODETYPE> *ptr) const
{
   if (ptr != 0) {
      inOrderHelper(ptr->leftPtr);
      cout << ptr->data << ' ';
      inOrderHelper(ptr->rightPtr);
   }
}


template<class NODETYPE>
void Tree<NODETYPE>::postOrderTraversal() const
   { postOrderHelper(rootPtr); }

template<class NODETYPE>
void Tree<NODETYPE>::postOrderHelper(TreeNode<NODETYPE> *ptr) const
{
   if (ptr != 0) {
      postOrderHelper(ptr->leftPtr);
      postOrderHelper(ptr->rightPtr);
      cout << ptr->data << ' ';
   }
}


template<class NODETYPE>
void Tree<NODETYPE>::outputTree() const
   { outputTreeHelper(rootPtr, 0); }


template<class NODETYPE>
void Tree<NODETYPE>::outputTreeHelper(TreeNode<NODETYPE> *ptr,
                                      int totalSpaces) const
{
   if ( ptr != 0 ) {
      outputTreeHelper(ptr->rightPtr, totalSpaces + 5);

      for (int i = 1; i <= totalSpaces; i++)
         cout << ' ';

      cout << ptr->data << endl;
      outputTreeHelper(ptr->leftPtr, totalSpaces + 5);
   }
}


template<class NODETYPE>
TreeNode<NODETYPE> *Tree<NODETYPE>::binarySearch(int val) const
   { return binarySearchHelper(rootPtr, val); }
```

```
template<class NODETYPE>
TreeNode<NODETYPE> *Tree<NODETYPE>::binarySearchHelper(TreeNode<NODETYPE>
                                            *ptr, int value) const
{
   if (ptr == 0)
      return 0;

   cout << "Comparing " << value << " to " << ptr->data;

   if ( value == ptr->data) {    // match
      cout << "; search complete" << endl;
      return ptr;
   }
   else if (value < ptr->data) { // search val less than current data
      cout << "; smaller, walk left" << endl;
      return binarySearchHelper(ptr->leftPtr, value);
   }
   else {                        // search val greater than current data
      cout << "; larger, walk right" << endl;
      return binarySearchHelper(ptr->rightPtr, value);
   }
}

template<class NODETYPE>
int Tree<NODETYPE>::getDepth() const
{
   int totalDepth = 0, currentDepth = 0;

   determineDepth(rootPtr, &totalDepth, &currentDepth);

   return totalDepth;
}

template<class NODETYPE>
void Tree<NODETYPE>::determineDepth(TreeNode<NODETYPE> *ptr,
                                    int *totPtr, int *currPtr) const
{
   if (ptr != 0) {
      ++*currPtr;

      if (*currPtr > *totPtr)
         *totPtr = *currPtr;

      determineDepth(ptr->leftPtr, totPtr, currPtr);
      determineDepth(ptr->rightPtr, totPtr, currPtr);
      --*currPtr;
   }
}

#endif
```

```
// TREENODE.H
// Definition of class TreeNode

#ifndef TREENODE_H
#define TREENODE_H

template<class NODETYPE>
class TreeNode {
   friend class Tree<NODETYPE>;
public:
   TreeNode(const NODETYPE &);  // constructor
   NODETYPE getData() const;    // return data
```

```
private:
   TreeNode *leftPtr;   // pointer to left subtree
   NODETYPE data;
   TreeNode *rightPtr;  // pointer to right subtree
};

// Constructor
template<class NODETYPE>
TreeNode<NODETYPE>::TreeNode(const NODETYPE &d)
{
   data = d;
   leftPtr = rightPtr = 0;
}

//Return a copy of the data value
template<class NODETYPE>
NODETYPE TreeNode<NODETYPE>::getData() const { return data; }

#endif
```

```
// Exercise 15.25 solution
#include <iostream.h>
#include <stdlib.h>
#include <time.h>
#include "tree.h"

main()
{
   srand(time(NULL));  // randomize the random number generator

   Tree<int> intTree;
   int intVal;

   cout << "The values being placed in the tree are:" << endl;

   for (int i = 1; i <= 15; i++) {
      intVal = rand() % 100;
      cout << intVal << ' ';
      intTree.insertNode(intVal);
   }

   cout << endl << endl << "The tree is:" << endl;
   intTree.outputTree();

   return 0;
}
```

```
The values being placed in the tree are:
81 86 85 48 42 24 66 73 12 90 49 57 51 9 29

The tree is:
            90
        86
            85
81
                73
            66
                    57
                        51
                49
        48
            42
                    29
                24
                    12
                        9
```

Special Section: Building Your Own Compiler

In Exercises 5.18 and 5.19, we introduced Simpletron Machine Language (SML) and you implemented a Simpletron computer simulator to execute programs written in SML. In this section, we build a compiler that converts programs written in a high-level programming language to SML. This section "ties" together the entire programming process. You will write programs in this new high-level language, compile these programs on the compiler you build, and run the programs on the simulator you built in Exercise 7.19. You should make every effort to implement your compiler in an object-oriented manner.

15.26   (*The Simple Language*) Before we begin building the compiler, we discuss a simple, yet powerful, high-level language similar to early versions of the popular language BASIC. We call the language *Simple*. Every Simple *statement* consists of a *line number* and a Simple *instruction*. Line numbers must appear in ascending order. Each instruction begins with one of the following Simple *commands*: **rem**, **input**, **let**, **print**, **goto**, **if/goto**, or **end** (see Fig. 15.20). All commands except **end** can be used repeatedly. Simple evaluates only integer expressions using the +, -, *, and / operators. These operators have the same precedence as in C. Parentheses can be used to change the order of evaluation of an expression.

Command	Example statement	Description
rem	50 rem this is a remark	Any text following the command **rem** is for documentation purposes only and is ignored by the compiler.
input	30 input x	Display a question mark to prompt the user to enter an integer. Read that integer from the keyboard and store the integer in **x**.
let	80 let u = 4 * (j - 56)	Assign **u** the value of 4 * (j - 56). Note that an arbitrarily complex expression can appear to the right of the equal sign.
print	10 print w	Display the value of **w**.
goto	70 goto 45	Transfer program control to line **45**.
if/goto	35 if i == z goto 80	Compare **i** and **z** for equality and transfer program control to line **80** if the condition is true; otherwise, continue execution with the next statement.
end	99 end	Terminate program execution.

Fig. 15.20 Simple commands.

Our Simple compiler recognizes only lowercase letters. All characters in a Simple file should be lowercase (uppercase letters result in a syntax error unless they appear in a **rem** statement in which case they are ignored). A *variable name* is a single letter. Simple does not allow descriptive variable names, so variables should be explained in remarks to indicate their use in a program. Simple uses only integer variables. Simple does not have variable declarations—merely mentioning a variable name in a program causes the variable to be declared and initialized to zero automatically. The syntax of Simple does not allow string manipulation (reading a string, writing a string, comparing strings, etc.). If a string is encountered in a Simple program (after a command other than **rem**), the compiler generates a syntax error. The first version of our compiler will assume that Simple programs are entered correctly. Exercise 15.29 asks the student to modify the compiler to perform syntax error checking.

Simple uses the conditional **if/goto** statement and the unconditional **goto** statement to alter the flow of control during program execution. If the condition in the **if/goto** statement is true, control is transferred to a specific line of the program. The following relational and equality operators are valid in an **if/goto** statement: <, >, <=, >=, ==, or !=. The precedence of these operators is the same as in C++.

Let us now consider several programs that demonstrate Simple's features. The first program (Fig. 15.21) reads two integers from the keyboard, stores the values in variables **a** and **b**, and computes and prints their sum (stored in variable **c**).

The program of Fig. 15.22 determines and prints the larger of two integers. The integers are input from the keyboard and stored in **s** and **t**. The **if/goto** statement tests the condition **s >= t**. If the condition is true, control is transferred to line **90** and **s** is output; otherwise, **t** is output and control is transferred to the **end** statement in line **99** where the program terminates.

```
10 rem    determine and print the sum of two integers
15 rem
20 rem    input the two integers
30 input a
40 input b
45 rem
50 rem    add integers and store result in c
60 let c = a + b
65 rem
70 rem    print the result
80 print c
90 rem    terminate program execution
99 end
```

Fig. 15.21 Simple program that determines the sum of two integers.

```
10 rem    determine the larger of two integers
20 input s
30 input t
32 rem
35 rem    test if s >= t
40 if s >= t goto 90
45 rem
50 rem    t is greater than s, so print t
60 print t
70 goto 99
75 rem
80 rem    s is greater than or equal to t, so print s
90 print s
99 end
```

Fig. 15.22 Simple program that finds the larger of two integers.

Simple does not provide a repetition structure (such as C++'s **for**, **while**, or **do/while**). However, Simple can simulate each of C++'s repetition structures using the **if/goto** and **goto** statements. Figure 15.23 uses a sentinel-controlled loop to calculate the squares of several integers. Each integer is input from the keyboard and stored in variable **j**. If the value entered is the sentinel **-9999**, control is transferred to line **99** where the program terminates. Otherwise, **k** is assigned the square of **j**, **k** is output to the screen, and control is passed to line **20** where the next integer is input.

```
10 rem    calculate the squares of several integers
20 input j
23 rem
25 rem    test for sentinel value
30 if j == -9999 goto 99
33 rem
35 rem    calculate square of j and assign result to k
40 let k = j * j
50 print k
53 rem
55 rem    loop to get next j
60 goto 20
99 end
```

Fig. 15.23 Calculate the squares of several integers.

Using the sample programs of Fig. 15.21, Fig. 15.22, and Fig. 15.23 as your guide, write a Simple program to accomplish each of the following:

a) Input three integers, determine their average, and print the result.

ANS:

```
5 rem      Exercise 15.26 Part A Solution
6 rem
10 input x
15 input y
20 input z
21 rem     calculate average a
25 let a = ( x + y + z ) / 3
26 rem
30 print a
99 end
```

b) Use a sentinel-controlled loop to input 10 integers and compute and print their sum.

ANS:

```
5 rem      Exercise 15.26 Part B Solution
6 rem
10 input n
12 rem     set up sentinel loop
15 if n == 9999 goto 40
16 rem
17 rem add n to the sum s
20 let s = s + n
21 rem
22 rem     loop to get next n
25 goto 10
36 rem     print sum s
40 print s
99 end
```

c) Use a counter-controlled loop to input 7 integers, some positive and some negative, and compute and print their average.

ANS:

```
5 rem      Exercise 15.26 Part C Solution
6 rem
10 input m
11 rem     increment counter by 1
12 rem     c is automatically initiated to 0
13 rem     when created
15 let c = c + 1
16 rem
17 rem     calculate sum s
20 let s = s + m
22 rem     loop to get next m
23 rem     if c is not yet 7
25 if c <= 7 goto 10
26 rem
27 rem     compute average a
30 let a = s / 7
31 rem
35 print a
99 end
```

d) Input a series of integers and determine and print the largest. The first integer input indicates how many numbers should be processed.

ANS:

```
5 rem      Exercise 15.26 Part D Solution
6 rem
7 rem      Enter the number of integers
8 rem      to be processed
10 input n
23 rem     begin entering numbers t
25 input t
26 rem     check if t is larger than l
```

```
27 rem    l's initial value is zero
30 if t <= l goto 50
31 rem    t must be larger than l
32 rem    so assign t as largest
35 let l = t
49 rem    decrement n
50 let n = n - 1
59 rem    test for loop exit condition (n = 0)
60 if  n == 0 goto 80
69 rem    loop to get next t
70 goto 25
79 rem    print largest value
80 print l
99 end
```

e) Input 10 integers and print the smallest.

ANS:
```
1 rem    Exercise 15.26 Part E Solution
2 rem
3 rem    set counter c equal to 1
5 let c = 1
6 rem    input integer m
7 rem    assign first entry to
8 rem    the smallest value s
9 input m
10 let s = m
11 rem    enter main loop
13 goto 20
14 rem    main loop
15 input m
18 rem    determine if m is smaller
19 rem    than current s
20 if m < s goto 50
29 rem    increment counter
30 let c = c + 1
34 rem    exit when c becomes 11
35 if  c == 11 goto 60
39 rem    loop for next m
40 goto 15
48 rem    assign m to s as
49 rem    smallest value
50 let s = m
51 rem    loop to counter increment
55 goto 30
59 rem    print smallest value
60 print s
99 end
```

f) Calculate and print the sum of the even integers from 2 to 30.

ANS:
```
5 rem    Exercise 15.26 Part F Solution
6 rem
7 rem
9 rem    initialize i to 2
10 let i = 2
14 rem   store sum in s
15 let s = s + i
19 rem   increment i by 2
20 let i = i + 2
28 rem   set loop terminating
29 rem   condition at 32
30 if i < 32 goto 15
39 rem   print sum
40 print s
99 end
```

g) Calculate and print the product of the odd integers from 1 to 9.

ANS:

```
 5 rem    Exercise 15.26 Part G Solution
 6 rem
 7 rem
 9 rem    initialize k to 1
10 let k = 1
11 rem    initialize p to 1
13 let p = 1
14 rem    store product in p
15 let p = p * k
19 rem    increment k by 1
20 let k = k + 2
28 rem    set loop terminating
29 rem    condition at 10
30 if k < 10 goto 15
39 rem    print product
40 print p
99 end
```

15.27 (*Building A Compiler; Prerequisite: Complete Exercises 5.18, 5.19, 15.12, 15.13, and 15.26*) Now that the Simple language has been presented (Exercise 15.26), we discuss how to build a Simple compiler. First, we consider the process by which a Simple program is converted to SML and executed by the Simpletron simulator (see Fig. 15.24). A file containing a Simple program is read by the compiler and converted to SML code. The SML code is output to a file on disk, in which SML instructions appear one per line. The SML file is then loaded into the Simpletron simulator, and the results are sent to a file on disk and to the screen. Note that the Simpletron program developed in Exercise 5.19 took its input from the keyboard. It must be modified to read from a file so it can run the programs produced by our compiler.

The Simple compiler performs two *passes* of the Simple program to convert it to SML. The first pass constructs a *symbol table* (object) in which every *line number* (object), *variable name* (object) and *constant* (object) of the Simple program is stored with its type and corresponding location in the final SML code (the symbol table is discussed in detail below). The first pass also produces the corresponding SML instruction object(s) for each of the Simple statements (object, etc.). As we will see, if the Simple program contains statements that transfer control to a line later in the program, the first pass results in an SML program containing some "unfinished" instructions. The second pass of the compiler locates and completes the unfinished instructions, and outputs the SML program to a file.

First Pass

The compiler begins by reading one statement of the Simple program into memory. The line must be separated into its individual *tokens* (i.e., "pieces" of a statement) for processing and compilation (standard library function **strtok** can be used to facilitate this task). Recall that every statement begins with a line number followed by a command. As the compiler breaks a statement into tokens, if the token is a line number, a variable, or a constant, it is placed in the symbol table. A line number is placed in the symbol table only if it is the first token in a statement. The **symbolTable** object is an array of **tableEntry** objects representing each symbol in the program. There is no restriction on the number of symbols that can appear in the program. Therefore, the **symbolTable** for a particular program could be large. Make the **symbolTable** a 100-element array for now. You can increase or decrease its size once the program is working.

Each **tableEntry** object contains three members. Member **symbol** is an integer containing the ASCII representation of a variable (remember that variable names are single characters), a line number, or a constant. Member **type** is one of the following characters indicating the symbol's type: **'C'** for constant, **'L'** for line number, or **'V'** for variable. Member **location** contains the Simpletron memory location (**00** to **99**) to which the symbol refers. Simpletron memory is an array of 100 integers in which SML instructions and data are stored. For a line number, the location is the element in the Simpletron memory array at which the SML instructions for the Simple statement begin. For a variable or constant, the location is the element in the Simpletron memory array in which the variable or constant is stored. Variables and constants are allocated from the end of Simpletron's memory backwards. The first variable or constant is stored in location at **99**, the next in location at **98**, etc.

The symbol table plays an integral part in converting Simple programs to SML. We learned in Chapter 5 that an SML instruction is a four-digit integer comprised of two parts—the *operation code* and the *operand*. The operation code is determined by commands in Simple. For example, the simple command **input** corresponds to SML operation code **10** (read), and the Simple command **print** corresponds to SML operation code **11** (write). The operand is a memory location containing the data on which the operation code performs its task (e.g., operation code **10** reads a value from the keyboard and stores it in the memory location specified by the operand). The compiler searches **symbolTable** to determine the Simpletron memory location for each symbol so the corresponding location can be used to complete the SML instructions.

The compilation of each Simple statement is based on its command. For example, after the line number in a **rem** statement is inserted in the symbol table, the remainder of the statement is ignored by the compiler because a remark is for documentation purposes only. The **input**, **print**, **goto** and **end** statements correspond to the SML *read, write, branch* (to a specific location) and *halt* instructions. Statements containing these Simple commands are converted directly to SML (note that a **goto** statement may contain an unresolved reference if the specified line number refers to a statement further into the Simple program file; this is sometimes called a forward reference).

When a **goto** statement is compiled with an unresolved reference, the SML instruction must be *flagged* to indicate that the second pass of the compiler must complete the instruction. The flags are stored in 100-element array **flags** of type **int** in which each element is initialized to **-1**. If the memory location to which a line number in the Simple program refers is not yet known (i.e., it is not in the symbol table), the line number is stored in array **flags** in the element with the same subscript as the incomplete instruction. The operand of the incomplete instruction is set to **00** temporarily. For example, an unconditional branch instruction (making a forward reference) is left as **+4000** until the second pass of the compiler. The second pass of the compiler will be described shortly.

Compilation of **if/goto** and **let** statements is more complicated than other statements—they are the only statements that produce more than one SML instruction. For an **if/goto** statement, the compiler produces code to test the condition and to branch to another line if necessary. The result of the branch could be an unresolved reference. Each of the relational and equality operators can be simulated using SML's *branch zero* and *branch negative* instructions (or possibly a combination of both).

For a **let** statement, the compiler produces code to evaluate an arbitrarily complex arithmetic expression consisting of integer variables and/or constants. Expressions should separate each operand and operator with spaces. Exercises 15.12 and 15.13 presented the infix-to-postfix conversion algorithm and the postfix evaluation algorithm used by compilers to evaluate expressions. Before proceeding with your compiler, you should complete each of these exercises. When a compiler encounters an expression, it converts the expression from infix notation to postfix notation, then evaluates the postfix expression.

How is it that the compiler produces the machine language to evaluate an expression containing variables? The postfix evaluation algorithm contains a "hook" where the compiler can generate SML instructions rather than actually evaluating the expression. To enable this "hook" in the compiler, the postfix evaluation algorithm must be modified to search the symbol table for each symbol it encounters (and possibly insert it), determine the symbol's corresponding memory location, and *push the memory location on the stack (instead of the symbol)*. When an operator is encountered in the postfix expression, the two memory locations at the top of the stack are popped and machine language for effecting the operation is produced using the memory locations as operands. The result of each subexpression is stored in a temporary location in memory and pushed back onto the stack so the evaluation of the postfix expression can continue. When postfix evaluation is complete, the memory location containing the result is the only location left on the stack. This is popped and SML instructions are generated to assign the result to the variable at the left of the **let** statement.

Second Pass

The second pass of the compiler performs two tasks: resolve any unresolved references and output the SML code to a file. Resolution of references occurs as follows:
1) Search the **flags** array for an unresolved reference (i.e., an element with a value other than **-1**).
2) Locate the object in array **symbolTable** containing the symbol stored in the **flags** array (be sure that the type of the symbol is **'L'** for line number).
3) Insert the memory location from member **location** into the instruction with the unresolved reference (remember that an instruction containing an unresolved reference has operand **00**).
4) Repeat steps 1, 2, and 3 until the end of the **flags** array is reached.

After the resolution process is complete, the entire array containing the SML code is output to a disk file with one SML instruction per line. This file can be read by the Simpletron for execution (after the simulator is modified to read its input from a file). Compiling your first Simple program into an SML file and then executing that file should give you a real sense of personal accomplishment.

A Complete Example

The following example illustrates a complete conversion of a Simple program to SML as it will be performed by the Simple compiler. Consider a Simple program that inputs an integer and sums the values from 1 to that integer. The program and the SML instructions produced by the first pass of the Simple compilerare illustrated in Fig. 15.25. The symbol table constructed by the first pass is shown in Fig. 15.26.

Simple program	SML location and instruction		Description
5 rem sum 1 to x		*none*	**rem** ignored
10 input x	00	+1099	read **x** into location **99**
15 rem check y == x		*none*	**rem** ignored
20 if y == x goto 60	01	+2098	load **y** (**98**) into accumulator
	02	+3199	sub **x** (**99**) from accumulator
	03	+4200	*branch zero to unresolved location*
25 rem increment y		*none*	**rem** ignored
30 let y = y + 1	04	+2098	load **y** into accumulator
	05	+3097	add **1** (**97**) to accumulator
	06	+2196	store in temporary location **96**
	07	+2096	load from temporary location **96**
	08	+2198	store accumulator in **y**
35 rem add y to total		*none*	**rem** ignored
40 let t = t + y	09	+2095	load **t** (**95**) into accumulator
	10	+3098	add **y** to accumulator
	11	+2194	store in temporary location **94**
	12	+2094	load from temporary location **94**
	13	+2195	store accumulator in **t**
45 rem loop y		*none*	**rem** ignored
50 goto 20	14	+4001	branch to location **01**
55 rem output result		*none*	**rem** ignored
60 print t	15	+1195	output **t** to screen
99 end	16	+4300	terminate execution

Fig. 15.25 SML instructions produced after the compiler's first pass.

Symbol	Type	Location
5	L	00
10	L	00
'x'	V	99
15	L	01
20	L	01
'y'	V	98
25	L	04
30	L	04
1	C	97
35	L	09
40	L	09
't'	V	95
45	L	14
50	L	14
55	L	15
60	L	15
99	L	16

Fig. 15.26 Symbol table for program of Fig. 15.25.

Most Simple statements convert directly to single SML instructions. The exceptions in this program are remarks, the **if/goto** statement in line **20**, and the **let** statements. Remarks do not translate into machine language. However, the line number for a remark is placed in the symbol table in case the line number is referenced in a **goto** statement or an **if/goto** statement. Line **20** of the program specifies that if the condition $y == x$ is true, program control is transferred to line **60**. Because line **60** appears later in the program, the first pass of the compiler has not as yet placed **60** in the symbol table (statement line numbers are placed in the symbol table only when they appear as the first token in a statement). Therefore, it is not possible at this time to determine the operand of the SML *branch zero* instruction at location **03** in the array of SML instructions. The compiler places **60** in location **03** of the **flags** array to indicate that the second pass completes this instruction.

We must keep track of the next instruction location in the SML array because there is not a one-to-one correspondence between Simple statements and SML instructions. For example, the **if/goto** statement of line **20** compiles into three SML instructions. Each time an instruction is produced, we must increment the *instruction counter* to the next location in the SML array. Note that the size of Simpletron's memory could present a problem for Simple programs with many statements, variables and constants. It is conceivable that the compiler will run out of memory. To test for this case, your program should contain a *data counter* to keep track of the location at which the next variable or constant will be stored in the SML array. If the value of the instruction counter is larger than the value of the data counter, the SML array is full. In this case, the compilation process should terminate and the compiler should print an error message indicating that it ran out of memory during compilation. This serves to emphasize that although the programmer is freed from the burdens of managing memory by the compiler, the compiler itself must carefully determine the placement of instructions and data in memory, and must check for such errors as memory being exhausted during the compilation process.

A Step-by-Step View of the Compilation Process

Let us now walk through the compilation process for the Simple program in Fig. 15.25. The compiler reads the first line of the program

```
5 rem sum 1 to x
```

into memory. The first token in the statement (the line number) is determined using **strtok** (see Chapters 5 and 16 for a discussion of C++'s string manipulation functions). The token returned by **strtok** is converted to an integer using **atoi** so the symbol **5** can be located in the symbol table. If the symbol is not found, it is inserted in the symbol table. Since we are at the beginning of the program and this is the first line, no symbols are in the table yet. So, **5** is inserted into the symbol table as type **L** (line number) and assigned the first location in SML array (**00**). Although this line is a remark, a space in the symbol table is still allocated for the line number (in case it is referenced by a **goto** or an **if/goto**). No SML instruction is generated for a **rem** statement, so the instruction counter is not incremented.

The statement

```
10 input x
```

is tokenized next. The line number **10** is placed in the symbol table as type **L** and assigned the first location in the SML array (**00** because a remark began the program so the instruction counter is currently **00**). The command **input** indicates that the next token is a variable (only a variable can appear in an **input** statement). Because **input** corresponds directly to an SML operation code, the compiler simply has to determine the location of **x** in the SML array. Symbol **x** is not found in the symbol table. So, it is inserted into the symbol table as the ASCII representation of **x**, given type **V**, and assigned location **99** in the SML array (data storage begins at **99** and is allocated backwards). SML code can now be generated for this statement. Operation code **10** (the SML read operation code) is multiplied by 100, and the location of **x** (as determined in the symbol table) is added to complete the instruction. The instruction is then stored in the SML array at location **00**. The instruction counter is incremented by 1 because a single SML instruction was produced.

The statement

```
15 rem    check y == x
```

is tokenized next. The symbol table is searched for line number **15** (which is not found). The line number is inserted as type **L** and assigned the next location in the array, **01** (remember that **rem** statements do not produce code, so the instruction counter is not incremented).

The statement

```
20 if y == x goto 60
```

is tokenized next. Line number **20** is inserted in the symbol table and given type **L** with the next location in the SML array **01**. Command **if** indicates that a condition is to be evaluated. The variable **y** is not found in the symbol table, so it is inserted and given the type **V** and the SML location **98**. Next, SML instructions are generated to evaluate the condition. Since there is no direct equivalent in SML for the **if/goto**, it must be simulated by performing a calculation using **x** and **y** and branching based on the result. If **y** is equal to **x**, the result of subtracting **x** from **y** is zero, so the *branch zero* instruction can be used with the result of the calculation to simulate the **if/goto** statement. The first step requires that **y** be loaded (from SML location **98**) into the accumulator. This produces the instruction **01 +2098**. Next, **x** is subtracted from the accumulator. This produces the instruction **02 +3199**. The value in the accumulator may be zero, positive, or negative. Since the operator is **==**, we want to *branch zero*. First, the symbol table is searched for the branch location (**60** in this case), which is not found. So, **60** is placed in the **flags** array at location **03**, and the instruction **03 +4200** is generated (we cannot add the branch location because we have not assigned a location to line **60** in the SML array yet). The instruction counter is incremented to **04**.

The compiler proceeds to the statement

        25 rem   increment y

The line number **25** is inserted in the symbol table as type **L** and assigned SML location **04**. The instruction counter is not incremented.

When the statement

        30 let y = y + 1

is tokenized, the line number **30** is inserted in the symbol table as type **L** and assigned SML location **04**. Command **let** indicates that the line is an assignment statement. First, all the symbols on the line are inserted in the symbol table (if they are not already there). The integer **1** is added to the symbol table as type **C** and assigned SML location **97**. Next, the right side of the assignment is converted from infix to postfix notation. Then the postfix expression (**y 1 +**) is evaluated. Symbol **y** is located in the symbol table and its corresponding memory location is pushed onto the stack. Symbol **1** is also located in the symbol table and its corresponding memory location is pushed onto the stack. When the operator **+** is encountered, the postfix evaluator pops the stack into the right operand of the operator and pops the stack again into the left operand of the operator, then produces the SML instructions

        04 +2098   *(load y)*
        05 +3097   *(add 1)*

The result of the expression is stored in a temporary location in memory (**96**) with instruction

        06 +2196   *(store temporary)*

and the temporary location is pushed on the stack. Now that the expression has been evaluated, the result must be stored in **y** (i.e., the variable on the left side of **=**). So, the temporary location is loaded into the accumulator and the accumulator is stored in **y** with the instructions

        07 +2096   *(load temporary)*
        08 +2198   *(store y)*

The reader will immediately notice that SML instructions appear to be redundant. We will discuss this issue shortly.

When the statement

        35 rem   add y to total

is tokenized, line number **35** is inserted in the symbol table as type **L** and assigned location **09**.

The statement

        40 let t = t + y

is similar to line **30**. The variable **t** is inserted in the symbol table as type **V** and assigned SML location **95**. The instructions follow the same logic and format as line **30**, and the instructions **09 +2095**, **10 +3098**, **11 +2194**, **12 +2094**, and **13 +2195** are generated. Note that the result of **t + y** is assigned to temporary location **94** before being assigned to **t** (**95**). Once again, the reader will note that the instructions in memory locations **11** and **12** appear to be redundant. Again, we will discuss this shortly.

The statement

        45 rem   loop y

is a remark, so line **45** is added to the symbol table as type **L** and assigned SML location **14**.

The statement

        50 goto 20

transfers control to line **20**. Line number **50** is inserted in the symbol table as type **L** and assigned SML location **14**. The equivalent of **goto** in SML is the *unconditional branch* (**40**) instruction that transfers control to a specific SML location. The compiler searches the symbol table for line **20** and finds that it corresponds to SML location **01**. The operation code (**40**) is multiplied by 100 and location **01** is added to it to produce the instruction **14 +4001**.

The statement

```
55 rem    output result
```

is a remark, so line **55** is inserted in the symbol table as type **L** and assigned SML location **15**.

The statement

```
60 print t
```

is an output statement. Line number **60** is inserted in the symbol table as type **L** and assigned SML location ·**15**. The equivalent of **print** in SML is operation code **11** (*write*). The location of **t** is determined from the symbol table and added to the result of the operation code multiplied by 100.

The statement

```
99 end
```

is the final line of the program. Line number **99** is stored in the symbol table as type **L** and assigned SML location **16**. The **end** command produces the SML instruction **+4300** (**43** is *halt* in SML) which is written as the final instruction in the SML memory array.

This completes the first pass of the compiler. We now consider the second pass. The **flags** array is searched for values other than -**1**. Location **03** contains **60**, so the compiler knows that instruction **03** is incomplete. The compiler completes the instruction by searching the symbol table for **60**, determining its location, and adding the location to the incomplete instruction. In this case, the search determines that line **60** corresponds to SML location **15**, so the completed instruction **03 +4215** is produced replacing **03 +4200**. The Simple program has now been compiled successfully.

To build the compiler, you will have to perform each of the following tasks:

a) Modify the Simpletron simulator program you wrote in Exercise 5.19 to take its input from a file specified by the user (see Chapter 14). The simulator should output its results to a disk file in the same format as the screen output. Convert the simulator to be an object-oriented program. In particular, make each part of the hardware an object. Arrange the instruction types into a class hierarchy using inheritance. Then execute the program polymorphically simply by telling each instruction to execute itself with an **executeInstruction** message.

b) Modify the infix-to-postfix evaluation algorithm of Exercise 15.12 to process multi-digit integer operands and single-letter variable name operands. Hint: Standard library function **strtok** can be used to locate each constant and variable in an expression, and constants can be converted from strings to integers using standard library function **atoi**. (Note: The data representation of the postfix expression must be altered to support variable names and integer constants.)

c) Modify the postfix evaluation algorithm to process multi-digit integer operands and variable name operands. Also, the algorithm should now implement the "hook" discussed above so that SML instructions are produced rather than directly evaluating the expression. Hint: Standard library function **strtok** can be used to locate each constant and variable in an expression, and constants can be converted from strings to integers using standard library function **atoi**. (Note: The data representation of the postfix expression must be altered to support variable names and integer constants.)

d) Build the compiler. Incorporate parts (b) and (c) for evaluating expressions in **let** statements. Your program should contain a function that performs the first pass of the compiler and a function that performs the second pass of the compiler. Both functions can call other functions to accomplish their tasks. Make your compiler as object oriented as possible.

ANS: **Note that this is NOT an object oriented version of the compiler. This is a structured program written in C++. In the next edition of the instructor's manual, the problem will be solved in an object-oriented manner.**

```
// compiler.h
#include <iostream.h>
#include <iomanip.h>
#include <fstream.h>
#include <string.h>
#include <ctype.h>
#include <stdlib.h>
#include "stack.h"
```

```
#define MAXIMUM 81              // maximum length for lines
#define SYMBOLTABLESIZE 100     // maximum size of symbol table
#define MEMORYSIZE 100          // maximum Simpletron memory

// Definition of structure for symbol table entries
struct TableEntry{
   int location;                // SML memory location 00 to 99
   char type;                   // 'C' = constant, 'V' = variable,
   int symbol;                  // or 'L' = line number
};

// Function prototypes for compiler functions
int checkSymbolTable(TableEntry *, int, char);
int checkOperand(TableEntry *, char *, int *, int *, int *);
void addToSymbolTable(char, int, int, TableEntry *, int);
void addLineToFlags(int, int, int *, int *, const int *);
void compile(ifstream &, char *);
void printOutput(const int [], char *);
void lineNumber(char *,TableEntry *, int, int);
void initArrays(int *, int *, TableEntry *);
void firstPass(int *, int *, TableEntry *, ifstream &);
void secondPass(int *, int *, TableEntry *);
void separateToken(char *, int *, int *, TableEntry *, int *, int *);
void keyWord(char *, int *, int *, TableEntry *, int *, int *);
void keyLet(char *, int *, TableEntry *, int *, int *);
void keyInput(char *, int *, TableEntry *, int *, int *);
void keyPrint(char *, int *, TableEntry *, int *, int *);
void keyGoto(char *, int *, int *, TableEntry *, int *);
void keyIfGoto(char *, int *, int *, TableEntry *, int *, int *);
void evaluateExpression(int, int, char *, int *, TableEntry *, int *,
                        int *, char *);
int createLetSML(int, int, int *, int *, int *, char);
void infixToPostfix(char *, char *, int, TableEntry *, int *,
                    int *, int *);
void evaluatePostfix(char *, int *, int *, int *, int, TableEntry *);
int isOperator(char);
int precedence(char, char);

// Simpletron Machine Language (SML) Operation Codes
enum SMLOperationCodes { READ = 10, WRITE = 11, LOAD = 20, STORE = 21,
                         ADD = 30, SUBTRACT = 31, DIVIDE = 32,
                         MULTIPLY = 33, BRANCH = 40, BRANCHNEG = 41,
                         BRANCHZERO = 42, HALT = 43};
```

```
// STACKND.H
// Definition of template class StackNode
#ifndef STACKND_H
#define STACKND_H

template <class T>
class StackNode {
   friend class Stack<T>;
public:
   StackNode(const T & = 0, StackNode * = 0);
   T getData() const;
private:
   T data;
   StackNode *nextPtr;
};
```

```
// Member function definitions for class StackNode
template <class T>
StackNode<T>::StackNode(const T &d, StackNode<T> *ptr)
{
   data = d;
   nextPtr = ptr;
}

template <class T>
T StackNode<T>::getData() const { return data; }

#endif
```

```
// STACK.H
// Definition of class Stack

#ifndef STACK_H
#define STACK_H

#include <iostream.h>
#include <assert.h>
#include "stacknd.h"

template <class T>
class Stack {
public:
   Stack();                 // default constructor
   ~Stack();                // destructor
   void push(T &);          // insert item in stack
   T pop();                 // remove item from stack
   int isEmpty() const;     // is the stack empty?
   T stackTop() const;      // return the top element of stack
   void print() const;      // output the stack
private:
   StackNode<T> *topPtr;     // pointer to fist StackNode
};

// Member function definitions for class Stack
template <class T>
Stack<T>::Stack() { topPtr = 0; }

template <class T>
Stack<T>::~Stack()
{
   StackNode<T> *tempPtr, *currentPtr = topPtr;

   while (currentPtr != 0) {
      tempPtr = currentPtr;
      currentPtr = currentPtr->nextPtr;
      delete tempPtr;
   }
}

template <class T>
void Stack<T>::push(T &d)
{
   StackNode<T> *newPtr = new StackNode<T>(d, topPtr);

   assert(newPtr != 0);   // was memory allocated?
   topPtr = newPtr;
}
```

```cpp
template <class T>
T Stack<T>::pop()
{
    assert(!isEmpty());

    StackNode<T> *tempPtr = topPtr;

    topPtr = topPtr->nextPtr;
    T poppedValue = tempPtr->data;
    delete tempPtr;
    return poppedValue;
}

template <class T>
int Stack<T>::isEmpty() const { return topPtr == 0; }

template <class T>
T Stack<T>::stackTop() const { return !isEmpty() ? topPtr->data : 0; }

template <class T>
void Stack<T>::print() const
{
    StackNode<T> *currentPtr = topPtr;

    if (isEmpty())                 // Stack is empty
        cout << "Stack is empty" << endl;
    else {                         // Stack is not empty
        cout << "The stack is:" << endl;

        while (currentPtr != 0) {
            cout << currentPtr->data << ' ';
            currentPtr = currentPtr->nextPtr;
        }

        cout << endl;
    }
}

#endif
```

```cpp
// Exercise 15.27 Solution
// Non-optimized version.
#include "compiler.h"

main()
{
    char inFileName[15] = "", outFileName[15] = "";
    int last = 0;

    cout << "Enter Simple file to be compiled: ";
    cin >> setw(15) >> inFileName;

    while (isalnum(inFileName[last]) != 0) {
        outFileName[last] = inFileName[last];
        last++;                 // note the last occurance
    }

    outFileName[last] = '\0';       // append a NULL character
    strcat(outFileName, ".sml");    // add .sml to name

    ifstream inFile(inFileName, ios::in);

    if (inFile)
        compile(inFile, outFileName);
    else
        cerr << "File not opened. Program execution terminating." << endl;

    return 0;
}
```

```
// compile function calls the first pass and the second pass
void compile(ifstream &input, char *outFileName)
{
   TableEntry symbolTable[SYMBOLTABLESIZE]; // symbol table
   int flags[MEMORYSIZE];            // array for forward references
   int machineArray[MEMORYSIZE];     // array for SML instructions

   initArrays(flags, machineArray, symbolTable);

   firstPass(flags, machineArray, symbolTable, input);
   secondPass(flags, machineArray, symbolTable);

   printOutput(machineArray, outFileName);
}




// firstPass constructs the symbol table, creates SML, and flags
// unresolved references for goto and if/goto statements.
void firstPass(int flags[], int machineArray[], TableEntry symbolTable[],
               ifstream &input)
{
   char array[MAXIMUM];                  // array to copy a Simple line
   int n = MAXIMUM;                      // required for fgets()
   int dataCounter = MEMORYSIZE - 1; // 1st data location in machineArray
   int instCounter = 0;          // 1st instruction location in machineArray

   input.getline(array, n);

   while (!input.eof()) {
      separateToken(array, flags, machineArray, symbolTable, &dataCounter,
                    &instCounter);
      input.getline(array, n);
   }
}




// Separate Tokens tokenizes a Simple statement, process the line number,
// and passes the next token to keyWord for processing.
void separateToken(char array[], int flags[], int machineArray[],
                   TableEntry symbolTable[], int *dataCounterPtr,
                   int *instCounterPtr)
{
   char *tokenPtr = strtok(array, " ");     // tokenize line
   lineNumber(tokenPtr, symbolTable, *instCounterPtr, *dataCounterPtr);
   tokenPtr = strtok(NULL, " \n");     // get next token
   keyWord(tokenPtr, flags, machineArray, symbolTable, dataCounterPtr,
           instCounterPtr);
}




// checkSymbolTable searches the symbol table and returns
// the symbols SML location or a -1 if not found.
int checkSymbolTable(TableEntry symbolTable[], int symbol, char type)
{
   for (int loop = 0; loop < SYMBOLTABLESIZE; loop++)
      if ( (symbol == symbolTable[loop].symbol) &&
           (type == symbolTable[loop].type))
         return symbolTable[loop].location;  // return SML location

   return -1;                                // symbol not found
}
```

```
// lineNumber processes line numbers
void lineNumber(char *tokenPtr, TableEntry symbolTable[],
                int instCounter, int dataCounter)
{
   const char type = 'L';
   int symbol;

   if ( isdigit(tokenPtr[0]) ) {
      symbol = atoi(tokenPtr);

      if ( -1 == checkSymbolTable(symbolTable, symbol, type) )
         addToSymbolTable(type, symbol, dataCounter,
                          symbolTable, instCounter);
   }
}


// keyWord determines the key word type and calls the appropriate function
void keyWord(char *tokenPtr, int flags[], int machineArray[],
             TableEntry symbolTable[], int *dataCounterPtr,
             int *instCounterPtr)
{
   if ( strcmp(tokenPtr, "rem") == 0 )
      ; // no instructions are generated by comments
   else if ( strcmp(tokenPtr, "input") == 0 ) {
      tokenPtr = strtok(NULL, " ");  // assign pointer to next token
      keyInput(tokenPtr, machineArray, symbolTable, dataCounterPtr,
               instCounterPtr);
   }
   else if ( strcmp(tokenPtr, "print") == 0 ) {
      tokenPtr = strtok(NULL, " ");  // assign pointer to next token
      keyPrint(tokenPtr, machineArray, symbolTable, dataCounterPtr,
               instCounterPtr);
   }
   else if ( strcmp(tokenPtr, "goto") == 0 ) {
      tokenPtr = strtok(NULL, " ");  // assign pointer to next token
      keyGoto(tokenPtr, flags, machineArray, symbolTable, instCounterPtr);
   }
   else if ( strcmp(tokenPtr, "if") == 0 ) {
      tokenPtr = strtok(NULL, " ");  // assign pointer to next token
      keyIfGoto(tokenPtr, flags, machineArray, symbolTable, dataCounterPtr,
                instCounterPtr);
   }
   else if ( strcmp(tokenPtr, "end") == 0 ) {
      machineArray[*instCounterPtr] = 43 * 100;
      ++(*instCounterPtr);
      tokenPtr = NULL;          // assign tokenPtr to NULL
   }
   else if ( strcmp(tokenPtr, "let") == 0 ) {
      tokenPtr = strtok(NULL, " ");  // assign pointer to next token
      keyLet(tokenPtr, machineArray, symbolTable, dataCounterPtr,
             instCounterPtr);
   }
}


// keyInput process input keywords
void keyInput(char *tokenPtr, int machineArray[], TableEntry symbolTable[],
              int *dataCounterPtr, int *instCounterPtr)
{
   const char type = 'V';

   machineArray[*instCounterPtr] = 10 * 100;
   int symbol = tokenPtr[0];
   int tableTest = checkSymbolTable(symbolTable, symbol, type);
```

```
        if ( -1 == tableTest ) {
            addToSymbolTable(type, symbol, *dataCounterPtr, symbolTable,
                            *instCounterPtr);
            machineArray[*instCounterPtr] += *dataCounterPtr;
            --(*dataCounterPtr);
        }
        else
            machineArray[*instCounterPtr] += tableTest;

        ++(*instCounterPtr);
    }

    // keyPrint process print keywords
    void keyPrint(char *tokenPtr, int machineArray[], TableEntry symbolTable[],
                    int *dataCounterPtr, int *instCounterPtr)
    {
        const char type = 'V';

        machineArray[*instCounterPtr] = 11 * 100;
        int symbol = tokenPtr[0];
        int tableTest = checkSymbolTable(symbolTable, symbol, type);

        if ( -1 == tableTest ) {
            addToSymbolTable(type, symbol, *dataCounterPtr, symbolTable,
                            *instCounterPtr);
            machineArray[*instCounterPtr] += *dataCounterPtr;
            --(*dataCounterPtr);
        }
        else
            machineArray[*instCounterPtr] += tableTest;

        ++(*instCounterPtr);
    }

    // keyGoto process goto keywords
    void keyGoto(char *tokenPtr, int flags[], int machineArray[],
                    TableEntry symbolTable[], int *instCounterPtr)
    {
        const char type = 'L';

        machineArray[*instCounterPtr] = 40 * 100;
        int symbol = atoi(tokenPtr);
        int tableTest = checkSymbolTable(symbolTable, symbol, type);
        addLineToFlags(tableTest, symbol, flags, machineArray, instCounterPtr);
        ++(*instCounterPtr);
    }

    // keyIfGoto process if/goto commands
    void keyIfGoto(char *tokenPtr, int flags[], int machineArray[],
                    TableEntry symbolTable[], int *dataCounterPtr,
                    int *instCounterPtr)
    {
        int operand1Loc = checkOperand(symbolTable, tokenPtr, dataCounterPtr,
                                        instCounterPtr, machineArray);

        char *operatorPtr = strtok(NULL, " ");    // get the operator

        tokenPtr = strtok(NULL, " ");   // get the right operand of operator

        int operand2Loc = checkOperand(symbolTable, tokenPtr, dataCounterPtr,
                                        instCounterPtr, machineArray);

        tokenPtr = strtok(NULL, " ");   // read in the goto keyword
```

```
        char *gotoLinePtr = strtok(NULL, " ");   // read in the goto line number

        evaluateExpression(operand1Loc, operand2Loc, operatorPtr, machineArray,
                           symbolTable, instCounterPtr, flags, gotoLinePtr);
}

// checkOperand ensures that the operands of an if/goto statement are
// in the symbol table.
int checkOperand(TableEntry symbolTable[], char *symPtr, int *dataCounterPtr,
                 int *instCounterPtr, int machineArray[])
{
    char type;
    int tableTest, operand, temp;

    if ( isalpha(symPtr[0]) ) {
        type = 'V';
        operand = symPtr[0];
        tableTest = checkSymbolTable(symbolTable, operand, type);

        if (tableTest == -1) {
            addToSymbolTable(type, operand, *dataCounterPtr, symbolTable,
                             *instCounterPtr);
            temp = *dataCounterPtr;
            --(*dataCounterPtr);
            return temp;
        }
        else
            return tableTest;
    }
    // if the symbol is a digit or a signed digit
    else if (isdigit(symPtr[0]) ||
             ( (symPtr[0] == '-' || symPtr[0] == '+') &&
                           isdigit(symPtr[1]) != 0) ) {
        type = 'C';
        operand = atoi(symPtr);
        tableTest = checkSymbolTable(symbolTable, operand, type);

        if (tableTest == -1) {
            addToSymbolTable(type, operand, *dataCounterPtr, symbolTable,
                             *instCounterPtr);
            machineArray[*dataCounterPtr] = operand;
            temp = *dataCounterPtr;
            --(*dataCounterPtr);
            return temp ;
        }
        else
            return tableTest;
    }

    return 0;          // default return for compilation purposes
}

// evaluateExpression creates SML for conditional operators
void evaluateExpression(int operator1Loc, int operator2Loc, char *operandPtr,
                        int machineArray[], TableEntry symbolTable[],
                        int *instCounterPtr, int flags[], char *gotoLinePtr)
{
    const char type = 'L';
    int tableTest, symbol;

    if ( strcmp(operandPtr, "==") == 0 ) {
        machineArray[*instCounterPtr] = LOAD * 100;
        machineArray[*instCounterPtr] += operator1Loc;
        ++(*instCounterPtr);
```

```
         machineArray[*instCounterPtr] = SUBTRACT * 100;
         machineArray[*instCounterPtr] += operator2Loc;
         ++(*instCounterPtr);

         machineArray[*instCounterPtr] = BRANCHZERO * 100;

         symbol = atoi(gotoLinePtr);
         tableTest = checkSymbolTable(symbolTable, symbol, type);
         addLineToFlags(tableTest, symbol, flags, machineArray, instCounterPtr);
         ++(*instCounterPtr);
      }
      else if (strcmp(operandPtr, "!=") == 0) {
         machineArray[*instCounterPtr] = LOAD * 100;
         machineArray[*instCounterPtr] += operator2Loc;
         ++(*instCounterPtr);

         machineArray[*instCounterPtr] = SUBTRACT * 100;
         machineArray[*instCounterPtr] += operator1Loc;
         ++(*instCounterPtr);

         machineArray[*instCounterPtr] = BRANCHNEG * 100;

         symbol = atoi(gotoLinePtr);
         tableTest = checkSymbolTable(symbolTable, symbol, type);

         addLineToFlags(tableTest, symbol, flags, machineArray, instCounterPtr);

         ++(*instCounterPtr);

         machineArray[*instCounterPtr] = LOAD * 100;
         machineArray[*instCounterPtr] += operator1Loc;
         ++(*instCounterPtr);

         machineArray[*instCounterPtr] = SUBTRACT * 100;
         machineArray[*instCounterPtr] += operator2Loc;
         ++(*instCounterPtr);

         machineArray[*instCounterPtr] = BRANCHNEG * 100;

         symbol = atoi(gotoLinePtr);
         tableTest = checkSymbolTable(symbolTable, symbol, type);

         addLineToFlags(tableTest, symbol, flags, machineArray, instCounterPtr);

         ++(*instCounterPtr);
      }
      else if (strcmp(operandPtr, ">") == 0) {
         machineArray[*instCounterPtr] = LOAD * 100;
         machineArray[*instCounterPtr] += operator2Loc;
         ++(*instCounterPtr);

         machineArray[*instCounterPtr] = SUBTRACT * 100;
         machineArray[*instCounterPtr] += operator1Loc;
         ++(*instCounterPtr);

         machineArray[*instCounterPtr] = BRANCHNEG * 100;

         symbol = atoi(gotoLinePtr);
         tableTest = checkSymbolTable(symbolTable, symbol, type);

         addLineToFlags(tableTest, symbol, flags, machineArray, instCounterPtr);
         ++(*instCounterPtr);
      }
```

```
        else if (strcmp(operandPtr, "<") == 0) {
           machineArray[*instCounterPtr] = LOAD * 100;
           machineArray[*instCounterPtr] += operator1Loc;
           ++(*instCounterPtr);

           machineArray[*instCounterPtr] = SUBTRACT * 100;
           machineArray[*instCounterPtr] += operator2Loc;
           ++(*instCounterPtr);

           machineArray[*instCounterPtr] = BRANCHNEG * 100;

           symbol = atoi(gotoLinePtr);
           tableTest = checkSymbolTable(symbolTable, symbol, type);

           addLineToFlags(tableTest, symbol, flags, machineArray, instCounterPtr);
           ++(*instCounterPtr);
        }

        else if (strcmp(operandPtr, ">=") == 0) {
           machineArray[*instCounterPtr] = LOAD * 100;
           machineArray[*instCounterPtr] += operator2Loc;
           ++(*instCounterPtr);

           machineArray[*instCounterPtr] = SUBTRACT * 100;
           machineArray[*instCounterPtr] += operator1Loc;
           ++(*instCounterPtr);

           machineArray[*instCounterPtr] = BRANCHNEG * 100;

           symbol = atoi(gotoLinePtr);
           tableTest = checkSymbolTable(symbolTable, symbol, type);

           addLineToFlags(tableTest, symbol, flags, machineArray, instCounterPtr);
           ++(*instCounterPtr);

           machineArray[*instCounterPtr] = BRANCHZERO * 100;

           addLineToFlags(tableTest, symbol, flags, machineArray, instCounterPtr);
           ++(*instCounterPtr);
        }

        else if (strcmp(operandPtr, "<=") == 0) {
           machineArray[*instCounterPtr] = LOAD * 100;
           machineArray[*instCounterPtr] += operator1Loc;
           ++(*instCounterPtr);

           machineArray[*instCounterPtr] = SUBTRACT * 100;
           machineArray[*instCounterPtr] += operator2Loc;
           ++(*instCounterPtr);

           machineArray[*instCounterPtr] = BRANCHNEG * 100;

           symbol = atoi(gotoLinePtr);
           tableTest = checkSymbolTable(symbolTable, symbol, type);

           addLineToFlags(tableTest, symbol, flags, machineArray, instCounterPtr);
           ++(*instCounterPtr);

           machineArray[*instCounterPtr] = BRANCHZERO * 100;

           addLineToFlags(tableTest, symbol, flags, machineArray, instCounterPtr);
           ++(*instCounterPtr);
        }
    }
```

454   Data Structures: Solutions   Chapter 15

```cpp
// secondPass resolves incomplete SML instructions for forward references
void secondPass(int flags[], int machineArray[], TableEntry symbolTable[])
{
   const char type = 'L';

   for (int loop = 0; loop < MEMORYSIZE; loop++) {
      if (flags[loop] != -1) {
         int symbol = flags[loop];
         int flagLocation = checkSymbolTable(symbolTable, symbol, type);
         machineArray[loop] += flagLocation;
      }
   }
}


// keyLet processes the keyword let
void keyLet(char *tokenPtr, int machineArray[], TableEntry symbolTable[],
            int *dataCounterPtr, int *instCounterPtr)
{
   const char type = 'V';
   char infixArray[MAXIMUM] = "", postfixArray[MAXIMUM] = "";
   int tableTest, symbol, location;
   static int subscript = 0;

   symbol = tokenPtr[0];
   tableTest = checkSymbolTable(symbolTable, symbol, type);

   if ( -1 == tableTest ) {
      addToSymbolTable(type, symbol, *dataCounterPtr, symbolTable,
                       *instCounterPtr);
      location = *dataCounterPtr;
      --(*dataCounterPtr);
   }
   else
      location = tableTest;

   tokenPtr = strtok(NULL, " ");      // grab equal sign
   tokenPtr = strtok(NULL, " ");      // get next token

   while (tokenPtr != NULL) {
      checkOperand(symbolTable, tokenPtr, dataCounterPtr,
                   instCounterPtr, machineArray);
      infixArray[subscript] = tokenPtr[0];
      ++subscript;
      tokenPtr = strtok(NULL, " ");   // get next token
   }

   infixArray[subscript] = '\0';

   infixToPostfix(infixArray, postfixArray, location, symbolTable,
                  instCounterPtr, dataCounterPtr, machineArray);

   subscript = 0;     // reset static subscript when done
}

void addToSymbolTable(char type, int symbol, int dataCounter,
                      TableEntry symbolTable[], int instCounter)
{
   static int symbolCounter = 0;

   symbolTable[symbolCounter].type = type;
   symbolTable[symbolCounter].symbol = symbol;

   if (type == 'V' || type == 'C')
      symbolTable[symbolCounter].location = dataCounter;
```

```
      else
         symbolTable[symbolCounter].location = instCounter;

      ++symbolCounter;
   }

   void addLineToFlags(int tableTest, int symbol, int flags[],
                       int machineArray[], const int *instCounterPtr)
   {
      if (tableTest == -1)
         flags[*instCounterPtr] = symbol;
      else
         machineArray[*instCounterPtr] += tableTest;
   }

   void printOutput(const int machineArray[], char *outFileName)
   {
      ofstream output(outFileName, ios::out);

      if ( !output )
         cerr << "File was not opened." << endl;
      else                       // output every memory cell
         for (int loop = 0; loop <= MEMORYSIZE - 1; loop++)
            output << machineArray[loop] << endl;
   }

   void initArrays(int flags[], int machineArray[], TableEntry symbolTable[])
   {
      TableEntry initEntry = {0, 0, -1};

      for (int loop = 0; loop < MEMORYSIZE; loop++) {
         flags[loop] = -1;
         machineArray[loop] = 0;
         symbolTable[loop] = initEntry;
      }
   }


   ///////////////////////////////////////////////////////////////////////////
   // INFIX TO POSTFIX CONVERSION and POSTFIX EVALUATION FOR LET STATEMENT //
   ///////////////////////////////////////////////////////////////////////////

   // infixToPostfix converts an infix expression to a postfix expression
   void infixToPostfix(char infix[], char postfix[], int getsVariable,
                       TableEntry symbolTable[], int *instCounterPtr,
                       int *dataCounterPtr, int machineArray[])
   {
      Stack<int> intStack;
      int infixCount, postfixCount, higher, popValue;
      char leftParen = '(';

      // push a left paren onto the stack and add a right paren to infix
      intStack.push(leftParen);
      strcat(infix, ")");

      // convert the infix expression to postfix
      for (infixCount = 0, postfixCount = 0; intStack.stackTop(); infixCount++) {
         if ( isalnum(infix[infixCount]) )
            postfix[postfixCount++] = infix[infixCount];
         else if ( infix[infixCount] == '(' )
            intStack.push(leftParen);
         else if ( isOperator(infix[infixCount]) ) {
            higher = 1;    // used to store value of precedence test
```

```
            while (higher) {
                if ( isOperator(intStack.stackTop()) )
                    if ( precedence(intStack.stackTop(), infix[infixCount]) )
                        postfix[postfixCount++] = intStack.pop();
                    else
                        higher = 0;    // false
                else
                    higher = 0;    // false
            }


            intStack.push(infix[infixCount]);
        }
        else if ( infix[infixCount] == ')' )
            while ( ( popValue = intStack.pop() ) != '(' )
                postfix[postfixCount++] = popValue;
    }

    postfix[postfixCount] = '\0';

    evaluatePostfix(postfix, dataCounterPtr, instCounterPtr,
                    machineArray, getsVariable, symbolTable);
}


// check if c is an operator
int isOperator(char c)
{
    if (c == '+' || c == '-' || c == '*' || c == '/' || c == '^')
        return 1;    // true
    else
        return 0;    // false
}


// If the precedence of operator1 is >= operator2,
// return 1 (true) else return 0 (false).
int precedence(char operator1, char operator2)
{
    if (operator1 == '^')
        return 1;
    else if (operator2 == '^')
        return 0;
    else if (operator1 == '*' || operator1 == '/')
        return 1;
    else if (operator1 == '+' || operator1 == '-')
        if (operator2 == '*' || operator2 == '/')
            return 0;
        else
            return 1;

    return 0;
}

// evaluate postfix expression and produce code
void evaluatePostfix(char *expr, int *dataCounterPtr,
                     int *instCounterPtr, int machineArray[],
                     int getsVariable, TableEntry symbolTable[])
{
    Stack<int> intStack;
    int popRightValue, popLeftValue, accumResult, symbolLocation, symbol;
    char type, array[2] = "";
    int i;

    strcat(expr, ")");
```

```
        for (i = 0; expr[i] != ')'; i++)
            if (isdigit(expr[i])) {
                type = 'C';
                array[0] = expr[i];
                symbol = atoi(array);

                symbolLocation = checkSymbolTable(symbolTable, symbol, type);
                intStack.push(symbolLocation);
            }
            else if (isalpha(expr[i])) {
                type = 'V';
                symbol = expr[i];
                symbolLocation = checkSymbolTable(symbolTable, symbol, type);
                intStack.push(symbolLocation);
            }
            else {
                popRightValue = intStack.pop();
                popLeftValue = intStack.pop();
                accumResult = createLetSML(popRightValue, popLeftValue, machineArray,
                                         instCounterPtr, dataCounterPtr, expr[i]);
                intStack.push(accumResult);
            }

            machineArray[*instCounterPtr] = LOAD * 100;
            machineArray[*instCounterPtr] += intStack.pop();
            ++(*instCounterPtr);
            machineArray[*instCounterPtr] = STORE * 100;
            machineArray[*instCounterPtr] += getsVariable;
            ++(*instCounterPtr);
    }


int createLetSML(int right, int left, int machineArray[],
                 int *instCounterPtr, int *dataCounterPtr, char oper)
{
    int location;

    switch(oper) {
        case '+':
            machineArray[*instCounterPtr] = LOAD * 100;
            machineArray[*instCounterPtr] += left;
            ++(*instCounterPtr);
            machineArray[*instCounterPtr] = ADD * 100;
            machineArray[*instCounterPtr] += right;
            ++(*instCounterPtr);
            machineArray[*instCounterPtr] = STORE * 100;
            machineArray[*instCounterPtr] += *dataCounterPtr;
            location = *dataCounterPtr;
            --(*dataCounterPtr);
            ++(*instCounterPtr);
            return location;
        case '-':
            machineArray[*instCounterPtr] = LOAD * 100;
            machineArray[*instCounterPtr] += left;
            ++(*instCounterPtr);
            machineArray[*instCounterPtr] = SUBTRACT * 100;
            machineArray[*instCounterPtr] += right;
            ++(*instCounterPtr);
            machineArray[*instCounterPtr] = STORE * 100;
            machineArray[*instCounterPtr] += *dataCounterPtr;
            location = *dataCounterPtr;
            --(*dataCounterPtr);
            ++(*instCounterPtr);
            return location;
```

```
      case '/':
         machineArray[*instCounterPtr] = LOAD * 100;
         machineArray[*instCounterPtr] += left;
         ++(*instCounterPtr);
         machineArray[*instCounterPtr] = DIVIDE * 100;
         machineArray[*instCounterPtr] += right;
         ++(*instCounterPtr);
         machineArray[*instCounterPtr] = STORE * 100;
         machineArray[*instCounterPtr] += *dataCounterPtr;
         location = *dataCounterPtr;
         --(*dataCounterPtr);
         ++(*instCounterPtr);
         return location;
      case '*':
         machineArray[*instCounterPtr] = LOAD * 100;
         machineArray[*instCounterPtr] += left;
         ++(*instCounterPtr);
         machineArray[*instCounterPtr] = MULTIPLY * 100;
         machineArray[*instCounterPtr] += right;
         ++(*instCounterPtr);
         machineArray[*instCounterPtr] = STORE * 100;
         machineArray[*instCounterPtr] += *dataCounterPtr;
         location = *dataCounterPtr;
         --(*dataCounterPtr);
         ++(*instCounterPtr);
         return location;
      default:
         cerr << "ERROR: operator not recognized." << endl;
         break;
   }

   return 0;     // default return
}
```

Contents of test.sim

```
10 rem    determine and print the sum of two integers
15 rem
20 rem    input the two integers
30 input a
40 input b
45 rem
50 rem    add integers and store result in c
60 let c = a + b
65 rem
70 rem    print the result
80 print c
90 rem    terminate program execution
99 end
```

Contents of test.sml

```
1099
1098
2099
3098
2196
2096
2197
1197
4300
0
0
0
...
```

Contents of test2.sim

```
10 rem    determine the larger of two integers
20 input s
30 input t
32 rem
35 rem    test if s >= t
40 if s >= t goto 90
45 rem
50 rem    t is greater than s, so print t
60 print t
70 goto 99
75 rem
80 rem    s is greater than or equal to t, so print s
90 print s
99 end
```

Contents of test2.sml

```
1099
1098
2098
3199
4108
4208
1198
4009
1199
4300
0
0
0
...
```

15.28 (*Optimizing the Simple Compiler*) When a program is compiled and converted into SML, a set of instructions is generated. Certain combinations of instructions often repeat themselves, usually in triplets called *productions*. A production normally consists of three instructions such as *load*, *add*, and *store*. For example, Fig. 15.27 illustrates five of the SML instructions that were produced in the compilation of the program in Fig. 15.25 The first three instructions are the production that adds **1** to **y**. Note that instructions **06** and **07** store the accumulator value in temporary location **96**, then load the value back into the accumulator so instruction **08** can store the value in location **98**. Often a production is followed by a load instruction for the same location that was just stored. This code can be *optimized* by eliminating the store instruction and the subsequent load instruction that operate on the same memory location, thus enabling the Simpletron to execute the program faster. Figure 15.28 illustrates the optimized SML for the program of Fig. 15.25. Note that there are four fewer instructions in the optimized code—a memory-space savings of 25%.

Modify the compiler to provide an option for optimizing the Simpletron Machine Language code it produces. Manually compare the non-optimized code with the optimized code, and calculate the percentage reduction.

```
04  +2098 (load)
05  +3097 (add)
06  +2196 (store)

07  +2096 (load)
08  +2198 (store)
```

Fig. 15.27 Unoptimized code from the program of Fig. 15.25.

15.29 (*Modifications to the Simple compiler*) Perform the following modifications to the Simple compiler. Some of these modifications may also require modifications to the Simpletron Simulator program written in Exercise 5.19.

a) Allow the modulus operator (%) to be used in **let** statements. Simpletron Machine Language must be modified to include a modulus instruction.

b) Allow exponentiation in a **let** statement using ^ as the exponentiation operator. Simpletron Machine Language must be modified to include an exponentiation instruction.

c) Allow the compiler to recognize uppercase and lowercase letters in Simple statements (e.g., **'A'** is equivalent to **'a'**). No modifications to the Simpletron Simulator are required.

d) Allow **input** statements to read values for multiple variables such as **input x, y**. No modifications to the Simpletron Simulator are required.

e) Allow the compiler to output multiple values in a single **print** statement such as **print a, b, c**. No modifications to the Simpletron Simulator are required.

f) Add syntax-checking capabilities to the compiler so error messages are output when syntax errors are encountered in a Simple program. No modifications to the Simpletron Simulator are required.

g) Allow arrays of integers. No modifications to the Simpletron Simulator are required.

h) Allow subroutines specified by the Simple commands **gosub** and **return**. Command **gosub** passes program control to a subroutine and command **return** passes control back to the statement after the **gosub**. This is similar to a function call in C++. The same subroutine can be called from many **gosub** commands distributed throughout a program. No modifications to the Simpletron Simulator are required.

i) Allow repetition structures of the form

```
for x = 2 to 10 step 2
    Simple statements
next
```

This **for** statement loops from **2** to **10** with an increment of **2**. The **next** line marks the end of the body of the **for** line. No modifications to the Simpletron Simulator are required.

Simple program	SML location and instruction		Description
5 rem sum 1 to x		*none*	**rem** ignored
10 input x	00	+1099	read **x** into location **99**
15 rem check y == x		*none*	**rem** ignored
20 if y == x goto 60	01	+2098	load **y** (**98**) into accumulator
	02	+3199	sub **x** (**99**) from accumulator
	03	+4211	branch to location **11** if zero
25 rem increment y		*none*	**rem** ignored
30 let y = y + 1	04	+2098	load **y** into accumulator
	05	+3097	add **1** (**97**) to accumulator
	06	+2198	store accumulator in **y** (**98**)
35 rem add y to total		*none*	**rem** ignored
40 let t = t + y	07	+2096	load **t** from location (**96**)
	08	+3098	add **y** (**98**) accumulator
	09	+2196	store accumulator in t (**96**)
45 rem loop y		*none*	**rem** ignored
50 goto 20	10	+4001	branch to location **01**
55 rem output result		*none*	**rem** ignored
60 print t	11	+1196	output **t** (**96**) to screen
99 end	12	+4300	terminate execution

Fig. 15.28 Optimized code for the program of Fig. 15.25.

j) Allow repetition structures of the form

```
for x = 2 to 10
     Simple statements
next
```

This **for** statement loops from **2** to **10** with a default increment of **1**. No modifications to the Simpletron Simulator are required.

k) Allow the compiler to process string input and output. This requires the Simpletron Simulator to be modified to process and store string values. Hint: Each Simpletron word can be divided into two groups, each holding a two-digit integer. Each two-digit integer represents the ASCII decimal equivalent of a character. Add a machine language instruction that will print a string beginning at a certain Simpletron memory location. The first half of the word at that location is a count of the number of characters in the string (i.e., the length of the string). Each succeeding half word contains one ASCII character expressed as two decimal digits. The machine language instruction checks the length and prints the string by translating each two-digit number into its equivalent character.

l) Allow the compiler to process floating-point values in addition to integers. The Simpletron Simulator must also be modified to process floating-point values.

15.30 (*A Simple interpreter*) An interpreter is a program that reads a high-level language program statement, determines the operation to be performed by the statement, and executes the operation immediately. The high-level language program is not converted into machine language first. Interpreters execute slowly because each statement encountered in the program must first be deciphered. If statements are contained in a loop, the statements are deciphered each time they are encountered in the loop. Early versions of the BASIC programming language were implemented as interpreters.

Write an interpreter for the Simple language discussed in Exercise 15.26. The program should use the infix-to-postfix converter developed in Exercise 15.12 and the postfix evaluator developed in Exercise 15.13 to evaluate expressions in a **let** statement. The same restrictions placed on the Simple language in Exercise 15.26 should be adhered to in this program. Test the interpreter with the Simple programs written in Exercise 15.26. Compare the results of running these programs in the interpreter with the results of compiling the Simple programs and running them in the Simpletron Simulator built in Exercise 5.19.

15.31 (*Insert/Delete Anywhere in a Linked List*) Our linked list class template allowed insertions and deletions at only the front and the back of the linked list. These capabilities were convenient for us when we used private inheritance and composition to produce a stack class template and a queue class template with a minimal amount of code simply by reusing the list class template. Actually linked lists are more general that those we provided. Modify the linked list class template we developed in this chapter to handle insertions and deletions anywhere in the list.

ANS:

```
// LIST.H
// Template List class definition
#ifndef LIST_H
#define LIST_H

#include <iostream.h>
#include <assert.h>
#include "listnd.h"

template<class NODETYPE>
class List {
public:
   List();                              // default constructor
   List(const List<NODETYPE> &);        // copy constructor
   ~List();                             // destructor
   void insertAtFront(const NODETYPE &);
   void insertAtBack(const NODETYPE &);
   void insertInOrder(const NODETYPE &);
   int removeFromFront(NODETYPE &);
   int removeFromBack(NODETYPE &);
   int deleteNode(const NODETYPE &, NODETYPE &);
   int isEmpty() const;
   void print() const;
```

```
private:
   ListNode<NODETYPE> *firstPtr;   // pointer to first node
   ListNode<NODETYPE> *lastPtr;    // pointer to last node

   // Utility function to allocate a new node
   ListNode<NODETYPE> *getNewNode(const NODETYPE &);
};


// Default constructor
template<class NODETYPE>
List<NODETYPE>::List() { firstPtr = lastPtr = 0; }


// Copy constructor
template<class NODETYPE>
List<NODETYPE>::List(const List<NODETYPE> &copy)
{
   firstPtr = lastPtr = 0;   // initialize pointers

   ListNode<NODETYPE> *currentPtr = copy.firstPtr;

   while (currentPtr != 0) {
      insertAtBack(currentPtr->data);
      currentPtr = currentPtr->nextPtr;
   }
}


// Destructor
template<class NODETYPE>
List<NODETYPE>::~List()
{
   if (!isEmpty()) {      // List is not empty
      cout << "Destroying nodes ... " << endl;

      ListNode<NODETYPE> *currentPtr = firstPtr, *tempPtr;

      while (currentPtr != 0) {  // delete remaining nodes
         tempPtr = currentPtr;
         cout << tempPtr->data << ' ';
         currentPtr = currentPtr->nextPtr;
         delete tempPtr;
      }
   }

   cout << endl << "All nodes destroyed" << endl << endl;
}


// Insert a node at the front of the list
template<class NODETYPE>
void List<NODETYPE>::insertAtFront(const NODETYPE &value)
{
   ListNode<NODETYPE> *newPtr = getNewNode(value);

   if (isEmpty())  // List is empty
      firstPtr = lastPtr = newPtr;
   else {          // List is not empty
      newPtr->nextPtr = firstPtr;
      firstPtr = newPtr;
   }
}
```

```cpp
// Insert a node at the back of the list
template<class NODETYPE>
void List<NODETYPE>::insertAtBack(const NODETYPE &value)
{
    ListNode<NODETYPE> *newPtr = getNewNode(value);

    if (isEmpty())  // List is empty
        firstPtr = lastPtr = newPtr;
    else {             // List is not empty
        lastPtr->nextPtr = newPtr;
        lastPtr = newPtr;
    }
}


// Insert a node in order
template<class NODETYPE>
void List<NODETYPE>::insertInOrder(const NODETYPE &value)
{
    if (isEmpty()) { // List is empty
        ListNode<NODETYPE> *newPtr = getNewNode(value);
        firstPtr = lastPtr = newPtr;
    }
    else {             // List is not empty
        if (firstPtr->data > value)
            insertAtFront(value);
        else if (lastPtr->data < value)
            insertAtBack(value);
        else {
            ListNode<NODETYPE> *currentPtr = firstPtr->nextPtr,
                               *previousPtr = firstPtr,
                               *newPtr = getNewNode(value);

            while (currentPtr != lastPtr && currentPtr->data < value) {
                previousPtr = currentPtr;
                currentPtr = currentPtr->nextPtr;
            }

            previousPtr->nextPtr = newPtr;
            newPtr->nextPtr = currentPtr;
        }
    }
}


// Delete a node from the front of the list
template<class NODETYPE>
int List<NODETYPE>::removeFromFront(NODETYPE &value)
{
    if (isEmpty())                 // List is empty
        return 0;                  // delete unsuccessful
    else {
        ListNode<NODETYPE> *tempPtr = firstPtr;

        if (firstPtr == lastPtr)
            firstPtr = lastPtr = 0;
        else
            firstPtr = firstPtr->nextPtr;

        value = tempPtr->data;  // data being removed
        delete tempPtr;
        return 1;               // delete successful
    }
}
```

```cpp
// Delete a node from the back of the list
template<class NODETYPE>
int List<NODETYPE>::removeFromBack(NODETYPE &value)
{
   if (isEmpty())
      return 0;   // delete unsuccessful
   else {
      ListNode<NODETYPE> *tempPtr = lastPtr;

      if (firstPtr == lastPtr)
         firstPtr = lastPtr = 0;
      else {
         ListNode<NODETYPE> *currentPtr = firstPtr;

         while (currentPtr->nextPtr != lastPtr)
            currentPtr = currentPtr->nextPtr;

         lastPtr = currentPtr;
         currentPtr->nextPtr = 0;
      }

      value = tempPtr->data;
      delete tempPtr;
      return 1;   // delete successful
   }
}

// Delete a node from anywhere in the list
template<class NODETYPE>
int List<NODETYPE>::deleteNode(const NODETYPE &val, NODETYPE &deletedVal)
{
   if (isEmpty())
      return 0;   // delete unsuccessful
   else {
      if (firstPtr->data == val) {
         removeFromFront(deletedVal);
         return 1;   // delete successful
      }
      else if (lastPtr->data == val) {
         removeFromBack(deletedVal);
         return 1;   // delete successful
      }
      else {
         ListNode<NODETYPE> *currentPtr = firstPtr->nextPtr,
                            *previousPtr = firstPtr;

         while (currentPtr != lastPtr && currentPtr->data < val) {
            previousPtr = currentPtr;
            currentPtr = currentPtr->nextPtr;
         }

         if (currentPtr->data == val) {
            ListNode<NODETYPE> *tempPtr = currentPtr;
            deletedVal = currentPtr->data;
            previousPtr->nextPtr = currentPtr->nextPtr;
            delete tempPtr;
            return 1;   // delete successful
         }
         else
            return 0;   // delete unsuccessful
      }
   }
}
```

```
// Is the List empty?
template<class NODETYPE>
int List<NODETYPE>::isEmpty() const { return firstPtr == 0; }

// Return a pointer to a newly allocated node
template<class NODETYPE>
ListNode<NODETYPE> *List<NODETYPE>::getNewNode(const NODETYPE &value)
{
   ListNode<NODETYPE> *ptr = new ListNode<NODETYPE>(value);
   assert(ptr != 0);
   return ptr;
}

// Display the contents of the List
template<class NODETYPE>
void List<NODETYPE>::print() const
{
   if (isEmpty()) {
      cout << "The list is empty" << endl << endl;
      return;
   }

   ListNode<NODETYPE> *currentPtr = firstPtr;

   cout << "The list is: " << endl;

   while (currentPtr != 0) {
      cout << currentPtr->data << ' ';
      currentPtr = currentPtr->nextPtr;
   }

   cout << endl << endl;
}

#endif
```

```
// LISTND.H
// ListNode template definition
#ifndef LISTND_H
#define LISTND_H

template<class NODETYPE>
class ListNode {
   friend class List<NODETYPE>; // make List a friend
public:
   ListNode(const NODETYPE &);  // constructor
   NODETYPE getData() const;    // return the data in the node
private:
   NODETYPE data;               // data
   ListNode *nextPtr;           // next node in the list
};

// Constructor
template<class NODETYPE>
ListNode<NODETYPE>::ListNode(const NODETYPE &info)
{
   data = info;
   nextPtr = 0;
}

// Return a copy of the data in the node
template<class NODETYPE>
NODETYPE ListNode<NODETYPE>::getData() const { return data;}

#endif
```

```
// Exercise 15.31 solution
#include <iostream.h>
#include <stdlib.h>
#include <time.h>
#include "list.h"

main()
{
    srand(time(NULL));   // randomize the random number generator

    List<int> intList;

    for (int i = 1; i <= 10; i++)
        intList.insertInOrder(rand() % 101);

    intList.print();

    int value, deletedValue;

    cout << "Enter an integer to delete (-1 to end): ";
    cin >> value;

    while ( value != -1) {
        if ( intList.deleteNode(value, deletedValue) ) {
            cout << deletedValue << " was deleted from the list" << endl;
            intList.print();
        }
        else
            cout << "Element was not found";

        cout << "Enter an integer to delete (-1 to end): ";
        cin >> value;
    }

    return 0;
}
```

```
The list is:
8 20 51 55 71 76 77 86 92 93

Enter an integer to delete (-1 to end): 8
8 was deleted from the list
The list is:
20 51 55 71 76 77 86 92 93

Enter an integer to delete (-1 to end): 93
93 was deleted from the list
The list is:
20 51 55 71 76 77 86 92

Enter an integer to delete (-1 to end): 92
92 was deleted from the list
The list is:
20 51 55 71 76 77 86

Enter an integer to delete (-1 to end): 20
20 was deleted from the list
The list is:
51 55 71 76 77 86

Enter an integer to delete (-1 to end): 71
71 was deleted from the list
```

continued

```
                                                      continued

The list is:
51 55 76 77 86

Enter an integer to delete (-1 to end): 55
55 was deleted from the list
The list is:
51 76 77 86

Enter an integer to delete (-1 to end): 77
77 was deleted from the list
The list is:
51 76 86

Enter an integer to delete (-1 to end): 76
76 was deleted from the list
The list is:
51 86

Enter an integer to delete (-1 to end): 51
51 was deleted from the list
The list is:
86

Enter an integer to delete (-1 to end): 86
86 was deleted from the list
The list is empty

Enter an integer to delete (-1 to end): -1

All nodes destroyed
```

15.32 *(List and Queues without Tail Pointers)* Our implementation of a linked list (Fig. 15.3) used both a `firstPtr` and a `lastPtr`. The `lastPtr` was useful for the `insertAtBack` and `removeFromBack` member functions of the `List` class. The `insertAtBack` function corresponds to the `enqueue` member function of the `Queue` class. Rewrite the `List` class so that it does not use a `lastPtr`. Thus, any operations on the tail of a list must begin searching the list from the front. Does this affect our implementation of the `Queue` class (Fig. 15.12)?

15.33 Use the composition version of the stack program (Fig. 15.11) to form a complete working stack program. Modify this program to inline the member functions. Compare the two approaches. Summarize the advantages and disadvantages of inlining member functions.

15.34 *(Performance of Binary Tree Sorting and Searching)* One problem with the binary tree sort is that the order in which the data is inserted affects the shape of the tree—for the same collection of data, different orderings can yield binary trees of dramatically different shapes. The performance of the binary tree sorting and searching algorithms is sensitive to the shape of the binary tree. What shape would a binary tree have if its data were inserted in increasing order? in decreasing orde? What shape should the tree have to achieve maximal searching performance?

15.35 *(Indexed Lists)* As presented in the text, linked lists must be searched sequentially. For large lists, this can result in poor performance. A common technique for improving list searching performance is to creatre and maintain an index to the list. An index is a set of pointers to various key places in the list. For example, an application that searches a large list of names could improve performance by creating an index with 26 entries—one for each letter of the alphabet. A search operation for a last name beginning with 'Y' would then first search the index to determine where the 'Y' entries begin, and then "jump into" the list at that point and search linearly until the desired name is found. This would be much faster than searching the linked list from the beginning. Use the `List` class of Fig. 15.3 as the basis of an `IndexedList` class. Write a program that demonstrates the operation of indexed lists. Be sure to include member functions `insertInIndexedList`, `seatrchIndexedList`, and `deleteFromIndexed-List`.

16

Bits, Characters, Strings, and Structures: Solutions

16.6 Provide the definition for each of the following structures and unions:

a) Structure **Inventory** containing character array **partName[30]**, integer **partNumber**, floating point **price**, integer **stock**, and integer **reorder**.

ANS:
```
struct Inventory {
   char partName[30];
   int partNumber;
   float price;
   int stock;
   int reorder;
};
```

b) A structure called **Address** that contains character arrays **streetAddress[25]**, **city[20]**, **state[3]**, and **zipCode[6]**.

ANS:
```
struct Address {
   char streetAddress[25];
   char city[20];
   char state[3];
   char zipCode[6];
};
```

c) Structure **Student** that contains arrays **firstName[15]** and **lastName[15]**, and variable **homeAddress** of type **struct Address** from part (b).

ANS:
```
struct Student {
   char firstName[15];
   char lastName[15];
   struct Address homeAddess;
};
```

d) Structure **Test** containing 16 bit fields with widths of 1 bit. The names of the bit fields are the letters **a** to **p**.

ANS:
```
struct Test {
   unsigned a:1, b:1, c:1, d:1, e:1, f:1, g:1, h:1,
            i:1, j:1, k:1, l:1, m:1, n:1, o:1, p:1;
};
```

16.7   Given the following structure definitions and variable declarations,

```
struct Customer {
    char lastName[15];
    char firstName[15];
    int customerNumber;

    struct {
        char phoneNumber[11];
        char address[50];
        char city[15];
        char state[3];
        char zipCode[6];
    } personal;

} customerRecord, *customerPtr;

customerPtr = &customerRecord;
```

write a separate expression that can be used to access the structure members in each of the following parts.

a) Member lastName of structure customerRecord.
ANS: customerRecord.lastName
b) Member lastName of the structure pointed to by customerPtr.
ANS: customerPtr->lastName
c) Member firstName of structure customerRecord.
ANS: customerRecord.firstName
d) Member firstName of the structure pointed to by customerPtr.
ANS: customerPtr->firstName
e) Member customerNumber of structure customerRecord.
ANS: customerRecord.customerNumber
f) Member customerNumber of the structure pointed to by customerPtr.
ANS: customerPtr->customerNumber
g) Member phoneNumber of member personal of structure customerRecord.
ANS: customerRecord.personal.phoneNumber
h) Member phoneNumber of member personal of the structure pointed to by customerPtr.
ANS: customerPtr->personal.phoneNumber
i) Member address of member personal of structure customerRecord.
ANS: customerRecord.personal.address
j) Member address of member personal of the structure pointed to by customerPtr.
ANS: customerPtr->personal.address
k) Member city of member personal of structure customerRecord.
ANS: customerRecord.personal.city
l) Member city of member personal of the structure pointed to by customerPtr.
ANS: customerPtr->personal.city
m) Member state of member personal of structure customerRecord.
ANS: customerRecord.personal.state
n) Member state of member personal of the structure pointed to by customerPtr.
ANS: customerPtr->personal.state
o) Member zipCode of member personal of structure customerRecord.
ANS: customerRecord.personal.zipCode
p) Member zipCode of member personal of the structure pointed to by customerPtr.
ANS: customerPtr->personal.zipCode

16.8   Modify the program of Fig. 16.14 to shuffle the cards using a high-performance shuffle (as shown in Fig. 16.2). Print the resulting deck in two column format as in Fig. 16.3. Precede each card with its color.
ANS:

```
// Exercise 16.8 Solution
#include <iostream.h>
#include <iomanip.h>
#include <stdlib.h>
#include <time.h>
```

```
struct bitCard {
   unsigned face : 4;
   unsigned suit : 2;
   unsigned color : 1;
};

typedef struct bitCard Card;

void fillDeck(Card *);
void shuffle(Card *);
void deal(Card *);

main()
{
   Card deck[52];

   srand(time(NULL));

   fillDeck(deck);
   shuffle(deck);
   deal(deck);
   return 0;
}

void fillDeck(Card *wDeck)
{
   for (int i = 0; i < 52; i++) {
      wDeck[i].face = i % 13;
      wDeck[i].suit = i / 13;
      wDeck[i].color = i / 26;
   }
}

void shuffle(Card *wDeck)
{
   int j;
   Card temp;

   for (int i = 0; i < 52; i++) {
      j = rand() % 52;

      temp = wDeck[i];
      wDeck[i] = wDeck[j];
      wDeck[j] = temp;
   }
}

void deal(Card *wDeck2)
{
   char *face[] = {"Ace", "Deuce", "Three", "Four", "Five", "Six", "Seven"
                  ,"Eight", "Nine", "Ten", "Jack", "Queen", "King"},
        *suit[] = {"Hearts", "Diamonds", "Clubs", "Spades"},
        *color[] = {"Red", "Black"};

   for (int i = 0; i < 52; i++) {

      cout << setw(5) << color[wDeck2[i].color] << ": "
           << setw(8) << face[wDeck2[i].face] << " of "
           << setiosflags(ios::left) << setw(8) << suit[wDeck2[i].suit]
           << resetiosflags(ios::left);

      cout.put( (i + 1) % 2 ? '\t' : '\n' );
   }
}
```

```
   Red: Eight of Diamonds        Red:   Ace of Hearts
 Black: Eight of Clubs         Black: Five of Spades
   Red: Seven of Hearts          Red: Deuce of Diamonds
 Black:   Ace of Clubs           Red:   Ten of Diamonds
 Black: Deuce of Spades          Red:   Six of Diamonds
 Black: Seven of Spades        Black: Deuce of Clubs
 Black:  Jack of Clubs         Black:   Ten of Spades
   Red:  King of Hearts          Red:  Jack of Diamonds
   Red: Three of Hearts          Red: Three of Diamonds
 Black: Three of Clubs         Black:  Nine of Clubs
   Red:   Ten of Hearts          Red: Deuce of Hearts
 Black:   Ten of Clubs          Red: Seven of Diamonds
 Black:   Six of Clubs        Black: Queen of Spades
   Red:   Six of Hearts       Black: Three of Spades
   Red:  Nine of Diamonds        Red:   Ace of Diamonds
 Black:  Jack of Spades       Black: Five of Clubs
   Red:  King of Diamonds     Black: Seven of Clubs
 Black:  Nine of Spades         Red:  Four of Hearts
 Black:   Six of Spades       Black: Eight of Spades
   Red: Queen of Diamonds        Red: Five of Diamonds
 Black:   Ace of Spades         Red:  Nine of Hearts
 Black:  King of Clubs          Red: Five of Hearts
 Black:  King of Spades         Red:  Four of Diamonds
   Red: Queen of Hearts         Red: Eight of Hearts
 Black:  Four of Spades         Red:  Jack of Hearts
 Black:  Four of Clubs        Black: Queen of Clubs
```

16.9   Write a program that right shifts an integer variable 4 bits. The program should print the integer in bits before and after the shift operation. Does your system place 0s or 1s in the vacated bits?

ANS:

```cpp
// Exercise 16.9 Solution
#include <iostream.h>
#include <iomanip.h>

void displayBits(unsigned);

main()
{
   unsigned val;

   cout << "Enter an integer: ";
   cin >> val;

   cout << "Before right shifting 4 bits is:" << endl;
   displayBits(val);
   cout << "After right shifting 4 bits is:" << endl;
   displayBits(val >> 4);
   return 0;
}
void displayBits(unsigned value)
{
   unsigned displayMask = 1 << 15;

   cout << setw(7) << value << " = ";

   for (unsigned c = 1; c <= 16; c++) {
      cout.put(value & displayMask ? '1' : '0');
      value <<= 1;

      if (c % 8 == 0)
         cout.put(' ');
   }

   cout.put('\n');
}
```

```
Enter an integer: 1234
Before right shifting 4 bits is:
   1234 = 00000100 11010010
After right shifting 4 bits is:
     77 = 00000000 01001101
```

16.10 If your computer uses 4-byte integers, modify the program of Fig. 16.5 so that it works with 4-byte integers.

16.11 Left shifting an **unsigned** integer by 1 bit is equivalent to multiplying the value by 2. Write function **power2** that takes two integer arguments **number** and **pow**, and calculates

> number * 2^{pow}

Use the shift operator to calculate the result. The program should print the values as integers and as bits.

ANS:
```cpp
// Exercise 16.11 Solution
#include <iostream.h>
#include <iomanip.h>

void displayBits(unsigned);
unsigned power2(unsigned, unsigned);

main()
{
   unsigned number, pow, result;

   cout << "Enter two integers: ";
   cin >> number >> pow;

   cout << "number:" << endl;
   displayBits(number);
   cout << endl << "power:" << endl;
   displayBits(pow);
   result = power2(number, pow);
   cout << endl << number << " * 2^" << pow << " = " << result << endl;
   displayBits(result);

   return 0;
}

unsigned power2(unsigned n, unsigned p) { return n << p; }

void displayBits(unsigned value)
{
   unsigned displayMask = 1 << 15;

   cout << setw(7) << value << " = ";

   for (unsigned c = 1; c <= 16; c++) {
      cout.put(value & displayMask ? '1' : '0');
      value <<= 1;

      if (c % 8 == 0)
         cout.put(' ');
   }

   cout << endl;
}
```

```
Enter two integers: 10 3
number:
      10 = 00000000 00001010

power:
       3 = 00000000 00000011

10 * 2^3 = 80
      80 = 00000000 01010000
```

16.12   The left shift operator can be used to pack two character values into a 2-byte unsigned integer variable. Write a program that inputs two characters from the keyboard and passes them to function **packCharacters**. To pack two characters into an **unsigned** integer variable, assign the first character to the **unsigned** variable, shift the **unsigned** variable left by 8 bit positions, and combine the **unsigned** variable with the second character using the bitwise inclusive OR operator. The program should output the characters in their bit format before and after they are packed into the **unsigned** integer to prove that the characters are in fact packed correctly in the **unsigned** variable.

ANS:
```cpp
// Exercise 16.12 Solution
#include <iostream.h>
#include <iomanip.h>

unsigned packCharacters(char, char);
void displayBits(unsigned);

main()
{
   char a, b;
   unsigned result;

   cout << "Enter two characters: ";
   cin.setf(ios::skipws);
   cin >> a >> b;

   cout << '\'' << a << '\'' << " in bits as an unsigned integers is: "
        << endl;
   displayBits(a);

   cout << '\'' << b << '\'' << " in bits as an unsigned integers is: "
        << endl;
   displayBits(b);

   result = packCharacters(a, b);

   cout << endl << '\'' << a << '\'' << " and " << '\'' << b << '\''
        << " packed in an unsigned integer: " << endl;

   displayBits(result);

   return 0;
}

unsigned packCharacters(char x, char y)
{
   unsigned pack = x;

   pack <<= 8;
   pack |= y;
   return pack;
}
```

```
void displayBits(unsigned value)
{
   unsigned displayMask = 1 << 15;

   cout << setw(7) << value << " = ";

   for (unsigned c = 1; c <= 16; c++) {
      cout.put(value & displayMask ? '1' : '0');
      value <<= 1;

      if (c % 8 == 0)
         cout.put(' ');
   }

   cout << endl;
}
```

```
Enter two characters: A B
'A' in bits as an unsigned integers is:
    65 = 00000000 01000001

'B' in bits as an unsigned integers is:
    66 = 00000000 01000010

'A' and 'B' packed in an unsigned integer:
  16706 = 01000001 01000010
```

16.13   Using the right shift operator, the bitwise AND operator, and a mask, write function `unpackCharacters` that takes the `unsigned` integer from Exercise 16.12 and unpacks it into two characters. To unpack two characters from an `unsigned` 2-byte integer, combine the unsigned integer with the mask `65280` (`11111111 00000000`) and right shift the result 8 bits. Assign the resulting value to a `char` variable. Then combine the `unsigned` integer with the mask `255` (`00000000 11111111`). Assign the result to another `char` variable. The program should print the `unsigned` integer in bits before it is unpacked, then print the characters in bits to confirm that they were unpacked correctly.

ANS:
```
// Exercise 16.13 Solution
#include <iostream.h>
#include <iomanip.h>

void unpackCharacters(char *, char *, unsigned);
void displayBits(unsigned);

main()
{
   char a, b;
   unsigned packed = 16706;

   cout << "The packed character representation is:" << endl;

   displayBits(packed);
   unpackCharacters(&a, &b, packed);

   cout << endl << "The unpacked characters are \'" << a
        << "\' and \'" << b << '\'' << endl;

   displayBits(a);
   displayBits(b);

   return 0;
}
```

```
void unpackCharacters(char *aPtr, char *bPtr, unsigned pack)
{
   unsigned mask1 = 65280, mask2 = 255;

   *aPtr = (pack & mask1) >> 8;
   *bPtr = (pack & mask2);
}

void displayBits(unsigned value)
{
   unsigned displayMask = 1 << 15;

   cout << setw(7) << value << " = ";

   for (unsigned c = 1; c <= 16; c++) {
      cout.put(value & displayMask ? '1' : '0');
      value <<= 1;

      if (c % 8 == 0)
         cout.put(' ');
   }

   cout << endl;
}
```

```
The packed character representation is:
  16706 = 01000001 01000010

The unpacked characters are 'A' and 'B'
    65 = 00000000 01000001
    66 = 00000000 01000010
```

16.14   If your system uses 4-byte integers, rewrite the program of Exercise 16.12 to pack 4 characters.

16.15   If your system uses 4-byte integers, rewrite the function **unpackCharacters** of Exercise 16.13 to unpack 4 characters. Create the masks you need to unpack the 4 characters by left shifting the value 255 in the mask variable by 8 bits 0, 1, 2, or 3 times (depending on the byte you are unpacking).

16.16   Write a program that reverses the order of the bits in an unsigned integer value. The program should input the value from the user and call function **reverseBits** to print the bits in reverse order. Print the value in bits both before and after the bits are reversed to confirm that the bits are reversed properly.

ANS:

```
// Exercise 16.16 Solution
#include <iostream.h>
#include <iomanip.h>

unsigned reverseBits(unsigned);
void displayBits(unsigned);

main()
{
   unsigned a;

   cout << "Enter an unsigned integer: ";
   cin >> a;

   cout << endl << "Before bits are reversed:" << endl;
   displayBits(a);
   a = reverseBits(a);
   cout << endl << "After bits are reversed:" << endl;
   displayBits(a);
   return 0;
}
```

```
unsigned reverseBits(unsigned value)
{
    unsigned mask = 1, temp = 0;

    for (int i = 0; i <= 15; i++) {
        temp <<= 1;
        temp |= (value & mask);
        value >>= 1;
    }

    return temp;
}


void displayBits(unsigned value)
{
    unsigned displayMask = 1 << 15;

    cout << setw(7) << value << " = ";

    for (unsigned c = 1; c <= 16; c++) {
        cout.put(value & displayMask ? '1' : '0');
        value <<= 1;

        if (c % 8 == 0)
            cout.put(' ');
    }

    cout << endl;
}
```

```
Enter an unsigned integer: 2127

Before bits are reversed:
  2127 = 00001000 01001111

After bits are reversed:
  61968 = 11110010 00010000
```

16.17   Modify the `displayBits` function of Fig. 16.5 so it is portable between systems using 2-byte integers and systems using 4-byte integers. Hint: Use the `sizeof` operator to determine the size of an integer on a particular machine.

ANS:
```
// Exercise 16.17 Solution
#include <iostream.h>
#include <iomanip.h>

void displayBits(unsigned);

main()
{
    unsigned x;

    cout << "Enter an unsigned integer: ";
    cin >> x;
    displayBits(x);

    return 0;
}
```

```
void displayBits(unsigned value)
{
    unsigned displayMask = 1 << ( sizeof(unsigned) * 8 - 1 );

    cout << setw(7) << value << " = ";

    for (unsigned c = 1; c <= sizeof(int) * 8; c++) {
        cout.put(value & displayMask ? '1' : '0');
        value <<= 1;

        if (c % 8 == 0)
            cout.put(' ');
    }

    cout << endl;
}
```

```
Enter an unsigned integer: 2345
2345 = 00001001 00101001
```

16.18 Write a program that inputs a character from the keyboard, and tests the character with each of the functions in the character handling library. The program should print the value returned by each function.

ANS:

```
// Exercise 16.18 Solution
#include <iostream.h>
#include <ctype.h>

main()
{
    char c;

    cout << "Enter a character: ";
    c = cin.get();

    cout << "isdigit(\'" << c << "\')  = " << isdigit(c) << endl
         << "isalpha(\'" << c << "\')  = " << isalpha(c) << endl
         << "isalnum(\'" << c << "\')  = " << isalnum(c) << endl;

    cout << "isxdigit(\'" << c << "\') = " << isxdigit(c) << endl
         << "islower(\'" << c << "\')  = " << islower(c) << endl
         << "isupper(\'" << c << "\')  = " << isupper(c) << endl
         << "tolower(\'" << c << "\')  = " << tolower(c) << endl
         << "toupper(\'" << c << "\')  = " << toupper(c) << endl
         << "isspace(\'" << c << "\')  = " << isspace(c) << endl;

    cout << "iscntrl(\'" << c << "\')  = " << iscntrl(c) << endl
         << "ispunct(\'" << c << "\')  = " << ispunct(c) << endl
         << "isprint(\'" << c << "\')  = " << isprint(c) << endl
         << "isgraph(\'" << c << "\')  = " << isgraph(c) << endl;

    return 0;
}
```

```
Enter a character: h
isdigit('h')  = 0
isalpha('h')  = 8
isalnum('h')  = 8
isxdigit('h') = 0
islower('h')  = 8
```
continued

```
                                                              continued
    isupper('h')  = 0
    tolower('h')  = 104
    toupper('h')  = 72
    isspace('h')  = 0
    iscntrl('h')  = 0
    ispunct('h')  = 0
    isprint('h')  = 8
    isgraph('h')  = 8
```

16.19 The following program uses function `multiple` to determine if the integer entered from the keyboard is a multiple of some integer **X**. Examine the function `multiple`, then determine the value of **X**.

```cpp
// This program determines if a value is a multiple of X
#include <iostream.h>

int multiple(int);

main()
{
   int y;

   cout << "Enter an integer between 1 and 32000: ";
   cin >> y;

   if (multiple(y))
      cout << y << " is a multiple of X" << endl;
   else
      cout << y << " is not a multiple of X" << endl;

   return 0;
}

int multiple(int num)
{
   int mask = 1, mult = 1;

   for (int i = 0; i < 10; i++, mask <<= 1)
      if ((num & mask) != 0) {
         mult = 0;
         break;
      }

   return mult;
}
```

ANS: X is 1024.

```
Enter an integer between 1 and 32000: 1024
1024 is a multiple of X
```

```
Enter an integer between 1 and 32000: 10
10 is not a multiple of X
```

16.20 What does the following program do?

```
#include <iostream.h>

int mystery(unsigned);

main()
{
   unsigned x;

   cout << "Enter an integer: ";
   cin >> x;
   cout << "The result is " << mystery(x) << endl;
   return 0;
}

int mystery(unsigned bits)
{
   unsigned mask = 1 << 15, total = 0;

   for (int i = 0; i < 16; i++, bits <<= 1)
      if ((bits & mask) == mask)
         ++total;

   return total % 2 == 0 ? 1 : 0;
}
```

ANS: The program prints 0 if the total number of 1s in the bit representation is an odd, and prints a 1 if the number of bits is even.

```
Enter an integer: 5678
The result is 0
```

```
Enter an integer: 65
The result is 1
```

16.21 Write a program that inputs a line of text with **istream** member function **getline** (see Chapter 11) into character array **s[100]**. Output the line in uppercase letters, then in lowercase letters.

ANS:
```
// Exercise 16.21 Solution
#include <iostream.h>
#include <ctype.h>

const int SIZE = 100;

main()
{
   char s[SIZE];

   cout << "Enter a line of text:" << endl;
   cin.getline(s, SIZE);

   cout << endl << "The line in uppercase is:" << endl;

   for (int i = 0; s[i] != '\0'; i++)
      cout.put(toupper(s[i]));

   cout << endl << endl << "The line in lowercase is:" << endl;

   for (i = 0; s[i] != '\0'; i++)
      cout.put(tolower(s[i]));

   return 0;
}
```

```
Enter a line of text:
Sentence in uppercase and lowercase

The line in uppercase is:
SENTENCE IN UPPERCASE AND LOWERCASE.

The line in lowercase is:
sentence in uppercase and lowercase.
```

16.22   Write a program that inputs 4 strings that represent integers, converts the strings to integers, sums the values, and prints the total of the 4 values.

ANS:

```cpp
// Exercise 16.22 Solution
#include <iostream.h>
#include <stdlib.h>

const int SIZE = 6;

main()
{
   char stringValue[SIZE];
   int sum = 0;

   for (int i = 1; i <= 4; i++) {
      cout << "Enter an integer string: ";
      cin >> stringValue;
      sum += atoi(stringValue);
   }

   cout << "The total of the values is " << sum << endl;
   return 0;
}
```

```
Enter an integer string: 43
Enter an integer string: 77
Enter an integer string: 120
Enter an integer string: 9999

The total of the values is 10239
```

16.23   Write a program that inputs 4 strings that represent floating-point values, converts the strings to double values, sums the values, and prints the total of the 4 values.

ANS:

```cpp
// Exercise 16.23 Solution
#include <iostream.h>
#include <iomanip.h>
#include <stdlib.h>

const int SIZE = 15;

main()
{
   char stringValue[SIZE];
   double sum = 0.0;

   for (int i = 1; i <= 4; i++) {
      cout << "Enter a floating point string: ";
      cin >> stringValue;
      sum += atof(stringValue);
   }
```

```
        cout.setf(ios::fixed | ios::showpoint);
        cout << endl << "The total of the values is " << setprecision(3)
             << sum << endl;
        return 0;
}
```

```
Enter a floating point string: 1.2
Enter a floating point string: 2.3
Enter a floating point string: 3.4
Enter a floating point string: 4.5

The total of the values is 11.400
```

16.24   Write a program that inputs a line of text and a search string from the keyboard. Using function **strstr**, locate the first occurrence of the search string in the line of text, and assign the location to variable **searchPtr** of type **char ***. If the search string is found, print the remainder of the line of text beginning with the search string. Then, use **strstr** again to locate the next occurrence of the search string in the line of text. If a second occurrence is found, print the remainder of the line of text beginning with the second occurrence. Hint: The second call to **strstr** should contain **searchPtr + 1** as its first argument.

  ANS:

```
// Exercise 16.24 Solution
#include <iostream.h>
#include <string.h>

const int SIZE1 = 80, SIZE2 = 15;

main()
{
    char text[SIZE1], search[SIZE2], *searchPtr;

    cout << "Enter a line of text:" << endl;
    cin.get(text, SIZE1);
    cout << "Enter a search string: ";
    cin >> search;
    searchPtr = strstr(text, search);

    if (searchPtr) {
        cout << endl << "The remainder of the line beginning with" << endl
             << "the first occurrence of " << endl << "\"" << search
             << "\":" << endl << searchPtr << endl;

        searchPtr = strstr(searchPtr + 1, search);

        if (searchPtr)
            cout << endl << "The remainder of the line beginning with"
                 << endl << "the second occurrence of " << endl << "\""
                 << search << "\":" << endl << searchPtr << endl;
        else
            cout << "The search string appeared only once." << endl;
    }
    else
        cout << "\"" << search << "\" not found." << endl;

    return 0;
}
```

```
Enter a line of text:
To be or not to be; that is the question.
Enter a search string: be
                                                                    continued
```

```
                                                                          continued
   The remainder of the line beginning with
   the first occurrence of "be":
   be or not to be; that is the question.

   The remainder of the line beginning with
   the second occurrence of "be":
   be; that is the question.
```

16.25   Write a program based on the program of Exercise 16.24 that inputs several lines of text and a search string, and uses function **strstr** to determine the total number of occurrences of the string in the lines of text. Print the result.

ANS:
```
// Exercise 16.25 Solution
#include <iostream.h>
#include <iomanip.h>
#include <string.h>
#include <ctype.h>

const int SIZE1 = 80, SIZE2 = 20;

main()
{
   char text[3][SIZE1], search[SIZE2], *searchPtr;
   int count = 0;

   cout << "Enter three lines of text:" << endl;

   for (int i = 0; i <= 2; i++)
      cin.getline(&text[i][0], SIZE1);

   // make all characters lowercase
   for (i = 0; i <= 2; i++)
      for (int j = 0; text[i][j] != '\0'; j++)
         text[i][j] = tolower(text[i][j]);

   cout << endl << "Enter a search string: ";
   cin >> search;

   for (i = 0; i <= 2; i++) {
      searchPtr = &text[i][0];

      while (searchPtr = strstr(searchPtr, search)) {
         ++count;
         ++searchPtr;
      }
   }

   cout << endl << "The total occurrences of \"" << search
        << "\" in the text is:" << setw(3) << count << endl;

   return 0;
}
```

```
   Enter three lines of text:
   This program inputs three lines of text
   and counts the number of occurrences of
   the search string in the three lines of text.

   Enter a search string: th

   The total occurrences of "th" in the text is 6
```

16.26 Write a program that inputs several lines of text and a search character, and uses function **strchr** to determine the total number of occurrences of the character in the lines of text.

ANS:
```
// Exercise 16.26 Solution
#include <iostream.h>
#include <iomanip.h>
#include <string.h>
#include <ctype.h>

const int SIZE = 80;


main()
{
   char text[3][SIZE], search, *searchPtr;
   int count = 0;

   cout << "Enter three lines of text:" << endl;

   for (int i = 0; i <= 2; i++)
      cin.getline(&text[i][0], SIZE);

   // convert all letters to lowercase
   for (i = 0; i <= 2; i++)
      for (int j = 0; text[i][j] != '\0'; j++)
         text[i][j] = tolower(text[i][j]);

   cout << endl << "Enter a search character: ";
   cin >> search;

   for (i = 0; i <= 2; i++) {
      searchPtr = &text[i][0];

      while (searchPtr = strchr(searchPtr, search)) {
         ++count;
         ++searchPtr;
      }
   }

   cout << "The total occurrences of \'" << search
        << "\' in the text is:" << setw(3) << count << endl;

   return 0;
}
```

```
Enter three lines of text:
This program inputs three lines of text
and counts the number of occurrences of
the specified search character in the text.

Enter a search character: e

The total occurrences of 'e' in the text is 15
```

16.27 Write a program based on the program of Exercise 16.26 that inputs several lines of text and uses function **strchr** to determine the total number of occurrences of each letter of the alphabet in the text. Uppercase and lowercase letters should be counted together. Store the totals for each letter in an array, and print the values in tabular format after the totals have been determined.

ANS:

```cpp
// Exercise 16.27 Solution
#include <iostream.h>
#include <iomanip.h>
#include <string.h>
#include <ctype.h>

const int SIZE1 = 80, SIZE2 = 26;

main()
{
   char text[3][SIZE1], *searchPtr, characters[SIZE2] = {'\0'};
   int count = 0;

   cout << "Enter three lines of text:" << endl;

   for (int i = 0; i <= 2; i++)
      cin.getline(&text[i][0], SIZE1);

   // convert letters to lowercase
   for (i = 0; i <= 2; i++)
      for (int j = 0; text[i][j] != '\0'; j++)
         text[i][j] = tolower(text[i][j]);

   for (i = 0; i <= 25; i++) {
      for (int j = 0, count = 0; j <= 2; j++) {
         searchPtr = &text[j][0];

         while (searchPtr = strchr(searchPtr, 'a' + i)) {
            ++count;
            ++searchPtr;
         }

      }

      characters[i] = count;
   }

   cout << endl << "The total occurrences of each character:" << endl;

   for (i = 0; i < SIZE2; i++)
      cout << setw(3) << 'a' + i << ':' << setw(3)
           << (int) characters[i] << endl;

   return 0;
}
```

```
Enter three lines of text:
This program inputs three lines of text
and determines the number of occurrences
of each character in the three lines.

The total occurrences of each character:
a:   5
b:   1
c:   6
d:   2
e:  17
f:   3
g:   1
h:   7
                                            continued
```

continued

```
i:    6
j:    0
k:    0
l:    2
m:    3
n:    8
o:    5
p:    2
q:    0
r:   10
s:    6
t:   10
u:    3
v:    0
w:    0
x:    1
y:    0
z:    0
```

16.28   The chart in Appendix D shows the numeric code representations for the characters in the ASCII character set. Study this chart and then state whether each of the following is true or false.

   a) The letter "**A**" comes before the letter "**B**."
   ANS: True.
   b) The digit "**9**" comes before the digit "**0**."
   ANS: False.
   c) The commonly used symbols for addition, subtraction, multiplication, and division all come before any of the digits.
   ANS: True.
   d) The digits come before the letters.
   ANS: True.
   e) If a sort program sorts strings into ascending sequence, then the program will place the symbol for a right parenthesis before the symbol for a left parenthesis.
   ANS: True.

16.29   Write a program that reads a series of strings and prints only those strings beginning with the letter "**b**."
   ANS:

```
// Exercise 16.29 Solution
#include <iostream.h>

const int SIZE = 20;

main()
{
   char array[5][SIZE];

   for (int i = 0; i <= 4; i++) {
      cout << "Enter a string: ";
      cin.getline(&array[i][0], SIZE);
   }

   cout << endl << "The strings starting with 'b' are:" << endl;

   for (i = 0; i <= 4; i++)
      if (array[i][0] == 'b')
         cout << &array[i][0] << endl;

   return 0;
}
```

```
Enter a string: the
Enter a string: big
Enter a string: bad
Enter a string: boy
Enter a string: sings

The strings starting with 'b' are:
big
bad
boy
```

16.30   Write a program that reads a series of strings and prints only those strings that end with the letters **"ED."**
ANS:

```
// Exercise 16.30 Solution
#include <iostream.h>
#include <string.h>

const int SIZE = 20;

main()
{
   int length;
   char array[5][SIZE];

   for (int i = 0; i <= 4; i++) {
      cout << "Enter a string: ";
      cin.getline(&array[i][0], SIZE);
   }

   cout << endl << "The strings ending with \"ed\" are:" << endl;

   for (i = 0; i <= 4; i++) {
      length = strlen(&array[i][0]);

      if (strcmp(&array[i][length - 2], "ed") == 0)
         cout << &array[i][0] << endl;
   }

   return 0;
}
```

```
Enter a string: walked
Enter a string: skipped
Enter a string: jumped
Enter a string: flew
Enter a string: drove

The strings ending with "ed" are:
walked
skipped
jumped
```

16.31   Write a program that inputs an ASCII code and prints the corresponding character. Modify this program so that it generates all possible three-digit codes in the range 000 to 255 and attempts to print the corresponding characters. What happens when this program is run?

ANS:
```
// Exercise 16.31 Solution
// NOTE: This solution is easily modified to print all
// possible three digit codes.
#include <iostream.h>

main()
{
   int c;

   cout << "Enter an ASCII character code (EOF to end): ";
   cin >> c;

   while ( c != EOF ) {
      if (c >= 0 && c <= 255)
         cout << "The corresponding character is '" << (char) c << "'"
              << endl;
      else
         cout << "Invalid character code" << endl;

      cout << endl << "Enter an ASCII character code (EOF to end): ";
      cin >> c;
   }

   return 0;
}
```

```
Enter an ASCII character code (EOF to end): 90
The corresponding character is 'Z'

Enter an ASCII character code (EOF to end): 116
The corresponding character is 't'

Enter an ASCII character code (EOF to end): 130
The corresponding character is 'Ç'

Enter an ASCII character code (EOF to end): 45
The corresponding character is '-'

Enter an ASCII character code (EOF to end): 40
The corresponding character is '('

Enter an ASCII character code (EOF to end):
```

16.32   Using the ASCII character chart in Appendix D as a guide, write your own versions of the character handling functions in Fig. 16.16.

ANS:
```
// Exercise 16.32 Solution
#include <iostream.h>

int isDigit(int);
int isAlpha(int);
int isAlNum(int);
int isLower(int);
int isUpper(int);
int isSpace(int);
int isPunct(int);
int isPrint(int);
int isGraph(int);
int toLower(int);
int toUpper(int);
```

```
main()
{
   int v;
   char array[2] = {'\0'}, header[] = "According to",
       *names[] = { "isDigit ", "isAlpha ", "isAlNum ",
                    "isLower ", "isUpper ", "isSpace ",
                    "isPunct ", "isPrint ", "isGraph ",
                    "toLower ", "toUpper " };

   cout << "Enter a character: ";
   cin >> &array[0];

   v = isDigit((int) array[0]);
   cout.write(header, 13);
   cout << names[0] << array[0]
       << (v == 0 ? " is not a digit" : " is a digit") << endl;

   v = isAlpha((int) array[0]);
   cout.write(header, 13);
   cout << names[1] << array[0]
       << (v == 0 ? " is not a letter" : " is a letter") << endl;

   v = isAlNum((int) array[0]);
   cout.write(header, 13);
   cout << names[2] << array[0]
       << (v == 0 ? " is not a letter or digit" :
                    " is a letter or digit") << endl;

   v = isLower((int) array[0]);
   cout.write(header, 13);
   cout << names[3] << array[0]
       << (v == 0 ? " is not a lowercase letter" :
                    " is a lowercase letter") << endl;

   v = isUpper((int) array[0]);
   cout.write(header, 13);
   cout << names[4] << array[0]
       << (v == 0 ? " is not an uppercase letter" :
                    " is an uppercase letter") << endl;


   v = isSpace((int) array[0]);
   cout.write(header, 13);
   cout << names[5] << array[0]
        << (v == 0 ? " is not a white-space character" :
                    " is a white-space character") << endl;

   v = isPunct((int) array[0]);
   cout.write(header, 13);
   cout << names[6] << array[0]
       << (v == 0 ? " is not a punctuation character" :
                    " is a punctuation character") << endl;

   v = isPrint((int) array[0]);
   cout.write(header, 13);
   cout << names[7] << array[0]
       << (v == 0 ? " is not a printing character" :
                    " is a printing character") << endl;

   v = isGraph((int)   __ay[0]);
   cout.write(header, 13);
   cout << names[8] << array[0]
       << (v == 0 ? " is not a printing character" :
                    " is a printing character") << endl;
```

```
        v = toLower((int) array[0]);
        cout.write(header, 13);
        cout << names[9] << (char) v
             << (v == array[0] ? " is unchanged" :
                        " has been converted to lowercase") << endl;

        v = toUpper((int) array[0]);
        cout.write(header, 13);
        cout << names[10] << (char) v
             << (v == array[0] ? " is unchanged" :
                        " has been converted to uppercase") << endl;

        return 0;
}


int isDigit(int c)
{
    return (c >= 48 && c <= 57) ? 1 : 0;
}

int isAlpha(int c)
{
    return ((c >= 65 && c <= 90) || (c >= 97 && c <= 122)) ? 1 : 0;
}

int isAlNum(int c)
{
    return (isDigit(c) == 1 || isAlpha(c) == 1) ? 1 : 0;
}

int isLower(int c)
{
    return (c >= 97 && c <= 122) ? 1 : 0;
}

int isUpper(int c)
{
    return (c >= 65 && c <= 90) ? 1 : 0;
}

int isSpace(int c)
{
    return ((c == 32) || (c >= 9 && c <= 13)) ? 1 : 0;
}

int isPunct(int c)
{
    return (isAlNum(c) == 0 && isSpace(c) == 0) ? 1 : 0;
}

int isPrint(int c)
{
    return (c >= 32 && c <= 126) ? 1 : 0;
}

int isGraph(int c)
{
    return (c >= 33 && c <= 126) ? 1 : 0;
}

int toLower(int c)
{
    return (isUpper(c) == 1) ? c + 32 : c;
}
```

```
int toUpper(int c)
{
   return (isLower(c) == 1) ? c - 32 : c;
}
```

```
Enter a character: m
According to isDigit m is not a digit
According to isAlpha m is a letter
According to isAlNum m is a letter or digit
According to isLower m is a lowercase letter
According to isUpper m is not an uppercase letter
According to isSpace m is not a white-space character
According to isPunct m is not a punctuation character
According to isPrint m is a printing character
According to isGraph m is a printing character
According to toLower m is unchanged
According to toUpper M has been converted to uppercase
```

```
Enter a character: *
According to isDigit * is not a digit
According to isAlpha * is not a letter
According to isAlNum * is not a letter or digit
According to isLower * is not a lowercase letter
According to isUpper * is not an uppercase letter
According to isSpace * is not a white-space character
According to isPunct * is a punctuation character
According to isPrint * is a printing character
According to isGraph * is a printing character
According to toLower * is unchanged
According to toUpper * is unchanged
```

16.33   Write your own versions of the functions in Fig. 16.20 for converting strings to numbers.

16.34   Write your own versions of the functions in Fig. 16.27 for searching strings.

16.35   Write your own versions of the functions in Fig. 16.34 for manipulating blocks of memory.

16.36   *(Project: A Spelling Checker)* Many popular word processing software packages have built-in spell checkers. We used the spell-checking capabilities of Microsoft Word 5.0 in preparing this book and discovered that no matter how careful we thought we were in writing a chapter, Word was always able to find a few more spelling errors than we were able to catch manually.

In this project, you are asked to develop your own spell-checker utility. We make suggestions to help get you started. You should then consider adding more capabilities. You may find it helpful to use a computerized dictionary as a source of words.

Why do we type so many words with incorrect spellings? In some cases, it is because we simply do not know the correct spelling, so we make a "best guess." In some cases, it is because we transpose two letters (e.g., "defualt" instead of "default"). Sometimes we double-type a letter accidentally (e.g., "hanndy" instead of "handy"). Sometimes we type a nearby key instead of the one we intended (e.g., "biryhday" instead of "birthday"). And so on.

Design and implement a spell-checker program in C++. Your program maintains an array **wordList** of character strings. You can either enter these strings or obtain them from a computerized dictionary.

Your program asks a user to enter a word. The program then looks up that word in the **wordList** array. If the word is present in the array, your program should print "**Word is spelled correctly**."

If the word is not present in the array, your program should print "**word is not spelled correctly**." Then your program should try to locate other words in **wordList** that might be the word the user intended to type. For example, you can try all possible single transpositions of adjacent letters to discover that the word "default" is a direct match to a word in **wordList**. Of course, this implies that your program will check all other single transpositions such as "edfault," "dfeault," "deafult," "defalut," and "defautl." When you find a new word that matches one in **wordList**, print that word in a message such as, "**Did you mean "default?"**."

Implement other tests such as replacing each double letter with a single letter and any other tests you can develop to improve the value of your spell checker.

17

The Preprocessor: Solutions

Exercises

17.4   Write a program that defines a macro with one argument to compute the volume of a sphere. The program should compute the volume for spheres of radius 1 to 10, and print the results in tabular format. The formula for the volume of a sphere is:

$$(4/3) * \pi * r^3$$

where π is 3.14159.

ANS:

```
// Exercise 17.4 Solution
#include <iostream.h>
#include <iomanip.h>

// define preprocessor directive sphere volume
#define SPHEREVOLUME(r) (4.0 / 3.0 * 3.14159 * (r) * (r) * (r))

main()
{
   // print header
   cout << setw(10) << "Radius" << setw(10) << "Volume" << endl;

   cout.setf(ios::fixed | ios::showpoint);
   for (int i = 1; i <= 10; i++)
      cout << setw(10) << i << setw(10) << setprecision(3)
           << SPHEREVOLUME(i) << endl;

   return 0;
}
```

```
    Radius    Volume
         1     4.189
         2    33.510
         3   113.097
         4   268.082
         5   523.598
         6   904.778
         7  1436.754
         8  2144.659
         9  3053.625
        10  4188.787
```

17.5   Write a program that produces the following output:

```
The sum of x and y is 13
```

The program should define macro **SUM** with two arguments, **x** and **y**, and use **SUM** to produce the output.

```
ANS:
// Exercise 17.5 Solution
#include <iostream.h>

#define SUM(x, y) ((x) + (y))

main()
{
    cout << "The sum of x and y is " << SUM(6, 4) << endl;

    return 0;
}
```

```
The sum of x and y is 10
```

17.6   Write a program that uses macro **MINIMUM2** to determine the smallest of two numeric values. Input the values from the keyboard.

```
ANS:
// Exercise 17.6 Solution
#include <iostream.h>
#include <iomanip.h>

#define MINIMUM2(x, y) ((x) < (y) ? (x) : (y))

main()
{
    int a, b;
    float c, d;

    cout << "Enter two integers: ";
    cin >> a >> b;
    cout << "The minimum of " << a << " and " << b << " is "
         << MINIMUM2(a,b) << endl << endl;

    cout << "Enter two floats: ";
    cin >> c >> d;

    cout.setf(ios::fixed | ios::showpoint);
    cout << "The minimum of " << setprecision(2) << c << " and " << d
         << " is " << MINIMUM2(c,d) << endl;

    return 0;
}
```

```
Enter two integers: 4 9
The minimum of 4 and 9 is 4

Enter two floats: 45.7 13.2
The minimum of 45.70 and 13.20 is 13.20
```

17.7   Write a program that uses macro **MINIMUM3** to determine the smallest of three numeric values. Macro **MINIMUM3** should use macro **MINIMUM2** defined in Exercise 17.6 to determine the smallest number. Input the values from the keyboard.

```
ANS:
// Exercise 17.7 Solution
#include <iostream.h>
#include <iomanip.h>
#define MINIMUM2(x, y) ((x) < (y) ? (x) : (y))
#define MINIMUM3(u, v, w) (MINIMUM2(w, MINIMUM2(u, v)))
```

```
main()
{
    int a, b, c;
    float d, e, f;

    cout << "Enter three integers: ";
    cin >> a >> b >> c;
    cout << "The minimum of " << a << ", " << b << ", and " << c
         << " is " << MINIMUM3(a, b, c) << endl << endl
         << "Enter three floats: ";

    cin >> d >> e >> f;
    cout.setf(ios::fixed | ios::showpoint);
    cout << "The minimum of " << setprecision(2) << d << ", " << e
         << ", and " << f << " is " << MINIMUM3(d, e, f) << endl;

    return 0;
}
```

```
Enter three integers: 7 2 10
The minimum of 7, 2, and 10 is 2

Enter three floats: 4.9 93.2 1.3
The minimum of 4.90, 93.20, and 1.30 is 1.30
```

17.8   Write a program that uses macro **PRINT** to print a string value.
ANS:
```
// Exercise 17.8 Solution
#include <iostream.h>
#define PRINT(string) cout << string

const int SIZE = 20;

main()
{
    char text[SIZE];

    PRINT("Enter a string: ");
    cin >> text;

    PRINT("The string entered was: ");
    PRINT(text);
    PRINT(endl);

    return 0;
}
```

```
Enter a string: Hello
The string entered was: Hello
```

17.9   Write a program that uses macro **PRINTARRAY** to print an array of integers. The macro should receive the array and the number of elements in the array as arguments.
ANS:
```
// Exercise 17.9 Solution
#include <iostream.h>
#include <iomanip.h>

#define PRINTARRAY(a, n)   for (int i = 0; i < (n); i++) \
                               cout << setw(3) << a[i]
```

```
const int SIZE = 10;

main()
{
    int b[SIZE] = {2, 4, 6, 8, 10, 12, 14, 16, 18, 20};

    cout << "The array values are:" << endl;
    PRINTARRAY(b, SIZE);
    return 0;
}
```

```
The array values are:
2 4 6 8 10 12 14 16 18 20
```

17.10   Write a program that uses macro **SUMARRAY** to sum the values in a numeric array. The macro should receive the array and the number of elements in the array as arguments.

ANS:
```
// Exercise 17.10 Solution
#include <iostream.h>

#define SUMMARRAY(a, s)    for (int c = 0; c < s; c++)
                               sum += a[c];
const int SIZE = 10;

main()
{
    int array[SIZE] = { 1, 2, 3, 4, 5, 6, 7, 8, 9, 10 }, sum = 0;

    SUMMARRAY(array, SIZE);
    cout << "Sum is " << sum << endl;
    return 0;
}
```

```
The sum of the elements of array b is 55
```

17.11   Rewrite the solutions to 17.4 to 17.10 as inline functions.

ANS:
```
// Exercise 17.11 Solution
// NOTE: Exercises 17.9 and 17.10 cannot be
// expanded inline because they require the
// use of for repetition structures
#include <iostream.h>
#include <iomanip.h>

inline float sphereVolume(int r) { return 4.0 / 3.0 * 3.14159 * r * r * r; }
inline int sum(int x, int y) { return x + y; }
inline int minimum2(int x, int y) { return x < y ? x : y; }
inline int minimum3(int x, int y, int z) { return minimum2(z, minimum2(x, y));}
inline void print(char *c) { cout << c; }

main()
{
    // print header
    cout << "Function sphereVolume as an inline function:" << endl
         << setw(10) << "Radius" << setw(10) << "Volume" << endl;

    cout.setf(ios::fixed | ios::showpoint);
    for (int i = 1; i <= 10; i++)
       cout << setw(10) << i << setw(10) << setprecision(3)
            << sphereVolume(i) << endl;
```

```
   int x = 6, y = 7;
   cout << endl << "Function sum as an inline function:" << endl
        << "The sum of " << x << " and " << y << " is "
        << sum(6, 7) << endl;

   cout << endl << "Function minimum2 as an inline function:" << endl
        << "The minimum of " << x << " and " << y << " is "
        << minimum2(x, y) << endl;

   int z = 4;
   cout << endl << "Function minimum3 as an inline function:" << endl
        << "The minimum of " << x << ", " << y << " and " << z << " is "
        << minimum3(x, y, z) << endl;

   char s[] = {"string..."};
   cout << endl << "Function print as an inline function:" << endl
        << "The output of print is: ";
   print(s);
   cout << endl;
   return 0;
}
```

```
Function sphereVolume as an inline function:
    Radius     Volume
         1       4.189
         2      33.510
         3     113.097
         4     268.082
         5     523.598
         6     904.778
         7    1436.754
         8    2144.659
         9    3053.625
        10    4188.787

Function sum as an inline function:
The sum of 6 and 7 is 13

Function minimum2 as an inline function:
The minimum of 6 and 7 is 6

Function minimum3 as an inline function:
The minimum of 6, 7 and 4 is 4

Function print as an inline function:
The output of print is: string...
```

18
Other Topics: Solutions

Exercises

18.2 Write a program that calculates the product of a series of integers that are passed to function **product** using a variable-length argument list. Test your function with several calls each with a different number of arguments.

    ANS:

```
// Exercise 18.2 Solution
#include <iostream.h>
#include <stdarg.h>

int sum(int, ...);

main()
{
   int a = 1, b = 2, c = 3, d = 4, e = 5;

   cout << "a = " << a << ", b = " << b << ", c = " << c << ", d = " << d
        << ", e = " << e << endl << endl;
   cout << "The sum of a and b is: " << sum(2, a, b) << endl
        << "The sum of a, b, and c is: " << sum(3, a, b, c) << endl
        << "The sum of a, b, c, and d is: " << sum(4, a, b, c, d) << endl
        << "The sum of a, b, c, d, and e is: " << sum(5, a, b, c, d, e)
        << endl;
   return 0;
}

int sum(int i, ...)
{
   int total = 0;
   va_list ap;

   va_start(ap, i);

   // calculate total
   for (int j = 1; j <= i; j++)
      total += va_arg(ap, int);

   va_end(ap);
   return total;
}
```

```
a = 1, b = 2, c = 3, d = 4, e = 5
The sum of a and b is: 3
The sum of a, b, and c is: 6
The sum of a, b, c, and d is: 10
The sum of a, b, c, d, and e is: 15
```

18.3   Write a program that prints the command-line arguments of the program.

ANS:

```
// Exercise 18.3 Solution
#include <iostream.h>

main(int argc, char *argv[])
{
    cout << "The command line arguments are:" << endl;

    for (int i = 0; i < argc; i++)
        cout << argv[i] << ' ';

    return 0;
}
```

```
C:\P18_3.EXE ARG1 ARG2 ARG3
```

18.4   Write a program that sorts an integer array into ascending order or descending order. The program should use command-line arguments to pass either argument **-a** for ascending order or **-d** for descending order. (Note: This is the standard format for passing options to a program in UNIX.)

ANS:

```
// Exercise 18.4 Solution
#include <iostream.h>
#include <iomanip.h>

const int SIZE = 100;

void swap(int *, int *);

main(int argc, char *argv[])
{
    int a[SIZE], temp, order;

    if (argc != 2)
        cout << "Usage: p18_4 -option" << endl;
    else {
        cout << "Enter up to " << SIZE << " integers (EOF to end input): ";

        for (int count = 0; !(cin.eof()) && count < SIZE; count++)
            cin >> a[count];

        // count is incremented before for loop continuation fails
        --count;

        order = (argv[1][1] == 'd') ? 1 : 0;

        for (int i = 1; i < count; i++)
            for (int j = 0; j < count - 1; j++)

                if (order == 1) {

                    if (a[i] > a[j])
                        swap(&a[i], &a[j]);

                }
                else
                    if (a[i] < a[j])
                        swap(&a[j], &a[i]);

        cout << endl << endl << "The sorted array is:" << endl;
```

```
            for (i = 0; i < count; i++)
                cout << setw(3) << a[i];

            cout << endl;
        }

        return 0;
    }

    void swap(int *xPtr, int *yPtr)
    {
        int temp;

        temp = *xPtr;
        *xPtr = *yPtr;
        *yPtr = temp;
    }
```

Command line:

```
p18_4 -a
```

```
The sorted array is:
1 2 4 5 7 8 9 11 13 19
```

Command line:

```
p18_4 -d
```

```
The sorted array is:
19 13 11 9 8 7 5 4 2 1
```

18.5   Read the manuals for your system to determine what signals are supported by the signal handling library (`signal.h`). Write a program with signal handlers for the signals **SIGABRT** and **SIGINT**. The program should test the trapping of these signals by calling function **abort** to generate a signal of type **SIGABRT**, and by typing <ctrl> c to generate a signal of type **SIGINT**.

18.6   Write a program that dynamically allocates an array of integers. The size of the array should be input from the keyboard. The elements of the array should be assigned values input from the keyboard. Print the values of the array. Next, reallocate the memory for the array to half of the current number of elements. Print the values remaining in the array to confirm that they match the first half of the values in the original array.

ANS:

```
// Exercise 18.6 Solution
#include <iostream.h>
#include <iomanip.h>
#include <stdlib.h>

main()
{
    int count, *array;

    cout << "This program dynamically allocates an array of integers."
         << endl <<  "Enter the number of elements in the array: ";
    cin >> count;
    // allocate memory
    array = (int *) calloc(count, sizeof(int));
```

```
      for (int i = 0; i < count; i++) {
         cout << "Enter an integer: ";
         cin >> array[i];
      }

      cout << endl << "The elements of the array are:" << endl;

      for (i = 0; i < count; i++)
         cout << setw(3) << array[i];

      // reallocate to half the original size
      realloc(array, count / 2 * sizeof(int));
      cout << endl << endl
           << "The elements of the array after reallocation are:" << endl;

      for (i = 0; i < count / 2; i++)
         cout << setw(3) << array[i];

      cout << endl;

      return 0;
   }
```

```
This program dynamically allocates an array of integers.
Enter the number of elements in the array: 10
Enter an integer: 1
Enter an integer: 2
Enter an integer: 3
Enter an integer: 4
Enter an integer: 5
Enter an integer: 6
Enter an integer: 7
Enter an integer: 8
Enter an integer: 9
Enter an integer: 10

The elements of the array are:
1 2 3 4 5 6 7 8 9 10

The elements of the array after reallocation are:
1 2 3 4 5
```

18.7   Write a program that takes two file name command-line arguments, reads the characters from the first file one at a time, and writes the characters in reverse order to the second file.

ANS:

```
// Exercise 18.7 Solution
#include <iostream.h>
#include <fstream.h>

void reverseFile(istream&, ostream&);

main(int argc, char *argv[])
{
   ifstream inFile(argv[1], ios::in);
   ofstream outFile(argv[2], ios::out);

   if (argc != 3)
      cout << "Usage: copy infile outfile" << endl;
```

```
         else
            if (inFile)
               if (outFile)
                  reverseFile(inFile, outFile);
               else
                  cerr << "File \"" << argv[2] << "\" could not be opened"
                       << endl;
            else
               cerr << "File \"" << argv[1] << "\" could not be opened"
                       << endl;

      return 0;
   }

   void reverseFile(istream &in, ostream &out)
   {
      int c;

      if ((c = in.get()) != EOF)
         reverseFile(in, out);

      out.put(c);
   }
```

Command line:

```
   c:\>p18_7 test.txt test.rev
```

Contents of "test.txt":

```
   Testing reverseFile in problem p18_7.cpp
```

Contents of "test.rev":

```
   ppc.7_81p melborp ni eliFesrever gnitseT
```

18.8   Write a program that uses **goto** statements to simulate a nested looping structure that prints a square of asterisks, as follows:

```
   *****
   *   *
   *   *
   *   *
   *****
```

The program should use only the following three output statements:

```
   cout << '*';
   cout << ' ';
   cout << endl;
```

ANS:
```
   // Exercise 18.8 Solution
   #include <iostream.h>
   main()
   {
      int size, row = 0, col;

      cout << "Enter the side length of the square: ";
      cin >> size;
```

```
    start:                    // label
        ++row;
        cout << endl;

        if (row > size)
            goto end;

        col = 1;

        innerLoop:            // label
            if (col > size)
                goto start;

            cout << (row == 1 || row == size || col == 1 ||
                    col == size ? '*':' ');

            ++col;
            goto innerLoop;

    end:                      // label

    return 0;
}
```

```
Enter the side length of the square: 10
**********
*        *
*        *
*        *
*        *
*        *
*        *
*        *
*        *
**********
```

18.9 Provide the definition for union **Data** containing **char c, short s, long l, float f**, and **double d**.
ANS:
```
union Data {
    char c;
    short s;
    long l;
    float f;
    double d;
};
```

18.10 Create union **Integer** with members **char c, short s, int i**, and **long l**. Write a program that inputs values of type **char, short, int** and **long**, and stores the values in union variables of type **union Integer**. Each union variable should be printed as a **char**, a **short**, an **int**, and a **long**. Do the values always print correctly?

ANS:
```
// Exercise 18.10 Solution
#include <iostream.h>

union Integer {
    char c;
    short s;
    int i;
    long l;
};
```

```
void printUnion(Integer);

main()
{
    Integer value;

    cout << "Enter a character: ";
    value.c = cin.get();
    printUnion(value);

    cout << "Enter a short: ";
    cin >> value.s;
    printUnion(value);

    cout << "Enter an int: ";
    cin >> value.i;
    printUnion(value);

    cout << "Enter a long: ";
    cin >> value.l;
    printUnion(value);

    return 0;
}

void printUnion(Integer x)
{
    cout << "Current values in union Integer are:" << endl
         << "char c  = " << x.c << endl
         << "short s = " << x.s << endl
         << "int i   = " << x.i << endl
         << "long l  = " << x.l << endl << endl;
}
```

```
Enter a character: y
Current values in union Integer are:
char c  = y
short s = 121
int i   = 121
long l  = 300744825

Enter a short: 12
Current values in union Integer are:
char c  =
short s = 12
int i   = 12
long l  = 300744716

Enter an int: 32444
Current values in union Integer are:
char c  = ¼
short s = 32444
int i   = 32444
long l  = 300777148

Enter a long: 2000000
Current values in union Integer are:
char c  =
short s = -31616
int i   = -31616
long l  = 2000000
```

18.11   Create union **FloatingPoint** with members **float f**, **double d**, and **long double l**. Write a program that inputs value of type **float**, **double**, and **long double**, and stores the values in union variables of type **union FloatingPoint**. Each union variable should be printed as a **float**, a **double**, and a **long double**. Do the values always print correctly?

ANS:

```
// Exercise 18.11 Solution
#include <iostream.h>

union FloatingPoint {
    float f;
    double d;
    long double l;
};

void printUnion(FloatingPoint);

main()
{
    FloatingPoint value;

    cout << "Enter a float: ";
    cin >> value.f;
    printUnion(value);

    cout << "Enter a double: ";
    cin >> value.d;
    printUnion(value);

    cout << "Enter a long double: ";
    cin >> value.l;
    printUnion(value);

    return 0;
}

void printUnion(FloatingPoint x)
{
    cout << "Current values in union Integer are:" << endl
         << "float f  = " << x.f << endl
         << "double d = " << x.d << endl
         << "long double l  = " << x.l << endl << endl;
}
```

```
Enter a float: 4.567897
Current values in union Integer are:
float f  = 4.567897
double d = 0
long double l  = 0.000002e-2004

Enter a double: 1234567.674844
Current values in union Integer are:
float f  = -5.529634e-12
double d = 1234567.674844
long double l  = 1.125582e-2004

Enter a long double: 9000000.322457
Current values in union Integer are:
float f  = -2.060075e-31
double d = -1.004884e-263
long double l  = 9000000.322457
```

OTHER TOPICS: SOLUTIONS   507

18.12   Given the union

```
union A {
    float y;
    char *z;
};
```

which of the following are correct statements for initializing the union?

    a) `A p = B; // B is of same type as A`
    b) `A q = x; // x is a float`
    c) `A r = 3.14159;`
    d) `A s = { 79.63 };`
    e) `A t = { "Hi There!" };`
    f) `A u = { 3.14159, "Pi" };`
    ANS: (a) and (d).

Appendix:
An Elevator Simulator

Section 2.22: Identifying the Objects in a Problem

1. building, elevator, person, door, floor, clock, scheduler, button, light, bell.

2. Building: The building contains two floors and an elevator.

    Elevator: The elevator begins the day on floor one with its doors open. The elevator takes 5 clock ticks to travel between floors and has a capacity of one person. The elevator has an up button and a down button. Upon arriving at a floor, the floor light is turned on, the bell sounds, and the elevator doors open. The elevator always knows what floor it is on and what floor it is going to.

    Person: People are created at randomly generated times to ride the elevator. When created, people arrive at either floor 1 or floor 2, then travel to the other floor.

    Door: The doors are open only when the elevator is stationary. The elevator doors close just before the elevator moves and remain closed in transit.

    Floor: Each floor has a call button that summons the elevator when pushed by a person. People are not permanent fixtures on a floor or in the elevator. When the elevator arrives at a floor, the person waiting enters the elevator.

    Clock: The clock will keep track of the elapsed time during the simulation. The elevator takes five ticks of the clock to move from floor to floor.

    Scheduler: The scheduler creates the arrival times of people in the building at given floors. In addition, the scheduler will create the people in this simulation.

    Button: There are buttons on each floor and in the elevator. Buttons on a floor call the elevator when pressed. Buttons in the elevator tell the elevator to move to a given floor when pressed. Buttons are reset when the elevator arrives on a floor.

Questions

1. The elevator's ability to handle the traffic can be measured by the number of people that are rescheduled immediately after arriving in the simulation. If the total rescheduled time is greater than

zero, it means that there are really lines of people waiting for the elevator at given times. The larger the total rescheduled time, the more people are waiting.

2. Efficiency and logic make this problem much more difficult for three or more floors. The elevator has many more decisions to make as the number of floors increases.

3. Once a building contains multiple elevators, the elevators must be coordinated for maximum efficiency. For example, in a building with 2 idle elevators on floor 1, when a person arrives on floor 2, both elevators should not go to pick up that person. Thus, there must be another set of controls that coordinates multiple elevators.

4. Larger capacities on the floors and in the elevator increases the possibility of queues (waiting lines) on each floor. If the queue for a particular floor is larger than the capacity of the elevator there will be some number of people that cannot enter the elevator when it arrives. These people will have to wait longer. However, if the elevator has a large capacity, it is possible that noone will ever have to wait for an elevator—particularly if there are multiple elevators in the building.

Section 3.22: Identifying an Object's Attributes

1.   A company intends to build a two-story office building and equip it with the "latest" in elevator technology. The company wants you to develop an object-oriented software simulator that models the operation of the elevator to determine if this elevator will meet their needs.

     The elevator, which has a capacity of one person, is designed to conserve energy, so it only moves when necessary. The elevator starts the day waiting with its doors shut on floor 1 of the building. The elevator, of course, alternates directions—first up, then down.

     Your simulator includes a clock that begins the day set to time 0 and that "ticks" once per second. The "scheduler" component of the simulator randomly schedules the arrival of the first person on each floor (you will learn how to schedule random arrivals in Chapter 3). When the clock's time becomes equal to the time of the first arrival, the simulator "creates" a new person for the specified floor, and places the person on that floor. The person then presses the up-button or the down-button on that floor. The person's destination floor is never equal to the floor on which that person arrives.

     If the first person of the day arrives at floor 1, the person can immediately get on the elevator (after pressing the up-button and waiting for the elevator's doors to open, of course!). If the first person arrives at floor 2, the elevator proceeds to floor 2 to pick up that person. The elevator requires five ticks of the clock to travel between floors. The elevator signals its arrival at a floor by turning on a light above the elevator door on that floor and by sounding a bell. The buttons on the floor and the buttons in the elevator for that floor are reset, the elevator opens its door, the passenger—if there is one whose destination is that floor—gets out of the elevator, another passenger—if there is one waiting on that floor—gets into the elevator and presses a destination button, and the elevator closes its doors. If the elevator needs to begin moving, it determines in which direction it should go (a simple decision on a two-story elevator!), and begins moving to the next floor. For simplicity, assume that all of the events that happen once the elevator reaches a floor, and until the elevator closes its doors on that floor, take zero time. The elevator always knows what floor it is on and what floor it is going to.

     At most, one person can be waiting on each floor at any time, so if a floor is occupied when a new person (i.e., not a person already on the elevator) is due to arrive at that floor, the new arrival is rescheduled for one second later. For simplicity, only one person can be "created" in the simulation at any given time, so there is never a duplicate arrival time for the next person in the building. Assume that people arrive at random on each floor every 5 to 20 seconds—in Chapter 3 you will learn how to use random number generation to simulate this arrival rate.

2.
- two-story office building
- elevator
- elevator capacity of one person

- person
- elevator only moves when necessary
- elevator starts the day waiting with its doors shut on floor 1
- doors
- floor 1
- elevator alternates directions--first up, then down
- clock
- clock begins the day set to time 0
- clock "ticks" once per second
- scheduler
- scheduler randomly schedules the arrival of the first person on each floor
- When the clock's time becomes equal to the time of the first arrival, the simulator "creates" a new person for the specified floor
- person placed on floor (i.e., person walks onto floor)
- person presses the up-button or the down-button
- destination floor
- arrival floor
- destination floor is never equal to the floor on which that person arrives
- elevator requires five ticks of the clock to travel between floors
- bell
- light
- buttons on the floor
- buttons in the elevator
- If first person of day arrives at floor 1, person can immediately get on elevator
- If first person of day arrives at floor 2, elevator proceeds to floor 2 to pick up that person
- elevator signals its arrival at a floor by turning on a light above the elevator door on that floor and by sounding a bell
- buttons on the floor and the buttons in the elevator for that floor are reset
- elevator opens its door
- passenger gets out of the elevator
- another passenger gets into the elevator
- presses a destination button
- elevator closes door
- if elevator needs to begin moving, elevator determines which direction it should go
- begins moving to the next floor
- all of the events that happen once the elevator reaches a floor, and until the elevator closes its doors on that floor, take zero time
- elevator always knows what floor it is on and what floor it is going to
- At most, one person can be waiting on each floor at any time
- if a floor is occupied when a new person (i.e., not a person already on the elevator) is due to arrive at that floor, the new arrival is rescheduled for one second later
- only one person can be "created" in the simulation at any given time, so there is never a duplicate arrival time for the next person
- people arrive at random on each floor every 5 to 20 seconds

3.
Building
    two floors
    elevator

Elevator
    maximum capacity of one person
    elevator only moves when necessary

elevator starts the day waiting with its doors shut on floor 1

doors

elevator alternates directions--first up, then down

elevator requires five ticks of the clock to travel between floors

bell

buttons in the elevator

elevator signals its arrival at a floor by turning on a light above the elevator door on that floor and by sounding a bell

buttons on the floor and the buttons in the elevator for that floor are reset

elevator opens its door

person presses a destination button

elevator closes door

if elevator needs to begin moving, elevator determines which direction it should go

elevator begins moving to the next floor

all of the events that happen once the elevator reaches a floor, and until the elevator closes its doors on that floor, take zero time

elevator always knows what floor it is on and what floor it is going to

Floor

At most, one person can be waiting on each floor at any time

doors

person presses the up-button or the down-button

light

buttons on the floor

buttons on the floor and the buttons in the elevator for that floor are reset

Person

person placed on floor (i.e., person walks onto floor)

person presses the up-button or the down-button

destination floor

arrival floor

destination floor is never equal to the floor on which that person arrives

If first person of day arrives at floor 1, person can immediately get on elevator

If first person of day arrives at floor 2, elevator proceeds to floor 2 to pick up that person

passenger gets out of the elevator

another passenger gets into the elevator

person presses a destination button

Light

turning on a light

Door

open or closed

elevator opens its door

elevator closes door

Button

buttons on the floor and the buttons in the elevator for that floor are reset

Bell

sounding a bell

Clock

clock begins the day set to time 0

clock "ticks" once per second

Scheduler

    scheduler randomly schedules the arrival of the first person on each floor

    When the clock's time becomes equal to the time of the first arrival, the simulator "creates" a new person for the specified floor

    if a floor is occupied when a new person (i.e., not a person already on the elevator) is due to arrive at that floor, the new arrival is rescheduled for one second later

    only one person can be "created" in the simulation at any given time, so there is never a duplicate arrival time for the next person

    people arrive at random on each floor every 5 to 20 seconds

4.

Building

Attributes:

    two floors

    elevator

    scheduler (to simulate people randomly arriving on floors in the building)

    clock (to keep track of the time of day in the building)

Other Facts:

Elevator

Attributes:

    doors

    occupied or unoccupied (maximum capacity of one person)

    location (elevator starts the day waiting with its doors shut on floor 1, elevator always knows what floor it is on and what floor it is going to)

    direction (elevator alternates directions--first up, then down)

    moving or stopped (elevator only moves when necessary)

    time of arrival at next floor (elevator requires five ticks of the clock to travel between floors)

    bell

    buttons in the elevator

Other Facts:

    elevator signals its arrival at a floor by turning on a light above the elevator door on that floor and by sounding a bell

    buttons on the floor and the buttons in the elevator for that floor are reset

    elevator opens its door

    person presses a destination button

    elevator closes door

    if elevator needs to begin moving, elevator determines which direction it should go

    elevator begins moving to the next floor

    all of the events that happen once the elevator reaches a floor, and until the elevator closes its doors on that floor, take zero time

Floor

Attributes:

    occupied or unoccupied (at most, one person can be waiting on each floor at any time)

    doors

    light

    buttons on the floor

Other Facts:

    person presses the up-button or the down-button

    buttons on the floor and the buttons in the elevator for that floor are reset

Person
Attributes:
   destination floor
   arrival floor
   sequence number in simulation (for control purposes)
Other Facts:
   person placed on floor (i.e., person walks onto floor)
   person presses the up-button or the down-button
   destination floor is never equal to the floor on which that person arrives
   If first person of day arrives at floor 1, person can immediately get on elevator
   If first person of day arrives at floor 2, elevator proceeds to floor 2 to pick up that person
   passenger gets out of the elevator
   another passenger gets into the elevator
   person presses a destination button

Light
Attributes:
   on or off
Other Facts:
   turning on a light

Door
Attributes:
   open or shut
Other Facts:
   elevator opens its door
   elevator closes door

Button
Attributes:
   on or off
Other Facts:
   buttons on the floor and the buttons in the elevator for that floor are reset
   person presses a destination button
   person presses the up-button or the down-button

Bell
Attributes:
   dinged or not dinged
Other Facts:
   sounding a bell

Clock
Attributes:
   current time in simulation
Other Facts:
   clock begins the day set to time 0
   clock "ticks" once per second

Scheduler
Attributes:
   time of arrival on each floor
Other Facts:
   scheduler randomly schedules the arrival of the first person on each floor

When the clock's time becomes equal to the time of the first arrival, the simulator "creates" a new person for the specified floor

if a floor is occupied when a new person (i.e., not a person already on the elevator) is due to arrive at that floor, the new arrival is rescheduled for one second later

only one person can be "created" in the simulation at any given time, so there is never a duplicate arrival time for the next person

people arrive at random on each floor every 5 to 20 seconds

Section 4.10: Identifying an Object's Behaviors

Building
Attributes:
two floors
elevator
scheduler (to simulate people randomly arriving on floors in the building)
clock (to keep track of the time of day in the building)
Behaviors:
runSimulation - starts the simulation

Elevator
Attributes:
doors
occupied or unoccupied (maximum capacity of one person)
location (elevator starts the day waiting with its doors shut on floor 1, elevator always knows what floor it is on and what floor it is going to)
direction (elevator alternates directions--first up, then down)
moving or stopped (elevator only moves when necessary)
time of arrival at next floor (elevator requires five ticks of the clock to travel between floors)
bell
buttons in the elevator
elevatorCalled (true if a person called the elevator from another floor)
elevatorName - string containing the name of the elevator
Behaviors:
ringBell - ding the bell to announce arrival at floor
wasYourBellRung - determine if bell dinged
pressButton - enable person to press button for destination
resetButton - turn destination floor button off
determineDirection - determine the elevator's direction
passengerEnters - indicate that a passenger has entered the elevator
passengerExits - indicate that the passenger left the elevator
shouldElevatorMove - determine if the elevator should move
shouldElevatorStop - determine if the elevator should stop
Other Facts:
all of the events that happen once the elevator reaches a floor, and until the elevator closes its doors on that floor, take zero time

Floor
Attributes:
occupied or unoccupied (at most, one person can be waiting on each floor at any time)
doors
light
buttons on the floor
floorNumber - the number of the floor

Behaviors:

    openDoorOnFloor - enable elevator to open the door on the floor

    closeDoorOnFloor - enable elevator to close the door on the floor

    turnLightOn - enable elevator to turn on the light on the floor that indicates elevator arrival

    turnLightOff - enable elevator to turn off the light on the floor that indicates elevator arrival

    isLightOn - enable person to check if light is on

    pressCallButton - enable person to press the call button that belongs to the floor

    resetCallButton - enable elevator to turn off call button on floor

    personArriving - indicate that a person is arriving on the floor

    personDeparting - indicate that a person is leaving the floor

Person

Attributes:

    destination floor

    arrival floor

    sequence number in simulation (for control purposes)

Behaviors:

    walkOntoFloor - person enters simulation

    enterElevator - enter the elevator

    exitElevator - exit the elevator

Other Facts:

    destination floor is never equal to the floor on which that person arrives

    If first person of day arrives at floor 1, person can immediately get on elevator

    If first person of day arrives at floor 2, elevator proceeds to floor 2 to pick up that person

Light

Attributes:

    on or off

Behaviors:

    lightOn - turn light on

    lightOff - turn light off

    isLightOn - determine if light is on

Door

Attributes:

    open or shut

    doorName - string containing door name (i.e., elevator door, floor 1 door, floor 2 door)

Behaviors:

    openDoor - open the door

    closeDoor - close the door

    isDoorOpen - determine if door is open

Button

Attributes:

    on or off

    buttonName - string containing the button name

Behaviors:

    buttonOn - turn the button on

    buttonOff - turn the button off

    isButtonOn - determine if a button is on

Bell

Attributes:

    dinged or not dinged

Behaviors:
    ding - ring the bell; set to dinged
    stopThatRingingSound - reset the bell to not dinged

Clock
Attributes:
    current time in simulation
Behaviors:
    tick - add one to the current time
    getTime - return the current time
Other Facts:
    clock begins the day set to time 0

Scheduler
Attributes:
    time of arrival on each floor
Behaviors:
    setInitialArrivalTimes - randomly set first arrival on floor 1 and first arrival on floor 2
    isPersonArriving - determine if a person is arriving at the current time
    createPerson - create a person for the simulation
    scheduleNextRandomArrival - pick a random arrival time for next person
    rescheduleConflictingArrival - set arrival time to arrival time + 1

Other Facts:
    only one person can be "created" in the simulation at any given time, so there is never a duplicate
        arrival time for the next person
    people arrive at random on each floor every 5 to 20 seconds

Section 5.13: Interactions Among Objects

Building
Attributes:
    floor 1
    floor 2
    elevator
    scheduler (to simulate people randomly arriving on floors in the building)
    clock (to keep track of the time of day in the building)
Behaviors:
    runSimulation - starts the simulation
Messages sent to Other Objects:
    getTime message sent to clock
    isMoving message sent to elevator
    shouldElevatorStop message sent to elevator
    stopElevator message sent to elevator
    checkIfPersonArriving message sent to scheduler
    shouldElevatorMove message sent to elevator
    tick message sent to clock

Elevator
Attributes:
    door
    pointer to a person - occupied or unoccupied (maximum capacity of one person)
    location (elevator starts the day waiting with its doors shut on floor 1, elevator always knows what
        floor it is on and what floor it is going to)

direction (elevator alternates directions--first up, then down)

moveState - moving or stopped (elevator only moves when necessary)

time of arrival at next floor (elevator requires five ticks of the clock to travel between floors)

bell

buttons in the elevator

call states (one for each floor; set to CALLED if elevator was called)

elevatorName - string containing the name of the elevator

Behaviors:

wasYourBellRung - determine if bell dinged

pressButton - enable person to press button for destination

resetButton - turn destination floor button off

determineDirection - determine the elevator's direction

passengerEnters - indicate that a passenger has entered the elevator

passengerExits - indicate that the passenger left the elevator

shouldElevatorMove - determine if the elevator should move

isMoving - is the elevator moving

shouldElevatorStop - determine if the elevator should stop

stopElevator - stop the elevator and process events

elevatorCalled - set the call state in the elevator for a specific floor

prepareToLeaveFloor - close doors, reset lights, etc.

getCurrentFloor - return the current floor number

Messages sent to Other Objects:

elevator sends resetCallButton message to floor

elevator sends turnLightOn message to floor

elevator sends turnLightOff message to floor

elevator sends openDoor message to floor

elevator sends closeDoor message to floor

elevator sends resetCallButton message to floor

elevator sends didBellRing message to bell

elevator sends buttonOn message to button

elevator sends buttonOff message to button

elevator sends isDoorOpen message to door

elevator sends ding message to bell

elevator sends stopThatRingingSound message to bell

Other Facts:

all of the events that happen once the elevator reaches a floor, and until the elevator closes its doors on that floor, take zero time

Floor

Attributes:

pointer to a person - occupied or unoccupied (at most, one person can be waiting on each floor at any time)

doors

light

call button

floorNumber - the number of the floor

pointer to the elevator - for messaging between the floor and the elevator

Behaviors:

openDoor - enable elevator to open the door on the floor

closeDoor - enable elevator to close the door on the floor

turnLightOn - enable elevator to turn on the light on the floor that indicates elevator arrival

turnLightOff - enable elevator to turn off the light on the floor that indicates elevator arrival

isLightOn - enable person to check if light is on

pressCallButton - enable person to press the call button that belongs to the floor

resetCallButton - enable elevator to turn off call button on floor
personArriving - indicate that a person is arriving on the floor
personDeparting - indicate that a person is leaving the floor
isOccupied - is there a person on the floor
getFloorNumber - return the floor number

Messages sent to Other Objects:
enterElevator message sent to person
lightOff message sent to light
lightOn message sent to light
isLightOn message sent to light
buttonOn message sent to button
buttonOff message sent to button
elevatorCalled message sent to elevator

Person
Attributes:
end floor
start floor
sequence number in simulation (for control purposes)
total number of people in simulation
Behaviors:
walkOntoFloor - person enters simulation
enterElevator - enter the elevator
exitElevator - exit the elevator
Messages sent to Other Objects:
person sends pressCallButton message to floor
person sends personArriving message to floor
person sends personDeparting message to floor
person sends passengerEnters message to elevator
person sends passengerExits message to elevator
person sends getFloorNumber message to floor
person sends pressButton message to elevator
Other Facts:
destination floor is never equal to the floor on which that person arrives
If first person of day arrives at floor 1, person can immediately get on elevator
If first person of day arrives at floor 2, elevator proceeds to floor 2 to pick up that person

Light
Attributes:
status - on or off
Behaviors:
lightOn - turn light on
lightOff - turn light off
isLightOn - determine if light is on
Messages sent to Other Objects:

Door
Attributes:
status - open or closed
doorName - string containing door name (i.e., elevator door, floor 1 door, floor 2 door)
Behaviors:
open - open the door
close - close the door
isDoorOpen - determine if door is open

Messages sent to Other Objects:
   Non

Button
Attributes:
   status - on or off
Behaviors:
   buttonOn - turn the button on
   buttonOff - turn the button off
   isButtonOn - determine if a button is on
Messages sent to Other Objects:
   None

Bell
Attributes:
   bell status - digned or not dinged
Behaviors:
   ding - ring the bell; set to dinged
   stopThatRingingSound - reset the bell to not dinged
   didBellRing - did the bell ring
Messages sent to Other Objects:
   exitElevator message sent to person

Clock
Attributes:
   time - elapsed time in simulation
Behaviors:
   tick - add one to the current time
   getTime - return the current time
Messages sent to Other Objects:
   None
Other Facts:
   clock begins the day set to time 0

Scheduler
Attributes:
   time of arrival on each floor
Behaviors:
   set initial arrival times - randomly set first arrival on floor 1 and first arrival on floor 2
   checkIfPersonArriving - determine if a person is arriving at the current time
   createPerson - create a person for the simulation
   scheduleNextRandomArrival - pick a random arrival time for next person
   rescheduleConflictingArrival - set arrival time to arrival time + 1
   getRandom - get a random interval time for next arrival
Messages sent to Other Objects:
   isOccupied message set to floor
Other Facts:
   only one person can be "created" in the simulation at any given time, so there is never a duplicate
      arrival time for the next person
   people arrive at random on each floor every 5 to 20 seconds

```cpp
// simulate.cpp
// Driver for the elevator simulation
#include <iostream.h>
#include <stdlib.h>
#include <time.h>
#include "building.h"

main()
{
    srand(time(NULL));

    cout << "Enter length of elevator simulation: ";

    int length;
    cin >> length;

    Building b;

    b.runSimulation(length);

    return 0;
}
```

```cpp
// building.h
// Definition of class Building
#ifndef BUILDING_H
#define BUILDING_H

#include "floor.h"
#include "elevator.h"
#include "clock.h"
#include "schedule.h"

class Building {
public:
    Building();               // constructor
    void runSimulation(int);  // start the simulation
private:
    Elevator elevator;        // the elevator
    Floor floorOne;           // first floor
    Floor floorTwo;           // second floor
    Scheduler scheduler;      // scheduler to create random arrivals
    Clock clock;              // Clock to time the simulation
};

#endif
```

```cpp
// building.cpp
// Member function definitions for class Building
#include <iostream.h>
#include <iomanip.h>
#include "building.h"

// constructor
Building::Building()
    : elevator("elevator 1"), floorOne(1, &elevator), floorTwo(2, &elevator)
{ }
```

```cpp
// start the simulation
void Building::runSimulation(int simulationLength)
{
   cout << "STARTING ELEVATOR SIMULATION" << endl;

   while ( clock.getTime() < simulationLength ) {
      cout << "Elapsed time:" << setw(5) << clock.getTime() << endl;

      if (elevator.isMoving()) {
         int result = elevator.shouldElevatorStop(clock.getTime());

         if (result)
            elevator.stopElevator( result == 1 ? &floorOne : &floorTwo);
      }

      scheduler.checkIfPersonArriving(clock.getTime(), floorOne, floorTwo);

      if (!elevator.isMoving())
         elevator.shouldElevatorMove(clock.getTime(),
                    elevator.getCurrentFloor() == 1 ? &floorOne : &floorTwo);

      clock.tick();
   }
}
```

```cpp
// elevator.h
// Definition of class Elevator
#ifndef ELEVATOR_H
#define ELEVATOR_H

#include "door.h"
#include "bell.h"
#include "button.h"
class Person;
class Floor;

class Elevator {
public:
   // enumerated types defined for use in class Elevator
   enum Location { FLOOR1, FLOOR2 };
   enum Direction { DOWN, UP };
   enum MovingOrStopped { STOPPED, MOVING };
   enum ElevatorCalled { NOTCALLED, CALLED };

   Elevator(char *);                           // constructor
   int wasYourBellRung() const;                // check if bell sounded
   void pressButton(short);                    // press a destination button
   void resetButton(short);                    // reset a destination button
   Direction determineDirection() const;       // determine the elevator's direction
   void passengerEnters(Person *);             // passenger entering elevator
   void passengerExits();                      // passenger exiting elevator
   void shouldElevatorMove(int, Floor *);      // determine if elevator should move
   int isMoving() const;                       // determine if elevator is moving
   int shouldElevatorStop(int);                // determine if elevator should stop
   void stopElevator(Floor *);                 // stop the elevator
   void elevatorCalled(Floor *);               // set the callState to CALLED
   void prepareToLeaveFloor(Floor *);          // close doors, turn off light, etc
   int getCurrentFloor() const;                // determine the current floor
private:
   Door elevatorDoor;                          // door to the elevator
   Person *passengerPtr;                       // passenger (if there is one)
   Location currentFloor;                      // elevator's current floor
```

```
    Direction direction;                    // elevator's direction
    MovingOrStopped moveState;              // is elevator moving
    short timeOfArrivalAtNextFloor;         // when elevator will arrive
    Bell ringyDingy;                        // bell
    Button destinationButtons[2];           // destonation buttons
    ElevatorCalled callState[2];            // has elevator been called
    char *elevatorName;                     // name of the elevator
};

#endif
```

```cpp
// elevator.cpp
// Member function definitions for class Elevator
#include <iostream.h>
#include "elevator.h"
#include "floor.h"
#include "person.h"

// constructor
Elevator::Elevator(char *name)
    : elevatorDoor("elevator"), passengerPtr(0), currentFloor(FLOOR1),
      direction(UP), moveState(STOPPED), timeOfArrivalAtNextFloor(0),
elevatorName(name)
{ callState[0] = callState[1] = NOTCALLED; }

// determine if bell sounded
int Elevator::wasYourBellRung() const { return ringyDingy.didBellRing(); }

// press the button for a specific floor
void Elevator::pressButton(short floorNum)
    { destinationButtons[floorNum].buttonOn(); }

// reset the button for a specific floor
void Elevator::resetButton(short floorNum)
    { destinationButtons[floorNum].buttonOff(); }

// determine the direction of the elevator
Elevator::Direction Elevator::determineDirection() const { return direction; }

// indicate that a passenger has entered the elevator; store the
// pointer to the person in passengerPtr.
void Elevator::passengerEnters(Person *ptr) { passengerPtr = ptr; }

// indicate that a passenger has exited the elevator; store 0 (null)
// in passengerPtr.
void Elevator::passengerExits() { passengerPtr = 0; }

// determine if elevator should move
// Subscripts 0 and 1 represent floors 1 and 2, respectively.
void Elevator::shouldElevatorMove(int time, Floor *floorPtr)
{
    if ( callState[ (currentFloor == FLOOR1 ? 1 : 0) ] == CALLED ||
         destinationButtons[ (currentFloor == FLOOR1 ? 1 : 0) ].isButtonOn() ) {
      prepareToLeaveFloor(floorPtr);
      moveState = MOVING;
      direction = ( currentFloor == FLOOR1 ? UP : DOWN );
      timeOfArrivalAtNextFloor = time + 5;
      cout << "Elevator starting to move " << ( direction == UP ? "up" : "down" )
           << endl;

      return;
    }
```

```cpp
   if ( elevatorDoor.isDoorOpen() )     // if not moving, close the doors, etc.
      prepareToLeaveFloor(floorPtr);

   cout << "Elevator waiting on floor "
        << ( currentFloor == FLOOR1 ? "floor 1" : "floor 2" )
        << " for passengers" << endl;
}


// determine if elevator is moving
int Elevator::isMoving() const { return moveState == MOVING; }


// determine if elevator should stop
// if so, return 1 to stop at floor 1 or return 2 to stop at floor 2
int Elevator::shouldElevatorStop(int time)
{
   if ( timeOfArrivalAtNextFloor == time )
      return currentFloor == FLOOR1 ? 2 : 1;
   else {
      cout << "Elevator moving " << ( direction == UP ? "up" : "down" )
           << endl;
      return 0;
   }
}


// stop the elevator
void Elevator::stopElevator(Floor *floorPtr)
{
   cout << "Elevator stopped" << endl;
   moveState = STOPPED;
   currentFloor = currentFloor == FLOOR1 ? FLOOR2 : FLOOR1;
   callState[ currentFloor == FLOOR1 ? 0 : 1 ] = NOTCALLED;
   floorPtr->openDoor();
   floorPtr->resetCallButton();
   destinationButtons[ currentFloor == FLOOR1 ? 0 : 1 ].buttonOff();
   elevatorDoor.open();
   ringyDingy.ding(passengerPtr, this);
   floorPtr->turnLightOn(this);
}


// set the callState to called to indicate that a call button was
// pressed on a floor.
void Elevator::elevatorCalled(Floor *floorPtr)
{
   short floor = floorPtr->getFloorNumber();

   cout << "Elevator called from floor " << floor << endl;

   // if elevator is waiting when person arrives
   if ( moveState == STOPPED && currentFloor == (floor == 1 ? FLOOR1 : FLOOR2) ) {
      floorPtr->openDoor();
      floorPtr->resetCallButton();
      elevatorDoor.open();
      floorPtr->turnLightOn(this);
   }
   else
      callState[ floor - 1 ] = CALLED;
}
```

```
// close door to elevator, close door on floor, turn off light
// above elevator, reset bell.
void Elevator::prepareToLeaveFloor(Floor *floorPtr)
{
   ringyDingy.stopThatRingingSound();
   floorPtr->turnLightOff();
   elevatorDoor.close();
   floorPtr->closeDoor();
}

// determine the current floor
int Elevator::getCurrentFloor() const
   { return currentFloor == FLOOR1 ? 1 : 2; }
```

```
// floor.h
// Definition of class Floor
#ifndef FLOOR_H
#define FLOOR_H

#include "door.h"
#include "light.h"
#include "button.h"
class Person;
class Elevator;

class Floor {
public:
   Floor(short, Elevator *);        // constructor
   void openDoor();                 // open the floor door
   void closeDoor();                // close the floor door
   void turnLightOn(Elevator *);    // turn light on
   void turnLightOff();             // turn light off
   int isLightOn() const;           // determine if light is on
   void pressCallButton();          // press the button to call elevator
   void resetCallButton();          // reset the button
   void personArriving(Person *);   // person arriving on floor
   void personDeparting();          // person departing from floor
   int isOccupied() const;          // is there a person here
   short getFloorNumber() const;    // retrieve the floor number

private:
   Person *personPtr;               // possible person on floor
   Door floorDoor;                  // door to elevator from floor
   Light light;                     // light to indicate elevator arrival
   Button callButton;               // button to call elevator
   short floorNumber;               // number of the floor
   Elevator *elevatorPtr;           // knowledge of elevator built into floor
};

#endif
```

```
// floor.cpp
// Member function definition for class Floor

#include <iostream.h>
#include "floor.h"
#include "elevator.h"
#include "person.h"

// constructor
Floor::Floor(short num, Elevator *ePtr)
   : personPtr(0), floorDoor("floor"), floorNumber(num), elevatorPtr(ePtr) { }
```

```
// open the floor door
void Floor::openDoor() { floorDoor.open(); }

// close the floor door
void Floor::closeDoor() { floorDoor.close(); }

// turn light on
void Floor::turnLightOn(Elevator *elevatorPtr)
{
   light.lightOn();

   if ( personPtr != 0)
      personPtr->enterElevator(this, elevatorPtr);
}

// turn light off
void Floor::turnLightOff() { light.lightOff(); }

// determine if light is on
int Floor::isLightOn() const { return light.isLightOn(); }

// press the button to call elevator
void Floor::pressCallButton()
{
   callButton.buttonOn();           // turn on the call button
   elevatorPtr->elevatorCalled(this); // set callState in elevator to CALLED
}

// reset the button
void Floor::resetCallButton()
{
   cout << "Call button reset" << endl;
   callButton.buttonOff();
}

// person arriving on floor
void Floor::personArriving(Person *ptr) { personPtr = ptr; }

// person departing from floor
void Floor::personDeparting()
{
   personPtr = 0;
   cout << "Person leaving floor " << floorNumber << endl;
}

// is there a person here
int Floor::isOccupied() const { return personPtr != 0; }

// retrieve the floor number
short Floor::getFloorNumber() const { return floorNumber; }
```

```
// person.h
// Definition of class Person
#ifndef PERSON_H
#define PERSON_H

#include "floor.h"
#include "elevator.h"

class Person {
public:
   Person(short, short, Floor &);          // constructor
   void walkOntoFloor(Floor &);            // walk into simulation
```

```cpp
    void enterElevator(Floor *, Elevator *);   // walk into elevator from floor
    void exitElevator(Elevator *);                     // walk out of elevator
private:
    short startFloor;                       // starting location
    short endFloor;                         // ending location
    short sequenceNumber;                   // person number in simulation
    static short totalPeople;               // total # of people processed
};

#endif
```

```cpp
// person.cpp
// Member function definitions for class Person
#include <iostream.h>
#include "person.h"

// initialize static data member for class Person
short Person::totalPeople = 0;

// constructor
Person::Person(short start, short end, Floor &floor)
    : startFloor(start), endFloor(end), sequenceNumber(++totalPeople)
{
    cout << "Person " << sequenceNumber << " created" << endl;
    walkOntoFloor(floor);
}

// walk into simulation
void Person::walkOntoFloor(Floor &floor)
{
    short num = floor.getFloorNumber();

    floor.personArriving(this);
    floor.pressCallButton();

    cout << "Person " << sequenceNumber << " walked onto floor " << num
         << " and pressed the " << (num == 1 ? "up" : "down") << " button "
         << endl;
}

// walk into elevator from floor
void Person::enterElevator(Floor *floorPtr, Elevator *elevatorPtr)
{
    cout << "Person " << sequenceNumber << " entered the elevator" << endl;
    floorPtr->personDeparting();
    elevatorPtr->passengerEnters(this);
    elevatorPtr->pressButton(endFloor);
}

// walk out of elevator
void Person::exitElevator(Elevator *elevatorPtr)
{
    cout << "Person " << sequenceNumber << " exited the elevator" << endl;
    delete this;
    elevatorPtr->passengerExits();
}
```

```cpp
// light.h
// Definition of class Light
#ifndef LIGHT_H
#define LIGHT_H
```

```
class Light {
public:
   // enumerated type defined for use in class Light
   enum LightState { OFF, ON };

   Light();                  // constructor
   void lightOn();           // turn light on
   void lightOff();          // turn light off
   int isLightOn() const;    // determine if the light is on
private:
   LightState status;        // state of the light
};

#endif
```

```
// light.cpp
// Member function definitions for class Light
#include <iostream.h>
#include "light.h"

// constructor
Light::Light() : status(OFF) { }

// turn light on
void Light::lightOn()
{
   cout << "Light turned on" << endl;
   status = ON;
}

// turn light off
void Light::lightOff()
{
   cout << "Light turned off" << endl;
   status = OFF;
}

// determine if the light is on
int Light::isLightOn() const { return status == ON; }
```

```
// bell.h
// Definition of class Bell
#ifndef BELL_H
#define BELL_H

class Elevator;
class Person;

class Bell {
public:
   // enumeration type defined for use in class Bell
   enum RingMyBell { NOTDINGED, DINGED };

   Bell();                            // constructor
   void ding(Person *, Elevator*);    // ring the bell
   void stopThatRingingSound();       // reset the bell
   int didBellRing() const;           // determine if bell sounded
private:
   RingMyBell bellStatus;             // status of bell
};

#endif
```

```
// bell.cpp
// Member function definitions for class Bell
#include <iostream.h>
#include "bell.h"
#include "person.h"
#include "elevator.h"

// Constructor
Bell::Bell() : bellStatus(NOTDINGED) { }

// ring the bell
void Bell::ding(Person *personPtr, Elevator *elevatorPtr)
{
   cout << "\aBell sounded" << endl;
   bellStatus = DINGED;

   if ( personPtr != 0 )
      personPtr->exitElevator(elevatorPtr);
}

// reset the bell
void Bell::stopThatRingingSound()
{
   cout << "Bell reset" << endl;
   bellStatus = NOTDINGED;
}

// determine if bell sounded
int Bell::didBellRing() const { return bellStatus == DINGED; }
```

```
// button.h
// Definition of class Button
#ifndef BUTTON_H
#define BUTTON_H

class Button {
public:
   // enumeration type defined for use in class Button
   enum ButtonState { OFF, ON };

   Button();                      // constructor
   void buttonOn();               // turn button on
   void buttonOff();              // turn button off
   int isButtonOn() const;        // determine if button is on
private:
   ButtonState status;
};

#endif
```

```
// button.cpp
// Member function definitions for class Button
#include <iostream.h>
#include "button.h"

// constructor
Button::Button() : status(OFF) { }

// turn button on
void Button::buttonOn() { status = ON; }
```

```
// turn button off
void Button::buttonOff() { status = OFF; }

// determine if button is on
int Button::isButtonOn() const { return status == ON; }
```

```
// clock.h
// Definition of class clock
#ifndef CLOCK_H
#define CLOCK_H

class Clock {
public:
   Clock();                   // constructor
   void tick();               // increment time
   short getTime() const;     // return time
private:
   short time;                // current time
};

#endif
```

```
// clock.cpp
// Member function definitions for class Clock
#include "clock.h"

// Constructor
Clock::Clock() : time(0) { }

// Increment the time by 1
void Clock::tick() { ++ time; }

// Return the current time
short Clock::getTime() const { return time; }
```

```
// door.h
// Definition of class Door
#ifndef DOOR_H
#define DOOR_H

class Door {
public:
   // enumeration type defined for use in class Door
   enum DoorState { CLOSED, OPEN };

   Door(char *);              // constructor
   void open();               // open the door
   void close();              // close the door
   int isDoorOpen() const;    // determine if the door is open
private:
   DoorState status;          // state of the door
   char *doorName;            // name of the door
};

#endif
```

```
// door.cpp
// Member function definitions for class Door
#include <iostream.h>
#include "door.h"
```

```cpp
// constructor
Door::Door(char *name) : doorName(name), status(CLOSED) { }

// open the door
void Door::open()
{
   cout << doorName << " door opened" << endl;
   status = OPEN;
}

// close the door
void Door::close()
{
   cout << doorName << " door closed" << endl;
   status = CLOSED;
}

// determine if the door is open
int Door::isDoorOpen() const { return status == OPEN; }
```

```cpp
// schedule.h
// Definition of class Scheduler
#ifndef SCHEDULE_H
#define SCHEDULE_H

#include "floor.h"
#include "person.h"

class Scheduler {
public:
   Scheduler();                                 // constructor
   void checkIfPersonArriving(int, Floor &, Floor &);  // determine if
                                                // person is arriving
private:
   short arrivalTimes[2];                       // array of two arrival times

   void createPerson(short, short, Floor &);        // create a Person
   void scheduleNextRandomArrival(short);    // schedule next arrival
   void rescheduleConflictingArrival(short); // reschedule an arrival
   int getRandom();                             // get random val in interval
};

#endif
```

```cpp
// schedule.cpp
// Member function definitions for class Scheduler
//
// person.h included here to enable creation of Person objects.
// floor.h included here to determine if a particular floor is occupied.
// Subscripts of 0 represent floor 1 and subscripts of 1 represent floor 2.
//
#include <iostream.h>
#include <stdlib.h>
#include "schedule.h"
#include "person.h"
#include "floor.h"

// constructor
Scheduler::Scheduler()
{
   arrivalTimes[0] = getRandom();
   arrivalTimes[1] = getRandom();
```

```
      while ( arrivalTimes[0] == arrivalTimes[1] )
         arrivalTimes[1] = getRandom();

      cout << "First person scheduled to arrive on floor 1 at time "
           << arrivalTimes[0] << endl
           << "First person scheduled to arrive on floor 2 at time "
           << arrivalTimes[1] << endl;
}

// determine if person is arriving
void Scheduler::checkIfPersonArriving(int time, Floor &floor1, Floor &floor2)
{
   short arrivalFloor = -1;

   if ( arrivalTimes[0] == time )
      arrivalFloor = 0;                      // arrival at floor 1
   else if ( arrivalTimes[1] == time )
      arrivalFloor = 1;                      // arrival at floor 2

   if ( arrivalFloor == -1 )
      return;                                // no arrival scheduled for this time

   if ( arrivalFloor == 0 )
      if ( !floor1.isOccupied() ) {
         createPerson(0, 1, floor1);              // arrive at 1, go to 2
         scheduleNextRandomArrival(0);      // schedule next arrival
      }
      else
         rescheduleConflictingArrival(0);   // reschedule arrival

   if ( arrivalFloor == 1 )
      if( !floor2.isOccupied() ) {
         createPerson(1, 0, floor2);              // arrive at 2, go to 1
         scheduleNextRandomArrival(1);      // schedule next arrival
      }
      else
         rescheduleConflictingArrival(1);   // reschedule arrival
}

// create a Person
void Scheduler::createPerson(short start, short end, Floor &floor)
   { new Person(start, end, floor); }

// schedule next arrival
void Scheduler::scheduleNextRandomArrival(short floor)
{
   arrivalTimes[floor] += getRandom();

   // If new arrival time is same as next arrival time on other floor,
   // add one to the new arrival time.
   if ( arrivalTimes[floor] == arrivalTimes[floor == 0 ? 1 : 0] )
      ++arrivalTimes[floor];

   cout << "Next person scheduled to arrive on floor " << floor + 1
        << " at time " << arrivalTimes[floor] << endl;
}

// reschedule an arrival
void Scheduler::rescheduleConflictingArrival(short floor)
{
   while ( ++arrivalTimes[floor] == arrivalTimes[floor == 0 ? 1 : 0] )
      ;  // empty body
```

```
    cout << "Next person to arrive on floor " << floor + 1
         << " rescheduled for time " << arrivalTimes[floor] << endl;
}

// get a random number in the specified interval
int Scheduler::getRandom() { return 5 + rand() % 16; }
```

OUTPUT

```
Enter length of elevator simulation: 100
First person scheduled to arrive on floor 1 at time 15
First person scheduled to arrive on floor 2 at time 7
STARTING ELEVATOR SIMULATION
Elapsed time:      0
Elevator waiting on floor floor 1 for passengers
Elapsed time:      1
Elevator waiting on floor floor 1 for passengers
Elapsed time:      2
Elevator waiting on floor floor 1 for passengers
Elapsed time:      3
Elevator waiting on floor floor 1 for passengers
Elapsed time:      4
Elevator waiting on floor floor 1 for passengers
Elapsed time:      5
Elevator waiting on floor floor 1 for passengers
Elapsed time:      6
Elevator waiting on floor floor 1 for passengers
Elapsed time:      7
Person 1 created
Elevator called from floor 2
Person 1 walked onto floor 2 and pressed the down button
Next person scheduled to arrive on floor 2 at time 18
Bell reset
Light turned off
elevator door closed
floor door closed
Elevator starting to move up
Elapsed time:      8
Elevator moving up
Elapsed time:      9
Elevator moving up
Elapsed time:     10
Elevator moving up
Elapsed time:     11
Elevator moving up
Elapsed time:     12
Elevator stopped
floor door opened
Call button reset
elevator door opened
Bell sounded
Light turned on
Person 1 entered the elevator
Person leaving floor 2
Bell reset
Light turned off
elevator door closed
floor door closed
Elevator starting to move down
Elapsed time:     13
Elevator moving down
Elapsed time:     14
```

```
Elevator moving down
Elapsed time:   15
Elevator moving down
Person 2 created
Elevator called from floor 1
Person 2 walked onto floor 1 and pressed the up button
Next person scheduled to arrive on floor 1 at time 22
Elapsed time:   16
Elevator moving down
Elapsed time:   17
Elevator stopped
floor door opened
Call button reset
elevator door opened
Bell sounded
Person 1 exited the elevator
Light turned on
Person 2 entered the elevator
Person leaving floor 1
Bell reset
Light turned off
elevator door closed
floor door closed
Elevator starting to move up
Elapsed time:   18
Elevator moving up
Person 3 created
Elevator called from floor 2
Person 3 walked onto floor 2 and pressed the down button
Next person scheduled to arrive on floor 2 at time 31
Elapsed time:   19
Elevator moving up
Elapsed time:   20
Elevator moving up
Elapsed time:   21
Elevator moving up
Elapsed time:   22
Elevator stopped
floor door opened
Call button reset
elevator door opened
Bell sounded
Person 2 exited the elevator
Light turned on
Person 3 entered the elevator
Person leaving floor 2
Person 4 created
Elevator called from floor 1
Person 4 walked onto floor 1 and pressed the up button
Next person scheduled to arrive on floor 1 at time 40
Bell reset
Light turned off
elevator door closed
floor door closed
Elevator starting to move down
Elapsed time:   23
Elevator moving down
Elapsed time:   24
Elevator moving down
Elapsed time:   25
Elevator moving down
Elapsed time:   26
Elevator moving down
Elapsed time:   27
```

```
Elevator stopped
floor door opened
Call button reset
elevator door opened
Bell sounded
Person 3 exited the elevator
Light turned on
Person 4 entered the elevator
Person leaving floor 1
Bell reset
Light turned off
elevator door closed
floor door closed
Elevator starting to move up
Elapsed time:    28
Elevator moving up
Elapsed time:    29
Elevator moving up
Elapsed time:    30
Elevator moving up
Elapsed time:    31
Elevator moving up
Person 5 created
Elevator called from floor 2
Person 5 walked onto floor 2 and pressed the down button
Next person scheduled to arrive on floor 2 at time 47
Elapsed time:    32
Elevator stopped
floor door opened
Call button reset
elevator door opened
Bell sounded
Person 4 exited the elevator
Light turned on
Person 5 entered the elevator
Person leaving floor 2
Bell reset
Light turned off
elevator door closed
floor door closed
Elevator starting to move down
Elapsed time:    33
Elevator moving down
Elapsed time:    34
Elevator moving down
Elapsed time:    35
Elevator moving down
Elapsed time:    36
Elevator moving down
Elapsed time:    37
Elevator stopped
floor door opened
Call button reset
elevator door opened
Bell sounded
Person 5 exited the elevator
Light turned on
Bell reset
Light turned off
elevator door closed
floor door closed
Elevator waiting on floor floor 1 for passengers
Elapsed time:    38
Elevator waiting on floor floor 1 for passengers
```

```
Elapsed time:    39
Elevator waiting on floor floor 1 for passengers
Elapsed time:    40
Person 6 created
Elevator called from floor 1
floor door opened
Call button reset
elevator door opened
Light turned on
Person 6 entered the elevator
Person leaving floor 1
Person 6 walked onto floor 1 and pressed the up button
Next person scheduled to arrive on floor 1 at time 60
Bell reset
Light turned off
elevator door closed
floor door closed
Elevator starting to move up
Elapsed time:    41
Elevator moving up
Elapsed time:    42
Elevator moving up
Elapsed time:    43
Elevator moving up
Elapsed time:    44
Elevator moving up
Elapsed time:    45
Elevator stopped
floor door opened
Call button reset
elevator door opened
Bell sounded
Person 6 exited the elevator
Light turned on
Bell reset
Light turned off
elevator door closed
floor door closed
Elevator waiting on floor floor 2 for passengers
Elapsed time:    46
Elevator waiting on floor floor 2 for passengers
Elapsed time:    47
Person 7 created
Elevator called from floor 2
floor door opened
Call button reset
elevator door opened
Light turned on
Person 7 entered the elevator
Person leaving floor 2
Person 7 walked onto floor 2 and pressed the down button
Next person scheduled to arrive on floor 2 at time 56
Bell reset
Light turned off
elevator door closed
floor door closed
Elevator starting to move down
Elapsed time:    48
Elevator moving down
Elapsed time:    49
Elevator moving down
Elapsed time:    50
Elevator moving down
Elapsed time:    51
```

```
Elevator moving down
Elapsed time:    52
Elevator stopped
floor door opened
Call button reset
elevator door opened
Bell sounded
Person 7 exited the elevator
Light turned on
Bell reset
Light turned off
elevator door closed
floor door closed
Elevator waiting on floor floor 1 for passengers
Elapsed time:    53
Elevator waiting on floor floor 1 for passengers
Elapsed time:    54
Elevator waiting on floor floor 1 for passengers
Elapsed time:    55
Elevator waiting on floor floor 1 for passengers
Elapsed time:    56
Person 8 created
Elevator called from floor 2
Person 8 walked onto floor 2 and pressed the down button
Next person scheduled to arrive on floor 2 at time 67
Bell reset
Light turned off
elevator door closed
floor door closed
Elevator starting to move up
Elapsed time:    57
Elevator moving up
Elapsed time:    58
Elevator moving up
Elapsed time:    59
Elevator moving up
Elapsed time:    60
Elevator moving up
Person 9 created
Elevator called from floor 1
Person 9 walked onto floor 1 and pressed the up button
Next person scheduled to arrive on floor 1 at time 77
Elapsed time:    61
Elevator stopped
floor door opened
Call button reset
elevator door opened
Bell sounded
Light turned on
Person 8 entered the elevator
Person leaving floor 2
Bell reset
Light turned off
elevator door closed
floor door closed
Elevator starting to move down
Elapsed time:    62
Elevator moving down
Elapsed time:    63
Elevator moving down
Elapsed time:    64
Elevator moving down
Elapsed time:    65
Elevator moving down
```

```
Elapsed time:   66
Elevator stopped
floor door opened
Call button reset
elevator door opened
Bell sounded
Person 8 exited the elevator
Light turned on
Person 9 entered the elevator
Person leaving floor 1
Bell reset
Light turned off
elevator door closed
floor door closed
Elevator starting to move up
Elapsed time:   67
Elevator moving up
Person 10 created
Elevator called from floor 2
Person 10 walked onto floor 2 and pressed the down button
Next person scheduled to arrive on floor 2 at time 86
Elapsed time:   68
Elevator moving up
Elapsed time:   69
Elevator moving up
Elapsed time:   70
Elevator moving up
Elapsed time:   71
Elevator stopped
floor door opened
Call button reset
elevator door opened
Bell sounded
Person 9 exited the elevator
Light turned on
Person 10 entered the elevator
Person leaving floor 2
Bell reset
Light turned off
elevator door closed
floor door closed
Elevator starting to move down
Elapsed time:   72
Elevator moving down
Elapsed time:   73
Elevator moving down
Elapsed time:   74
Elevator moving down
Elapsed time:   75
Elevator moving down
Elapsed time:   76
Elevator stopped
floor door opened
Call button reset
elevator door opened
Bell sounded
Person 10 exited the elevator
Light turned on
Bell reset
Light turned off
elevator door closed
floor door closed
Elevator waiting on floor floor 1 for passengers
Elapsed time:   77
```

```
Person 11 created
Elevator called from floor 1
floor door opened
Call button reset
elevator door opened
Light turned on
Person 11 entered the elevator
Person leaving floor 1
Person 11 walked onto floor 1 and pressed the up button
Next person scheduled to arrive on floor 1 at time 85
Bell reset
Light turned off
elevator door closed
floor door closed
Elevator starting to move up
Elapsed time:    78
Elevator moving up
Elapsed time:    79
Elevator moving up
Elapsed time:    80
Elevator moving up
Elapsed time:    81
Elevator moving up
Elapsed time:    82
Elevator stopped
floor door opened
Call button reset
elevator door opened
Bell sounded
Person 11 exited the elevator
Light turned on
Bell reset
Light turned off
elevator door closed
floor door closed
Elevator waiting on floor floor 2 for passengers
Elapsed time:    83
Elevator waiting on floor floor 2 for passengers
Elapsed time:    84
Elevator waiting on floor floor 2 for passengers
Elapsed time:    85
Person 12 created
Elevator called from floor 1
Person 12 walked onto floor 1 and pressed the up button
Next person scheduled to arrive on floor 1 at time 105
Bell reset
Light turned off
elevator door closed
floor door closed
Elevator starting to move down
Elapsed time:    86
Elevator moving down
Person 13 created
Elevator called from floor 2
Person 13 walked onto floor 2 and pressed the down button
Next person scheduled to arrive on floor 2 at time 103
Elapsed time:    87
Elevator moving down
Elapsed time:    88
Elevator moving down
Elapsed time:    89
Elevator moving down
Elapsed time:    90
Elevator stopped
```

```
floor door opened
Call button reset
elevator door opened
Bell sounded
Light turned on
Person 12 entered the elevator
Person leaving floor 1
Bell reset
Light turned off
elevator door closed
floor door closed
Elevator starting to move up
Elapsed time:    91
Elevator moving up
Elapsed time:    92
Elevator moving up
Elapsed time:    93
Elevator moving up
Elapsed time:    94
Elevator moving up
Elapsed time:    95
Elevator stopped
floor door opened
Call button reset
elevator door opened
Bell sounded
Person 12 exited the elevator
Light turned on
Person 13 entered the elevator
Person leaving floor 2
Bell reset
Light turned off
elevator door closed
floor door closed
Elevator starting to move down
Elapsed time:    96
Elevator moving down
Elapsed time:    97
Elevator moving down
Elapsed time:    98
Elevator moving down
Elapsed time:    99
Elevator moving down
```